VISUALIZING
TECHNOLOGY

VISUALIZING
TECHNOLOGY

Debra Geoghan
Bucks County Community College

Prentice Hall

Boston   Columbus   Indianapolis   New York   San Francisco
Upper Saddle River   Amsterdam   Cape Town   Dubai   London
Madrid   Milan   Munich   Paris   Montreal   Toronto   Delhi   Mexico City
Sao Paulo   Sydney   Hong Kong   Seoul   Singapore   Taipei   Tokyo

Editor in Chief: Michael Payne
AVP/Executive Acquisitions Editor: Stephanie Wall
Product Development Manager: Eileen Bien Calabro
Development Editor: Linda Harrison
Editorial Project Manager: Virginia Guariglia
Editorial Assistant: Nicole Sam
Director of Marketing: Kate Valentine
Marketing Manager: Tori Olson Alves
Marketing Coordinator: Susan Osterlitz
Marketing Assistant: Darshika Vyas
Senior Managing Editor: Cynthia Zonneveld
Managing Editor: Camille Trentacoste
Production Project Manager: Mike Lackey
Operations Director: Nick Sklitsis
Operations Specialist: Natacha Moore
Manager of Design Development: John Christiana
Art Director: Kathy Mrozek
Manager, Visual Research: Karen Sanatar
Photo Researcher: David Tietz
Manager, Rights and Permissions: Zina Arabia
Cover Art: iStockphoto—alptraum and Shutterstock—AlexRoz
Text Researcher: Doreen Crotty
Permissions Project Manager: Hessa Albader
Media Development Manager: Cathi Profitko
VP, Director of Digital Development: Zara Wanless
Media Project Manager, Editorial: Alana Coles
Media Project manager, Production: John Cassar
Supplements Editor: Vonda Keator
Full-Service Project Management: PreMediaGlobal
Composition: PreMediaGlobal
Printer/Binder: Courier
Cover Printer: Lehigh/Phoenix
Text Font: 10/12 Helvetica Neue LT Std Roman

Credits and acknowledgments borrowed from other sources and reproduced, with permission, in this textbook appear in the Rear Matter of this book.

Microsoft® and Windows® are registered trademarks of the Microsoft Corporation in the U.S.A. and other countries. Screen shots and icons reprinted with permission from the Microsoft Corporation. This book is not sponsored or endorsed by or affiliated with the Microsoft Corporation.

Copyright © 2012 Pearson Education, Inc., publishing as Prentice Hall. All rights reserved. Manufactured in the United States of America. This publication is protected by Copyright, and permission should be obtained from the publisher prior to any prohibited reproduction, storage in a retrieval system, or transmission in any form or by any means, electronic, mechanical, photocopying, recording, or likewise. To obtain permission(s) to use material from this work, please submit a written request to Pearson Education, Inc., Permissions Department, 1 Lake Street, Upper Saddle River, New Jersey, 07458.

Many of the designations by manufacturers and seller to distinguish their products are claimed as trademarks. Where those designations appear in this book, and the publisher was aware of a trademark claim, the designations have been printed in initial caps or all caps.

Library of Congress Cataloging-in-Publication Data
Control number is on record at the Library of Congress.

10 9 8 7 6 5 4 3

Prentice Hall is an imprint of

PEARSON

www.pearsonhighered.com

ISBN 10: 0-13-137625-X
ISBN 13: 978-0-13-137625-0

Brief Contents

Chapter 1: What Is a Computer? 2
Chapter 2: Hardware 40
Chapter 3: File Management 98
Chapter 4: Digital Devices and Multimedia 138
Chapter 5: Application Software 178
Chapter 6: System Software 222
Chapter 7: The Internet 254
Chapter 8: Communicating and Sharing:
　　　　　　　The Social Web 292
Chapter 9: Networks and Communication 334
Appendix 376

Contents

Chapter 1

What Is a Computer? 2

What Does a Computer Do? 4
- Objective 1: Explain the functions of a computer. 4
  - Necessity Is the Mother of Invention 4
  - The Information Processing Cycle 5

A Brief History of Computers 6
- Objective 2: Describe the evolution of computer hardware, and explain the importance of Moore's Law. 6
  - History of Computers 6
  - Moore's Law 8

Let's Get Personal 10
- Objective 3: List the various types and characteristics of personal computers. 10
  - Desktop Computers 10
  - Notebook Computers 11
  - Mac or PC? 12

Multiuser Computers—More Power to You 14
- Objective 4: List the various types and characteristics of multiuser computers. 14
  - Servers 14
  - Supercomputers 16
  - Distributed and Grid Computing 16

It's Not Your Father's Desktop Anymore 18
- Objective 5: Give examples of other computing devices. 18
  - Handheld and Mobile Devices 18
  - Video Game Systems 20

Comfort and Safety 22
- Objective 6: List several ways ergonomics can improve the comfort and safety of a computer user. 22
  - Ergonomics 22

Computers are Everywhere: Ubiquitous Computing 24
- Objective 7: Explain the terms "ubiquitous computing" and "convergence." 24
  - Embedded Computers 24
  - Convergence 25

What Can I Do With Knowledge About Computers? 28
- Objective 8: Identify the certifications and careers related to computers. 28
  - Bioinformatics 28
  - Auto Mechanic 29
  - MCDST 29
  - Volunteer 29

How To: Create Screenshots of Your Desktop Using the Windows Snipping Tool 30

Objectives Recap 32

Key Terms 32

Summary 33

End of Chapter Exercises 34

Chapter 2

Hardware 40

The CPU: The Brains of the Operation   42

Objective 1: Explain the function of the CPU.   42
Instruction Cycle   42
CPU Performance   43
Cooling System: Air Conditioning for the Processor   45

Getting to Know Your System Unit and Motherboard   46

Objective 2: Identify the parts of a system unit and motherboard.   46
The Motherboard   46
Memory   50

Bits and Bytes   52

Objective 3: Describe how computers present data using binary codes.   52
Binary Code   52
Measuring Data   54

A Place for Everything . . . and Everything in its Place   56

Objective 4: Compare different types of storage devices.   56
Optical Discs   56
Solid-State Storage   57
Hard Drives   58

What Goes In . . .   60

Objective 5: List different input devices and their uses.   60
Keyboards   60
Mouse and Other Pointing Devices   63
Digital Cameras and Webcams   64
Scanners   64
Microphones and Game Controllers   66

. . . Must Come Out   68

Objective 6: List the different video and audio output devices and their uses.   68
Video Output Devices   68
Audio Output Devices   72

Pick a Printer   74

Objective 7: Compare the features of different types of printers.   74
Inkjet Printers   74
Photo Printers   74
Dye-Sublimation Printers   75
Thermal Printers   75
Laser Printers   76
Multifunction Devices   77
Plotters   77

Adaptation: Making Technology Work for You   78

Objective 8: Explain and provide examples of the concept of adaptive technology.   78
Adaptive Input Devices   79
Adaptive Output Devices   80

Communicate, Communicate, Communicate   82

Objective 9: Discuss the different communication devices that can be used.   82
Network Adapters   82
Modems   82
Fax Devices   83

What Can I Do With Knowledge About Hardware?   84

Objective 10: Identify the certifications and careers related to computer hardware.   84
A+ Certification   84
Computer Sales and Technical Support Careers   85

How To: Assess Your Computer Hardware   86

Objectives Recap   88

Key Terms   89

Summary   90

End of Chapter Exercises   91

Chapter 3

File Management..................98

A Place for Everything   100

Objective 1: Create folders to organize files.   100
- Navigating Your Computer   100
- Creating and Using Folders   104

What's in a Name?   108

Objective 2: Explain the importance of file extensions.   108
- File Names and Extensions   108
- File Properties   109

Back It Up   112

Objective 3: Explain the importance of backing up files.   112
- Windows Backup   112
- Other Backup Software   114
- Online Backups   115

Shrink It   116

Objective 4: Demonstrate how to compress files.   116
- Types of File Compression   116
- Working with File Compression   117

How To: Create a Compressed (Zipped) Folder   120

It's Always in the Last Place You Look   122

Objective 5: Use advanced search options to locate files.   122
- Using Windows to Search For Files   122
- Using Boolean Logic to Refine Searches   125

That's Not the Program I Want to Open This File Type   126

Objective 6: Change the default program associated with a file type.   126
- Setting Program Defaults   126
- Managing File Type Associations   127

What Can I Do With Knowledge About File Management?   128

Objective 7: Identify the certifications and careers related to file management.   128
- Life Sciences   128
- Federal Records Managment   129

Objectives Recap   130

Key Terms   130

Summary   131

End of Chapter Exercises   132

Chapter 4

Digital Devices and Multimedia..........................138

The 4-1-1 on Digital Cameras   140

Objective 1: Explain the features of various types of digital cameras.   140
- Key Features   140
- Types of Digital Cameras   142

Bridging the Gap: Transferring Photos   144

Objective 2: Compare different methods for transferring images from a digital camera.   144
- Memory Cards   144
- USB or FireWire Cables   145
- Wireless Transfer   145

A Picture Is Worth a Thousand Words: Editing, Printing, and Sharing Photos   148

Objective 3: List several ways to edit and print photos.   148
- Editing Photos   148
- Printing and Sharing Photos   149

Making Sense of Sound 152

Objective 4: Recognize different audio file types. 152
- Audio File Types 152
- Media Software 153
- Speech Recognition 155

You Ought to Be in Pictures 156

Objective 5: Describe several ways to create videos. 156
- Screen Capture 156
- Webcams and Video Conferencing 156
- Video Cameras 157
- Sharing Video 158

How To: Use Windows Movie Maker 160

On the Move With Technology 164

Objective 6: Compare portable media players, PDAs, and smartphones. 164
- Portable Media Players 164
- PDA and Smartphones 166

What Can I Do With Knowledge About Digital Devices and Multimedia? 168

Objective 7: Identify careers related to digital devices and multimedia. 168
- Health Care 168
- Graphics 168
- Engineering and Science 169
- Photojournalism 169

Objectives Recap 170

Key Terms 170

Summary 171

End of Chapter Exercises 172

Chapter 5

Application Software 178

Making Business Work 180

Objective 1: Identify types and uses of business productivity software. 180
- Office Suites 180
- Other Types of Business Software 186

Making It Personal 188

Objective 2: Identify types and uses of personal software. 188
- Office Applications 188
- Finance and Tax Preparation Software 190
- Entertainment and Multimedia Software 191
- Educational and Reference Software 195
- Portable Apps 197

How To: Create a Document Using Wordpad 198

Will It Run? 202

Objective 3: Assess a computer system for software compatibility. 202
- Your System Specs 202
- System Requirements 204

Where to Get It 206

Objective 4: Compare various ways of obtaining software. 206
- Licensing 206
- Free or Fee 207
- Sources of Software 208

Your Head in the Cloud 210

Objective 5: Discuss the importance of cloud computing. 210
- Cloud Computing 210

What Can I Do With Knowledge About Application Software? 212

Objective 6: Identify the certifications and careers related to application software. 212
- Microsoft Certified Application Specialist (MCAS) 212
- Other Software Certifications 213
- Software Trainer 213

Objectives Recap 214

Key Terms 214

Summary 215

End of Chapter Exercises 216

Chapter 6

System Software 222

Who's Being Bossy Now? 224

Objective 1: Explain what an operating system does. 224
- Provides User Interface 224
- Manages Resources 225
- Manages and Controls Hardware 226
- Interacts with Software 227

Running the Show on Personal Computers 228

Objective 2: Compare the most common stand-alone operating systems. 228
- Windows 228
- MAC 229
- Linux 230

How To: Keep Windows Up to Date 232

The NOS Knows 234

Objective 3: Compare the most common operating systems. 234
- Network Operating Systems 234

Something Special for You 236

Objective 4: Compare specialized operating systems. 236
- Embedded Operating Systems 236
- Web Operating Systems 238

Utilities You Should Use 240

Objective 5: List and explain important disk utility software. 240
- Why Use Utilities? 240
- Utilities for Disk Health 241
- Disk Defragmenter 241
- Disk Cleanup 242

What Can I Do With Knowledge About System Software? 244

Objective 6: Identify the certifications and careers related to system software. 244
- Microsoft Certified Technology Specialist Certification 244
- Microsoft Certified IT Professional 245
- Linux and MAC Certifications 245
- Job Opportunities 245

Objectives Recap 246

Key Terms 246

Summary 247

End of Chapter Exercises 248

Chapter 7

The Internet 254

Did Al Gore Invent the Internet? 256

Objective 1: Recognize the importance of the Internet. 256
- How it All Got Started 256
- World Wide Web 257
- Internet2 (I2) 258

Get Connected 260

Objective 2: Compare the types of Internet connections. 260

- So, How Do You Get Connected? 260
- Connecting Without a Computer? 264

Surf's Up 266

Objective 3: Compare popular Web browsers. 266

- Browsers 266
- Configuring Your Web Browser 269
- Add-ons, Plug-ins, and Toolbars 270

How To: Create a Custom Home Page Using iGoogle 272

Navigating the Net 276

Objective 4: Demonstrate how to navigate the Web. 276

- Web Addresses 276
- Smart Searching 278

Would I Lie to You? 280

Objective 5: Discuss how to evaluate the credibility of information found on the Web. 280

- Who Wrote It? 280
- What About the Design? 281

What Can I Do With Knowledge About The Internet? 282

Objective 6: Identify the certifications and careers related to the Internet. 282

- Web Designer 282
- Web Developer 283
- CIW (Certified Internet Web Professional) 283

Objectives Recap 284

Key Terms 284

Summary 286

End of Chapter Exercises 286

Chapter 8

Communicating and Sharing: The Social Web 292

Talk to Me 294

Objective 1: Compare different forms of synchronous online communication. 294

- Chat and IM 294
- VoIP 297

Leave a Message 298

Objective 2: Demonstrate how to use e-mail effectively. 298

- How Do You Read and Send E-mail? 298
- Forums and Discussion Boards 302

There's a Place for Everyone . . . 304

Objective 3: Discuss the roles of social media in today's society. 304

- Social Network Sites 304
- Social Video, Image, and Music Sites 307

How To: Create an Avatar 310

Get Your Word Out 314

Objective 4: Locate user-generated content in the form of a blog or podcast. 314

- Blogs 314
- Podcasts 316
- RSS 317

The Wisdom of the Crowd 318

Objective 5: Discuss how wikis and other social media sites rely on the wisdom of the crowd. 318

- Wikis 318
- Social Review Sites 319
- Social Bookmarking and News Sites 320

E-Commerce 322

Objective 6: Explain the influence of social media on e-commerce. 322

Types of e-Commerce 322
How Safe is My Credit Card 323

What Can I Do With Knowledge About Online Communication? 324

Objective 7: Identify the careers related to online communication. 324

Blogger 324
Social Media Marketer 324

Objectives Recap 326

Key Terms 326

Summary 327

End of Chapter Exercises 328

Chapter 9

Networks and Communication 334

From Sneakernet to HotSpots 336

Objective 1: Discuss the importance of computer networks. 336

Peer-to-Peer Networks 336
Client-Server Networks 340

How To: Share Files and Printers Using a Windows Homegroup 342

LANS and WANS 348

Objective 2: Compare different types of LANs and WANs. 348

Small Networks 348
Large Networks 349

The Networking Hardware Store 352

Objective 3: List and describe the hardware used in both wired and wireless networks. 352

Network Adapters 352
Network Hardware 354

The Softer Side   358

Objective 4: List and describe the software and protocols used in both wired and wireless networks.   358

- Peer-to-Peer Network Software   358
- Client-Server Network Software   359
- Network Protocols   361

Protecting Your Network   364

Objective 5: Explain how to protect a network.   364

- Layer 1—The Fence   364
- Layer 2—Door Locks   364
- Layer 3—Alarm Systems   365
- Layer 4—Guard Dogs   365

What Can I Do With Knowledge About Computer Networks?   366

Objective 6: Identify the certifications and careers related to computer networks.   366

- CompTIA Certifications   366
- Microsoft Certifications   366
- Cisco Certifications   367
- Network Adminstrator   367

Objectives Recap   368

Key Terms   368

Summary   370

End of Chapter Exercises   371

Appendix 376

Appendix A: Blogger 376

Appendix B: Mind Maps 378

Appendix C: Google Docs 380

Glossary 382
Index 392
Photo Credits 402

Visual Walkthrough

VISUALIZING TECHNOLOGY

- Addresses visual and kinesthetic learners—images help students to learn and retain content while hands-on projects allow students to practice and apply what they learned.
- Easy to read—it has the same amount of text as other concepts books but broken down into smaller chunks of text to aid in comprehension and retention.
- Clear, easy-to-follow organization—each chapter is broken into a series of articles that correspond to chapter objectives.
- Highly visual—students will want to read!

Link to Facebook page

Become our friend on Facebook

CHAPTER 3
File Management

Running Project

In this chapter, you learn about the importance of file management. Look for instructions as you complete each article. For most, there's a series of questions for you to research or a set of tasks to perform. At the conclusion of this chapter you're asked to submit your responses to the questions raised and the results of the tasks you've performed.

OBJECTIVES

1. Create folders to organize files. (p. 100)
2. Explain the importance of file extensions. (p. 108)
3. Explain the importance of backing up files. (p. 112)
4. Demonstrate how to compress files. (p. 116)
5. Use advanced search options to locate files. (p. 122)
6. Change the default program associated with a file type. (p. 126)
7. Identify the certifications and careers related to file management. (p. 128)

IN THIS CHAPTER

The concepts of file management are not unique to computing. We use file cabinets, folders, boxes, drawers, and piles to manage our paper files. This can be anything from bills to photographs to homework assignments to coupons. In this chapter, we look at managing our electronic files.

Summary of the running project for that chapter

Objectives clearly outlined in chapter opener and restated at the beginning of each article

Catchy headlines begin each article

The CPU: The Brains OF THE OPERATION

OBJECTIVE
Explain the function of the CPU.

The brain of a computer is called the **central processing unit (CPU)**, or **processor**, and is housed inside the system unit on the motherboard (see Figure 2.1). The CPU consists of two parts: the arithmetic logic unit and the control unit.

The **arithmetic logic unit (ALU)** performs arithmetic (addition and subtraction) and logic (AND, OR, and NOT) calculations. The **control unit** manages the movement of data through the CPU. Together, these units perform three main functions: executing program instructions, performing calculations, and making decisions.

FIGURE 2.1 The central processing unit fits into the motherboard inside the system unit.

INSTRUCTION CYCLE

In order to perform the three functions, the CPU utilizes the **instruction cycle**, which is also known as the "fetch-and-execute cycle" or the "machine cycle." Here's how it works (see Figure 2.2).

FIGURE 2.2 The four steps of the instruction cycle: fetch, decode, execute, and store.

- The instruction is retrieved from main memory.
- **STORE** The results are written back to memory (stored).
- **DECODE** The control unit translates the instruction into a computer command.
- **EXECUTE** The ALU processes the command.

CPU PERFORMANCE

The instruction cycle happens so quickly that you don't realize what's happening. In fact, the processor executes billions of cycles each second. When you evaluate processors for performance, one of the variables you look at is **clock speed**, which is the speed at which the processer executes the cycles. Today, that speed is measured in **gigahertz (GHz)**—billions of cycles per second. A 3 GHz processor has 3 billion data cycles per second.

So far, we've looked at how a processor executes one instruction at a time. Modern computers are capable of processing multiple instructions simultaneously, which increases the efficiency of the processor and the performance of the computer.

PIPELINING Pipelining is used by a single processor. As soon as the first instruction has moved from the fetch to the decode stage, the processor fetches the next instruction. The process is much like an assembly line in a factory (see Figure 2.3).

FIGURE 2.3 Commands are fed to the processor as the previous command completes a phase—like the stations on this assembly line.

Find Out MORE

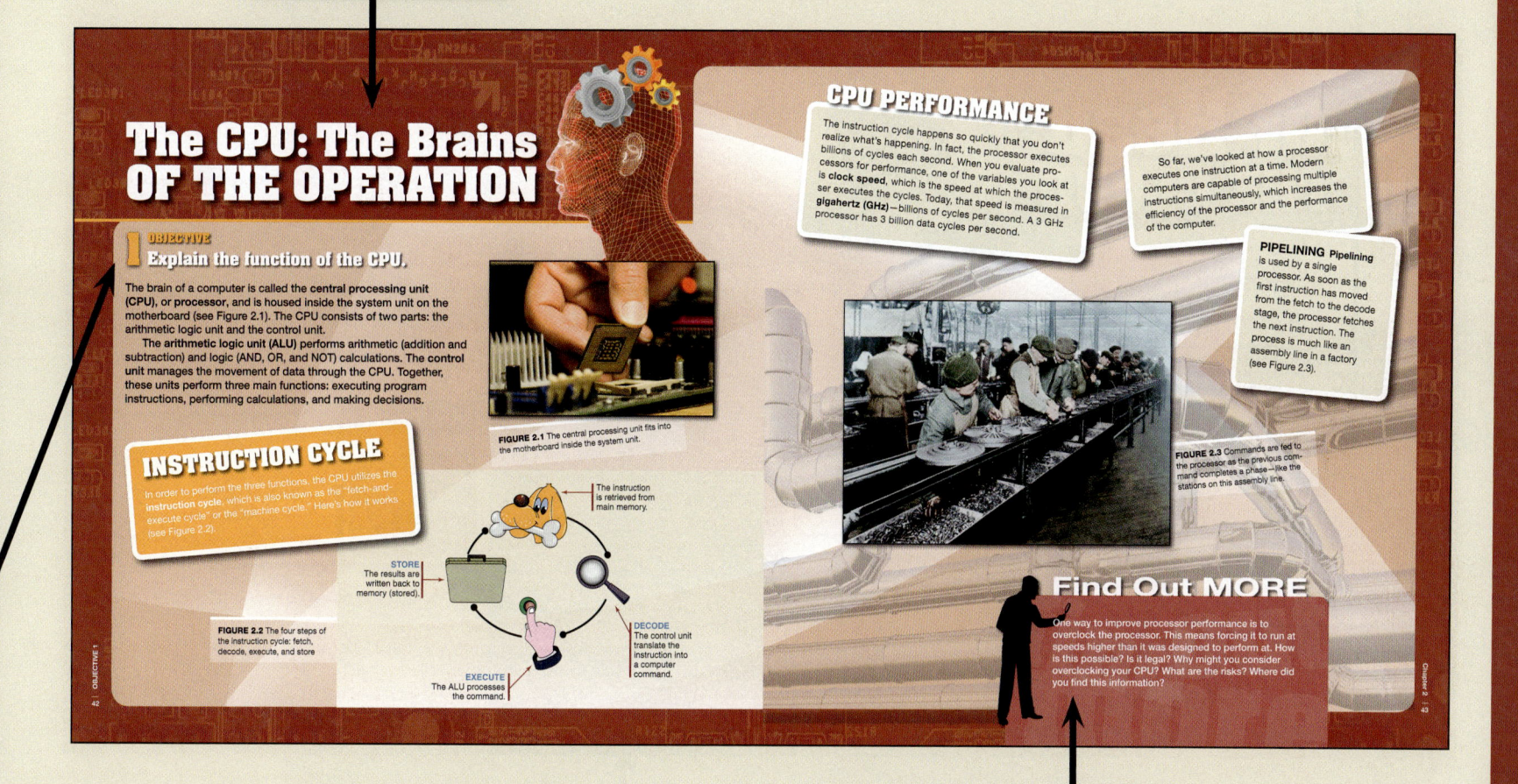

One way to improve processor performance is to overclock the processor. This means forcing it to run at speeds higher than it was designed to perform at. How is this possible? Is it legal? Why might you consider overclocking your CPU? What are the risks? Where did you find this information?

Find Out More—prompts for additional research on a given topic

> Images are used to represent concepts that help students learn and retain ideas

Your Head IN THE CLOUD

5 OBJECTIVE
Discuss the importance of cloud computing.

You may have heard the term "cloud computing." The cloud refers to the Internet. In this chapter, we've already discussed some online applications. Cloud computing takes the processing and storage off your desktop and business hardware and puts it in the cloud—on the Internet. As the need for storage, security, and collaboration has grown, cloud computing has become an important part of business and personal systems.

CLOUD COMPUTING

There are three types of services that can be delivered through the cloud: Infrastructure-as-a-Service, Platform-as-a-Service, and Software-as-a-Service. Together, these three services can provide a business with an integrated system for delivering applications and content using the cloud.

INFRASTRUCTURE-AS-A-SERVICE (IAAS) Infrastructure-as-a-Service (IaaS) means that a company uses servers in the cloud instead of purchasing and maintaining the hardware. This saves both hardware costs and in personnel. Even small companies that don't have the hardware can have sophisticated servers to house large databases, centralized document management, and security using and paying for just what they need.

PLATFORM-AS-A-SERVICE (PAAS) Platform-as-a-Service (PaaS) provides a programming environment to develop, test, and deploy custom Web applications. This gives businesses the ability to build applications without installing software on their computers. PaaS also makes collaboration easier and requires less programming knowledge. Three popular PaaS programs are: AppEngine from Google, Force.com from SalesForce, and Microsoft Azure Services Platform.

SOFTWARE-AS-A-SERVICE (SAAS) Software-as-a-Service (SaaS) means the delivery of applications over the Internet—or Web apps. This is the most visible to the user. Any time you open your browser to access your e-mail, upload photos, use Facebook, or share a file, you're using SaaS.

GREEN COMPUTING

ONLINE AND DOWNLOADED PROGRAMS VS. STORE-BOUGHT SOFTWARE

We've talked about your options for purchasing software from a convenience and cost standpoint, but there are also environmental issues to consider.

When you walk into a store and pick up software in a box or order from an online retailer and have the package shipped to you, there are several environmental impacts. First, there's the packaging material used to ship the product and product packaging. While cardboard and paper are recyclable, the EPA estimates that only about 70 percent of it is actually recycled. The rest of it—and other materials, such as plastic shrink-wrap and packing peanuts—ends up in our landfills. Then, there's the media inside the package. What happens to the CD or DVD when the software is no longer needed? It ends up in the trash—and into the landfill it goes. Finally, the transportation costs of shipping the product to you or to the store—air pollution, fuel consumption, and emission of greenhouse gases—all add up.

All these environmental impacts are eliminated using online applications or purchasing software online and downloading it to your computer. No packaging, no transportation costs, no obsolete media, and the convenience of having the software delivered to you on the spot make these alternatives the better choices for the environment.

SaaS has several advantages over installing software locally. Because SaaS is delivered on demand, it's available anytime from any computer with Internet access. In addition to the convenience, SaaS also eliminates the need to apply updates to local software installations. You use SaaS whenever you use Web mail. Using Web mail means that you don't download your e-mail messages to your personal computer. They're stored and accessed from a hosted e-mail server, providing backup and security for you, giving you access from anywhere, and eliminating the need to install and configure an e-mail program on your computer. Figure 5.28 illustrates some common SaaS applications you probably already use.

> E-mail
> Word processing
> Photo editing
> Facebook & Twitter
> Online file storage and sharing
> Collaboration

FIGURE 5.28 Commonly used SaaS applications

SaaS may not be a term most people use very often, but the services it provides are used every day by individuals and businesses alike. As cloud computing continues to mature, we'll find more and more of our computing up in the cloud.

Key Terms
cloud computing
Infrastructure-as-a-Service (IaaS)
Platform-as-a-Service (PaaS)
Software-as-a-Service (SaaS)

Running Project
Does your school use cloud computing (also known as above-campus computing)? If so, which services do you access from the cloud (for example: e-mail, apps)? Give two examples of your personal use of cloud computing.

3 Things You Need to Know
- The cloud is the Internet.
- Cloud computing uses hardware and software resources that are in the cloud instead of local.
- Cloud computing consists of three types of services: Infrastructure-as-a-Service (IaaS), Platform-as-a-Service (PaaS), and Software-as-a-Service (SaaS).

> Green Computing provides eco-friendly tips for using technology

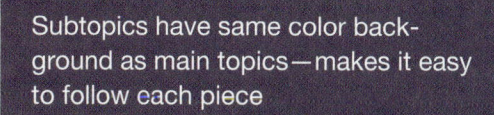

Subtopics have same color background as main topics—makes it easy to follow each piece

Ethics boxes provide thought-provoking questions about the use of technology

SOCIAL BOOKMARKING AND NEWS SITES

Social bookmarking sites allow you to save and share your bookmarks or favorites online. Delicious allows you to not only save and share your bookmarks online but to also search the bookmarks of others. It's a great way to quickly find out what other people find interesting and important right now. Figure 8.24 shows the Delicious Web page with the current list of most recently bookmarked sites. StumbleUpon discovers websites based on your interests. When you sign up, you indicate topics that interest you. Then, as you visit websites, you can click the StumbleUpon button to be taken to a similar site. You can click I like this to improve the pages you stumble onto.

Social news sites are different than traditional media news sites in that at least some of the content is submitted by users. It's interactive in a way that traditional media isn't. It's like having millions of friends sharing their finds with you. Content that's submitted more frequently or gets the most votes is promoted to the front page.

Relying on the wisdom of the crowd is much like asking your friends, family, and co-workers for advice. Did you enjoy the movie? Where should I go for the best ice cream? How do you change the oil in your car? Everybody's an expert in something. The Web just makes it easier for us to find and share that expertise with each other. But just a word of caution: Like anything else you read on the Web, be critical in your evaluation of the credibility and reliability of its author.

FIGURE 8.24 The Delicious Fresh Bookmarks tab shows the most recent items that users have bookmarked.

Two of the most popular social news sites are reddit and Digg. Digg doesn't publish any content but allows the community to submit content they discover on the Web and puts it in one place for everyone to see and to discuss. Slashdot, which focuses primarily on technology topics, does produce its content but also accepts submissions from its readers. Boudica is a social news site for women that works very much like Digg. Whatever your interests, there's probably a social news site for you.

ETHICS

Some people create multiple accounts on social bookmarking and news sites so they can promote their own content. For example, a blogger might create several accounts on Digg and use each one to Digg a blog post, thereby artificially raising its popularity on Digg and driving more traffic to it. This violates the Digg terms of use. But what if the blogger had all his friends and family members create accounts and Digg his post? Is it ethical? Does it violate the terms of use? Is it fair to other bloggers?

Key Terms
social bookmarking site
social news site
social review site
wiki

Running Project
Go to the Wikipedia home page. Locate the page Editorial administration, oversight, and management. How does Wikipedia assure that the content is correct? What procedures are in place to remove or correct mistakes?

3 Things You Need to Know
- Social media relies on the wisdom of the crowd rather than that of an expert.
- A wiki can be edited by anybody.
- Social bookmarking and news helps users find content that others recommend.

Articles end with the same elements: a list of key terms, a piece of the Running Project, the Things You Need to Know—takeaway points from the article

Visual Walkthrough | xvii

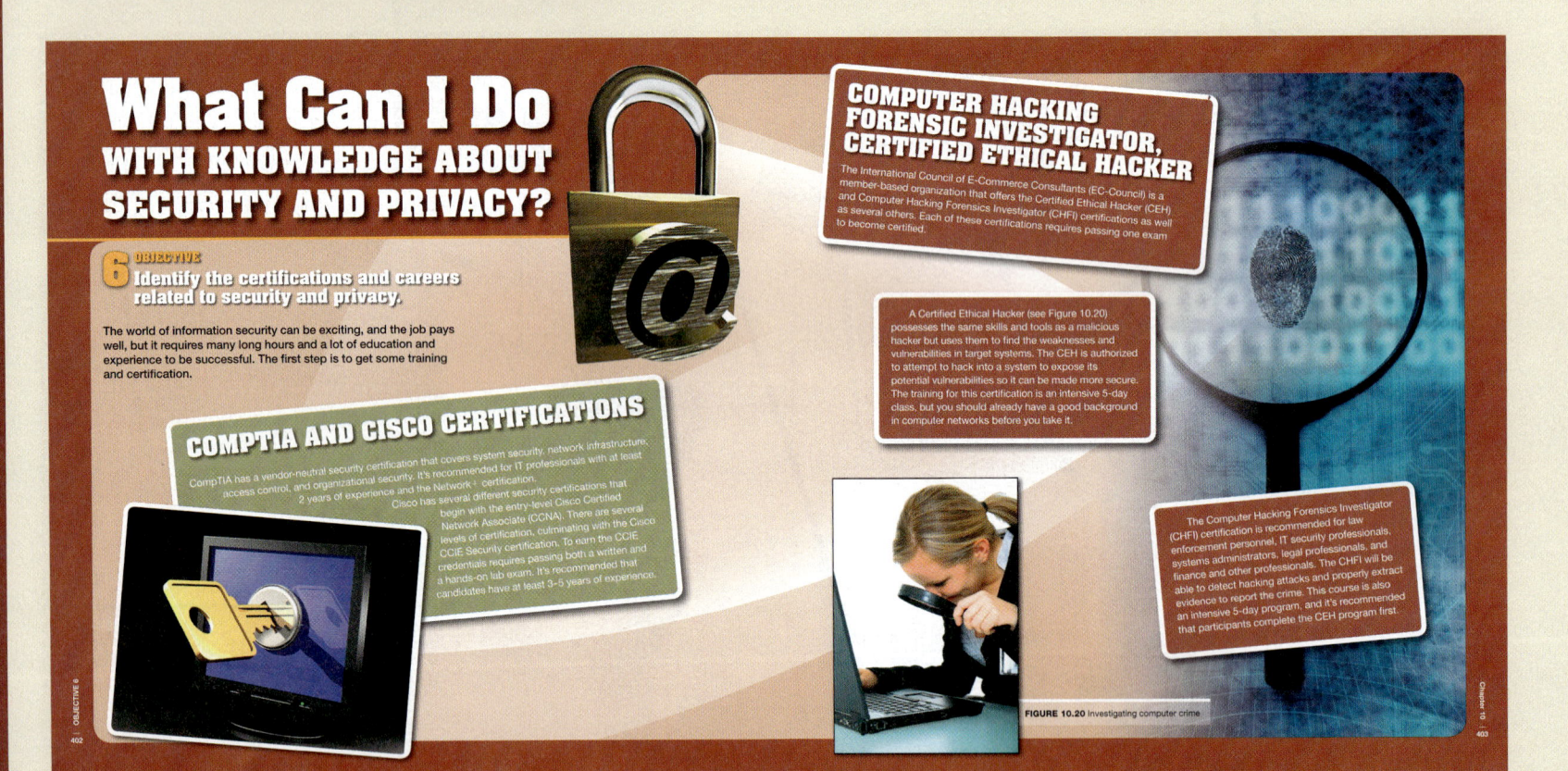

Certifications and Careers—the last article in every chapter provides interesting career options based on chapter content

What Can I Do WITH KNOWLEDGE ABOUT SECURITY AND PRIVACY?

6 OBJECTIVE Identify the certifications and careers related to security and privacy.

The world of information security can be exciting, and the job pays well, but it requires many long hours and a lot of education and experience to be successful. The first step is to get some training and certification.

COMPTIA AND CISCO CERTIFICATIONS

CompTIA has a vendor-neutral security certification that covers system security, network infrastructure, access control, and organizational security. It's recommended for IT professionals with at least 2 years of experience and the Network+ certification. Cisco has several different security certifications that begin with the entry-level Cisco Certified Network Associate (CCNA). There are several levels of certification, culminating with the Cisco CCIE Security certification. To earn the CCIE credentials requires passing both a written and a hands-on lab exam. It's recommended that candidates have at least 3–5 years of experience.

COMPUTER HACKING FORENSIC INVESTIGATOR, CERTIFIED ETHICAL HACKER

The International Council of E-Commerce Consultants (EC-Council) is a member-based organization that offers the Certified Ethical Hacker (CEH) and Computer Hacking Forensics Investigator (CHFI) certifications as well as several others. Each of these certifications requires passing one exam to become certified.

A Certified Ethical Hacker (see Figure 10.20) possesses the same skills and tools as a malicious hacker but uses them to find the weaknesses and vulnerabilities in target systems. The CEH is authorized to attempt to hack into a system to expose its potential vulnerabilities so it can be made more secure. The training for this certification is an intensive 5-day class, but you should already have a good background in computer networks before you take it.

The Computer Hacking Forensics Investigator (CHFI) certification is recommended for law enforcement personnel, IT security professionals, systems administrators, legal professionals, and finance and other professionals. The CHFI will be able to detect hacking attacks and properly extract evidence to report the crime. This course is also an intensive 5-day program, and it's recommended that participants complete the CEH program first.

FIGURE 10.20 Investigating computer crime.

How To projects—step-by-step project with visual instructions to create something personal and unique

HOW TO Create an Avatar

Most social websites allow you to upload a picture for your profile, but what if you don't want to use an actual image of yourself? You can use a website like WeeWorld to create an avatar that you can use instead.

1 Go to **weeworld.com** and click *Create your WeeMee*.

2 Select your body features and click *Get dressed now*.

3 Dress your avatar using the menu on the left and choosing items from the middle of the screen.

4 Click on *More stuff* and add accessories and change your environment. Click *Save me now!*

5 Register your WeeMee.

FILL OUT THE REGISTRATION FORM.

The End of Chapter content ranges from traditional review exercises to hands-on projects that have students working independently, collaboratively, and online

Mind maps—visual outlines of the chapter content, organized by objectives. Helps students organize and remember the information they learned

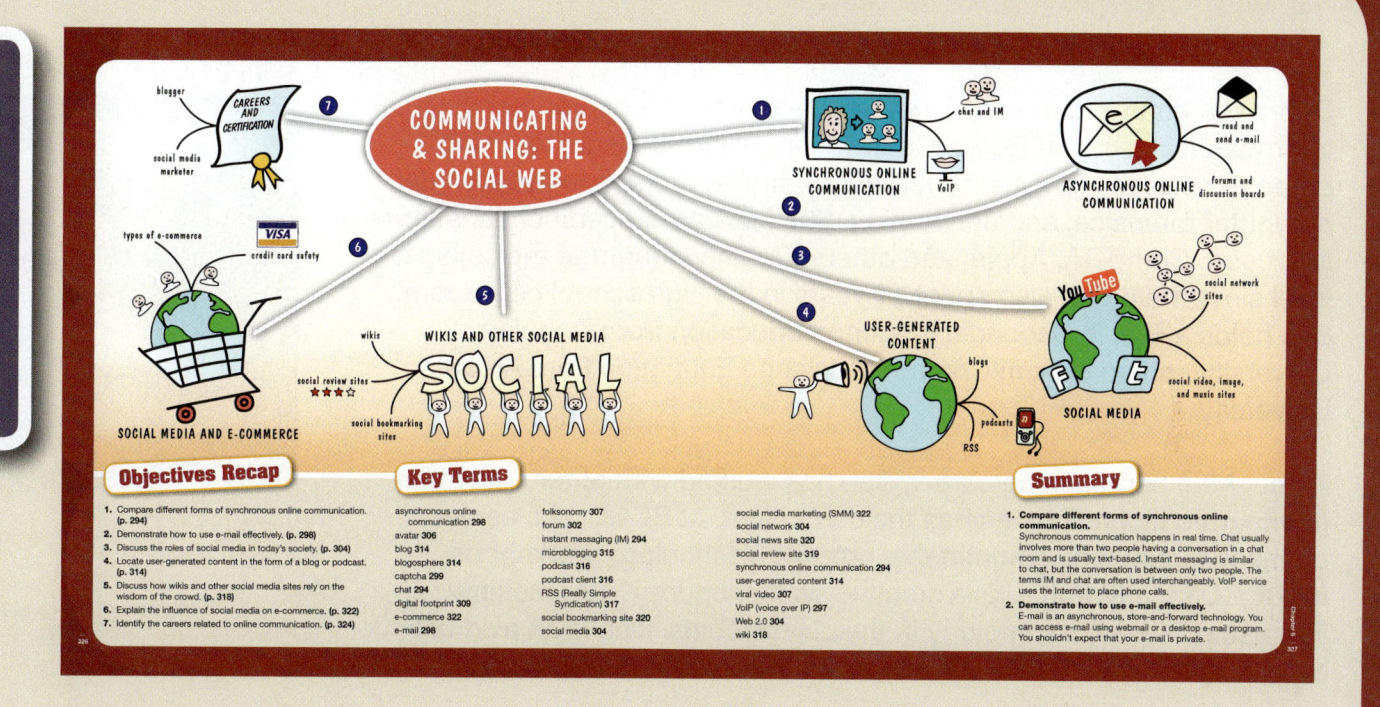

Instructor Materials

- Annotated Instructor's Edition
  - Chapter tabs with article and special feature summaries, as well as a correlation guide between chapter objectives and end of chapter projects
  - Social Media tabs for each chapter with Facebook, Twitter, Blogger and polleverywhere.com assignments
- An Instructors Resource CD:
  - PowerPoints
  - End of Chapter solutions
  - Testbanks

Student Materials

- Facebook site for the latest updates in technology
- Student CD with data files for End of Chapter projects
- Companion Website
  - Online Study Guide
  - Jeopardy games
  - Crosswords

Visual Walkthrough | xxi

About the Author

Debra Geoghan is currently an associate professor of computer and information science at Bucks County Community College, teaching computer classes ranging from basic computer literacy to cybercrime, computer forensics, and networking. She has earned certifications from Microsoft, CompTIA, Apple, and others. Deb has taught at the college level since 1996 and also spent 11 years in the high school classroom. She holds a B.S. in Secondary Science Education from Temple University and an M.A. in Computer Science Education from Arcadia University.

Throughout her teaching career, Deb has worked with other educators to integrate technology across the curriculum. At BCCC, she serves on many technology committees, presents technology workshops for BCCC faculty, and runs a summer workshop for K-12 teachers interested in using technology in their classrooms. Deb is an avid user of technology, which has earned her the nickname "gadget lady."

Dedication

This project would not have been possible without the help and support of many people. I cannot express how grateful I am to all of you. Thank you.

My team at Pearson—Stephanie, Virginia, Michael, Linda, Mike, and everyone else: you have been amazing, helping to bring my vision to reality and teaching me so much along the way.

My colleagues and students at Bucks County Community College: for your suggestions and encouragement throughout this process.

And most importantly—my husband and sons for your patience, help, and love—even when it meant taking a photo "right this minute", or reading a chapter when you wanted to be doing something else, or missing me while I was away. I couldn't have done this without your love and support.

And finally my dad—who taught me to love technology and not be afraid to try new things. I miss you and love you daddy.

Reviewers

We would like to thank the following people for their work on *Visualizing Technology*. We couldn't publish the book without their contributions.

Karen Allen   Bunker Hill Community College
Beverly Amer   Northern Arizona University
Michael Beddoes   Salt Lake Community College
Leilani Benoit   New Mexico State University
Gina Bowers   Harrisburg Area Community College
Linda Collins   Mesa Community College
Fred D'Angelo   Pima Community College
Robert Devoe Peterson   Fresno City College
Hedy Fossenkemper   Paradise Valley Community College
Rachelle Hall   Glendale Community College
Terri Helfand   Chaffey College
Ilga Higbee   Black Hawk College
Kay Johnson   Community College of Rhode Island
Darrel Karbginsky   Chemeketa Community College
Susan Katz   University of Bridgeport
Sherry Kersey   Hillsborough Community College
Ellen Kessler   Harrisburg Area Community College
Kate Legrand   Broward Community College
Mike Lehrfeld   Brevard Community College
Jian Lin   Eastern Connecticut State University
Nicole Lytle   California State University, San Bernadino
Peggy Menna   Community College of Rhode Island
Deborah Meyer   Saint Louis Community College, Forest Park
Pam Silvers   Asheville-Buncombe Technical Community College
Will Smith   Tulsa Community College
Lynne Stuhr   Trident Technical College
Ann Taff   Tulsa Community College
Jim Taggart   Atlantic Cape Community College
Michelle Vlaich Lee   Greenville Technical College

CHAPTER 1
What Is a Computer

Running Project

In this project, you'll explore computers that are used in everyday life. Look for instructions as you complete each article. For most, there's a series of questions for you to research. At the conclusion of the chapter, you're asked to submit your responses to the questions raised.

OBJECTIVES

1. Explain the functions of a computer. (p. 4)
2. Describe the evolution of computer hardware, and explain the importance of Moore's Law. (p. 6)
3. List the various types and characteristics of personal computers. (p. 10)
4. List the various types and characteristics of multiuser computers. (p. 14)
5. Give examples of other computing devices. (p. 18)
6. List several ways ergonomics can improve the comfort and safety of a computer user. (p. 22)
7. Explain the terms "ubiquitous computing" and "convergence." (p. 24)
8. Identify the certifications and careers related to computers. (p. 28)

Become our friend on Facebook

IN THIS CHAPTER

If you've gone grocery shopping, put gas in your car, watched the weather report on TV, or used a microwave oven today, then you've interacted with a computer. Most of us use computers every day, often without even realizing it. Computers have become so commonplace that we don't even consider them computers. In this chapter, we discuss what a computer is and look at the development of computers in the last few centuries.

What Does a Computer Do?

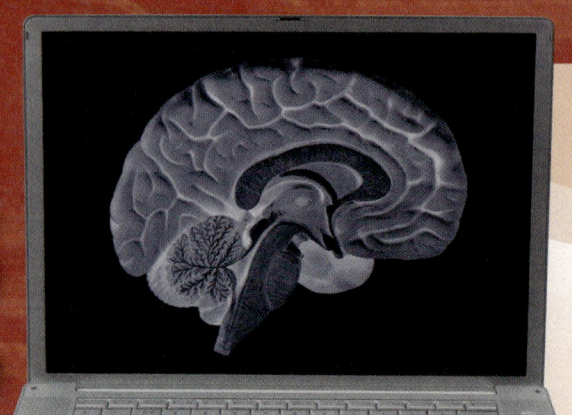

OBJECTIVE 1
Explain the functions of a computer.

A **computer** is a programmable machine that converts raw data into useful information. A toaster can never be anything more than a toaster—it has one function—but a computer can be a calculator, a media center, a communications center, and so much more. The ability to change its programming is what distinguishes a computer from any other machine.

NECESSITY IS THE MOTHER OF INVENTION

The original computers were people, not machines, and the mathematical tables they computed tended to be full of errors. The technical and scientific advancements of the Industrial Revolution led to a growing need for this type of hand-calculated information, and the first mechanical computers were developed to automate the tedious work of computing such things as tide charts and navigation tables.

In the early 19th century, mathematician Charles Babbage designed a machine called an Analytical Engine, a mechanical computer that could be programmed using punched cards, which were originally developed by Joseph Marie Jacquard as part of the Jacquard loom to manufacture textiles with complex patterns. Had the Analytical Engine actually been built, it would have been the first mechanical computer, but the technology simply didn't exist at the time to build the machine. In his 1864 book *Passages from the Life of a Philosopher*, Babbage wrote: "The whole of the development and operations of analysis are now capable of being executed by machinery. As soon as an Analytical Engine exists, it will necessarily guide the future course of science."

Mathematician Ada Lovelace (see Figure 1.1), a contemporary of Babbage, wrote a program for the Analytical Engine to calculate a series of Bernoulli numbers. Because of her efforts, she's considered by many to be the first computer programmer. Lovelace never tested the program because there were no machines capable of running it; however, when run on a computer today, the program yields the correct mathematical results. In 1979, the Ada computer language was named in her honor.

FIGURE 1.1 Augusta Ada King, Countess of Lovelace

STORAGE: The raw data is stored temporarily until it can be processed. The processed information is stored for later retrieval.

INPUT: Data is collected from customers who submit a form on a website.

OUTPUT: The processed data—now information—is output as reports and charts that managers can use to help make decisions.

PROCESSING: The data is then manipulated, or processed, so it can be used to evaluate the customer's needs.

THE INFORMATION PROCESSING CYCLE

Computers convert data into information using the **information processing cycle (IPC)**. The four steps of the IPC are input, processing, storage, and output. Raw **data** is entered into the system during the input stage. The data is processed, or manipulated, to create useful **information**. The information is then stored for later retrieval and is returned to the user in the output stage. An example of how this works is illustrated in Figure 1.2.

FIGURE 1.2 The information processing cycle converts raw data, perhaps collected from a form on a website, into useful information.

As amazing as it may seem, it took nearly a century after Babbage designed his Analytical Engine before the first working mechanical computers were built. From that point, it took only about 40 years to go from those first-generation machines to the current fourth-generation designs. Since the first working computers became a reality, the computer has become an integral part of our modern lives.

Key Terms

computer

data

information

information processing cycle (IPC)

Running Project

Many developments of the Industrial Revolution helped pave the way for modern computers. In this article, we discussed the Jacquard loom. Use the Internet to find out how the following people also contributed: George Boole, Vannevar Bush, Nikola Tesla, and Gottfried Wilhelm Leibniz.

3 Things You Need to Know

- Computers are programmable machines.
- The four steps of the information processing cycle (IPC) are: input, processing, storage, output.
- The IPC converts raw data into useful information.

A Brief History OF COMPUTERS

2 OBJECTIVE
Describe the evolution of computer hardware, and explain the importance of Moore's Law.

In this article, we look at the evolution of computers in the past century—from the first-generation massive machines of the 1930s and 1940s to the modern fourth-generation devices—and how Moore's Law has predicted the exponential growth of technology.

HISTORY OF COMPUTERS

Computers have come a long way since Babbage and Lovelace. Between the mid-19th and mid-20th centuries, the Industrial Revolution gave way to the Information Age. Since that time, technology has grown at an amazing rate. The pace of technology change is growing exponentially—faster than it ever has before.

FIRST-GENERATION COMPUTERS
During the 1930s and 1940s, several electromechanical and electronic computers were built. These first-generation computers were massive in size and used vacuum tubes and manual switches. **Vacuum tubes**, which resemble incandescent light bulbs, give off a lot of heat and are notoriously unreliable. Some of the most important first-generation computers include the Z1 and Z3 built in Germany; the Colossus machines in the United Kingdom; and the Atanasoff-Berry Computer (ABC), the Harvard Mark 1, ENIAC, and UNIVAC in the United States (see Figure 1.3).

FIGURE 1.3 Important first-generation computers

DATE	COMPUTER	ORIGIN	CREATOR	DESCRIPTION
1936–41	Z1–Z3	Germany	Konrad Zuse	The Z1 through Z3 were mechanical, programmable computers. Working in isolation in Germany, Konrad Zuse didn't receive the support of the Nazi government, and his computers were destroyed during the war.
1944	Colossus	United Kingdom	Tommy Flowers	Used by code-breakers to translate encrypted German messages, these computers were destroyed after the war and kept secret until the 1970s.
1942	Atanasoff-Berry Computer (ABC)	United States	Professor John Atanasoff and graduate student Clifford Berry at Iowa State College	The ABC was never fully functional, but Atanasoff won a patent dispute against John Mauchly (ENIAC), declaring Atanasoff the inventor of the electronic digital computer.
1944	Harvard Mark 1	United States	Designed by Howard Aiken and programmed by Grace Hopper at Harvard University	Used by the U.S. Navy for gunnery and ballistic calculations until 1959
1946	ENIAC	United States	Presper Eckert and John Mauchly at the University of Pennsylvania	The first working, digital, general-purpose computer
1951	UNIVAC	United States	Eckert/Mauchly	The world's first commercially available computer; famous for predicting the outcome of the 1952 presidential election

ENIAC (Electronic Numerical Integrator and Computer), built at the University of Pennsylvania from 1943–1946, was the first working, digital, general-purpose computer. It used about 18,000 vacuum tubes, weighed almost 30 tons, and occupied about 1,800 square feet. Originally created to calculate artillery firing tables, ENIAC wasn't actually completed until after the war ended. Fortunately, the computer was capable of being reprogrammed to solve a range of other problems, such as atomic energy calculations, weather predictions, and wind-tunnel design. The programming was done by manipulating switches and took six programmers several days to complete (see Figure 1.4)

FIGURE 1.4 Two women are shown operating the ENIAC's main control panel while the machine was still located at the Moore School. U.S. Army photo from the archives of the ARL Technical Library. Left: Betty Jennings (Mrs. Bartik). Right: Frances Bilas (Mrs. Spence)

SECOND-GENERATION COMPUTERS

Transistors, tiny electronic switches, were invented in 1947 and led to second-generation computers in the 1950s and 1960s. The use of transistors in place of vacuum tubes allowed these newer computers to be more powerful, smaller, and more reliable. Equally important, they could be reprogrammed in far less time. Figure 1.5 illustrates the difference between the size of a vacuum tube and a transistor.

FIGURE 1.5 The vacuum tube and the transistor

THIRD-GENERATION COMPUTERS

Developed in the 1960s, **integrated circuits** (see Figure 1.6) are silicon chips that contain large numbers of tiny transistors. Third-generation computers using integrated circuits were even smaller, faster, and more reliable than their predecessors, although there was much overlap between second- and third-generation technologies in the 1960s. The Apollo Guidance Computer, used in the moon landing missions, was originally designed using transistors, but over time, the design was modified to use integrated circuits instead. The 2000 Nobel Prize in physics was awarded for the invention of the integrated circuit.

FIGURE 1.6 Two integrated circuits on a circuit board

FOURTH-GENERATION COMPUTERS

The integrated circuit made the development of the microprocessor possible in the 1970s. A **microprocessor** is the chip that contains the central processing unit (CPU) of a computer. The first microprocessor was developed in 1971 and was as powerful as ENIAC. Today's personal computers use microprocessors and are considered fourth-generation computers. Microprocessors can be found in everything from alarm clocks to automobiles to refrigerators.

MOORE'S LAW

In 1965, Intel co-founder Gordon Moore observed that the number of transistors that could be placed on an integrated circuit had doubled roughly every 2 years. **Moore's Law** predicted this exponential growth would continue. The current trend is closer to doubling every 18 months and is expected to continue for another 10 to 20 years (see Figure 1.7). The increase in the capabilities of integrated circuits directly affects the processing speed and storage capacity of modern electronic devices.

Moore stated in a 1996 article: "More than anything, once something like this gets established, it becomes more or less a self-fulfilling prophecy. The Semiconductor Industry Association puts out a technology road map, which continues this [generational improvement] every three years. Everyone in the industry recognizes that if you don't stay on essentially that curve they will fall behind. So it sort of drives itself." Thus, Moore's Law really became a technology plan that guides the industry.

Find Out MORE

Play the integrated circuit game at www.Nobelprize.org/educational_games/physics/integrated_circuit to learn more about this invention. Who invented the integrated circuit? Where might you still find a vacuum tube today? How did the invention of the transistor affect the radio? What's the significance of the hand-held calculator?

Over the last several decades, the end of Moore's Law has been predicted. Each time, new technological advances have kept it going. Moore himself admits that exponential growth can't continue forever, but there's no denying the impact his law has had on the pace of technology in the last 45 years (see Figure 1.8).

In less than a century, computers have gone from massive, unreliable, and costly machines to being an integral part of almost everything we do. As technology has improved, the size and costs have dropped as the speed, power, and reliability have grown. Today, the chip inside your cell phone has more processing power than that first microprocessor developed in 1971. Technology that was science fiction just a few decades ago is now commonplace.

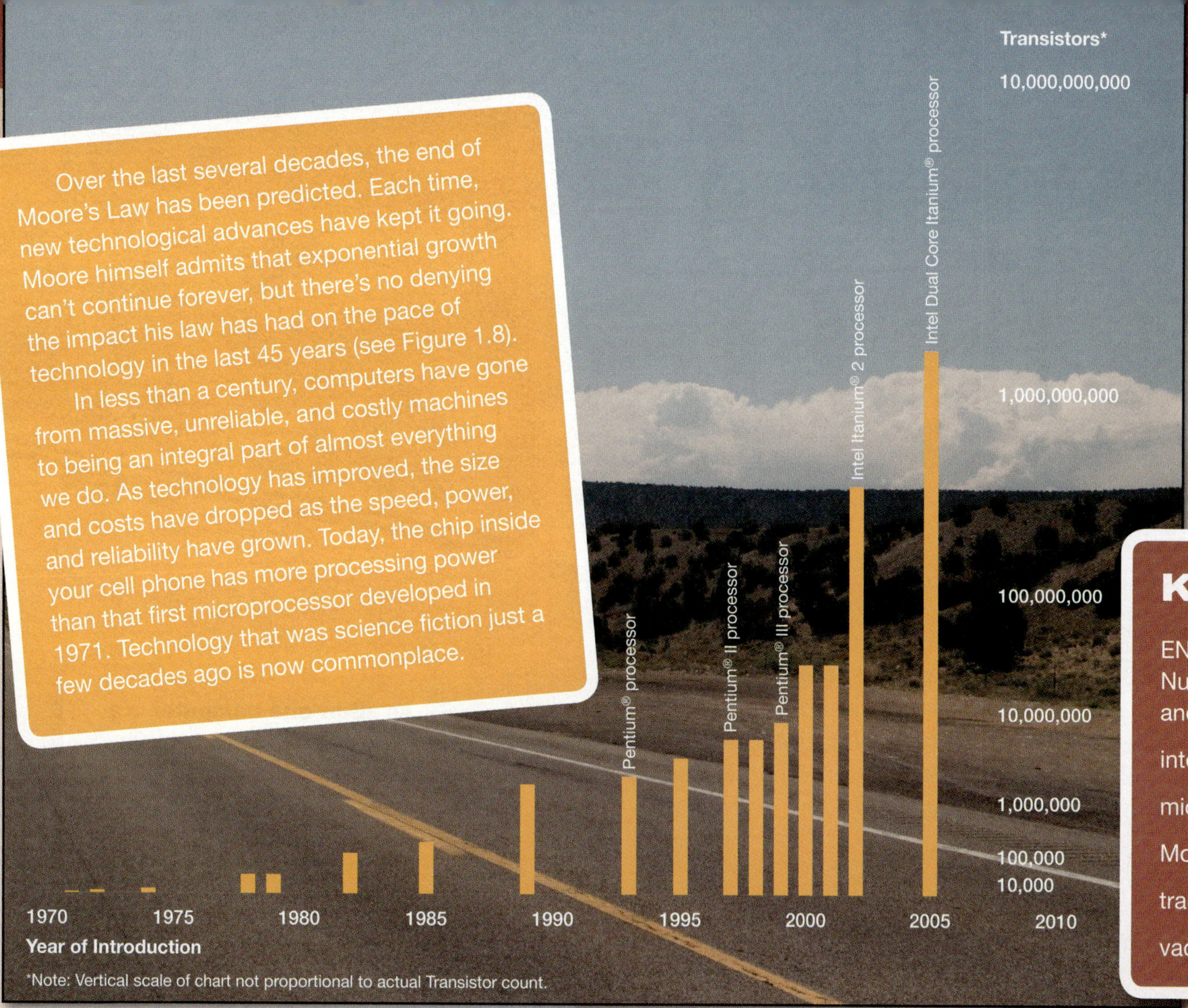

FIGURE 1.7 Moore's Law graphically represented

FIGURE 1.8 In 2005, to celebrate its 40th anniversary, Intel released some interesting statistics that illustrate Moore's Law.

Because electricity travels a shorter distance in a smaller transistor, smaller transistors mean faster chips. It would take you about 25,000 years to turn a light switch on and off 1.5 trillion times, but Intel has developed transistors that can switch on and off that many times each second.

In 1978, a commercial flight between New York and Paris cost around $900 and took seven hours. If the principles of Moore's Law had been applied to the airline industry the way they have to the semiconductor industry since 1978, that flight would now cost about a penny and take less than one second.

Key Terms

ENIAC (Electronic Numerical Integrator and Computer)

integrated circuit

microprocessor

Moore's Law

transistor

vacuum tube

Running Project

Use the Internet to look up vacuum tubes and transistors. What are some of the places they're still used today?

5 Things You Need to Know

- First-generation computers used vacuum tubes.
- Second-generation computers used transistors.
- Third-generation computers used integrated circuits (chips).
- Fourth-generation computers use microprocessors.
- Moore's Law states that the number of transistors that can be placed on an integrated circuit doubles roughly every 2 years.

Let's Get PERSONAL

3 OBJECTIVE
List the various types and characteristics of personal computers.

A **personal computer (PC)** is a small microprocessor-based computer designed to be used by one person at a time. Today, the term **PC** usually refers to a computer running a Windows operating system; however, Macintosh computers and those running Linux operating systems are also personal computers.

DESKTOP COMPUTERS

Desktop computers are designed to sit on a user's desk. They range in price from under $500 for basic personal systems to thousands of dollars for cutting-edge machines that can be used for video editing, gaming, and number crunching. Desktop computers offer the most speed, power, and upgradability for the lowest cost. The term **workstation** is used in a business environment to refer to a high-end desktop computer or one that's attached to a network.

An **all-in-one computer** is a compact desktop computer with an integrated monitor (see Figure 1.9). Some systems have a touch-screen monitor and are wall-mountable. All-in-ones save desktop real estate but may be difficult to upgrade because of their small size. They are popular in places where space is at a premium, such as emergency rooms, bank teller windows, and business cubicles.

FIGURE 1.9 An all-in-one desktop computer with the components mounted behind the monitor is popular in settings in which desktop space is limited.

NOTEBOOK COMPUTERS

Notebook, or laptop, computers are portable personal computers. Today's notebook computers rival desktops in power and storage capacity—but at a price. A notebook can cost about twice as much as a comparable desktop system. However, the cost of all computers has come down dramatically, and notebook computers are becoming more popular as a result. Once used primarily by business travelers, notebooks are now common on college campuses, in living rooms, and in coffee shops. Modern notebook computers typically come with built-in wireless networking capabilities, webcams, and bright widescreen displays. Desktop replacements are high-end notebooks with large screens and powerful processors.

A **tablet PC** is a type of notebook computer that has a screen that can swivel to fold into what resembles a notepad or tablet. They include a special digital pen or stylus that allows the user to write directly on the screen. Tablet PCs are useful for taking notes or drawing diagrams and for making information such as sales catalogs portable. Windows 7 includes a feature called Windows Touch, which offers multi-touch capability. Newer all-in-ones and tablets that support multi-touch allow you to interact with your computer using not just one finger but two or even four!

The newest type of notebook computer is called a **netbook**. These lightweight, inexpensive computers are designed primarily for Internet access. Netbooks have built-in wireless capabilities but have small screens and offer limited computing power and storage. With prices starting under $200, netbooks are becoming popular quickly (see Figure 1.10).

FIGURE 1.10 A large desktop replacement notebook and a tiny netbook are two types of notebook computers.

MAC OR PC?

You've seen the commercials on TV and perhaps have used different types of computers at work or in school. In the personal computer market, there are two main types of PCs to choose from: Macs and PCs. So, the question is: What's the difference between the two, and which one should you choose? All the types of hardware discussed in this chapter apply to both types of computers. The primary difference between them is the operating system they run. We'll discuss operating systems in detail in another chapter.

Mac computers are built by Apple and run the Mac OS X Snow Leopard operating system. Using a program called Boot Camp that's included with Snow Leopard, users can also run Windows. Macs have a reputation for being secure, stable, and fun. They come with a variety of useful programs already installed and are very user-friendly. Macs are often used in creative businesses, such as advertising and graphic design.

FIGURE 1.11 Comparing Mac and PC computers

MAC

PROS
- Easy to set up and use
- Great multimedia capabilities
- More secure and stable
- iLife software suite included

CONS
- More expensive than a comparable PC
- Less software availability

PC

PROS
- Less expensive for similar capabilities
- Preferred platform in most businesses

CONS
- Prone to security problems and virus attacks
- Problem with operating system (Windows) stability

Personal computers, designed to be used by one person at a time, have become so commonplace that even in the tough economy of 2008, it was estimated that U.S. sales topped 302.2 million units, and roughly 80 percent of U.S. households had at least one personal computer.

PCs can be built by any number of companies, including Dell, Hewlett-Packard, Acer, and Toshiba. PCs that run some version of Windows or Linux constitute over 90 percent of the U.S. market share. Because they're produced by many manufacturers, PCs are available in numerous models, configurations, and price ranges. They also have a much larger selection of software applications available.

The type of computer you choose depends on many factors, including personal preferences, the types of software you need to run, compatibility with school or work computers, and, of course, cost.

Figure 1.11 highlights some of the features of both types of computers.

Key Terms

all-in-one computer

desktop computer

Mac

netbook

notebook

PC (personal computer)

tablet PC

workstation

Running Project

It's hard to imagine a job that doesn't require a working knowledge of personal computers. Look up the term "computer literacy." Use several different websites to get an idea of what this term means. Then, write up a description of computer literacy for the career that you plan to pursue.

5 Things You Need to Know

- Desktop computers give you the most bang for your buck.
- All-in-one computers are smaller but less upgradable desktops.
- Notebook computers are portable and have dramatically dropped in price.
- Tablet PCs and netbooks are specialized notebook computers.
- The primary difference between a Mac and a PC is the operating system, not the hardware.

Multiuser Computers— MORE POWER TO YOU

4 OBJECTIVE
List the various types and characteristics of multiuser computers.

Multiuser computers are systems that allow multiple, simultaneous users to connect to them. The advantages to multiuser systems include centralized resources and security. Multiuser computers are also more powerful than personal computers.

SERVERS

Servers are computers that provide services, such as Internet access, e-mail, or file and print services, to client systems. They range in size and cost from very small servers costing a few hundred dollars to massive enterprise servers costing hundreds of thousands of dollars (see Figure 1.12).

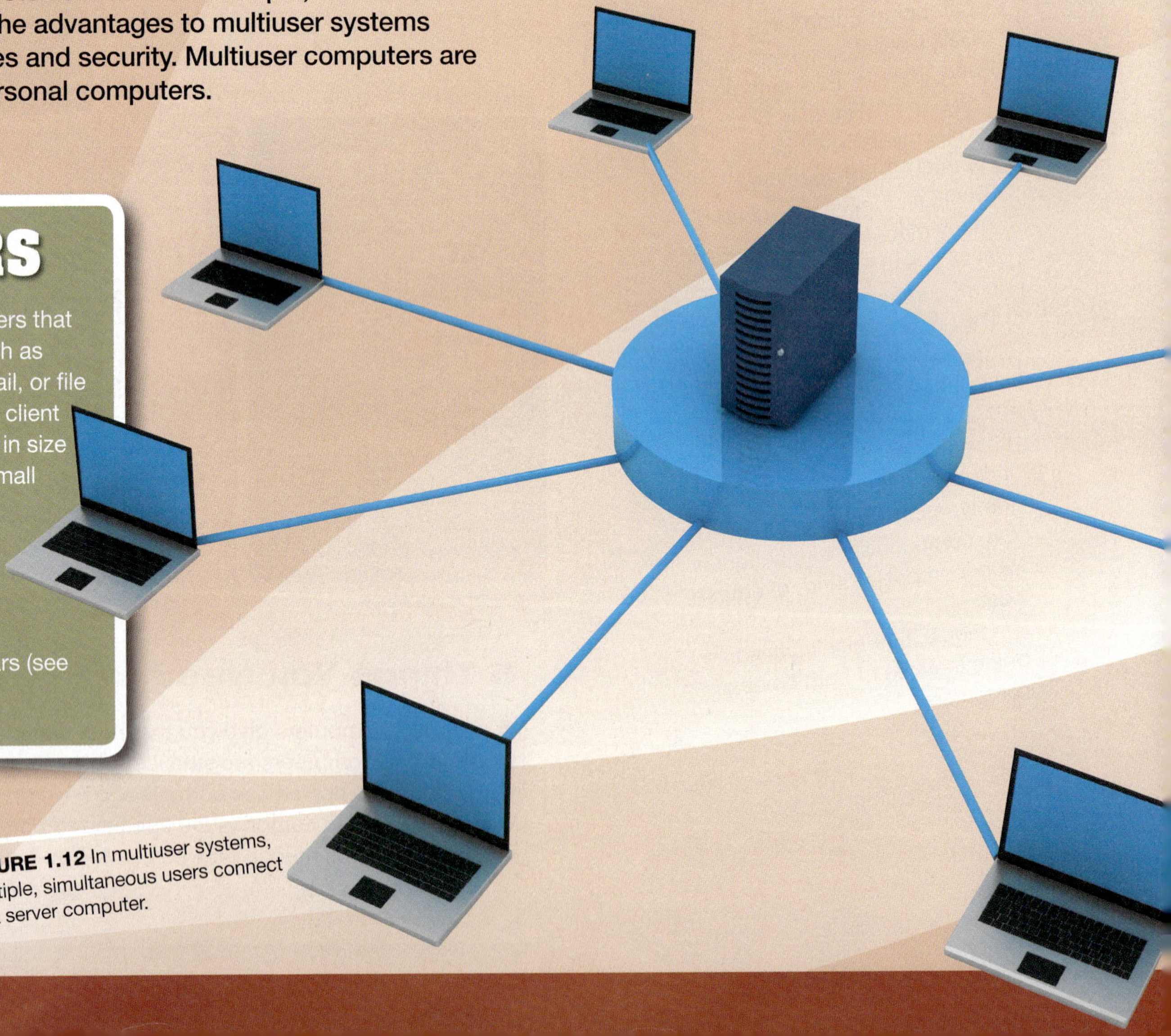

FIGURE 1.12 In multiuser systems, multiple, simultaneous users connect to a server computer.

The smallest multiuser computers are called **minicomputers**. Users connect to minicomputers via dumb terminals, which have no processing capabilities of their own. Today, minicomputers have been largely replaced by midrange servers that users connect to via personal computers called **clients**. Midrange servers can be used to perform complex calculations, store customer information and transactions, or host an e-mail system for an organization. They can support hundreds of simultaneous users and are scalable, allowing for growth as a company's needs change.

Mainframes are large computers that can perform millions of transactions in a day. These are most commonly found in businesses that have massive amounts of data or transactions to process, such as banks and insurance companies. Mainframe computers have largely been replaced by enterprise servers, and the terms are sometimes used synonymously (see Figure 1.13). These systems allow thousands of users to utilize the system concurrently.

FIGURE 1.13 Enterprise servers can allow thousands of simultaneous users and perform millions of transactions every day.

SUPERCOMPUTERS

Supercomputers are very expensive computer systems that are used to perform complex mathematical calculations, such as those used in weather forecasting and medical research. Designed to perform a limited number of tasks as quickly as possible, supercomputers can consist of a single computer with multiple processors or a group of computers that work together. The world's top supercomputers can be found at major universities and research institutes around the world. Figure 1.14 provides a sampling from the listing of the top 500 supercomputers, which is located at **www.top500.org**.

FIGURE 1.14 Key supercomputers

RESEARCH INSTITUTE	LOCATION	USES
Los Alamos National Security Laboratory	United States	• Nuclear deterrents • Energy-climate nexus • Protecting against weapons of mass destruction
Shanghai Supercomputer Center	China	• Weather forecast • Oil exploration • Bio-medical • Gene research • Aviation and aeronautics
NASA Advanced Supercomputing (NAS) Division	United States	• Critical NASA missions • Scientific discoveries for the benefit of humankind www.nas.nasa.gov
CERN European Organization for Nuclear Research	Switzerland	• Physics—the fundamental particles www.cern.ch

DISTRIBUTED AND GRID COMPUTING

Distributed computing distributes the processing of a task across a group of computers. This can be done on a fairly small scale, using a few computers in one location (known as **grid computing**) or on a much larger scale. Some of these projects rely on **volunteer computing**, using the processing power of hundreds or thousands of personal computers. At **boinc.berkeley.edu**, a volunteer can choose from a variety of projects to join.

A volunteer interested in astronomy might join SETI@home. One of the first volunteer computing projects, SETI@home was launched in 1999 and has close to 200,000 volunteers. A volunteer downloads and installs a program that runs as a screensaver when the computer is idle. This allows SETI to utilize the processing abilities of the individual's computer without having to pay for processing time and without compromising the user's ability to complete his or her own projects. The SETI screensaver is actually a complex piece of software that downloads and analyzes radio telescope data to Search for Extraterrestrial Intelligence (see Figure 1.15).

FIGURE 1.15 The SETI@home screen gives you a picture of what your computer's doing.

Multiuser systems allow users to leverage the power of computers that far exceed what a PC can do. The ability to centrally manage information and security and to distribute the processing across multiple systems has given the scientific and business communities the power to solve many of our most pressing problems in an extremely short amount of time.

Key Terms

client
distributed computing
grid computing
mainframe
minicomputer
multiuser computer
server
supercomputer
volunteer computing

Running Project

Select one supercomputer from the list in this chapter, and use the Internet to find out more about the type of work it is used for. Write two or three paragraphs highlighting some of its achievements.

5 Things You Need to Know

- Servers provide services such as file and print sharing and e-mail to client computers.
- Minicomputers have largely been replaced by mid-sized servers that can support hundreds of concurrent users.
- Mainframes/enterprise servers can process millions of transactions in a day.
- Supercomputers perform complex mathematical calculations for such things as weather forecasting and medical research.
- Distributed computing distributes processing tasks across multiple computers.

It's Not Your FATHER'S DESKTOP ANYMORE

5 OBJECTIVE
Give examples of other computing devices.

Today, the term "computer" no longer refers only to those desktop devices used for office work. We carry computers with us everywhere we go. In some countries, mobile devices have become the primary computing devices that many people have access to.

HANDHELD AND MOBILE DEVICES

Handheld and **mobile devices** are portable computers used for business and entertainment and come in many different shapes and sizes—from pocket-sized PDAs to heart-rate monitors that you wear on your wrist. Some of these devices serve specialized functions, such as GPS navigation, while others, such as smartphones, are more general-purpose devices. These devices have more features and capabilities with every new model introduced, and costs continue to drop.

PDAS AND SMARTPHONES Mobile devices such as PDAs (personal digital assistants) and smartphones are pocket-sized computers we carry with us wherever we go. They may include such features as Internet and e-mail access, built-in cameras, GPS and mapping tools, and even the ability to edit documents. Also referred to as **handhelds**, these devices are useful when carrying a regular notebook computer isn't practical. Once primarily the tool of the business professional, devices such as the Apple iPhone and Palm Pre have made themselves indispensible to rest of us.

GPS AND WEARABLES

Commonly found on cell phones today, another familiar handheld device is a GPS unit. Originally built by the military, **GPS (global positioning system)** consists of 24 satellites (see Figure 1.16) that transmit signals that can be picked up by a GPS receiver on the ground and used to determine its current location, time, and velocity through triangulation of the signals. Today, GPS is used in cars, boats, and, yes, cell phones.

FIGURE 1.17 Modern technology is incorporated into the equipment worn by soldiers.

Computers designed to be worn on the body are called **wearables**. Today, wearable computers are used for health monitoring, communications, military operations, and entertainment (see Figure 1.17).

FIGURE 1.16 The Global Positioning System (GPS) is a satellite-based navigation system composed of a network of 24 satellites placed into orbit by the U.S. Department of Defense.

Find Out MORE

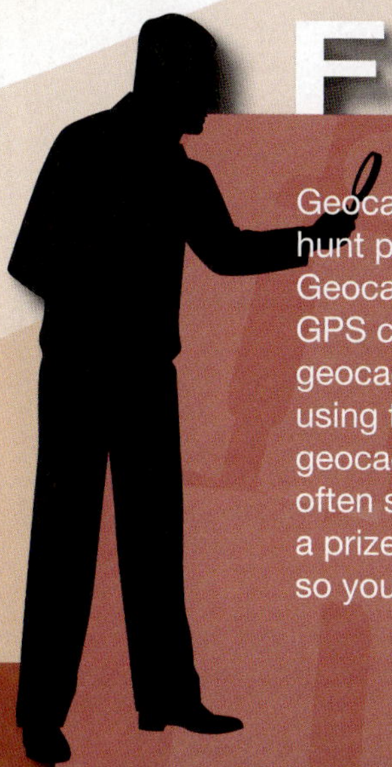

Geocaching is an electronic scavenger hunt played around the world. Geocachers hide geocaches and post GPS coordinates on the Internet. Other geocachers can then find geocaches using their own GPS devices. The geocaches have logbooks to sign and often small prizes. Geocachers that find a prize leave something else in return, so you never know what you'll find!

Use the Internet to find geocaches near you. What website(s) did you use? How many geocaches are there near you? Are they in an urban or rural area? How many are there globally? What is "Cache In Trash Out"? What are Geocoins and Travel Bugs?

Chapter 1 | 19

VIDEO GAME SYSTEMS

A **video game system** is a computer that's designed primarily to play games. The first arcade video games were released in the early 1970s, and video game systems for the home soon followed. Magnavox released its Odyssey game console in 1972. It was programmed to play 12 different games. Atari released a home version of PONG (see Figure 1.18) for the 1975 holiday season, sold exclusively through Sears. For many people, video game consoles were the first computers they had in their homes.

FIGURE 1.18 Atari released a home version of PONG, an electronic ping-pong game, in 1975. It became one of the hottest gifts of the year.

Today's systems are considered seventh-generation video games and have high-end processing and graphic capabilities, the ability to play movies and music, enable online game play, and even allow users to browse the Internet. Game consoles, such as Microsoft Xbox 360 and Sony Playstation 3, have built-in hard-drives, can play DVDs, and offer high-definition resolution. Nintendo's Wii is less powerful and less expensive than either the Xbox 360 or the Playstation 3, but it's also more popular. The Wii has unique motion-sensing controllers, giving players new gameplay experiences and interactivity. The Wii has reached out to nontraditional markets, such as senior citizens and suburban moms, by offering such unique games as bowling, tennis, Wii Fit, and Brain Age. All three systems offer some level of backward-compatibility with older systems.

FIGURE 1.19 Kids young and old play video games today.

Handheld video games, such as the Nintendo DS and DSi and Playstation Portable (PSP), allow you to take your games wherever you go. Newer versions even allow you to view photos and listen to music. You can download and watch movies on the PSP. The DSi has two built-in cameras for taking pictures and built-in photo-editing software. Both systems also include Internet capabilities (see Figure 1.19).

Key Terms

GPS (global positioning system)

handheld

mobile device

video game system

wearable

Running Project

Video game systems aren't just for entertainment anymore. Use the Internet to find out how medical students are using video games to learn to be better doctors. What are some of the medical schools using such systems? How are they used? How do professors and students feel about them?

4 Things You Need to Know
- PDAs and smartphones are handheld, mobile computers.
- GPS is a satellite-based navigation system.
- Wearables are computers designed to be worn on the body.
- Today's video game consoles are seventh-generation systems with high-end graphics and processing.

Comfort and SAFETY

6 OBJECTIVE
List several ways ergonomics can improve the comfort and safety of a computer user.

Using a computer for hours on end can literally be a pain in the neck. How you design your workspace can have a big impact on your comfort and health. It definitely requires some research and effort on your part—but it's well worth it.

ERGONOMICS

Ergonomics is the study of the relationship between workers and their workspaces. An improperly set up workspace can affect your health, comfort, and productivity. Ergonomic design creates a work environment designed to reduce illnesses and musculoskeletal disorders. The furniture you use, the lighting in the room, and the position of your equipment all impact your work environment.

Ergonomics should be personalized to you. If you share a workspace with others, make sure it's adjustable. Your basic goals should be to keep your body in a neutral body position, without twisting or turning to reach or see your screen. You should not need to lean forward, and your feet should be flat on the ground or on a footrest. Your monitor should be at or below eye level so you don't need to tilt your neck to see it, and the lighting shouldn't cause glare on your screen. The keyboard and mouse should be positioned so your arms are in a relaxed position (see Figure 1.20). One important step that many people forget is to take regular breaks to stretch and move around. Whether you're writing a report for school, doing your income taxes, or playing a video game, following ergonomic design principles will help you work more comfortably and reduce strain on your body.

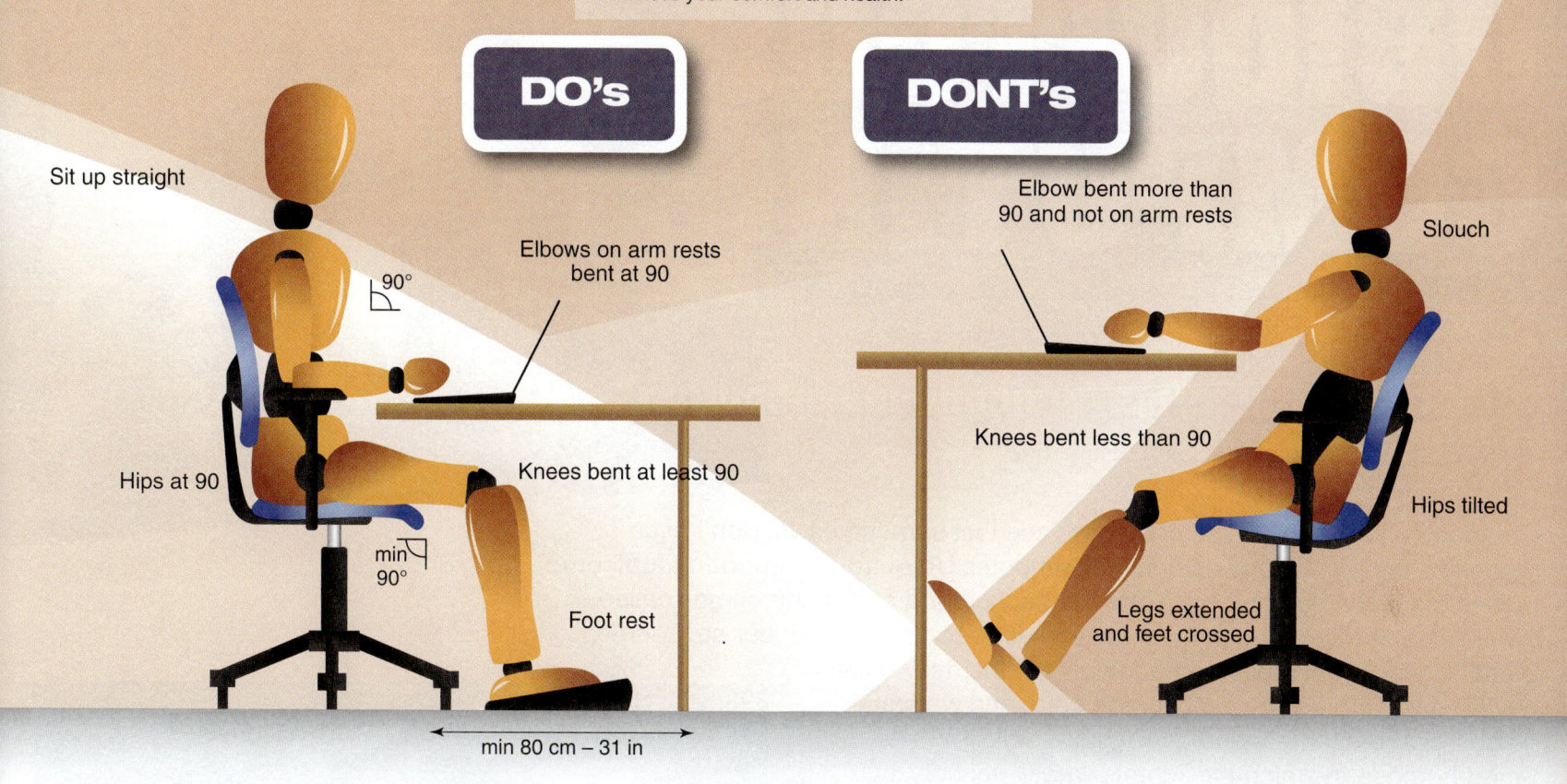

FIGURE 1.20 A properly designed workspace enhances your comfort and health.

DO's

- Sit up straight
- Elbows on arm rests bent at 90
- 90°
- Hips at 90
- Knees bent at least 90
- min 90°
- Foot rest
- min 80 cm – 31 in

DONT's

- Elbow bent more than 90 and not on arm rests
- Slouch
- Knees bent less than 90
- Hips tilted
- Legs extended and feet crossed

Key Term
ergonomics

Running Project
Ergonomics is big business. Research ergonomically designed desk chairs. What are some of the features they have in common? What is the price range for these chairs? What features do the more expensive chairs include? Do you think they're worth the money?

2 Things You Need to Know
- Ergonomics is your relationship to your workspace.
- A poorly designed workspace can cause health problems and make you less productive.

Computers are Everywhere: UBIQUITOUS COMPUTING

7 OBJECTIVE
Explain the terms "ubiquitous computing" and "convergence."

Computers have become so commonplace that sometimes we don't even recognize the technology as being a computer. **Ubiquitous computing (ubicomp)** means the technology recedes into the background and is sometimes called invisible computing. The technology actually becomes part of our environment. Digital signage has replaced traditional billboards, we can pay for gas with the wave of a credit card, and we can upload pictures to Facebook from our mobile phones. Smart homes—in which the lights, climate, security, and entertainment are automated—are a glimpse into the future of ubiquitous computing.

EMBEDDED COMPUTERS

Embedded computers are present at the gasoline pump, in home appliances, in traffic lights, and at the self-checkout line at the supermarket (see Figure 1.21). Computer chips regulate the flow of gas in your car and the temperature of water in your dishwasher. All serve to make our modern lives easier. These specialized computers have become so common that it would be hard for us to imagine living without them, yet we don't really even think of them as computers.

FIGURE 1.21 Embedded computers can be found in many objects that we come in contact with every day.

CONVERGENCE

The **convergence** or integration of technology on multifunction devices, such as smartphones, has accustomed us to carrying technology with us. We no longer need to carry around several different devices because these devices now incorporate cell phones, personal information management tools, e-mail, Web browsing, document editing, MP3 players, cameras, GPS, games, and more (see Figure 1.22). In many parts of the world, there are more mobile phones than people, and this has resulted in the rapid development of technologies such as mobile payment systems. In many cases, mobile phones have replaced personal computers.

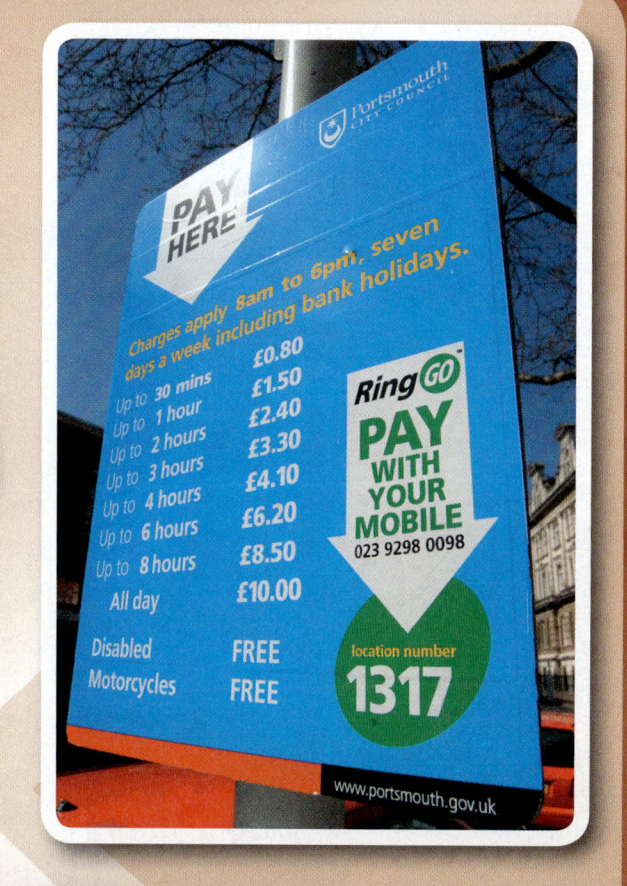

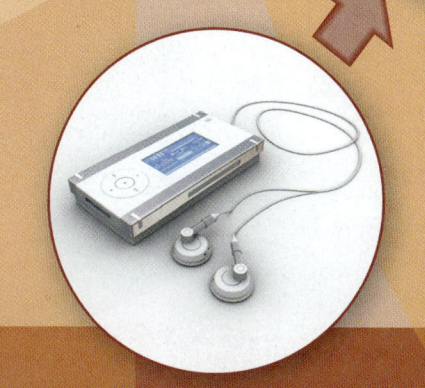

FIGURE 1.22 The convergence of technology on a smartphone

GREEN COMPUTING

SMART HOMES

The efficient and eco-friendly use of computers and other electronics is called **green computing**. Smart homes and smart appliances help save energy and, as a result, are good for both the environment and your pocketbook.

Smart homes use home automation to control lighting, heating and cooling, security, entertainment, and appliances in a home. The system can be programmed to turn various components on and off at set times to maximize energy efficiency. So, the heat can turn up, and the house can be warm right before you get home from work while not wasting the energy to keep it warm all day while you're away. If you're away on vacation or have to work late, a smart home can be remotely activated by phone or over the Internet. Some utility companies offer lower rates during off-peak hours, so programming your dishwasher and other appliances to run during these times can save you money and help energy utility companies better manage the power grid, potentially reducing the need for new power plants.

So, you can't make your home a smart home overnight. No worries! There are some small steps you can take without investing in a whole smart home system. Try installing a programmable thermostat, putting lights on timers or motion sensors, and running appliances during off-peak hours.

Smart appliances go one step further. They plug into the smart grid and can actually monitor signals from the power company. When the electric grid system is stressed, appliances can react by cutting back on their power consumption.

As we rely more and more on technology, we come to expect it to just work. We take for granted that the traffic light timing will protect us, the microwave won't burn our food, GPS will guide us to our destination, and the ATM will dispense our funds only to us. Ubiquitous computing is only in its infancy, and we've already made it an integral part of our lives. It will be interesting to see where ubicomp takes us in the not-too-distant future.

Key Terms

convergence

embedded computer

green computing

ubiquitous computing (ubicomp)

Running Project

Science fiction meets science fact? Many of our modern devices were envisioned by famous science fiction writers, such as Gene Roddenberry. Use the Internet to research some of the Star Trek technologies that do exist today. Write a paragraph about at least three of them.

3 Things You Need to Know

- Ubiquitous computing is technology that's invisible to us.
- Embedded computers are found in everything from traffic lights to dishwashers.
- The convergence of technology allows us to carry a single multifunction device that can do the job of many separate devices.

What Can I Do WITH KNOWLEDGE ABOUT COMPUTERS?

8 OBJECTIVE
Identify the certifications and careers related to computers.

Computers are everywhere, and being computer fluent will help you in most career paths you might take. What's your career goal, and how can knowledge of technology help you? In this article, we look at just a few careers and an entry-level certification where that knowledge is important.

BIOINFORMATICS

Computers have become integral in almost every modern career. Nowhere is this more evident than in the field of biology. **Bioinformatics** is the application of information technology to the field of biology. Computers are used to analyze data, predict how molecules will behave, and maintain and search massive databases of information (Figure 1.23). The rapid growth of biological information over the past few decades has created a demand for new technologies and people that know how to use them. This field requires at least a four-year degree. If you have a strong interest in science and technology, bioinformatics might be a good career choice for you.

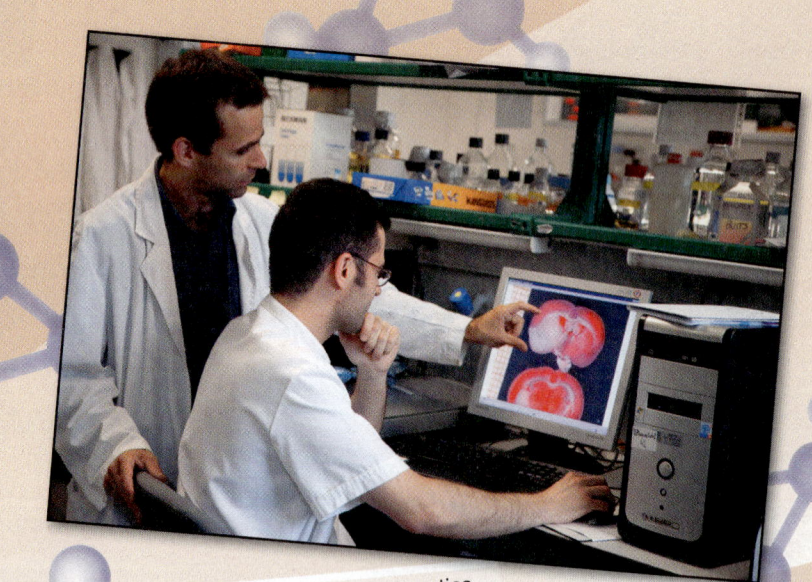

FIGURE 1.23 Bioinformatics includes genome mapping.

AUTO MECHANIC

Since the early 1980s, cars have used computer chips to regulate emissions, fuel injection, and timing. Modern cars have GPS units, entertainment units, automatic parallel parking systems, and many other computer-controlled features. One of the main diagnostic tools of an auto mechanic plugs into a car's onboard diagnostics port (OBD) to read the data from the car's computer systems (see Figure 1.24). There are even chip upgrades that can enhance your car's performance. A good auto mechanic needs to be comfortable with new technologies, and ongoing training is a must.

FIGURE 1.24 An auto mechanic needs a solid understanding of the computers that control a modern car.

MCDST

A good way to show a prospective employer your skills is to earn a certification. The Microsoft Certified Desktop Support Technician (MCDST) certification is a technical certification that includes both the technical skills necessary to support and troubleshoot desktop computers and the soft skills needed to educate and communicate effectively with the users of those systems. The certification requires you to pass two certification exams and is geared toward someone with only 6 to 12 months of work experience.

VOLUNTEER

It's a catch-22—you can't get a job because they require experience, but you can't get experience because you can't get a job. If you're looking for a computer-related job, one way to get some experience is to volunteer, perhaps at your school, library, or local community organization. Volunteer experience not only looks good on your résumé but can also help you make contacts and connections that may serve as references and may even result in a job offer down the line—not to mention the good feeling you get from helping others.

No matter what field you eventually choose, knowledge of computers is sure to be helpful. As ubiquitous as computers have become in the past 20 years, imagine how much more important they'll become in the future.

Key Term
bioinformatics

HOW TO Create Screenshots of Your Desktop Using the Windows Snipping Tool

Throughout this book, you're asked to provide screenshots of the work you've done. This is quite easy to do and is also useful in other situations. For example, it's very helpful for providing someone else with directions on how to do something or for keeping a record of an error message that appears on your screen.

Windows 7 includes a nifty little utility called the Snipping Tool. To access it, type **snip** in the search box in the Start menu, and under Programs, click *Snipping Tool*. This opens the Snipping Tool window.

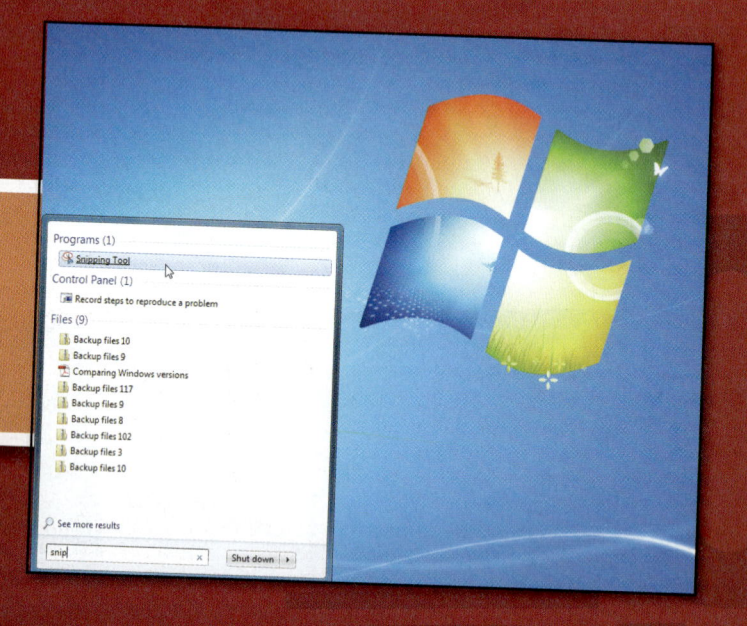

Click the arrow next to New to set the options for the snip, or capture, you wish to take:
Free-form Snip: Allows you to draw the boundaries around an object for a snip
Rectangular Snip: Allows you to draw a rectangle around an object for a snip
Window Snip: Captures a selected window for a snip
Full-screen Snip: Captures the whole screen for a snip

30 | HOW TO

Drag the mouse around the object for a Free-form or Rectangular Snip. Click the object for a Window or Full-screen Snip.

You can save your screenshots, e-mail them, paste them into documents, and even annotate and highlight them using the buttons on the Snipping Tool toolbar.

1. Open your word processor and type your name and date in the document.
2. Insert your student CD and open the Chapter 01 folder. Double-click the file ch01_friend to open it.
3. Open the Start menu and type **snip** in the search box. Start the Windows Snipping Tool from the Start menu search results.
4. In the Snipping Tool window, click the drop-down arrow next to New and select *Free-form snip*.
5. Draw a line around the dog's head with the Snipping Tool scissors. Paste the snip into your document and type **Free-form Snip** under it.
6. Use the same procedure to capture a rectangular snip of the dog's head, paste it into your document, and type **Rectangular Snip** under it.
7. Use the Snipping Tool to capture a Window Snip and a Full-screen snip of the dog, pasting and labeling each in your document.
8. In a paragraph, describe the difference between each of the snips you took. Save the file as **Lastname_Firstname_ch01_HowTo**, and submit your file as directed by your instructor.

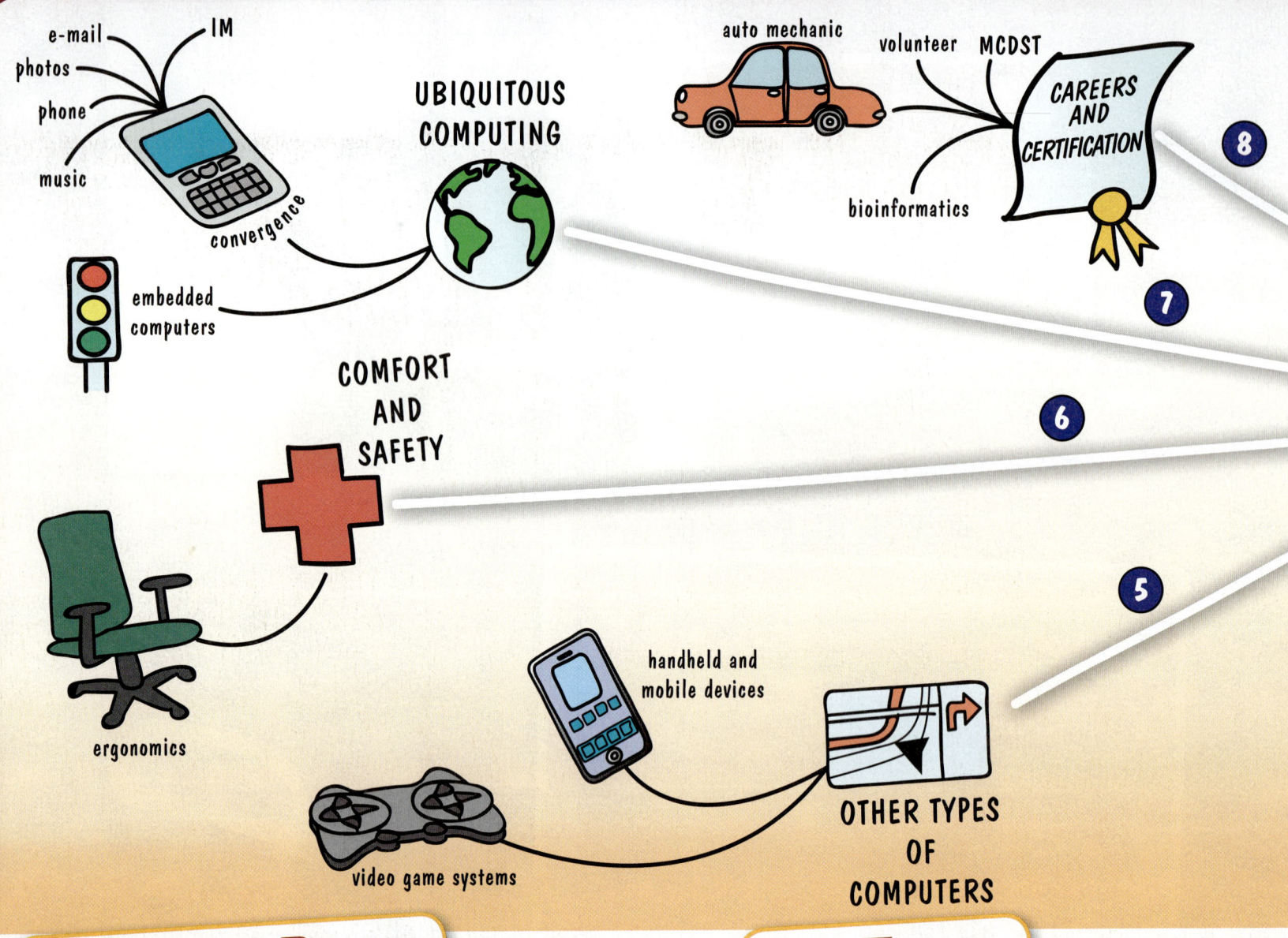

Objectives Recap

1. Explain the functions of a computer. (p. 4)
2. Describe the evolution of computer hardware, and explain the importance of Moore's Law. (p. 6)
3. List the various types and characteristics of personal computers. (p. 10)
4. List the various types and characteristics of multiuser computers. (p. 14)
5. Give examples of other computing devices. (p. 18)
6. List several ways ergonomics can improve the comfort and safety of a computer user. (p. 22)
7. Explain the terms "ubiquitous computing" and "convergence." (p. 24)
8. Identify the certifications and careers related to computers. (p. 28)

Key Terms

all-in-one computer **10**
bioinformatics **28**
client **15**
computer **4**
convergence **25**
data **5**
desktop computer **10**
distributed computing **16**
embedded computer **24**
ENIAC (Electronic Numerical Integrator and Computer) **7**
ergonomics **22**
GPS (global positioning system) **19**
green computing **26**
grid computing **16**
handheld **18**
information **5**
information processing cycle (IPC) **5**
integrated circuit **8**
Mac **12**
mainframe **15**

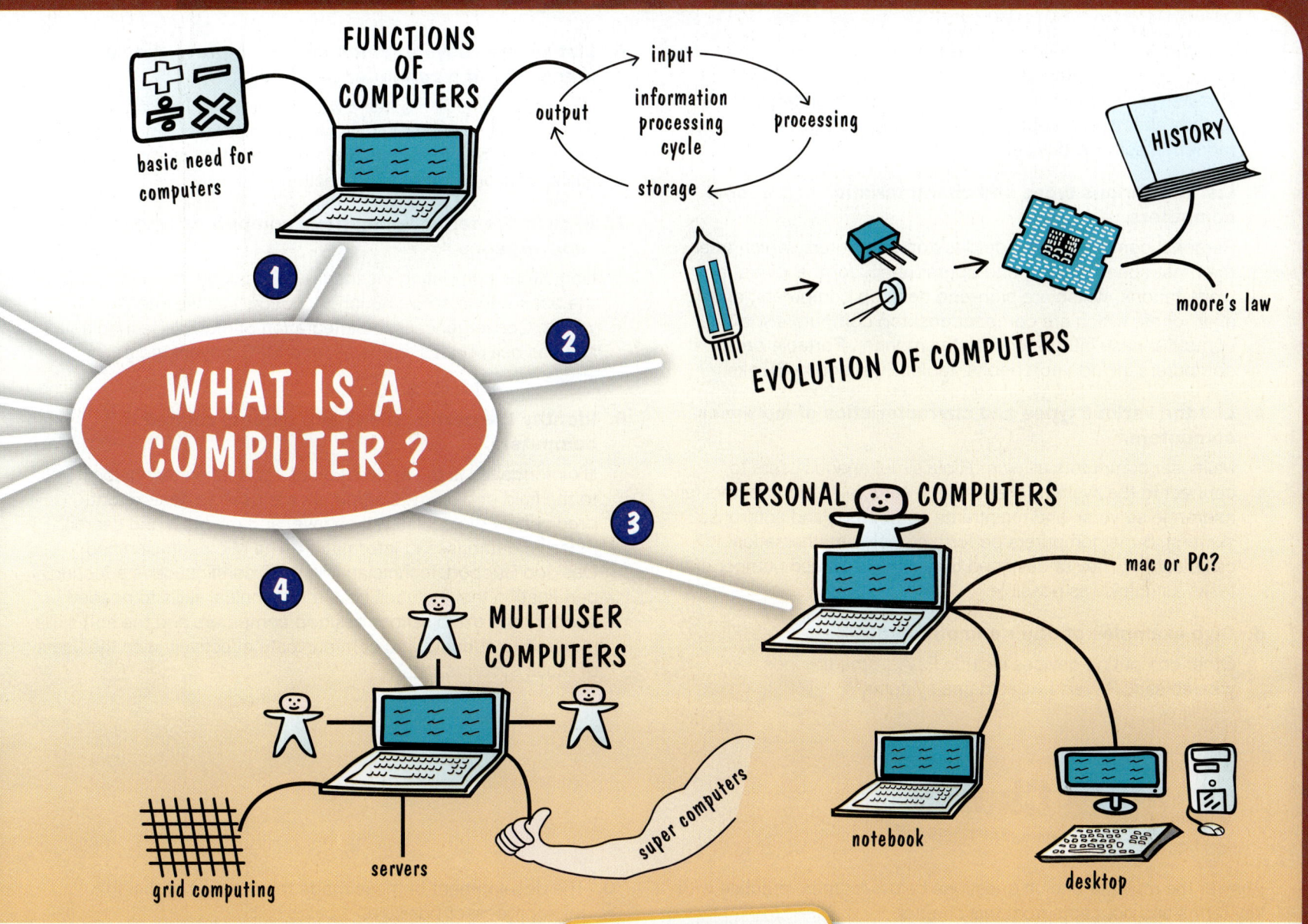

WHAT IS A COMPUTER?

1. FUNCTIONS OF COMPUTERS
- basic need for computers
- information processing cycle: input → processing → storage → output

2. EVOLUTION OF COMPUTERS
- HISTORY
- moore's law

3. PERSONAL COMPUTERS
- mac or PC?
- notebook
- desktop

4. MULTIUSER COMPUTERS
- grid computing
- servers
- super computers

Summary

microprocessor 8
minicomputer 15
mobile device 18
Moore's Law 8
multiuser computer 14
netbook 11
notebook 11
PC 10
personal computer 10
server 14
supercomputer 16
tablet PC 11
transistor 8
ubiquitous computing (ubicomp) 24
vacuum tube 6
video game system 20
volunteer computing 16
wearable 19
workstation 10

1. Explain the functions of a computer.

A computer is a device that converts raw data into information using the information processing cycle. Computers can be programmed to perform different tasks.

2. Describe the evolution of computer hardware, and explain the importance of Moore's Law.

The earliest computers used vacuum tubes, which are inefficient, large, and prone to failure. Second-generation computers used transistors, which are small electric switches. Third-generation computers used integrated circuits, which are chips that contain multiple tiny transistors. Fourth-generation computers use microprocessors.

Moore's Law states that the number of transistors that can be placed on an integrated circuit has doubled roughly every 2 years. The increase in the capabilities of integrated circuits directly affects the processing speed and storage capacity of modern electronic devices.

3. **List the various types and characteristics of personal computers.**

   Personal computers include desktop computers, which offer the most speed, power, and upgradability for the lowest cost; workstations, which are high-end desktop computers; and all-in-ones, which are compact desktop computers with the computer case integrated into the monitor. Portable personal computers include notebooks, tablet PCs, and netbooks.

4. **List the various types and characteristics of multiuser computers.**

   Multiuser computers allow multiple simultaneous users to connect to the system. They include servers, minicomputers (and midrange servers), and mainframe computers (and enterprise servers). Supercomputers perform complex mathematical calculations. They're designed to perform a limited number of tasks as quickly as possible.

5. **Give examples of other computing devices.**

   Other computing devices include PDAs, smartphones, wearables, GPS, and video game systems.

6. **List several ways ergonomics can improve the comfort and safety of a computer user.**

   Ergonomic design creates a work environment configured to reduce illnesses and musculoskeletal disorders. The furniture you use, the lighting in the room, and the position of your equipment all impact your comfort and health.

7. **Explain the terms "ubiquitous computing" and "convergence."**

   Ubiquitous computing means the technology recedes into the background so we no longer notice it as we interact with it. Convergence is the integration of multiple technologies, such as cell phones, cameras, and MP3 players, on a single device.

8. **Identify the certifications and careers related to computers.**

   Bioinformatics is the application of information technology to the field of biology. Computers are used to analyze data, predict how molecules will behave, and maintain and search massive databases of information. The Microsoft Certified Desktop Support Technician (MCDST) certification is a technical certification that includes both the technical skills to needed support and troubleshoot desktop computers and the soft skills required to educate and communicate effectively with the users of those systems.

Multiple Choice

Answer the multiple-choice questions below for more practice with key terms and concepts from this chapter.

1. _____ is considered to be the first computer programmer.
   a. Charles Babbage
   b. Ada Lovelace
   c. Grace Hopper
   d. John Atanasoff

2. Originally created to calculate artillery firing tables, _____ was the first working, digital, general-purpose computer.
   a. Analytical Engine
   b. Colossus
   c. Mark 1
   d. ENIAC

3. The development of these made the creation of the microprocessor possible.
   a. Vacuum tubes
   b. Transistors
   c. Integrated circuits
   d. Silicons

4. Today's personal computers are considered _____ -generation computers.
   a. first
   b. second
   c. third
   d. fourth

5. Which of the following is a high-end desktop computer in a business environment?
   a. Minicomputer
   b. All-in-one
   c. Mainframe
   • d. Workstation

6. What type of portable computer allows a user to write directly on the screen?
   • a. Tablet PC
   b. Netbook
   c. Laptop
   d. Desktop replacement

7. Personal computers that connect to servers are known as
   a. dumb terminals.
   • b. minicomputers.
   c. clients.
   d. mainframes.

8. _____ share(s) the processing of a task across multiple computer systems.
   • a. Distributed computing
   b. Mainframe
   c. Enterprise servers
   d. Multitasking

9. Computers in traffic lights, at supermarket checkouts, and in appliances are examples of _____ computers.
   a. personal
   b. portable
   c. ubiquitous
   • d. embedded

10. A _____ is an example of ubiquitous computing.
    a. smart home
    • b. traffic light
    c. video game console
    d. smartphone

True or False

Answer the following questions with T for true or F for false for more practice with key terms and concepts from this chapter.

F 1. Computers convert information into data.
T 2. First-generation computers used vacuum tubes.
___ 3. Today's computers use transistors and microprocessors.
T 4. Moore's Law is expected to hold true for another 10–20 years.
F 5. An all-in-one is a high-end notebook computer.
T 6. Notebook computers cost significantly more than comparable desktop computers.
___ 7. Users connect to servers via minicomputers.
T 8. GPS was originally built by the military.
T 9. Ergonomics allows you to design a workspace for your comfort and health.
F 10. The idea that computers are all around us is called embedded computing.

Fill in the Blank

Fill in the blanks with key terms and concepts from this chapter.

1. Computers convert data into information using the __IPC__. Information Processing Cycle

2. _____, which resemble incandescent light bulbs, give off a lot of heat and are notoriously unreliable.

3. The use of __transistors__ in place of vacuum tubes allowed second-generation computers to be more powerful, smaller, more reliable, and able to be reprogrammed in far less time.

4. A __PC__ is a small microprocessor-based computer designed to be used by one person at a time. *Personal Computer*

5. A __netbook__ is a lightweight, inexpensive computer designed primarily for Internet access.

Fill in the Blank

6. _____ computers are built by Apple and run the OS X Snow Leopard operating system. Using a program called Boot Camp that's included with Snow Leopard, they can also run Windows.

7. _____ are computers that provide services, such as Internet access, e-mail, or file and print services, to client systems.

8. Very expensive computer systems that are used to perform complex mathematical calculations, such as those used in weather forecasting and medical research, are _____.

9. Personal digital assistants (PDAs), Pocket PCs, and smartphones are handheld or _____ we carry with us wherever we go.

10. _____ design creates a work environment designed to reduce illnesses and musculoskeletal disorders.

Running Project

. . . The Finish Line

Use your answers from the previous sections of the running project to discuss the evolution of computers in the past few centuries.

Write a report responding to the questions raised. Save your file as **Lastname_Firstname_ch01_Project,** and submit it to your instructor as directed.

Critical Thinking 1

Visit a place that could be considered a gathering place for many people, such as a school cafeteria, park, coffee shop, or mall. For 15 minutes, observe people's use of technology.

1. Of those that you observe, how many are alone? How many of them are in groups? What are the approximate ages of people you see using technology? Are they texting? Talking? Viewing something? Did you use your phone or notebook during these 15 minutes? For what?

2. Write a paragraph that expresses your perspective on this scene. Were you surprised at what you saw? Did you see exactly what you were expecting? Did anything disappoint you? Do you think this scene will be different in 5 years? How?

3. Type up your answers, save the file as **Lastname_Firstname_ch01_Technology**, and submit it as directed by your instructor.

Critical Thinking 2

Convergence has led to smaller devices that cost less and do more. Today, a handheld or smartphone has the same processing power of a PC from a few years ago. Compare features and costs in a table like the one on the next page.

1. Research three of the newest smartphones or handhelds on the market. Create a table like the one below, comparing the features of each device, to organize your research. Use this research to decide which device would best meet your personal needs.

2. Write up your decision in a two- to three-paragraph essay. Which device should you buy and why? What other accessories will you need to purchase? Do you need to purchase a service plan to take advantage of all the device's features?

3. Save your file as **Lastname_Firstname_ch01_Convergence**, and submit both your table and essay as directed by your instructor.

	Device 1	Device 2	Device 3
Website or store			
Brand			
Model			
Price			
Phone			
Calendar			
Camera/video			
GPS			
Games			
Video player			
MP3 player			
Internet			
Additional features			
Additional purchases required to meet your needs			

Do It Yourself 1

Ergonomics is the study of the relationship between workers and their workspaces. Ergonomic design creates a work environment designed to reduce illnesses and musculoskeletal disorders. The OSHA website has a computer workstation checklist available at **www.osha.gov/SLTC/etools/computerworkstations**.

1. Download the checklist, and use it to evaluate your computer workstation (the form is also provided on your CD). How did your workstation fare? What are some areas for improvement? How could you improve your score?

2. Type up your answers, save the file as **Lastname_Firstname_ch01_Ergonomics**, and submit your work as directed by your instructor.

Do It Yourself 2

Check out all the features of the mobile device you use the most.

1. What device did you choose? How long have you had it? Did you research the device before you made your purchase? What made you purchase it?

2. What are the five features you use most frequently? Why? What are the five you use the least? Why?

3. How could your device be improved to make your life more convenient? Give one reason life would be easier without all this technology. Give one way your life would be more difficult without all this technology.

4. Type up your answers, save the file as **Lastname_Firstname_ch01_My_Device,** and submit it as directed by your instructor.

Ethical Dilemma

The term "digital divide" was coined in the 1990s. It refers to the gap in technology access and literacy. There have been many types of programs designed to close this gap, including the federal e-rate program, state and local government programs, and private initiatives from companies such as Microsoft, Sun, and AOL. But is there really still such a gap? Have these programs served their purpose? Is it still economically viable for the government to spend millions of dollars on these programs? Who should be responsible for closing the gap? Does putting the technology in classrooms and community centers really close the gap or do we need to have a computer in every home? What about Internet access? What about other forms of technology (such as cell phones)?

1. Use the Internet to research these questions. Pay close attention to the dates of the Web pages and articles you find. Much of the information is from the period from 2000–2004 and isn't current. What sources did you use?

2. Type up your answers, save the file as **Lastname_Firstname_ch01_Digital_Divide**, and submit your work as directed by your instructor.

On the Web 1

The World Community Grid has projects benefiting humanity that depend on volunteer computing. Volunteer computing provides massive computing power to researchers without passing on much of the cost and allows volunteers to participate in projects they care about.

1. Go to **www.worldcommunitygrid.org**. What are some of the projects currently available? Select one project of interest to you, and write a short summary of the project. What's the mission of the project? What's the current status? Why did you select this project?
2. Type up your answers, save the file as **Lastname_Firstname_ch01_Grid**, and submit your work as directed by your instructor.

On the Web 2

Supercomputers make possible much of the current scientific research. Visit the website of the International Supercomputing Conference (**www.supercomp.de/isc09**). Look at the events for the next (or previous) conference.

1. What are some of the topics? Select two sessions that you think are interesting or important, and write a short summary of each. Why did you select these?
2. Type up your answers, save the file as **Lastname_Firstname_ch01_Supercomp**, and submit your work as directed by your instructor.

Collaboration 1

With a group of three to five students, research a famous person mentioned in this chapter. Write and perform a news interview of this person. If possible, video record the interview. Present your newscast to the class.

Instructors: Divide the class into groups of three to four students, and assign each group a famous person mentioned in this chapter.

The Project: Each team is to prepare a dialogue depicting a news reporter interviewing this person. Teams must use at least three references, only one of which may be this textbook. Use Google Docs to prepare the final version of your presentation, and provide documentation that all team members have contributed to the project. For more on using Google Docs, see Appendix C.

Students: Before beginning this project, discuss the roles each group member will play. Choose a team name, which you'll use in submitting your presentation. Be sure to divide the work among your members, and pick someone to present your project. You may find it helpful to elect a team leader who can direct your activities and ensure that all team contributions are collated through Google Docs.

Outcome: Perform the interview in a newscast format using the dialogue you have written. The interview should be 3 to 5 minutes long. If possible, videotape the interview, and share the newscast with the rest of the class. Save this video as **Teamname_ch01_Interview_Video**.

Turn in a final text version of your presentation named as **Teamname_ch01_Interview** and your Google Docs file showing your collaboration named as **Teamname_ch01_Interview_Collaboration**. Be sure to include the name of your presentation and a list of all team members. Submit your presentation to your instructor as directed.

Collaboration 2

With a group of three to five students, research the history of the personal computer. Create a timeline showing five to seven important milestones of this development. Use a free online timeline generator, a drawing program, a word processor, or a presentation tool to create your timeline. Present your findings to the class.

Instructors: Divide the class into groups of three to five students.

The Project: Each team is to research the history of the personal computer. Create a timeline showing five to seven important milestones of this development. Teams must use at least three references, only one of which may be this textbook. Use Google Docs to plan the presentation, and provide documentation that all team members have contributed to the project. For more on using Google Docs, see Appendix C.

Students: Before beginning this project, discuss the roles each group member will play. Choose a team name, which you'll use in submitting your presentation. Be sure to divide the work among your members, and pick someone to present your project. You may find it helpful to elect a team leader who can direct your activities and ensure that all team contributions are collated through Google Docs.

Outcome: Use a free online timeline generator, a drawing program, a word processor, or a presentation tool to create your timeline, and present it to your class. The presentation may be no longer than 3 minutes and should contain 5 to 7 milestones. Turn in a final version of your presentation named as **Teamname_ch01_Timeline** and your Google Docs file showing your collaboration named as **Teamname_ch01_Timeline_Collaboration**. Be sure to include the name of your presentation and a list of all team members. Submit your presentation to your instructor as directed.

Blogging

1. Blog about the pace of technology change in your lifetime. In your write-up, talk about the technology that has been developed since you were born. What do you expect to change in the next 10 years? The next 20 years?

2. Visit at least two of your classmates' blogs on this topic. On the blogs you visit, comment on their ideas, and compare them to what you've written.

3. Create a document that includes your blog URL and the URLs of the two blogs you commented on. Save the file as **Lastname_Firstname_ch01_Pace_Blog**. Submit the document to your instructor as directed.

CHAPTER 2
Hardware

Running Project

In this chapter, you'll explore the key hardware components of the computer and put them together to create a computer you could use to complete your academic career. Look for instructions as you complete each article. For most, there's a series of questions for you to research. At the conclusion of the chapter, you're asked to submit your responses to the questions raised and present and justify the computer system you selected.

OBJECTIVES

1. Explain the function of the CPU. (p. 42)
2. Identify the parts of a system unit and motherboard. (p. 46)
3. Describe how computers represent data using binary codes. (p. 52)
4. Compare different types of storage devices. (p. 56)
5. List different input devices and their uses. (p. 60)
6. List different video and audio output devices and their uses. (p. 68)
7. Compare the features of different types of printers. (p. 74)
8. Explain and provide examples of the concept of adaptive technology. (p. 78)
9. Discuss the different communication devices that can be used. (p. 82)
10. Identify the certifications and careers related to computer hardware. (p. 84)

f Become our friend on Facebook

IN THIS CHAPTER

Hardware refers to the physical components of a computer. Computers perform four tasks: input, processing, output, and storage. The computer itself consists of the components that process data. The components that serve the input, output, and storage functions are called **peripheral devices**. Peripherals can be external devices or they can be integrated into the system unit.

The CPU: The Brains OF THE OPERATION

OBJECTIVE 1
Explain the function of the CPU.

The brain of a computer is called the **central processing unit (CPU)**, or **processor**, and is housed inside the system unit on the motherboard (see Figure 2.1). The CPU consists of two parts: the arithmetic logic unit and the control unit.

The **arithmetic logic unit (ALU)** performs arithmetic (addition and subtraction) and logic (AND, OR, and NOT) calculations. The **control unit** manages the movement of data through the CPU. Together, these units perform three main functions: executing program instructions, performing calculations, and making decisions.

FIGURE 2.1 The central processing unit fits into the motherboard inside the system unit.

INSTRUCTION CYCLE

In order to perform the three functions, the CPU utilizes the **instruction cycle**, which is also known as the "fetch-and-execute cycle" or the "machine cycle." Here's how it works (see Figure 2.2).

FETCH
The instruction is retrieved from main memory.

DECODE
The control unit translates the instruction into a computer command.

EXECUTE
The ALU processes the command.

STORE
The results are written back to memory (stored).

FIGURE 2.2 The four steps of the instruction cycle: fetch, decode, execute, and store

CPU PERFORMANCE

The instruction cycle happens so quickly that you don't realize what's happening. In fact, the processor executes billions of cycles each second. When you evaluate processors for performance, one of the variables you look at is **clock speed**, which is the speed at which the processer executes the cycles. Today, that speed is measured in **gigahertz (GHz)**—billions of cycles per second. A 3 GHz processor has 3 billion data cycles per second.

So far, we've looked at how a processor executes one instruction at a time. Modern computers are capable of processing multiple instructions simultaneously, which increases the efficiency of the processor and the performance of the computer.

PIPELINING Pipelining is used by a single processor. As soon as the first instruction has moved from the fetch to the decode stage, the processor fetches the next instruction. The process is much like an assembly line in a factory (see Figure 2.3).

FIGURE 2.3 Commands are fed to the processor as the previous command completes a phase—like the stations on this assembly line.

Find Out MORE

One way to improve processor performance is to overclock the processor. This means forcing it to run at speeds higher than it was designed to perform at. How is this possible? Is it legal? Why might you consider overclocking your CPU? What are the risks? Where did you find this information?

Chapter 2   43

PARALLEL PROCESSING

Parallel processing uses multiple processors, or multi-core processors, to divide up the work (see Figure 2.4). It can dramatically increase computer performance when running processor-intensive programs, such as system scans or multiple simultaneous programs. Each processor may also use pipelining to further boost the processing efficiency of the system.

Parallel processing is most effective when software developers write programs that can take advantage of multiple processors. Modern operating systems, such as Microsoft Windows 7, Mac OS X, and Linux, were all developed with parallel processing in mind.

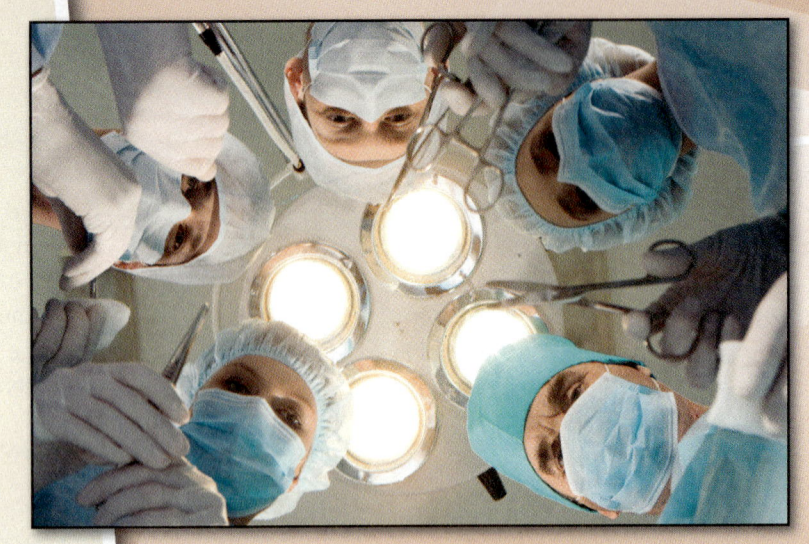

FIGURE 2.4 Parallel processing is like a surgical team, with each member performing a part of the operation.

Multiple processors are typically found in servers, which may have anywhere from two to several hundred processors (see Figure 2.5). Supercomputers are considered "massively multiprocessor" computers and may have thousands of processors, just as the massively multiplayer online game *World of Warcraft* has thousands of players.

FIGURE 2.5 Multiple processors on a server motherboard

A **multi-core processor** consists of two or more processors that are integrated on a single chip. Multi-core processing increases the processing speed over single-core processors and reduces energy consumption over multiple separate processors. Today, dual-core and quad-core processors are found on most personal computers. In 2010, Intel released the first six-core processor for desktop computers.

COOLING SYSTEM: AIR CONDITIONING FOR THE PROCESSOR

Of course, working quickly and using multiple processors or processing paths generates a great deal of heat. Excessive heat can damage a processor or cause it to fail; thus, modern computers provide cooling systems for the CPU.

To keep the processor from overheating, a heat sink and cooling fan are generally installed above the processor to dissipate the heat the processor produces. The heat sink is composed of metal or ceramic and draws heat away from the processor. The cooling fan simply moves the heat away (see Figure 2.6).

FIGURE 2.6 A copper heat sink and a small fan are installed above the CPU to keep it cool.

FIGURE 2.7 In this high-performance system, tubes from the liquid cooling system can be seen inside the case.

Some computers have a liquid cooling system that works like a car radiator by circulating liquid through tubes in the system, carrying heat away from the processor. The advantage to liquid cooling is that it's more efficient and quieter than a fan. The biggest disadvantage is that the liquid cooling system takes up much more space in the system unit (see Figure 2.7).

The ability to process instructions is what makes a computer different from a toaster. The CPU is what makes this possible. Without the CPU, a computer is nothing more than a big night-light.

Key Terms

- arithmetic logic unit (ALU)
- central processing unit (CPU)
- clock speed
- control unit
- gigahertz (GHz)
- instruction cycle
- multi-core processor
- parallel processing
- pipelining
- processor

Running Project

Use the Internet to research current processors. What is the fastest processor available today for desktop computers? What about notebooks? Netbooks? What are the two main manufacturers of processors today?

4 Things You Need to Know

- The CPU consists of the arithmetic logic unit (ALU) and the control unit.
- The four steps of the instruction cycle are: fetch, decode, execute, and store.
- Modern processors use pipelining and parallel processing to improve performance.
- A multi-core processor consists of more than one processor on a single chip.

Getting to Know YOUR SYSTEM UNIT AND MOTHERBOARD

2 OBJECTIVE
Identify the parts of a system unit and motherboard.

The **system unit** is the case that encloses and protects the power supply, motherboard, processor (CPU), and memory of a computer. It also has drive bays to hold the storage devices and openings for peripheral devices to connect to expansion cards on the motherboard (see Figure 2.8). All-in-one systems and notebook computers may also have the keyboard and monitor integrated into the system unit. The system unit is what holds everything together.

- Power supply
- Processor and cooling fan
- Expansion cards
- Drive bays

FIGURE 2.8 In this typical desktop system unit with the cover removed, the processor is hidden under the cooling fan. The motherboard is mostly obscured by the other components.

THE MOTHERBOARD

The main circuit board of your computer is the **motherboard**. In addition to housing the processor (CPU), it contains drive controllers and interfaces, expansion slots, data buses, ports and connectors, BIOS, and memory. A motherboard may also include integrated peripherals, such as video, sound, and network cards. The motherboard provides the way for devices to attach to your computer.

46 | OBJECTIVE 2

DRIVE CONTROLLERS AND INTERFACES A **drive controller** on the motherboard provides a drive interface, which connects disk drives to the processor. **SATA (Serial ATA)** has become the standard internal drive interface, but the **EIDE (enhanced integrated drive electronics)** interface is still found on older computers. SATA is up to three times faster than EIDE and has smaller, thinner cables that take up less room and allow for better airflow inside the system unit (see Figure 2.9).

FIGURE 2.9 A SATA cable (left) takes up less room in the system unit than an EIDE cable (right).

PCI slots
PCIe slot
Memory slots
EIDE controller
SATA Controllers
Sound card
Network card

FIGURE 2.10 A motherboard with PCI expansion slots (white), PCIe slot (blue), EIDE disk controller (green), SATA disk controllers (orange), and memory slots (yellow/red) and examples of expansion cards: sound card and network card

EXPANSION CARDS Also called "adapter cards," **expansion cards** plug directly into expansion slots on the motherboard and allow you to connect additional peripheral devices to a computer. Video cards, sound cards, network cards, TV tuners, and modems are common expansion cards (see Figure 2.10). Most expansion cards plug into a **PCI (peripheral component interconnect)** slot on the motherboard. Video cards and some other devices use the faster **PCI express (PCIe)** slots. Systems manufactured before 2009 used an **AGP (accelerated graphics port)** for video.

DATA BUSES Information flows between the components of the computer over wires on the motherboard called **data buses**. Local buses connect the internal devices on the motherboard, while external buses connect the peripheral devices to the CPU and memory of the computer. The speed of the data bus is an important factor in the performance of the system.

PORTS AND CONNECTORS Ports are used to connect peripheral devices to the motherboard (see Figure 2.11). The most common types of ports found today are USB and FireWire. **Serial and parallel ports** are legacy ports that aren't typically found on modern computers. **PS/2 ports** used to connect a keyboard and mouse have also been widely replaced by USB. Bluetooth is a technology designed to connect peripherals wirelessly.

FIGURE 2.12 Multiple USB cables connected through a hub can share a single USB port on your computer.

Audio | Ethernet (network) | Parallel | PS/2 Keyboard and mouse
USB | FireWire | Standard (VGA) video | HDMI video

FIGURE 2.11 Various ports on a motherboard are often color coded.

USB (Universal Serial Bus) is a standard port type that is used to connect many kinds of devices, including printers, mice, keyboards, digital cameras, cell phones, and external drives. Up to 127 devices can share a single USB port by using a **USB hub** (see Figure 2.12). Most computers today have six to eight USB ports that provide enough connections for all the peripheral devices you might have. USB also provides power to some devices, which allows this type of connection to be used to charge a media player or cell phone and power devices such as webcams. Another advantage of USB devices is that they are **hot-swappable**, meaning they can be plugged and unplugged without turning off the computer.

USB 1.0 was introduced in 1996 and was replaced by USB 2.0 (2000), which is called Hi-Speed USB and is 40 times faster than its predecessor. The USB 3.0 (SuperSpeed) standard, released in 2008, is about 10 times faster. This additional speed is particularly valuable for hard drives and digital video applications.

There are several types of USB connectors. The standard connection to the computer or hub is called USB-A. USB-B and various mini, micro, and proprietary formats are used to connect to USB devices (see Figure 2.13).

FIGURE 2.13 USB connectors: Type A (top) connects to a computer or hub, and type B (bottom) connects to a USB device, such as a printer or external drive.

FireWire, also known as **IEEE 1394**, was originally released by Apple in 1995. FireWire is hot-swappable and can connect up to 63 devices per port. It also allows for peer-to-peer communication between devices, such as two video cameras, without the use of a computer. The original FireWire 400 is roughly equal to USB 2.0 in speed, and FireWire 800 is twice as fast. Today, FireWire is primarily used to connect high-end digital camcorders, which benefit from its superior speed. There are three types of FireWire connectors: 4-circuit and 6-circuit alpha connectors used in FireWire 400 (see Figure 2.14) and a 9-circuit beta connector used in FireWire 800. Both the 6-circuit and 9-circuit connector can supply power to some devices.

FIGURE 2.14 FireWire 400 connectors: 4-circuit (or 4-pin) connector (left) and 6-circuit (or 6-pin) connector (right)

Bluetooth is a short-range wireless technology that's used to connect many types of peripheral devices. It's commonly used to connect cell phones, PDAs, mice, keyboards, and printers to personal computers. Bluetooth is also used in game consoles, such as the Nintendo Wii and Sony PlayStation 3 to connect game controllers. A computer must have an adapter to communicate with Bluetooth-enabled devices.

Several other ports may be found on a computer, such as Ethernet ports to connect to a network, audio ports for speakers and microphones, and video ports to connect monitors and projectors. These are covered in more detail later in this chapter.

BIOS The **BIOS (basic input output system)** is a program stored on a chip on the motherboard that's used to start up the computer. The BIOS chip is **ROM (read-only memory)**, a nonvolatile form of memory that does not need power to keep its data. The BIOS uses settings that are stored on the **CMOS (complementary metal oxide semiconductor)** chip, which is also on the motherboard. CMOS is volatile memory and uses a small battery to provide it with power to keep the data in memory even when the computer is turned off.

MEMORY

Memory is temporary storage that's used by the computer to hold instructions and data. It's sometimes referred to as primary storage. In this section, we look at two types of memory used by a computer: random access memory and cache memory.

RANDOM ACCESS MEMORY The operating systems, programs, and data the computer is currently using are stored in **RAM (random access memory)**. You can think of it as your workspace. A computer that doesn't have enough RAM will be very slow and difficult to use. This type of memory is volatile memory, meaning that any information left in memory is lost when the power is turned off. For this reason, any unsaved work is lost when you close a program or turn off your computer.

Memory boards are small circuit boards that contain memory chips. Most desktop memory uses a DIMM (dual in-line memory module), and notebooks use the SODIMM (small outline dual in-line memory module) configuration (see Figure 2.15). There are several types of RAM available today. Older computers used SDRAM (synchronous dynamic random access memory) and DDR (double data rate) SDRAM. Newer computers use DDR2 and DDR3. Each type of memory is faster and more efficient than its predecessor.

RAM is fairly easy to install, and adding more memory to a computer is an inexpensive way to increase its performance. Installing additional RAM in an older computer can significantly extend its useful life.

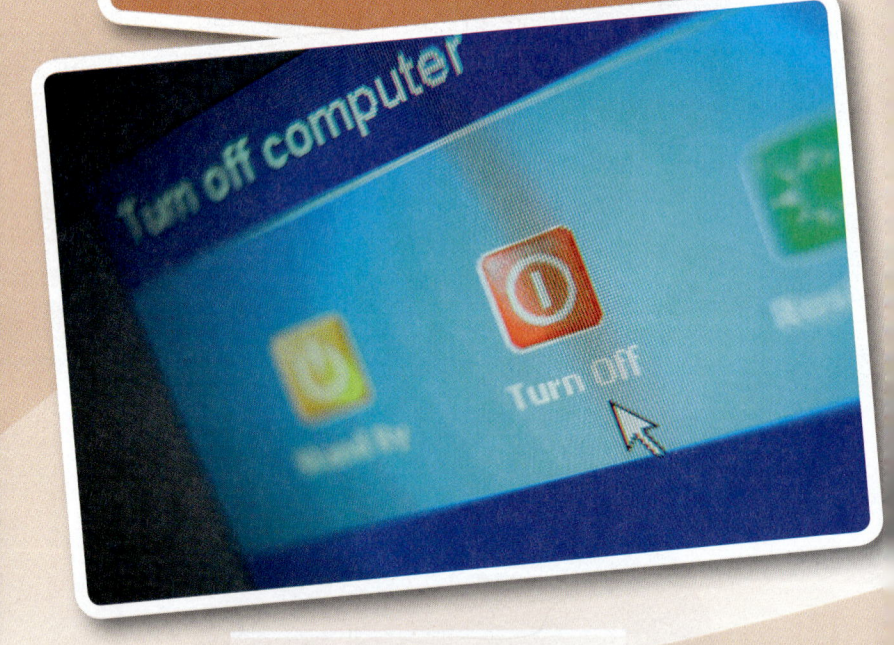

FIGURE 2.15 A desktop DIMM is about twice the physical size of a notebook SODIMM.

CACHE MEMORY

Most computers have a small amount of very fast memory that's used to store frequently accessed information close to the processor. This type of memory is called **cache memory**. Because it's located so close to the processor, it speeds up the time it takes to access the data and improves the processor performance. Level 1 (L1) cache is actually built into the processor, and Level 2 (L2) cache is on a separate chip and takes slightly longer to access. Modern processors may actually have L2 cache built in and have a Level 3 (L3) cache on the motherboard. Each progressive level of cache is farther from the CPU and takes longer to access.

Although it's commonly referred to as the CPU, the system unit is so much more. The system unit is the case that holds the components inside your system, including the CPU and the motherboard. The motherboard provides the ports and connectors for devices to attach to the system. Together, they allow you to build a system that's powerful and versatile in a relatively small package.

Key Terms

- AGP (accelerated graphics port)
- BIOS (basic input output system)
- Bluetooth
- cache memory
- CMOS (complementary metal oxide semiconductor)
- data bus
- drive controller
- EIDE (enhanced integrated drive electronics)
- expansion card
- FireWire
- hot-swappable
- IEEE 1394
- memory
- motherboard
- PCI (peripheral component interconnect)
- PCI express (PCIe)
- port
- PS/2 port
- RAM (random access memory)
- ROM (read-only memory)
- SATA (serial ATA)
- serial and parallel ports
- system unit
- USB (Universal Serial Bus)
- USB hub

Running Project

Use the Internet to research RAM. What's the fastest RAM available today for desktop computers? What about notebooks? Look at computer ads on some current retail websites. What is the average amount of RAM in desktop computers? In notebooks? What type of RAM is found in the most expensive systems?

5 Things You Need to Know

- The motherboard is the main circuit board in a computer.
- A motherboard provides the way for devices to attach to a computer.
- Information flows between the components of a computer over data buses.
- The BIOS is a program stored on a chip on the motherboard that's used to start up the computer.
- RAM is volatile memory that holds the operating systems, programs, and data the computer is currently using.

Bits and BYTES

3 OBJECTIVE
Describe how computers represent data using binary codes.

Humans have 10 digits (fingers), which is why we find the decimal, or base 10, number system to be natural. (Remember how you used your fingers and toes to do math when you were a kid?) Computers don't have fingers; they have switches and use the **binary number system (base 2)**, which has only two digits (0 and 1).

BINARY CODE

Computers don't speak English (or Spanish, Chinese, or Greek for that matter), so how does a computer understand what we enter? On a typewriter, when you press the A key, you get an A, but computers only understand 0s and 1s, so when you press the A key, it must somehow be represented by 0s and 1s. Digital data is represented using a binary code.

A **binary code** works like a bank of light switches, as illustrated in Figure 2.16. If you have only a single light switch in a room, there are two possible states—the light can either be on or it can be off. This code can be used for situations with only two possibilities, such as yes/no, true/false, boy/girl, but it fails when there are more than two choices (yes/no/maybe). Adding another switch, or bit, increases the possible combinations by a factor of two (2^2), which equals 4 possibilities. A third bit (switch) gives us 2^3 or 8 possibilities and so on. A **bit** (short for binary digit) is the smallest unit of digital information. Eight bits equals a **byte** and gives us 2^8 or 256 possibilities. A byte is used to represent a single character in modern computer systems. For example, when you press the A key, the binary code 01000001 (which equals 65 in decimal) is sent to the computer.

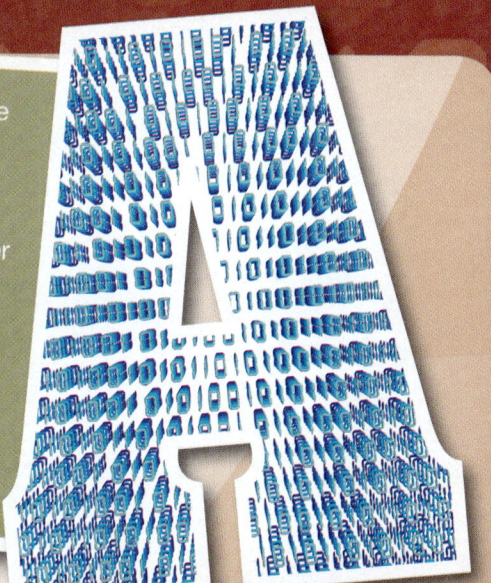

FIGURE 2.16 A binary code using 8 switches, or bits, has 256 different possible combinations.

Number of Bits (switches)	Possibilities	Power of two
	2	2^1
	4	2^2
	8	2^3
	16	2^4
	32	2^5
	64	2^6
	128	2^7
	256	2^8

ASCII (American Standard Code for Information Interchange) was originally developed in the 1960s using a 7-bit system that represented 128 characters and included English alphabet symbols (upper- and lowercase), numbers 0 through 9, punctuation, and a few special characters. It was later expanded to an 8-bit extended set with 256 characters. ASCII needed to be adapted to be used for other languages, and many extended sets were developed. The most common extended ASCII set is **Unicode**. It has become the standard on the Internet and includes codes for most of the world's written languages, mathematical systems, and special characters. It has codes for over 100,000 characters. The first 256 characters are the same in both ASCII and Unicode; however, the characters in the last columns in Figure 2.17 include Latin, Greek, and Cyrillic symbols, which are represented only in Unicode.

CHARACTER	ASCII	UNICODE	CHARACTER	ASCII	UNICODE	CHARACTER	ASCII	UNICODE
"	34	34	A	65	65	ő		337
#	35	35	B	66	66	œ		339
$	36	36	C	67	67	ŕ		341
0	48	48	a	97	97	ə		399
1	49	49	b	98	98	λ		411
2	50	50	c	99	99	α		945

FIGURE 2.17 ASCII and Unicode representations

MEASURING DATA

Today, bits (b) are used to measure data transfer rates (such as your Internet connection), and bytes (B) are used to measure file size and storage capacity. The decimal prefixes of kilo (10^3), mega (10^6), giga (10^9), etc., are added to the base unit to indicate larger values. Binary prefixes kibi (2^{10}), mebi (2^{20}), and gibi (2^{30}) have been adopted, although their use isn't widespread. A megabyte (MB) is equal to 1,000,000 bytes, and a mebibyte (MiB) is equal to 1,048,576 bytes, a slightly larger value. Figure 2.18 compares the two systems.

FIGURE 2.18 A comparison of decimal and binary storage capacity prefixes

DECIMAL PREFIX	SYMBOL	DECIMAL VALUE EXPONENTIAL	DECIMAL VALUE NUMERIC	BINARY PREFIX	SYMBOL	BINARY VALUE	DECIMAL VALUE
kilo	K or k	10^3	1,000	kibi	Ki	2^{10}	1,024
mega	M	10^6	1,000,000	mebi	Mi	2^{20}	1,048,576
giga	G	10^9	1,000,000,000	gibi	Gi	2^{30}	1,073,741,824
tera	T	10^{12}	1,000,000,000,000	tebi	Ti	2^{40}	1,099,511,627,776
peta	P	10^{15}	1,000,000,000,000,000	pebi	Pi	2^{50}	1,125,899,906,842,624
exa	E	10^{18}	1,000,000,000,000,000,000	exbi	Ei	2^{60}	1,152,921,504,606,846,976
zetta	Z	10^{21}	1,000,000,000,000,000,000,000	zebi	Zi	2^{70}	1,180,591,620,717,411,303,424
yotta	Y	10^{24}	1,000,000,000,000,000,000,000,000	yobi	Yi	2^{80}	1,208,925,819,614,629,174,706,176

A megabyte (MB) can hold about 500 pages of plain text, but a single picture taken with a modern digital camera can be several megabytes in size. As the types of files we save have changed from plain text to images, music, and video, the file sizes have become larger, and the need for storage has grown dramatically—but, fundamentally, all files are still just 0s and 1s.

Key Terms

ASCII (American Standard Code for Information Interchange)

binary code

binary number system (base 2)

bit

byte

Unicode

4 Things You Need to Know

- Computers use the binary (base 2) number system.
- ASCII and Unicode are binary code character sets.
- A bit is the smallest unit of digital information.
- A byte is equal to 8 bits and represents one character.

A Place for Everything...
AND EVERYTHING IN ITS PLACE

4 OBJECTIVE
Compare different types of storage devices.

There are two ways to think about the storage of data: how it's physically stored on disks and how we organize the files we store. In this article, we'll look at physical storage devices.

OPTICAL DISCS

Optical discs are a form of removable storage and include CDs, DVDs, and Blu-ray discs. The spelling *d-i-s-c* refers to optical discs. Data is stored on these discs using a laser to either melt the disc material or change the color of embedded dye. A laser can read the variations as binary data (see Figure 2.19).

Optical disc drives are mounted in the system unit in external drive bays, which enables you to access them to insert or eject discs. They can also be peripheral devices connected by USB or FireWire. Optical discs can take several forms: read-only (ROM), recordable (+R/–R), or rewritable (+RW/–RW). The type of disc you should purchase depends on the type of drive you have. This is usually labeled on the front of the drive, as seen in Figure 2.20.

FIGURE 2.19 The data on an optical disc is read by a laser.

FIGURE 2.20 The type of disc supported is labeled on the front of the disc drive.

CDS A **CD (compact disc)** is the oldest type of optical disc in use today and has a storage capacity of about 700 MB. CDs are still used to distribute software and music and to store photos and data, but they have, for the most part, been replaced by larger capacity DVDs to distribute movies and some software.

DVDS A **digital versatile disc** or **digital video disc**, more commonly known as a **DVD**, has the same dimensions as a CD but stores more than six times as much data. Single-layer (SL) DVDs can hold about 4.7 GB of information. Double-layer (DL) DVDs have a second layer to store data and can hold about 8.5 GB.

BLU-RAY A **Blu-ray disc** is an optical disc with about five times the capacity of a DVD, which it was designed to replace. The single-layer disc capacity is 25 GB, and double-layer disc capacity is 50 GB. Today, Blu-ray is mainly used for high-definition video and data storage. BD-R discs are recordable, and BD-RE discs can be erased and re-recorded multiple times. Figure 2.21 provides a comparison of the storage capacities of the various optical media.

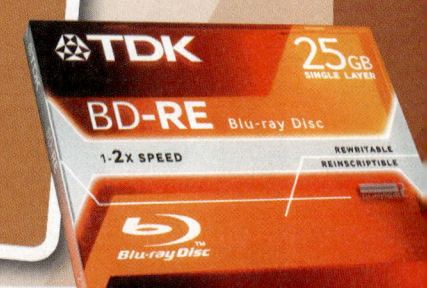

FIGURE 2.21 Comparison of the capacities of optical disc formats

OPTICAL DISC	CAPACITY	NUMBER OF 3.5 MB PHOTOS	VIDEO	HIGH-DEFINITION VIDEO
CD-ROM	700 MB	200	35 minutes	—
DVD single layer	4.7 GB	1,343	2 hours	—
DVD dual layer	8.5 GB	2,429	4 hours	—
Blu-ray single layer	25 GB	7,143	—	4.5 hours
Blu-ray dual layer	50 GB	14,286	—	9 hours

SOLID-STATE STORAGE

Unlike optical (and magnetic) storage, **solid-state storage** is nonmechanical. The data is stored using **flash memory** on a chip. Because there are no moving parts, solid-state drives are quiet and durable. Solid-state drives are often used in small electronic devices, such as media players and cell phones, as well as in netbooks.

FLASH DRIVES

Sometimes called "*key drives*," "*thumb drives*," "*pen drives*," or "*jump drives*," **flash drives** are small, portable, solid-state drives that can hold up to 128 GB of information. They have become the standard for transporting data. Flash drives connect to a computer by a USB port and come in a variety of shapes and sizes, including pens, watches, toys, and Swiss Army knives (see Figure 2.22).

FIGURE 2.22 Zip Zip's Memory Bricks connect together when not in use as a flash drive. You can also get a Swiss Flash USB knife with an integrated flash drive.

MEMORY CARDS

You can expand the storage of digital cameras, video games, and other devices with **memory cards**. The type of memory card you use is dependent upon the device. The most common formats include Secure Digital (SD), CompactFlash (CF), Memory Stick (MS), and xD-Picture Card (xD). Figure 2.23 provides a comparison of these formats.

Card readers are used to transfer data, such as photos and music, between a card and a computer or printer. Personal computers and photo printers may have built-in card readers, but you can use USB card readers on computers that don't have them (see Figure 2.24).

HARD DRIVES

Hard drives are the main mass-storage devices in a computer. They are sometimes called "hard disks" or "hard disk drives." Hard drives are a form of nonvolatile storage; when the computer is powered off, the data isn't lost. The primary hard drive holds the operating system, programs, and data files. Hard drives are measured in hundreds of gigabytes and even terabytes and can hold hundreds of thousands of files.

Hard drives can be either internal or external. Internal drives are located inside the system unit in an internal drive bay and are not accessible from the outside. External drives may be attached as a peripheral device using a USB or FireWire connection. The advantages of external drives are that they can be installed without opening the system unit and can be easily moved to another computer.

FIGURE 2.23 Comparison of flash memory card formats

TYPE OF MEMORY CARD	CAPACITY	DETAILS
Secure Digital (SD)/ SDHC (SD High Capacity)	The most common format, SD cards come in capacities up to 4 GB. SDHC cards can be from 4–32 GB in size.	Micro and mini SD cards are small cards and are typically used in cell phones.
CompactFlash (CF)	CompactFlash has capacities of up to 100 GB and is used by many high-end digital cameras, from Nikon, Canon, Sony, and Olympus.	CF+ is a magnetic form of CompactFlash used in microdrives (tiny, 1-inch hard drives).
Memory Stick (MS)	Memory sticks are more expensive and have a smaller capacity (currently up to 16 GB) than other formats.	Memory sticks are a proprietary format developed by Sony for use with their digital cameras.
xD-Picture Card (xD)	Picture cards have capacities up to 2 GB.	xD cards are a proprietary format of Olympus and Fujifilm that's used by most Olympus digital cameras.

FIGURE 2.24 A photo printer with a built-in card reader (right) and a USB card reader with slots for several different memory card formats (left) are tools to transfer files from device to device.

The capacity of storage has grown dramatically over the past few years, as the operating systems and software we use have gotten more sophisticated and the files we save have become larger and more numerous. A decade ago, a floppy disk could hold 1.4 MB of information—roughly 750 pages of text. Today, the 500 GB hard drive in your personal computer can store about 250,000,000 pages of text, 90 hours of high-definition video, or over 140,000 high-quality photos. That's a lot of photo albums!

Hard drives store data magnetically on metal platters. The platters are stacked, and read/write heads move across the surface of the platters, reading data and writing it to memory (see Figure 2.25). The drives spin at up to 15,000 revolutions per minute, allowing for very fast data transfer.

Read/write head

FIGURE 2.25 The read/write head is visible above the disk surface in this view of the inside of a hard drive.

Key Terms

Blu-ray disc (BD)

CD (compact disc)

DVD (digital video disc; digital versatile disc)

flash drive

flash memory

hard drive

memory card

optical disc

solid-state storage

Running Project

Look at computer ads on some current retail websites. What is the average size of a hard drive in desktop computers? In notebooks? Netbooks? What type of optical disc drive is found in most desktops? Notebooks? Netbooks? What other types of storage devices are listed in the ads? Think about your needs. What type(s) of storage do you need and how much? Can you easily add more storage later?

3 Things You Need to Know

- Lasers read the data on optical discs (CDs, DVDs, Blu-rays).
- Hard drives store data magnetically on metal platters.
- Solid-state storage stores data on a chip.

What GOES IN...

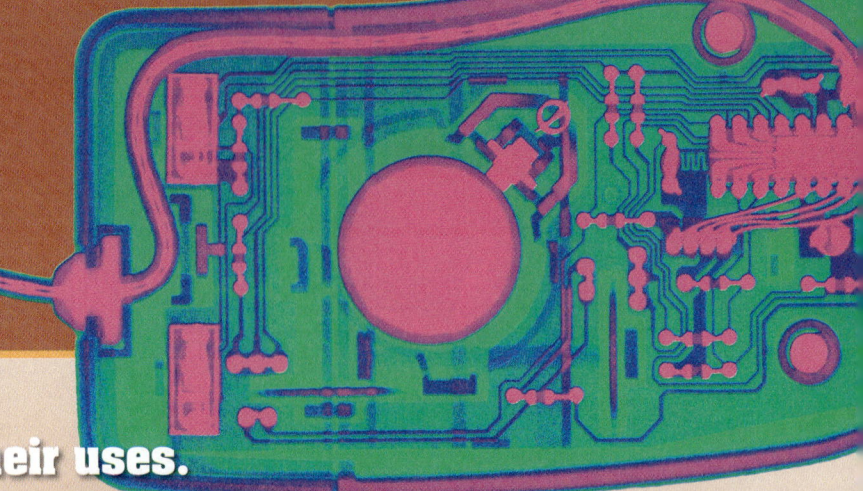

5 OBJECTIVE: List different input devices and their uses.

An **input device** is a device that's used to get data into the computer system so it can be processed. There are many types of input devices, but the most common are keyboards and mice. Input devices allow us to interact with technology in many different ways, from playing a guitar in a video game to typing out an e-mail to checking for the best price on an item using our cell phones. In this article, we'll look at some of the many input devices you can use.

KEYBOARDS

The first thing that comes to mind when we discuss input devices is the **keyboard**. As basic as that seems, there are many different types of keyboards available. The most common type of keyboard is the standard QWERTY format, so called because Q-W-E-R-T-Y are the first alphabetic keys on the keyboard. The QWERTY design was originally developed by Christopher Sholes in 1874 to reduce the number of key jams, which can occur when keys that are next to each other on the keyboard are pressed quickly and interfere with each other on a mechanical typewriter (see Figure 2.26). While it may reduce the interference, it's an inefficient typing layout that's no longer needed because computer keyboards aren't mechanical. We have become so accustomed to the QWERTY layout that many cell phones now feature a QWERTY keyboard for faster texting.

FIGURE 2.26 A mechanical typewriter is prone to key jams when keys that are close together are pressed too quickly.

In addition to the alphabet and number keys, keyboards have specialized keys (see Figure 2.27). Some keys, such as Esc and the Function keys, have specific actions associated with them. Other keys, such as Ctrl, Alt, and Shift, are modifiers and are pressed in conjunction with other keys. Toggle keys, such as Caps Lock and Num Lock, turn a feature on or off when pressed. Full-sized keyboards contain 101 or 104 keys, but notebook computer keyboards are smaller and do not typically include a separate numeric keypad.

FIGURE 2.27 Special keys on a keyboard

KEY	TYPE	ACTION
Esc		Cancel
F1	Function	Help
F5	Function	Refresh
Caps Lock	Toggle	Turns capitalization on/off
Shift	Modifier—pressed with at least one other key	Activates uppercase or alternate-key assignment
Ctrl (Windows)/Command (Mac)	Modifier—pressed with at least one other key	Modifies the behavior of a key press
Alt (Windows)/Option (Mac)	Modifier—pressed with at least one other key	Modifies the behavior of a key press
Windows logo		Opens the Start menu

Keyboards can also have alternate layouts or be customized for a particular application. The Dvorak Simplified Keyboard was designed to put the most commonly used letters where they're more easily accessed to increase efficiency and reduce fatigue (see Figure 2.28). Most modern operating systems include support for the Dvorak layout, but it's not been widely adopted.

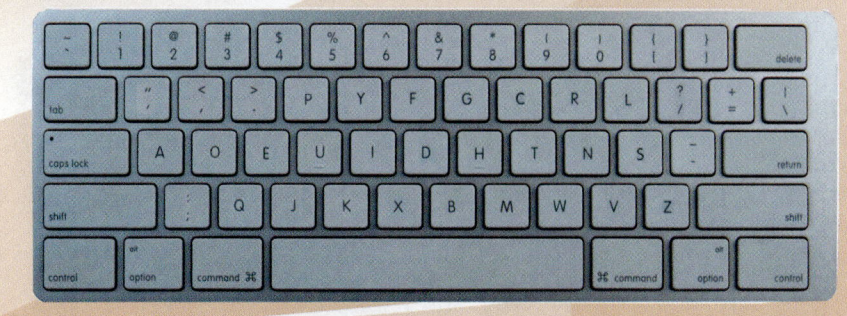

FIGURE 2.28 The QWERTY keyboard layout (top) and the Dvorak keyboard layout (bottom)

Find Out MORE

There are many standard keystroke combinations that can be used to perform common tasks. For example: Ctrl + P is a command to print, Ctrl + C copies highlighted material, and Alt + F4 closes a window. Research useful keystroke shortcuts that can be used with your favorite application and present them in a table. Which application did you research? Where did you find your information? Are there any keystroke shortcuts you already use? Is there a way to create your own keystroke shortcuts in this application? If so, what additional tasks would you create them for?

Ergonomic keyboards are full-sized keyboards that have a curved shaped and are designed to position the wrists in a more natural position to reduce strain (see Figure 2.29). They may look funny, but many people that spend a lot of time on the computer rely on them to prevent injuries.

FIGURE 2.29 The curved shape of an ergonomic keyboard reduces wrist strain.

Another alternative keyboard is a **keypad**, a small keyboard that doesn't contain all the alphabet keys. This type of input device is typically found in Point-of-Sale (POS) terminals (see Figure 2.30). People that enter a lot of numbers, such as teachers, accountants, and telemarketers, might find it useful to attach a USB keypad to a notebook computer.

FIGURE 2.30 Keypads typically contain numbers and are used in such applications as Point-of-Sale (POS) terminals and as peripherals for personal computers. The model on the right is designed like a telephone keypad to speed up dialing phone numbers.

62 | OBJECTIVE 5

MOUSE AND OTHER POINTING DEVICES

Pointing devices, such as mice and touchpads (see Figure 2.31), are input devices that allow a user to interact with objects by moving a pointer, also called a cursor, on the computer screen. Many different versions of each of these devices are available. They allow us to point and click instead of typing in text commands.

FIGURE 2.31 A mouse and touchpad are common pointing devices found on personal computers.

MOUSE A **mouse** may include one or more buttons and a scroll wheel and works by moving across a smooth surface to signal movement of the pointer. Older mechanical mice had a ball that rolled across the surface. The ball tended to get dirty, which caused the mouse to become difficult to use. Modern optical mice detect motion by bouncing light from a red LED (light-emitting diode) off the surface below it. Because they have fewer moving parts, optical mice are less prone to failure than mechanical mice.

TOUCHPAD Most notebook computers include a built-in **touchpad** instead of a mouse. With this device, motion is detected by moving your finger across the touch-sensitive surface. Touchpads also have buttons that function like mouse buttons and special areas that enable you to quickly scroll through documents, Web pages, and images.

TOUCH INPUT A **stylus** is a special pen-like input tool used by tablet computers, graphic design tablets (see Figure 2.32), PDAs, and other handheld devices. These devices might also have a **touch screen** that can accept input from a finger. Interactive whiteboards are large interactive displays used in classrooms and businesses. They have touch-sensitive surfaces and allow the user to control the computer from the screen as well as capture what's written on the screen with special pens.

FIGURE 2.32 A graphic design tablet with a stylus is a specialized input device used in graphic arts, CAD (computer-aided design), and other applications.

DIGITAL CAMERAS AND WEBCAMS

Digital cameras can capture still images or video. The cameras can be built in or directly connected to a computer by USB or FireWire cable or the files can be transferred to the computer via a removable flash card. **Webcams** are specialized video cameras that provide visual input for online communication, such as Web conferencing or chatting, as seen in Figure 2.33. Look for more detailed information about different types of digital cameras when we discuss multimedia and digital devices.

FIGURE 2.33 A boy and his grandfather talk over the Internet using the webcam built into this monitor.

SCANNERS

Scanners are used in many types of businesses, from grocery stores to libraries to law enforcement. The use of scanners increases the speed and accuracy of data entry and converts information into a digital format that can be saved, copied, and manipulated.

OPTICAL SCANNERS You can convert a photo or document into a digital file with an optical scanner. Flatbed scanners are the most common type of optical scanner used in homes and offices. You simply place the document or photo you wish to scan on a glass screen, and the scanner head moves underneath the glass to convert the image to a digital file. Business card readers and photo scanners typically have a sheet-feed format that moves the page to be scanned and keeps the scanner head stationary. Handheld scanners such as bar code readers are small and portable (see Figure 2.34). You see these in supermarket checkout lines, library circulation desks, and shipping operations.

FIGURE 2.34 A bar code reader quickly scans the label on this carton, saving time and reducing data entry errors.

RFID SCANNERS An RFID scanner can read the information in an **RFID tag**, which contains a tiny antenna for receiving and sending a radio-frequency signal. RFID (radio frequency identification) is used in inventory tracking, electronic toll collection, and contactless credit card transactions, such as Exxon Mobil Speedpass and MasterCard PayPass. It's also the technology used in passports). There have been some security and privacy concerns over the United States' decision to use RFID passports.

Another type of scanner that's used frequently is a magnetic strip reader. Such scanners can read information encoded in the magnetic strip on plastic cards, such as drivers' licenses, gift cards, library cards, credit cards, and even hotel door keys (see Figure 2.35).

FIGURE 2.36 A fingerprint scanner built into a notebook computer can be used for added security.

BIOMETRIC SCANNERS Used in banks to identify patrons, in theme parks to assure that tickets aren't transferred to other guests, and in corporate security systems, **biometric scanners** measure human characteristics such as fingerprints and eye retinas. Some notebook computers even use a fingerprint scanner to ensure that the person trying to access the computer is an authorized user (see Figure 2.36).

RFID symbol

FIGURE 2.35 An RFID chip is embedded in this U.S. passport (above). On the left, a magnetic strip reader reads the information on the magnetic strip on the back of the card to open an electronic door lock.

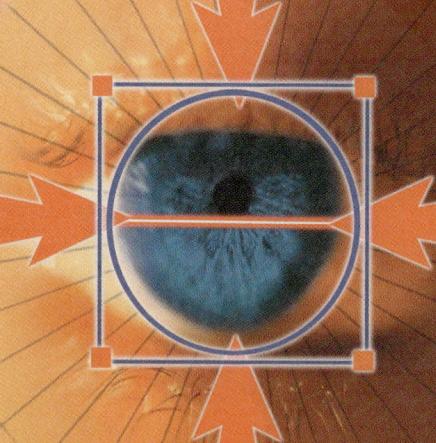

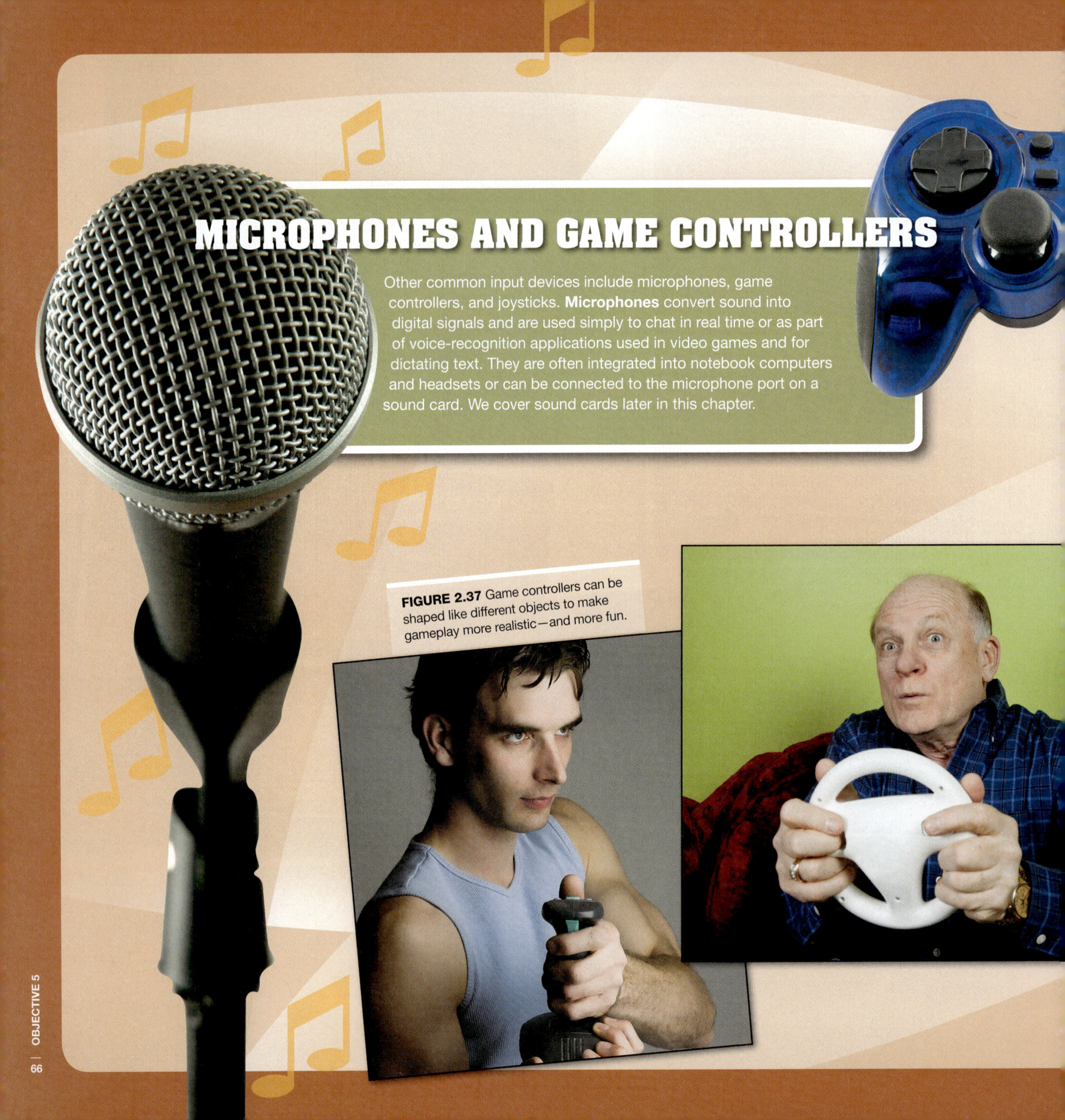

MICROPHONES AND GAME CONTROLLERS

Other common input devices include microphones, game controllers, and joysticks. **Microphones** convert sound into digital signals and are used simply to chat in real time or as part of voice-recognition applications used in video games and for dictating text. They are often integrated into notebook computers and headsets or can be connected to the microphone port on a sound card. We cover sound cards later in this chapter.

FIGURE 2.37 Game controllers can be shaped like different objects to make gameplay more realistic—and more fun.

Game controllers provide a way to interact with video games. Special game controllers include steering wheels, tennis rackets, guns, musical instruments, and pressure-sensitive mats. These controllers make the gameplay more realistic (see Figure 2.37). A **joystick**, which is mounted on a base, consists of a stick, buttons, and sometimes a trigger. Typically used as a game controller, especially in flight-simulator games, a joystick also may be used for such tasks as controlling robotic machinery in a factory.

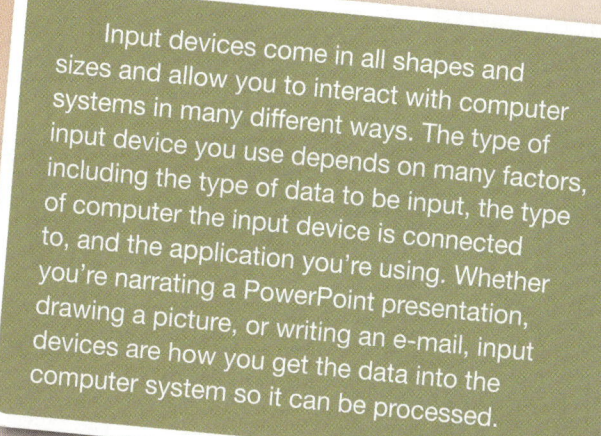

Input devices come in all shapes and sizes and allow you to interact with computer systems in many different ways. The type of input device you use depends on many factors, including the type of data to be input, the type of computer the input device is connected to, and the application you're using. Whether you're narrating a PowerPoint presentation, drawing a picture, or writing an e-mail, input devices are how you get the data into the computer system so it can be processed.

Key Terms

biometric scanner

game controller

input device

joystick

keyboard

keypad

microphone

mouse

RFID tag

scanner

stylus

touchpad

touch screen

webcam

Running Project

A mouse or touchpad and keyboard are standard input devices. Think about how you might use your computer in the future. What other input devices might you need? Pick at least one additional input device, and research current models and costs. Which model would you choose and why?

4 Things You Need to Know

- The mouse and keyboard are the most common input devices.
- Digital cameras and webcams input images and video.
- Scanners convert information into a digital format.
- Microphones are audio input devices.

...Must COME OUT

6 OBJECTIVE
List different video and audio output devices and their uses.

Information is returned to the user through **output devices**. The most common output devices provide video or paper document output. Other devices provide audio output or other types of hard copy, such as x-rays and maps. This article focuses on video and audio output. Printers are discussed in the next article.

VIDEO OUTPUT DEVICES

What you see on your computer screen is video output. There are a variety of video output devices that provide visual output to the user. The most popular types of monitors and projectors come in many different sizes, technologies, and price ranges.

MONITORS Similar to television screens, **monitors** work by lighting up **pixels** (short for picture elements) on the screen. Each pixel contains three colors: red, green, and blue (RGB). From that base, all colors can be created by varying the intensities of the three colors. Display **resolution** indicates the number of horizontal pixels by vertical pixels, for example 1280×1024 or 1024×768. The higher the resolution, the sharper the image is. The size of a monitor is measured diagonally across the screen.

Older **CRT monitors**, such as televisions, use a cathode ray tube to excite phosphor particles coating the glass TV screen to light up the pixels. CRT monitors are big and use a lot of energy. As a result, they've been replaced by smaller and more energy-efficient flat-panel monitors. CRT monitors are considered **legacy technology**, which is old technology that's still used alongside its more modern replacement, typically because it still works and is cost-effective.

Most modern desktop and notebook computers have flat-panel monitors, which create bright, crisp images without using traditional picture tubes. Instead, such displays use LCD or plasma panels (see Figure 2.38).

FIGURE 2.38 An LCD monitor is much thinner than a CRT monitor of the same screen size.

LCD (liquid crystal display) panels are found on most desktop and notebook computers. They consist of two layers of glass that are glued together with a layer of liquid crystals between them. When electricity is passed through the individual crystals, it causes them to pass or block light to create an image. LCDs do not give off any light, so they need to be backlit by a light source, typically CCFLs (cold cathode fluorescent lamps). Some LCD monitors are backlit by LEDs. The LED versions are generally thinner and more energy efficient, but they're also more expensive.

Available in larger screen sizes that you wouldn't use with a desktop computer, plasma screen monitors are typically included in media center systems or are used in conference rooms. **Plasma monitors** work by passing an electric current through gas sealed in thousands of cells inside the screen. The current excites the gas, which in turn excites the phosphors that coat the screen to pass light through an image.

Chapter 2 | 69

The next technology in monitors is **OLED (organic light-emitting diode)**. These monitors are composed of extremely thin panels of organic molecules sandwiched between two electrodes. The prototypes of these monitors are less than 1-inch thick and are even bendable. OLEDs use very little energy and are expected to be at least 10 times more energy efficient than today's LCDs, but OLED technology has a way to go before consumer level products reach the market.

Choosing between an LCD and plasma screen monitor depends on many factors, including size and cost. Figure 2.39 provides a comparison of the advantages and disadvantages of LCD and plasma flat-panel monitors.

PROJECTORS When making a presentation or sharing media with a group in such places as classrooms, businesses, and home theaters, **projectors** are more practical than monitors because they produce larger output. They can be classified as video projectors, which are typically used in home media centers to display movies on a wall or screen, and data projectors, which are designed for presentations in a business or classroom setting. The two main types of projectors used today are DLP and LCD projectors.

DLP (digital light-processing) projectors have hundreds of thousands of tiny swiveling mirrors that are used to create an image. They produce high-contrast images with deep blacks but are limited by having weaker reds and yellows. The most portable projectors on the market today are DLP projectors, which weigh less than 3 pounds. DLPs also are very popular home theater projectors because of the higher contrast and deeper blacks that they produce.

FIGURE 2.39 The advantages and disadvantages of flat-panel monitor formats

DISPLAY TYPE/SIZE	ADVANTAGES	DISADVANTAGES
LCD Size: 13" to 65" and larger	• Panels weigh less than plasma • Use less energy than CRTs or plasmas • Better in bright-light situations	• Picture is slightly less natural than top plasmas • More expensive than comparable plasmas • Screens larger than 52" are very expensive.
Plasma Size: 32" to 61"	• The screen's phosphor coating creates lifelike color and truer blacks that are closest to conventional tube TVs.	• Not available in sizes smaller than 32" • Heavy and fragile, plasmas are difficult to install.

LCD projectors pass light through a prism, which divides the light into three beams—red, green, and blue—which are then passed through an LCD screen. These projectors display richer colors but produce poorer contrast and washed-out blacks. LCDs tend to have sharper images than DLPs and are better in bright rooms, making them ideal for presentations in conferences and classrooms.

Each technology has distinct advantages and disadvantages. The choice between them depends on many factors, including the primary use, the room the projector is in, whether it needs to be portable, and cost. Figure 2.40 compares some features of DLP and LCD projectors.

FIGURE 2.40 A comparison of DLP and LCD projectors

PROJECTOR TYPE	ADVANTAGES	DISADVANTAGES
DLP projectors	• Smoother video • Smaller and lighter • Truer blacks • Higher contrast	• Some noise created by moving parts • Weaker reds and yellows • Need more lumens than LCD
LCD projectors	• Richer color for better results in bright rooms • More energy efficient • Gives off less heat • Quieter	• More visible pixels • Larger and heavier • Poorer contrast • Washed-out blacks

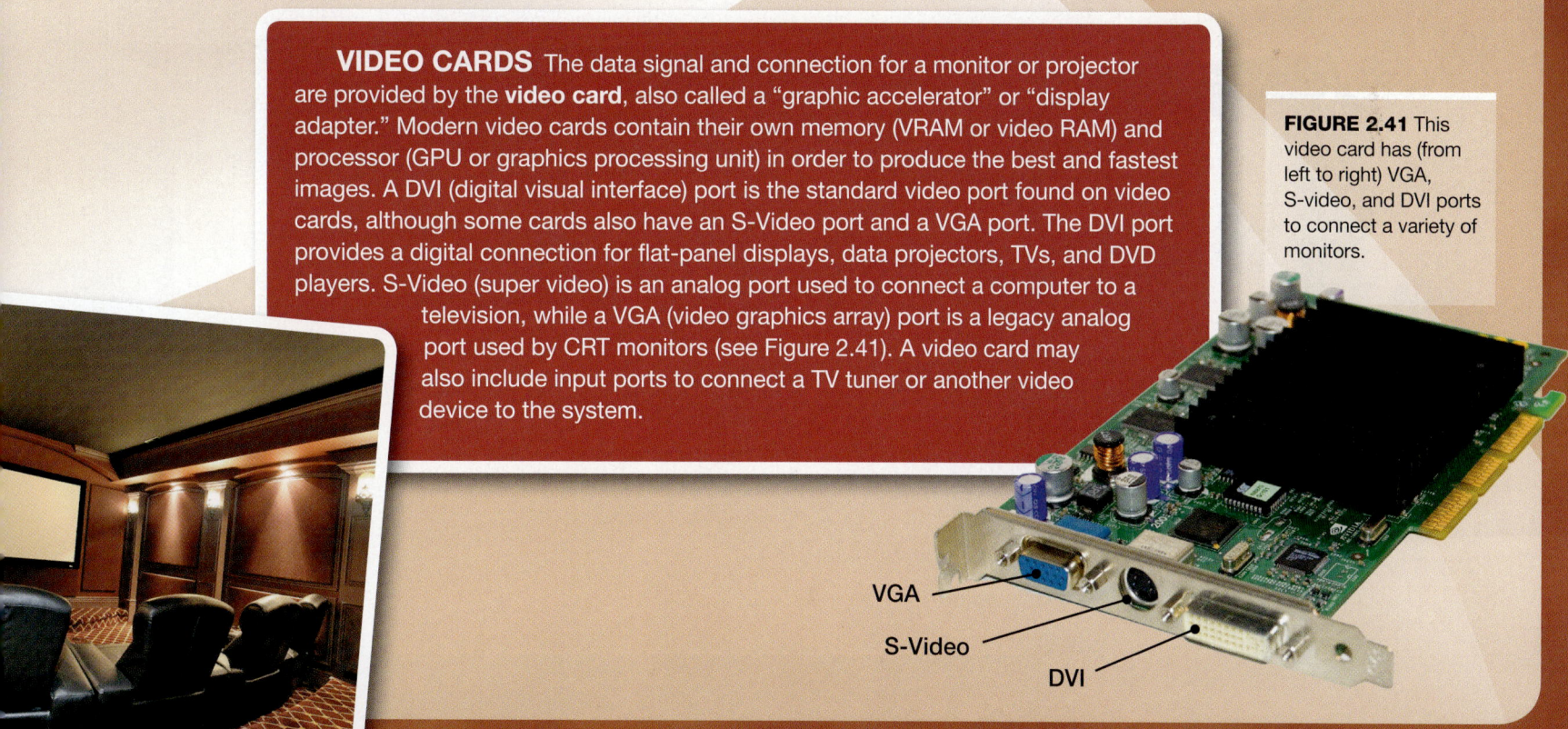

VIDEO CARDS The data signal and connection for a monitor or projector are provided by the **video card**, also called a "graphic accelerator" or "display adapter." Modern video cards contain their own memory (VRAM or video RAM) and processor (GPU or graphics processing unit) in order to produce the best and fastest images. A DVI (digital visual interface) port is the standard video port found on video cards, although some cards also have an S-Video port and a VGA port. The DVI port provides a digital connection for flat-panel displays, data projectors, TVs, and DVD players. S-Video (super video) is an analog port used to connect a computer to a television, while a VGA (video graphics array) port is a legacy analog port used by CRT monitors (see Figure 2.41). A video card may also include input ports to connect a TV tuner or another video device to the system.

FIGURE 2.41 This video card has (from left to right) VGA, S-video, and DVI ports to connect a variety of monitors.

VGA
S-Video
DVI

AUDIO OUTPUT DEVICES

Audio output can be anything from your favorite song to sound effects in a video game to an e-mail alert chime. The sound can be heard through speakers or headphones.

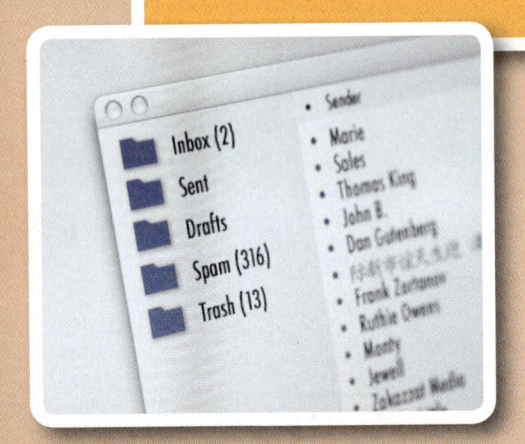

SPEAKERS Speakers convert digital signals from a computer or media player into sound. They may be integrated into notebook computers and monitors or connected to the speaker ports on a sound card. Typical desktop speaker systems include two or three speakers, but speaker systems designed for gaming or home theater uses include as many as eight speakers and can cost hundreds of dollars.

HEADPHONES
Like speakers, **headphones** convert digital signals into sound. They come in several different sizes and styles, ranging from tiny earbuds that fit inside your ear to full-size headphones that completely cover your outer ear. High-quality headphones can cost hundreds of dollars and incorporate up to eight speakers in the design. Noise-cancelling headphones reduce the effect of ambient noise and are especially useful in noisy environments, such as in airplanes. Headphones can plug into the headphone or speaker port of a computer, the headphone port on a speaker, or USB ports and can connect wirelessly via Bluetooth. Headphones that also include a microphone are called "headsets."

SOUND CARDS A **sound card** provides audio connections for both input devices (microphones and synthesizers) and output devices (speakers and headphones), as shown in Figure 2.42. Sound cards can be integrated into the motherboard (onboard) or connected through expansion cards or external USB or FireWire boxes. High-end sound cards support surround sound and may have connections for up to eight speakers.

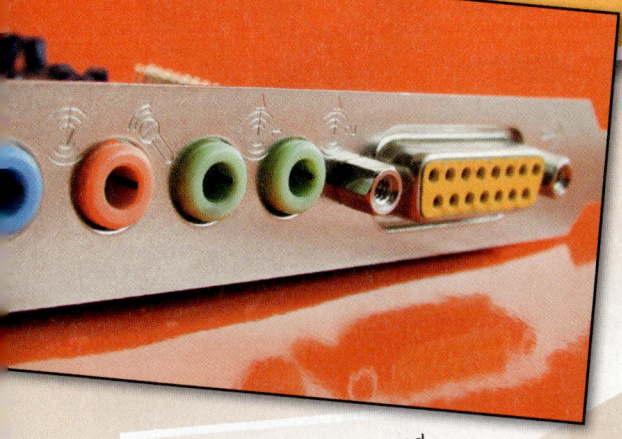

FIGURE 2.42 A basic sound card with color-coded connections: line-in (Blue), microphone (Pink), speakers or headphone (Green), MIDI [Musical Instrument Digital Interface] (Gold)

Computer output comes in two basic forms: tangible and intangible. In this article, we looked at intangible outputs: video and audio. The output devices in this section allow us to listen to Beethoven or the White Stripes and to view a Picasso painting or watch some idiot fall off his skateboard on YouTube. Video and audio output has changed computers from simply being calculators of data to being an integral part of our education and entertainment experiences.

Key Terms

CRT monitor	output device
DLP (digital light-processing projector)	pixel
headphones	plasma monitor
LCD (liquid crystal display)	projector
LCD projector	resolution
legacy technology	sound card
monitor	speakers
OLED (organic light-emitting diode)	video card

Running Project

If you were going to purchase a new desktop computer today, one decision you would have to make is what type and size of monitor to get. Think about the room you would put the system in and what you might use it for. Would you be watching movies on the screen? Is the room really bright? Does the screen need to be large enough for several people to view at once? Using the answers to these questions, determine the type and size of monitor you would need. Use the Internet to compare several models, and select the one that best fits your needs.

6 Things You Need to Know

- Most personal and notebook computers have LCD monitors.
- Large plasma monitors are found in media centers and conference rooms.
- Resolution is the number of horizontal pixels by the number of vertical pixels on a screen.
- The two types of video projectors are DLP and LCD.
- Video cards connect monitors and projectors to your computer.
- Speakers and headphones are audio output devices that connect to a sound card.

Pick a PRINTER

7 OBJECTIVE
Compare the features of different types of printers.

Hard copies (printouts) of documents and photos are produced by printers. There are many different types of printers that generate everything from photos to blueprints to ID cards. In this article, we'll look at some of the most common types of printers used in homes and businesses.

INKJET PRINTERS

The most common personal printers are **inkjet printers**. They work by spraying droplets of ink onto paper. Some printers use one ink cartridge; others may use two, three, four, or even more. The standard ink colors are cyan, magenta, yellow, and key (black), abbreviated as **CMYK**. Printers mix these colors to form every color (see Figure 2.43). Inkjets are inexpensive to purchase, but the cost of ink can quickly add up. When purchasing a printer, you should factor in the cost of ink, which is responsible for a large portion of the cost per page.

FIGURE 2.43 CMYK (cyan, magenta, yellow, black) are the colors used by inkjet and dye-sublimation printers.

PHOTO PRINTERS

A **photo printer** is a printer designed to print high-quality photos on special photo paper. Photo printers can be inkjet printers that use special ink cartridges or dye-sublimation printers, which produce lab-quality prints.

Some photo printers connect directly to a PictBridge-enabled digital camera or read data from a memory card. **PictBridge** is an industry standard that allows a camera to connect directly to a printer, usually by a USB connection or special dock, as seen in Figure 2.44.

FIGURE 2.44 You can print directly from a PictBridge-enabled camera or cell phone connected by a USB cable to a compatible printer.

DYE-SUBLIMATION PRINTERS

Dye-sublimation printers (or dye-sub printers) use heat to turn solid dye into a gas that's then transferred to special paper. The dye comes on a three- or four-color ribbon that prints a single color at a time. After all colors have been printed, the print is then coated with a clear protective layer to produce a high-quality photo that lasts longer than those printed on an inkjet printer. Dye-subs aren't general-purpose printers. They're limited to printing photos and some specialty items, such as ID badges and medical scans.

THERMAL PRINTERS

The receipts you receive from gas pumps, ATMs, and many cash registers are printed by **thermal printers**. They create an image by heating specially coated heat-sensitive paper, which changes color where the heat is applied. Thermal printers can print in one or two colors and can also be used to print bar codes, postage, and labels (see Figure 2.45).

FIGURE 2.45 A thermal printer uses special thermal paper to print receipts that you might get at a gas pump.

The most common type of printers found in schools and businesses are **laser printers**. Laser printers produce the sharpest text at a much lower cost per page than inkjet printers. Although they initially cost more that inkjets, the lower cost per page makes them less expensive for high-volume printing. Laser printers use a laser beam to draw an image on a drum. The image is electrostatically charged and attracts a dry ink called toner (see Figure 2.46). The drum is then rolled over paper, and the toner is deposited on the paper. Finally, the paper is heated, bonding the ink to it.

FIGURE 2.46 Static electricity causes this balloon to attract this little guy's hair, much like toner is attracted to the drum in a laser printer.

GREEN COMPUTING

SHOP SMART

The efficient and eco-friendly use of computers and other electronics is called green computing. Green computing is good for the environment, but it also saves money, making it a win-win proposition.

Choose Energy Star–rated devices. Energy Star (www.energystar.gov) is a rating system that's awarded to devices that use an average of 20–30% less energy than comparable devices. Saving energy saves money and reduces greenhouse gas emissions that contribute to global warming.

The Green Electronics Council has a program called the EPEAT (Electronic Product Environmental Assessment Tool; www.epeat.net) that can help you choose systems with environmentally friendly designs. The assessment is based on industry standards and ranks the devices as bronze, silver, or gold depending on the number of environmental performance criteria they meet.

MULTIFUNCTION DEVICES

Also known as "all-in-one printers," **multifunction devices** have built-in scanners and sometimes have fax capabilities. They can also be used as copy machines and eliminate the need for several different devices, saving both space and money. The disadvantage to using an all-in-one device is that if it needs to be repaired, all of its functions are unavailable.

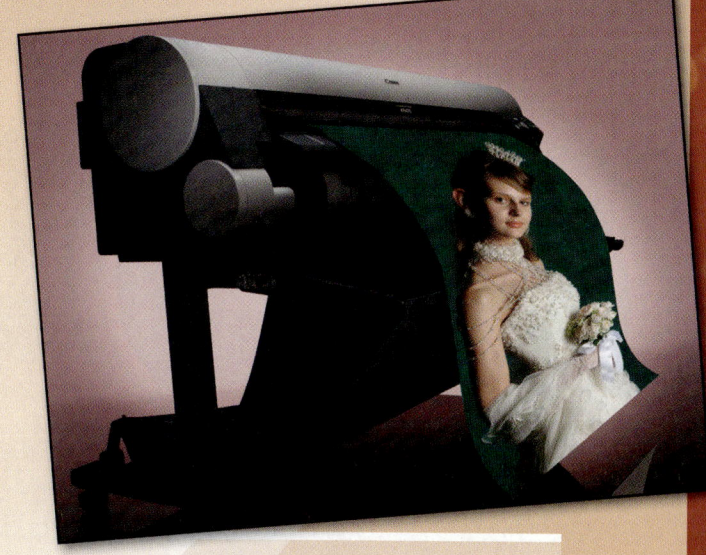

FIGURE 2.47 A plotter can create much larger printouts than a typical desktop printer can.

PLOTTERS

To produce very large printouts, such as blueprints, posters, and maps, **plotters** use one or more pens to draw an image on a roll of paper. Large inkjet and laser printers have mostly replaced pen plotters (see Figure 2.47).

Printers produce tangible output. The type of printer you choose depends on many things, including the type and size of output you need, cost, and size. Businesses might have several different types of printers on hand to meet all their needs. For a home user, a multifunction device might be the best choice. As the technology grows and the costs decrease, home users have the ability to have high-quality prints at home.

Key Terms

CMYK

dye-sublimation printer

inkjet printer

laser printer

multifunction device

photo printer

PictBridge

plotter

thermal printer

Running Project

What type of printer will you need? Think about the types of documents you'll print. Will you need to print mostly text? Do you print a lot of photos? Do you want to be able to connect your camera or memory card directly to the printer? Do you want to be able to scan and fax? Using the answers to these questions, decide which type of printer is right for you. Use the Internet to compare several models, and select the one that best fits your needs.

4 Things You Need to Know

- The most common personal printer is an inkjet.
- The most common office printer is a laser.
- Dye-subs, thermal printers, and plotters are specialized printers.
- PictBridge is a standard that lets you connect a digital camera directly to a printer.

ADAPTATION: Making Technology WORK FOR YOU

OBJECTIVE 8
Explain and provide examples of the concept of adaptive technology.

The Americans with Disabilities Act of 1990 requires employers with 15 or more employees "to make a reasonable accommodation to the known disability of a qualified applicant or employee if it would not impose an 'undue hardship' on the operation of the employer's business. Reasonable accommodations are adjustments or modifications provided by an employer to enable people with disabilities to enjoy equal employment opportunities." As a result of the ADA, many hardware and software vendors have developed adaptive technology.

Adaptive technology, also called "assistive technology," is used by individuals with disabilities to interact with technology (see Figure 2.48). It includes both hardware and software, and in many cases, everyday input and output devices can be adapted to the user. For example, a computer monitor screen image can be enlarged for a visually impaired user, and a hearing impaired user might have lights flash when an audio signal would normally be heard. Modern operating systems include accessibility settings that you can easily change.

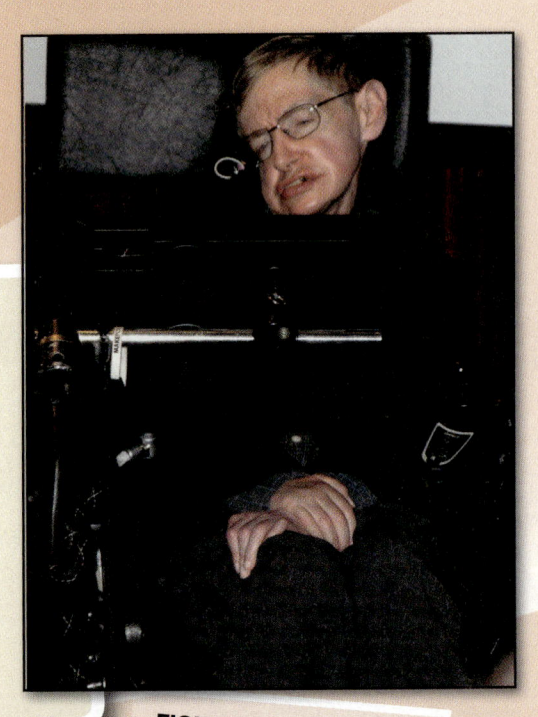

FIGURE 2.48 Many talented professionals, including physicist Stephen Hawking, use adaptive technology.

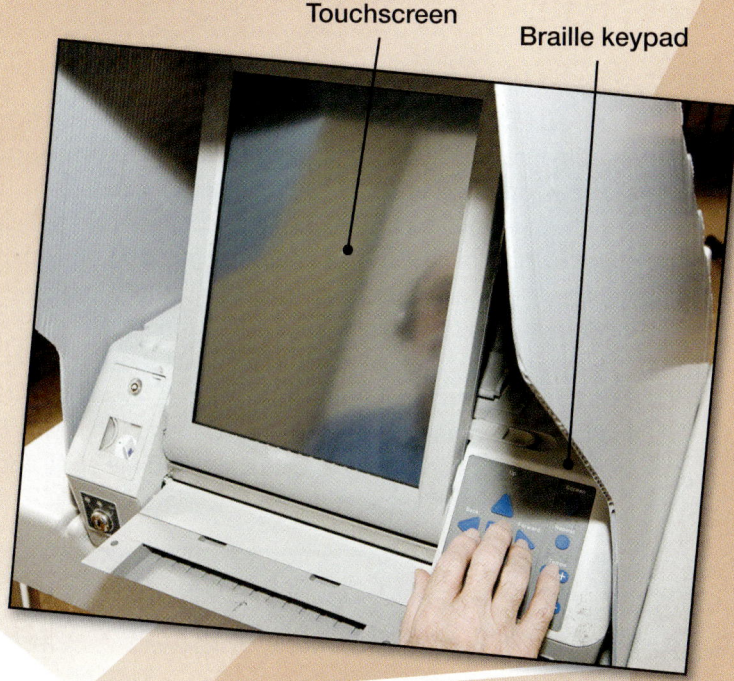

FIGURE 2.49 Introduced in 2008, this touch-screen voting machine is wheelchair-accessible and equipped for visual, auditory, and other disabilities.

ADAPTIVE INPUT DEVICES

Alternate input devices include Braille-writing devices, eye-driven keyboards, and keyboards that have locator dots on commonly used keys or large-print key labels. On-screen keyboards can be typed on using a pointing device or a touch screen. Such devices are being used in many public locations, such as libraries, schools, and polling places (see Figure 2.49). Trackballs, head wands, mouth sticks, and joysticks are all alternatives to the standard mouse.

Voice-recognition software allows a user to verbally control a computer and dictate text. Dragon NaturallySpeaking and MacSpeech Dictate are two of the most popular voice-recognition programs, and Windows 7 includes built-in speech recognition. Software settings, such as Sticky Keys and Mouse Keys on a Windows computer, adapt a standard keyboard for users with limited fine-motor control and allow the user to use arrow keys on the keyboard to move the pointer.

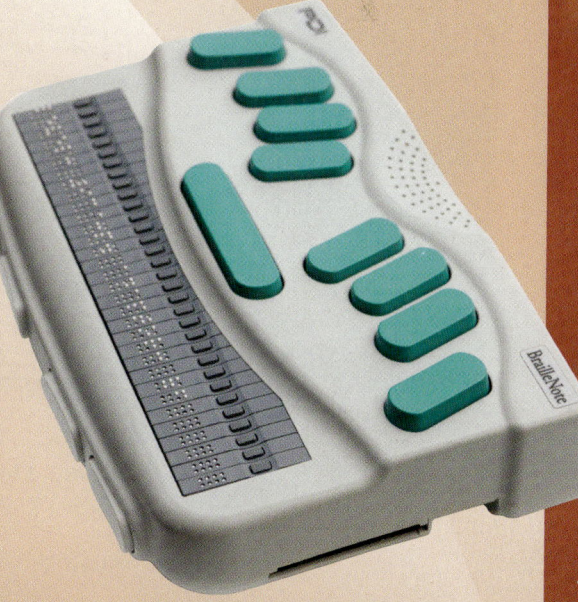

ADAPTIVE OUTPUT DEVICES

Standard monitors can be adapted by magnifying the screen (see Figure 2.50) and adjusting color and contrast settings. Speech synthesis screen-reader software and audio alerts aid visually and learning disabled users, while closed captions and visual notifications, such as flashing lights, aid those with auditory disabilities. Braille embossers are special printers that translate text to Braille. They're impact printers that create dots in special heavy paper that can be read by touch by visually impaired users.

While adaptive technology can make technology more accessible for individuals with disabilities, it also benefits those without disabilities. Enlarging the screen, touch-sensitive surfaces, easy-to-read buttons, and other accommodations make accessing technology easier for everybody. Businesses benefit by gaining the skills and talents of disabled employees.

OUT

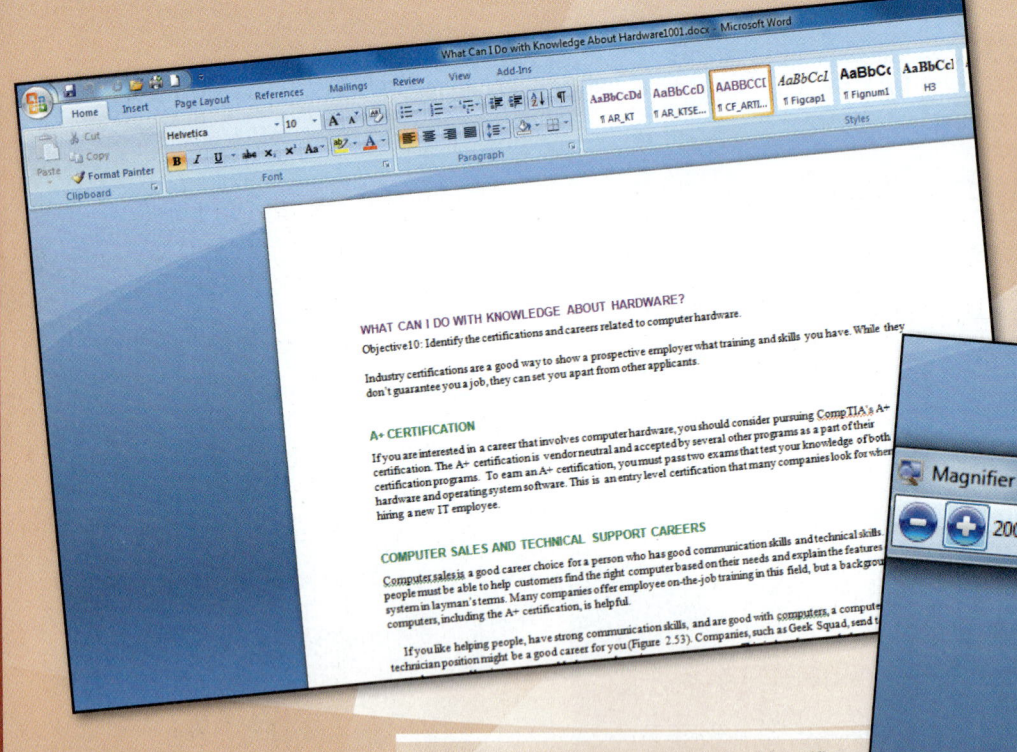

FIGURE 2.50 Windows 7 includes Magnifier, a screen magnification program that can be used to enlarge portions of the screen, as it has in the Word document on the right.

ETHICS

The Americans with Disabilities Act (see www.ada.gov) requires businesses with 15 or more employees to provide reasonable accommodation for all employees who have—or who have a record of having—a disability. A disability is any condition that limits one or more major life activities. Are there questionable conditions that fall into that category? As an employer, how would you address such a condition?

Should small businesses be required to provide adaptive technology to all employees, regardless of cost? Should they have to provide the technology the employee wants? Or can they choose other methods of addressing the issue of concern? What if the disability becomes so great that it causes the business financial hardship? Is the business then legally required to provide accommodation? What is the moral responsibility?

Key Terms

adaptive technology

Running Project

Are there any adaptive technology devices that you would include to meet the needs of any of the users of this computer?

3 Things You Need to Know

- Adaptive technology helps individuals with disabilities to interact with technology.
- The Americans with Disabilities Act (ADA) requires employers to make reasonable accommodations for disabled employees.
- Adaptive technology includes both hardware and software.

Communicate, Communicate, COMMUNICATE

OBJECTIVE 9
Discuss the different communication devices that can be used.

Communication devices serve as both input and output devices and allow you to connect to other devices on a network or to the Internet. These include network adapters, modems, and fax devices.

NETWORK ADAPTERS

Used to establish a connection with a network, **network adapters** may be onboard expansion cards or USB devices and may be wired or wireless. Wired cards are sometimes referred to as Ethernet cards and have a port that resembles a telephone jack, while wireless cards are used to connect to WiFi networks at home and in hot spots in airports and cafes, as shown in Figure 2.51.

FIGURE 2.51 A blue Ethernet cable can plug into the onboard network adapter on this notebook computer (left), while a wireless adapter connects this notebook to a hot spot at an airport (right).

MODEMS

Modems are used to connect a computer to a telephone line and are most often used for dial-up Internet access. Modem is short for *modulator-demodulator*. A modem modulates digital data into an analog signal that can be transmitted over a phone line and, on the receiving end, demodulates the analog signal back into a digital data.

We use the terms "analog" and "digital" devices throughout this book. The difference is in the way the data is encoded and transmitted (see Figure 2.52). Analog input devices convert data signals into continuous electronic waves or pulses, while analog output devices, such as telephones, televisions, and CRT monitors, translate the electronic pulses back into audio and video signals. In digital devices, the audio or video data is represented by a series of 0s and 1s. Digital signals can carry more data and are less prone to interference than analog signals.

FIGURE 2.52 An analog signal is a continuous wave, while a digital signal is an on/off transmission.

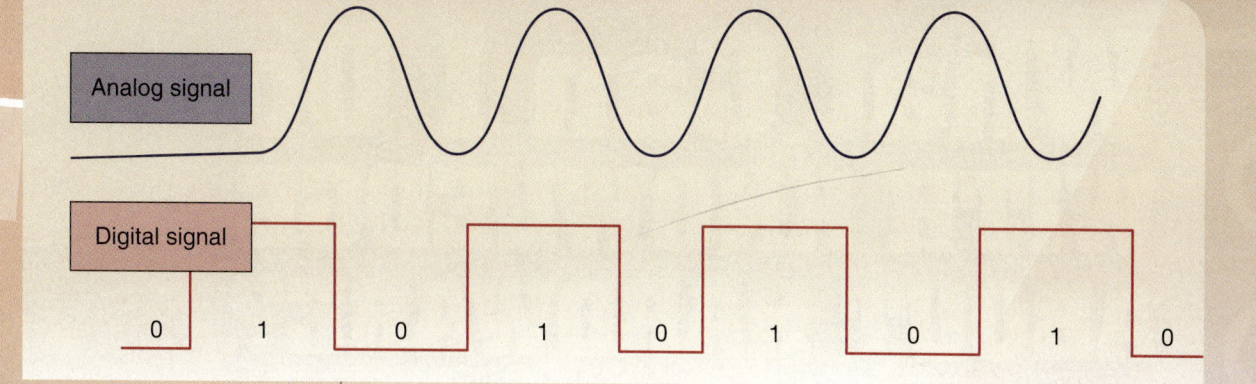

Analog signal

Digital signal

0 1 0 1 0 1 0 1 0

Some modems also include the capability to send and receive faxes. With fax software and a fax modem, a computer can be used as a fax machine. A cable modem is a special type of modem that connects to the cable system instead of a telephone line to provide fast Internet access. DSL (digital subscriber line) modems, which are used to provide broadband services, aren't really modems at all because the DSL line is already digital and there's no need to modulate the signal to analog.

FAX DEVICES

A fax device can be a stand-alone fax machine, part of a multifunction device, or built into a modem. A fax device (or facsimile) works by scanning a document and converting it into a digital format that can then be transmitted over telephone lines to a receiving fax device, which then outputs the document.

Communication devices allow us to connect our computers to other devices in our own homes and to the world, enabling us to access resources that just a few short years ago were unimaginable.

Key Terms

communication device

modem

network adapter

Running Project

Think about the location for this computer. What type of communications devices do you need to connect this system to the Internet? Will it connect to a network? Is it wired or wireless? Do you need fax capabilities?

Find Out MORE

In 2009, broadcast television was converted to digital TV (DTV). Older televisions now require a DTV converter box to convert the digital TV signal into an analog signal the TV can display. Why was the switch made? Was is strictly an economic decision or does it benefit society in some ways? What are the advantages of DTV over analog TV? Try checking www.dtv.gov for answers.

4 Things You Need to Know

- Network adapters connect a computer to a network.
- A modem is used for dial-up Internet access.
- Digital signals carry more data and are less prone to interference than analog signals.

What Can I Do WITH KNOWLEDGE ABOUT HARDWARE?

10 OBJECTIVE **Identify the certifications and careers related to computer hardware.**

Industry certifications are a good way to show a prospective employer what training and skills you have. While they don't guarantee you a job, they can set you apart from other applicants.

A+ CERTIFICATION

If you're interested in a career that involves computer hardware, you should consider pursuing CompTIA's A+ certification. The A+ certification is vendor-neutral and accepted by several other programs as a part of their certification programs. To earn an A+ certification, you must pass two exams that test your knowledge of both hardware and operating system software. This is an entry-level certification that many companies look for when hiring a new IT employee.

COMPUTER SALES AND TECHNICAL SUPPORT CAREERS

Computer sales is a good career choice for a person who has good communication skills and technical skills. Salespeople must be able to help customers find the right computer based on their needs and explain the features of a system in layman's terms. Many companies offer employee on-the-job training in this field, but a background in computers, including the A+ certification, is helpful.

If you like helping people, have strong communication skills, and are good with computers, a computer technician position might be a good career for you (see Figure 2.53). Companies, such as Geek Squad, send technicians out to homes and businesses to troubleshoot and repair computer systems. This is hands-on work that may involve travel and working nights and weekends. A+ certification is usually the minimum requirement at the entry-level positions in this field. Much of the training in this field takes place on the job.

Even if you're not looking for a technical career, understanding how computer hardware works and being able to make decisions about the hardware purchases you might make will help you be a better consumer and enable you to succeed in many different careers. For example, an office worker might need to make decisions about the type of printer to buy or a teacher might need help choosing the type of projector to install in a classroom. There are very few careers today that don't involve the use of some computer technology.

FIGURE 2.53 A computer technician needs to be good with people as well as computers.

HOW TO Assess Your Computer Hardware

Computer performance is affected by many things. In this tutorial, you'll learn a little bit about your own computer and how you might improve its performance by upgrading hardware components.

Windows 7 can provide many details about your computer's hardware through a variety of built-in utilities. For this exercise, you'll use the System Control Panel and Computer window.

1 Click the Start button and right-click *Computer*. From the context menu, choose *Properties*.

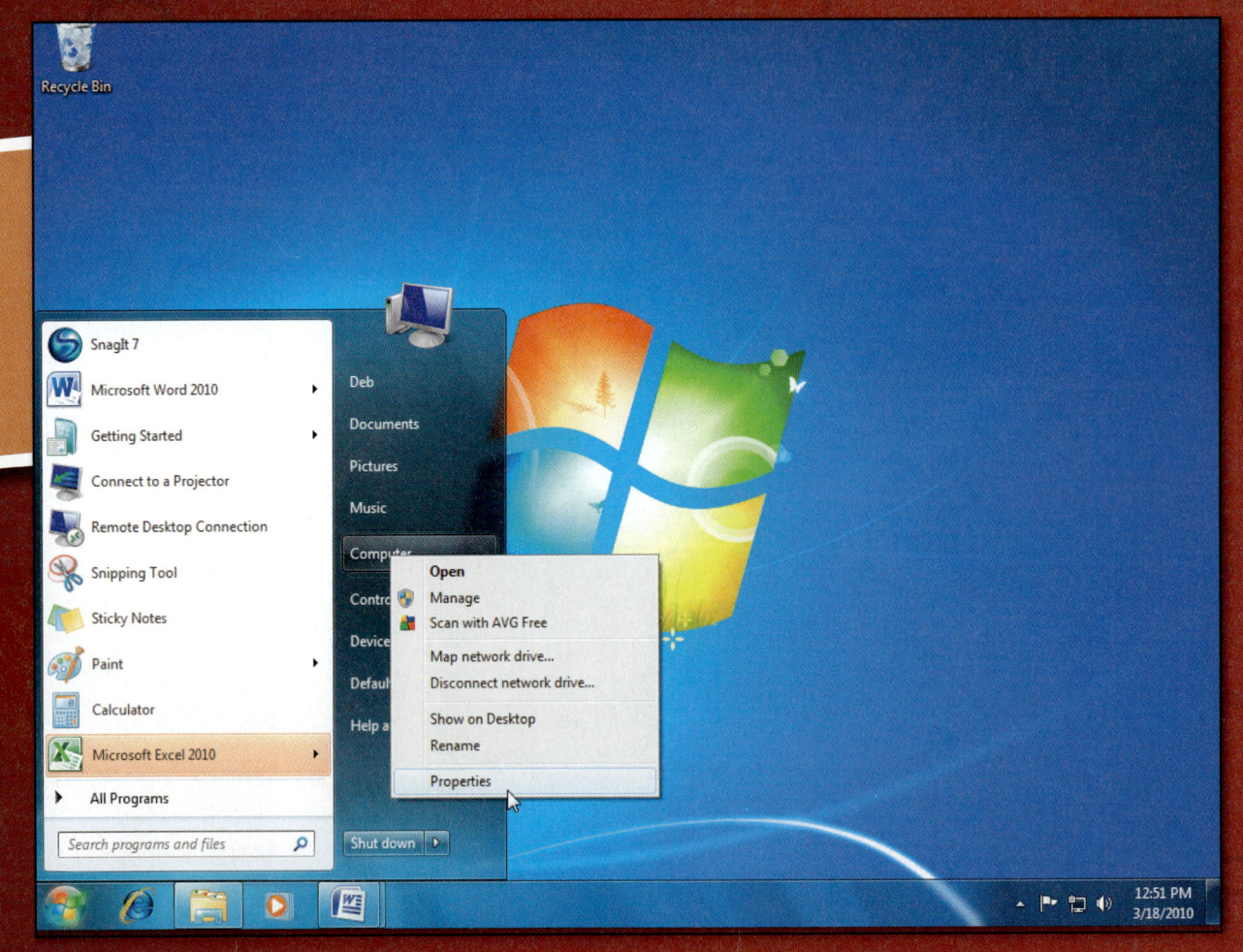

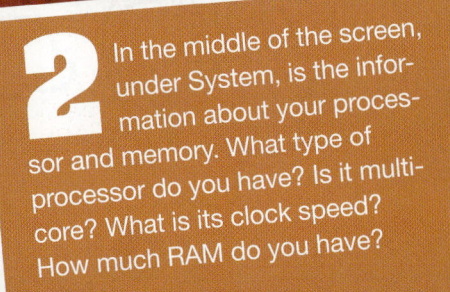

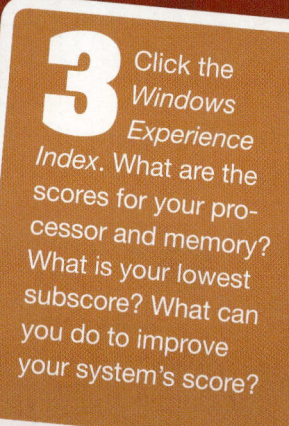

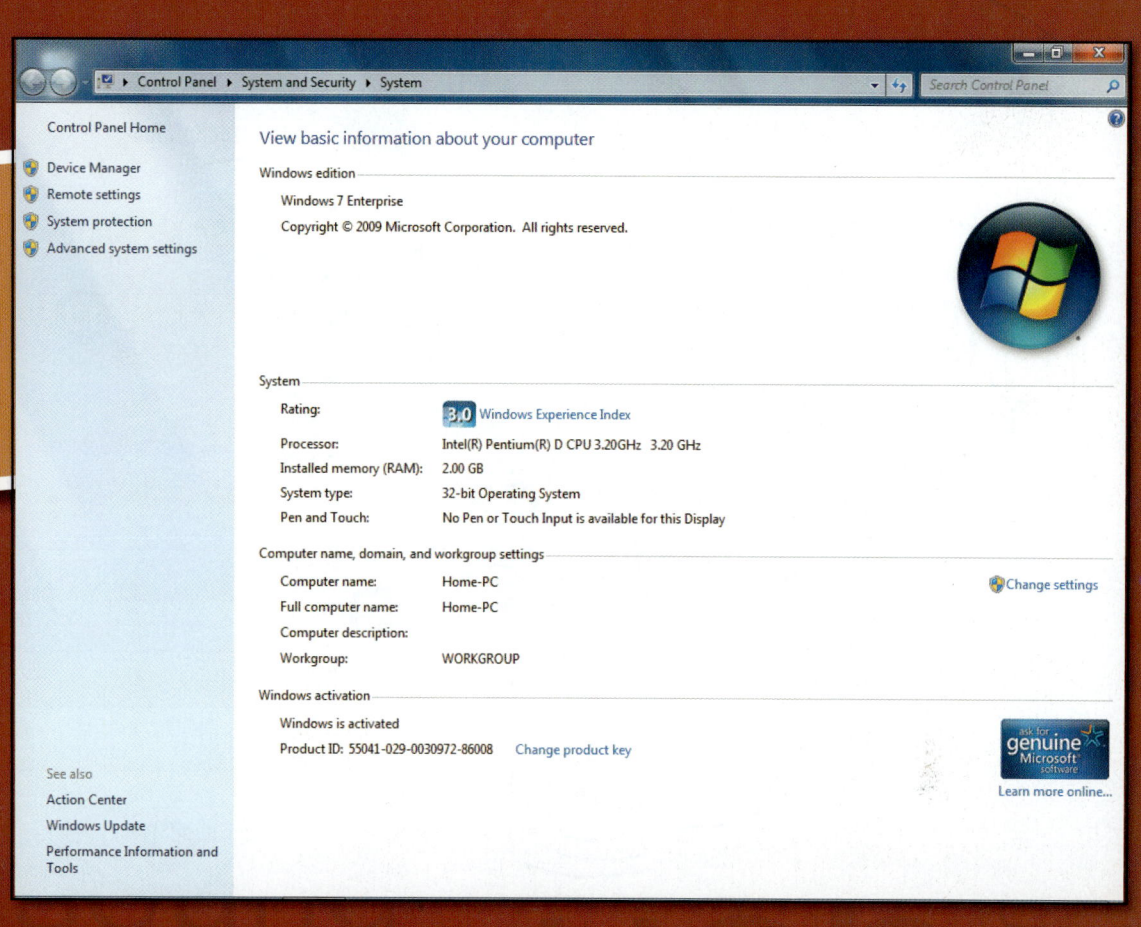

2 In the middle of the screen, under System, is the information about your processor and memory. What type of processor do you have? Is it multi-core? What is its clock speed? How much RAM do you have?

3 Click the *Windows Experience Index*. What are the scores for your processor and memory? What is your lowest subscore? What can you do to improve your system's score?

4 Click the Start button and click *Computer*. List all hard disk drives and devices with removable storage that are displayed. Include any additional information, such as size and free space, for each.

5 Click the Start button and click *Help and Support*. Click the *Learn about Windows Basics* link. Click the *Using your mouse* link. Scroll down to the section *Tips for using your mouse safely*. List three tips to prevent injury. Do you follow these tips? Click the Back button and click the *Using your keyboard* link. What are the three odd keys, and what do they do?

6 Type up your answers, save the file as **Lastname_Firstname_ch02_HowTo,** and submit it as directed by your instructor.

Objectives Recap

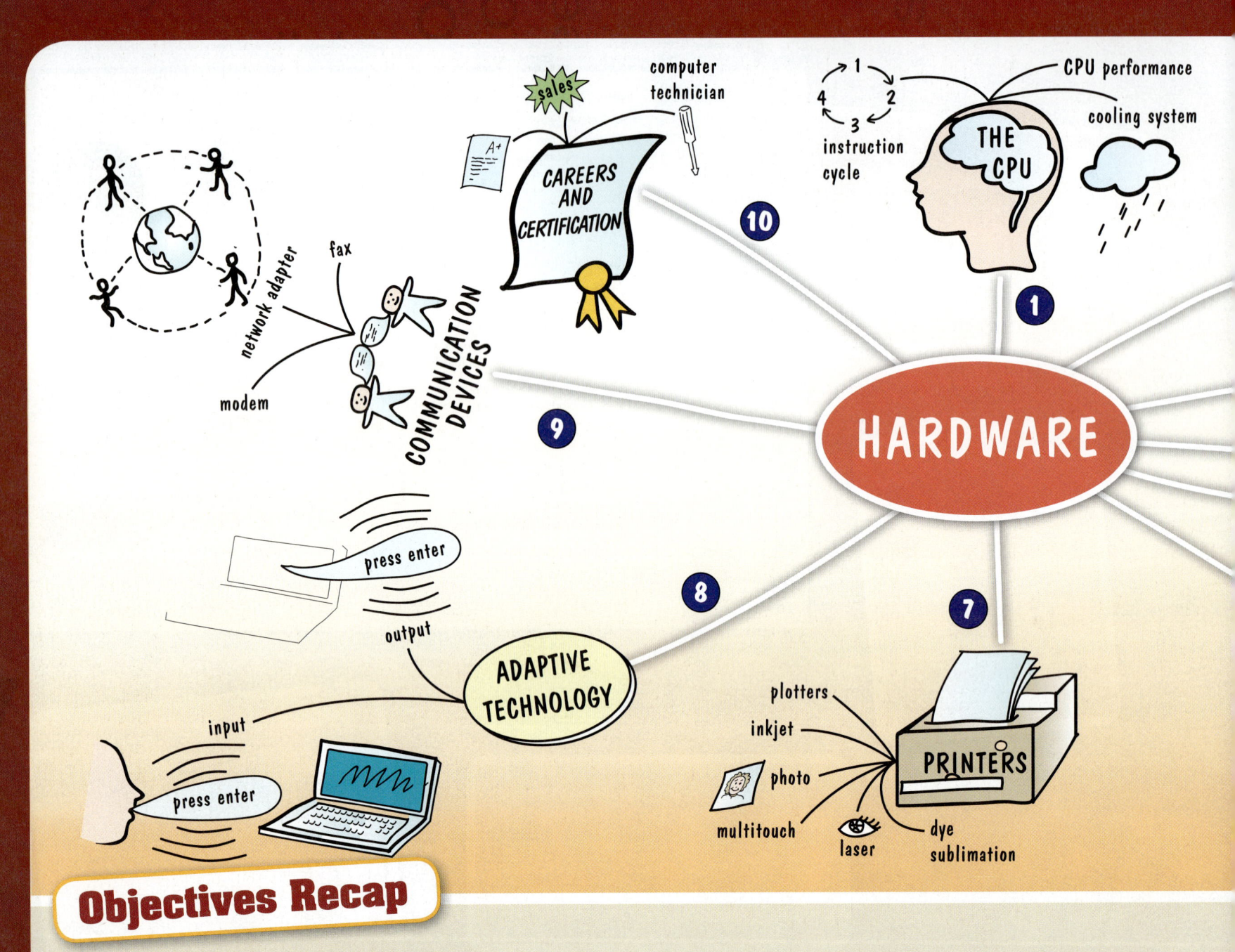

1. Explain the function of the CPU. **(p. 42)**
2. Identify the parts of a system unit and motherboard. **(p. 46)**
3. Describe how computers represent data using binary codes. **(p. 52)**
4. Compare different types of storage devices. **(p. 56)**
5. List different input devices and their uses. **(p. 60)**
6. List different video and audio output devices and their uses. **(p. 68)**
7. Compare the features of different types of printers. **(p. 74)**
8. Explain and provide examples of the concept of adaptive technology. **(p. 78)**
9. Discuss the different communication devices that can be used. **(p. 82)**
10. Identify the certifications and careers related to computer hardware. **(p. 84)**

② SYSTEM UNIT
- motherboard
- memory

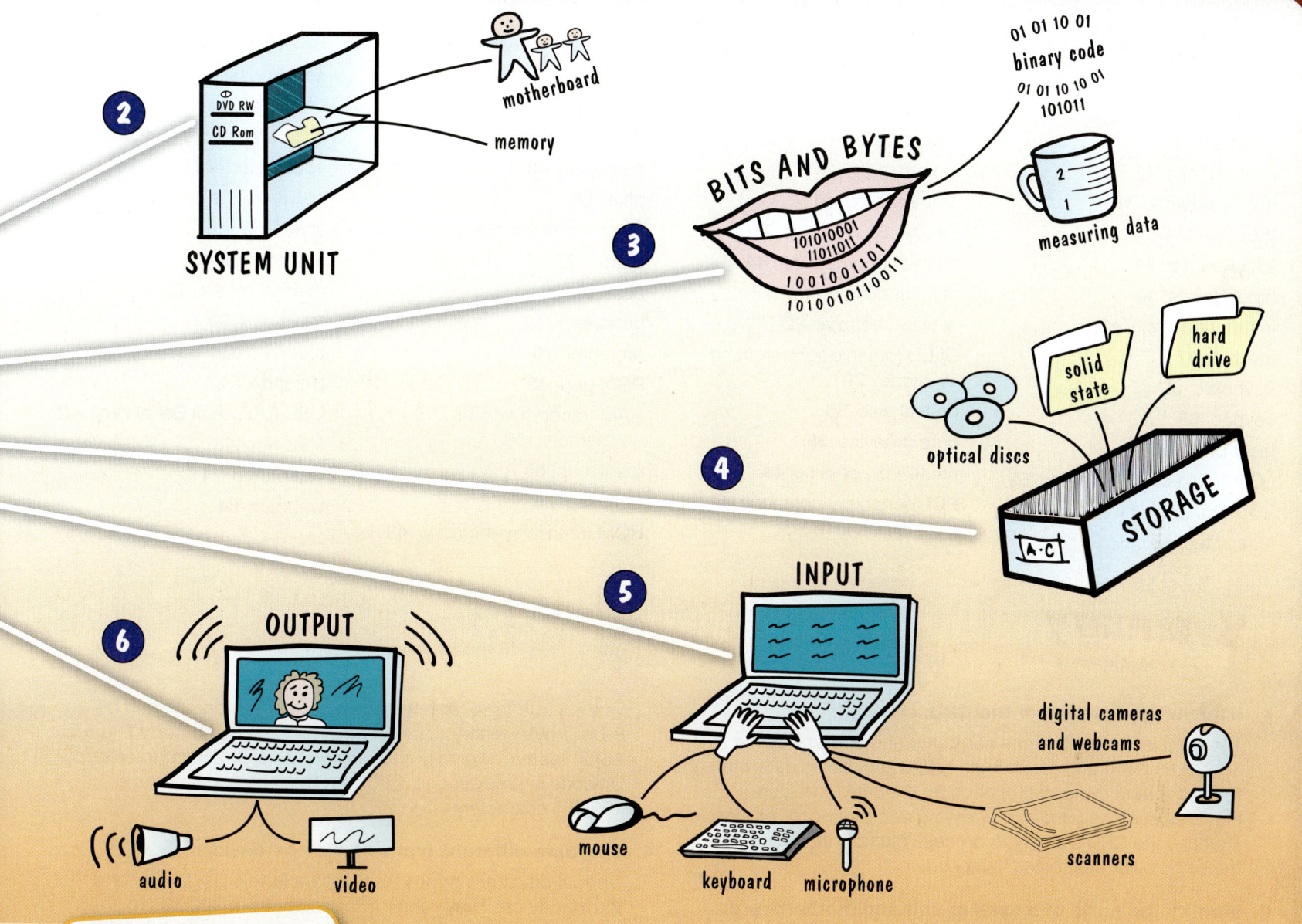

③ BITS AND BYTES
- binary code
- measuring data

④ STORAGE
- optical discs
- solid state
- hard drive

⑤ INPUT
- mouse
- keyboard
- microphone
- digital cameras and webcams
- scanners

⑥ OUTPUT
- audio
- video

Key Terms

AGP (accelerated graphics port) **47**
adaptive technology **78**
arithmetic logic unit (ALU) **42**
ASCII (American Standard Code for Information Interchange) **54**
binary code **53**
binary number system (base 2) **52**
biometric scanner **65**

BIOS (basic input output system) **49**
bit **53**
Bluetooth **49**
Blu-ray disc (BD) **57**
byte **53**
cache memory **51**
CD (compact disc) **57**
central processing unit (CPU) **42**

clock speed **43**
CMOS (complementary metal oxide semiconductor) **49**
CMYK **74**
communication device **82**
control unit **42**
CRT monitor **69**
data bus **47**
DLP (digital light-processing) projector **70**

DVD (digital video disc/digital versatile disc) **57**
drive controller **47**
dye-sublimation printer **75**
EIDE (enhanced integrated drive electronics) **47**
expansion card **47**
FireWire **49**
flash drive **58**
flash memory **57**

game controller 67
gigahertz (GHz) 43
hard drive 58
hardware 41
headphones 72
hot-swappable 48
IEEE 1394 49
inkjet printer 74
input device 60
instruction cycle 42
joystick 67
keyboard 60
keypad 62
laser printer 76
LCD (liquid crystal display) 69
LCD projector 71
legacy technology 69
memory 50
memory card 58
microphone 66
modem 82
monitor 68
motherboard 46
mouse 63
multi-core processor 44
multifunction device 77
network adapter 82
OLED (organic light-emitting diode) 70
optical disc 56
output device 68
parallel processing 44
PCI (peripheral component interconnect) 47
PCI express (PCIe) 47
peripheral device 41
photo printer 74
PictBridge 74
pipelining 43
pixel 68
plasma monitor 69
plotter 77
port 48
processor 42
projector 70
PS/2 port 48
RAM (random access memory) 50
resolution 68
RFID tag 65
ROM (read-only memory) 49
SATA (serial ATA) 47
scanner 64
serial and parallel ports 48
solid-state storage 57
sound card 73
speakers 72
stylus 63
system unit 46
thermal printer 75
touchpad 63
touch screen 63
Unicode 54
USB (Universal Serial Bus) 48
USB hub 48
video card 71
webcam 64

Summary

1. **Explain the function of the CPU.**

   The CPU is the brain of the computer and consists of the control unit and arithmetic logic unit. It processes data through the instruction cycle: fetch, decode, execute, and store. Features such as parallel processing and multi-core processing increase the CPU's ability to process multiple instructions at the same time, increasing its speed.

2. **Identify the parts of a system unit and motherboard.**

   The system unit is the case that houses the power supply, motherboard, processor (CPU), heat sink and cooling fan, and memory of a computer. It also has drive bays to hold the storage devices and openings for peripheral devices to connect to expansion cards on the motherboard. The motherboard is the main circuit board of a computer. In addition to housing the CPU, it contains: drive controllers and interfaces, expansion slots, data buses, ports and connectors, BIOS, and memory. A motherboard may also include integrated peripherals, such as video, sound, and network cards.

3. **Describe how computers represent data using binary codes.**

   A single bit (or switch) has two possible states—on or off—and can be used for situations with two possibilities, such as yes/no, true/false, or boy/girl. Digital data is represented by 8-bit (1 byte) binary code on most modern computers. The 8-bit ASCII system originally had binary codes for 256 characters. Unicode is an extended ASCII set that has codes for over 100,000 characters.

4. **Compare different types of storage devices.**

   Optical discs are removable and include CDs, DVDs, and Blu-ray discs. They range in capacity from 700 MB to 50 GB and are used to distribute music, programs, and movies as well as to archive data. Solid-state storage is a nonmechanical form of storage found in small flash drives, memory cards, personal media players, and netbooks. Hard disks are a form of magnetic storage and can be mounted in the system unit or connected via USB or FireWire cable. They have the largest capacities of any current storage device and hold the operating systems, programs, and data on the computer.

5. **List different input devices and their uses.**

   Input devices include keyboards and keypads for entering text; pointing devices, such as the mouse, touchpad, stylus, and touch-sensitive screens that move the cursor on the screen; cameras and webcams for video input; optical scanners, RFID scanners, magnetic strip readers, and biometric scanners that read data and convert it into digital form; microphones that convert sound into digital signals; and video game controllers and joysticks to interact with games and other software programs.

6. **List different video and audio output devices and their uses.**

   The most common output devices are monitors (LCD and plasma) and projectors (LCD and DLP) attached to video cards that produce video output; printers that produce hard copies; and speakers and headphones attached to sound cards that produce audio output.

7. **Compare the features of different types of printers.**

   The most common personal printer is the inkjet, which works by spraying droplets of ink onto paper. Photo printers can be either inkjet or dye-sub printers and are specifically designed to produce high-quality photo prints. Dye-sublimation printers use heat to turn solid dye into a gas that's then transferred to special paper to primarily produce photos. Thermal printers use special heat-sensitive paper to produce receipts, postage, and bar code labels. Laser printers produce the sharpest text at a much lower cost per page than inkjet printers. A multifunction device combines a printer with a scanner and sometimes a fax machine. A plotter produces very large printouts, such as blueprints, posters, and maps.

8. **Explain and provide examples of the concept of adaptive technology.**

   Adaptive technology enables users with a variety of disabilities to access technology through special hardware and software. Input devices include head wands, mouth sticks, voice-recognition software, and on-screen keyboards. Output devices include Braille embossers (printers), screen readers, and enlarged screens.

9. **Discuss the different communication devices that can be used.**

   Communication devices serve as both input and output devices and include network adapters, modems, and fax devices. A network adapter connects a computer to a network. A modem connects a computer to a telephone line for dial-up Internet access. The cable and DSL modems are special modems that enable access to high-speed Internet. Fax devices, which can be stand-alone fax machines, part of a multifunction device, or built into a modem, scan and convert a document into a digital form that can be transmitted over telephone lines.

10. **Identify the certifications and careers most closely related to computer hardware.**

    The CompTIA A+ certification is the most common entry-level certification for those that are interested in working in the computer support field. Computer sales and technical support are careers that require an in-depth knowledge of computer hardware.

Multiple Choice

Answer the multiple-choice questions below for more practice with key terms and concepts from this chapter.

1. A computer's clock speed is measured in
   a. gigabytes.
   b. gigahertz.
   c. gibibytes.
   d. gigabits.

2. The wires that transfer data across the motherboard are known as the
   a. system clock.
   b. CPU.
   c. CMOS.
   d. data buses.

3. _____ is a short-range, wireless technology used to connect peripheral devices to a computer.
   a. Blu-ray
   b. PS/2
   c. Bluetooth
   d. WiFi

4. The binary code that can represent most currently used language characters as well as mathematical and graphic symbols is known as
   a. Unicode.
   b. ASCII.
   c. international standards.
   d. There is no such code.

5. What is the standard internal drive interface in use today?
   a. SATA ✓
   b. EIDE
   c. USB
   d. IEEE 1394

6. Pointing devices, such as the mouse and _____, work by moving a cursor on the screen.
   a. scroll wheel
   b. touchpad ✓
   c. ball
   d. LED

7. _____ scanners read human characteristics such as fingerprints and retinas.
   a. Optical
   b. RFID
   c. Magnetic
   d. Biometric ✓

8. What type of monitor is found on most desktop and notebook computers?
   a. CRT
   b. LCD ✓
   c. Plasma
   d. DLP

9. What type of printer produces the highest-quality photo prints?
   a. Inkjet
   b. Color laser
   c. Dye-sublimation ✓
   d. Thermal

10. Digital signals are superior to analog signals because
    a. they're less prone to interference.
    b. they can carry more information.
    c. they don't have to be converted for use by computers and other digital devices.
    d. All the above ✓

True or False

Answer the following questions with T for true or F for false for more practice with key terms and concepts from this chapter.

F 1. The terms "CPU" and "system unit" mean the same thing.
T 2. Random access memory (RAM) loses the information stored in it when the power is turned off.
T 3. Computers use the decimal number system to store data.
F 4. ASCII contains codes for all the languages in use today.
____ 5. CDs and DVDs store data magnetically.
T 6. Mice and touchpads move a pointer, called a cursor, on the screen.
____ 7. LCD monitors are big, use a lot of energy, and are considered legacy technology.
T 8. Adaptive technology includes the hardware and software used by individuals with disabilities to interact with technology.
F 9. Network adapters are used to connect a computer to a telephone line for dial-up Internet access.
T 10. Energy Star is a rating system that's awarded to devices that use an average of 20–30 percent less energy than comparable devices.

Fill in the Blank

Fill in the blanks with key terms and concepts from this chapter.

1. The hardware components that serve the input, output, and storage functions of a computer are called ~~BIOS~~ _peripheral devices_.

2. The __ALU__ performs arithmetic (addition and subtraction) and logic (AND, OR, and NOT) calculations, and the __Control Unit__ manages the movement of data through the CPU.

3. A(n) __multi-core processor__ consists of two or more processors on a single chip.

4. __Expansion cards__ plug directly into expansion slots on the motherboard and allow you to connect additional peripheral devices to a computer.

5. USB and FireWire devices are __hot-swappable__, meaning they can be plugged and unplugged without turning off the computer.

6. The operating systems, programs, and data the computer is currently using are stored in __RAM__.

7. _____ are the main mass storage devices in a computer system.

8. The use of __scanners__ increases the speed and accuracy of data entry and converts information into a digital format that can be saved, copied, and manipulated.

9. __Plasma__ monitors work by passing an electric current through gas sealed in thousands of cells inside the screen. The current excites the gas, which in turn excites the phosphors that coat the screen to pass light through an image.

10. __Laser__ printers produce the sharpest text at a much lower cost per page than __inkjet__ printers.

Running Project

... The Finish Line

Use your answers to the previous sections of the Running Project to determine what you would need in a desktop system. Look at computer ads on some current retail websites and select a computer system that meets your needs. Pick a system in the $500–800 price range. Does it include everything you need? What's missing? What additional features does it have that you will find useful? Does it have extras that you could do without? Is it reasonably priced? What features would you get if you spent more money? What would you lose if you spent less? Justify why the system you chose is a good choice for you.

Write a report describing your selection and responding to the questions raised. Save your file as **Lastname_Firstname_ch02_Project**, and submit it to your instructor as directed.

Critical Thinking 1

You work for a small real estate office of 20 people. A new agent, Chris, is blind and needs assistive technology to do her job. Your boss asks you to help set up Chris's computer.

1. What are some of the accommodations that the office will need to make for Chris?

2. Windows implements assistive technology through accessibility features. To access these settings, click the Start button, click Control Panel, and under Ease of Access, click *Let Windows suggest settings*.

3. Answer the questions the wizard asks, and review the recommended settings. What are the recommended settings for Chris? What hardware is needed to implement the suggestions? What other assistive devices might be useful for Chris? Visit **www.microsoft.com/enable** for more information and suggestions.

4. Does the ADA apply in this situation? Explain your answer. Type up your answers, save the file as **Lastname_Firstname_ch02_Accessibility**, and submit it as directed by your instructor.

Critical Thinking 2

Michael is a freshman at a local community college. He's looking for a computer for doing schoolwork. He needs to run Microsoft Office 2010 and needs network access. Mike's also an avid computer gamer and wants a machine that can handle the latest computer games. He's looking for a machine that will get him through the next couple of years until he graduates and can afford to upgrade. Because you're taking this class, Mike has enlisted your help in choosing a computer that meets his needs. He has $750 to spend.

1. Evaluate three computer choices from current newspaper ads or websites and compare them with respect to Mike's requirements.

2. Use a word processor to create a table like the one on the next page, comparing the features of each computer, to organize your research.

3. In the same document, write up your recommendation for Mike in a two- to three-paragraph essay. Which computer should he buy and why? What other peripherals and software will he need to purchase? You should also recommend necessary peripherals, including a monitor and printer. Remember your budget is fixed, so you can't exceed $750.

4. Save your file as **Lastname_Firstname_ch02_750**, and submit both your table and essay as directed by your instructor.

	Computer 1	Computer 2	Computer 3
Website or store providing sales information (support issues)			
Brand			
Model			
Price			
Processor type			
Processor speed			
Memory type			
Memory amount			
Hard drive capacity			
Additional equipment/features			
Additional purchases required to meet Mike's needs			

Do It Yourself 1

1. Windows 7 ClearType Text Tuner is a program that helps make the text on your screen easier to read over long periods of time. In this activity, you'll use the ClearType Text Tuner to fine-tune your screen. Click the Start button and click *Help and Support*. Type **ClearType** in the search box and press Enter. Click *ClearType: frequently asked questions.* What is it? How does it work? What type of monitor is best suited for ClearType?

2. Click the Start button and type **clear** in the search box. Select *Adjust ClearType text* from the search results list.

3. If necessary, click *Turn on ClearType* and click *Next*. In each of the next four screens, select the text box that looks the clearest to you. Click *Finish*. Did you make any changes? Do you notice any difference?

4. Type up your answers, save the file as **Lastname_Firstname_ch02_ClearType,** and submit it as directed by your instructor.

Do It Yourself 2

Windows provides several ways to reduce the energy consumption of your computer. In this activity, you'll examine the Power Settings on your computer.

1. Click the Start button and click Control Panel. Click *System and Security* and click *Power Options.*

2. Click *Change plan settings* for each of the plans. Compare the settings to turn off the display and put the computer to sleep. Which power plan is your computer currently using? Is this the appropriate plan for your computer?

3. Click the Start button and click *Help and Support*. In the search box, type **sleep** and press Enter. Click *Sleep and hibernation: frequently asked questions*. What is sleep mode?

4. Close the Help window. Type up your answers, save the file as **Lastname_Firstname_ch02_Power**, and submit it as directed by your instructor.

Ethical Dilemma

The United States now issues RFID passports to its citizens. Many individuals and groups, such as the American Civil Liberties Union, have criticized this decision, claiming the passports pose security and privacy risk. In February 2009, Chris Paget, an "ethical hacker," used $250 worth of equipment to scan and copy the information on RFID passport cards (wallet-sized passport cards that can be used only to enter the United States from Canada, Mexico, the Caribbean, and Bermuda at land border crossings or sea ports-of-entry) and enhanced driver's licenses while he drove around San Francisco. Paget claims he did this to demonstrate the security weakness in the technology. You can watch the video of his experiment by searching for Chris Paget on YouTube.

1. What Paget did is illegal, but does the end justify the means?
2. Should the United States consider scrapping the RFID passport program? Why or why not?
3. There are several websites that suggest microwaving your passport to disable the RFID chip. Is this legal? Would you do it if you thought it would work? (By the way, it doesn't; but it will ruin your passport.) Are there other, legal ways to protect your information?
4. Type up your answers, save the file as **Lastname_Firstname_ch02_RFID,** and submit it as directed by your instructor.

On the Web 1

The EPEAT website provides information to help you "evaluate, compare and select electronic products based on their environmental attributes." Visit the site **www.epeat.net**, and answer the following questions:

1. What types of devices are included in the system? How are they placed into the registry? What testing do they undergo?
2. What are the environmental performance criteria the devices must meet?
3. What manufacturers participate in the program? How is it funded? Is there any conflict of interest? Type up your answers, save the file as **Lastname_Firstname_ch02_Epeat,** and submit it as directed by your instructor.

On the Web 2

Your aunt just purchased a new notebook computer, and she has given you her old desktop. You need to upgrade some components to improve its performance. The system is a Dell Inspiron 530 with 1 GB of RAM and a 120 GB hard drive. You know that one of the best steps you can take is to upgrade the memory by adding RAM. You also need more hard drive space.

1. Go to Dell's website (**www.dell.com**), and search for these components. Add an additional 1 GB of RAM and at least a 500 GB hard drive.
2. What is the total cost for these upgrades? Are they worth the cost? Type up your answers, save the file as **Lastname_Firstname_ch02_Upgrade**, and submit it as directed by your instructor.

Collaboration 1

Instructors: Divide the class into five groups, and assign each group one topic for this project. The topics include: system unit, storage, input devices, output devices, and communication devices.

The Project: Each team is to prepare a written presentation that includes an explanation of its topic, examples of devices in that category (including adaptive/assistive devices), and examples of devices that aren't included in this book. Use pictures, text, key terms, and color to enhance the presentation. Teams must use at least three references, only one of which may be this textbook. Use Google Docs to prepare the final version of your presentation, and provide documentation that all team members have contributed to the project. For more on using Google Docs, see Appendix C.

Collaboration 2

Students: Before beginning this project, discuss the roles each group member will play. Choose a team name, which you'll use in submitting your presentation. Be sure to divide the work among your members, and pick someone to present your project. You may find it helpful to elect a team leader who can direct your activities and ensure that all team contributions are collated through Google Docs.

Outcome: You're to prepare a presentation on your assigned topic in Word. The presentation may be no longer than two pages, double-spaced. On the first page, be sure to include the name of your presentation and a list of all team members. Turn in a version of your presentation showing revisions named as **Teamname_ch02_Hardware_Draft**. In addition, turn in a final version of your presentation with all revisions accepted named as **Teamname_ch02_Hardware_Final**. Submit your presentation to your instructor as directed.

Instructors: Divide the class into five groups, and assign each group one type of printer for this project. The topics include: inkjet, dye-sublimation, laser, multifunction, and plotter.

The Project: Each team is to prepare a multimedia commercial for its printer type. The presentation should be designed to convince a consumer to buy the team's printer. Teams must use at least three references, only one of which may be this textbook. Use Google Docs to plan the presentation, and provide documentation that all team members have contributed to the project. For more on using Google Docs, see Appendix C.

Students: Before beginning this project, discuss the roles each group member will play. Choose a team name, which you'll use in submitting your presentation. Be sure to divide the work among your members, and pick someone to present your project. You may find it helpful to elect a team leader who can direct your activities and ensure that all team contributions are collated through Google Docs.

Outcome: You're to prepare a multimedia presentation on your assigned topic in PowerPoint (or another tool, if approved by your instructor) and present it to your class. The presentation may be no longer than 3 minutes and should contain five to seven slides. On the first slide, be sure to include the name of your presentation and a list of all team members. Turn in a final version of your presentation named as **Teamname_ch02_Printers** and your Google Docs file showing your collaboration named as **Teamname_ ch02_Printers_Collaboration**. Submit your presentation to your instructor as directed.

Blogging

1. Blog about your evaluation of the computer you're currently using. In your write-up, provide the type of computer you have and the operating system you're using. Outline the things your computer does well and the challenges you face in using your computer for school, work, and recreation. Also, note areas you feel need to be upgraded and why.

2. Visit at least two of your classmates' blogs on this topic. On the blogs you visit, provide three to five sentences with suggestions of how the blog owner could upgrade his or her system or improve performance.

3. Create a document that includes your blog URL and the URLs of the two blogs you commented on. Save the file as **Lastname_Firstname_ch02_Hardware_Blog**. Submit the document to your instructor as directed.

CHAPTER 3
File Management

Running Project

In this chapter, you learn about the importance of file management. Look for instructions as you complete each article. For most, there's a series of questions for you to research or a set of tasks to perform. At the conclusion of this chapter you're asked to submit your responses to the questions raised and the results of the tasks you've performed.

Become our friend on Facebook

OBJECTIVES

1. Create folders to organize files. (p. 100)
2. Explain the importance of file extensions. (p. 108)
3. Explain the importance of backing up files. (p. 112)
4. Demonstrate how to compress files. (p. 116)
5. Use advanced search options to locate files. (p. 122)
6. Change the default program associated with a file type. (p. 126)
7. Identify the certifications and careers related to file management. (p. 128)

IN THIS CHAPTER

The concepts of file management are not unique to computing. We use file cabinets, folders, boxes, drawers, and piles to manage our paper files. This can be anything from bills to photographs to homework assignments to coupons. In this chapter, we look at managing our electronic files.

A Place for EVERYTHING

OBJECTIVE 1
Create folders to organize files.

One of the most important things that you need to do when working with computers is called **file management**. This means opening, closing, saving, naming, deleting, and organizing digital files. In this article, we discuss organizing your digital files, creating new folders, and navigating through the folder structure of your computer.

NAVIGATING YOUR COMPUTER

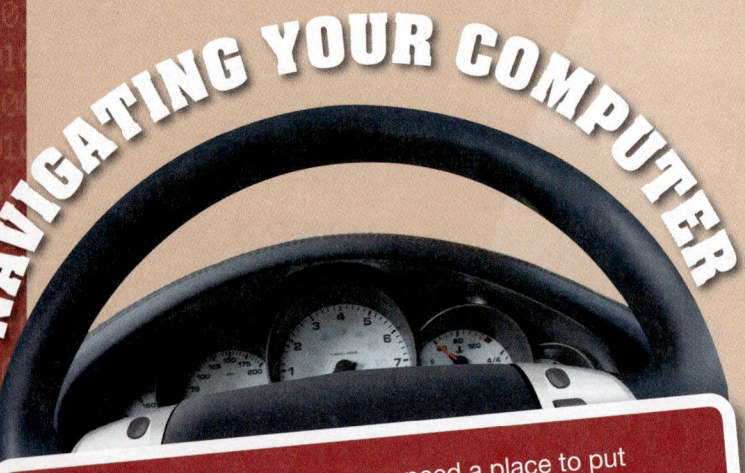

Before you can create files, you need a place to put them. Let's start with the existing folder structure of your computer and how to navigate through it.

THE USER AND PUBLIC FOLDERS By default, Windows comes with certain files and folders already created. When a user account is added to a Windows computer, Windows will automatically create a personal user folder for that username and the subfolders inside it (see Figure 3.1). You can access your user folder through the Windows Start menu or it may appear on the desktop. **Folders** are containers that are used to organize files on your computer. Your user folder is normally only accessible by you. If another person logs on to the computer using another username, they won't see your files. Windows also creates **Public folders** that are common to all users and provide an easy way to share files between them. You can also share files across computers that are on a network or in the same homegroup (computers on your home network running Windows 7).

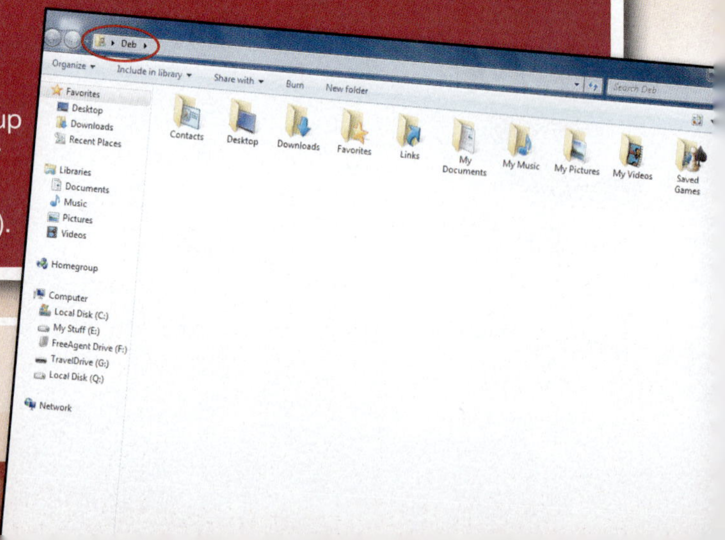

FIGURE 3.1 The user folder for my account (Deb) consists of subfolders that I use to organize my files.

OBJECTIVE 1 | 100

What folders are located under your username? The folder structure created by Windows is a **hierarchy**. There are folders within folders, known as subfolders or children, which allow you to further organize your files. Windows creates a set of folders to help you sort out your files. The My Documents folder is the place to store files such as word processing files, spreadsheets, presentations, and text files. There are also folders set up for pictures, music, and videos. These specialized folders are the best places to save your pictures, music, and videos so they're easy to find. Without this folder structure, all your files would be lumped together, making it much harder to keep track of what you have, similar to dumping all your snapshots into a shoebox. The sequence of folders to a file or folder is known as its **path**.

LIBRARIES Windows 7 introduced **libraries** to help you organize your files. There are four libraries: Documents, Music, Pictures, and Videos, and you can create more to suit your needs. Each library includes the matching user subfolder and the corresponding Public folder. This gives you quick access to both your personal files and the public shared files in one place. You can also customize libraries by adding other locations to the list. For example, if you store pictures on an external hard drive, you can add its location to the Picture library by right-clicking on the location (see Figure 3.2).

FIGURE 3.2 Libraries gather files that are located in different locations. In this example, the Digital camera pics folder on the My Stuff (D:) drive is added to the Pictures library.

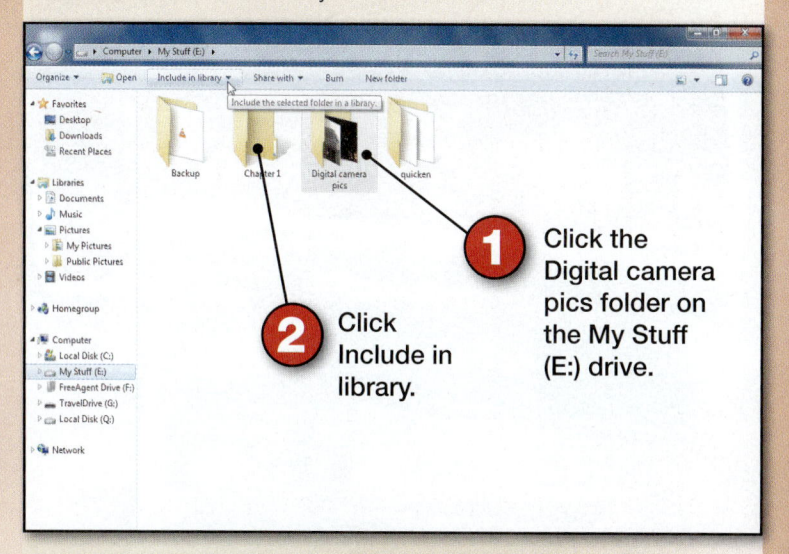

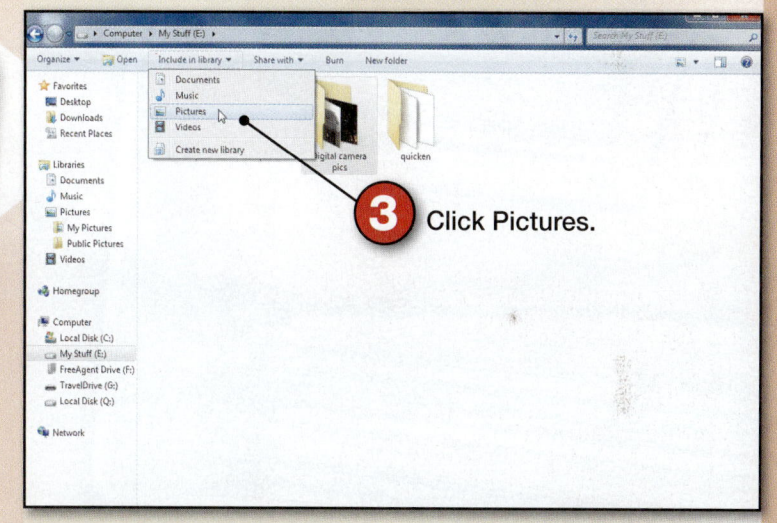

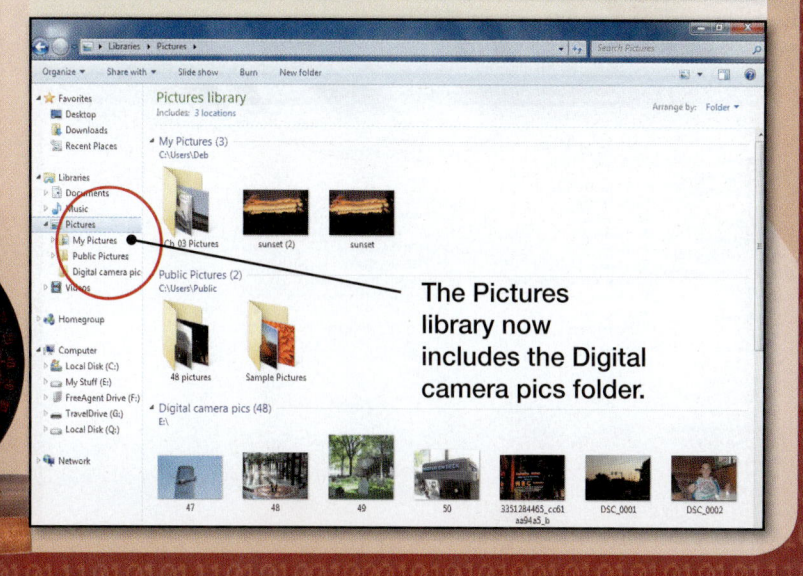

1. Click the Digital camera pics folder on the My Stuff (E:) drive.

2. Click Include in library.

3. Click Pictures.

The Pictures library now includes the Digital camera pics folder.

Chapter 3 | 101

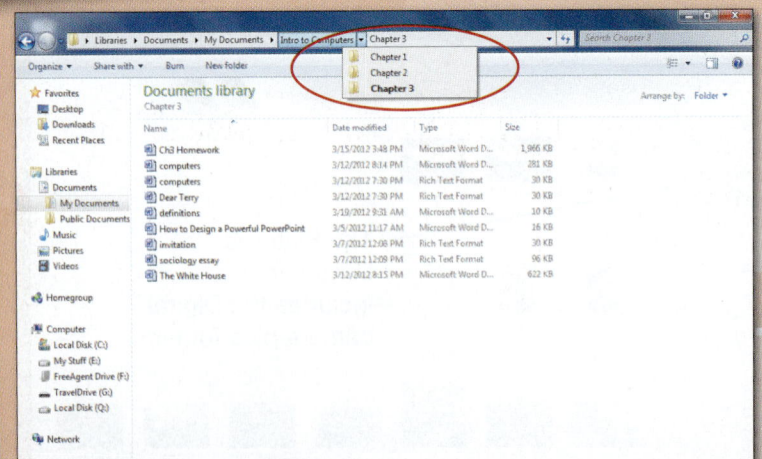

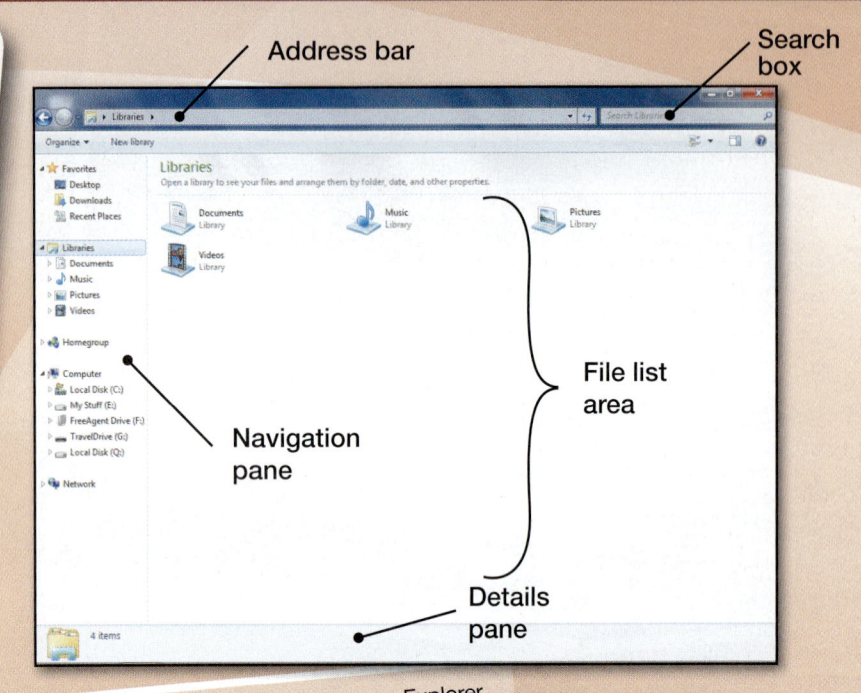

WINDOWS EXPLORER The window you use to look at a library or folder is called **Windows Explorer**. You can open it by clicking the Windows Explorer icon on the taskbar. You can use Windows Explorer to navigate through the folders and drives on your system and to handle most file management tasks. Figure 3.3 identifies some of the parts of the Explorer window.

FIGURE 3.3 The parts of Windows Explorer

- The search box is used to search for files located in the current Explorer window. Windows searches the files in your current location for the text you type into the Search box. We explore searching in more detail later in this chapter.
- The toolbar contains buttons for common tasks to be performed on the items in the file list area. These buttons change depending on the objects displayed.
- The file list area takes up most of the window and displays the contents of the current library or folder displayed in the Explorer window.
- The Address bar contains the path to the current location in the Explorer window and is used to navigate through folders and libraries. You can move down in the folder hierarchy by clicking the arrow after your location. You can move back up in the folder hierarchy by clicking the arrows or links before your location in the Address bar (see Figure 3.4).

FIGURE 3.4 The Address bar in Windows Explorer is used to move up and down the folder hierarchy and contains the path to the current location.

- The Navigation pane is used to navigate the folders, libraries, and drives available on a computer. The Navigation pane is divided into several sections: Favorites, which is a list of your favorite/common locations, Libraries, Homegroup, Computer, and Network. Clicking on any of these sections changes the contents in the right pane. Clicking the small triangle before an item in the Navigation pane expands it to display the locations it contains (see Figure 3.5).

FIGURE 3.5 The Navigation pane makes it easy to navigate through the libraries, folders, and drives available on your computer.

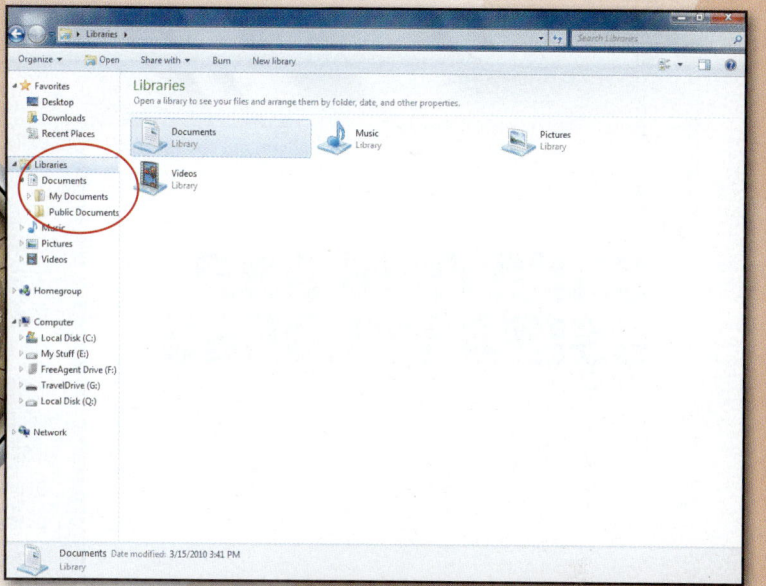

- The Details pane shows properties of the item selected in the file list area. For some files, you can use this area to modify certain properties, such as Tags and Rating (see Figure 3.6).

- The Views button allows you to change the way the file list objects are displayed in the file list area. For picture files, choosing Large Icons, as in Figure 3.7, displays a small preview, or thumbnail, of the image. Selecting Details from the Views menu displays a list of files with some of their properties. You can change the view by dragging the slider bar up and down.

FIGURE 3.6 The Details pane displays properties of the selected file, and you can use it to modify some of those properties. If the file is a picture or video, there is also a small preview of the image.

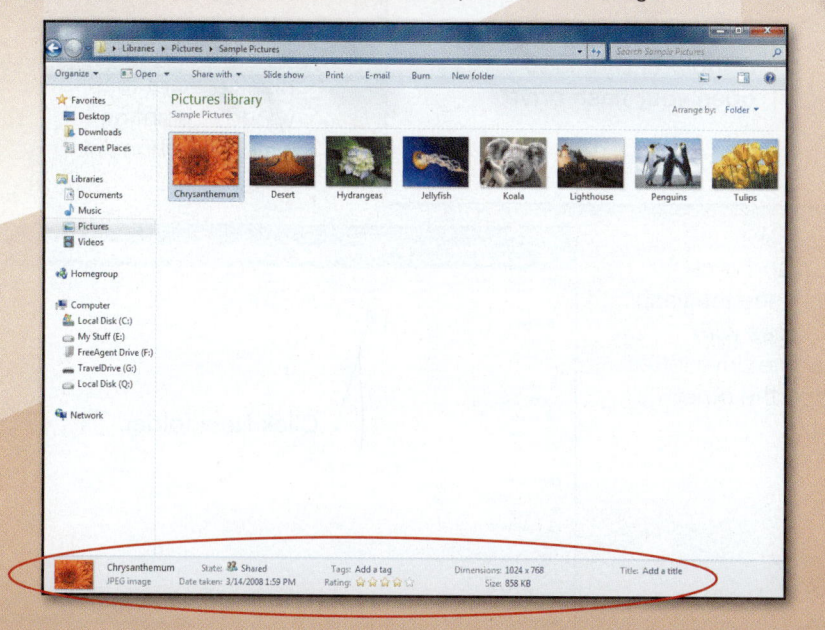

FIGURE 3.7 The Large Icons view displays small previews of image files.

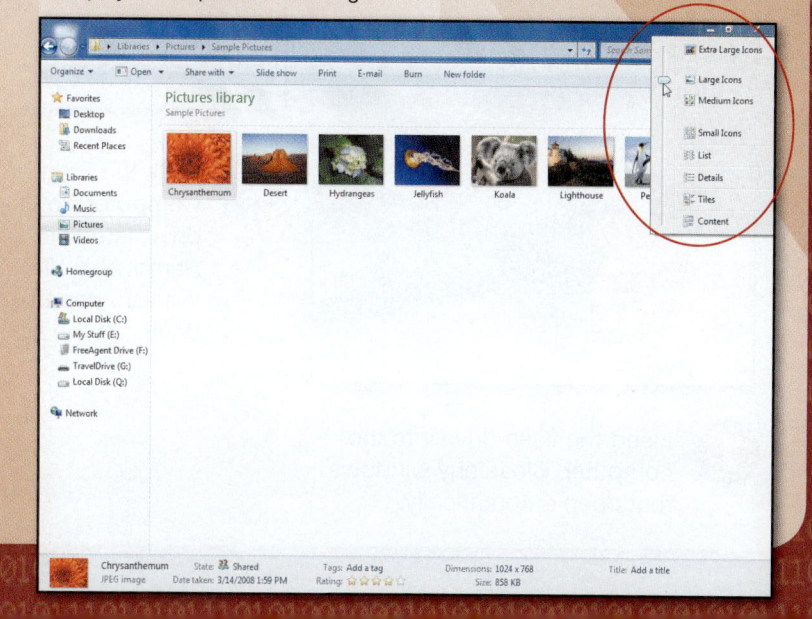

Chapter 3 | 103

CREATING AND USING FOLDERS

Of course, you're not limited to using the folder structure that's created by Windows. You can create your own organization scheme to fit your needs. This is especially useful when you use flash drives and other locations that aren't part of the user folder hierarchy. Suppose you print 25–30 photos a month (or 300–360 photos a year). How would you keep track of them? If you put them in a big box, in a few years, you'd have thousands of photos in the box. It would be nearly impossible to keep track of them or find anything unless you organized them into photo albums. The same is true of the files on your computer. Creating folders to organize your files will make storing and finding them easier to do. **Figure 3.8** demonstrates how to create a new folder on a flash drive.

FIGURE 3.8 The steps to create a new folder on a flash drive

1 Insert the flash drive into the computer. Close any windows that open automatically.

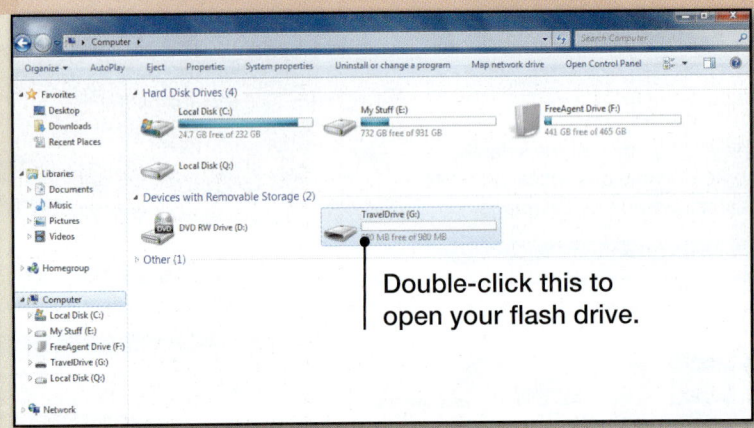

2 Click the Start button and click Computer. You should see the flash drive listed under *Devices with Removable Storage*. The drive letter will vary depending on the other drives on the system.

Double-click this to open your flash drive.

3 Double-click the icon for the flash drive to open it. On the toolbar, click New folder. (You can also create a folder by right-clicking on a blank area of the window, pointing to New, and choosing Folder.)

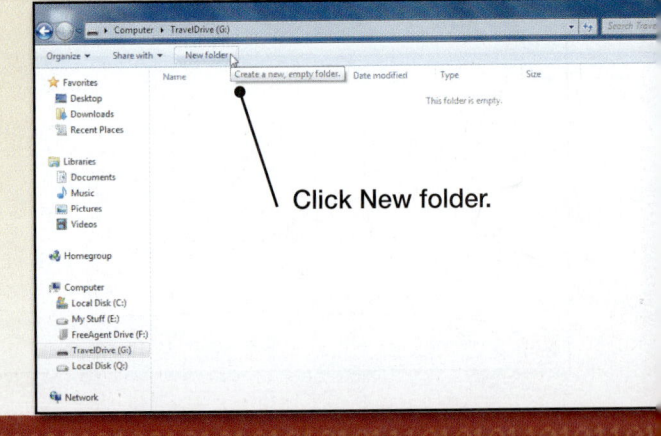

Click New folder.

OBJECTIVE 1

You can also create a new folder when you save a file. This allows you to organize your files as they're created instead of after the fact. The Save As dialog box that opens when you save a file looks very much like Windows Explorer and includes the New folder button (see **Figure 3.9**).

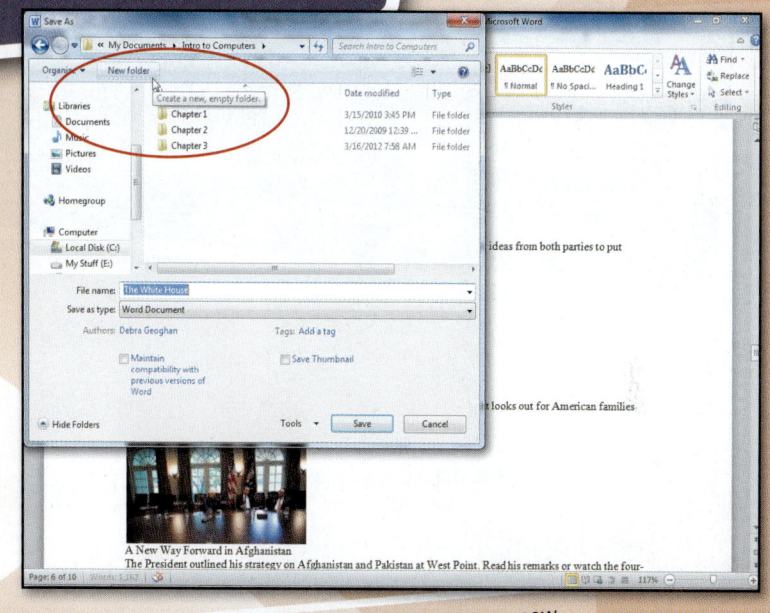

FIGURE 3.9 You can create a new folder from the Save As dialog box.

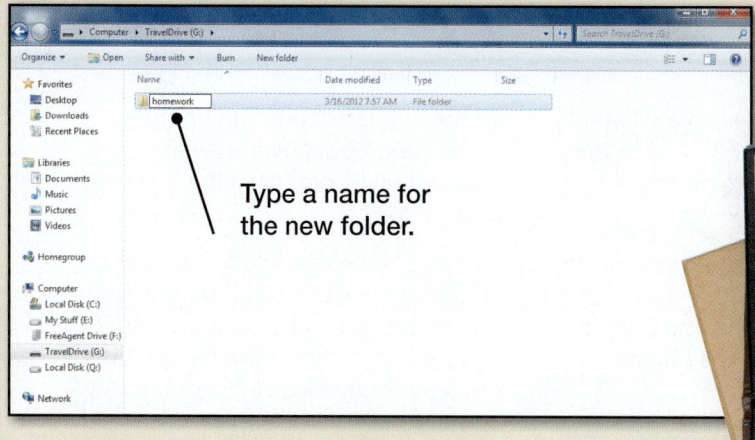

Type a name for the new folder.

4 Type a name for the folder and press Enter. You have created a new folder to store your files.

Chapter 3 | 105

Organizing your files into folders is easy once the folders have been created. You can use Windows Explorer to copy and move files to different locations on your computer. When you copy a file, you make a duplicate that can be put in another location, leaving the original file intact. Moving a file changes the location of the file. Both of these tasks can be accomplished in several ways, as explained in **Figure 3.10**. To select multiple files to copy or move, hold down the Ctrl key as you click on each file. If the files are adjacent, you can click the first file, hold down the Shift key, and click the last file. To select all of the files in a window, press Ctrl + A.

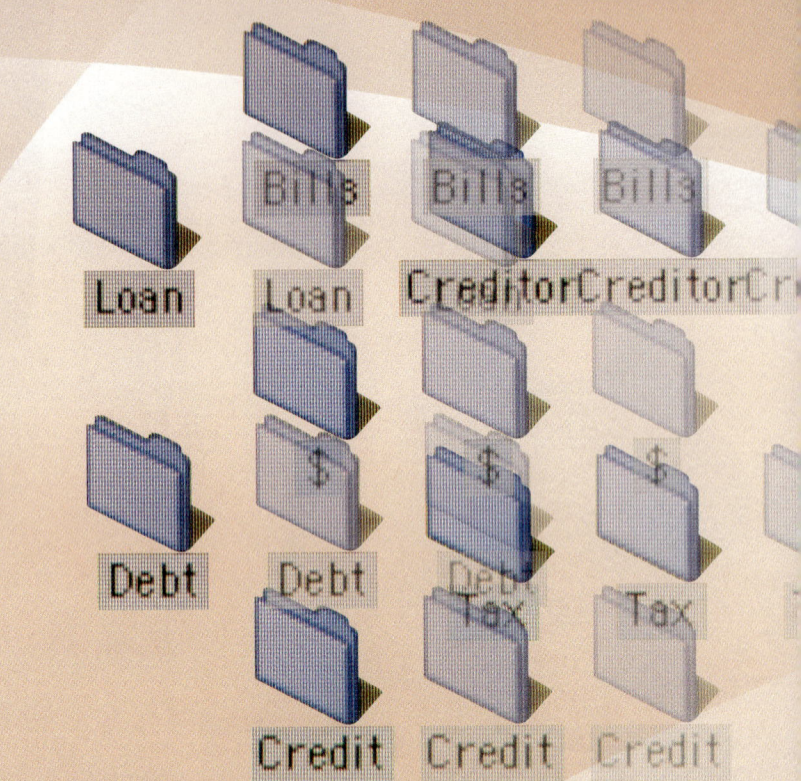

FIGURE 3.10 Copying and moving files using Windows Explorer

METHOD	COPY	MOVE
Mouse click: Click the right mouse button to display the context menu.	To copy a file, right-click on the file and click Copy. Navigate to the destination folder, right-click on it, and choose Paste from the context menu.	To move a file, right-click on the file and click Cut. Navigate to the destination folder, right-click on it, and choose Paste from the context menu.
Mouse drag: Hold down the left mouse button while moving the file to the destination location.	To copy a file to a folder on a different disk, hold down the left mouse button and drag the file to its destination. To copy a file to a folder on the same disk, hold down the right mouse button and drag the file to its destination. Release the mouse button and choose Copy here from the context menu.	To move a file to a folder on the same disk, hold down the left mouse button and drag the file to its destination. To move a file to a folder on a different disk, hold down the right mouse button and drag the file to its destination. Release the mouse button and choose Move here from the context menu.
Keyboard shortcut: Hold down [Ctrl] while pressing the designated letter.	Select the file to be copied and press [Ctrl] + C to copy the file. Navigate to the destination location and press [Ctrl] + V to paste the file.	Select the file to be copied and press [Ctrl] + X to copy the file. Navigate to the destination location and press [Ctrl] + V to paste the file.

Running Project

To complete the steps of this project, you first need to copy files from your student CD to your computer. Place the CD in your drive and close any windows that open. Click the Start button and click Computer. Right-click on your CD drive in the file list area and select Open. Navigate to the data files for this chapter. Drag the *Ch_03 Pictures* folder to the Pictures library in the Navigation pane. Drag the *Ch_03 Music* folder to the Music library.

1. On your flash drive, create a folder for this class, and create a folder for Chapter 3 inside the class folder. Use this folder to save your work for this chapter.
2. In the Navigation pane on the left, under Libraries, click *Music*. In the file list on the right, double-click the *Ch_03 Music* folder. If it's not been customized, the default view is Music Details. Click the down arrow next to the Views button (on the toolbar) and, if necessary, move the slider to Details (see Figure 3.11). What are the headings of the columns in this view? Click the Title column heading. What happens to the files in the window? Click the Name column heading. What happens?
3. In the Navigation pane, under Libraries, click *Pictures*. The default view for this folder is Large Icons. Use the Views menu, if necessary, to change the view to Large Icons. How is the view in this folder different from the Music folder? Double-click on *Ch_03 Pictures*.
4. Select one image (but do not open it) and look at the Details pane at the bottom of the window (Figure 3.12). What information is found in this pane? Change the rating of the file. What other information can you change?
5. On the Address bar, click the arrow to the right of Libraries, and choose Documents from the menu. What two locations are included in this view? Click the Start button and click *Help and Support*. In the Search box, type **public folder** and press Enter. Click *File sharing essentials*. What is the purpose of public folders? Where are they located?
6. Use the Views menu to change the view of the Document folder to Details. How is the Details view of this folder different from the Music Details view? Click the Type column heading. Click *Organize*, point to Layout, and choose *Preview pane*. Scroll down and select various files from this folder. What file types display their contents in the Preview pane?

Learning to work with folders and libraries will make organizing your files much easier and more efficient. Windows Explorer gives you the ability to navigate and view your files in several different ways so you can use the methods that you find the most useful.

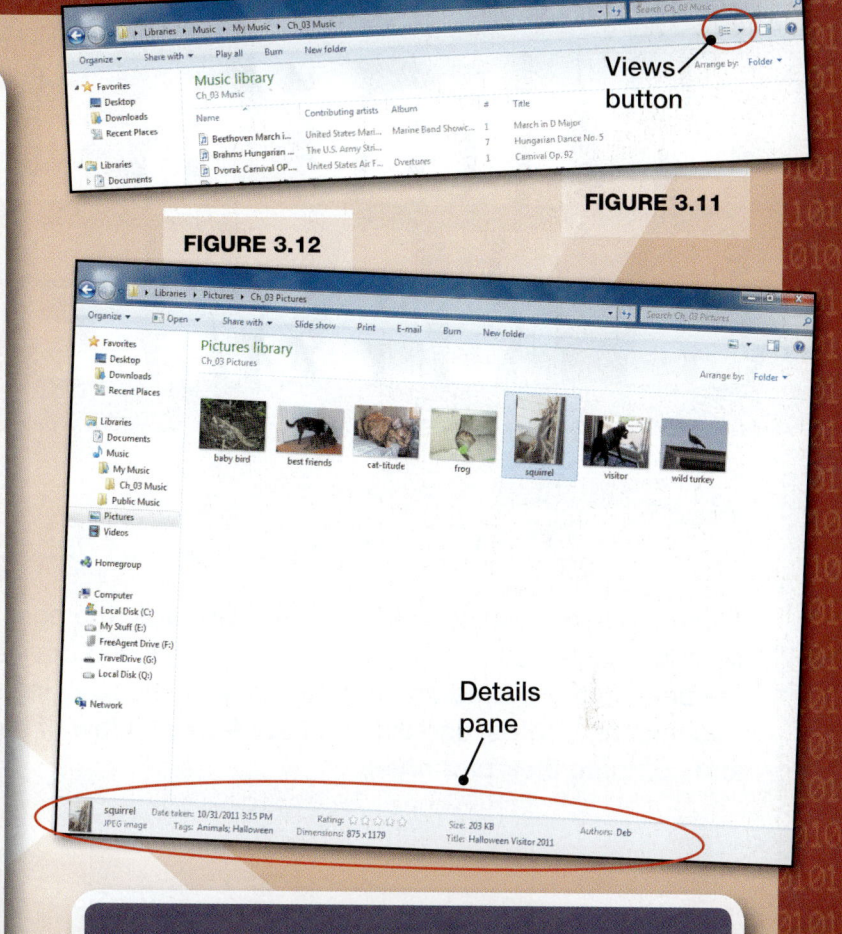

FIGURE 3.11

FIGURE 3.12

Key Terms

file management	path
folder	Public folders
hierarchy	Windows Explorer
library	

4 Things You Need to Know

- Windows creates a folder hierarchy for storing files.
- Each user has his or her own folder structure for storing documents, pictures, music, videos, and more.
- Libraries gather files that are located in different locations.
- Windows Explorer is used to navigate through folders and drives.

What's in A NAME?

OBJECTIVE 2
Explain the importance of file extensions.

There are two types of files on every computer: the ones that the computer uses to function, such as programs and device drivers, and the ones that are used and created by you, the user, including music, documents, photos, and videos. Let's look at a few of these user files and compare their properties.

FILE NAMES AND EXTENSIONS

Every file has a **file name** that consists of a name and an extension. The name is useful to the user and describes the contents of the file. When creating your own files, you decide the name. In the example in Figure 3.13, ch03_homework is the name of the file. On early PCs, file names were limited to eight characters with a three-letter extension and were often cryptic. Today, file names on Windows computers can be up to 260 characters long (including the extension and the path to the file) and can include spaces and special characters. The only illegal characters in a file name are the \ / ? : * " > < | characters.

filename
ch 03_homework

ch 03_homework.docx

file extension
.docx

FIGURE 3.13 A file name includes a name and an extension to identify the contents and type of file.

108 | OBJECTIVE 2

The second part of the file name is the **file extension**. In this example, .docx is the extension. The extension is assigned by the program that's used to create the file. Microsoft Word 2007/2010 files have the extension .docx when you save them. Windows maintains an association between a file extension and a program, so double-clicking on a .docx file opens Microsoft Word. The extension helps the operating system determine the type of file. If you change the file extension of a file, you may no longer be able to open it. Figure 3.14 lists some common file types and programs associated with them.

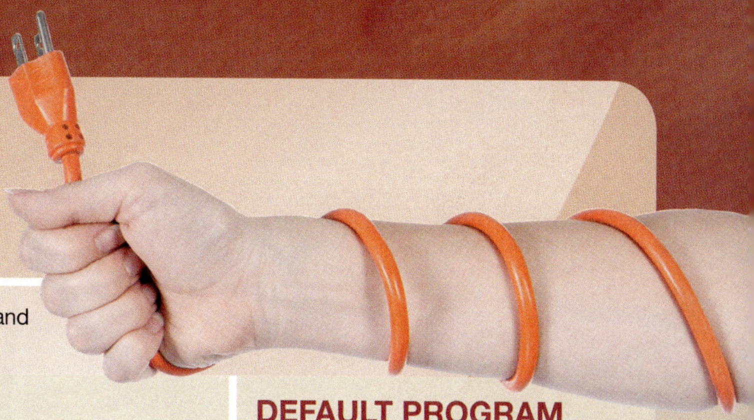

FIGURE 3.14 Common file extensions and default program associations

EXTENSION	TYPE OF FILE	DEFAULT PROGRAM ASSOCIATION
.docx	Word document	Microsoft Word 2007/2010
.bmp	bitmap image	Microsoft Paint
.mp3	audio file	Windows Media Player
.mov	video file	Apple QuickTime
.pdf	portable document format	Adobe Acrobat and Reader

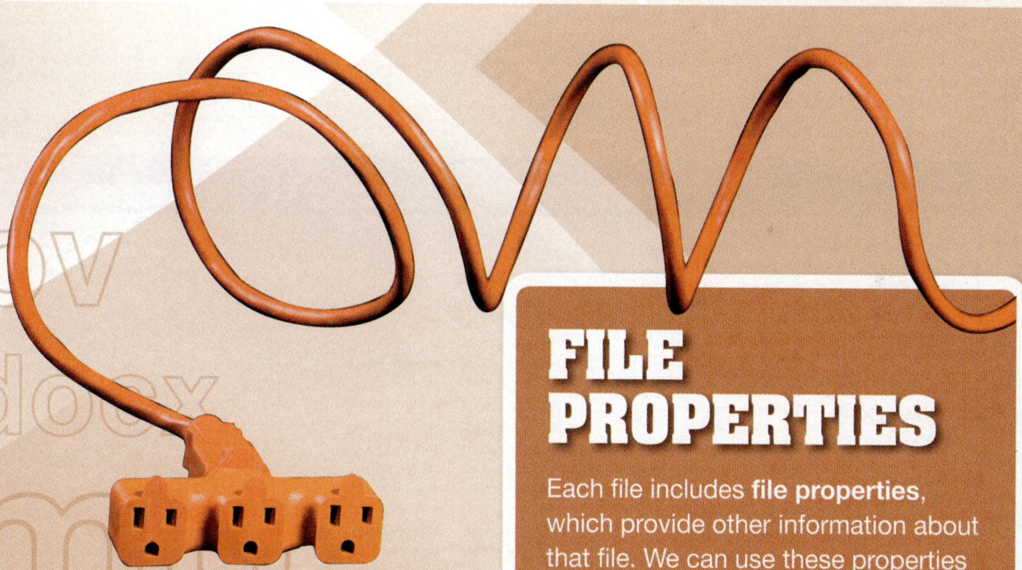

Find Out MORE

The characters \ / ? : * " > < | can't be used in a file name because they each have a special meaning in Windows. For example, the : is used when you indicate the letter of a drive (such as C: for your hard drive or D: for your DVD drive). Use the Internet to research the remaining illegal characters. What does each of these symbols represent?

FILE PROPERTIES

Each file includes **file properties**, which provide other information about that file. We can use these properties to organize, sort, and find files more easily. Some file properties, such as type, size, and date, are automatically created along with the file. Others, such as title and authors, can be added or edited by the user.

Figure 3.15 shows the properties of a file in the Details pane of Windows Explorer. The Details pane at the bottom of the Explorer window gives you a preview of the file. You can modify some of these properties, such as Title and Authors, right in the Details pane.

When the files are displayed in Details view, as they are in this figure, you can use the column headings to sort files by their properties. For example, clicking on the Name column heading lists the files in alphabetical order. The properties that display in this view depend on the type of files in the folder.

You can view more information about a file by right-clicking the file in Windows Explorer and choosing *Properties* from the context menu. This opens the Properties dialog box for the file. The four tabs of the Properties dialog box contain a lot of information, but you'll probably find the General and Details tabs to be the most useful. The General tab makes it easy to change the name of a file. The Details tab lists information about the content of the file, such as word count. Figure 3.16 shows these two tabs for the same file. Notice that the Details tab contains too much information to display on the page. You'll need to scroll down to see the rest of it. The type of information that's displayed depends on the type of file you're viewing.

FIGURE 3.15 Windows Explorer allows you to view and modify some file properties.

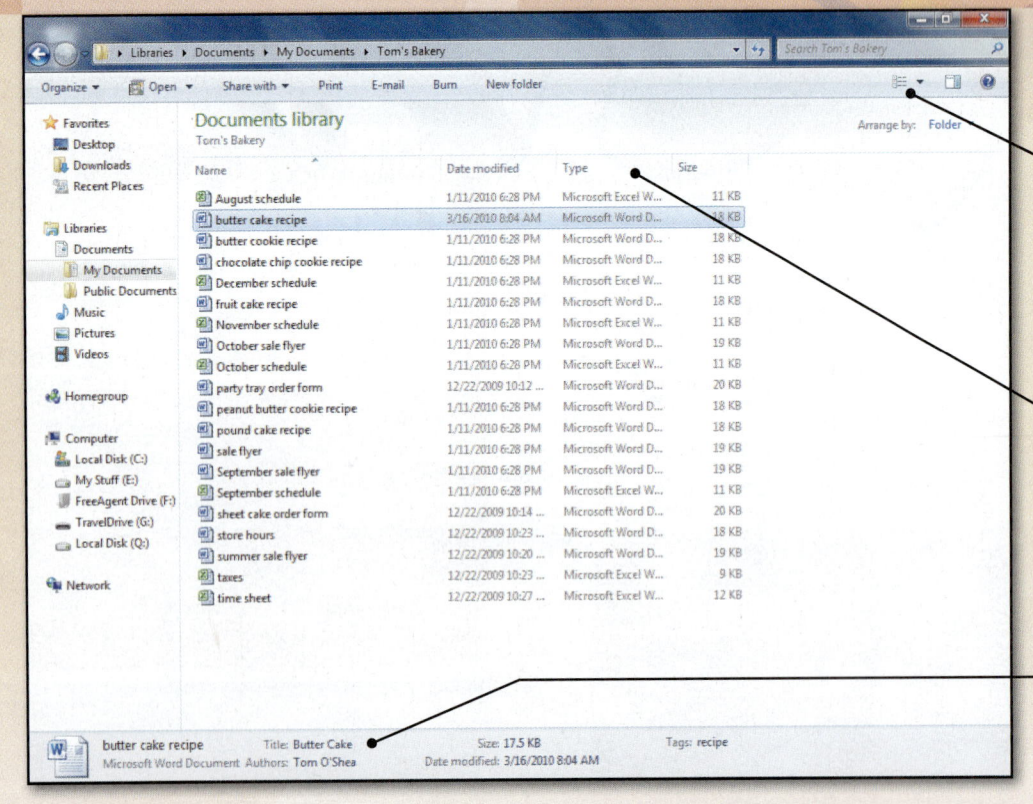

Use the Views button to change the Explorer window to the Details view and display the columns.

Properties such as Date modified and Type are applied by the operating system.

Title, Authors, and Tags are properties of a file that can be modified in the Details pane.

OBJECTIVE 2

110

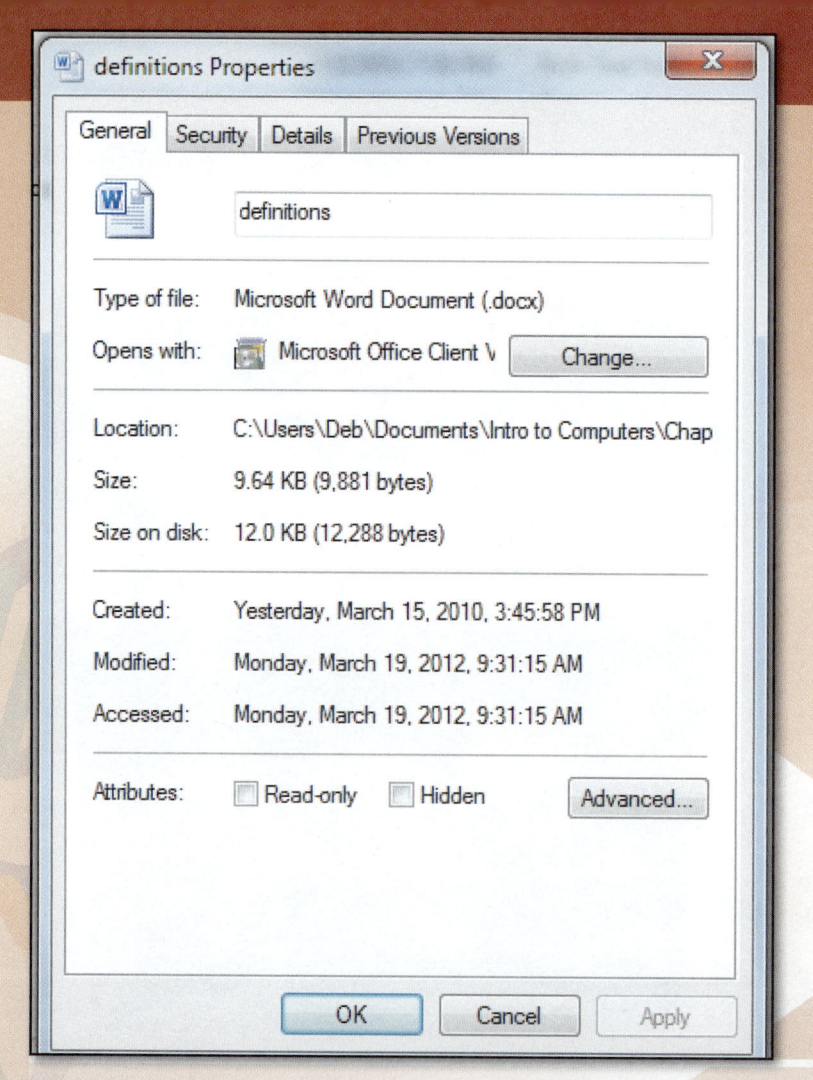

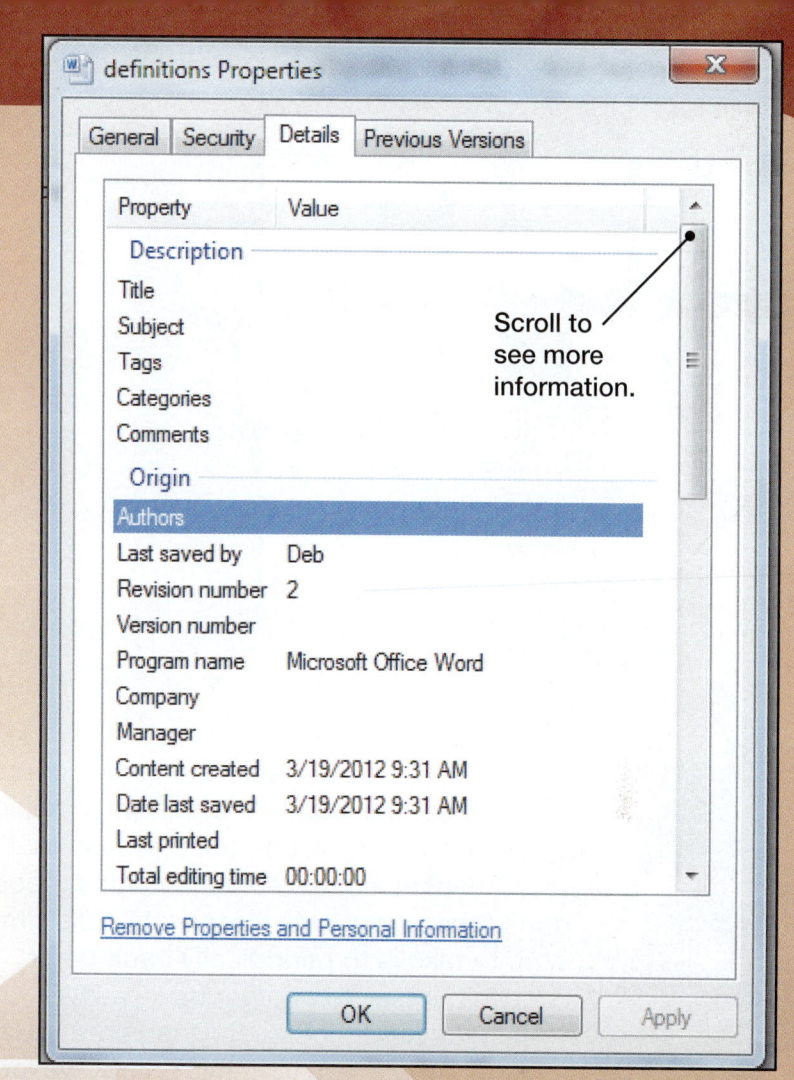

FIGURE 3.16 Right-clicking on a file in Windows Explorer allows you to open the Properties dialog box for the file. The four tabs on this sheet contain more information about the file.

> File names and other properties give us more information about files, making them more useful and easier to manage and locate. They also save us time and give us more control over our computer systems.

Key Terms

file extension

file name

file property

Running Project

In this article, we discussed how to add properties to a file, but how would you remove them? Which properties can you remove? Use Windows Help and Support to find the answers.

4 Things You Need to Know

- File names can be up to 260 characters long, including the path.
- File names can't include \ / ? : * " > < |
- File extensions indicate the type of file.
- File properties, such as size, type, date, and author, can be used to sort and search for files.

Back IT UP

3 OBJECTIVE
Explain the importance of backing up files.

Closing the barn door after the horse got out—an old adage that's often too true when talking about losing files on a computer system that wasn't backed up. It's something most people don't think about until it's too late. One simple step to take is to periodically **back up** or copy your files to another drive, a DVD, or a flash drive. Of course, this requires you to remember to do it. In this article, we look at how easy it is to automatically back up your files for protection.

WINDOWS BACKUP

Windows 7 includes a backup utility that automatically backs up your files on a regular basis. It requires you to set it up once. After that, the utility runs routinely without prompting you. The key is to remember to set it up in the first place. The Windows Action Center will remind you to set it up (see Figure 3.17).

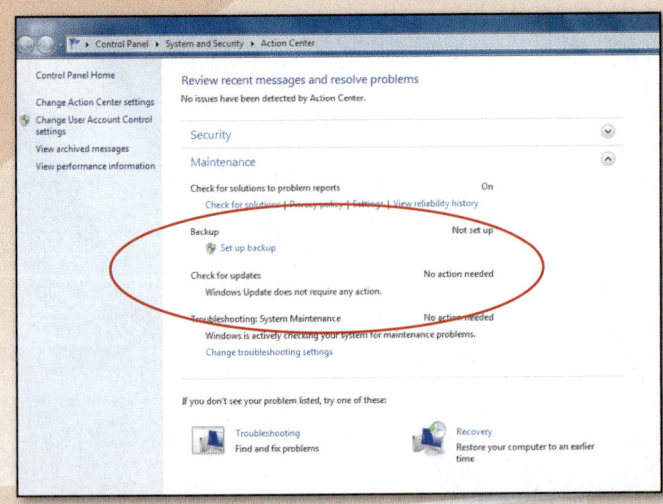

FIGURE 3.17 The Windows Action Center warns you if you've not set up a backup for your system.

When you click on *Set up backup*, it opens the Windows Backup utility. The first screen asks you to choose where to save the backup. You can't back up a disk to itself; you have to put the backup on a different drive. Your options are internal hard drives, external hard drives, optical drives, flash drives, and network locations. Tape drives and floppy drives are no longer supported. The options available to you depend on the drives that you have access to. Figure 3.18 lists the pros and cons of each choice. Also, to keep your files safe from flood, fire, or theft, you should keep your backup files in a different physical location than your working files.

FIGURE 3.18 Comparing backup storage types

STORAGE TYPE	PROS	CONS
Internal hard drive	• The price per GB is relatively low. • The speed of transfer is fastest. • The drive is secure inside the system unit.	• You need to open the system unit to install it. • Because it's in same physical location as the original files, backing up to the internal hard drive doesn't keep files safe from fire, flood, or other damage.
External hard drive	• The price per GB is relatively low. • The speed of transfer is fast. • The drive is easy to move and secure in another location.	• If the external hard drive is stored in another location, it must be transported back to the system location to perform a backup. • If the backup storage device is left in the same physical location as the original files, the files aren't safe from fire, flood, or other damage.
Optical drive (CD/DVD)	• Media (discs) are inexpensive and easy to purchase. • Media is easy to move to store in another location. • New discs for each backup means the discs don't have to be returned to the system to complete future backups.	• Disc capacity is small compared to hard drives and may require several (or many) discs to complete a backup.
Flash drive	• It's small and easy to move and store in another location. • It's a good solution for quickly moving files between systems.	• The capacity is still small compared to hard drives. • If it's stored in another location, the flash drive must be transported back to the system to complete a backup. • If the flash drive is left in the same physical location as the original files, the files aren't safe from fire, flood, or other damage.
Network	• A shared folder or drive on another Windows 7 (Professional, Enterprise, or Ultimate) computer can be used for backup. • Placing the files on another system protects them.	• Using a network as a backup location requires some advanced setup of the network. • The network location must be available when the backup runs.

FIGURE 3.19 Determine what information to include in the backup. Once you click the Save settings and exit button, the backup will automatically run on a regular schedule.

After you choose the backup location, you have to decide what to back up. It's not practical to back up your entire computer system every time. Windows gives you two options (see Figure 3.19): Let Windows choose or Let me choose. If you select the recommended Let Windows choose option, Windows automatically backs up your data files stored in libraries and on the desktop and creates a system image that can be used to restore your system if it stops working. If you select the Let me choose option, then you can specify which files and folders should be included in the backup. Once set up, the backup will run on a regular schedule.

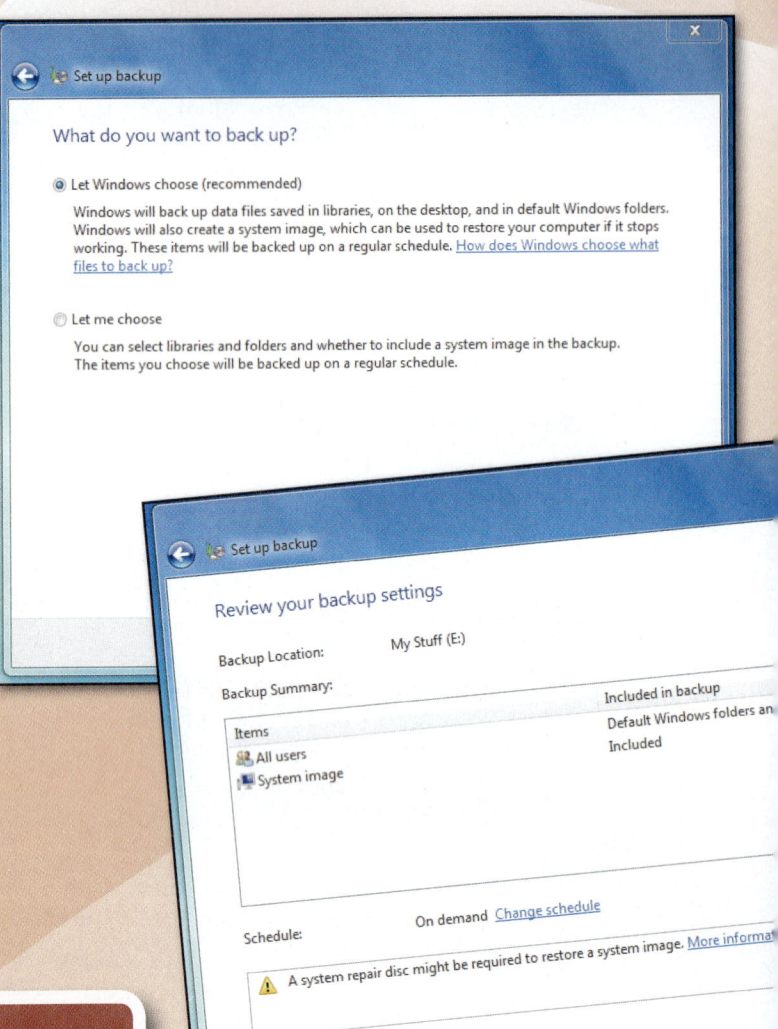

OTHER BACKUP SOFTWARE

External hard drives are an inexpensive place to back up your files. Many of these drives include a backup program that you can use for automatic or one-touch back-ups of your system. For example, Seagate FreeAgent external drives include Seagate Manager software, and Western Digital's Passport drives include WD SmartWare software. You can purchase a large-capacity external hard drive for less than $100.

Another alternative is commercial software. There are literally dozens of programs on the market, including many that are free or cost less than $50. DVD-burning software, such as Roxio Creator and Nero BackItUp & Burn, also include backup features.

ONLINE BACKUPS

The use of online backup services is becoming increasingly popular. Many sites offer free personal storage of 1 or 2 GB or unlimited storage for about $5–10 per month. Business solutions can cost thousands of dollars, depending on the amount of storage needed.

Using an online backup service has the advantage of keeping your backups at another location—but easily accessible—thus protecting your assets from fire, flood, or damage to your main location. Professional backup companies make setup easy and are very safe and reliable. Once the initial setup is complete, the backup process is automatic, and your backed-up files are then accessible from any Internet-connected computer. As with any service, you should do your homework before trusting online backup services with your files.

However you choose to back up your files, you can rest easy knowing that your files are safe and that if the inevitable hard drive failure strikes, you won't lose your important work and precious photos.

Key Term

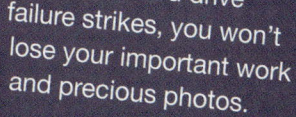

back up

Running Project

Research two online backup sites, and investigate their cost, reliability, storage size, and features. Write a brief report to convince your boss of the importance of backing up files and how backups should be handled. Should the company use online storage? Explain your thoughts. In the report, be sure to describe the type and size of the business you're working for.

4 Things You Need to Know

- You should use a backup program to regularly back up your important files.
- Keep your backup files in a different physical location than your working files.
- Back up (verb) is the process of creating a backup (noun).
- Online backup services are free or inexpensive for personal use.

Shrink it

4 OBJECTIVE
Demonstrate how to compress files.

Some of the files we use today can be quite large, especially media files, such as photos, music, and videos. File **compression** is the process of making files smaller to conserve disk space and make them easier to transfer.

TYPES OF FILE COMPRESSION

There are two types of file compression: lossless and lossy. The type of compression depends on the type of file you're trying to compress.

Lossless compression takes advantage of the fact that files contain a lot of redundant information. This is especially true of files that contain text and numbers. With lossless compression, the compressed file can be decompressed with no loss of data. A lossless compression **algorithm** (procedure for solving a problem) looks for the redundancy in the file and creates an encoded file using that information to remove the redundant information. When the file is decompressed, all the information from the original file is restored. Lossless compression is used in ZIP files.

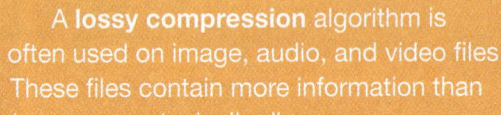

A **lossy compression** algorithm is often used on image, audio, and video files. These files contain more information than humans can typically discern, and that extra information can be removed from the file. An image file taken with a digital camera on its highest setting can yield a file of 5 to 10 MB in size (or more), while the normal quality setting yields a file of 1 to 2 MB. If the file is going to be used to create a large high-quality print, then the high-quality information is important, but most people couldn't tell the difference between the two when viewing them on a computer screen. The high-quality setting results in a uncompressed BMP or TIF file. An image taken at the lower quality setting results in a JPG file—a BMP file with lossy compression. It's possible to compress a BMP or TIF file after it's been taken, but it's not possible to decompress a JPG file because the information has been removed from the file.

WORKING WITH FILE COMPRESSION

Windows includes the ability to compress and decompress files using the ZIP format. This is a common format that's used to send files by e-mail or download them from the Internet. A ZIP file, known as an "archive", can contain multiple files zipped together. The files in the archive may be compressed using different algorithms and can be browsed and extracted from the archive. This makes transferring multiple files easier.

To zip files using Windows, you simply right-click on the file or folder that you want to zip, point to Send to, and choose *Compressed (zipped) folder* from the context menu (see Figure 3.20). In this example, the Chapter 3 folder was compressed from 3.50 MB down to 1615 KB. This ZIP file can more easily be sent as an e-mail attachment or uploaded to the Web and takes up less than half the space on a disk.

FIGURE 3.20 The Chapter 3 folder (3.50 MB) is compressed. The resulting ZIP file is 1615 KB.

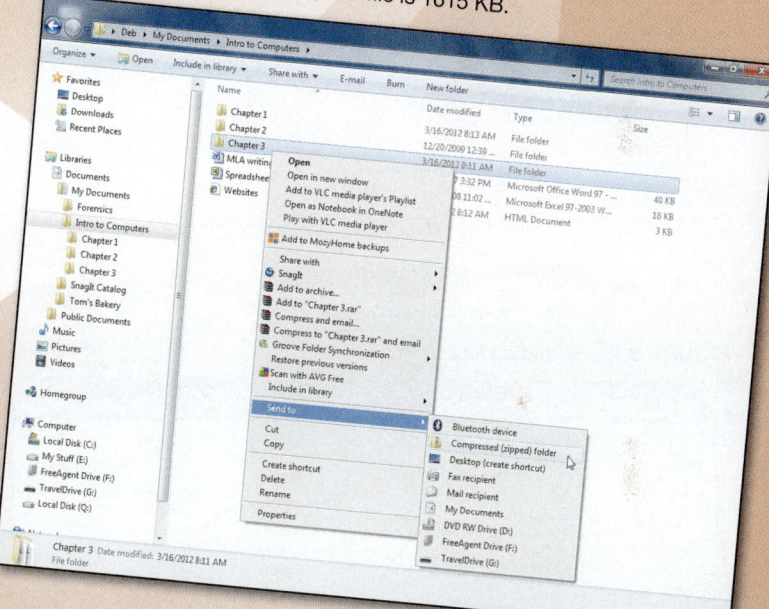

Original file size

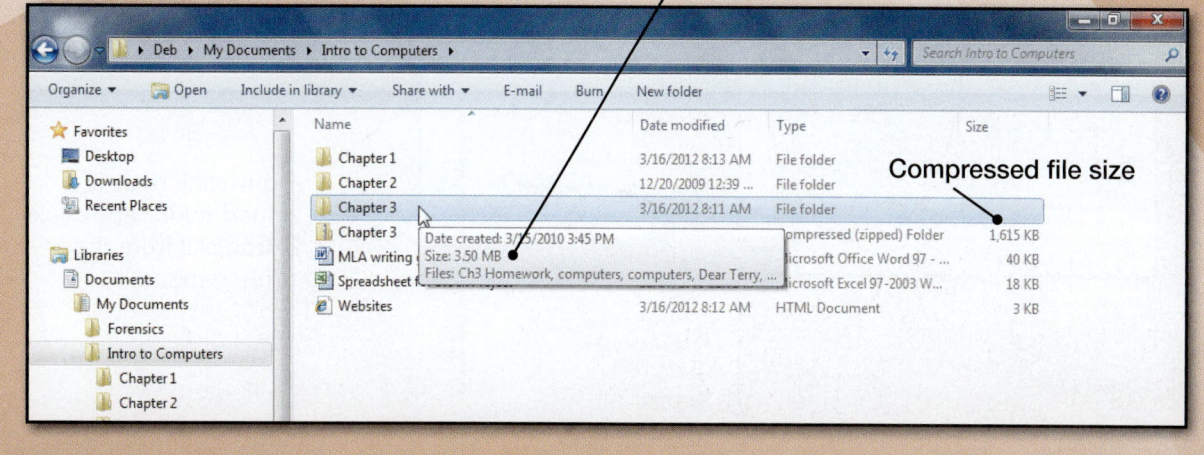

Compressed file size

Chapter 3 | 117

Windows can open and browse the files in a ZIP archive. Figure 3.21 shows the Chapter 3.zip file and the compression ratio for each file inside it. Because each file contains different types and amounts of information, the compression ratio varies.

FIGURE 3.21 A look inside a ZIP file using Windows Explorer shows the compression ratios for each file.

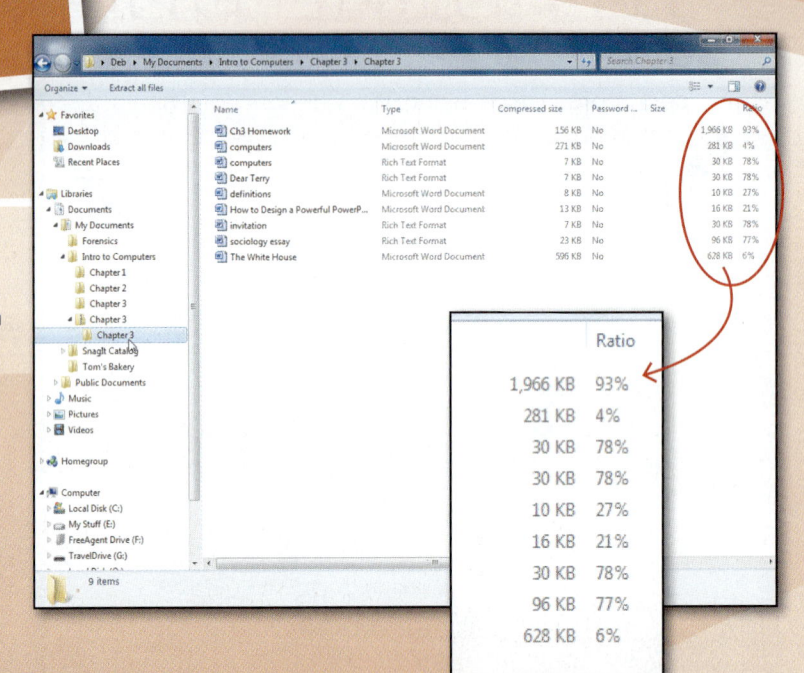

FIGURE 3.22 Extracting files from a ZIP archive

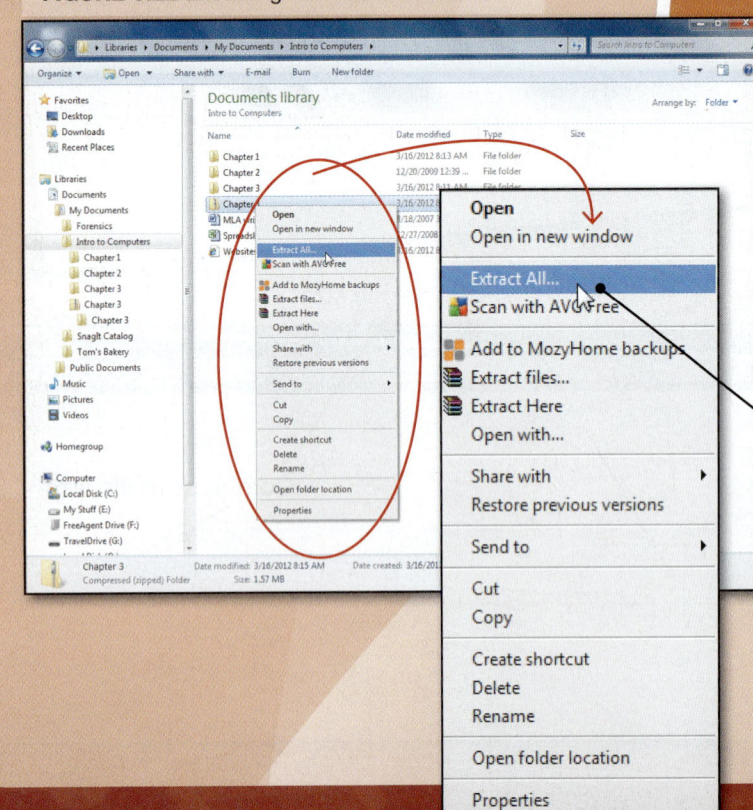

Windows can browse and use files inside a zipped folder, but sometimes, you need to decompress or extract the files. In Windows, you simply right-click on the ZIP file and choose *Extract All* from the context menu (see Figure 3.22). There are other programs that you can use to compress and decompress ZIP files, and there are other compressed formats, such as TAR and RAR, that Windows can't create or open. Some of the more popular programs available are 7-Zip (free), WinRAR, WinZip, and StuffIt.

Right-click on a zipped folder and click Extract All from the context menu.

118

File compression has become increasingly common as the size of files we use has increased, along with our need to transfer files by e-mail or to websites. Working with compression using Windows or another program is a fairly easy and important skill to have, notably when it comes to submitting your homework for this class.

Key Terms

algorithm

compression

lossless compression

lossy compression

Running Project

An MP3 file is a compressed audio file that uses a lossy compression algorithm. Many audiophiles say that they can hear a noticeable difference in the quality of the sound. Use the Internet to research ways to improve the quality of MP3 files.

4 Things You Need to Know

- File compression saves disk space and makes transferring files easier.
- A file compressed with lossless compression can be decompressed back to the original file.
- A file compressed with lossy compression can't be decompressed because information has been removed from the file.
- Windows has the ability to create and extract ZIP archives.

HOW TO Create a Compressed (Zipped) Folder

Did you ever try to e-mail a bunch of photos to a friend? If you want to send more than a couple images, you usually wind up sending multiple messages. But you could compress the files into a single zipped folder and send them all at once. In this activity, we'll compress a folder that contains several files to make it easier to e-mail them or to submit them electronically to your teacher.

1 Insert your flash drive into your computer and close any windows that open. Insert your student CD in the drive and navigate to the folder for Chapter 3. Locate the folder Jessica's Bookstore. Copy this folder to your flash drive (right-click on it, point to Send to, and choose your flash drive from the list).

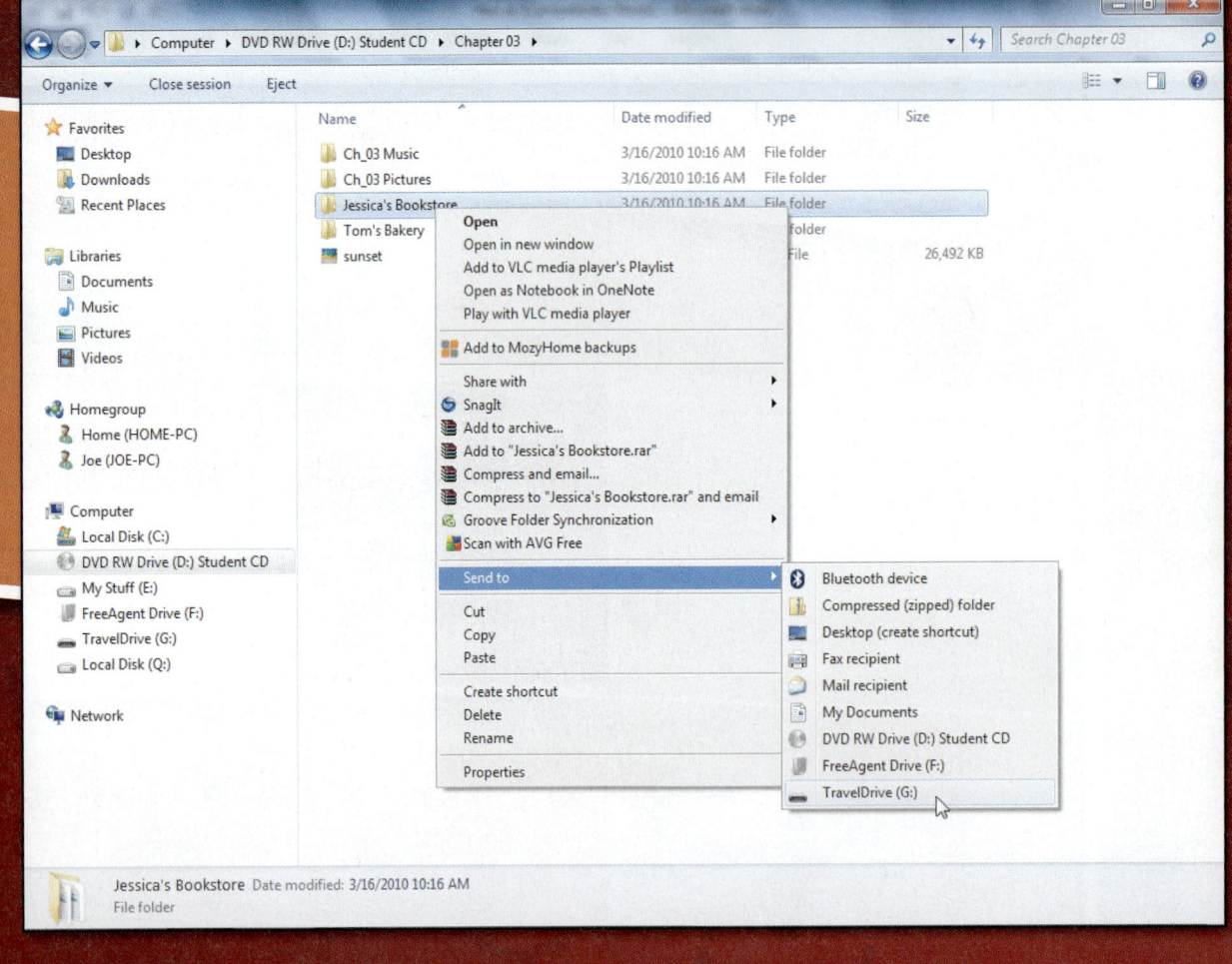

2 From the Computer window, open your flash drive. Right-click on the Jessica's Bookstore folder and choose *Properties* from the context menu. How big is the folder? How many files and folders does it contain?

3 Close the Properties dialog box. Right-click on Jessica's Bookstore, point to Send to, and choose *Compressed (zipped) folder* from the context menu to create a zipped archive.

4 Right-click on the compressed folder and choose *Properties* from the context menu. Compare the size to the original folder.

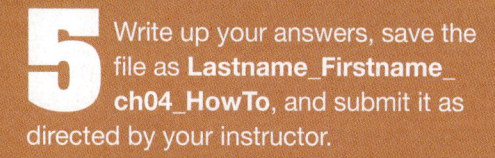

5 Write up your answers, save the file as **Lastname_Firstname_ch04_HowTo**, and submit it as directed by your instructor.

It's Always IN THE LAST PLACE YOU LOOK

5 OBJECTIVE
Use advanced search options to locate files.

An average computer contains thousands of files, and finding what you need among them can be like looking for the proverbial needle in a haystack. If you follow the principles of good file management, create folders, and save your files in an organized way, then you'll have a much easier time keeping track of your materials. In this article, we look at how Windows can help you find what you're looking for.

USING WINDOWS TO SEARCH FOR FILES

We know that our files contain properties that we can use to help organize and find them. Using the Windows Search feature can help us do just that. Notice that there's a search box in almost every place you go in Windows. It's in the Start menu, the Help and Support window, every Control Panel window (such as the Default Programs control panel), and every Explorer window. When you begin to type something in the search box, Windows immediately begins searching for you.

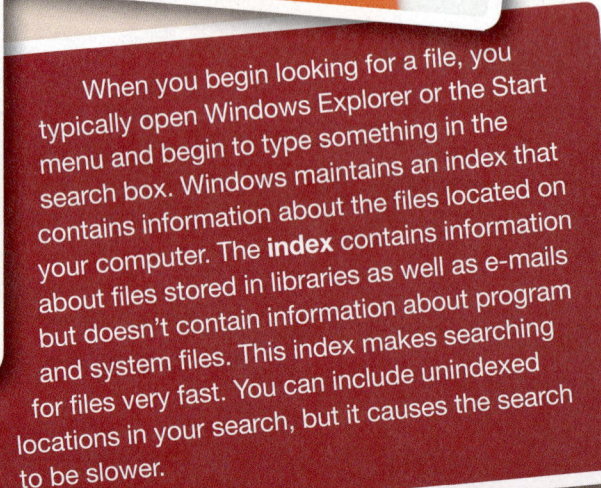

When you begin looking for a file, you typically open Windows Explorer or the Start menu and begin to type something in the search box. Windows maintains an index that contains information about the files located on your computer. The **index** contains information about files stored in libraries as well as e-mails but doesn't contain information about program and system files. This index makes searching for files very fast. You can include unindexed locations in your search, but it causes the search to be slower.

In Figure 3.23, the search began as soon as I typed the letter "f" in the Search box. The search results include files in the current location and the folders below it in the hierarchy. Notice in the Search Results that Windows found the letter "f" in file names and in the contents and other properties of the file, such as tags and author. The search results can be further refined by typing more letters or by adding a search filter, such as Type or Name. You can also save a search to be repeated later.

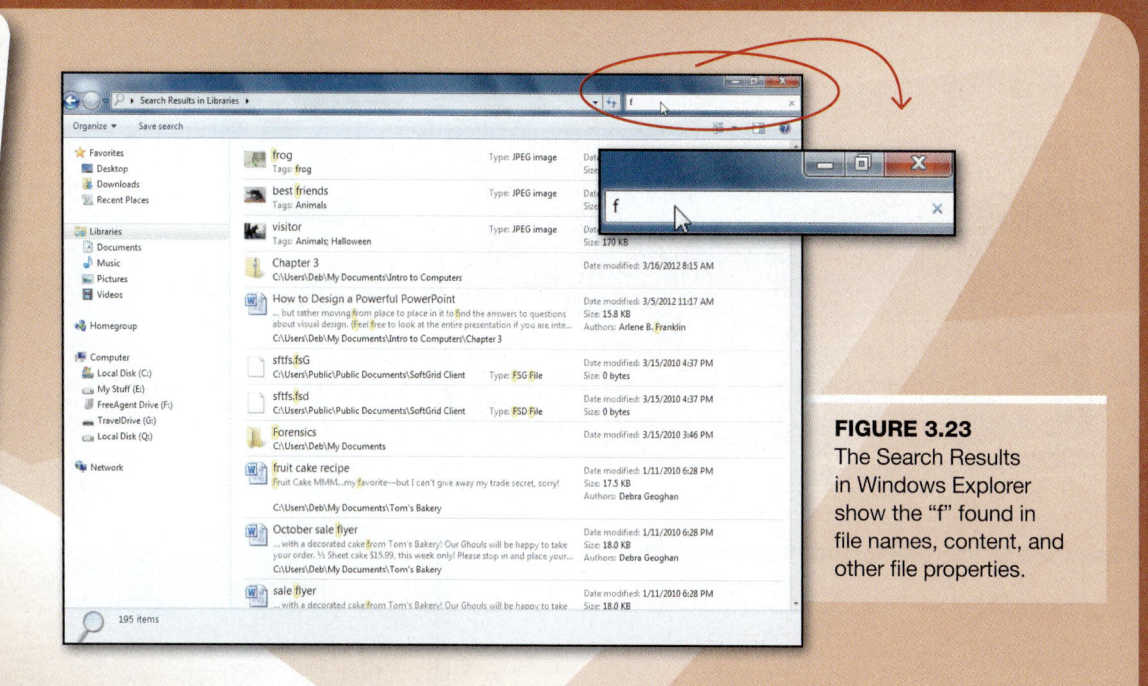

FIGURE 3.23 The Search Results in Windows Explorer show the "f" found in file names, content, and other file properties.

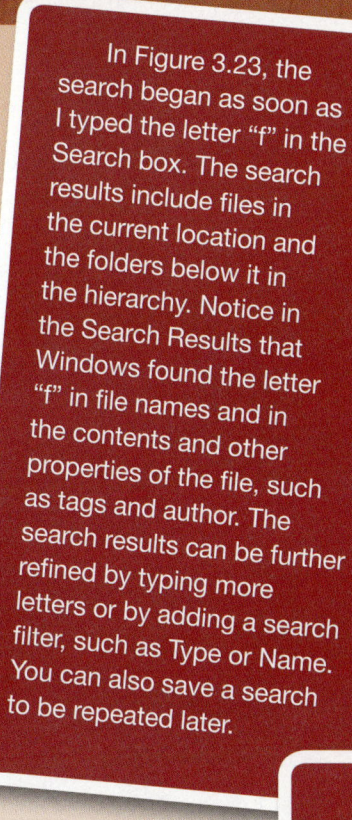

If you don't find what you're looking for from your initial search, adjust your criteria. One way to do that is to expand the search to include other locations. As illustrated in Figure 3.24, you can click on the appropriate location to include in the search at the bottom of the Search Results page.

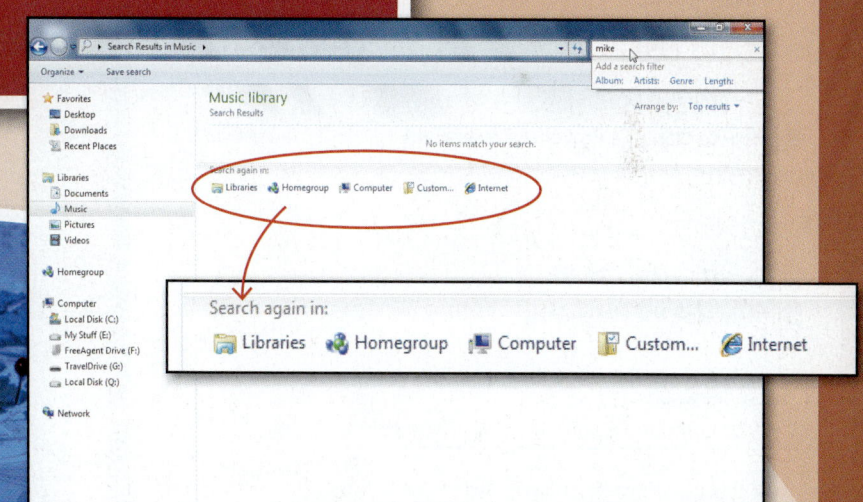

FIGURE 3.24 Expand the search to include other locations by clicking on the icon at the bottom of the Search Results window.

Chapter 3 | 123

Searching from the Start menu yields different results than searching from Windows Explorer because using the Start menu will automatically search programs, the Control Panel, and files (see Figure 3.25), and it will search in all indexed locations. In addition to locating a file, you can quickly launch a program by typing the name of the program in the Start menu's search box.

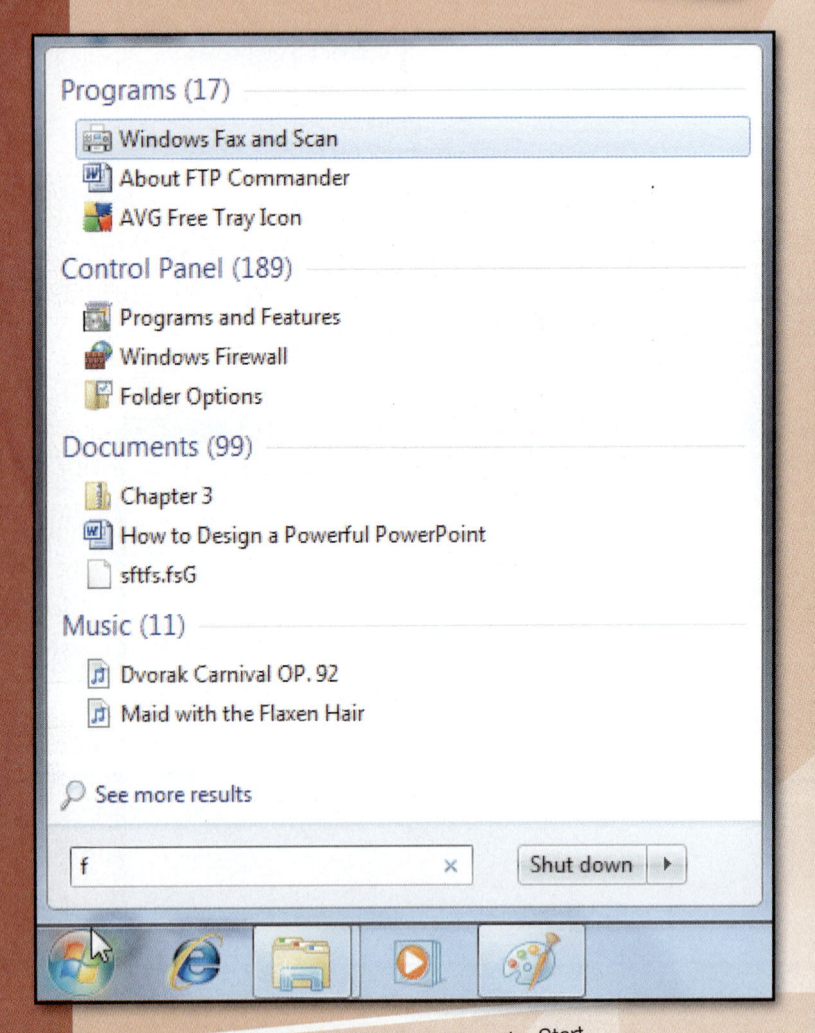

FIGURE 3.25 Searching from the Start menu locates programs as well as files.

GREEN COMPUTING

THE PAPERLESS OFFICE

The promise of the paperless office hasn't quite become a reality. In fact, we're buried under more paper today than ever. According to the U.S. Environmental Protection Agency (EPA), in 2008, paper and paperboard made up 31% of our municipal solid waste generated each year.

The process of making paper uses water and energy in addition to trees and results in greenhouse emissions, air and water pollution. Reduce your paper usage to help the environment.

Source: http://www.epa.gov/epawaste/nonhaz/municipal/msw99.htm.

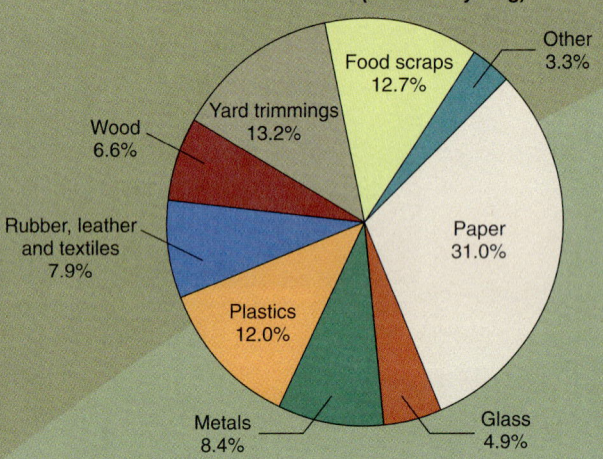

Total MSW Generation (by material), 2008
250 Million Tons (before recycling)

- Food scraps 12.7%
- Other 3.3%
- Yard trimmings 13.2%
- Wood 6.6%
- Rubber, leather and textiles 7.9%
- Plastics 12.0%
- Metals 8.4%
- Glass 4.9%
- Paper 31.0%

The prospect of going paperless has advantages for the environment and for your bottom line. So, how do you achieve it? The reality is you probably can't go totally paperless, but here are a few ways to reduce your paper usage:

1. Send e-mails and make phone calls instead of sending greeting cards and letters.
2. Pay your bills online and opt for paperless billing from your billers and banks.
3. Don't print out electronic documents unless absolutely necessary.
4. Read magazines and books in electronic formats.
5. Opt out of receiving junk mail at the DMA website **(www.dmachoice.org.)** and catalogs at Catalog Choice **(www.catalogchoice.org.)**.

USING BOOLEAN LOGIC TO REFINE SEARCHES

You can further refine your searches by using Boolean filters. George Boole was a 19th century mathematician that we can thank for creating this system. While it can seem complex, there are basically only three **Boolean operators**: AND, OR, and NOT. Notice that they're written in uppercase. You can use these operators to create search filters in Windows and most other databases and Web searches. Figure 3.26 illustrates the effect of Boolean filters on the search using the terms John and Kennedy:

FIGURE 3.26 Boolean operators can be used to filter search results. The blue areas represent the search results for each Boolean filter.

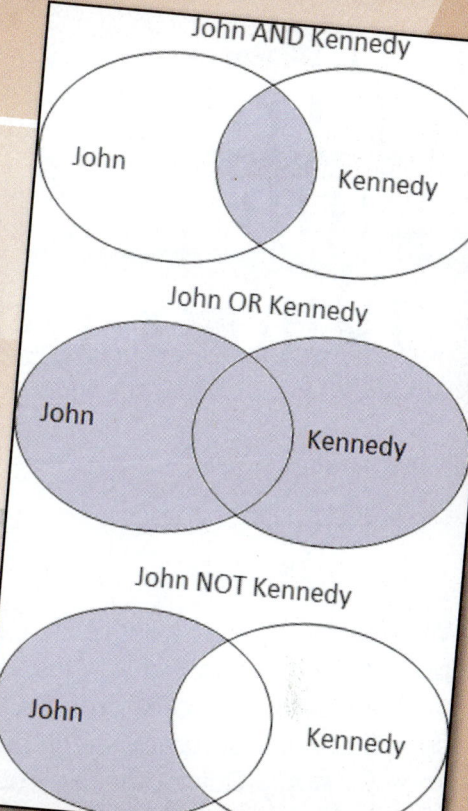

AND
Search results must include both words: John AND Kennedy. This filter excludes files that don't include both terms.

OR
Search results must include either word: John OR Kennedy. This filter includes all files that contain either or both terms.

NOT
Search results must include the first term and must not include the second term: John NOT Kennedy. This filter excludes files that include the term Kennedy.

Using the Search feature of Windows can make locating a file or program quick and easy, saving you both time and aggravation. The combination of good file management and good searching skills will serve you well.

Key Terms
Boolean operators
index

3 Things You Need to Know
- There's a search box in the Start menu, most windows, control panels, and help screens.
- The Boolean operators AND, OR, and NOT can be used to create search filters.
- Windows maintains an index that contains information about the files located on your computer.

That's Not the PROGRAM I WANT TO OPEN THIS FILE TYPE

OBJECTIVE 6
Change the default program associated with a file type.

Windows maintains a list of file extensions and associated **default programs** that enables Windows to automatically open the correct program when you click on a file. This is fine for file types that are specific to one program—such as .docx for Microsoft Word and .mov for Apple QuickTime. However, it can be a problem with more generic file types that can be opened with several different programs. For example, take the file extension .mp3. By default, Windows associates MP3 files with Windows Media Player, but if you install another program that can play music files, such as Apple iTunes or Winamp, the association may be changed. In this article, we look at how to manage default programs and file type associations in Windows.

You can manage these settings via the Default Programs control panel (see Figure 3.27). To access it, click the Start button and click Default Programs.

FIGURE 3.27 The Default Programs control panel has options to work with programs or file types.

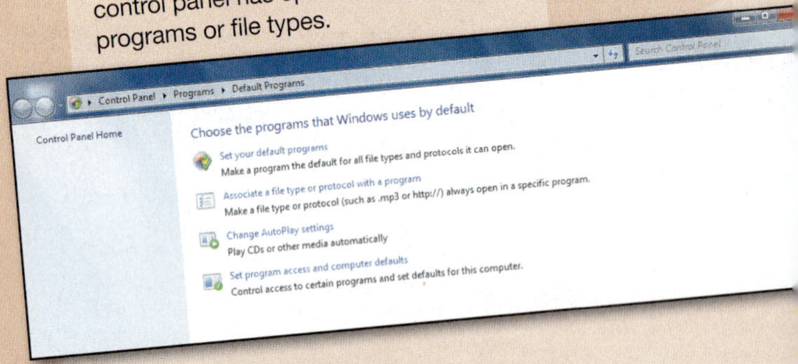

FIGURE 3.28 The Set Default Programs window for Windows Live Photo Gallery

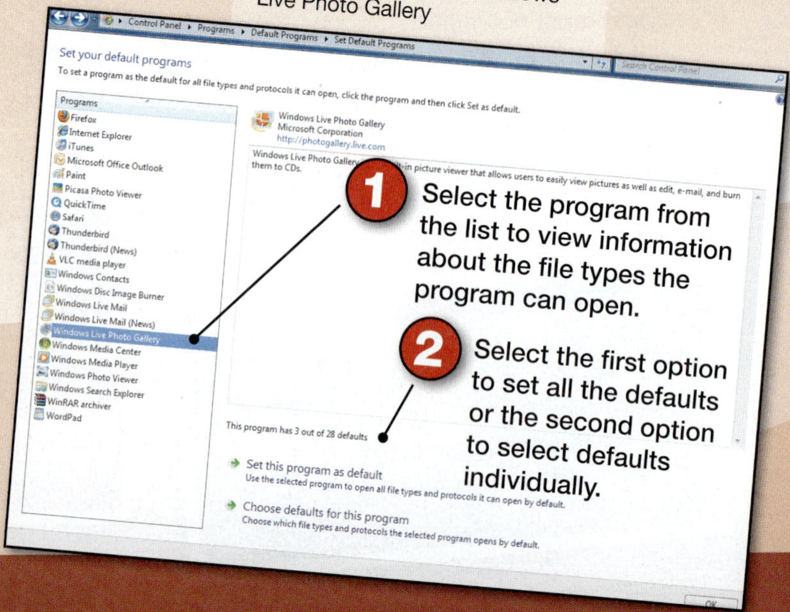

1. Select the program from the list to view information about the file types the program can open.

2. Select the first option to set all the defaults or the second option to select defaults individually.

SETTING PROGRAM DEFAULTS

In the Default Programs control panel, click the *Set your default programs* option to work with the programs on your computer. This opens the Set Default Programs window (see Figure 3.28). This window allows you to view and modify the file types the program opens by default.

To restore all the program's defaults at once, click *Set this program as default* or click *Choose defaults for this program* to modify them individually. This allows you to specify which file types should be automatically opened by this program.

If you select the *Choose defaults for this program* option, a new window opens and allows you to pick items individually (see Figure 3.29). For example, Windows Live Photo Gallery is capable of viewing many types of image files, such as JPG and GIF files, but in this example, the default association for GIF files has been changed to Picasa Photo Viewer. You can use this dialog box to change the association back to Windows Live Photo Gallery.

FIGURE 3.30 Associating the .bmp file extension with Windows Live Photo Gallery.

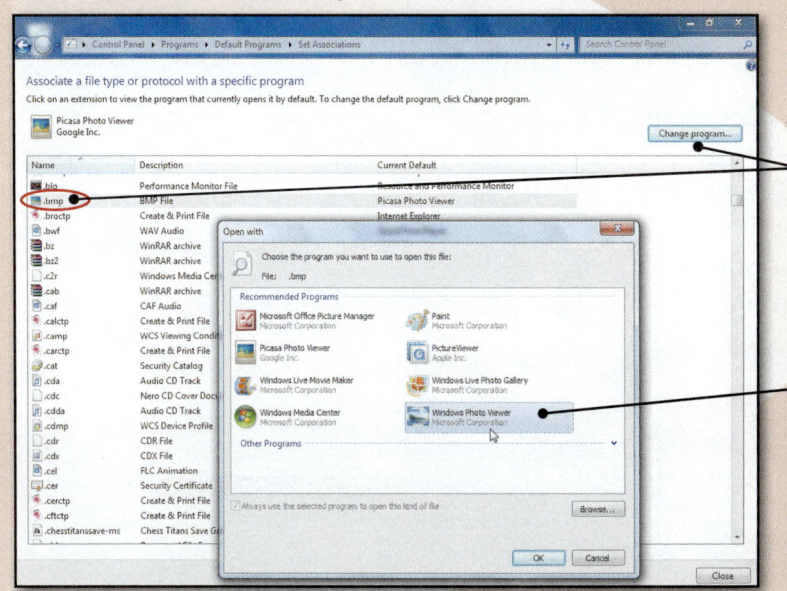

FIGURE 3.29 Click the check box next to each file type you want this program to open by default and click Save.

① Click the file extension you wish to modify and then click the Change program button.

② Select the program that you want to use to open the file type or click the Browse button to locate it and then click OK.

MANAGING FILE TYPE ASSOCIATIONS

To manage file type associations directly, in the Default Programs control panel, click *Associate a file type or protocol with a program*. This opens the window shown in Figure 3.30. This example shows the process for associating .bmp files, which are currently associated with Picasa Photo Viewer, with Windows Live Photo Gallery.

Key Term

default program

Running Project

Use the Default Programs control panel on your computer to complete this section of the project. What program is currently associated with MP3 files? What other files types can this program open by default? What other programs are installed on your computer that can open MP3 files by default?

2 Things You Need to Know

- Windows maintains a list of file extensions and associated default programs.
- You can use the Default Programs control panel to change these associations.

What Can I Do WITH KNOWLEDGE ABOUT FILE MANAGEMENT?

7 OBJECTIVE
Identify the certifications and careers related to file management.

It's hard to imagine a career today that doesn't require you to have some file-management skills. Any work that deals with documents—from traditional office work to doctor's offices, flower shops, contractors, and teachers—has files that need to be managed. Many industries, such as health care, finance, and government agencies, have document management regulations that require individuals with excellent file-management skills to complete.

LIFE SCIENCES

The Document Management Certified Professional (DMCP) offered by the Center for Professional Innovation & Education is a certification track for professionals in the life sciences (pharmacy, medical device, and biotech) that need to manage documents and regulatory compliance. To earn the DMCP, you must complete three required courses in document management, writing process and procedures documents, and regulatory and clinical information systems; complete an elective course from a list that covers life science—related documentation needs and procedures; and pass the four corresponding exams.

FEDERAL RECORDS MANAGEMENT

The U.S. National Archives and Records Administration (NARA) offers a certification track for federal employees. To receive the Certification of Federal Records Management, you must complete five Knowledge Area courses and exams. The organization offers an overview course in records management that's optional. Required courses include Creating and Maintaining Agency Business Information; Records Scheduling; Records Schedule Implementation; Asset and Risk Management; and Records Management Program Development. The NARA certification focuses on federal record management and regulations.

If you're looking for a job, you'll often find file management listed as a required skill. Typing **file management** into the keyword search on Monster.com resulted in a listing of over 500 jobs in industries that included airlines, pharmacy, sales, and loan services. Other sites return similar results (see Figure 3.31). Having a solid knowledge of file management will serve you well in almost any career you choose.

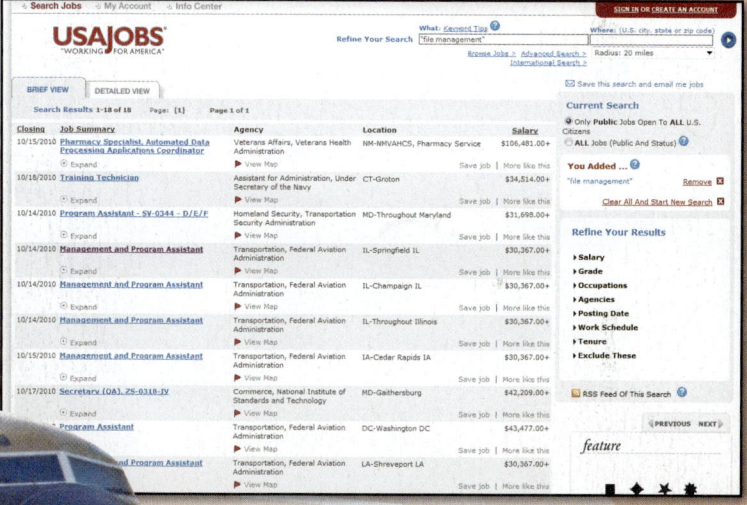

FIGURE 3.31 Many job listings include file management as a required skill.

Chapter 3 | 129

FILE MANAGEMENT

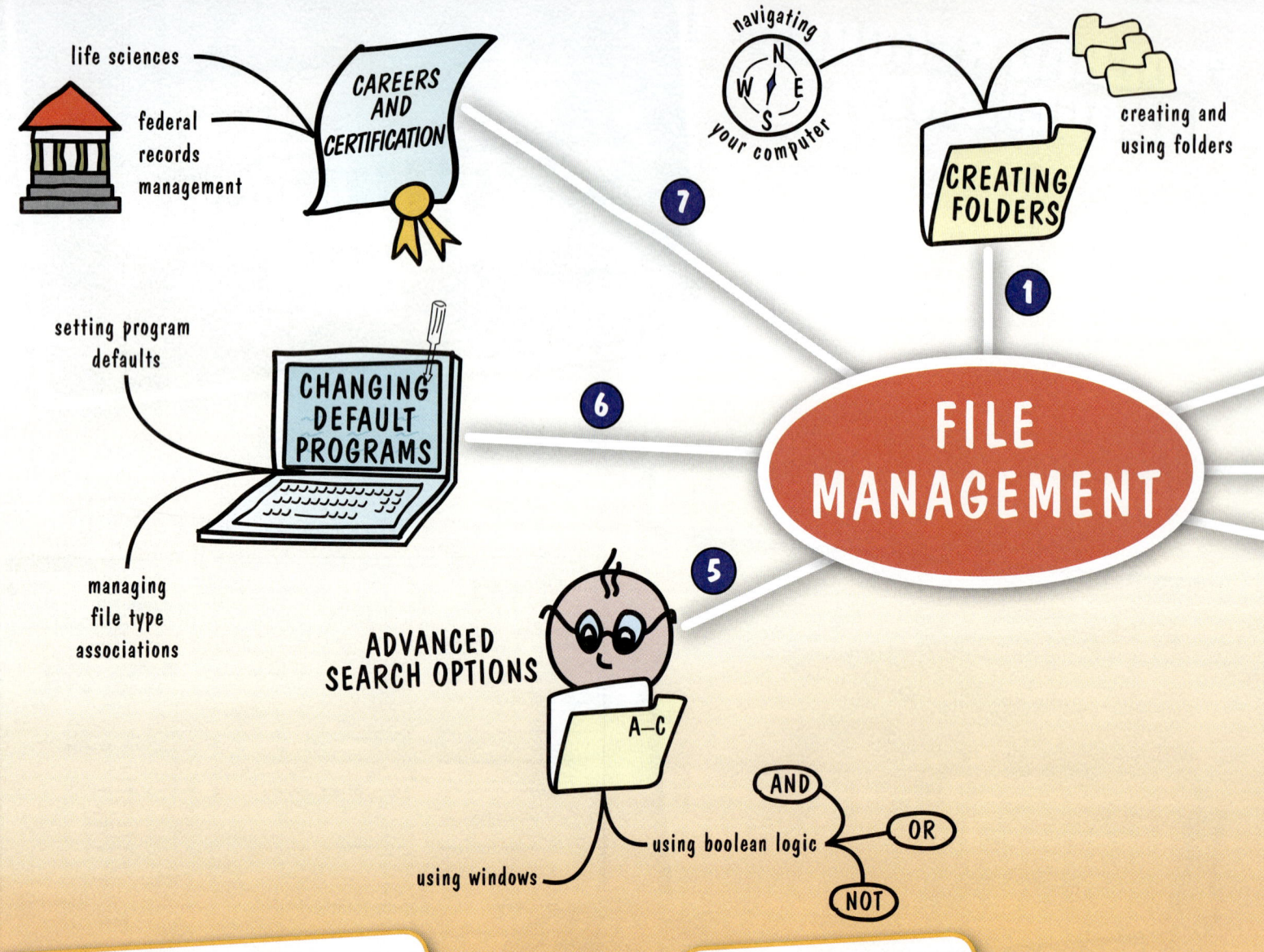

- life sciences
- federal records management
- **CAREERS AND CERTIFICATION** (7)
- navigating your computer
- **CREATING FOLDERS** — creating and using folders (1)
- setting program defaults
- **CHANGING DEFAULT PROGRAMS** (6)
- managing file type associations
- **ADVANCED SEARCH OPTIONS** (5)
  - using windows
  - using boolean logic — AND, OR, NOT

Objectives Recap

1. Create folders to organize files. (p. 100)
2. Explain the importance of file extensions. (p. 108)
3. Explain the importance of backing up files. (p. 112)
4. Demonstrate how to compress files. (p. 116)
5. Use advanced search options to locate files. (p. 122)
6. Change the default program associated with a file type. (p. 126)
7. Identify the certifications and careers related to file management. (p. 128)

Key Terms

algorithm 116
back up 112
Boolean operators 125
compression 116
default program 126
file extension 109
file management 100
file name 108
file property 109

folder 100
hierarchy 101
index 122
library 101
lossless compression 116
lossy compression 116
path 101
Public folder 100
Windows Explorer 102

file names and extensions

FILE EXTENSIONS

file properties

②

③

FILE BACKUP

windows backup

other backups

online backup

hard drive

④

COMPRESSING FILES

working with file compression

types of compression

Summary

1. **Create folders to organize files.** Windows creates a user folder hierarchy for you to use to store your files. You can create new folders in this hierarchy and in other locations, such as a flash drive, to organize and store your files. Libraries are used to gather several locations together and make locating files easier. Windows Explorer is a tool you can use to work with these folders and libraries.

2. **Explain the importance of file extensions.** A file name consists of two parts: the name that's used by people to describe the contents of the file and the extension that's used by the operating system to identify the type of file and determine which program should be used to open it.

3. **Explain the importance of backing up files.** Scheduling a regular, automatic backup of important files ensures that you won't lose your files if something happens to your computer. For the greatest protection, keep the backup files in a different physical location.

4. **Demonstrate how to compress files.** Files can be compressed using several methods. The easiest method is to use Windows, right-click a file or folder, point to Send to in the context menu, and choose *Compressed (zipped) folder*.

5. **Use advanced search options to locate files.** Windows creates an index of common files found on your computer that's used when you use the Search box in the Start menu or in an Explorer window. You can add filters, such as Type and Author, to your search as well as use Boolean operators (AND, OR, or NOT) to further refine it.

6. **Change the default program associated with a file type.** Windows provides a Default Programs control panel that can be used to modify the programs associated with specific file types. This tool allows you to control which program to open automatically when you click on a file.

7. **Identify the certifications and careers related to file management.** Almost every career today requires file management skills, but many industries also have regulatory concerns. Certifications in document management include the Document Management Certified Professional (DMCP) in the life sciences and the Certification of Federal Records Management for federal employees.

Multiple Choice

Answer the multiple-choice questions below for more practice with key terms and concepts from this chapter.

1. An easy way to share files with other users is to put them
    a. on the desktop.
    b. in a library.
    c. in a Public folder.
    d. in your user folder.

2. To select multiple files in Windows Explorer,
    a. press Ctrl + A.
    b. press Ctrl and click on each file.
    c. click the first file, press Shift, and click on the last file.
    d. All the above

3. Which of the following contains an illegal character and therefore isn't a legal file name?
    a. hello.goodbye.hello.txt
    b. make_my_day.bmp
    c. homework 11/04/12.docx
    d. homework (ch_03).xlsx

4. Which storage location can't be used by the Windows Backup utility?
    a. Tape drive
    b. Optical drive
    c. Internal hard drive
    d. Flash drive

5. Online backup services
    a. are very expensive for the average user.
    b. are for large businesses only.
    c. are complicated and unreliable.
    d. can automatically back up your files.

6. Which type of image uses lossy compression to reduce file size?
    a. JPG
    b. BMP
    c. TIF
    d. RAW

7. Which compressed file type can be decompressed using Windows?
    a. TAR
    b. RAR
    c. ZIP
    d. CF

8. Which Boolean operator can be used to exclude certain words from the search results?
    a. AND
    b. OR
    c. NOT
    d. EXCLUDE

9. What is the default file extension of Word 2007/2010 files?
   a. .doc
   (b.) .docx
   c. .word
   d. .txt

10. Which part of an Explorer window contains buttons for common tasks?
    (a.) Toolbar
    b. Address bar
    c. Views button
    d. Details pane

True or False

Answer the following questions with T for true or F for false for more practice with key terms and concepts from this chapter.

__F__ 1. You must create your user folder.

____ 2. You can customize a library by adding additional locations to it.

__F__ 3. Windows Explorer is a tool used to navigate the Internet.

__T__ 4. File extensions are assigned by the program that's used to create the file.

__T__ 5. If you change the file extension of a file, you may be unable to open it.

____ 6. All properties of a file can be modified using the Details pane in Windows Explorer.

__F__ 7. A file compressed with a lossless compression algorithm can't be decompressed to its original form.

__T__ 8. You can't perform a search on files that Windows hasn't indexed.

__T__ 9. The default program that opens a file can be easily changed.

__T__ 10. Searching from the Windows Start menu yields the same results as searching from Windows Explorer.

Fill in the Blank

Fill in the blanks with key terms and concepts from this chapter.

1. The processes of opening, closing, saving, naming, deleting, and organizing digital files are collectively called __file management__

2. A(n) __folder__ is a container used to store files.

3. The user folder structure of subfolders within folders is organized in a(n) __hierarchy__

4. Windows 7 introduced the __libraries__ which is used to gather files from several locations.

5. The utility you use to look at a library or folder is called __Windows Explorer__.

6. File __compression__ is the process of making files smaller to conserve disk space and make them easier to transfer.

7. Windows maintains a(n) __index__ of files on your computer to speed up searching.

8. The __file extension__ at the end of a file name is used by the operating system to determine which program to use to open it.

9. A set of steps designed to solve a problem is a(n) __algorithm__

10. You should automatically __back up__ your files for ease of recovering files in case of computer damage.

Running Project

... The Finish Line

Using your answers to the previous projects questions, write a report describing the importance of file management. Explain how to organize, protect, and manage the files you save on your computer. Save your file as **Lastname_Firstname_ch03_Project**, and submit it to your instructor as directed.

Critical Thinking 1

Tom owns a bakery in your neighborhood. He's overwhelmed by all the information he has to keep track of. He has hired you to help him get organized. All his files are stored on one flash drive, and he needs you to sort them out for him.

1. Locate the data files for this course. Copy the folder *Tom's Bakery* onto your flash drive. Examine the file names to determine the contents of each.

2. Use a word processor to create a table like the one below. Create columns with appropriate categories to organize the files on the disk (such as recipes, payroll, and so on). In each column, list the files that belong in each category.

3. In the same document, write a two- to three-paragraph essay for Tom to explain why he should organize his files in this way and what other ways he could organize the files.

4. Use Windows Explorer to create a folder that represents each category. Move the files into the appropriate folders. Use the Windows Snipping Tool to take screenshots that show the contents of each folder you create and paste these into your document.

5. Save your file as **Lastname_Firstname_ch03_Bakery**, and submit it as directed by your instructor.

RECIPES	CATEGORY 2	CATEGORY 3
Pound cake.docx		

Critical Thinking 2

You work for Jackie, a wedding photographer who has many gigabytes of image files on his computer. He asks you to help set up automatic backups to protect them.

1. Write a proposal explaining the difference between using Windows Backup on an external hard drive and using an online backup service.
2. Research the current cost of a 2 TB external drive and 2 TB of online storage, and include these costs in your proposal.
3. What are your recommendations for Jackie? What hardware and software are needed to implement your suggestions?
4. Type up your answers, save the file as **Lastname_Firstname_ch03_Backup**, and submit it as directed by your instructor.

Do It Yourself 1

Let's set up the folders you can use to store the work you complete in this class. This activity assumes you're using a USB flash drive to save your work for this class. If you're storing your files on your own computer, you can store them in the user's My Documents folder. If you didn't complete the steps in the Running Project to create a class folder and a Chapter 3 folder, do so now.

1. As you complete more work for this course, you may find it useful to organize your files by creating folders for each chapter. Let's do that now. Navigate to the folder that you created for this class. Create new folders for each chapter. Take a screenshot of the Explorer window showing these folders.
2. Open your word processor, and type your name and date in the document. Paste the screenshot into this document. Write a brief note to a friend explaining how to create a folder and why it is useful.
3. If you're using Microsoft Word 2007, click the Office button, choose *Save As*, and click *Word Document*. For most other programs, including Word 2010, choose *File* and click *Save As*.
4. When the Save As dialog box opens, in the left pane, click *Computer* and click your flash drive. Open the class folder and the Chapter 03 folder. In the File name text field, type the file name **Lastname_Firstname_ch03_File_Management** and click Save. Close your word processor. Submit the file as directed by your instructor.

Do It Yourself 2

Lossy compression is used when a BMP or TIF file is converted into a JPG file. Most people can't tell the difference between the two when viewing them on the computer screen. To complete this exercise, you need to have Windows Live Photo Gallery installed on your Windows 7 computer. If it's not, you can download it from **download.live.com** or you can use a different photo editing program.

Insert your student CD into your computer, and navigate to the data files folder for this chapter. Locate the sunset image file. This is a TIF file taken with the camera's highest setting. Drag this file to the Pictures library. Open the Pictures library, and locate the sunset file. Select the file, and look at the properties in the Details pane of the window.

1. How big is the image file? What are the dimensions of the image? What is the file type?
2. Click the More Options arrow next to the Preview button on the toolbar, and choose *Windows Live Photo Gallery*. Click *Fix* on the toolbar to open the editing window for the image.
3. Click File and click Make a copy.
4. Change the file type in the Save As dialog box to JPG, and save the file with the suggested name.
5. Open the Pictures library in Windows Explorer, and select the new .jpg version of the file. Look in the Details pane, and notice the new file size, dimensions, and file type. How much was the file compressed by converting it from a TIF to a JPG? Open the image files and look at them carefully. Compare both files. Can you tell the difference? If so, what differences do you notice? Is the JPG file acceptable for viewing on the screen or is the image quality too poor?
6. Type up your answers, save the file as **Lastname_Firstname_ch03_Lossy**, and submit the file as directed by your instructor.

Ethical Dilemma

The Public folders are accessible by all users of a computer system and provide an easy way to share files among them.

1. You log in to the computer in the lab at school and notice that another student has stored his or her homework assignments in the Public folder. It's the same class that you're taking, so the work could help you. What is the ethical thing to do?
2. Type up your answers, save the file as **Lastname_Firstname_ch03_Public_Files**, and submit it as directed by your instructor.

On the Web 1

1. Use the Internet to search for jobs that have file management listed as a required skill. Use at least two websites. What websites did you use? How many jobs were listed with your criteria? What were some of the industries that require this skill?
2. Type up your answers, save the file as **Lastname_Firstname_ch03_Careers,** and submit it as directed by your instructor.

On the Web 2

Your dad just purchased a second computer, and he wants to use online file storage to access his files from both computers.

1. Use the Internet to research two online file storage sites from the list below. Compare costs, features, security, and storage size.
   - box.net
   - livedrive.com
   - Windows Live SkyDrive
   - Office Live Workspace
   - Google Docs
2. What's the difference between using online file storage and using an online backup service? Which of these services do you recommend for your dad? Why?
3. Type up your answers, save the file as **Lastname_Firstname_ch03_Online_Files**, and submit it as directed by your instructor.

Collaboration 1

Instructors: Divide the class into five groups, and assign each group one topic for this project. The topics include: Windows libraries, user folders, Windows search, file type associations, and compression.

The Project: Each team is to prepare a written presentation that includes an explanation of its topic and examples of how to use the tool. Use pictures, text, key terms, and color to enhance the presentation. Teams must use at least three references, only one of which may be this textbook. Use Google Docs to prepare the final version of your presentation, and provide documentation that all team members have contributed to the project. For more on using Google Docs, see Appendix C.

Students: Before beginning this project, discuss the roles each group member will play. Choose a team name, which you'll use in submitting your presentation. Be sure to divide the work among your members, and pick someone to present your project. You may find it helpful to elect a team leader who can direct your activities and ensure that all team contributions are collated through Google Docs.

Outcome: You're to prepare a presentation on your assigned topic in using a word processor. The presentation may be no longer than two pages, double-spaced. On the first page, be sure to include the name of your presentation and a list of all team members. Turn in a version of your presentation showing revisions named as **Teamname_ch03_File_Managment_Draft**. In addition, turn in a final version of your presentation with all revisions accepted named as **Teamname_ch03_File_Management_Final**. Submit your presentation to your instructor as directed.

Collaboration 2

Instructors: Divide the class into five groups, and assign each group one topic for this project. The topics include: WMA and MP3; TIF and JPG; MP4 and WMV; AAC and MP3; and MOV and AVI.

The Project: Each team is to prepare a presentation comparing its file types. The presentation should explain both the pros and cons of each file type and include examples of when it's appropriate to use them. Teams must use at least three references, only one of which may be the textbook. Use Google Docs to plan the presentation, and provide documentation that all team members have contributed to the project. For more on using Google Docs, see Appendix C.

Students: Before beginning this project, discuss the roles each group member will play. Choose a team name, which you'll use in submitting your presentation. Be sure to divide the work among your members, and pick someone to present your project. You may find it helpful to elect a team leader who can direct your activities and ensure that all team contributions are collated through Google Docs.

Outcome: You're to prepare a multimedia presentation on your assigned topic in PowerPoint (or another tool, if approved by your instructor) and present it to your class. The presentation may be no longer than 3 minutes and should contain five to seven slides. On the first slide, be sure to include the name of your presentation and a list of all team members. Turn in a final version of your presentation named as **Teamname_ch03_File_Types** and your Google Docs file showing your collaboration named as **Teamname_ch03_File_Types_Collaboration**. Submit your presentation to your instructor as directed.

Blogging

1. Blog about your comparison of the TIF and JPG images in the Do It Yourself activity. In your write-up, provide the steps you took to compress the TIF file into a JPG, the size difference between them, and your evaluation of the quality of the JPG file. Explain how lossy compression is used to create a JPG file.

2. Visit at least two of your classmates' blogs on this topic. On the blogs you visit, provide three to five sentences with suggestions of when it might be best to work with an uncompressed TIF file.

3. Create a document that includes your blog URL and the URLs of the two blogs you commented on. Save the file as **Lastname_Firstname_ch03_File_Management_Blog**. Submit the document to your instructor as directed.

CHAPTER 4
Digital Devices and Multi...

Running Project

In this chapter, you explore how to purchase and use different types of digital devices and share multimedia content you create. Look for instructions as you complete each article. For most, there's a series of questions for you to research. At the conclusion of the chapter, you're asked to submit your responses to the questions raised.

media

Become our friend on Facebook

OBJECTIVES

1. Explain the features of various types of digital cameras. (p. 140)
2. Compare different methods for transferring images from a digital camera. (p. 144)
3. List several ways to edit and print photos. (p. 148)
4. Recognize different audio file types. (p. 152)
5. Describe several ways to create videos. (p. 156)
6. Compare portable media players, PDAs, and smartphones. (p. 164)
7. Identify the careers related to digital devices and multimedia. (p. 168)

IN THIS CHAPTER

Digital devices, such as digital cameras and portable media players, have become commonplace in our lives. **Multimedia**, which is the integration of text, graphics, video, animation, and sound, describes the type of content we view and create with these devices. In this chapter, we discuss digital devices and multimedia content and how we use these every day.

The 4-1-1 on DIGITAL CAMERAS

OBJECTIVE 1: Explain the features of various types of digital cameras.

Over the past few years, digital cameras have become increasingly popular because they've dropped in price and gotten easier to use. In fact, you don't even need to have a computer to use one. In this article, we'll look at the different types of digital cameras on the market, the features that distinguish them, and how to use them to capture your memories.

KEY FEATURES

Choosing a digital camera can be bewildering with all the choices available today. Three important features that can help you sort it all out are:

- resolution
- storage type
- zoom and lenses

RESOLUTION The quality of the images that a camera can take is determined by the resolution. **Resolution** is the measure of the number of pixels in an image and is expressed in megapixels. A 10-megapixel camera can take a picture containing 10 million pixels of information. The higher the resolution, the more detail in the image and the larger the prints you can make before the image quality suffers. Figure 4.1 lists the best resolution for various photo print sizes. Images that will only be viewed on a computer screen can be taken at a lower resolution (lower quality) than those intended for photo quality prints. This is important because resolution also affects file size: The higher the resolution, the larger the file. A very high resolution image isn't appropriate for use on a Web page because the larger file size takes longer to load on the screen. This also impacts storage. Many cameras allow you to select the image quality before you take a picture. Setting the camera to take lower resolution pictures will allow you to fit more pictures on your memory card.

RESOLUTION	PHOTO QUALITY PRINT SIZE
1–2 megapixel	Up to 4 x 6
2–3 megapixel	Up to 5 x 7
4–5 megapixel	Up to 8 x 10
6–7 megapixel	Up to 11 x 14
8 megapixel	Up to 16 x 20
10 megapixel	Up to 20 x 30

FIGURE 4.1 Image Resolution for Photo Quality Prints

STORAGE Digital cameras can store images internally or on removable memory cards. The internal memory on most cameras is relatively small compared to the capacity of removable media. The type of card you choose will depend on the camera. Flash memory cards come in capacities up to 100 GB in size, depending on the type of card. The cost of these cards has dropped dramatically, and many people now carry multiple cards with their cameras. The advantage to carrying these cards is that they can be easily read by most computers and in kiosks in many stores. In fact, consumers that don't have a computer can still use a digital camera and simply bring their memory cards to their local grocery or drug store to have the pictures printed or use a photo printer that can read memory cards. Once the images have been printed, saved to your computer, or transferred to a CD, the memory card can be erased and reused.

ZOOM AND LENSES Most digital cameras have the ability to zoom in on an object before taking the picture. **Zoom** can be either optical or digital, and some cameras will combine both. Optical zoom uses a zoom lens to change the focal length of the camera, making objects appear closer (telephoto) or farther (wide-angle) away. Typical low-end digital cameras have an optical zoom of 3–5x, while more advanced (and expensive) cameras may have 20–24x zoom. Some cameras have a macro setting, or close-focus, for taking pictures of objects that are very close. Digital SLRs (DSLRs), covered in detail later, allow you to change the lens. Zoom, telephoto, macro, and wide-angle lenses can cost hundreds or even thousands of dollars.

Digital zoom crops the image and enlarges a portion of it, resulting in a zoomed image of lower quality. Total zoom on a camera is determined by multiplying its optical by its digital zoom. Thus, a camera with a 3x optical zoom and a 10x digital zoom has a total zoom of 300x. Because digital zoom lowers the image quality, it's better to rely on optical zoom when taking pictures. You can always use software to crop and enlarge the image later (see Figure 4.2).

FIGURE 4.2 These images illustrate how zoom can make the subject appear closer.

TYPES OF DIGITAL CAMERAS

Not so long ago, digital cameras were expensive niche items. Today, they range from disposable cameras you can buy in a drugstore for under $20 to high-performance digital SLR cameras costing thousands. Most fall somewhere between the two. Choosing the camera that's right for you will depend on a number of factors, including the types of pictures you plan to take, ease of use, and cost.

POINT-AND-SHOOT The easiest cameras to use are point-and-shoot. They range from very simple and inexpensive cameras with limited features to high-end prosumer cameras with all the bells and whistles—and a price tag to match. Basic **point-and-shoot** cameras are the simplest, least expensive, and have the fewest features. You can purchase one for as little as $20 or spend hundreds of dollars for more features. Basic cameras may not have a flash or viewfinder and limited or no optical zoom. Another drawback to these cameras is that they often suffer from noticeable **shutter lag**—the time between pressing the button and the camera snapping the picture. When your subject is smiling and waiting for the flash to go off, several seconds can seem like a long time, and shutter lag can cause you to miss that action shot. Some basic point-and-shoots have the ability to capture limited video.

Single-use disposable cameras are basic point-and-shoot cameras that can be purchased in drugstores and supermarkets. These are great to carry on trips, send to school with your kids, and put out on tables at weddings and other celebrations for the guests to take pictures. Keep one in your car for that once in a life-time shot, or to document a fender-bender.

Basic point-and-shoot cameras take good pictures under normal conditions, but for better quality images and more features you'll need a more advanced camera. Advanced point-and-shoot cameras are moderate in price, features, and quality. While still easy to use, they include better zoom, macro functions, viewfinders, and other special effects. Most also include the ability to capture video and may have other features like image stabilization, which accounts for camera shake and results in sharper images, and burst mode, which allows you to take several pictures in a burst by holding down the shutter button. Although more expensive than basic cameras, advanced point-and-shoots are still relatively inexpensive.

PROSUMER A contraction of "professional" and "consumer", **prosumer** refers to someone that's not a professional photographer but has enough interest or expertise to require a camera with some professional features. Prosumer cameras are still technically point-and-shoot cameras but with some of the features of professional DSLR cameras, such as the ability to adjust speed and exposure settings.

Figure 4.3 compares features of different types of point-and-shoot cameras: basic, advanced, and prosumer. Deciding which camera to purchase can be a difficult task with all the options available today.

FIGURE 4.3 Comparison of point-and-shoot digital cameras

	BASIC POINT-AND-SHOOT	**ADVANCED POINT-AND-SHOOT**	**PROSUMER**
GENERAL	Tiny; fits in a pocket or part of a cell phone	Better pictures but still easy to use	More control, zoom, and features but still lets you point and shoot
RESOLUTION	1–8 megapixels	5 megapixels and up	5 megapixels and up
PRICE	$20–200 Good for snapshots, especially outdoors, and Web/e-mail	$150–600 Good for snapshots, portraits, and enlargements up to about 8 x 10 and larger; Web/e-mail	$200–900 Good for all types of pictures and larger enlargements
SPECIAL FEATURES		May capture short video clips and include macro (close-up) and other special effects	May include ability to manually control settings, image stabilization, burst mode; less shutter lag
ZOOM	Usually has little optical zoom; may not have a flash or a viewfinder	Typically 3–8x optical and additional digital zoom and a built-in flash	Up to 24x optical zoom; built-in and hot shoe flash options

DIGITAL SINGLE-LENS REFLEX (DSLR) If you really want control and a more traditional type camera, then you'll want to look at a **digital single-lens reflex (DSLR)** camera. With DSLRs, you can change the lens, which can cost hundreds or even thousands of dollars, to get the exact zoom you need. DSLRs can be manually focused, allowing you to create artistic images that autofocusing point-and-shoots can't. There's almost no shutter lag, so they're the best type of digital camera for shooting action stills. Older DSLRs didn't have the ability to shoot video, but processing power has increased, and many newer DSLRs can now shoot HD video. All this comes at a steep cost—from $700 to $5000, plus hundreds or thousands of dollars for additional lenses. See Figure 4.4

Key Terms

digital single-lens reflex (DSLR) camera

point-and-shoot camera

prosumer

resolution

shutter lag

zoom

Running Project

Use the Internet to research digital cameras.

WHAT is the highest resolution available today in point-and-shoot cameras?

WHAT about DSLRs? Choose one point-and-shoot and one DSLR camera with the same resolution.

HOW do they compare in terms of price, features, and reviews? **WHAT** other factors affect the price?

FIGURE 4.4 A basic point-and-shoot digital camera (left) and a DSLR camera with an attached lens (right)

4 Things You Need to Know

- **RESOLUTION** determines the quality of the print you can make and the size of the file.
- **OPTICAL ZOOM** is better than digital zoom.
- **POINT-AND-SHOOT CAMERAS** are the easiest to use.
- **DSLRS** take the best pictures and cost the most.

Bridging the Gap: TRANSFERRING PHOTOS

2 OBJECTIVE
Compare different methods for transferring images from a digital camera.

Imagine you just came home from a vacation and have a camera full of pictures. What do you do next? If you have a computer, you'll want to transfer the pictures from the camera to your computer so you can view, edit, store, share, and print them. There are several ways to transfer your images to your computer.

MEMORY CARDS

If your camera uses memory cards to store the images, you can take the card out of the camera and put it in a card reader attached to your computer. Many computers have a card reader built in, but removable card readers can be purchased for just a few dollars and plugged into a USB port. When you put the memory card into the reader, Windows will detect it, and it will appear in the Computer window as a removable device. You can copy, move, and delete the pictures just like any other type of file (see Figure 4.5.) Depending on your settings, Windows might automatically start the transfer process as described in the next section.

FIGURE 4.5 A memory card appears in the Computer window as a Removable Disk.

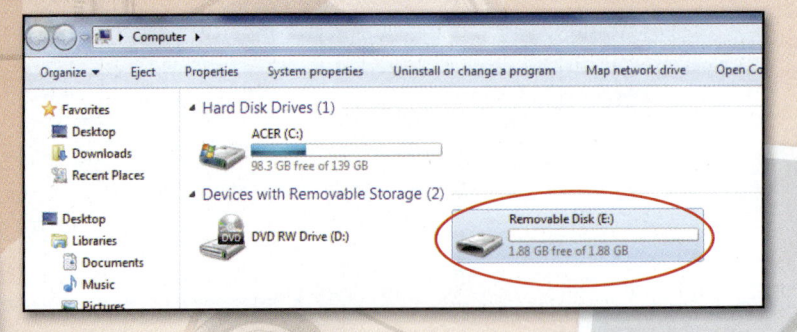

144

USB OR FIREWIRE CABLES

Digital cameras typically have a USB or FireWire connection that can be used to connect the camera directly to the computer, which requires you to install device driver software in order for the computer to be able to talk to the camera. The driver installation might happen through software that comes with your camera or through the operating system itself. Once the driver has been installed, the computer and camera can communicate, and you can transfer the pictures.

Windows 7 automatically starts the process of transferring your pictures when you connect the camera to a computer (see Figure 4.6, next page). You have the options of **tagging** the images with keywords and erasing them from the memory card. If you're using Windows, the operating system will automatically create a new folder inside your Pictures folder and copy the pictures into it. The folder will be named based on the tags you provided and the date of the transfer so you can easily find your pictures later.

WIRELESS TRANSFER

Wireless-enabled digital cameras can transfer photos using WiFi wireless technology, allowing you to connect to a computer network and save photos to your computer or even print photos without cables or card readers. For cameras that don't have wireless built in, a company called Eye-Fi makes a WiFi-enabled SD (secure digital) card that's compatible with over 1,000 camera models. The Eye-Fi card is set up once using a standard card reader and is then inserted into your camera. The wireless transmission range is about 45 feet indoors. If you are in range of the stored network, your images will automatically "fly" to your computer.

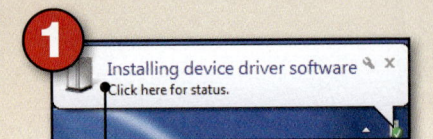

FIGURE 4.6 The Windows picture transfer process

1 Windows installs a device driver the first time you connect a device such as a digital camera.

2 After Windows is able to communicate with a device, it may open the AutoPlay dialog box, depending upon your settings. Clicking *Import pictures and videos* will start the process. If you check the *Always do this for pictures* box, the process will begin automatically.

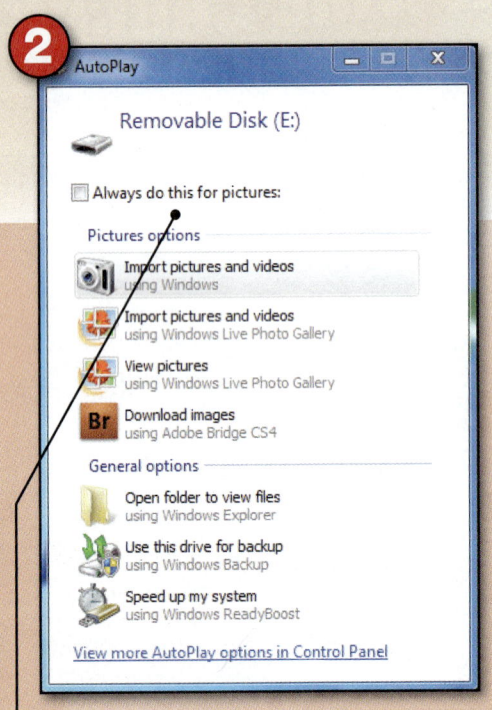

3 Tagging your pictures is optional and provides another way to organize and search for files later.

4 You can choose to have the pictures erased after importing them. You can also erase the pictures from your camera menu.

5 Your pictures display as thumbnails.

We take photos for many reasons: to remember a special occasion, a vacation, friends and family, pets, and for more practical reasons, such as documenting an accident or taking apart (and putting back together) a car engine. Once the pictures have been transferred to your computer, they can be saved, edited, printed, and shared, and moving the photos off the memory card of your camera frees up space to go out and take some more pictures.

Key Term

tagging

Running Project

DO any of the cameras you researched in the last section include wireless capabilities? **IF SO,** how fast can they transfer images? **WHAT** are the limitations?

If the cameras didn't include wireless, look up the current Eye-Fi card. **IS** your camera compatible with the card? **HOW** much will it cost to purchase the card?

FIND a similar model camera that includes wireless. **HOW** does the price compare to adding the Eye-Fi card instead?

3 Things You Need to Know

- **MEMORY CARDS** can be transported from camera to computer.
- **USB** and **FIREWIRE CABLES** connect a camera directly to a computer.
- **WIRELESS TRANSFER** uses a WiFi network to transfer photos to your computer.

A Picture Is Worth a Thousand Words:
EDITING, PRINTING, AND SHARING PHOTOS

3 OBJECTIVE
List several ways to edit and print photos.

The beauty of digital photography is what you can do with the images after you transfer them from your camera. With film photography, unless you invest in expensive darkroom equipment, you're pretty limited to choosing the size and finish of your prints and maybe ordering double prints to share with someone else. Cropping an image means taking a pair of scissors to it. Today, anyone can create amazing-looking photos using a home computer and free or inexpensive software.

EDITING PHOTOS

One of the biggest advantages of digital photography over film is the ability to edit the images. This can mean doing something as simple as cropping out unwanted parts of the image or removing red-eye or as advanced as using sophisticated software to create works of art—or anything in between.

EDITING SOFTWARE Photo editing software is available in simple, free programs, such as Picasa from Google, up to very sophisticated (and expensive) professional programs, such as Adobe Photoshop. These programs are covered in more detail elsewhere. Windows Vista includes the ability to perform basic editing on your pictures using the Windows Photo Gallery, but Windows 7 doesn't include this feature by default. Instead, Microsoft has a free download called Windows Live Essentials that includes Windows Live Photo Gallery, which allows you to edit, organize, and share your digital photos. Programs such as Windows Live Photo Gallery and Picasa also integrate online photo sharing.

ONLINE EDITING Many online photo services, such as Kodak Gallery (see Figure 4.7), Shutterfly, and Flickr, include basic editing tools you can use, including cropping, resizing, and red-eye removal. Editing options also often include special effects, such as making the picture look black and white and adding special borders. You can also order photo prints and create personalized gifts, such as calendars, books, and coffee mugs.

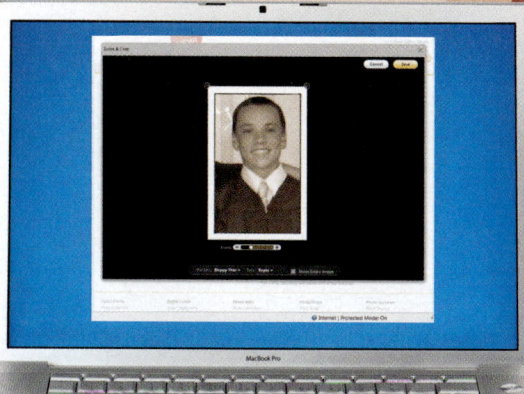

FIGURE 4.7 Online photo editing tools, such as Kodak Gallery, allow you to edit your images without installing software on your computer.

PRINTING AND SHARING PHOTOS

The cost of creating prints of your photos varies depending on the paper, ink, and type of printer you use. At home, printing can cost 50–70 cents per print. Less expensive prints using regular ink and paper have a lower quality and shorter lifespan. Photo printers are discussed in more detail in the chapter on hardware.

PICTBRIDGE PictBridge is an industry standard that allows a camera to connect directly to a printer, usually by a USB connection or special dock. Cameras that are compatible with this system don't require connecting to a computer. You can use a small portable printer to print photos on the spot. You may also be able to do some limited editing—either on the camera or printer—before you print.

KIOSKS Photo kiosks in retail stores have built-in editing capabilities and are very easy to use. Gone are the days of having a whole roll of film developed only to find that most of the pictures are bad. The printing kiosks allow you to print only the pictures you want and to fine-tune your images without needing to use your own computer. You can connect your camera via USB or FireWire or insert a memory card into the kiosk. These prints typically cost 15–59 cents per print.

Chapter 4 | 149

ONLINE PRINTING AND SHARING Websites such as Kodak Gallery, Snapfish, and Shutterfly are personal image sharing sites. Their main goal is to get you to buy prints and other merchandise they offer. The advantage to using these sites is that you can share your photos with your friends and family, and they can directly order the items they want. The prints can be e-mailed or picked up at local retail partners. Companies such as Walgreens and Walmart allow you to upload your pictures at home and pick up the prints in the store. The standard prints from these sites cost about 15 cents.

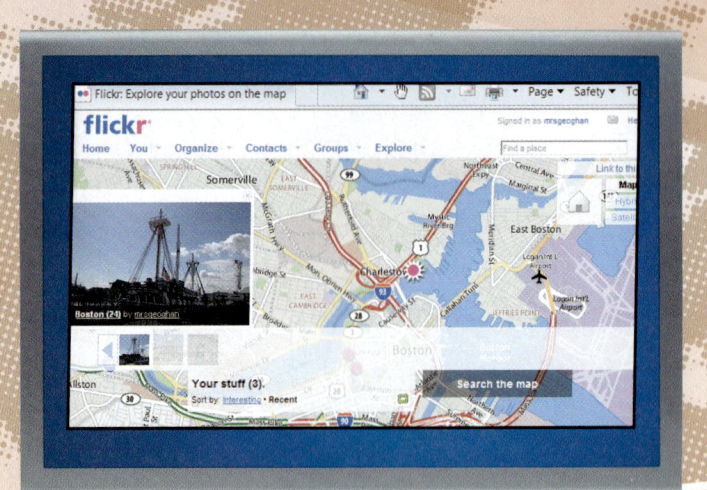

FIGURE 4.8 Geotagging images on Flickr

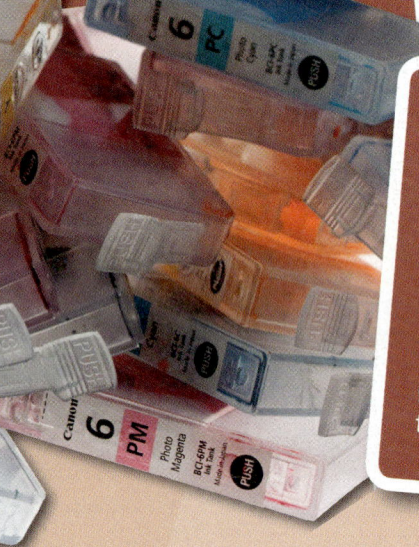

Flickr is an online photo sharing community owned by Yahoo! Flickr has millions of users and millions of images in its vast repository. When you upload images to Flickr, you're able to tag them with keywords that you define. The tags link your images to other Flickr images with the same tag, and while you can choose to keep you pictures private, the majority of the images on Flickr are publically available. Another feature is geotagging (see Figure 4.8), which allows you to add your photo to a location on a map. Flickr also gives you the ability to control how other people can use your pictures legally by applying Creative Commons licensing (CC).

Find Out MORE

Creative Commons **(creativecommons.org)** is a project that has been developed as a way to increase sharing and collaboration by specifying how images and other materials can be used.

According to the Creative Commons website, Creative Commons "tools give everyone from individual creators to large companies and institutions a simple, standardized way to grant copyright permissions to their creative work. The Creative Commons licenses enable people to easily change their copyright terms from the default of 'all rights reserved' to 'some rights reserved.'"

You can visit the Creative Commons website to learn more about how it works.

One of the first institutions to embrace this idea was the Smithsonian Institution, which made hundreds of images available on Flickr under Creative Commons. Visit **flickr.com/photos/smithsonian** to see them. What copyright restrictions are in place on these images? How can they be used legally? How did you find this information? Are there any other public institutions that have made CC images available on Flickr? How did you find them?

A number of years ago, when my son was little, I took a picture of his baseball team. Of course, every one of the 14 families wanted a copy, so off I went to the store to order 8 x 10 copies of the picture to give each of them. This year, I took a new team picture. I edited it on my computer, cropped out the distractions, enhanced the color, and added a caption. Next, I posted it on a sharing website and e-mailed the parents the link. Each parent was able to decide what to do with the image. That process was so much easier and faster—and much less expensive!

Key Term

PictBridge

Running Project

USE the Internet to compare the cost and quality of photo prints from several home photo printers, online services, and local retailers in your area.

CREATE a chart comparing them. Include the following information: cost per print, sizes available, finish available, expected lifespan of prints, water resistance, and any other details you think might be important. When might you choose to use each of these methods for prints?

4 Things You Need to Know

- **PHOTO EDITING SOFTWARE** can be used to enhance and fix your photos.
- **PRINTING PHOTOS AT HOME** is easy but can be expensive.
- **KIOSKS** in stores allow you to edit and print better quality photos less expensively than you could print them at home.
- **ONLINE PRINTING AND SHARING SITES** enable you to easily edit and share your photos and are the least expensive way to print quality photos.

Chapter 4

151

Making Sense OF SOUND

OBJECTIVE 4
Recognize different audio file types.

Sound plays an important role in the multimedia experience. We listen to songs on our portable media players, use speech to control our computers and video games, and are alerted to new e-mail with a ding. In this article, we examine the differences in several audio files types, and compare various media player programs and speech recognition programs.

AUDIO FILE TYPES

There are many different audio file types. Music files are typically **MP3** (MPEG-1 Audio Layer 3) files. These files are a compressed format, allowing them to maintain excellent quality while being reasonably small. When you rip a CD, you transfer your music files to your computer. The files on an audio CD are very large, which is why there are typically only 10–12 songs per disc. An MP3 file is about 1/10th the size of a CD file. MP3 utilizes lossy compression, in which some of the detail is removed. There's a trade-off between file size and quality. MP3 files have the file extension .mp3.

The default file type used by Apple's iTunes software is AAC (advanced audio coding), which are files compressed in a manner similar to MP3s. Because AAC files are somewhat higher in quality than MP3 files, support for them is growing on other devices, such as the Sony Playstation3, Nintendo Wii, and newer cell phones and media players.

iTunes Application

There are several other common file types that you may run into. Most commonly, you'll find Windows Media Audio files (WMA), synthesized digital media files you might hear as a soundtrack to a video game (MIDI files), and real media files (RAM).

Digital rights management (DRM) is a technology that's applied to digital media files, such as music, eBooks, and videos, to impose restrictions on the use of these files. This may mean that you can't transfer the file from one device to another or make a backup copy or that your access to the file will expire in a set amount of time. The companies that apply DRM to media files argue that it's necessary to protect the copyright holder. The Digital Millennium Copyright Act (DMCA) made it illegal to remove DRM from protected files. Opponents of DRM argue that it not only prevents copyright infringement but also restricts other lawful uses of the media.

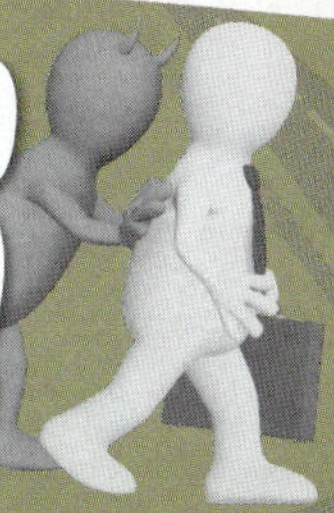

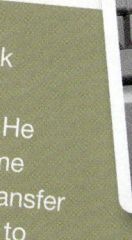

ETHICS

Joe purchased an eBook to use for his creative writing course at school. He downloaded it to his home computer, intending to transfer it to his iPod to take it to class with him. To his surprise, the DRM protection on the file prevented him from reading it on any device other than the one he originally downloaded the file to. Because he can't bring his computer to class, Joe sees no way to bring the eBook to school. His buddy Matt has a solution—a free program that he can use to strip the DRM from the file, making a new copy that Joe can easily transfer to his iPod. Because Joe is really in a bind, he takes Matt's advice, makes the copy of the book, and brings it to class with him. Joe feels that this is OK because he did pay for the file.
Was stripping the DRM rights from the book legal? Was it ethical? Was Joe justified in what he did? Did he have any other alternatives?

MEDIA SOFTWARE

Media software is used to organize and play multimedia files, such as music, videos, and podcasts. You can transfer (rip) your music CDs to your computer; organize your songs into playlists for working out, driving, or dancing; and find new music that you might like using the online store feature. You can watch a movie trailer, a professor's lecture, or a music video. The content available to you grows daily. We'll discuss three media programs: Apple iTunes, Windows Media Player, and Winamp Media Player.

Apple's iTunes is a program that you can use to organize your music if you have an iPod or even if you don't. If you do have an iPod, then you'll need to use iTunes to transfer music from your computer to your iPod. iTunes allows you to organize your music, videos, and other media files. You can use iTunes to shop for new music, find podcasts to subscribe to, rip your music CDs to your computer, and watch a movie trailer. **Podcasts** are prerecorded radio- and TV-like shows you can download and listen to or watch anytime. There are literally thousands of podcasts you can subscribe to. Your instructors may even have podcasts of their class lectures. Figure 4.9 shows my iTunes U homepage, where students can find and subscribe to my classroom podcasts.

FIGURE 4.9 My iTunesU page

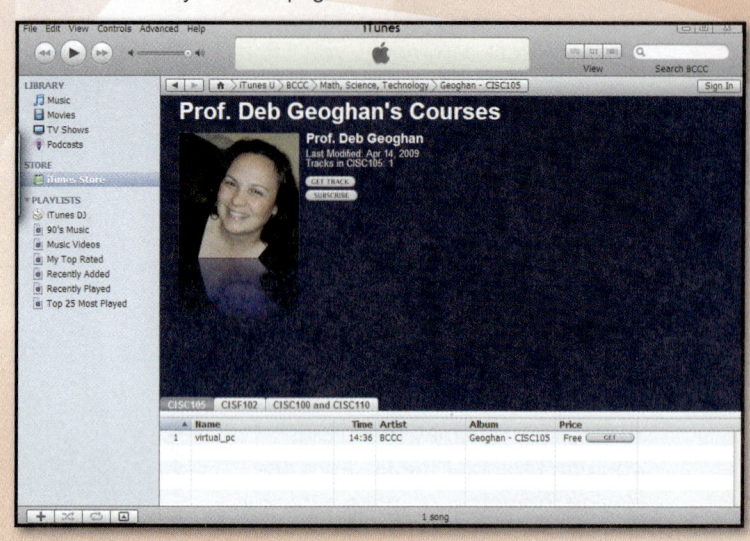

Windows Media Player is included with Windows, and like iTunes, it can be used to organize and play all your media files, find media on the Web to download and purchase, rip CDs, and transfer your media files to your media player (except if it's an iPod). The Windows 7 version of Media Player has the ability to stream media files to computers and other devices on your home network. You can also burn CDs of your music.

Another option is Winamp. This free media player has a Pro version you can purchase if you need more features. It's been around a long time and has recently added support for syncing iPods and sharing your media with all your devices through its website using a feature called Winamp Remote (see Figure 4.10).

Find Out MORE

We've discussed three of the most popular media player programs, but there are many others. Use Wikipedia or another website to find a list of current media player programs. How many did you find? What are some of the features they all have in common? Which of them have you used?

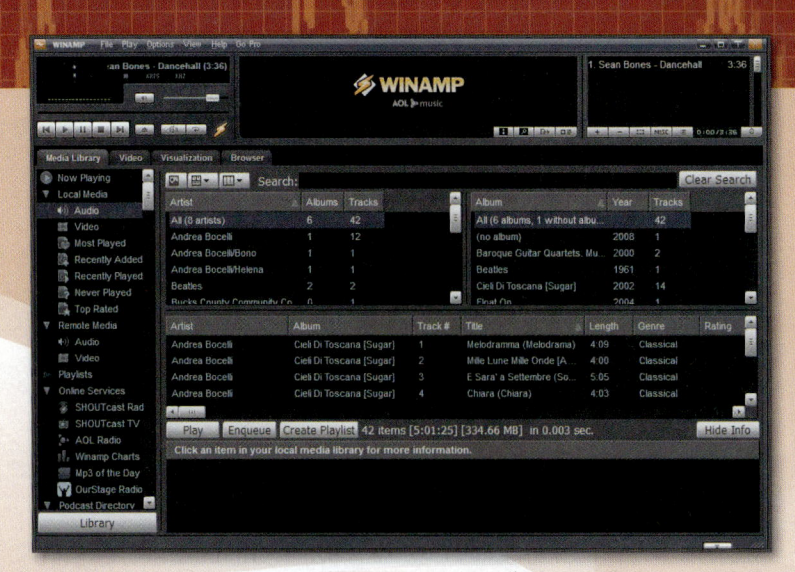

FIGURE 4.10 The Winamp media player is an alternative to using Apple iTunes or Windows Media Player.

To use speech recognition software, you generally need to train it to recognize your speech patterns. The more you use it, the better the software becomes at recognizing what you're saying. It takes time to use speech recognition efficiently to control your computer.

Sound is an important component of multimedia content. Speech recognition allows us to interact with our systems with voice commands, making for easy access and increasing safety. The use of compression allows us to convert our music collection into digital files that are small enough to enable us to carry thousands of songs on a media player or cell phone while still maintaining a high-quality sound. Media player software gives us control over how and what we listen to. How many songs do you have on your playlist?

SPEECH RECOGNITION

Speech recognition has gone from a feature used in expensive software to a way to automatically provide customer service through a call center, dial a cell phone, or even dictate a term paper. Speech recognition allows disabled users to use a computer without a keyboard. Windows 7 has built-in speech recognition, but there are also other software packages that provide similar services. The most recent releases of such software are becoming much more accurate and sophisticated. Speech recognition is often built into video games, allowing the player to control the action using voice commands.

Key Terms

digital rights management (DRM)

MP3

podcast

speech recognition

Running Project

Use Windows Help and Support to research speech recognition.

WHAT are three ways you can use speech recognition on your computer?

WHAT advantages can you see to using this feature?

WHAT disadvantages? Think about your everyday interactions with technology, and give an example of speech recognition that you use.

4 Things You Need to Know

- **MP3** is the most common music file type.
- **DIGITAL RIGHTS MANAGEMENT** imposes restrictions on the use of DRM-protected media files.
- **MEDIA PROGRAMS,** such as iTunes and Windows Media Player, organize and play multimedia files.
- **SPEECH RECOGNITION** allows you to interact with your systems using voice commands.

You Ought to BE IN PICTURES

5 OBJECTIVE
Describe several ways to create videos.

It's estimated that one-third of all Internet traffic is video, and that number is only expected to rise. Creating, viewing, and sharing video isn't very different from handling any other media, except that video files tend to be larger and require more storage and bandwidth.

SCREEN CAPTURE

There are several ways to create videos. **Screen capture** software tools allow you to create a video of what happens on your computer screen. This is a handy way to create a how-to video or to capture a video of a problem that you're having. You don't need a camera to do it. Some programs, such as Jing and Screencast-O-Matic (both free), even allow you to share the video online. Machinima, the art of creating videos using screens captured from video games, is one creative use of screen capture software.

WEBCAMS AND VIDEO CONFERENCING

Webcams can be used in live video chat sessions through an instant messaging (IM) tool, such as AIM or Skype, or through more sophisticated video conferencing software. **Webcams** allow you to have virtual meetings with people miles away, connect classrooms on different campuses, collaborate on projects with others in real time, or say goodnight to your family when you're far away. Such two-way interactions require both ends to have webcams and software setups that allow them to communicate with each other. Webcams are relatively inexpensive and come built-in to many notebooks today.

Broadcasting on the Web, or **webcasting,** can be used to monitor a child in daycare, stream a live performance or lecture, check out the waves on your favorite surfing beach, or watch a panda eat its lunch (see Figure 4.11). Webcasting isn't interactive—it's a one-way process. The broadcast, known as a video stream, can be live or prerecorded. **Streaming** means that the media begins to play immediately as it's being received and doesn't require the whole file to be downloaded to your computer first.

FIGURE 4.11 The view from the PandaCam at the National Zoo in Washington, D.C.

VIDEO CAMERAS

You can also use webcams to record video, but if you want to record something that's not right in front of your computer, you will need a video camera. Today, many basic digital cameras and cell phones include a video mode. However, for the best quality, you'll probably want a stand-alone video camera. A digital video camera will allow you to record video that can be easily uploaded to your computer, where it can be edited, stored, and, of course, shared. The features of video cameras (megapixels, storage, zoom) are similar to regular digital cameras, and the more money you spend, the more features you get.

An important thing to consider when buying a digital video camera is the media it records to. Some video cameras have a built-in hard drive and don't use any removable media. While this is convenient, it also means that once the hard drive is full, you'll need a computer nearby to upload the video to before you can record any more. Cameras that record right to mini-DVD are popular because you can pop the disc out of the camera and play it in a DVD player on your TV without using a computer. Of course, the video can't be edited on the disc, so you still need to upload it to your computer if you want to edit it or share it online. Also, the discs can be quite expensive. Like other DVDs, the mini discs come in recordable and rewritable formats. A third option is a camera that uses flash memory cards. Memory cards come in large capacities, are relatively inexpensive, and can be easily reused. In addition, it's easy to carry several with you. Cost, convenience, and the amount of storage you need will all affect your decision.

Chapter 4 | 157

SHARING VIDEO

As with photos, many people create videos intending to share them. This can mean using an online service or burning the video onto a DVD or Blu-ray disc. Regardless of how you decide to share your video, you may want to do some editing before you share it.

FIGURE 4.12
YouTube video: Belt Test

DVD AUTHORING Video editing software, like photo editing software, comes in a variety of forms. Video editing software ranges from free programs, such as Microsoft Movie Maker and Apple iMovie, to very expensive professional-quality programs, such as Adobe Premiere and Sony Vegas. All video editing software will capture, edit, and export video. Most programs have cool features you can add, including captions, credits and titles, fades between scenes, music, and more. The software allows you to burn your creation to DVD or upload it to the Web. If you want more than the free programs offer but don't want to spend the hundreds of dollars for professional software, programs in the $50–$200 range usually have all the features an amateur would need.

DVD authoring is a feature of most video editing software. Basic programs typically have design templates you can use to create attractive titles and menus and allow you to burn your creation to a DVD that can be played in any DVD player.

YOUTUBE YouTube (see Figure 4.12) is the most popular video sharing site on the Internet. In 2009, it was estimated to have over 160 million videos, growing at a rate of 10 hours of video per minute. The quality ranges from awful, cell phone videos to professionally created music videos and movie trailers. You can upload your videos to YouTube and other video sharing sites and share them with friends and family—or the world. Some of the photo sites will allow you to upload video too.

Find Out MORE

YouTube not only includes home videos of kids singing and dogs riding skateboards, but it has also become a place where professional videos are hosted. Go to **youtube.com/news**. What are the top stories today? What news organizations have videos on YouTube? Are there any news organizations that you're not familiar with?

In 1888, Thomas Edison filed a caveat with the U.S. Patent Office describing his plan to invent a motion-picture camera that would "do for the eye what the phonograph does for the ear." In 1892, he opened a motion-picture production studio to create motion pictures. One of the first motion pictures made there was called "Fred Ott's Sneeze," a recording of an Edison employee sneezing for the camera. You can watch the clip on YouTube today. Little could Edison have imagined the impact that video would have on society a century later.

Key Terms

screen capture

streaming

webcam

webcasting

Running Project

Use the Internet to research digital video cameras.

SELECT a model in the same price range as the point-and-shoot camera you researched earlier.

COMPARE the video capabilities of the two cameras. What features does a dedicated video camera have that the point-and-shoot doesn't? Is the video camera capable of taking still images? How do still images taken with a video camera compare to the image quality of a point-and-shoot camera? Do you think it's worth the money to purchase both types of camera? Explain your answer.

4 Things You Need to Know

- **SCREEN CAPTURE SOFTWARE** records what happens on your computer screen.
- **WEBCAMS** allow you to video conference with others.
- **WEBCASTING** is broadcasting on the Web.
- **YOUTUBE** is the most popular video sharing site on the Web.

HOW TO Use Windows Movie Maker

Windows 7 no longer includes Movie Maker, but it's available as part of the free Windows Live download. To download it and other free programs, go to the Windows Live Essentials website (**download.live.com**), and click on Movie Maker. Follow the directions to download and install it on your computer.

1 To start Movie Maker, click the Windows Start button, click *All Programs*, scroll down to Windows Live, and click to open the folder. Click on *Windows Live Movie Maker*.

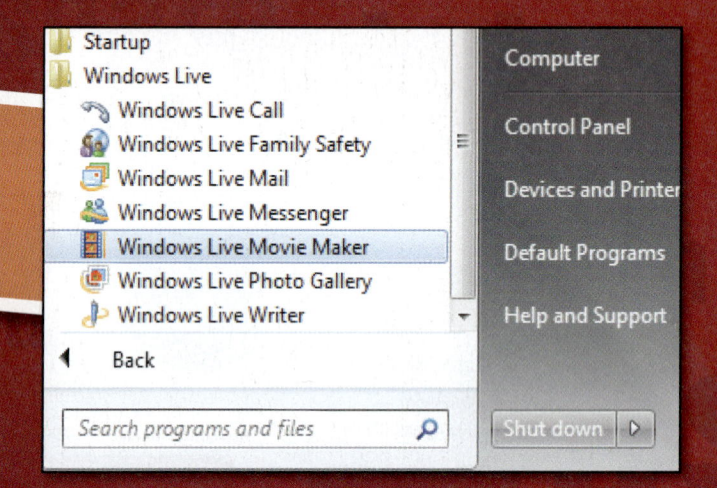

STORYBOARD AREA

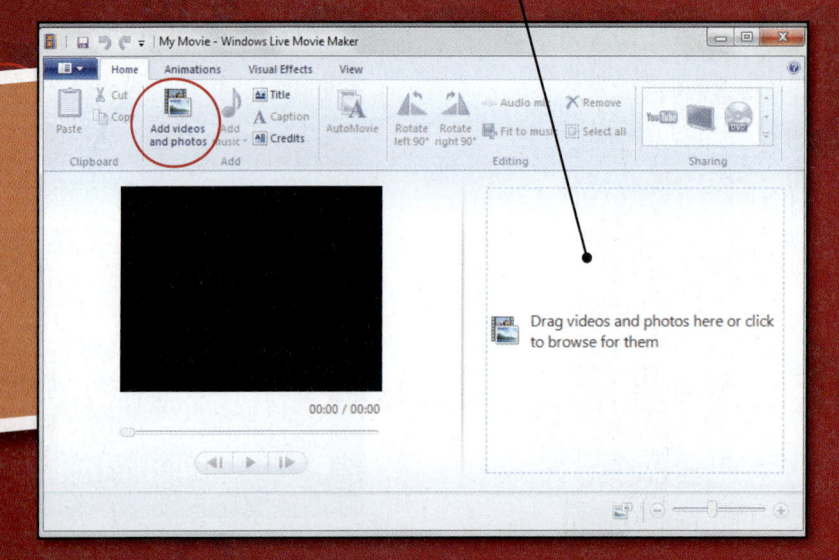

2 The Movie Maker Home screen has three ways to add content: You can click the Add videos and photos button, drag files to the Storyboard area on the right, or click the Storyboard to browse for files. You can add both photos and video files that are stored on your computer.

160 | HOW TO

3 Be sure your student CD is in the drive. On the Home tab, click the Add videos and photos button and, if necessary, scroll down to your CD in the left pane. Locate the files for the Chapter 4 How To. Select and open the **beach.wmv** file.

4 We're going to add some content to this short video. On the Home tab, click *Title* to add a title before the clip. Type **A Day at the Beach**. Notice that the Text Tools become visible and that you can format the Title text. You can change the formatting color, font, and size. In this example, the background has been changed to olive green. Adjust the Text Duration time to 7.00 seconds, and choose the Scroll effect. Move to the end of the video, and follow the same procedure to add your name to the Credits. Click the Play button to preview your work.

TEXT DURATION

SCROLL EFFECT

REWIND, PLAY, AND FAST FORWARD BUTTONS

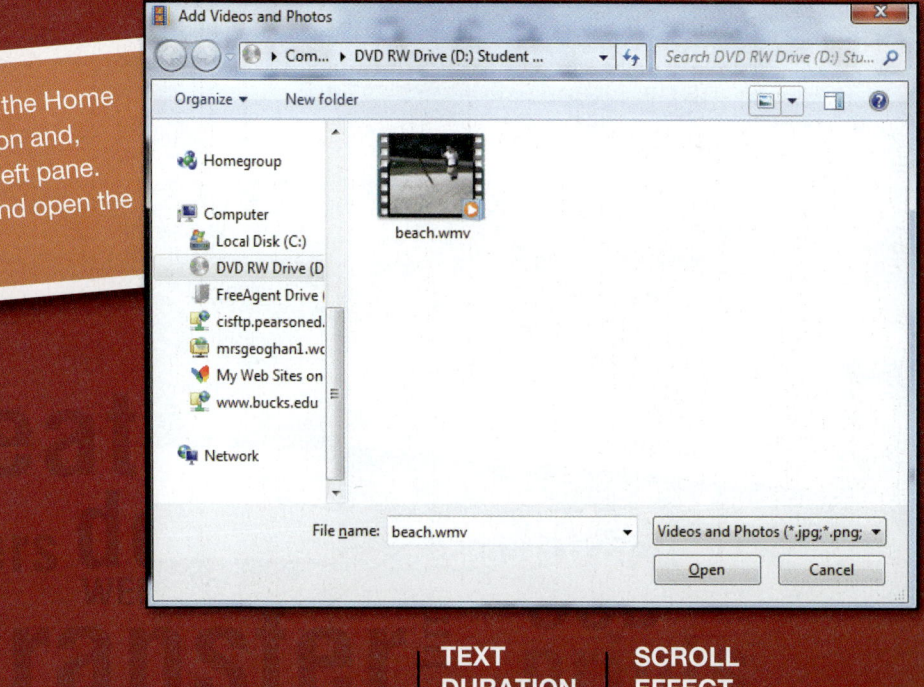

5 Next, let's place a picture between the title and video clip. On the Home tab, click the Add videos and photos button and, if necessary, click your student CD in the left pane. Locate and select the picture of a boat. Click *Open*. If necessary, drag the picture between the Title and video clip. Follow the same procedure to add the seagull photo before the credits.

APPLY THE WHEELS TRANSITION.

DRAG THE BOAT PICTURE BETWEEN THE TITLE AND VIDEO CLIP.

6 Click the boat image, click the Animation tab, and select the Wheel transition (in the Patterns and Shapes row). Click the seagull image, click the Visual Effects tab, and apply the 3D ripple effect (in the Motion and Fades row).

7 Drag the slider in the preview area to 17 seconds at the point when the scene changes from swings to the beach. Right-click this point on the Storyboard, and choose *Split* to split the clip into two parts. Drag the image of the boat between the clips.

DRAG THE SLIDER TO 17 SECONDS.

RIGHT-CLICK ON THE VERTICAL MARK ON THE CLIP.

SLIDE THE VIDEO VOLUME ALL THE WAY TO THE LEFT.

8 Preview the movie. The audio is very poor and will break up where the image is inserted. Select the first video clip, click the Edit tab, and slide the Video volume button all the way to the left to turn off the sound. Do the same for the second video clip.

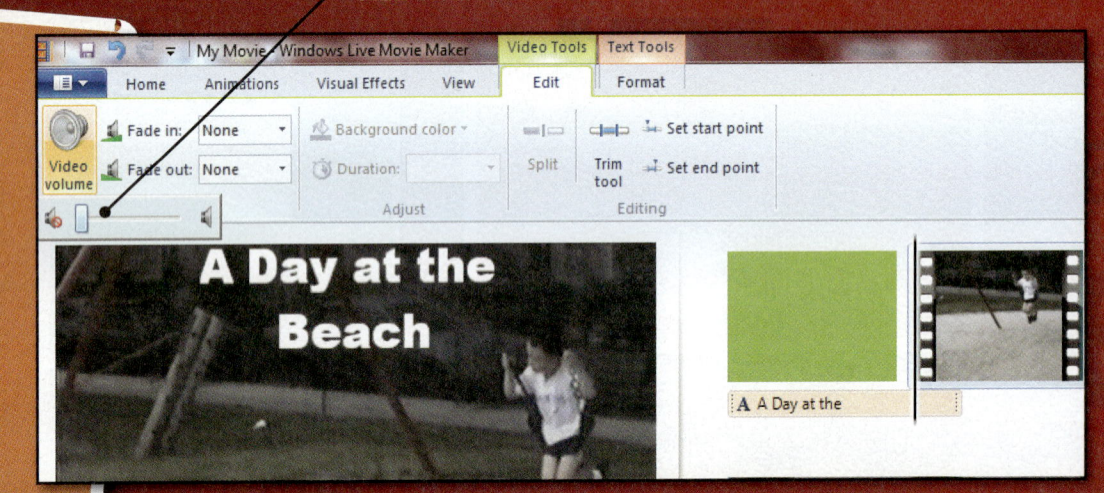

MUSIC ADDED

9 Click the Home tab, click the Add Music arrow, and click *Add Music*. Add the slapstick. mp3 file from your CD.

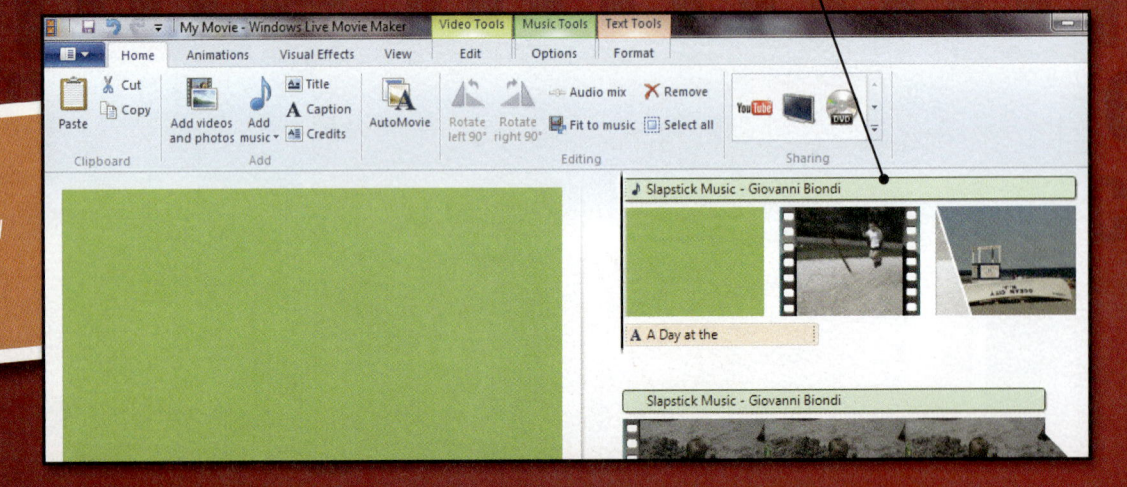

10 Movie Maker doesn't alter the contents of the video, photo, and music files you use. The project keeps all the directions you gave it. When you save the project file, you can open it and edit it again. To share the finished product, you need to save or publish the file. On the Home tab, in the Sharing group, select the settings based on the purpose of your movie. For this exercise, choose *For e-mail or instant messaging*. This will create a small file.

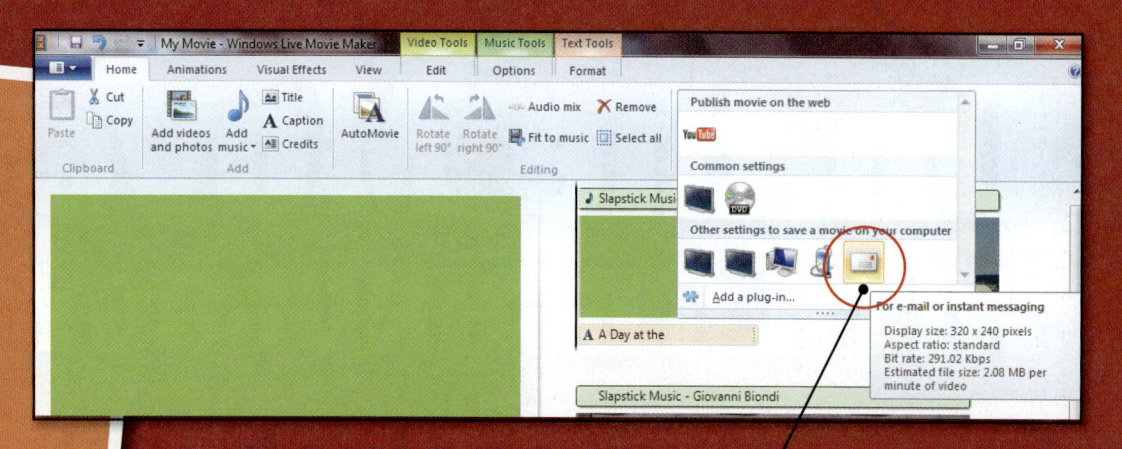

CHOOSE FOR E-MAIL OR INSTANT MESSAGING

11 Save your file as **Lastname_Firstname_ch04_MyMovie.wmv** when it's finished. Click *Play* to preview your work. Close Movie Maker. Save the project as **Lastname_Firstname_ch04_MyMovie.wlmp.** Submit your materials to your instructor as directed.

On the Move WITH TECHNOLOGY

6 OBJECTIVE
Compare portable media players, PDAs, and smartphones.

Digital mobile devices allow us to take technology with us everywhere we go. These mobile devices range from small inexpensive MP3 players to multifunction devices costing hundreds of dollars. The rate at which technology advances is staggering. Apple's release of the iPod in 2001 changed the way we listen to music forever, and less than a decade later, the iPod is also changed how we watch videos, share photos, and much more.

PORTABLE MEDIA PLAYERS

Today, **MP3 players**, or **portable media players**, have become commonplace. These handheld devices allow you to carry with you thousands of songs and podcasts (and perhaps photos, videos, and games) so you can access them wherever you are. You can plug portable media players into your computer, your home stereo, and even your car. Your cell phone may also have a built-in media player.

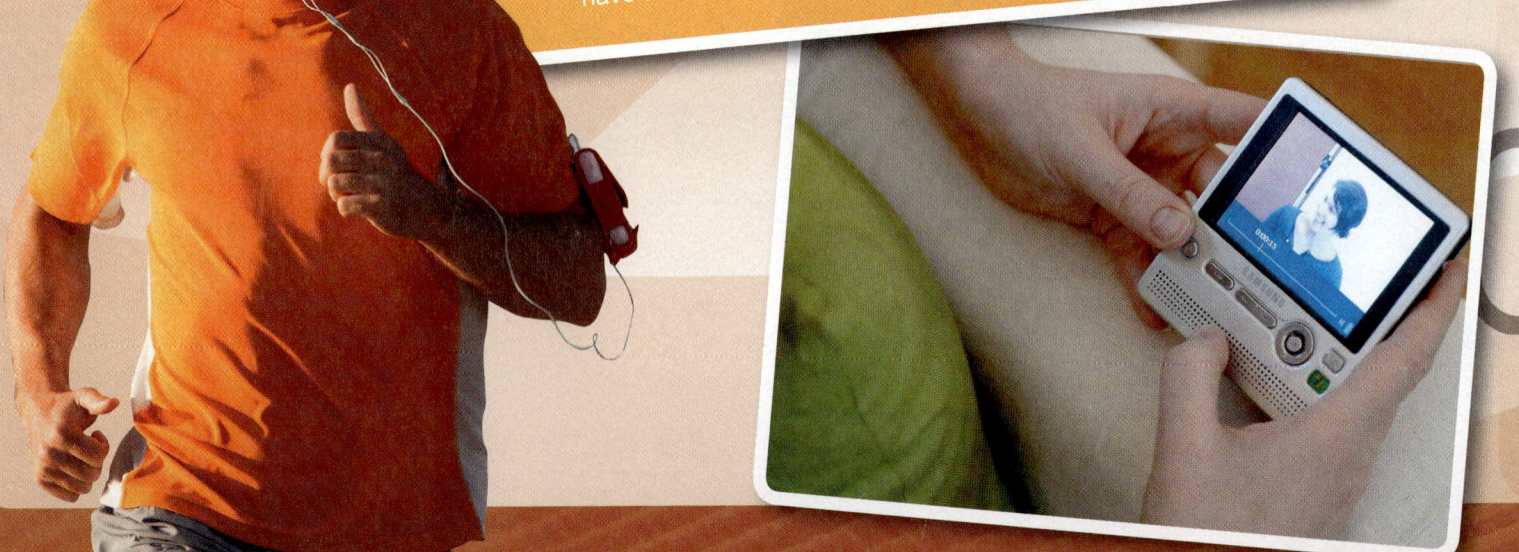

The simplest MP3 players, such as the iPod Shuffle and SanDisk Sansa Clip, have flash memory capacities from less than 1 GB to up to 4 GB, are inexpensive, and have limited features. Midrange flash media players, with capacities ranging from 8 GB to 32 GB, can hold up to 2 days worth of music and may have more features, such as video and photo support. Because they use flash memory, they have no moving parts, which makes them ideal for high-impact activities, such as jogging. Higher-end media players, such as the iPod Touch, Microsoft Zune, and Creative ZEN, can hold many days-worth of music, video, and photos on flash memory up to 32 GB or hard drives up to 160 GB in size. These players also have other features, including built-in games and Internet access. Figure 4.13 compares some of the popular media players as of this writing.

FIGURE 4.13 Hard drive and flash-based media players from Apple and Microsoft

APPLE iPOD CLASSIC	MICROSOFT ZUNE	APPLE iPOD TOUCH	MICROSOFT ZUNE HD
120 GB hard drive Stores up to 30,000 songs or 150 hours of video	**120 GB hard drive** Stores 30,000 songs, up to 25,000 pictures, or up to 375 hours of video	**8–32 GB flash memory** Stores up to 7,000 songs, up to 40,000 iPod viewable digital photos, or up to 40 hours of video	**32 GB flash memory** Stores up to 10 hours of high-definition video, up to 48 hours of standard-definition video, 25,000 pictures, or 8,000 songs
Large capacity holds lots of media	Built-in FM tuner; WiFi transfer of content from PC; Zune-to-Zune sharing.	Multi-touch interface, WiFi Web browsing.	Built-in FM tuner; WiFi transfer of content from PC and Web browsing.

Chapter 4

165

PDA AND SMARTPHONES

PDAs (personal digital assistants) and smartphones are small handheld computers that differ from portable media players in that they're designed for business instead of entertainment. A smartphone is a cell phone with PDA features built in. A PDA will typically have a calendar, contacts organizer, calculator, and other business applications. PDAs are small enough to fit in a pocket, generally have a longer battery life than a notebook, and are powerful enough to handle many basic business tasks, making them ideal for people in many different occupations. Many business people use the BlackBerry to keep their business at their fingertips.

FIGURE 4.14 Apple's iPhone and T-Mobile's G1 Google smartphone are devices that merge a cell phone, portable media player, and PDA into a single device. They have the ability to download additional software, or apps, to extend their capabilities.

Smartphones are multifunction devices that blend phone, PDA, and portable media player features and are popular in both the business and personal markets. There are several different platforms of smartphone available today. Figure 4.14 shows the Apple iPhone and the T-Mobile G1 from HTC. Both of these phones—and others like them—have the ability to download additional programs to extend their capabilities, making them true convergence devices. The cellular networks offered by major carriers have improved dramatically and now offer data transfer speeds that rival home connections. This improved connection speed allows us to watch TV, video chat, and play online games from our phones.

GREEN COMPUTING

E-WASTE

The efficient and ecofriendly use of computers and other electronics is called green computing. Green computing is good for the environment, but it also saves money, making it a win-win proposition.

The amount of **e-waste** (electronic waste) generated every year is staggering. Old computers, cell phones, TVs, VCRs, and other electronic devices make up e-waste, some of which is considered hazardous. CRT monitors can contain more than eight pounds of lead and, by EPA regulations, can't be disposed of in landfills. eCyling, or recycling electronics, is one way to reduce the amount of e-waste and hazardous materials that end up in landfills as well as to reduce the cost of having it hauled away. The EPA provides information on its website about eCycling in your community **(epa.gov/epawaste/conserve/materials/ecycling)**.

You can also dispose of e-waste in an altruistic manner by donating working electronics to worthwhile charities. Your donations of working electronics not only help reduce e-waste, but they also benefit the recipients.

The trend toward mobility has resulted in new specialized, entertainment devices. The Amazon Kindle, Sony Reader, and Barnes and Noble Nook allow you to carry thousands of books with you and download new ones wirelessly. The Apple iPad and similar tablets fall somewhere between a PDA and a notebook and feature Web browsing, e-book readers, video displays, and games.

For most of us, mobile devices have become a part of our everyday lives. Even the simplest cell phone is likely to have a built-in camera, the ability to send and receive text messages via Short Message Service (SMS) and multimedia text messages via Multimedia Messaging Service (MMS), and perhaps a game or two. Many people find that they're so plugged-in that they can never really relax. Sometimes, it makes sense to just turn your mobile device off. Hey leave a message. Beep.

Key Terms

e-waste

MP3 player

PDA (personal digital assistant)

portable media player

smartphone

Running Project

USE the Internet to research the latest and greatest smartphones.

SELECT two models you'd like to purchase.

CREATE a table comparing the features of each. Include the following information: cost, carrier, contract length, camera type, media player, video, games, Internet, e-mail, and any other information you think is important. How do the devices stack up?

WRITE up a summary explaining which one you'd buy and why.

4 Things You Need to Know

- **PORTABLE MEDIA PLAYERS** can carry music, videos, photos, and games.
- **FLASH-BASED** media players have small capacities—up to 32 GB.
- **HARD DRIVE** media players have larger capacities—up to 160 GB.
- **MULTIFUNCTION DEVICES,** such as PDAs and smartphones, combine the features of different devices.

What Can I Do With Knowledge about DIGITAL DEVICES AND MULTIMEDIA?

7 OBJECTIVE
Identify careers related to digital devices and multimedia.

Digital mobile devices have become so integral to the way we communicate and do business that the list of careers in this chapter could go on for many pages. This is just a brief list of them.

HEALTH CARE

The use of technology has become commonplace in many careers. Nowhere is this more evident than in health care. Many medical schools and nursing programs now require their students to learn to use PDAs (Figure 4.15), which give them instant access to vast amounts of clinical information in one small mobile device. PDAs can be loaded with drug and diagnostics manuals, calculators, and other medical reference materials—and they can also be used for patient tracking, ordering laboratory tests, and even billing. PDAs and other computing technology is a have changed the way health care providers practice medicine. Knowing how to use digital technologies is a critical skill for practitioners to have.

FIGURE 4.15 Health care practitioners use PDAs to track patients, review test results, check drug interactions, and access diagnostic information.

GRAPHICS

Graphic designers (see Figure 4.16) are commercial artists that use a variety of tools and media to create their designs, which are used in both print and electronic media. The tools they use include computers, graphic tablets, digital cameras, and drawing and graphic software. A college degree is usually required in this field and includes courses in the use of many of the digital devices discussed in this chapter. The old-fashioned portfolio has also gone electronic. Many graphic artists are authoring a DVD showcasing their work and uploading it to the Internet for maximum exposure.

ENGINEERING AND SCIENCE

The scientific applications of digital devices are numerous. Engineers and scientists that work in the field utilize digital cameras and specialized handheld equipment for collecting data and monitoring conditions (see Figure 4.17). An environmental engineer might monitor air conditions, calculate water currents, and measure pH and alkalinity. A civil engineer might collect traffic and accident data of an intersection or stretch of highway. Meteorologists gather weather data, and geologists monitor for earthquakes.

FIGURE 4.17 An engineer inspects a construction site using a handheld device.

FIGURE 4.16 A graphic artist uses technology to create designs.

PHOTOJOURNALISM

Photojournalism is the use of still images to tell a story. Photojournalists are reporters that travel all over the world to document the news stories of the day in photos. Some photojournalists are embedded with U.S. armed forces at locations around the world and bring us firsthand experiences through their photographs (see Figure 4.18). In the United States, many photojournalists are members of the NPPA (National Press Photographers Association) and the ASMP (American Society of Media Photographers).

FIGURE 4.18 A photographer embedded with U.S. troops in Panama

With a thorough knowledge of the available technology, there are many careers open to you. You're limited only by your own aspirations!

Chapter 4 | 169

Digital Media Devices

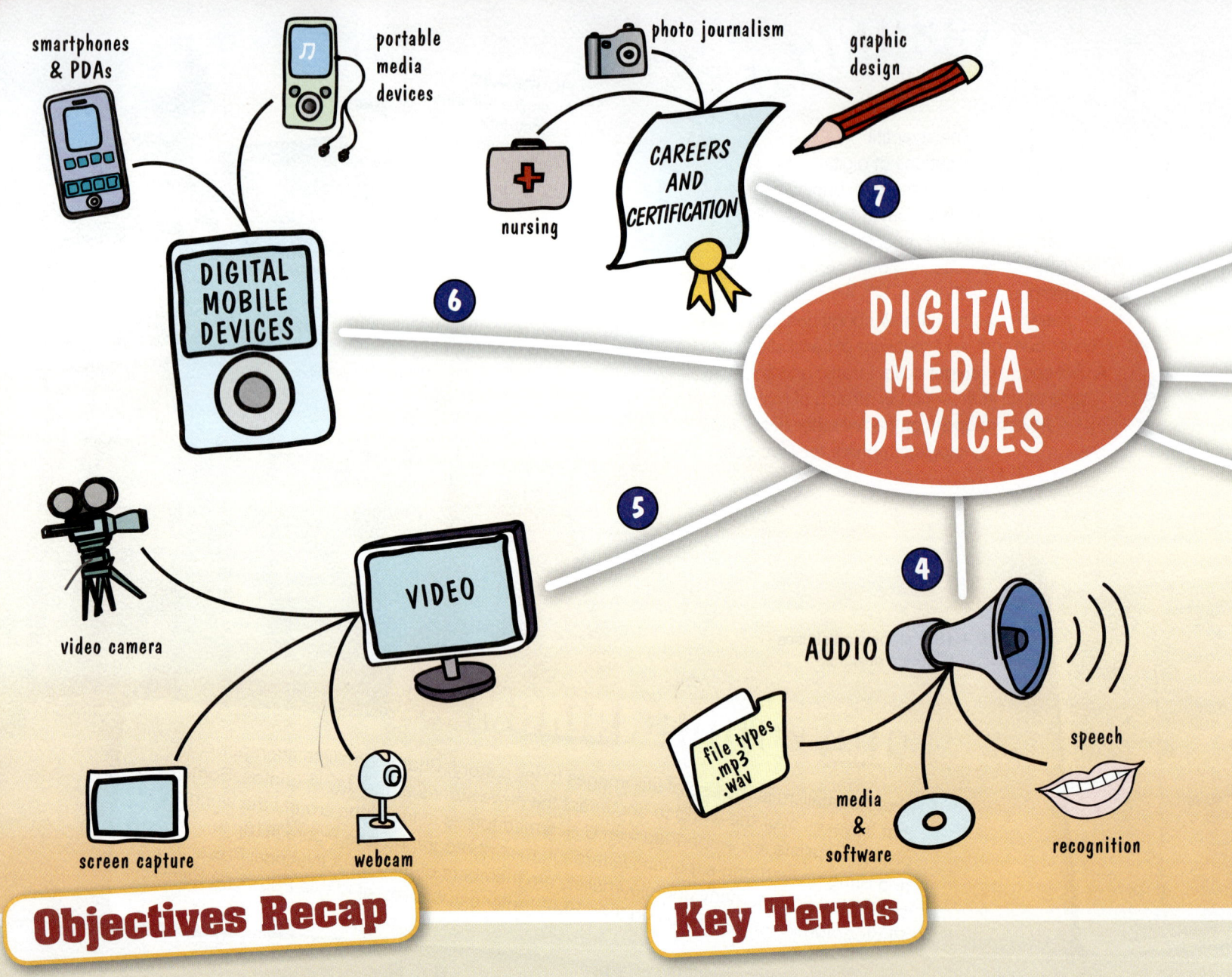

- smartphones & PDAs
- portable media devices
- photo journalism
- graphic design
- nursing
- **CAREERS AND CERTIFICATION** (7)
- **DIGITAL MOBILE DEVICES** (6)
- **VIDEO** (5)
  - video camera
  - screen capture
  - webcam
- **AUDIO** (4)
  - file types .mp3 .wav
  - media & software
  - speech recognition

Objectives Recap

1. Explain the features of various types of digital cameras. (p. 140)
2. Compare different methods for transferring images from a digital camera. (p. 144)
3. List several ways to edit and print photos. (p. 148)
4. Recognize different audio file types. (p. 152)
5. Describe several ways to create videos. (p. 156)
6. Compare portable media players, PDAs, and smartphones. (p. 164)
7. Identify the careers related to digital devices and multimedia. (p. 168)

Key Terms

digital rights management (DRM) 153
digital single-lens reflex (DSLR) 143
e-waste 166
MP3 152
MP3 player 164
multimedia 139
PDA (personal digital assistant) 166
PictBridge 149
podcast 154
point-and-shoot camera 142
portable media player 164
prosumer 142
resolution 140
screen capture 156
shutter lag 142
smartphone 166
speech recognition 155
streaming 157
tagging 145
webcam 156
webcasting 157
zoom 141

Summary

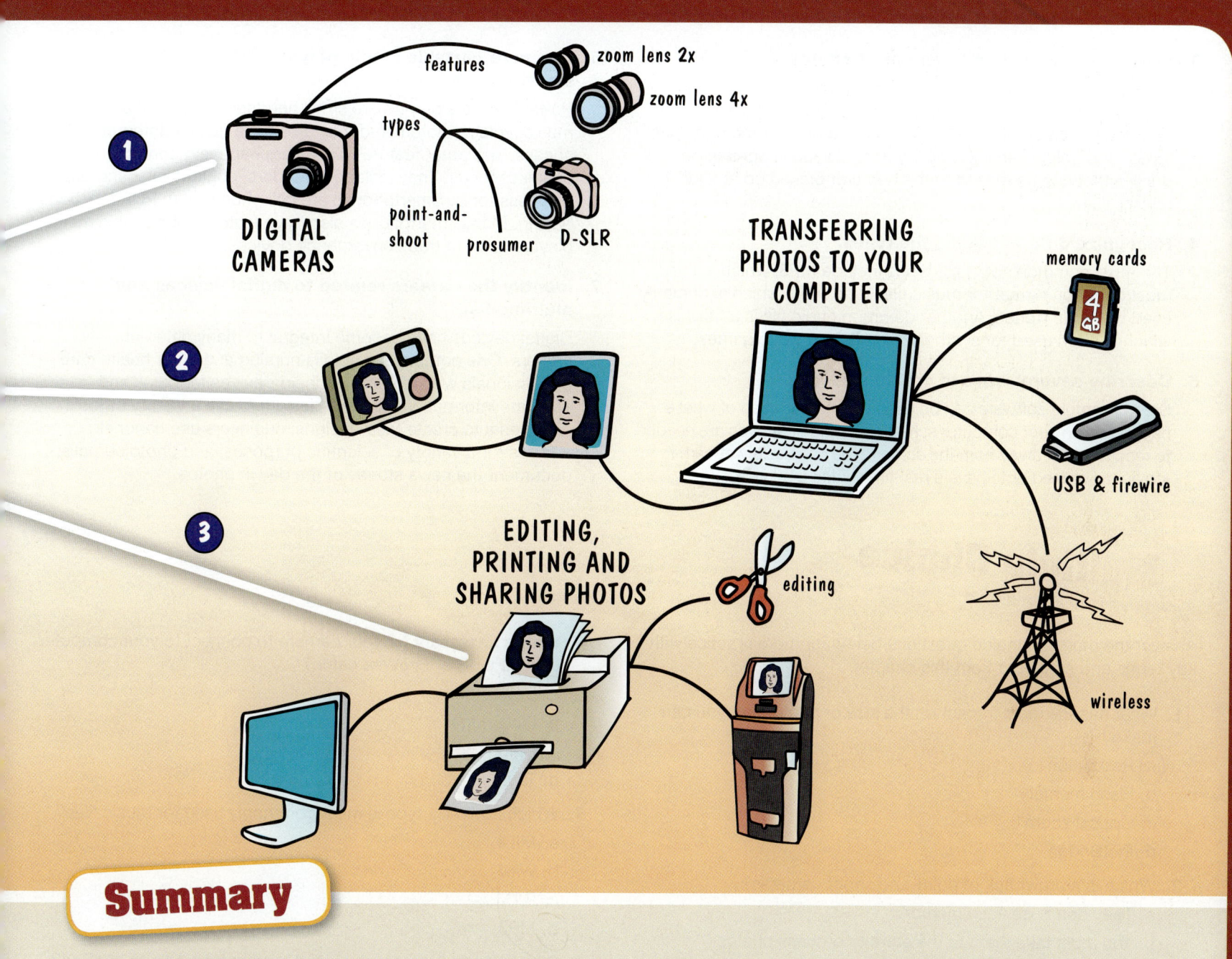

1. Explain the features of various types of digital cameras.

The four main types of digital cameras are basic and advanced point-and-shoot, prosumer, and DSLR. Each type is progressively more expensive and complex. Resolution is the measure of pixels in an image, and higher-resolution cameras can take higher-quality pictures. Storage includes internal camera storage as well as flash memory cards. Zoom and lenses are important features that can make an object appear closer (telephoto) or farther away (wide-angle).

2. Compare different methods for transferring images from a digital camera.

Flash memory cards can be removed from a camera and plugged directly into a card reader in a computer or at a kiosk in a store. Most cameras can also be connected to a computer via USB or FireWire cable. The images can then be copied to a CD or computer or made into prints. Wireless-enabled digital cameras can also transfer photos using WiFi technology.

3. **List several ways to edit and print photos.**

   At home, you can print photos by first transferring the images to a computer or by directly connecting a PictBridge-enabled printer and camera. In-store kiosks can read most memory card types, and online services allow you to upload images to be printed that can be mailed to the home or picked up at a local retailer.

4. **Recognize different audio file types.**

   The most common audio file types include MP3, which is the most common format for music files, and AAC, which is primarily used by Apple iTunes. Another common audio file is a MIDI file, which is often used for synthesized music in video games.

5. **Describe several ways to create videos.**

   Screen capture software can be used to create a video of what's happening on your computer screen, but video cameras are needed to record action away from the screen. You can use a webcam to stream a live feed or to have a real-time video conference.

6. **Compare portable media players, PDAs, and smartphones.**

   Portable media players are small handheld devices that play music, video, photos, and may also have games, Internet access, and other features. PDAs are handheld computers with a business focus. They include calendars, contact lists, and other business tools. Smartphones are cell phones with PDA functions built in. Many smartphones also have features of portable media players and are true convergence devices.

7. **Identify the careers related to digital devices and multimedia.**

   Digital devices have become integral to many different careers. One notable example is nursing and other health care professionals who rely on handheld devices for quick and accurate information. Graphic designers use a variety of tools and media to create their designs; engineers use handheld devices for a variety of scientific purposes; and photojournalists document the news stories of the day in photos.

Multiple Choice

Answer the multiple-choice questions below for more practice with key terms and concepts from this chapter.

1. What has the most impact on the size of photo print you can make?
   a. Resolution
   b. Flash memory
   c. Optical zoom
   d. PictBridge

2. Which is a drawback of point-and shoot cameras?
   a. They don't use flash memory.
   b. You must take them to the store to process photos.
   c. They're expensive.
   d. They're subject to shutter lag.

3. Which type of camera allows you to change lenses?
   a. Point-and-shoot
   b. Prosumer
   c. DSLR
   d. Digital video

4. What's necessary for your camera to connect to your computer using a USB or FireWire cable?
   a. Device driver
   b. PictBridge
   c. Card reader
   d. Tags

5. Which audio file type is most commonly used for music files?
   a. MIDI
   b. WAV
   c. RAM
   d. MP3

6. Which media player is designed to transfer media to an iPod?
   a. Windows Media Player
   b. Real Player
   c. iTunes
   d. Winamp

7. What process allows media to begin to play immediately as it's being received?
   a. *Streaming* ✓
   b. Webcasting
   c. Downloading
   d. Machinima

8. What type of portable media player has the largest capacity?
   a. Flash memory player
   b. *Hard drive player* ✓
   c. MP3 player
   d. PDA

9. Why might you carry a PDA instead of a notebook?
   a. *Longer battery life* ✓
   b. To listen to music
   c. To take pictures
   d. To play games

10. Why is a smartphone considered a convergence device?
    a. It includes support for multiple users.
    b. It includes support for multiple computers.
    c. It can connect users to other smartphones.
    d. *It has features of a PDA and a portable media player.* ✓

True or False

Answer the following questions with T for true or F for false for more practice with key terms and concepts from this chapter.

- **F** 1. You can change the lens on a point-and-shoot camera.
- **T** 2. Some DSLR cameras can shoot HD video.
- **F** 3. Before you can print an image, you must first transfer the image to a computer.
- **F** 4. Once full, memory cards can't be reused.
- **F** 5. Editing digital images requires expensive software.
- **F** 6. Once you post an image on an online photo sharing site, anyone can view it.
- **T** 7. Webcasts can be live or prerecorded.
- **F** 8. iTunes allows you to transfer music and other media to an iPod.
- **T** 9. Portable media players that use flash memory for storage have lower capacities than those that have hard drives.
- **T** 10. PDAs typically have business applications, such as calendars and contact lists.

Fill in the Blank

Fill in the blanks with key terms and concepts from this chapter.

1. *Resolution* is the measure of the number of pixels in an image and is expressed in megapixels.
2. The time between pressing the button and the camera snapping the picture is called *shutter lag*.
3. *Prosumer* refers to someone that's not a professional photographer but has enough interest or expertise to require a camera with some professional features.
4. Labeling images with keywords, or *tagging* them, makes it easier to find your pictures later.
5. An industry standard that allows a camera to connect directly to a printer is *PictBridge*.
6. To use *speech recognition* software, you generally need to train it to recognize your speech patterns.
7. *Podcasts* are prerecorded radio- and TV-like shows that you can download and listen to or watch any time.
8. Broadcasting on the Web, or *webcasting*, can be used to stream a live performance or lecture.
9. A prerecorded radio- and TV-like show that you can download and listen to or watch any time is called a *podcast / video stream*.
10. *MP3 players* allow you to carry with you thousands of songs and podcasts (and perhaps photos, videos, and games) so you can listen to them wherever you are.

Running Project

... The Finish Line

In this chapter, you researched a number of digital devices. Think about the career you're planning to pursue. What's one such device that would be important in your career? Using your answers to the previous sections of the Running Project, write a report describing your selections and responding to the questions raised. Save your file as **Lastname_Firstname_ch04_Project**, and submit it to your instructor as directed.

File Management

Files stored on your computer have properties attached to them that make searching for and organizing files easier. In this exercise, you'll examine the properties of several files, modify the tags, and use the Search feature to locate files.

1. Locate the data files for this chapter.
2. Select but don't open the file *show_me_the_tags.jpg*.
3. Click *Add a tag* in the Details pane at the bottom of the window, and type **logo**. Then, click *Save*. Take a screen shot of this window, and paste it into a word processor document.
4. Click *Libraries* in the folder pane on the left. In the Search Libraries box, type **logo**. As you typed each letter, what happened? What filter options are available? Answer these questions in the file with your screen shot from the previous step.
5. Did the Search locate the correct file? Did it locate any other files? If the Search didn't yield the results you wanted, what other options are available? Take a screen shot of the Search results window, and paste it into your answers document. Save your file as **Lastname_Firstname_ch04_Tags**, and submit it as directed by your instructor.

Critical Thinking 1

Your friend owns a small flower shop and wants to set up a website with photos of some of the arrangements available in the shop. She also wants to print large poster-sized photos to hang in the window. She needs to purchase a digital camera to take the pictures without spending too much money, so she asked for your advice.

1. What features should she look for in order to take closeup pictures with lots of detail? How many megapixels does she need to print the poster-sized photos? Explain why this is important.
2. Explain the differences between an inexpensive basic point-and-shoot, a prosumer camera, and a DSLR. What type of camera do you recommend for your friend, and how much should she expect to spend?
3. Write up a one-page summary that includes the answers to the questions above. Save the file as **Lastname_Firstname_ch04_Flowershop**, and submit it as directed by your instructor.

Critical Thinking 2

You're excited about the idea of using speech recognition to type your term papers for you, but before you begin, you need to do some homework to decide what the best option is for you.

1. Use the Internet to research the speech recognition built into Windows 7 and MAC OS X. What are the basic features of each? Do they require any special hardware or software to be installed?
2. Examine your own computer. Does it have all the hardware you'll need? If not, what will you need to purchase?
3. Look up two commercial speech recognition programs. How do their features compare to the built-in programs? Are there any additional hardware needs? Are they worth the cost?
4. Write up a one-page summary that includes the answers to the questions above. Save the file as **Lastname_Firstname_ch04_Speech**, and submit your assignment as directed by your instructor.

Do It Yourself 1

Purchasing a point-and-shoot digital camera can be a difficult task, as there are so many different models to choose from. In this exercise, you'll create a mindmap to compare the features of three categories of point-and-shoot digital cameras that you'll use to help a friend decide which type of camera is right for them.

1. Using a word processor, website, or paper and pencil, create a mindmap that compares the features of four categories of digital cameras: basic and advanced point-and-shoot, prosumer, and DSLR. Use the figure below as a starting point.

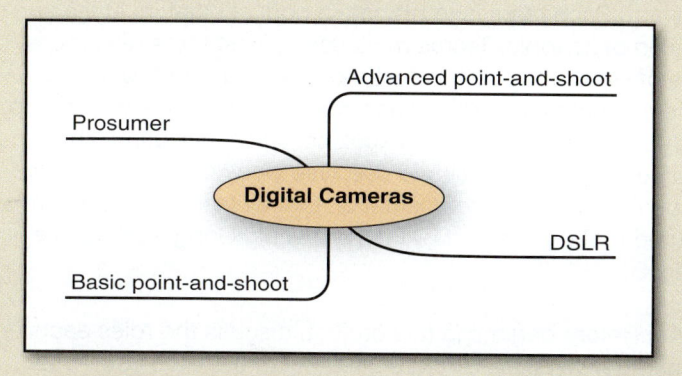

2. For each category of camera, be sure to include the following information:
   - cost
   - resolution
   - zoom
   - pros
   - cons

3. Use the Internet or a newspaper to find at least one camera model that falls into each of these categories and include it in the map. Include the source and date of this information. Save your file as **Lastname_Firstname_ ch04_Cameramap**, and submit your work as directed by your instructor.

Do It Yourself 2

In this exercise, you'll perform some basic editing on a photo. To complete this exercise, you'll need to have Windows Live Photo Gallery installed on your Windows 7 computer. If it's not, you can download it from **download.live.com** or you can use an online editing tool.

1. Locate the data files for this chapter. Right-click *Taz_needs_editing*, point to Open with > and click *Windows Live Photo Gallery*.

2. Click *Fix* on the menu bar. Click *Adjust exposure* in the right pane, and adjust the Brightness bar by moving it to the left until the image looks more natural. Follow the same procedure to adjust the Contrast. Click *Adjust color* in the right pane to adjust the color settings

3. Crop the image so that most of the table leg is removed. Use the red eye tool to clean up the eyes.

4. Save the image as **Lastname_Firstname_ ch04_Taz**, and submit your work as directed by your instructor.

Ethical Dilemma

Alaina received some music CDs of her favorite band for her birthday. She likes to listen to her music on her iPod, so she used iTunes to rip the music to her computer and transfer the songs to her iPod. Because she no longer needs the CDs to listen to her music, her roommate Jessica suggested that she sell them on eBay. This would free up some space in their cramped apartment and generate some much needed cash.

1. Alaina thinks this is a great idea, but is it? Is it ethical to sell the CDs and still keep the music? Is it legal?

2. Because Alaina and Jessica share a computer, is it OK for both of them to transfer the music files to their iPods?

3. Write up a one-page summary that includes the answers to the questions above. Save the file as **Lastname_Firstname_ ch04_Music**, and submit it as directed by your instructor.

On the Web 1

In this activity, you'll search the Web for podcasts using a podcast directory.

1. Open your Internet browser, and go to **podomatic.com**.
2. Click the Podcasts tab. What categories are listed on the Podcast page? Where would you find podcasts to help you with this course?
3. Click *Technology*, and browse through some of the featured podcasts. Select one that interests you, and listen to it. What show did you pick and why? Is this an audio or video podcast? Is there a subscribe section on the Podcast page? If so, what options are listed for subscribing to the podcast? Take a screen shot to capture the Podcast page.
4. Type up your answers, and include the screen shot from step 3. Save the file as **Lastname_Firstname_ ch04_Pods**. Submit your work as directed by your instructor.

On the Web 2

Webcams have become common tools for scientists to use to monitor animals, weather conditions, and even volcanoes.

1. Search the Web for a webcam that's streaming a live feed of a wild animal. Choose a webcam that's sponsored by a reputable scientific organization. Visit the site, and take a screen shot of the webcam feed.
2. What is the address of the webcam you chose? What animal is being observed? What organization sponsors the webcam? How did you locate it?
3. Type up your answers, and include the screen shot from step 1. Save the file as **Lastname_Firstname_ ch04_Webcam**. Submit your file as directed by your instructor.

Collaboration 1

In this project, you'll create your own audio podcast. You may use Sound Recorder or Audacity (**audacity.soundforge.net**) to record or edit your podcast. Help and tutorials are available at **audacity.soundforge.net/manual-1.2/**.

Instructors: Divide the class into small groups of two to four students, and assign each group one topic for this project. The topics include digital cameras, printing and sharing photos, YouTube, personal media players, and PDAs.

The Project: Each team is to prepare a podcast that includes an explanation of its topic. Teams must use at least three references, only one of which may be this textbook. Write a script for a 2- to 5-minute presentation. Choose a format that best suits your group. For example, it can be a news magazine, talk show, game show, or any other format you'd like to use. Use Google Docs to prepare the script, and provide documentation that all team members have contributed to the project. For more on using Google Docs, see Appendix C.

Students: Before beginning this project, discuss the roles each group member will play. Choose a team name, which you'll use in submitting your presentation. Be sure to divide the work among your members, and pick someone to present your project. You may find it helpful to elect a team leader who can direct your activities and ensure that all team contributions are collated through Google Docs.

Decide how you're going to record and edit your show as well as download and install any necessary software. If you're using a Windows PC, you can use the built-in program Sound Recorder to record your podcast, but you'll need another program to edit it. A good, free program for editing is Audacity, and it's available for Windows, MAC, and Linux operating systems.

Outcome: You're to prepare a podcast on your assigned topic. Submit an electronic copy of the script. On the first page, be sure to include the name of your podcast and a list of all team members. Save the file as **Teamname_Podcast_ ch04_Script**. The podcast will be 2 to 5 minutes in length, be in MP3 format, and have been edited to length. It should include at least one special audio effect and requires participation from everyone in the group. Save the final project as **Teamname_ ch04_Podcast.mp3**, and submit it as directed by your instructor.

Collaboration 2

In this project, you'll create a Public Service Announcement (PSA) to educate the community about the e-waste problem.

Instructors: Divide the class into groups of three to five students. The topic for this project is electronic waste disposal.

The Project: Each team is to prepare a Public Service Announcement (PSA) that teaches your community about the e-waste problem and how responsible computer users can dispose of their outdated hardware. You may use any multimedia tool that you're comfortable with. Here are just a few ideas:
- Create a video. You can write a script and cast your group members in it. Use Movie Maker (part of Windows Live Essentials) if you have a PC or iMovie (part of iLife) if you have a Mac.
- Use an online presentation tool, such as SlideRocket, Google Docs, or Zoho.
- Use a screen capture tool, such as like Screencast-O-Matic or Jing.
- Create a PowerPoint presentation.
- Don't be limited by the above suggestions; just remember to pay attention to both the content and the delivery method.

Students: Before beginning this project, discuss the roles each group member will play. Choose a team name, which you'll use in submitting your presentation. Be sure to divide the work among your members. For example, if you're making a video, one member may run the camera and direct, two or three other members may star in the video, still another member may be responsible for editing, and the whole group may collaborate on the script.

You may find it helpful to elect a team leader who can direct your activities and ensure that all team contributions are collated through Google Docs.

Outcome: Your presentation must stand alone, meaning it should not need you to be there to explain it. Your presentation should be 1 to 3 minutes long. Submit an electronic copy of the script. On the first page, be sure to include the name of your presentation and a list of all team members. Save the file as **Teamname_ewaste_ch04_Script**. Submit your presentation to your instructor as directed.

Blogging

Blog about a handheld device (portable media player, PDA, or smartphone) that you're currently using. Provide the type of device you have and why you bought it. Outline the things your device does well and the challenges you face in using your device. Also note areas you feel need to be upgraded and why.

Visit at least two of your classmates' blogs. On the blogs you visit, provide three to five sentences of suggestions on how the blog owner could upgrade his or her device or improve performance.

Create a *word processing document* that includes your blog URL and the URLs of the two blogs you commented on. Save the file as **Lastname_Firstname_ ch04_Handheld_Blog**. Submit the document to your instructor as directed.

CHAPTER 5
Application Software

Running Project

In this chapter, you learn about different kinds of application software and how to obtain it. Look for instructions as you complete each article. For most, there's a series of questions for you to research. At the conclusion of this chapter, you're asked to submit your responses to the questions raised.

Become our friend on Facebook

OBJECTIVES

1. Identify types and uses of business productivity software. (p. 180)
2. Identify types and uses of personal software. (p. 188)
3. Assess a computer system for software compatibility. (p. 202)
4. Compare various ways of obtaining software. (p. 206)
5. Discuss the importance of cloud computing. (p. 210)
6. Identify the certifications and careers related to application software. (p. 212)

IN THIS CHAPTER

A computer is a programmable machine that converts raw data into useful information. Programming—in particular, application software—is what makes a computer different than a toaster. In this chapter, we look at a variety of different software applications for both business and personal use.

Making BUSINESS WORK

OBJECTIVE 1
Identify types and uses of business productivity software.

Today, companies large and small rely on computers for virtually every aspect of running a business—from billing to inventory to payroll to sales. Most businesses depend on a variety of software applications to complete tasks.

OFFICE SUITES

The most commonly used application software in business (and often at home) is an **office application suite**, such as Microsoft Office or OpenOffice.org. These suites include several applications that are designed to work together to manage and create different types of documents and include features that allow multiple users to collaborate. In this article, we look at the office applications used most frequently in a business environment. We discuss other options for the home user, including online alternatives, in the other articles.

WORD PROCESSING A **word processor** is an application that's used to create, edit, and format text documents; the documents can also contain images. A full-featured word processor, such as Microsoft Word or OpenOffice.org Writer, can create everything from simple memos to large complex documents.

In Figure 5.1, some of the more commonly used features of a word processor were used to create a document. The page number in the header was automatically generated, and a word processor renumbers the pages of a long document as the content changes. The Heading 1 Style was used to format the title of the essay. Styles allow you to apply a predefined set of formatting steps to text. The title and image are center-aligned on the page, but the rest of the text is left-aligned. The spell-checker put a red squiggly line under the word Geoghan, indicating that the word wasn't found in the spell-check dictionary. It's possible to add words to the dictionary and even to create a custom dictionary that contains words you commonly use that aren't spelled incorrectly, such as your last name.

FIGURE 5.1 A simple essay that uses some Microsoft Word 2010 features

- Header with automatically generated and formatted page number
- Title and image center-aligned
- Page number and word count statistics
- Geoghan not in the Microsoft Word dictionary
- Heading 1 style used to format text

Some standard features of modern word processors include:

- **What you see is what you get:** The layout on the computer screen shows the document layout as it would appear when printed. This is sometimes referred to as **WYSIWYG**.
- **Formatting styles:** Text style, font, color, size, alignment
- **Spelling (and sometimes grammar) checkers:** Includes the ability to have custom dictionaries
- **Graphics:** The ability to insert and format images
- **Text organization tools:** Tables, bullets, lists
- **Statistics:** Includes such features as word count
- **Content guides:** Footnotes, indexes, tables of contents
- **Page layout:** Headers and footers, page numbers, margins
- **Mail merge:** The ability to generate mail labels or form letters for lists of people

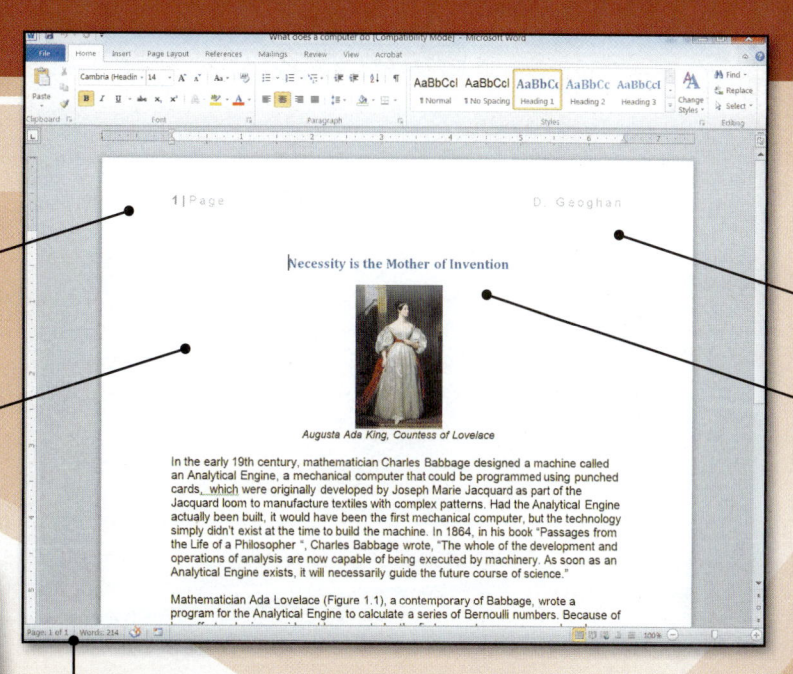

Most home users utilize the basic features, but businesses take advantage of the more advanced features—such as track changes, mail merge, and document protection—to create many kinds of business documents. Figure 5.2 shows comments from multiple reviewers working on the same document. This is one way that users can collaborate on a project.

Most businesses today rely on word processing for all types of documents; however, when calculations are involved, a spreadsheet program is necessary.

FIGURE 5.2 Microsoft Word 2010 allows multiple reviewers to collaborate on a document.

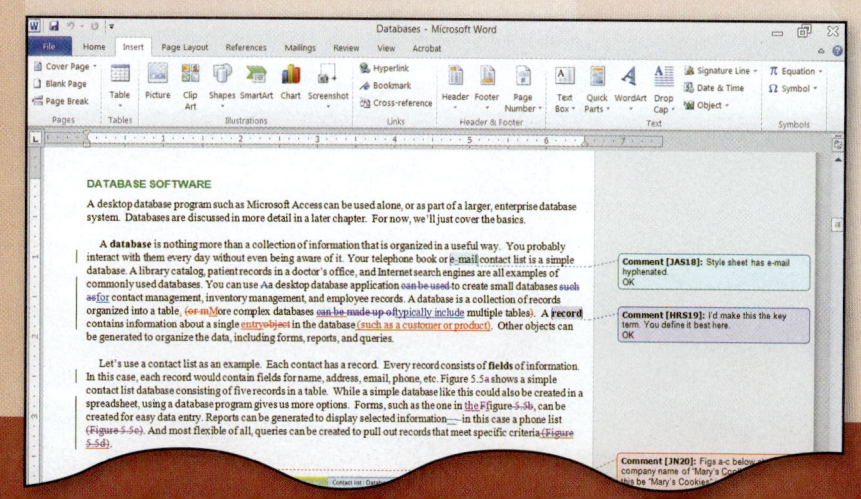

Chapter 5 | 181

SPREADSHEET SOFTWARE A **spreadsheet** application, such as Microsoft Excel, creates electronic worksheets composed of rows and columns. Spreadsheets are used for applications, such as budgeting, grade books, and inventory. They are very useful tools for managing business expenses, payroll, and billing, although large companies may use tools that are specifically made for such tasks.

In a spreadsheet, the intersection of a row and a column is called a **cell**. Cells can contain numbers, text, or formulas. Three-dimensional spreadsheets can have multiple worksheets that are linked together, making them very flexible and powerful. Most spreadsheet applications also have the ability to create charts or graphs to visually represent data. Although there are other spreadsheet programs available, in a business environment, you'll find Microsoft Excel almost exclusively.

One advantage to using a spreadsheet program is that it can be customized. For example, a teacher might use a spreadsheet instead of a grade book tool so he or she can create his or her own formulas and calculations rather than having to adjust his or her grading methods to fit into a commercial grade book program's format. Another advantage is cost savings. Because most office computers already have a spreadsheet program installed as part of an software suite, there's no need to purchase additional software. Also, users will have some familiarity with the program interface and need less training to use it.

Spreadsheets are also very good at organizing data so it can be sorted, filtered, and rearranged, making them useful for things that don't involve calculations at all—such as address lists and schedules. Figure 5.3 shows a spreadsheet created for a U.S. history course that lists all the U.S. presidents and their political parties. As you can see, the number of presidents in each party was calculated, and a pie chart showing that information was generated.

FIGURE 5.3 A simple spreadsheet illustrating text, numbers, a formula, and a pie chart.

The formula in cell A49 used to calculate the number of presidents in the Federalist party

The cell reference A49 indicates the active cell: column A, row 49.

A pie chart was created to visually represent the data.

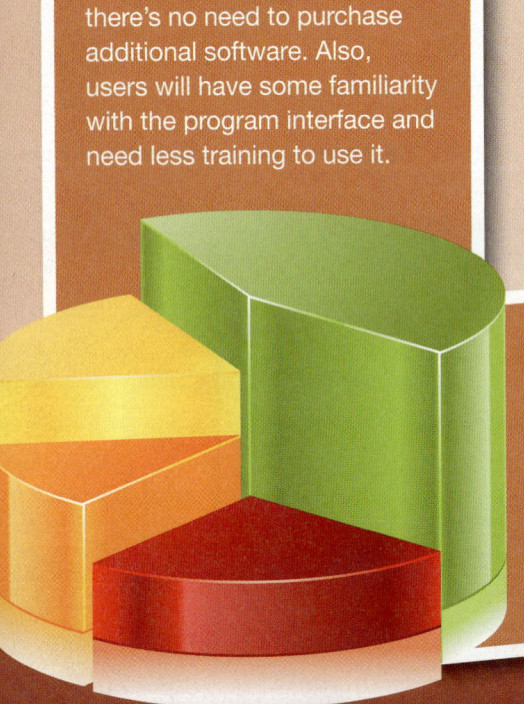

PRESENTATION SOFTWARE A presentation application, such as Microsoft PowerPoint or iWork Keynote (for Mac), is used to create electronic presentations. If you want to present facts, figures, and ideas and engage your audience at the same time, you need visual aids. With PowerPoint, it's easy to create them. Each slide can contain text, graphics, video, audio, or any combination of these, making your visual aids dynamic and enhancing your presentation. A good speaker creates a presentation that audiences will be interested in and will remember.

Figure 5.4 shows a PowerPoint presentation on digital cameras. The presentation here is shown in Slide Sorter view, which allows the author to see how the slides look in order and easily change the order by dragging the slides into position. This presentation contains 15 slides—some containing images—and uses a built-in design template with predefined colors, fonts, and layouts. The star symbol beneath the slides indicates that dynamic transitions between slides and animation of slide elements are used. Good design principles for presentations include using easy-to-see color schemes and large font sizes, limiting the amount of text on each slide, limiting the use of slide transitions and animations, and using images to enhance your words.

Animations and transitions make slides dynamic.

Animations and/or transitions are used on this slide.

The Title slide is formatted with built-in design style and layout.

Slides can contain images and text (as well as audio and video).

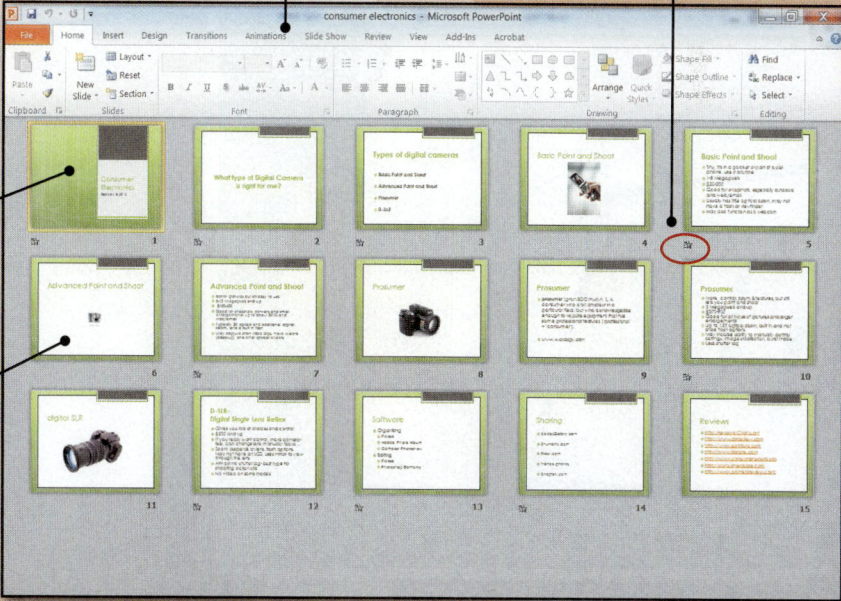

FIGURE 5.4 This PowerPoint presentation contains many commonly used elements.

Chapter 5 | 183

DATABASE SOFTWARE A desktop database program such as Microsoft Access can be used alone or as part of a larger enterprise database system. For now, we just cover the basics.

A **database** is nothing more than a collection of information that is organized in a useful way. You probably interact with databases every day without even realizing it. Your telephone book or e-mail contact list is a simple database. A library catalog, patient records in a doctor's office, and Internet search engines are all examples of commonly used databases. You can use a desktop database application to create small databases for contact management, inventory management, and employee records. A database is a collection of records organized into a table. More complex databases typically include multiple tables. A **record** contains information about a single entry in the database (such as a customer or product). Other objects can be generated to organize the data, including forms, reports, and queries.

Let's use a contact list as an example. Each contact has a record. Every record consists of **fields** of information. In this case, each record would contain fields for name, address, e-mail, phone, etc. Figure 5.5 shows a simple contact list database consisting of five records in a table. While a simple database like this could also be created in a spreadsheet, using a database program gives us more options. Forms, such as the one in the figure, can be created for easy data entry. Reports can be generated to display selected information—in this case, a phone list. And most flexible of all, queries can be created to pull out records that meet specific criteria.

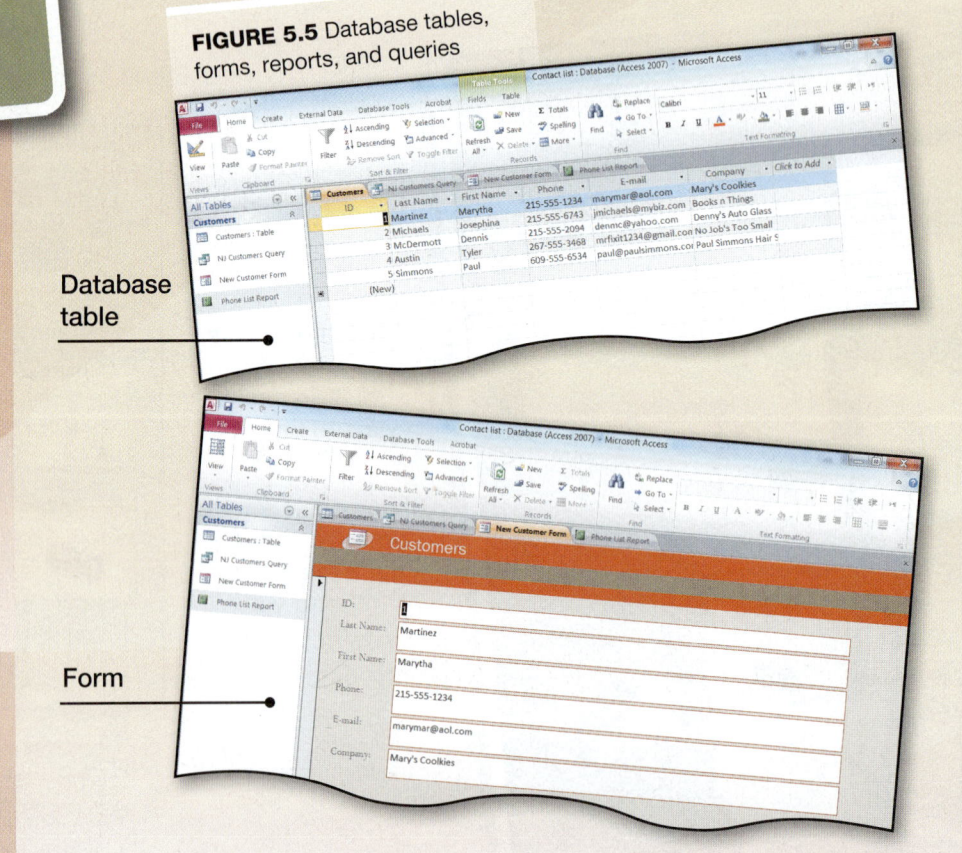

FIGURE 5.5 Database tables, forms, reports, and queries

Database table

Form

184 | OBJECTIVE 1

FIGURE 5.6 Microsoft Outlook 2010 PIM manages your e-mail, contacts, calendar, and tasks in one place.

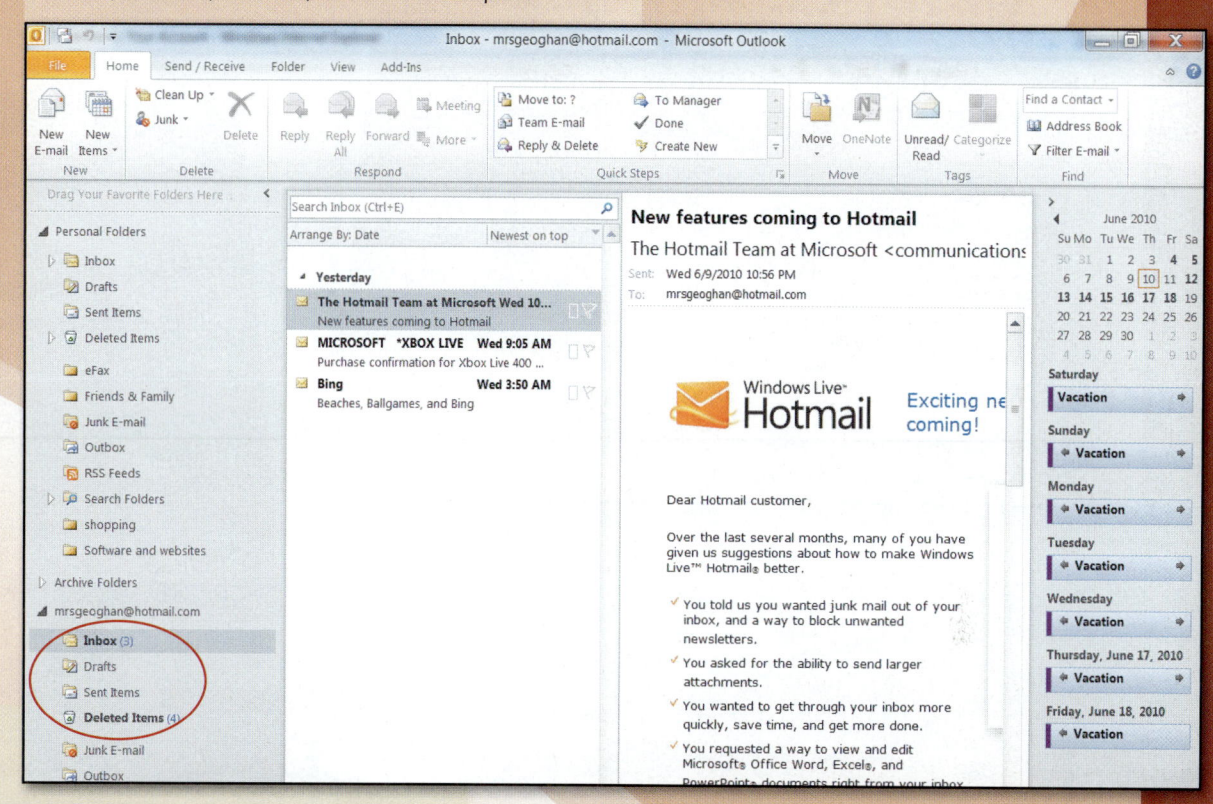

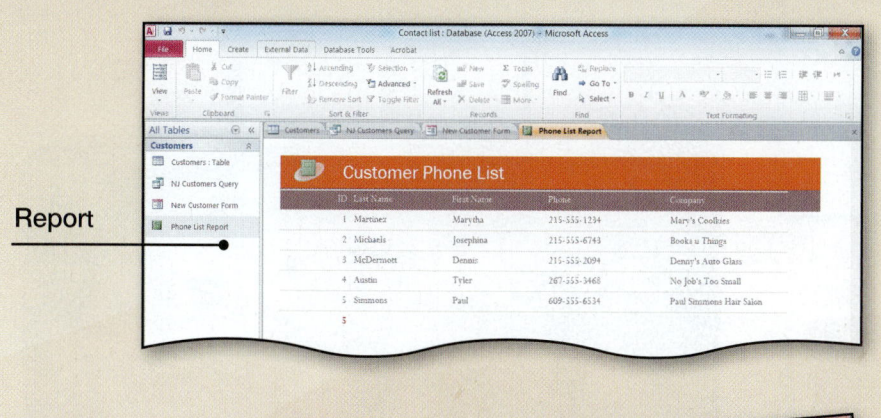

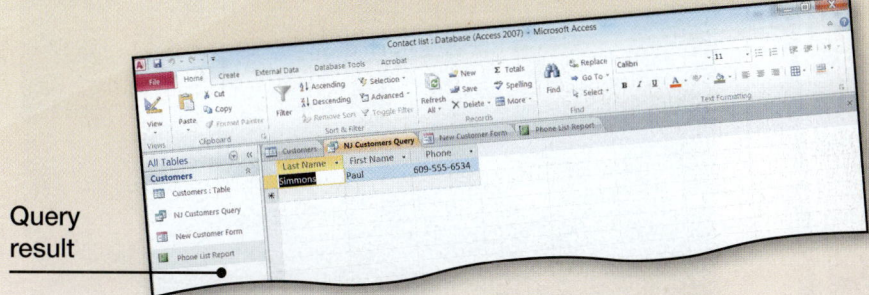

PERSONAL INFORMATION MANAGER

A **personal information manager (PIM)** may be a stand-alone program or part of an office suite. The most widely used of these programs is Microsoft Outlook (see Figure 5.6). A PIM manages your e-mail, calendar, contacts, and tasks all in one place. It includes the ability to share calendars and schedule meetings.

Report

Query result

OTHER TYPES OF BUSINESS SOFTWARE

While office suites cover the majority of business documents, other software is often used for more complex and larger scale management and projects. Keeping track of finances, projects, and the sheer number of documents even the smallest business might have can be a daunting task. Specialized software can help make these tasks easier and more efficient.

FIGURE 5.7 The home screen of QuickBooks Simple Start 2010 edition

FINANCIAL Even small businesses have to keep track of expenses and taxes. While an Excel spreadsheet system might work for very simple situations, most businesses find the need for basic accounting software such as Intuit QuickBooks (see Figure 5.7) or Sage Peachtree. Accounting software allows you to track your business finances and generate reports and graphs to help you make business decisions. You can use QuickBooks for expense tracking, invoicing, payroll, and inventory management. By organizing all your financial information in one place, it makes it easy to see the big picture and to handle year-end tasks such as income tax returns.

DOCUMENT MANAGEMENT For both practical and often legal reasons, even the smallest business needs document management capabilities—the ability to save, share, search, and audit electronic documents throughout their life cycle. Keeping track of all the documents in a business, ensuring that the right people have access to them, and ensuring that the correct version is available are all part of **document management systems (DMS)** such as Microsoft SharePoint, KnowledgeTree, and Alfresco. One of the keys to using DMS is storage. Instead of keeping files on local drives, the files are stored on a server or on the Web, making them more accessible and secure.

OBJECTIVE 1

186

PROJECT MANAGEMENT Project management software helps you complete projects, keep within your budget, stay on schedule, and even collaborate with others. The most popular project management program is Microsoft Project, and the leading Web-based application is Basecamp. Both of these tools excel at helping your projects run smoothly. Figure 5.8 shows a workshop planning project in Microsoft Project. The left column contains the tasks and dates for the project, and the right side shows those tasks in a graphic known as a **Gantt chart**.

FIGURE 5.8 Planning a workshop using Microsoft Project software

There are literally thousands of software applications used in businesses, including many that are created in-house or made for a specific type of business, but the programs discussed in this article are fairly universal. Modern businesses depend on both people and technology to remain competitive.

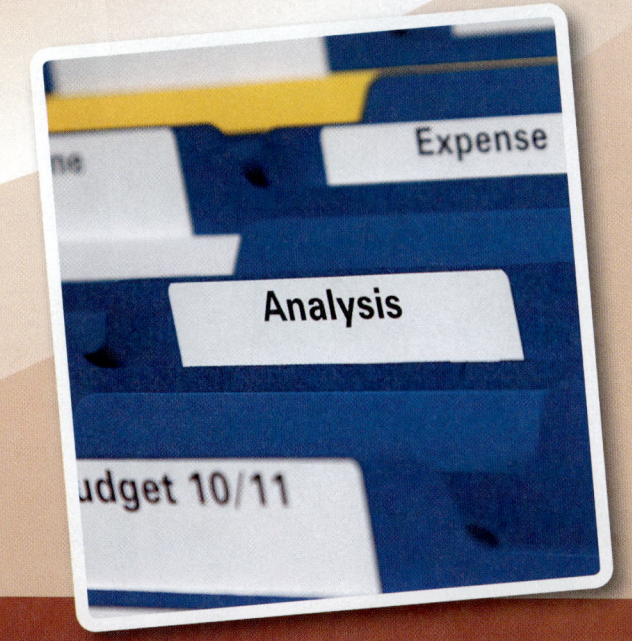

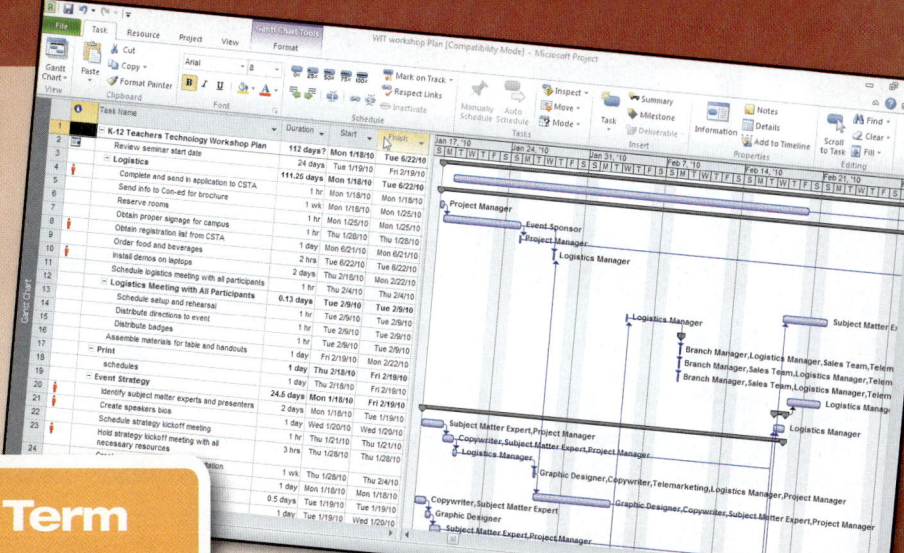

Key Term

cell

database

document management system

field

Gantt chart

office application suite

personal information manager (PIM)

project management software

record

spreadsheet

word processor

WYSIWYG

Running Project

Microsoft Office is a full suite of programs, but not every user needs the whole package. Use the Internet to research the versions of Microsoft Office 2010 that are available. Write a two- to three-paragraph essay comparing the versions. Explain which applications are in each, the cost, the number of licenses available, and any other details you deem important.

4 Things You Need to Know

- Office application suites include word processing, spreadsheet, presentation, and database software.
- Personal information manager software manages e-mail, contacts, calendars, and tasks.
- Document management systems allow businesses to save, share, search, and audit electronic documents.
- Project management software helps businesses keep projects on schedule.

Making It PERSONAL

OBJECTIVE 2: Identify types and uses of personal software.

Software is what makes our computers useful. The variety of software available today is vast, but it only takes a couple of programs to make our computers indispensible to us—and even fun to use. In this article, we look at some of the software you might want to install on your own system.

FIGURE 5.9 The OpenOffice.org welcome screen allows you to choose an application with which to work.

OFFICE APPLICATIONS

A full office application suite, which typically includes word processing, spreadsheet, database, presentation, and personal information management applications, is usually more than the average home user needs or wants. A basic word processor and perhaps a spreadsheet and presentation program are often included in home or student versions of the software. Microsoft Office comes in several different versions, allowing you to purchase just the applications you actually need. Nevertheless, commercial software can become expensive. There are many free or low-cost alternatives if you're willing to spend some time finding them and learning how to use them.

OpenOffice.org is a free, open source alternative office program. **Open source** means that the source code is published and made available to the public, enabling anyone to copy, modify, and redistribute it without paying fees. Some open source websites, such as OpenOffice.org, ask for donations to support the development of the product. OpenOffice.org contains word processor, spreadsheet, presentation, drawing, database, and formula writer applications. It can open and work with documents created in other programs, such as Microsoft Office, and can save files in its own format or Microsoft formats so you can work with your files in either system. Figure 5.9 shows the welcome screen of OpenOffice.org 3.1.

DONATION

FIGURE 5.10 A comparison of a Google Docs spreadsheet and a Zoho Docs sheet

Google Docs

Zoho Docs

Online alternative office suites are another solution. The two most popular are Google Docs and Zoho Docs. Both of these websites offer easy to use interfaces, with word processing, spreadsheet, presentation, and communication applications. You access them through a Web browser and don't need to install anything on your computer. The beauty of these websites is that you can access and edit your files from anywhere. While Google Docs is a free service, Zoho Docs is a "freemium" service. It is available for free for a single user with storage limit of 1GB. Figure 5.10 shows a spreadsheet in Google Docs and in Zoho Docs.

Microsoft has recently introduced Office Web Apps, which includes Word Web App, Excel Web App, PowerPoint Web App, and OneNote Web App. Figure 5.11 shows a PowerPoint presentation being edited using the Web App version. You'll notice that it is not a full-featured version of PowerPoint.

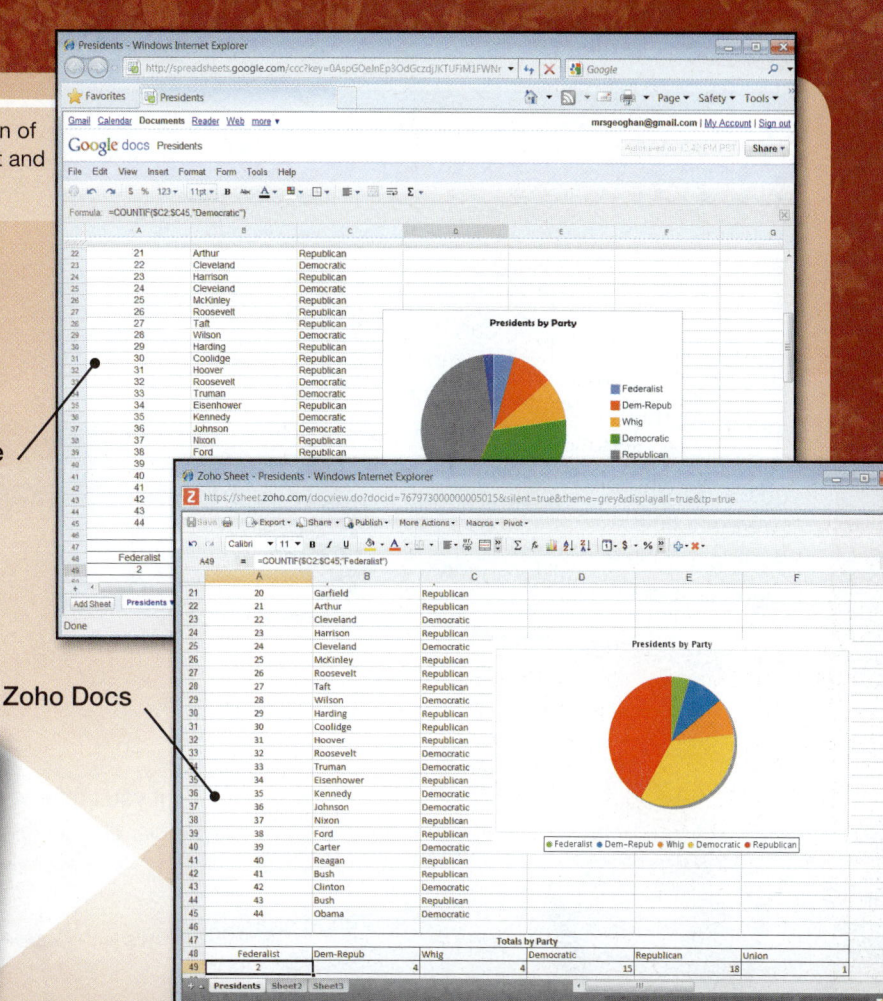

The market for free and inexpensive application software has grown exponentially as computers have become ubiquitous in our lives. Take the time to decide which options are best for you before spending a lot of money on a complicated software package that you may not even need.

FIGURE 5.11 The Microsoft PowerPoint Web App

FINANCE AND TAX PREPARATION SOFTWARE

Personal finance software can help you keep track of your bank accounts, monitor your investments, create and stick to a budget, and file your income taxes. As with office applications, personal finance software ranges from expensive commercial packages to free and online options.

Two of the most popular commercial packages are Intuit Quicken and Moneydance from The Infinite Kind. Both of these programs include advanced features, such as online banking and bill payment, investment portfolio tracking, and budgeting. You can also generate reports, calculate loan interest, and even write checks. When tax time comes around, you can easily gather the information you need from these applications.

If you prefer to use an online application, Mint.com has become a very popular choice. Once you enter all your accounts, you can use Mint.com to track your spending. Figure 5.12 shows a Mint account.

Tax preparation software allows you to complete your income tax returns yourself on your computer. This reduces the chance of making errors in your calculations and makes it easy to save—and later retrieve—your returns. You can file your return electronically or print and mail it. Previous years' returns can be imported into a new return and generate year-to-year comparisons. Tax preparation programs walk you through the process step-by-step and provide you with suggestions and help throughout. The three main tax preparation programs are TurboTax from Intuit, H&R Block At Home, and TaxACT. For simple tax returns, there are free online options. For more complex returns, you can install the full programs on your computer or use online versions. In general, the more complicated your return is, the more expensive the software you need is. Figure 5.13 shows the TurboTax Online free edition. If you start a free return and later discover that you need to upgrade to a full version, you can do so without losing any of the information you have already input.

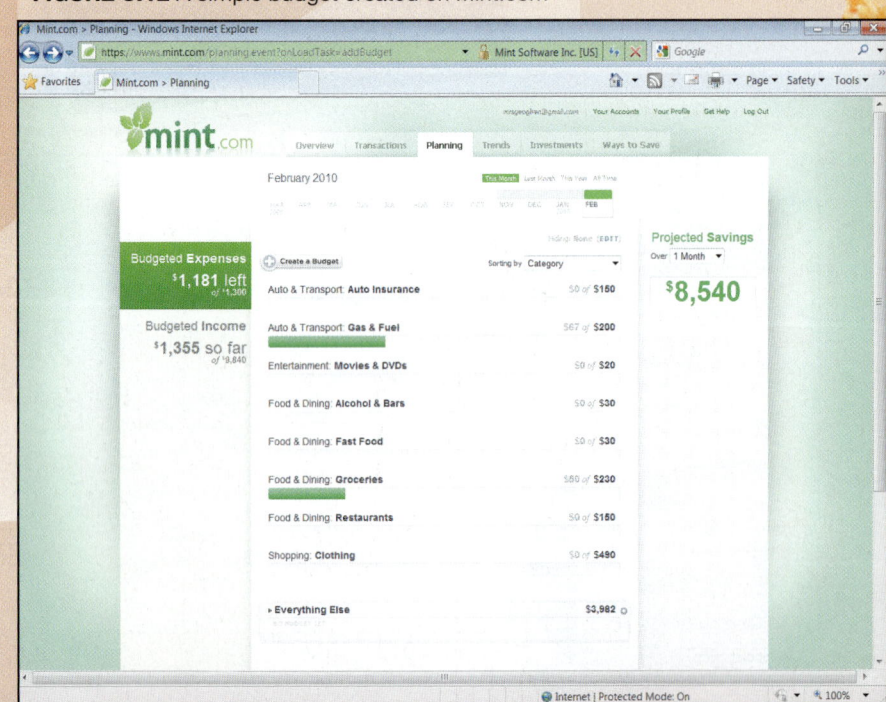

FIGURE 5.12 A simple budget created on Mint.com

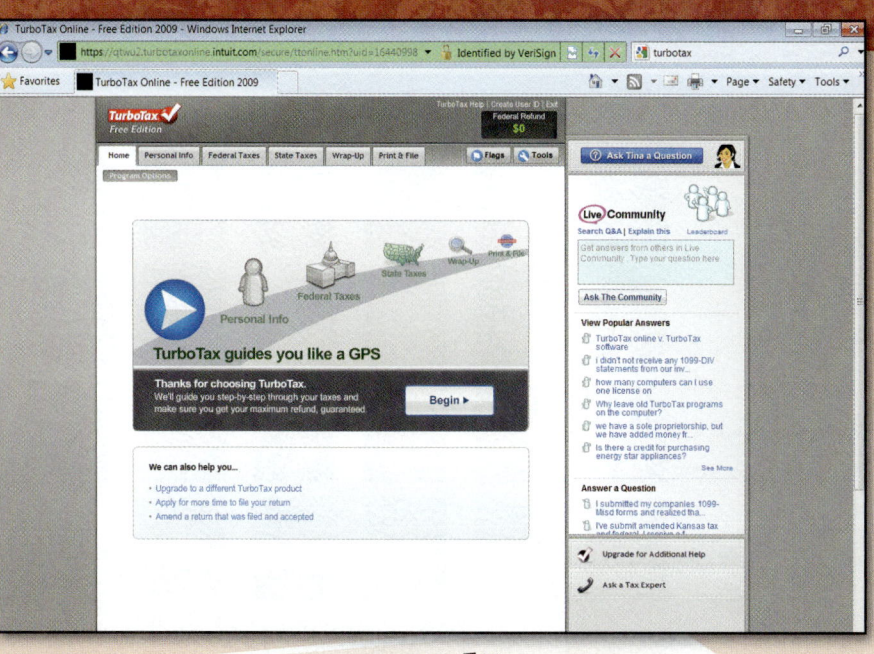

FIGURE 5.13 The TurboTax Online free edition

ENTERTAINMENT AND MULTIMEDIA SOFTWARE

Office applications and personal finance software aside, entertainment and multimedia software make our computers fun to use. There are literally thousands of programs available to educate and entertain us.

MEDIA MANAGEMENT Media management software is what we use to keep track of and play all the multimedia files on our computers—photos, music, TV shows, and videos. Media player software, such as Windows Media Player, Apple iTunes, and Winamp, are all examples of media management software. Windows 7 (except the Home Starter edition) includes Windows Media Center, which you can use to organize your photos, music, and videos and to watch and record TV shows on the Internet (see Figure 5.14).

FIGURE 5.14 You can watch and record Internet TV programs using Windows Media Center.

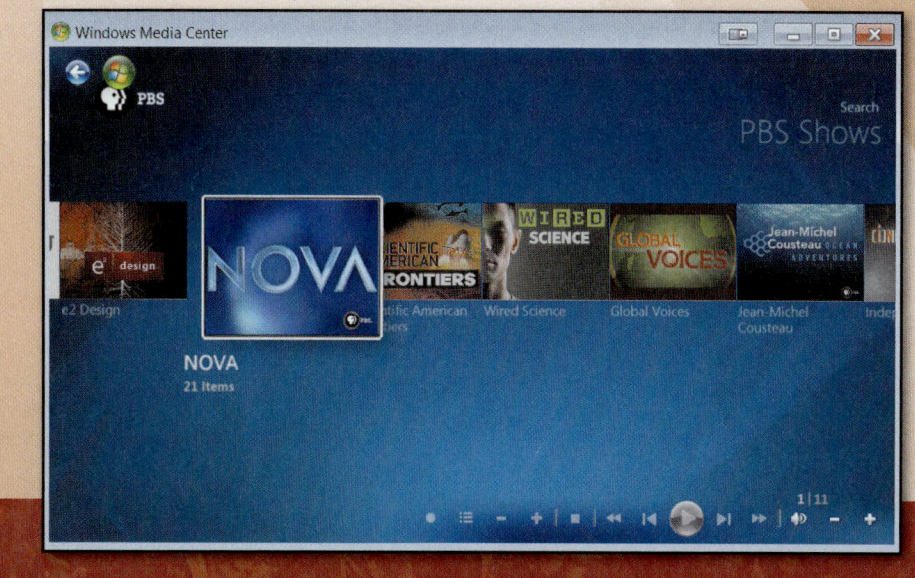

Chapter 5 | 191

VIDEO AND PHOTO EDITING Video and photo editing software allows you to create masterpieces from your personal photos and videos. You can spend hundreds of dollars for professional programs, but for most people, free or low-cost alternatives have all the features they need.

Picasa is a free program that you can download from Google. One really cool feature is facial recognition (see Figure 5.15). Picasa learns from the tags you apply to images and makes suggestions when it discovers other images with the same person, making it easy for you to locate pictures of that person later on.

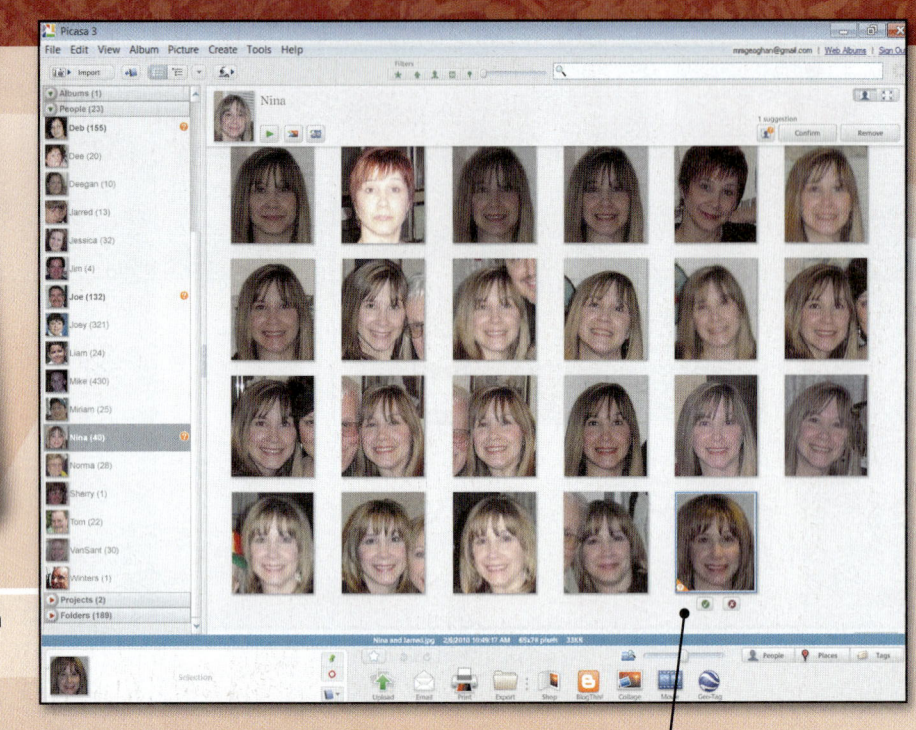

FIGURE 5.15 Picasa's facial recognition has identified a possible match.

Picasa suggested an image based on facial recognition.

Image editing tools in Picasa

Picasa can also edit your images. You can crop, straighten, adjust contrast and color, and apply various effects, such as sepia or black and white—most of the tasks you'd want to accomplish. In Figure 5.16, the image has been cropped and the sepia effect has been applied. Picasa saves your edits in a separate file, and you can always reset the image to its original state if you change your mind.

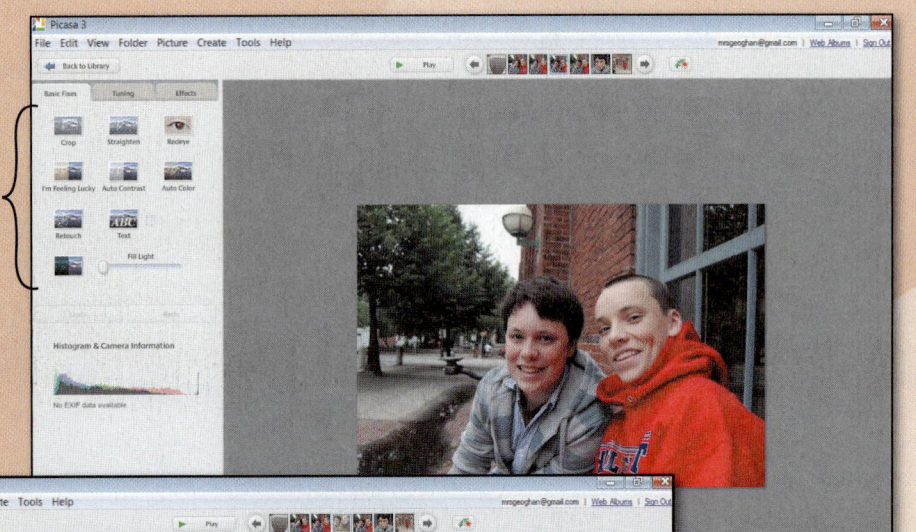

FIGURE 5.16 The original photo has been cropped and has the sepia effect applied.

You can also create some interesting projects using Picasa, such as a screensaver, a gift CD, a movie, and the collage shown in Figure 5.17. You can upload your images to Picasa Web Albums right from within the program, and share the link with others. You can Geo-Tag your photos using the Places panel.

FIGURE 5.17 It's easy to create a collage with just a few mouse clicks in Picasa.

You can create different projects using your own images.

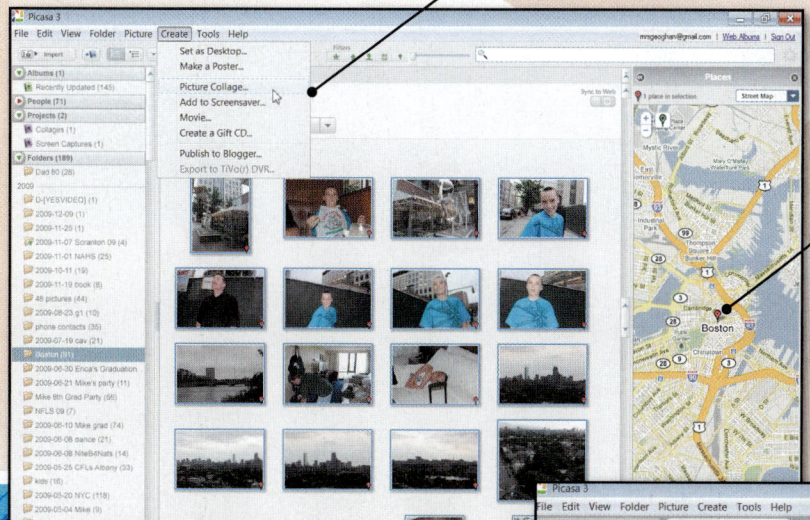

Images can be Geo-Tagged on a Google map.

Chapter 5 | 193

Picasa has some limited ability to organize and work with your videos, but you need a video editing program to really edit and create the movies you want. Windows Live Movie Maker is free, and Apple iMovie comes preloaded on Mac computers. If you want something else, several commercial products are available for about $100. Two of the most popular are Sony Vegas Movie Studio and Adobe Premiere Elements. Because video editing requires a lot of system resources, there are few online options available. Figure 5.18 shows a movie created using the Adobe Premiere Elements InstantMovie feature.

FIGURE 5.18 The Adobe Premiere Elements InstantMovie feature

FIGURE 5.19 World of Warcraft

GAMES When you think of someone who plays video games, do you picture a young man shooting aliens? What about the grandmother playing solitaire, or the dad playing online poker, or the preschooler learning colors and shapes? Games and simulations are more than just first-person shooters, and they're played by all sorts of people. Video game sales in 2009 reached $20 billion, with computer games sales accounting for about $500 million of that total. While the average age of a video game player is 32 to 35 years old, 20 percent are over 50. In addition, about 40 percent are female. So much for stereotypes.

Games (see Figure 5.19) are one type of software for which you really need to pay attention to the system requirements for installation. They take a lot of processing, memory, and video power to run well, and trying to play a game on an inadequate system will just frustrate you.

EDUCATIONAL AND REFERENCE SOFTWARE

Educational and reference software is a broad category of software. There's software to study, plan, design, and create just about anything you are interested in. Let's look at a few of the most popular offerings.

TRIP PLANNING When I was a little girl and the family planned a vacation, we had to go to the store to buy maps, tour books, and yellow highlighters. We would spend hours mapping out our route, planning our stops based on the often outdated information in the tour books, and hoping the food would be decent and the hotel rooms would be clean. Today, we still spend hours researching and planning our trips, but we use online mapping software, such as Microsoft Streets & Trips or Google Maps, read reviews from other travelers, and can easily reroute our trip if the unexpected happens.

FIGURE 5.20 Family Tree Maker

GENEALOGY There are many genealogy tools on the market today. The most popular is Family Tree Maker (see Figure 5.20), which integrates with Ancestry.com. You can create family trees and slideshows of your photos, view timelines and maps, and search through millions of historical records on the Internet.

Chapter 5 | 195

HOME AND LANDSCAPE DESIGN

Want to build a deck? Plant a garden? Remodel your kitchen? Rearrange your furniture? Paint the dining room? Home and landscape design software has you covered. Free or retail, online or installed on your system, there are programs to help you design and plan all your home improvement projects.

There are several online apps to compare paint colors. Just upload a picture of your room, and experiment with the color choices until you find your favorites. Behr Paint Your Place (**behr.com**), Sherwin-Williams Color Visualizer (**sherwin-williams.com**), and the Benjamin Moore Personal Color Viewer (**benjaminmoore.com**) all allow you to upload and color your own photos for free and will help you select the colors from their particular paint lines. Colorjive (**colorjive.com**) (see Figure 5.21) isn't affiliated with any brand and includes colors across multiple brands. You should use whatever program has the color codes for the brand of paint you plan to buy.

FIGURE 5.21 Colorjive.com lets me "paint" my garage a new color.

Find Out MORE

One place to learn about free software alternatives is MakeUseOf.com. This website is a daily blog that includes a directory of hundreds of useful websites and apps. Go to the Directory (**makeuseof.com/dir**), and select a category that interests you. Select two articles to read, and write a one- to two-paragraph summary of the article. Did you decide to try the application described? Why or why not? If so, did you find it useful? Would you recommend it to a friend?

PORTABLE APPS

We sometimes find ourselves without our own computers—at work, school, travel, or a friend's house. **Portable apps** are programs that you can carry and run from a flash drive. They need no installation, so you can run them on just about any computer system. Your settings and data are on your flash drive—not the host computer—and when you remove your drive, there's no personal information left behind. One place to find portable apps is at **portableapps.com** (see Figure 5.22). The Portable Apps platform is open source, and the apps are free. The same apps you use on your computer—OpenOffice.org, Mozilla Firefox, e-mail clients, games, utilities, and even operating systems—can be run as portable apps.

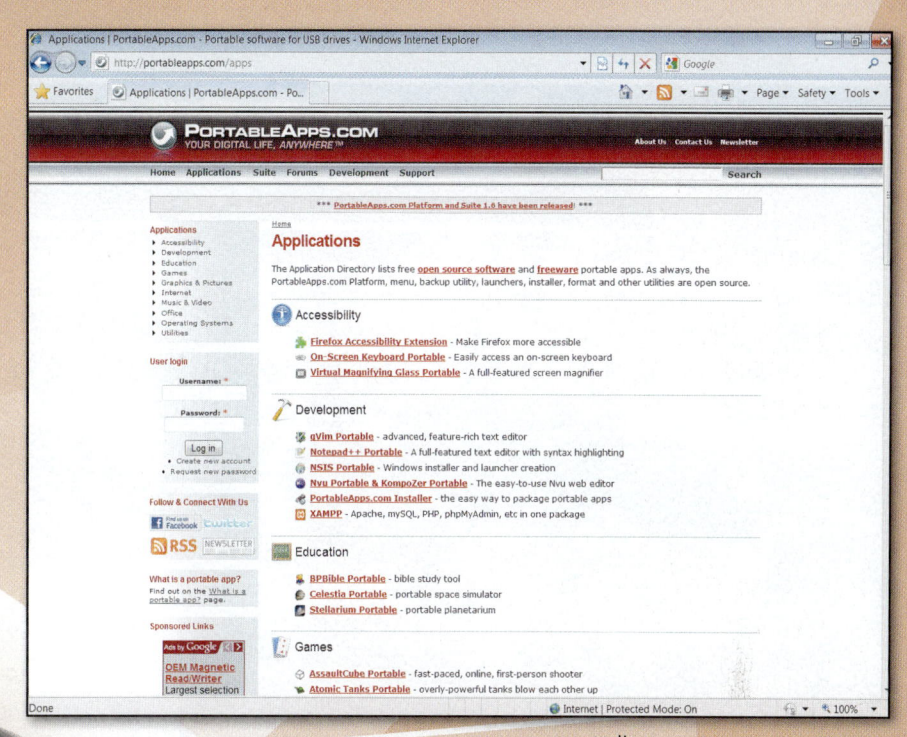

FIGURE 5.22 The Portable Apps website

No matter what you need or want to do, there is probably at least one program that can do it. Choosing the right option often requires a bit of research and comparison shopping, but when you find the program, you'll expand the usefulness of your computer.

Key Terms

open source

portable apps

Running Project

Use the Internet to learn about OpenOffice.org. Is it available in different versions? What applications are included? Compare it to the Microsoft Office versions you researched in the previous project. Does OpenOffice.org offer everything that Microsoft Office does? If not, what is missing?

4 Things You Need to Know

- Personal productivity software includes office applications as well as financial and reference software.
- Entertainment software includes media management software, photo and video editing software, and games.
- Educational and reference software is available to cover a variety of interests, including trip planning, genealogy, and landscaping.
- Portable apps can be stored on and run from a flash drive.

HOW TO

How to Create a Document Using Wordpad

Microsoft Windows includes a word processing application called WordPad. This is a basic program that can be used to create simple documents, such as homework assignments, even if you don't have a full word processor such as Microsoft Word installed.

LET'S CREATE A SIMPLE DOCUMENT

1 To access WordPad, click the Windows Start button, click *All Programs*, click the *Accessories* folder, and then click *WordPad*. You could also type **wordpad** in the Search box.

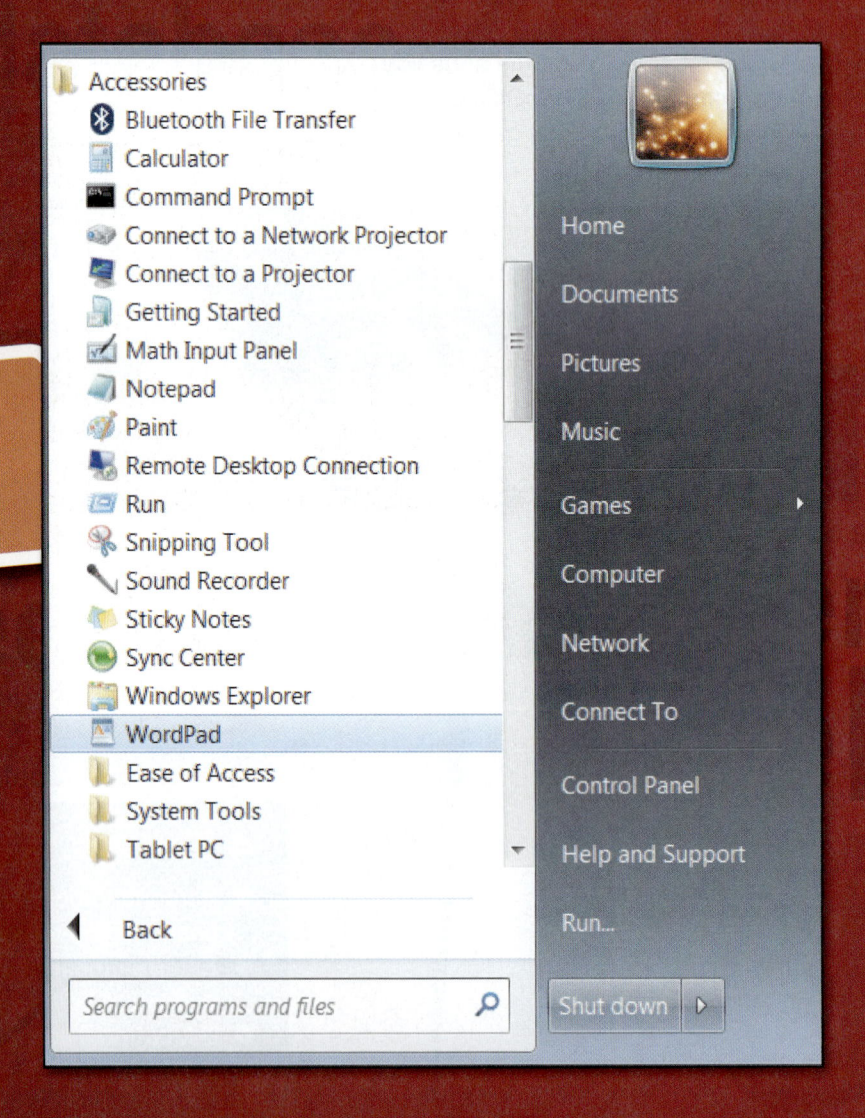

2 When WordPad opens, it begins with a blank document open. The WordPad button contains commands to open, save, print, and e-mail your documents. The right column contains a list of the nine most recent documents, making it easy to reopen them. The Quick Access Toolbar has buttons for Save, Undo and Redo by default, but you can customize it by clicking the arrow on the right. The Ribbon has two tabs: Home and View. The Home tab contains the commands for formatting the document and inserting objects; the View tab contains commands to change the way the document displays on your screen.

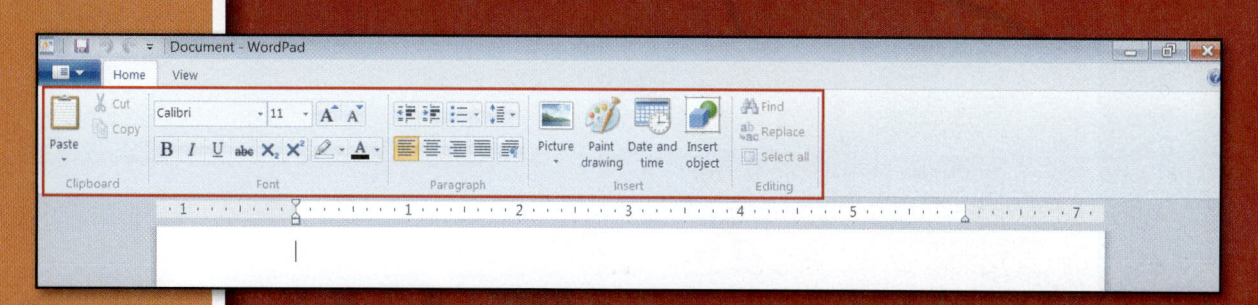

3 If necessary, open WordPad. In the blank document area of the WordPad screen type **Chapter 5 How To Use WordPad** and press *Enter*. On the next line, type your name and press *Enter* twice. Type the following paragraph:

WordPad is a basic word processor that is included with Windows. I can use it to type homework assignments and other documents that are compatible with most word processing programs.

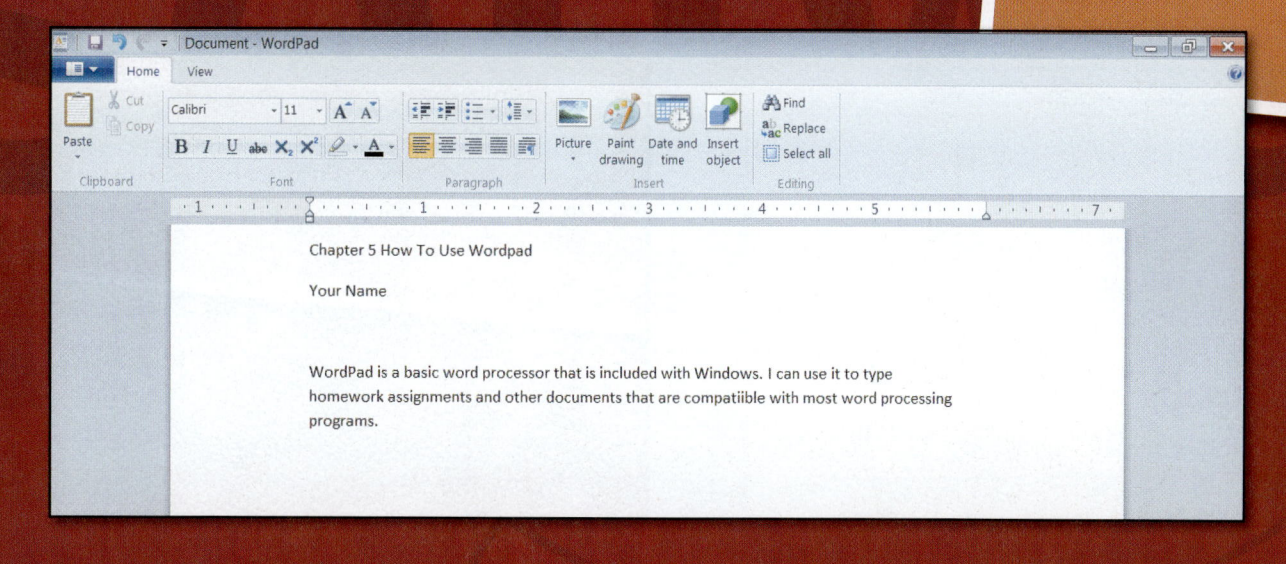

4 Press *Enter*. Click the *Start a list* button and type the following three bullet points (press Enter after each): **Free**, **Easy to use**, **Compatible**. Press *Enter* again to exit the bulleted list. Click the *Date and time* button in the Insert group; select a date format that includes the day of the week, and then click *OK*.

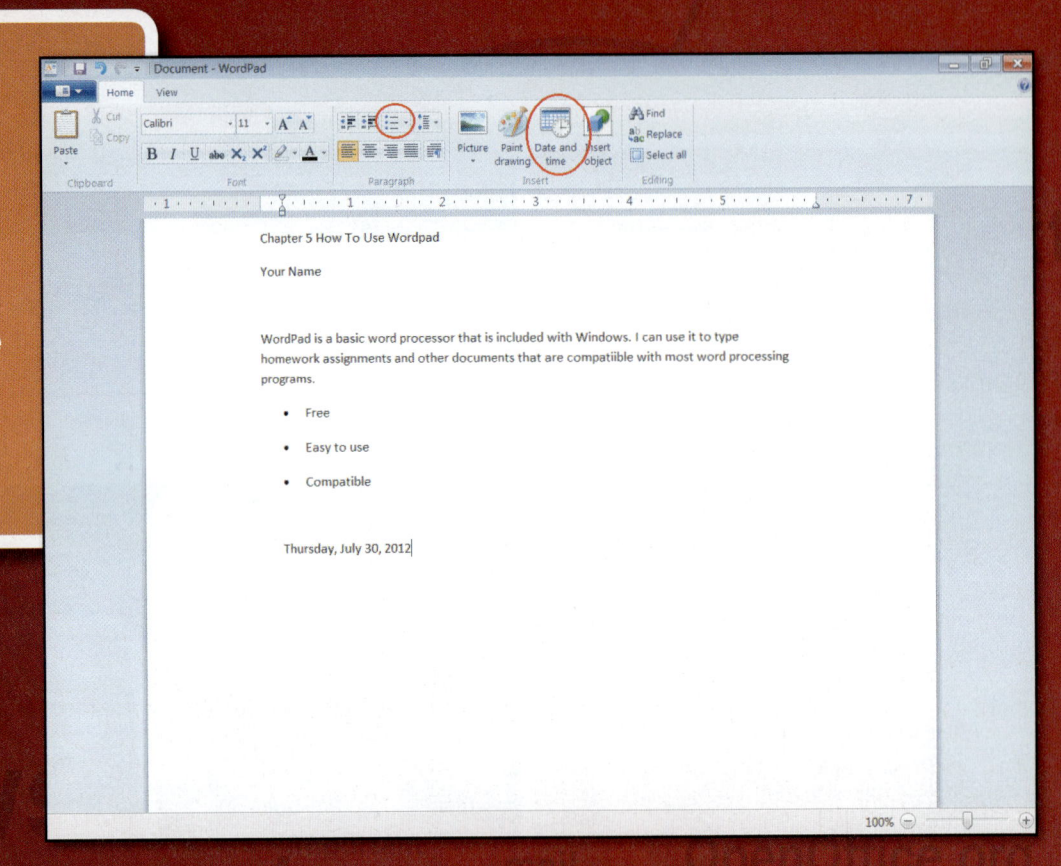

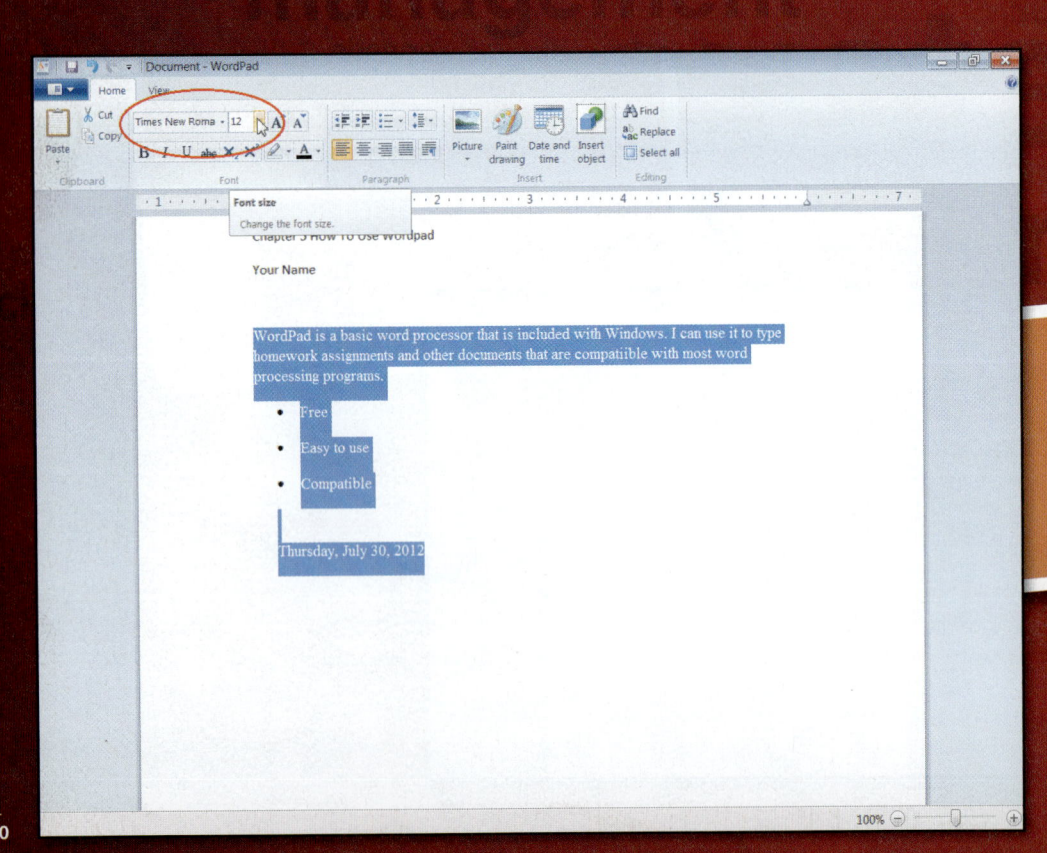

5 Drag your mouse to select the paragraph of text, the bulleted list, and the date. In the Font group, click the Font family arrow and change the font from Calibri to Times New Roman. Click the Font size arrow and change the font size to 12.

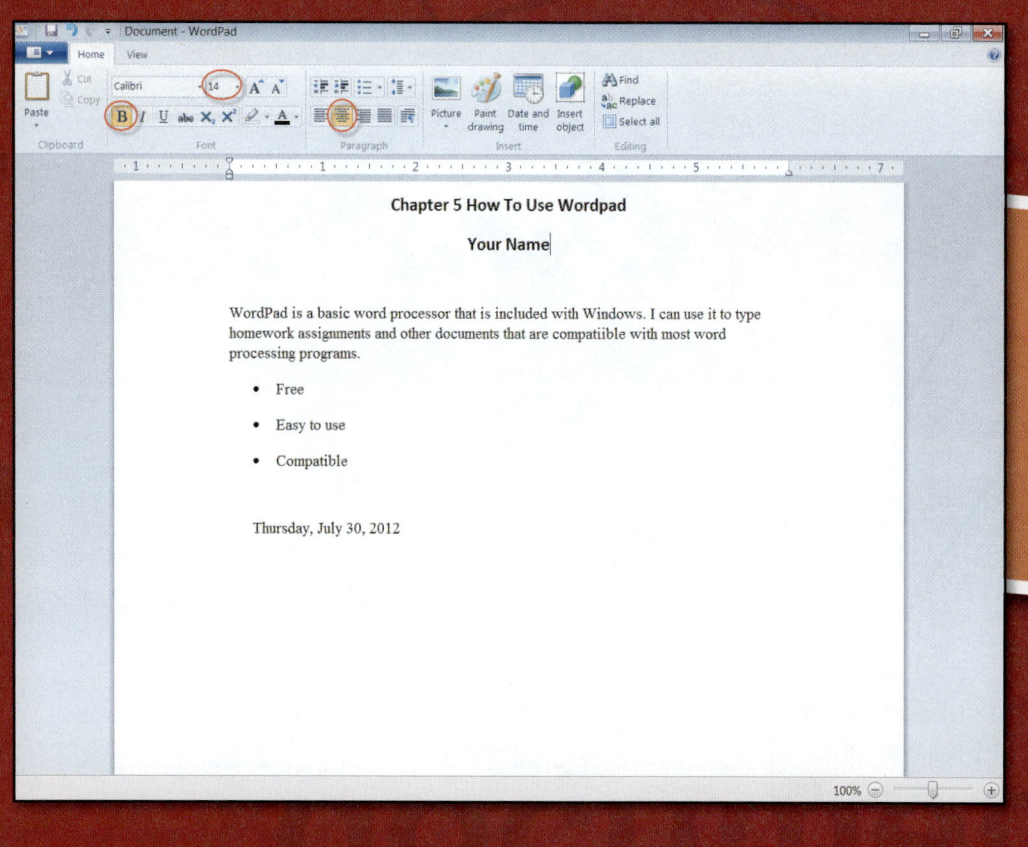

6 Select the first two lines and use the buttons on the WordPad Ribbon to format them. In the Paragraph group, click the *Center* button. In the Font group, change the font size from 11 to 14 and click the *B* button to make the text bold. Compare your document to the figure.

7 To save the file, click the WordPad button, point to *Save as* and select the appropriate format. The default format is Rich Text document, which is compatible with all word processors. If you are required to submit your work in Microsoft Word format, select *Office Open XML document* from the list instead. Navigate to the folder that you created for your Chapter 5 work and save the file as **Lastname_Firstname_ch05_HowTo**. Submit this file as directed by your instructor.

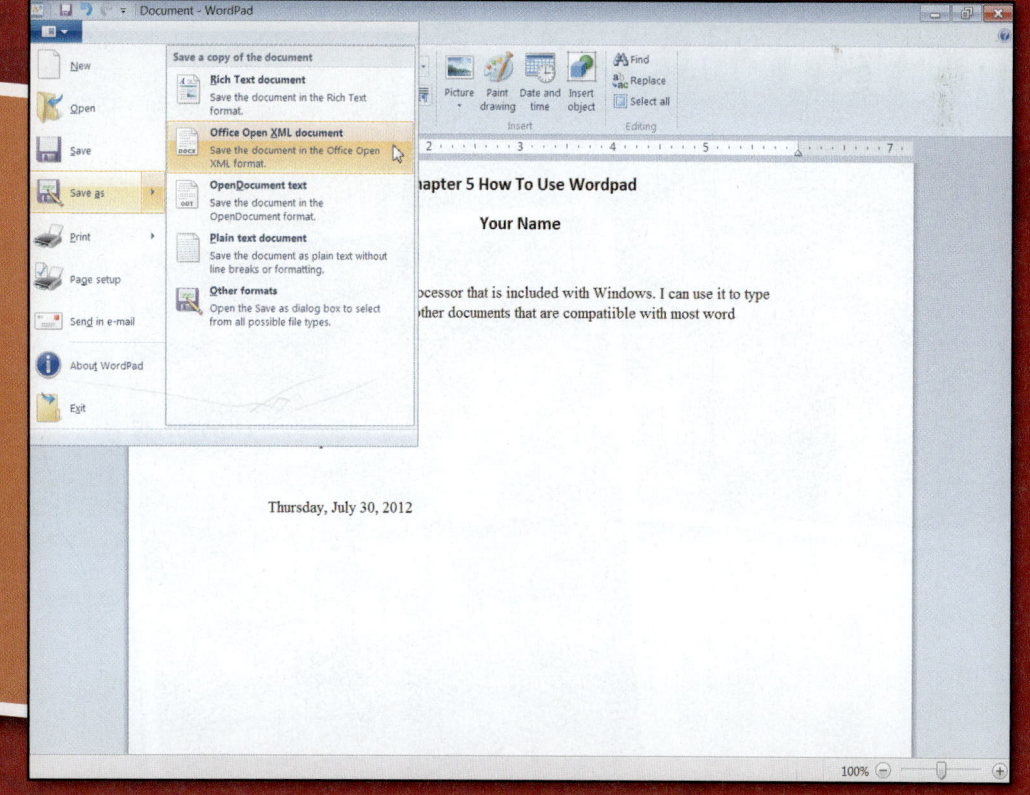

Will It RUN?

3 OBJECTIVE
Assess a computer system for software compatibility.

Your best friend just told you about an awesome new game she bought. Should you run right out and buy it too? At $60, the game is an investment that warrants at least a little bit of research on your part, as do most software purchases. So, what do you need to know?

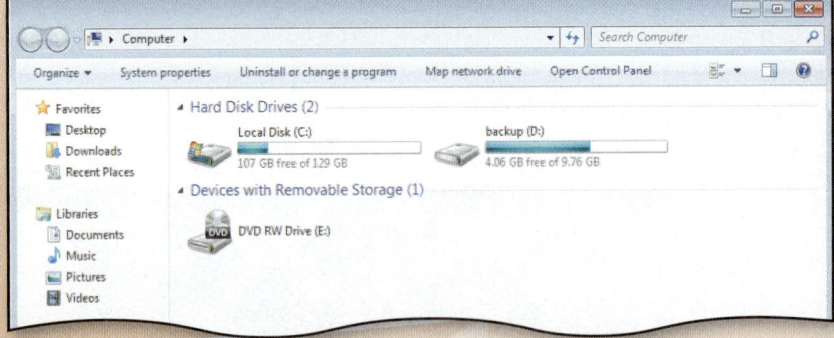

FIGURE 5.23 Open the Computer window to verify the space available on the drives on your system.

YOUR SYSTEM SPECS

Before you rush out (or go online) to buy software, you need to do a little bit of work. You need to document your system specs so you can compare them to the system requirements of the software. That is the only way you'll know your system can run the program. If you're using a Windows computer, you can get the information you need with just a few mouse clicks.

Let's start with drives. For most software you buy in a store, you'll need a DVD drive to do the installation. While a few programs will run from a DVD (or flash drive), most programs are installed on your hard drive. The amount of drive space required is listed in the system requirements. You can verify that you have enough free space by simply opening the Computer window from the Windows Start menu. The computer in Figure 5.23 has a DVD drive and 107 GB of free space on the hard drive (C):.

One of the easiest ways to obtain the other information you need is to open the System Control Panel in Windows. To do this, you can right-click on Computer in the Windows Start menu and choose Properties (see Figure 5.24).

FIGURE 5.24 Right-click on Computer in the Windows Start menu and choose *Properties* to open the System Control Panel.

Most of the information you need is found on this page: operating system version, processor type and speed, and amount of memory installed. The **Windows Experience Index** (see Figure 5.25) is a rating system that assesses these traits as well as your video card performance to determine the types of software that your computer can run. When you click on the index, it will show you a list of subscores for the components assessed. Some software packages list Windows Experience Index ratings under system requirements.

FIGURE 5.25 You can use the System Control Panel and Windows Experience Index to determine if a computer meets the system requirements for software.

Windows Experience Index and other System information

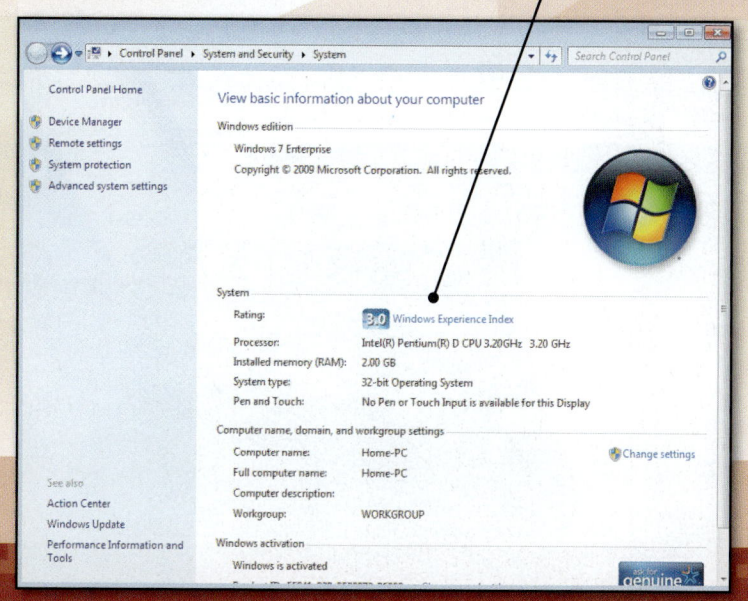

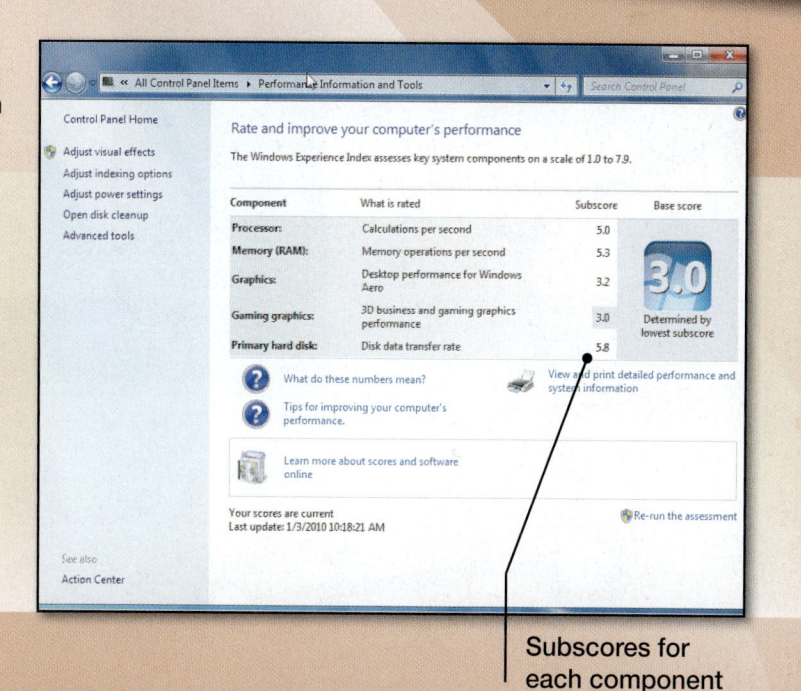

Subscores for each component

Chapter 5 | 203

SYSTEM REQUIREMENTS

System requirements for software are usually right on the box. These are *minimum requirements* to get the program running, but exceeding the requirements will give you better performance. These requirements list both the hardware and software specifications the computer must meet in order to run the program. Sometimes, you may need to upgrade your system to meet or exceed these requirements. As software becomes more sophisticated, the system requirements go up. Figure 5.26 shows the system requirements for running World of Warcraft, a popular online game that has high hardware requirements.

FIGURE 5.26 The system requirements for Office 2010, the Home and Student Edition, available on Microsoft's website

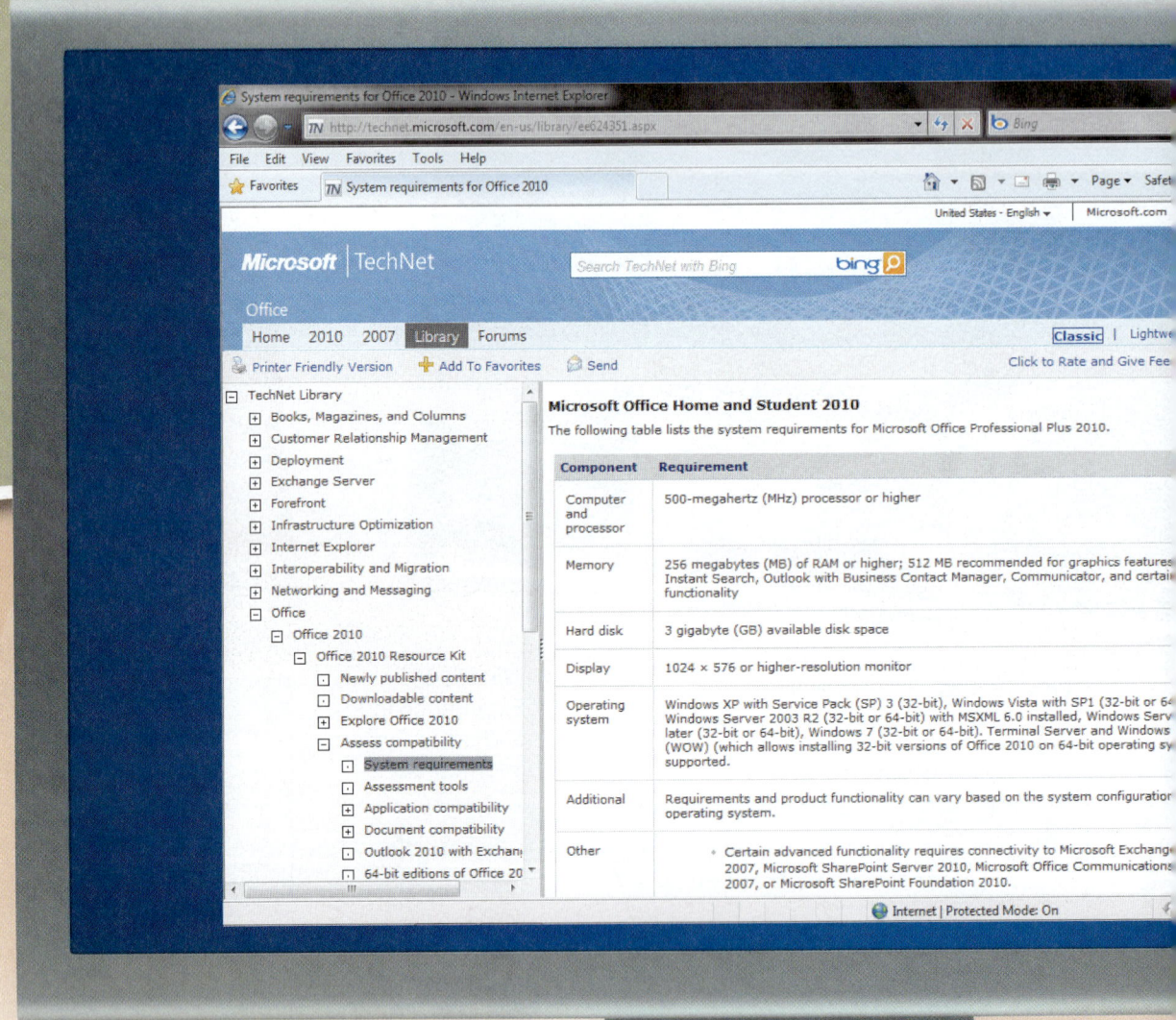

Microsoft Office Home and Student 2010

The following table lists the system requirements for Microsoft Office Professional Plus 2010.

Component	Requirement
Computer and processor	500-megahertz (MHz) processor or higher
Memory	256 megabytes (MB) of RAM or higher; 512 MB recommended for graphics features, Instant Search, Outlook with Business Contact Manager, Communicator, and certain functionality
Hard disk	3 gigabyte (GB) available disk space
Display	1024 × 576 or higher-resolution monitor
Operating system	Windows XP with Service Pack (SP) 3 (32-bit), Windows Vista with SP1 (32-bit or 64-bit), Windows Server 2003 R2 (32-bit or 64-bit) with MSXML 6.0 installed, Windows Server later (32-bit or 64-bit), Windows 7 (32-bit or 64-bit). Terminal Server and Windows (WOW) (which allows installing 32-bit versions of Office 2010 on 64-bit operating systems) supported.
Additional	Requirements and product functionality can vary based on the system configuration operating system.
Other	• Certain advanced functionality requires connectivity to Microsoft Exchange 2007, Microsoft SharePoint Server 2010, Microsoft Office Communications 2007, or Microsoft SharePoint Foundation 2010.

It's important to know what the system requirements are for a program before you buy it so you're not stuck with a purchase that you can't use. Spending a few minutes verifying that your system meets the requirements will help ensure that you can actually use the software you buy or let you know if a system upgrade is necessary.

Key Terms

system requirements

Windows Experience Index

Running Project

Research a game that you would like to run on your computer. What are the system requirements for the game? Does your computer meet the minimum requirements to run the game? In what ways does it exceed them?

3 Things You Need to Know

- You can find out your system specifications using the Computer window and System Control Panel.
- The Windows Experience Index can help you determine the software that your system can run.
- System requirements are the minimum requirements needed to run software and include hardware and software specifications.

Where to GET IT

4 OBJECTIVE **Compare various ways of obtaining software.**

There are many different ways to obtain software. You can go out to the store and buy it, order it online and have it shipped to you, or download it from a website. In this article, we look at software licensing and how to obtain software.

LICENSING

When you purchase and install software on your computer, you do not actually *own* the program. Instead, you license it. The software is owned by the company that created it. There are several different software license types. Carefully read the **EULA** (end-user license agreement)—the agreement between the user and the software publisher—on all software to know your rights before you install it, including the number of computers you can legally install it on, the length of time you have access to it, and any privacy notices. You should also look for important hidden information in the fine print. For example, by clicking I Agree on some EULAs, you allow the installation of additional "features," such as toolbars and spyware on your computer.

The two most common software licenses are:

- Proprietary software license: Grants a license to use one or more copies of software, but ownership of those copies remains with the software publisher. This is the type of license found on most commercial software and is the most restrictive in terms of your right to distribute and install the software.
- Open source software license: Grants ownership of the copy to the end-user. The source code for that software must be made freely available. The end-user has the right to modify and redistribute the software under the same license. Open source software is growing in popularity, and there are more offerings available all the time.

In both cases, there may or may not be a fee for the use of the software. The cost of software is a big factor in choosing which programs to install.

FREE OR FEE

Not all proprietary software has a fee, and not all open source software is free. The cost of software is determined by the publisher. There are four basic models for software distribution:

- **Retail software:** User pays a fee to use the software for an unlimited period of time. Microsoft Office, Adobe Photoshop, and TurboTax are all examples of retail software.
- **Freeware:** Can be used at no cost for an unlimited period of time. Some popular freeware includes Apple iTunes, Mozilla Firefox, and 7-Zip.
- **Shareware:** Software offered in trial form or for a limited period that allows the user to try it out before purchasing a license. It's sometimes referred to as trialware. This marketing model of selling software has become so popular that you can purchase most retail software this way. You can download a 30- or 60-day free trial of products from Microsoft, Adobe, and many other publishers.
- **Donationware:** A form of freeware where the developers accept donations, either for themselves or for a nonprofit organization. OpenOffice.org is an example of donationware.

Find Out MORE

Visit The Open Source Initiative (OSI; **opensource.org**). Who are they, and what do they do? How do they define open source?

SOURCES OF SOFTWARE

Software is available in a variety of places. Where you choose to obtain it will depend on the type of software you're looking for and the time frame in which you need it.

RETAIL BRICK-AND-MORTAR STORES You can purchase software in specialized computer and electronics stores, office supplies stores, mass merchandise stores, and even drugstores. The price and variety of programs available in these places will vary widely. If you're looking for a popular piece of software, such as game or tax preparation software, then you'll likely find it for a good price. But if you're looking for something less popular, you may have a hard time finding it on the shelf.

RETAIL WEBSITES You'll find a much larger selection of software available through online retailers, such as Amazon.com or Buy.com. These sites sell the same software in a box and ship it to you. Some software may also be available for immediate download. Online retailers often have a larger selection of software than retail stores, and prices are comparable.

PUBLISHER WEBSITES When you purchase software directly from the software publisher's website, you can usually immediately download the software. The cost can be competitive with retailers, but it pays to shop around.

SOFTWARE DOWNLOAD WEBSITES Websites such as cnet.com, tucows.com, and zdnet.com have vast libraries of freeware and shareware to download. For open source software, go to sourceforge.net. An advantage to using sites like these is that they include editor and user reviews to help you choose the program that is right for you. Also, these websites test the programs for malicious intent. The CNET website states: "We will not list software that contains viruses, Trojan horses, malicious adware, spyware, or other potentially harmful components." Figure 5.27 shows the most popular downloads as of this writing.

When you download software from a website, it's good practice to back up the downloaded file and license should you ever need to reinstall the program. Wherever you finally decide to purchase software, be sure that you understand the license terms before you click the I Accept button.

FIGURE 5.27 The most popular downloads from CNET's download.com as of January 2010

Key Terms

donationware

EULA (end-user license agreement)

freeware

retail software

shareware

Running Project

Use the Internet to find out what the terms "shrink-wrap license" and "click-wrap license" mean. What are they? How are they alike? Are they legal and binding?

3 Things You Need to Know

- When you purchase software, you don't own it but are only licensing it—unless it's open source.
- You should read the EULA (end-user license agreement) to determine the restrictions and potential add-on features related to the software before you install it.
- Not all proprietary software has a fee, and not all open source software is free.

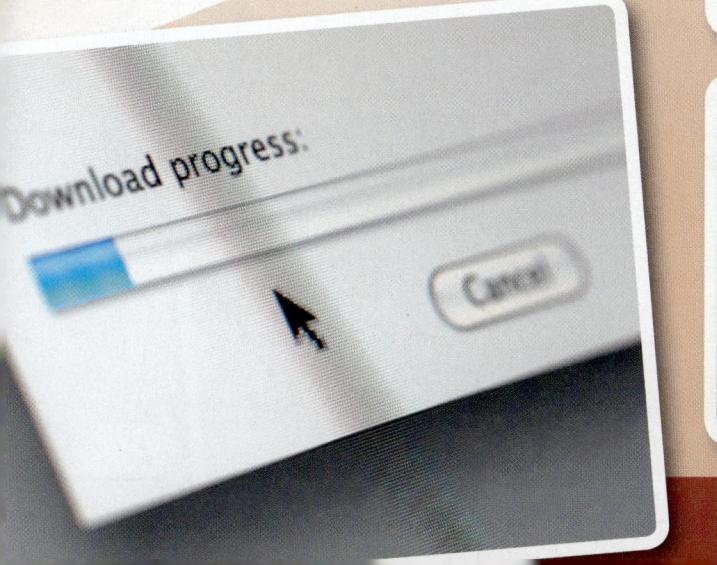

Your Head IN THE CLOUD

OBJECTIVE 5
Discuss the importance of cloud computing.

You may have heard the term "cloud computing." The cloud refers to the Internet. In this chapter, we've already discussed some online applications. **Cloud computing** takes the processing and storage off your desktop and business hardware and puts it in the cloud—on the Internet. As the need for storage, security, and collaboration has grown, cloud computing has become an important part of business and personal systems.

CLOUD COMPUTING

There are three types of services that can be delivered through the cloud: Infrastructure-as-a-Service, Platform-as-a-Service, and Software-as-a-Service. Together, these three services can provide a business with an integrated system for delivering applications and content using the cloud.

INFRASTRUCTURE-AS-A-SERVICE (IAAS)
Infrastructure-as-a-Service (IaaS) means that a company uses servers in the cloud instead of purchasing and maintaining the hardware. This saves both in hardware costs and in personnel. Even small companies that don't have the expertise in-house can have sophisticated servers to house large databases, centralized document management, and security using and paying for just what they need.

PLATFORM-AS-A-SERVICE (PAAS)
Platform-as-a-Service (PaaS) provides a programming environment to develop, test, and deploy custom Web applications. This gives businesses the ability to build applications without installing software on their computers. PaaS also makes collaboration easier and requires less programming knowledge. Three popular PaaS programs are: AppEngine from Google, Force.com from SalesForce, and Microsoft Azure Services Platform.

SOFTWARE-AS-A-SERVICE (SAAS) Software-as-a-Service (SaaS) means the delivery of applications over the Internet—or Web apps. This is the most visible to the user. Any time you open your browser to access your e-mail, upload photos, use Facebook, or share a file, you're using SaaS.

SaaS has several advantages over installing software locally. Because SaaS is delivered on demand, it's available anytime from any computer with Internet access. In addition to the convenience, SaaS also eliminates the need to apply updates to local software installations. You use SaaS whenever you use Web mail. Using Web mail means that you don't download your e-mail messages to your personal computer. They're stored and accessed from a hosted e-mail server, providing backup and security for you, giving you access from anywhere, and eliminating the need to install and configure an e-mail program on your computer. Figure 5.28 illustrates some common SaaS applications you probably already use.

> E-mail
> Word processing
> Photo editing
> Facebook & Twitter
> Online file storage and sharing
> Collaboration

FIGURE 5.28 Commonly used SaaS applications

SaaS may not be a term most people use very often, but the services it provides are used every day by individuals and businesses alike. As cloud computing continues to mature, we'll find more and more of our computing up in the cloud.

GREEN COMPUTING

ONLINE AND DOWNLOADED PROGRAMS VS. STORE-BOUGHT SOFTWARE

We've talked about your options for purchasing software from a convenience and cost standpoint, but there are also environmental issues to consider.

When you walk into a store and pick up software in a box or order from an online retailer and have the package shipped to you, there are several environmental impacts. First, there's the packaging material used to ship the product and product packaging. While cardboard and paper are recyclable, the EPA estimates that only about 70 percent of it is actually recycled. The rest of it—and other materials, such as plastic shrink-wrap and packing peanuts—ends up in our landfills. Then, there's the media inside the package. What happens to the CD or DVD when the software is no longer needed? It ends up in the trash—and into the landfill it goes. Finally, the transportation costs of shipping the product to you or to the store—air pollution, fuel consumption, and emission of greenhouse gases—all add up.

All these environmental impacts are eliminated using online applications or purchasing software online and downloading it to your computer. No packaging, no transportation costs, no obsolete media, and the convenience of having the software delivered to you on the spot make these alternatives the better choices for the environment.

Key Terms

cloud computing

Infrastructure-as-a-Service (IaaS)

Platform-as-a-Service (PaaS)

Software-as-a-Service (SaaS)

Running Project

Does your school use cloud computing (also known as above-campus computing)? If so, which services do you access from the cloud (for example: e-mail, apps)? Give two examples of your personal use of cloud computing.

3 Things You Need to Know

- The cloud is the Internet.
- Cloud computing uses hardware and software resources that are in the cloud instead of local.
- Cloud computing consists of three types of services: Infrastructure-as-a-Service (IaaS), Platform-as-a-Service (PaaS), and Software-as-a-Service (SaaS).

What Can I Do with Knowledge about APPLICATION SOFTWARE?

6 OBJECTIVE
Identify the certifications and careers related to application software.

Today, you'd be hard-pressed to find a career in which the use of application software isn't important. Knowledge of office applications, such as word processors and spreadsheets, is expected in almost any type of business. If you work in any type of office—from a real estate office to a doctor's office to a landscape contractor's office—you'll find these skills are critical to your success.

MICROSOFT CERTIFIED APPLICATION SPECIALIST (MCAS)

One way to prove to an employer that you have these skills is to earn the Microsoft Certified Application Specialist (MCAS) certification. MCAS is a series of six certification exams—Word, Excel, PowerPoint, Outlook, Access, and Windows. You earn a separate certification for each exam that you pass. If you pass the Word, Excel, PowerPoint, and Outlook exams, you receive the Microsoft Office Master certificate.

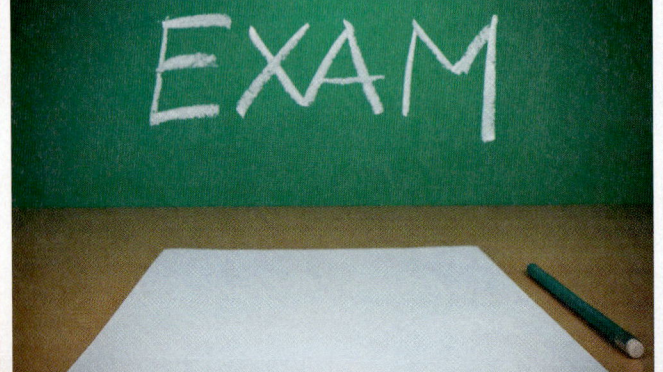

OTHER SOFTWARE CERTIFICATIONS

There are also certifications offered for other software applications. A bookkeeper might pursue a QuickBooks certification. Adobe has two levels of certification—Adobe Certified Associate (ACA) and Adobe Certified Expert (ACE)—for many of its products, including Photoshop and Flash. Sun even offers OpenOffice.org specialist certifications in Writer (word processing), Calc (spreadsheets), and Impress (presentation).

FIGURE 5.29 Software trainers are in demand in many fields.

SOFTWARE TRAINER

Software trainers (see Figure 5.29)—sometimes called corporate trainers—are in demand as companies deploy more software programs. This high-paying career may involve some travel and requires good computer skills, organization, and communication skills. Software trainers usually have at least a bachelor's degree and on-the-job training. Some companies offer train-the-trainer courses that can lead to a certification. You might work for a training company, in the training department of a large company, or as a consultant to many companies.

One important thing to realize is that the skills you learn when using one software application will often translate to another. The more you know, the easier you'll find it is to pick up something new, so even knowing just office applications will help you more easily pick up a new program specific to your job—whatever that may be.

Running Project

What career are you pursuing? Explain how knowledge of application software will help you get your first job in your field.

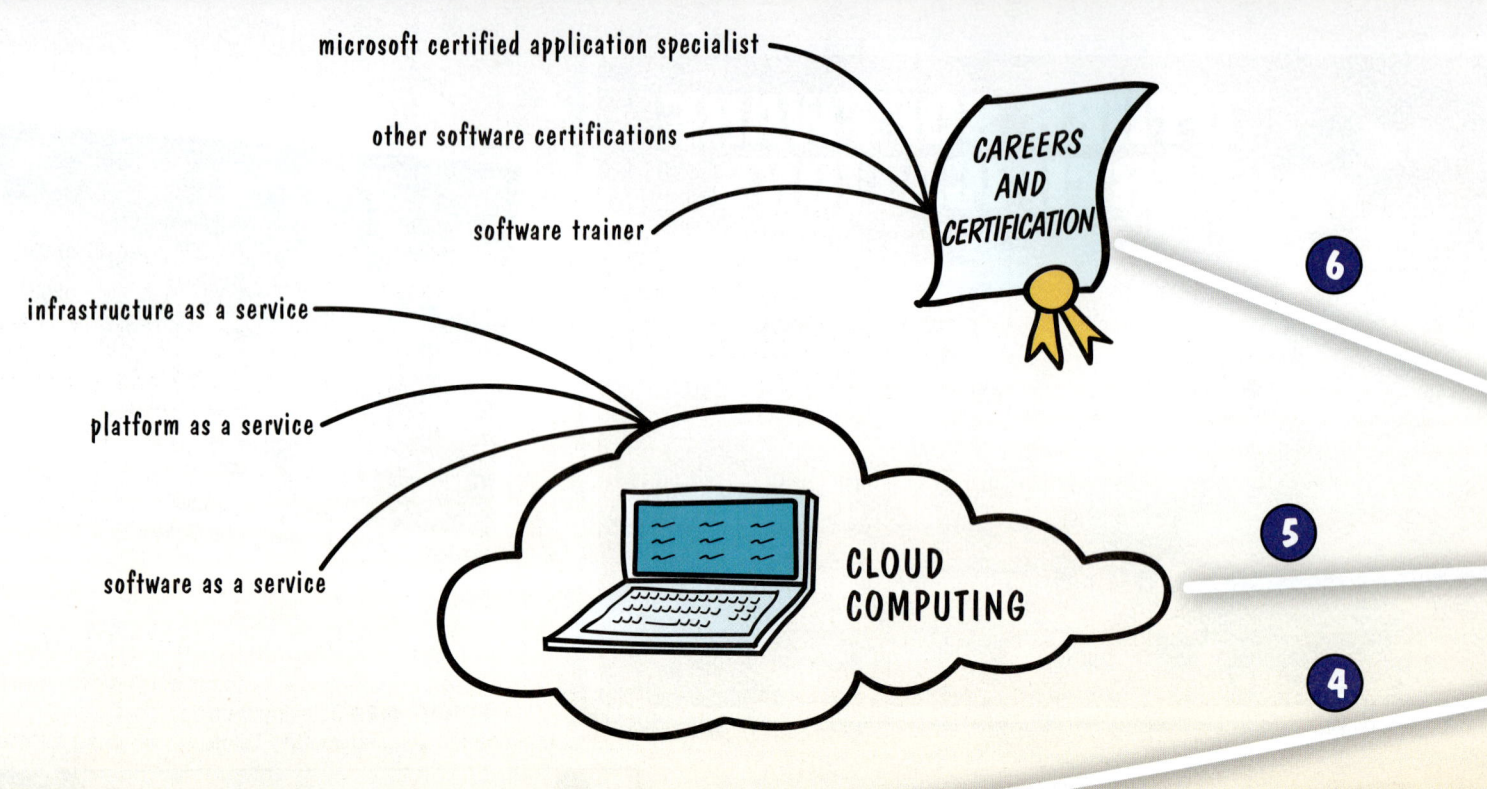

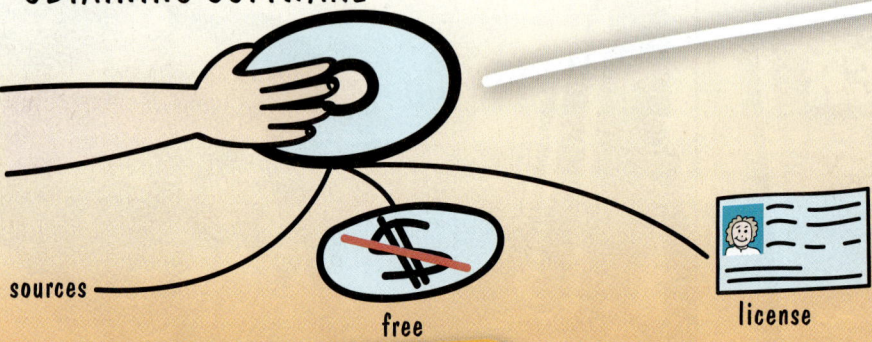

microsoft certified application specialist
other software certifications
software trainer

CAREERS AND CERTIFICATION

infrastructure as a service
platform as a service
software as a service

CLOUD COMPUTING

OBTAINING SOFTWARE

sources
free
license

Objectives Recap

1. Identify types and uses of business productivity software. (p. 180)
2. Identify types and uses of personal software. (p. 188)
3. Assess a computer system for software compatibility. (p. 202)
4. Compare various ways of obtaining software. (p. 206)
5. Discuss the importance of cloud computing. (p. 210)
6. Identify the certifications and careers related to application software. (p. 212)

Key Terms

cell **182**
cloud computing **210**
database **184**
document management system **186**
donationware **207**
EULA (end-user license agreement) **206**
field **184**
freeware **207**

Gantt chart **187**
Infrastructure-as-a-Service (IaaS) **210**
office application suite **180**
open source **188**
personal information manager (PIM) **185**
Platform-as-a-Service (PaaS) **210**
portable apps **197**
project management software **187**

APPLICATION SOFTWARE

1. **BUSINESS PRODUCTIVITY SOFTWARE**
   - office suites
   - other business software
     - financial
     - document management
     - project management

2. **PERSONAL SOFTWARE**
   - office apps
   - finance $
   - entertainment
   - education and reference
   - portable

3. **SOFTWARE COMPATIBILITY**
   - system specs
   - system requirements

Summary

record **184**
retail software **207**
shareware **207**
Software-as-a-Service (SaaS) **211**
spreadsheet **182**
system requirements **204**
Windows Experience Index **203**
word processor **180**
WYSIWYG **181**

1. **Identify types and uses of business productivity software:** The most common business software is an office application suite—including a word processor, spreadsheet, presentation program, database, and personal information manager. Other business applications include financial software, document management, and project management software.

2. **Identify types and uses of personal software:** Personal software includes office applications, especially word processors, spreadsheets, and presentation programs. Other personal applications include entertainment and multimedia software such as media managers, video and photo editing software, and video games. Financial and tax preparation software as well as educational and reference software are also popular. You can run portable apps from a flash drive and take them with you.

3. **Assess a computer system for software compatibility:** Before purchasing and installing software, you should research the system requirements needed to run the program and compare them to your system specifications using the System Control Panel.
4. **Compare various ways of obtaining software:** You can obtain software from brick-and-mortar and online stores, publisher websites, and download websites. It's important to read the EULA to understand the restrictions the software license puts on you.
5. **Discuss the importance of cloud computing:** Cloud computing moves hardware and software into the cloud, or Internet. Cloud computing allows you to access applications and data from any Web-connected computer. Some benefits include lower cost, easier maintenance, security, and collaboration.
6. **Identify the certifications and careers related to application software:** Virtually every career today uses application software. As businesses deploy more software, the demand for software trainers grows. The Microsoft Certified Application Specialist (MCAS) certification is a series of six certification exams: Word, Excel, PowerPoint, Outlook, Access, and Windows. You earn a separate certification for each exam that you pass and a Master certification for passing the first four. Other software certifications are also available. The increased use of software in businesses large and small has created a growing need for software trainers.

Multiple Choice

Answer the multiple-choice questions below for more practice with key terms and concepts from this chapter.

1. Which application would be the best choice for creating a budget?
   a. Word processor
   b. Spreadsheet
   c. Database
   d. Personal information manager

2. Software that has the source code published and made available to the public—enabling anyone to copy, modify and redistribute it without paying fees—is called _____ software.
   a. freeware
   b. free source
   c. open source
   d. trial version

3. What is the intersection of a row and a column called in a spreadsheet?
   a. Field
   b. Record
   c. Chart
   d. Cell

4. _____ is an online alternative to office application suites.
   a. Zoho Docs
   b. Mint.com
   c. OpenOffice.org
   d. WordPad

5. _____ software helps you to complete projects, keep within your budget, stay on schedule, and collaborate with others.
   a. Project management
   b. Document management
   c. Personal information management
   d. Word processing

6. Programs that can run from a flash drive are known as _____.
   a. suites
   b. SaaS
   c. portable apps
   d. open source software

7. The Windows Experience Index _____.
   a. evaluates the fun factor of video games
   b. refers to the Windows Media Center
   c. refers to your personal computing experience
   d. evaluates the computer's ability to run software

8. _____ is software offered in trial form or for a limited period that allows the user to try it out before purchasing a license.
   a. Retail
   b. Freeware
   (c.) Shareware
   d. Donationware

9. Which acronym refers to the delivery of applications over the Internet—or Web apps?
   a. Waps   c. PaaS
   b. IaaS   (d.) SaaS

10. Which word processor comes with Windows?
    (a.) Word
    b. WordPad
    c. Writer
    d. Docs

True or False

Answer the following questions with T for true or F for false for more practice with key terms and concepts from this chapter.

F 1. In a business environment, you'll find Microsoft Excel almost exclusively as the spreadsheet application.
F 2. Each database can have only one table of records.
F 3. OpenOffice.org can't open and work with documents created in Microsoft Office.
T 4. Documents created with a word processor can also contain images.
F 5. Free software versions are trial versions of retail software.
F 6. The average video game player is between the ages of 14 and 20.
F 7. If your computer doesn't meet the minimum system requirements for a piece of software, the software will probably still run on your system.
T 8. A proprietary software license grants a license to use one or more copies of software, but ownership of those copies remains with the software publisher.
T 9. Web mail is an example of SaaS.
F 10. You must pass all six Microsoft Certified Application Specialist (MCAS) certification exams to become certified.

Fill in the Blank

Fill in the blanks with key terms and concepts from this chapter.

1. A(n) **word processor** is an application that's used to create, edit, and format text documents.
2. **WYSIWYG** means the layout on the computer screen shows the document layout as it would be printed.
3. A(n) **database** is a collection of records organized in a useful way.
4. A(n) **PIM** is a program that's used to manage e-mail, calendar, and tasks and is often part of an office suite.
5. A(n) **Gantt Chart** is used in project management to illustrate a project schedule.
6. **Document Management** is used to save, share, search, and audit electronic documents throughout their life cycle.
7. **Freeware** can be used at no cost for an unlimited period of time.
8. The license agreement between the software user and the software publisher is the **EULA**.
9. **Cloud Computing** takes the processing and storage off your desktop and business hardware and puts it on the Internet.
10. Part of cloud computing, **SAAS** is the delivery of applications over the Internet—or Web apps.

Running Project

... The Finish Line

Assume that you just got a new computer with no software on it. Use your answers to the previous sections of the project to help you select five pieces of software that you consider indispensable to have. Which programs did you pick and why? If you could only afford to buy one program, which would it be?

Write a report describing your selections and responding to the questions raised. Save your file as **Lastname_Firstname_ch05_Project** and submit it to your instructor as directed.

File Management

1. Open your user folder from the Windows Start menu. Locate the Downloads folder. Are there any files in this folder? If so, what types of files are they?

2. Search Help and Support for **Downloads folder**. Click on *Downloading files from the Internet: frequently asked questions* and then click *Where are downloaded files saved?* What's the purpose of the Downloads folder?

3. Type up your answers, save the file as **Lastname_Firstname_ch05_Downloads**, and submit the assignment as directed by your instructor.

Critical Thinking 1

You're starting a small home business. You want to be sure to keep good records and will need to use finance software to help you. You'll be the only employee of your business, so you need something basic and easy to use. Compare two small business finance programs:

1. Evaluate two programs from current newspaper ads and websites and compare them with respect to your requirements.

2. Use a word processor to create a table like the one below, comparing the features of each program, to organize your research. (Note: WordPad does not include the ability to create tables.)

3. In the same document, write your conclusion in a two- to three-paragraph essay. Which program should you buy and why? Is there anything else (hardware, software, office supplies) that you'll need to purchase to use the program?

4. Save your file as **Lastname_Firstname_ch05_Smallbiz** and submit both your table and essay as directed by your instructor.

	Program 1	Program 2
Name of program		
Cost		
Local install or online?		
Important features		
Online ratings (website)		
Support		

Critical Thinking 2

You work for a nonprofit animal shelter that has very limited funds. Your boss wants to find a free or inexpensive program to help keep track of the Friends of Animals member contact information so it can be used to send out invitations to the annual charity ball. She would also like to access this information when she's working from home.

1. What type of application could she use for this task? Word processor? Spreadsheet? Database? Which would you recommend she use and why?

2. Assuming the shelter has Internet access, recommend two websites that the shelter could use to manage this information.

3. Read the EULA for each. Are there different restrictions for personal users vs. nonprofit and business users? What are they? Write up your answers, save the file as **Lastname_Firstname_ch05_Shelter**, and submit the assignment as directed by your instructor.

Do It Yourself 1

System requirements for new software often require a computer system with lots of available processing power, storage space, and memory. In this activity, you learn a little bit about your own computer to help you make smart software purchases.

Windows 7 provides many details about your computer through a variety of built-in utilities. For this exercise, you'll use the System Control Panel and Computer window.

1. Click the Windows Start button and click *Computer*.

2. In the right pane is a listing of all the drives available on your computer. Create a table like the one below to record details about your system—include the name, capacity, and free space for each drive. (Note: WordPad does not include the ability to create tables.)

3. Right-click on *Computer* in the navigation pane and choose *Properties* to open the System Control Panel. Click on *Windows Experience Index*. What is your lowest subscore? What can you do to improve your system's score?

4. Type up your answers, save the file as **Lastname_Firstname_ch05_Index**, and submit the assignment as directed by your instructor.

Hard Disk Drives	Devices with Removable Storage	Network Locations	Other Locations

Do It Yourself 2

Windows provides several applications beside WordPad. In this activity, you'll examine these accessories.

1. Click the Windows Start button, click *All Programs*, and click *Accessories*. What programs are listed?
2. Use Windows Help and Support to look up Calculator, Math Input Panel, Paint, and Sticky Notes. Write a one- to two-paragraph summary of each application.
3. Close the Help window. Save the file as **Lastname_Firstname_ch05_Accessories** and submit it as directed by your instructor.

Ethical Dilemma

You decided to buy an expensive photo editing program and look on eBay for a good deal. You find a listing from a seller that has good ratings, so you bid on and buy the software. When the software arrives, you're disappointed to find that it is a pirated copy and includes a program to generate a license key to unlock the program—a key gen program.

1. You bought the software in good faith and really need it to complete your homework assignment. What do you do? Would you install the software? Why or why not?
2. Is it acceptable to install the software for the assignment and uninstall it when you're finished?
3. Type up your answers, save the file as **Lastname_Firstname_ch05_eBay**, and submit it as directed by your instructor.

On the Web 1

The CNET website provides information to help you evaluate and compare both hardware and software. Visit the site **reviews.cnet.com/software** and answer the following questions:

1. Click the *Best applications* link. What are the Best 5 applications?
2. Select an application category from the menu on the left. Choose one application that you do not already use and read the review. How do the editor's and average user's ratings compare? What are the strengths and weaknesses of the program?
3. Type up your answers, save the file as **Lastname_Firstname_ch05_CNET**, and submit it as directed by your instructor.

On the Web 2

Microsoft Project is the most popular project management program. Its main online rival is Basecamp.

1. Go to the Basecamp website (**basecamphq.com**). What are some of the companies that use Basecamp? Research the pricing plans.
2. Research the price for Microsoft Project. How does it compare to Basecamp? Which would you recommend for a small business and why?
3. Compare the total cost for these applications. Are they worth the cost? Type up your answers, save the file as **Lastname_Firstname_ch05_Basecamp**, and submit it as directed by your instructor.

Collaboration 1

Instructors: Divide the class into five groups, and assign each group one topic for this project. The topics include: Web apps, personal finance software, photo editing software, trip planning software, and home and landscape design software.

The Project: Each team is to prepare a written presentation that includes an explanation of its topic and examples of programs in that category that aren't included in this book. Use pictures, text, key terms, and color to enhance the presentation. Teams must use at least three references, only one of which may be this textbook. Use Google Docs to prepare the final version of your presentation, and provide documentation that all team members have contributed to the project. For more on using Google Docs, see Appendix C.

Students: Before beginning this project, discuss the roles each group member will play. Choose a team name, which you'll use in submitting your presentation. Be sure to divide the work among your members, and pick someone to present your project. You may find it helpful to elect a team leader who can direct your activities and ensure that all team contributions are collated through Google Docs.

Outcome: You're to prepare a presentation on your assigned topic. The presentation may be no longer than two pages, double-spaced. On the first page, be sure to include the name of your presentation and a list of all team members. Turn in a version of your presentation showing revisions named as **Teamname_Software_ch05_Draft**. In addition, turn in a final version of your presentation with all revisions accepted named as **Teamname_Software_ch05_Final**. Submit your presentation to your instructor as directed.

Collaboration 2

Instructors: Divide the class into five groups, and assign each group one software license topic for this project. The topics include: freeware, shareware, donationware, open source software, and EULAs.

The Project: Each team is to prepare a multimedia presentation for their license type. The presentation should be designed to educate consumers about the license type. Teams must use at least three references, only one of which may be this textbook. Use Google Docs to plan the presentation, and provide documentation that all team members have contributed to the project. For more on using Google Docs, see Appendix C.

Students: Before beginning this project, discuss the roles each group member will play. Choose a team name, which you'll use in submitting your presentation. Be sure to divide the work among your members, and pick someone to present your project. You may find it helpful to elect a team leader who can direct your activities and ensure that all team contributions are collated through Google Docs.

Outcome: You're to prepare a multimedia presentation on your assigned topic in PowerPoint (or another tool approved by your instructor) and present it to your class. The presentation may be no longer than three minutes and should contain five to seven slides. On the first slide, be sure to include the name of your presentation and a listing of all team members. Turn in a final version of your presentation named as **Teamname_ch05_Licenses** and your Google Docs file showing your collaboration named as **Teamname_License_ch05_Collaboration**. Submit your presentation to your instructor as directed.

Blogging

1. Blog about your favorite computer game or program. In your blog, provide the type of computer you have and the operating system you're using. Outline the things your program does well and things it could do better.

2. Visit at least two of your classmates' blogs on this topic. On the blogs you visit, provide three to five sentences to convince your classmate to try your program.

3. Create a document that includes your blog URL and the URLs of the two blogs you commented on. Save the file as **Lastname_Firstname_ch05_Software_Blog**. Submit the document to your instructor as directed.

CHAPTER 6
System Softwa

Running Project

In this chapter, you'll learn about different kinds of system software and how to obtain it. Look for instructions as you complete each article. For most, there's a series of questions for you to research. At the conclusion of the chapter, you're asked to submit your responses to the questions raised.

Become our friend on Facebook

OBJECTIVES

1. Explain what an operating system does. (p. 224)
2. Compare the most common stand-alone operating systems. (p. 228)
3. Compare the most common network operating systems. (p. 234)
4. Compare specialized operating systems. (p. 236)
5. List and explain important disk utility software. (p. 240)
6. Identify the certifications and careers related to system software. (p. 244)

IN THIS CHAPTER

A computer is a programmable machine that converts raw data into useful information. Programming is what makes a computer different from a toaster. In this chapter, we look at the system software used to make computers run smoothly and securely.

Who's Being BOSSY NOW?

1 OBJECTIVE
Explain what an operating system does.

We often hear about application software—software for the user. Software that makes the computer run is **system software**. The **operating system (OS)** is the most important type of system software because it provides the user with the interface to communicate with the hardware and other software on the computer and manages system resources. Without an operating system, a personal computer is useless.

PROVIDES USER INTERFACE

The user interface is the part of the operating system that you see and interact with. Modern operating systems, such as Windows, Linux, and MAC OS X, have a **graphical user interface**, or **GUI**. Graphical because we interact with graphic objects such as icons and buttons to control the computer, a GUI allows a user to point to and click on objects to initiate commands. Older operating systems used a command-line interface, which required the user to type out all commands. If you look at the interface on most personal computers, you'll see that they have a lot in common. Figure 6.1 shows how the interface changed from command line to GUI in Microsoft operating systems from the 1980s through today. This change made PCs more user-friendly, which helped them increase in popularity. A similar evolution occurred in the Apple systems. In fact, in 1988, Apple sued Microsoft for copyright infringement, but the case was later dismissed.

All user interfaces serve the same basic function: to allow the user to control the computer. If you want to play a game, you navigate to the icon for the game and click (or double-click) on it to begin. The clicking tells the computer to open the file—in this case, to run the game. The procedure to open a Word document is very much the same. All these tasks require the OS user interface. GUIs use icons, menus, dialog boxes, and windows, and in many cases, there are multiple ways to perform the same task.

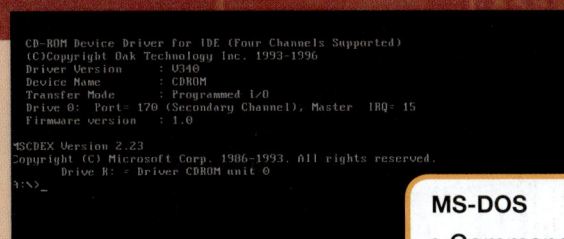

MS-DOS
- Command line
- 80s and early 90s

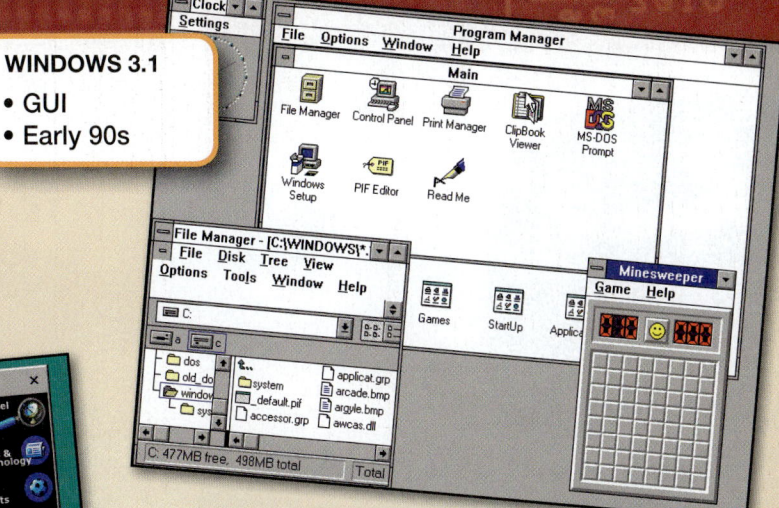

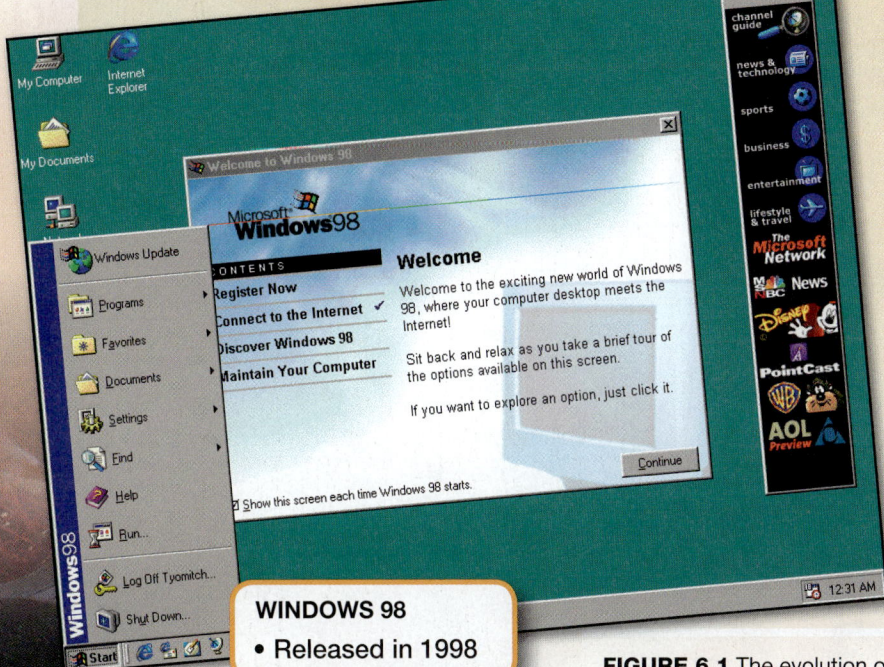

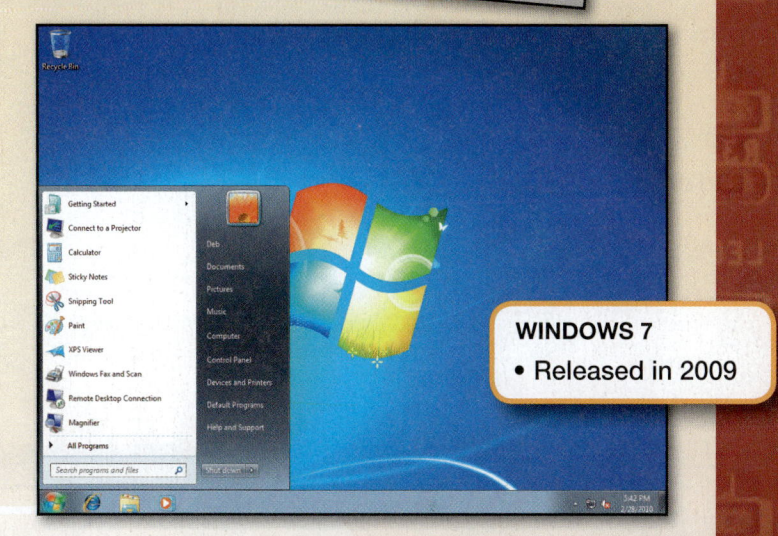

WINDOWS 3.1
- GUI
- Early 90s

WINDOWS 98
- Released in 1998

WINDOWS 7
- Released in 2009

FIGURE 6.1 The evolution of the user interface in Microsoft operating systems

MANAGES RESOURCES

The resources on your system include the processor and the memory. The operating system has the very important job of managing how these resources are allocated to both hardware and software. The operating system makes sure that each process is allocated its own memory and manages the instructions that are sent to the processor (see Figure 6.2). Modern operating systems support **multitasking**, which is the ability to do more than one task at a time. A single processor can't actually do more than one thing at a time but switches between the tasks so quickly that it's transparent to the user. Each running application is assigned its own area of memory and is prevented from accessing the memory area of other programs. This prevents a program crash from affecting other processes running in other areas of memory.

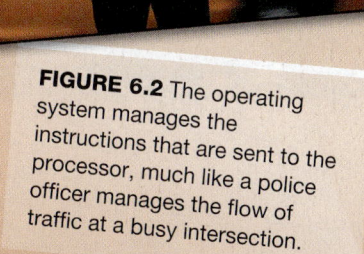

FIGURE 6.2 The operating system manages the instructions that are sent to the processor, much like a police officer manages the flow of traffic at a busy intersection.

Chapter 6 | 225

MANAGES AND CONTROLS HARDWARE

The operating system manages and controls the hardware. Early PCs were simple devices that had limited hardware: a keyboard, a monochrome monitor, a disk drive, and not much else. Today, we have a wide variety of peripheral devices, including printers, scanners, cameras, media players, video and sound cards, and storage devices. Windows 95 introduced a feature known as Plug and Play. **Plug and Play (PnP)** allows you to easily add new hardware to a computer system. When you plug in a new piece of hardware, the OS detects it and helps you set it up. An OS communicates with hardware by means of a device driver, which acts like a translator between the two. A **device driver** is software that enhances the capabilities of the operating system. It's what allows you to expand your computer with new hardware. If it were not for device drivers, there would be no way for you to install new hardware on your system. Figure 6.3 shows how Windows 7 notifies you of the installation of new hardware. When you first connect the hardware, Windows detects it and informs you that it's installing the device driver software. If Windows cannot locate the device driver, it asks you for permission to search the Web or instructs you to insert the manufacturer's disc. The message *Device driver software installed successfully* indicates your new hardware is now ready to use.

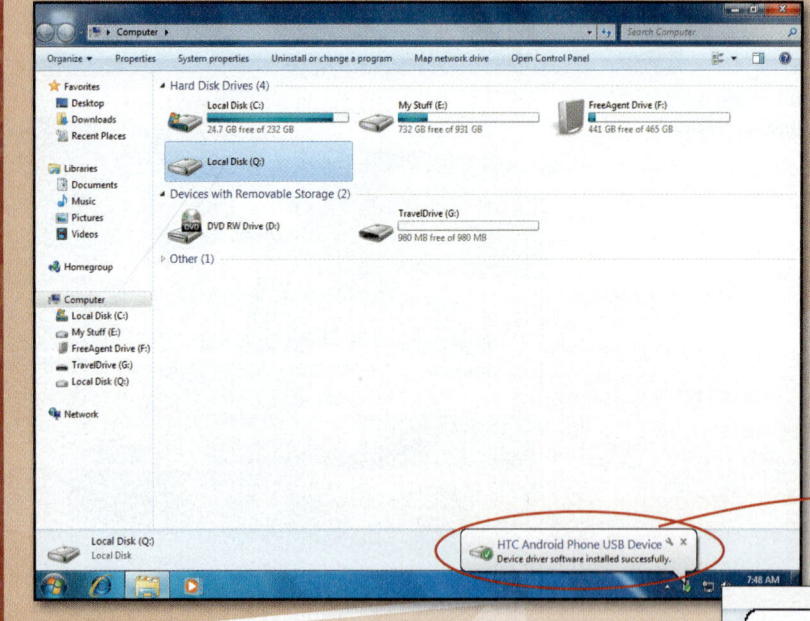

FIGURE 6.3 Windows automatically installs the device driver for new hardware—in this case, an HTC Android phone.

INTERACTS WITH SOFTWARE

When you look at the system requirements to install software, you'll always see a list of supported operating systems. The OS on a computer interacts directly with the software you install, giving it access to resources it needs to run. This happens through the use of an **application programming interface (API)**, which allows the application to request services from the operating system, such as a request to print or save a file. An API lets a computer programmer write a program that will run on computers with different hardware configurations by sending such service requests to the OS to handle. Figure 6.4 shows applications using the API to request the save services from Windows 7.

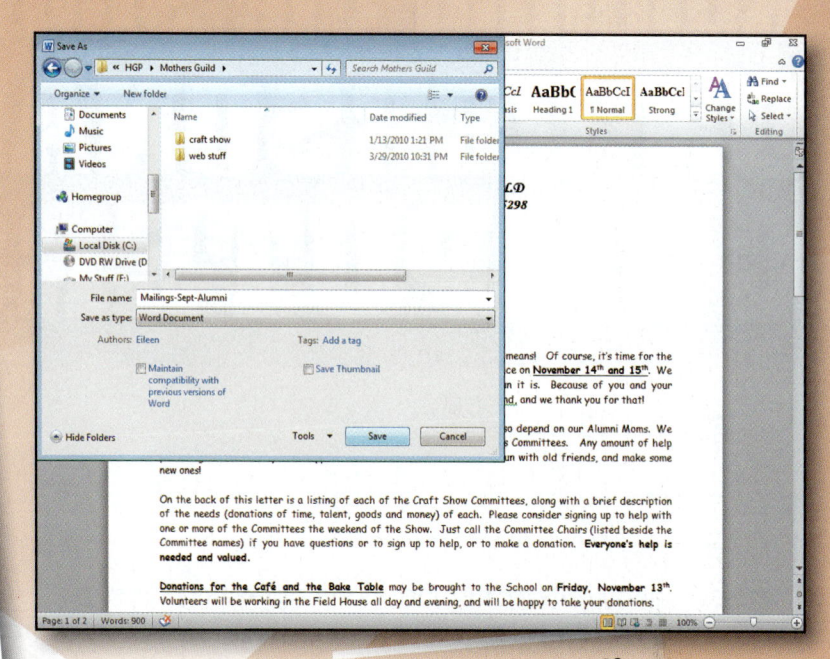

FIGURE 6.4 Programs use the API to save files.

An operating system manages interactions between the user, the software, and the hardware of a computer. These critical functions make the computer more user-friendly, flexible, and expandable. The OS is the most important piece of software on the computer because without it, the computer won't run at all.

Key Terms

application programming interface (API)

device driver

graphical user interface (GUI)

multitasking

operating system (OS)

Plug and Play (PnP)

system software

Running Project

What operating system is on your computer? You can check a Windows computer by right-clicking on *Computer* in the Start menu and choosing *Properties*. Is it the latest version? If you have not upgraded yet, why not? If you could change the OS, would you? Which OS would you use instead?

Four Things You Need to Know

- A GUI allows you to point and click to control your computer.
- The OS manages the system resources: processing and memory.
- PnP allows you to add new hardware easily.
- Application software communicates with the OS through an API.

Running the Show ON PERSONAL COMPUTERS

2 OBJECTIVE
Compare the most common stand-alone operating systems.

There are many different stand-alone operating systems. In this article, we look at some of the most popular operating systems used on personal computers today.

WINDOWS

The most common desktop operating system is **Microsoft Windows**. Figure 6.5 shows a timeline of the release of successive versions of the Windows desktop operating systems. The current version is Windows 7, although you'll still find many computers running previous versions of Windows, such as Vista or XP. It's estimated that over 90 percent of personal computers are running one of these versions of Windows. Windows XP was released in 2001 and was still the most widely used operating system in the world in 2010. However, sales of Windows XP ended in 2008. All Microsoft support for Windows XP will end in 2014. Windows Vista was released in 2006 (2007 to consumers) but was met with much resistance from both the public and business customers. The hardware requirements to install Vista are much more stringent than those for XP. In addition, software and device driver compatibility were problematic when Vista was first released, adding to the cost of upgrading. Windows 7 was greeted much more favorably, and both home and business users that were still using XP began to upgrade to it. Since its release in 2008 (2009 to consumers), Windows 7 has been steadily gaining, and the number of PCs running Windows XP and Vista has been declining. In this book, the Windows screen shots and exercises are based on Windows 7 (see Figure 6.6).

FIGURE 6.5 Windows release timeline

- Windows 7 — 2009
- Windows Vista — 2007
- Windows XP — 2001
- Windows Me / Windows 2000 — 2000
- Windows 98 — 1998
- Windows NT 4.0 — 1996
- Windows 95 — 1995
- Windows NT 3.5 — 1994
- Windows NT 3.1 — 1993
- Windows 3.0 — 1990
- Windows 2.0 — 1987
- Windows 1.0 — 1985

Each release of Windows added new features and security measures and was designed to be easier to use, more secure, and able to incorporate the new technologies.

- Windows 95 introduced Plug and Play (PnP), enhanced support for CD-ROMs, and the right mouse click.
- Windows 98 included Internet Explorer, better PnP support, and more multimedia features.
- Windows XP introduced a new interface, automatic updates, easier networking and Internet connectivity, and increased reliability.
- Windows Vista once again introduced a new interface, gadgets, enhanced networking, entertainment, and accessibility features.
- Windows 7 includes a redesigned taskbar, new ways to manipulate windows, Remote Media Streaming, and Windows Touch multi-touch technology.

Moving from one version of Windows to the next usually requires a fairly small learning curve, and users adapt quickly to the changes.

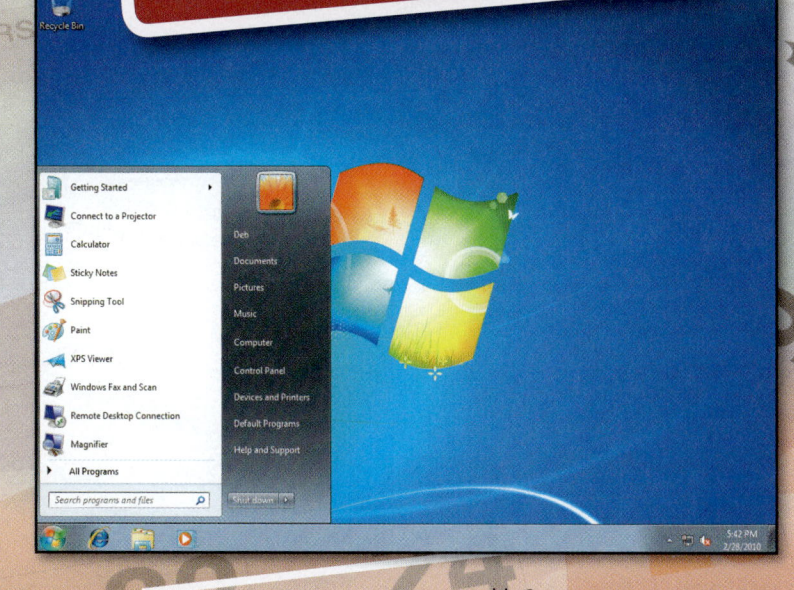

FIGURE 6.6 The Windows 7 desktop with the Start menu opened

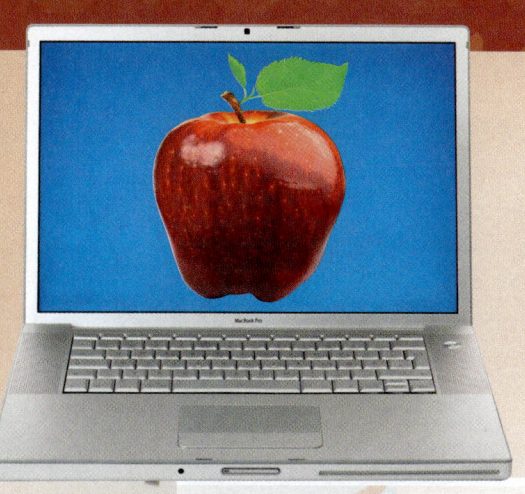

FIGURE 6.7 Timeline of Mac operating system releases from 1984–2009

MAC

In 1984, Apple introduced its first Macintosh computer, which had a GUI interface. The OS at the time was called Mac System Software. New versions and updates that improved stability and hardware support were released between 1984 and 1991. Figure 6.7 shows a timeline of Mac releases.

- System 7 was released in 1990 with an updated GUI, multitasking support, built-in networking, better hardware and memory management, and new applications. Beginning with version 7.6, the name was changed to Mac OS.
- Mac OS 8 was released in 1997 and included a new interface, a better file system, searching, and Internet browsing.
- Mac OS 9 had improved wireless networking support, a better search tool, and the ability to be updated over the Internet. Mac OS 9 is referred to today as Mac Classic.

- Mac OS X 10.6 Snow Leopard 2009
- Mac OS X 10.5 Leopard 2007
- Mac OS X 10.4 Tiger 2004
- Mac OS X 10.3 Panther 2003
- Mac OS X 10.2 Jaguar 2002
- Mac OS X 10.0 Cheetah
- Mac OS X 10.1 Puma 2001
- Mac OS 9 Mac Classic 1999
- Mac OS 8 1997
- System 7 1991
- System 6 1988
- System 5 System 4 1987
- System 3 1986
- System 2 1985
- System 1 1984

The **Mac OS X** operating system was first released in 2001 as Mac OS X 10.0, also called Cheetah. This OS isn't an updated version of the classic Mac OS but is an entirely new operating system. Early versions of OS X included a Mac OS 9 emulation to run older applications. Cheetah introduced iMovie and iTunes; Puma added iDVD. Each new version included more integrated applications for e-mail, chat, Internet, and multimedia. The current version—Mac OS X 10.6 Snow Leopard (see Figure 6.8)—is faster, more reliable, and easier to use. The interface has been updated and includes the Time Machine backup utility, better file sharing and networking capabilities, and exceptional multimedia applications.

The Mac OS is a secure, feature-rich operating system that only runs on Mac computers. If you don't have a Mac, then you can't use the Mac OS. Currently, Macs have about a 5 percent share of the personal computer market.

FIGURE 6.8 Mac OS X Snow Leopard

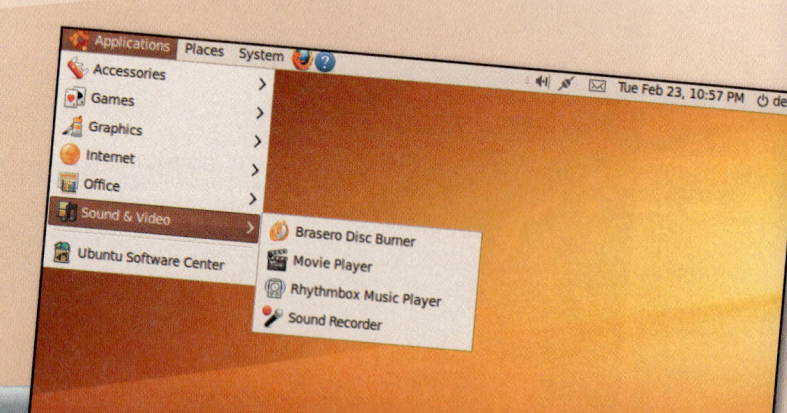

LINUX

Unlike Windows and Mac, Linux doesn't refer to a single operating system but rather many different versions, or distributions, that use the same kernel OS: Linux. **Linux** was first developed in 1991 by Linus Torvalds, then a graduate student at the University of Helsinki. It was designed to be similar to UNIX and is sometimes called UNIX-like. Unlike UNIX (and Windows and Mac OS), however, Linux is **open source**. The code is publically available, and developers all over the world have created hundreds of Linux distributions (distros) with all kinds of features. Distros include the OS, various utilities, and software applications, such as Internet browsers, games, entertainment software, and an office suite. The most popular personal version of Linux is currently Ubuntu. Figure 6.9 shows the Ubuntu desktop with the Applications menu expanded. Most Linux distros come with a GUI that's similar to a Windows or Mac OS, and users can easily navigate through the system. Linux desktops make up a very small percentage of personal computers, but the number is growing all the time. Linux has found a niche in the netbook market. On machines with limited memory and processing power, Linux shines.

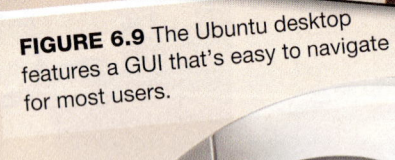

FIGURE 6.9 The Ubuntu desktop features a GUI that's easy to navigate for most users.

FIGURE 6.10 The beta version of Google Chrome OS

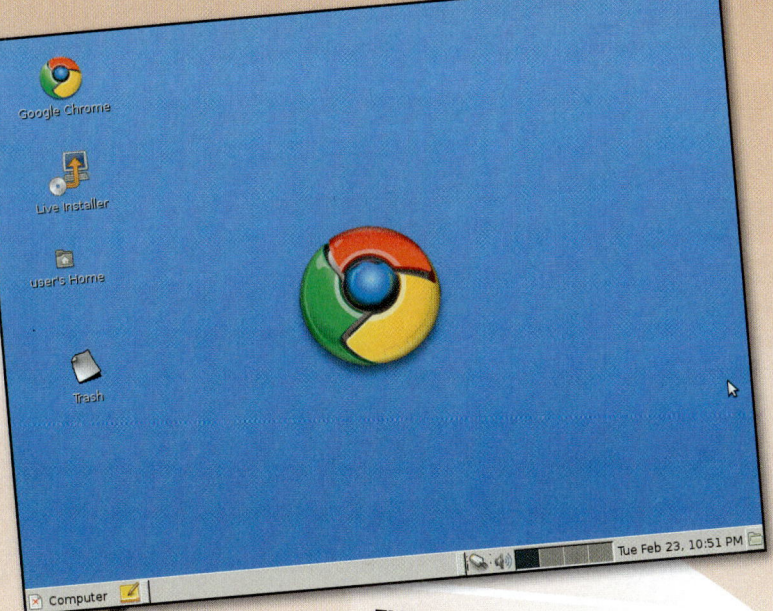

ETHICS

Older versions of Mac OS only ran on Mac hardware with PowerPC processors, but modern Macs now use Intel processors just like most PCs. With a bit of tweaking, it's possible to get the Mac OS to run on a PC. "Hackintosh" is the name given to a PC that's been modified so Mac OS X can be run on it. The question is, is it legal? Is it ethical? What are the restrictions on the Mac OS X EULA? Why do people do it? Would you?

In 2009, Google released a pre-release, or **beta version**, of its Chrome OS. "Chromium OS is an open source project that aims to provide a fast, simple, and more secure computing experience for people who spend most of their time on the web." The full release of this Linux distro is set for the end of 2010. Figure 6.10 shows the desktop of the beta version.

In businesses, Linux has a very small market share of desktop computers (less than 2 percent), but it has a larger share of the server market. Red Hat Enterprise Linux is the world's leading open source application platform—at least according to their website (redhat.com/rhel). We'll discuss Linux servers in the next article.

The operating system that you run largely depends on the hardware you have, but running the most recent version of your OS of choice ensures the best features and security.

Key Terms

beta version

Linux

Mac OS X

Microsoft Windows

open source

Running Project

Microsoft Windows is the primary desktop operating system installed on new personal computers, but not every consumer is happy with that choice. Some manufacturers sell Linux computers. Use the Internet to research the versions of Linux currently available preinstalled on new computers. Write a two- to three-paragraph essay summarizing your findings, which applications are included, the cost, and any other details you deem important.

Three Things You Need to Know

- Microsoft Windows is the primary OS installed on PCs.
- Mac OS X is the proprietary Mac OS.
- Linux is an open source kernel OS that's distributed as part of many versions or distros.

HOW TO Keep Windows up to Date

One of the most important things you can do to protect your system is to keep your software up to date. Some programs will check automatically and prompt you when a new version or update is available. Windows includes Windows Update to do just that. It's important to set the utility up correctly and monitor it to be sure that your updates are being installed. Complete each step, and compare your screen to the figures that accompany each step.

1 Open Windows Update through the Start menu or Action Center (the white flag on the taskbar).

2 In the left pane, click *Change settings* to verify that you're getting the updates you need. In a business or school, this is likely handled centrally, and these settings might be disabled.

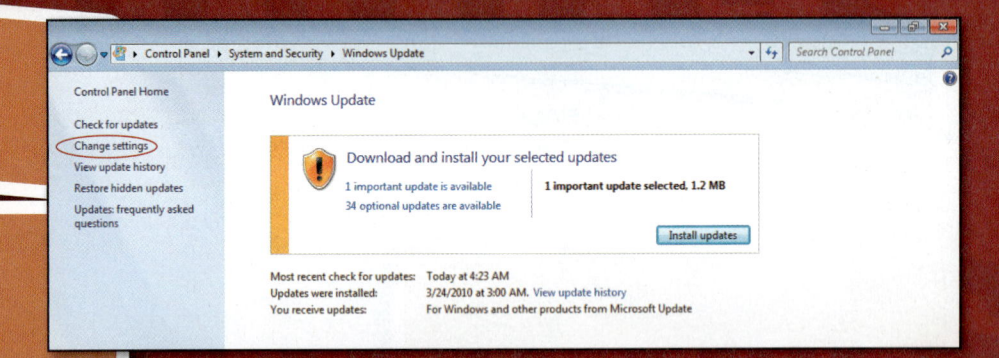

3 Important updates can be installed automatically (the default) or you can change the settings by clicking the drop-down arrow on the right. I sometimes change this to *Check for updates but let me choose whether to download and install them* when I'm traveling and not connected to my broadband Internet connection at home. This prevents Windows from downloading files while I'm working on a slow dial-up or public WiFi connection.

4 Click the check boxes for the other options you want. If you enable *Recommended updates*, you'll get additional items, such as new device drivers. Microsoft Update will also get you updates for other Microsoft products, such as Office. When you're finished making your selections, take a screen shot of your choices, and click *OK* to save your changes or *Cancel* to discard them. Open a new document, and paste the screen shot in it.

5 When you close the *Change settings* window, you're returned to the Windows Update screen. Notice that in this example, there are many updates ready to be installed. You can click the links for more information. The first figure shows the important updates ready to be installed. Notice that they're all checked by default. You can click on each for more information. Take another screen shot of the Important updates, and paste it in your document below the previous screen shot.

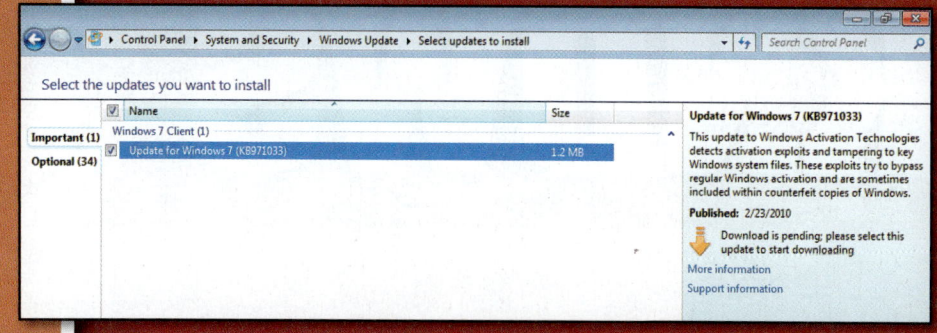

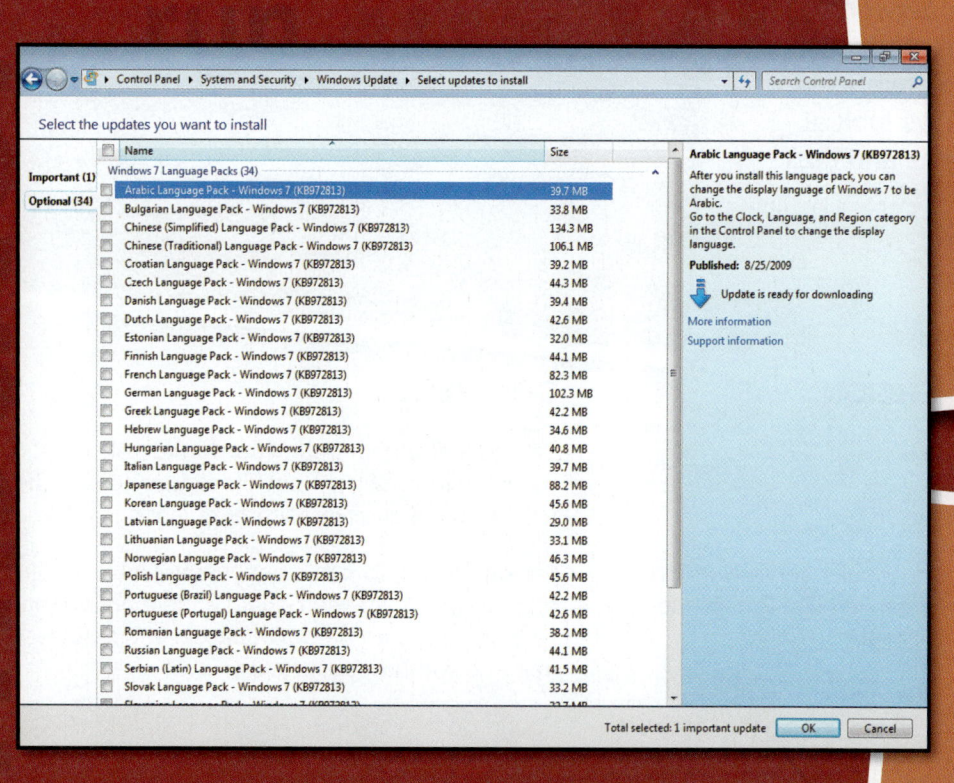

6 The optional updates in this example are all Windows 7 Language Packs. Because I don't use any other language on this computer, I chose not to install them. Click the Optional tab, take another screen shot, and paste it below the others in your document. Unlike the recommended updates, optional updates are not checked by default.

7 If Windows is set to automatically install updates, you don't need to install them yourself, but you can choose to manually install them if there are updates available by clicking the Install updates button in the Windows Update window. Save your file as **Lastname_Firstname_ch06_HowTo**, and submit it as directed by your instructor.

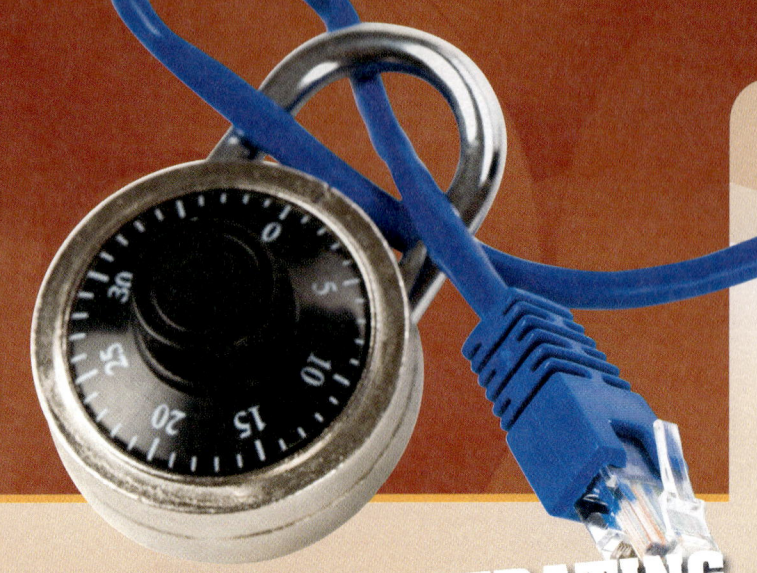

The NOS KNOWS

3 OBJECTIVE
Compare the most common network operating systems.

In a business or school environment, a network server centralizes resources, storage, and, most importantly, security in what is known as a client-server network. These servers run a specialized operating system called a network operating system. We'll discuss networks in more detail in a later chapter. In this article, we look at the most common network operating systems and their basic functions.

NETWORK OPERATING SYSTEMS

A **network operating system (NOS)** is a multiuser operating system that controls the software and hardware that runs on a network. It allows multiple computers (clients) to communicate with the server and each other, to share resources, run applications, and send messages. A NOS centralizes resources and security and provides services such as file and print services, communication services, Internet and e-mail services, and backup and database services to the client computers. Figure 6.11 details the most common network operating systems found today.

FIGURE 6.11 Comparing modern network operating systems

NETWORK (NOS)	CURRENT VERSION	COMMENTS
Windows Server: First released as Windows NT in 1993	Windows 2008 R2	Scalable; found on many corporate networks; available in versions from Small Business edition to Enterprise and Datacenter editions
Linux: Linux kernel is part of many different distros	Some of the most popular server versions used in business are Red Hat Enterprise Linux and Novell SUSE.	It's impossible to know how many Linux servers are currently installed because there are so many versions that can be downloaded and installed for free and without registration.
UNIX: Developed in 1969; the oldest NOS	UNIX itself is not an OS but a set of standards that are used to create a UNIX OS. Apache Web server is the most widely used NOS found on Web servers. Apache can run on UNIX or Linux servers.	Found on servers from HP (HP-UX), IBM (AIX), and Sun (Solaris)
Novell	SUSE Linux Enterprise Server	Novell was a leader in business servers throughout the 1980s and 1990s with its Netware products but moved to open source in the past decade.

Your school network is most likely a client-server network. When you log in to the network, you're given access to certain resources, such as printers and file storage. Figure 6.12 shows my Windows 7 welcome screen for my network login. The first part of the username HOMENET\ indicates the network domain. The second part, mom, is me. When I enter my password, I'm granted access to network resources on the HOMENET network.

FIGURE 6.12 Windows 7 welcome screen for a client-server network

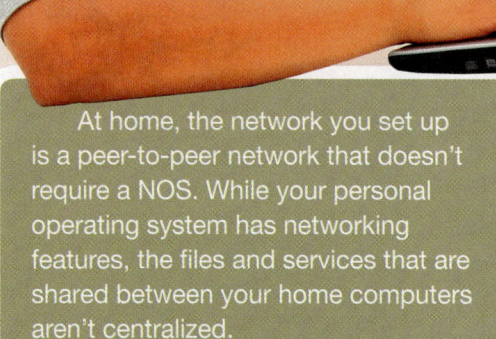

At home, the network you set up is a peer-to-peer network that doesn't require a NOS. While your personal operating system has networking features, the files and services that are shared between your home computers aren't centralized.

A NOS centralizes important security and resource management in a business environment. Without a NOS, businesses would have to rely on peer-to-peer networks, which are just not practical for more than a few computers.

Key Term

network operating system (NOS)

Running Project

The one area of NOS usage that can be easily monitored is activity on Web servers. These are the servers that serve up Web pages when you go to a URL, such as amazon.com. Netcraft **(netcraft.com)** does a monthly survey of Web servers. Go to the Netcraft website and look at the current report. What are the three most popular Web servers for this month? How much has it changed in the past month? Are there any servers not mentioned in this chapter?

Three Things You Need to Know

- A NOS controls the software and hardware that runs on a client-server network.
- The most common NOSs are Windows Server, UNIX, and Linux.
- A NOS isn't necessary on a peer-to-peer network.

Something SPECIAL FOR YOU

4 OBJECTIVE
Compare specialized operating systems.

So far, we've discussed the most mainstream operating systems that run on personal computers and servers. In this article, we look at embedded and Web operating systems.

EMBEDDED OPERATING SYSTEMS

Devices such as ATM machines, GPS devices, video game consoles, ultrasound machines, and even the communication and entertainment system in your car run **embedded operating systems**. Because they have very specialized and limited functions, these operating systems can be very small and are able to run on simpler hardware.

FIGURE 6.13 Smartphone operating systems

Symbian

Proprietary; largest market share globally but small impact in the United States; recently became open source

BlackBerry® OS from Research In Motion® (RIM®)

Proprietary; the standard for business users

Apple iPhone OS/ Mac OS X

Proprietary; found only on iPhones

Microsoft Windows Mobile

Based on Windows Embedded CE

Google Android

Linux kernel

Palm webOS

Linux kernel

The Windows Embedded OS has been around since 1996. It can be found on many devices from set-top cable boxes and GPS devices to complex industrial automation controllers and medical devices. The advantage to using an embedded version of Windows is that users recognize the familiar interface. Windows Mobile is based on Windows Embedded CE version and can be found on many PDAs and cell phones. The iPhone runs a scaled-down version of Mac OS X, and Android is an embedded version of Linux that runs on many phones. These small operating systems have familiar interfaces and features, including touch-screen support, e-mail, and Web browsers.

The most popular smartphone operating systems are illustrated in Figure 6.13. The market changes quite rapidly as new technologies are released.

Chapter 6 | 237

WEB OPERATING SYSTEMS

What do you spend the most time doing on your computer? For most people, the answer involves using the Internet. Enter the idea of a Web operating system. A **Web OS** is a virtual desktop that you interact with through your browser. It doesn't matter what desktop operating system you're running. As long as you have a Web browser, you can even use an old, obsolete computer to access your documents, pictures, contacts, and other files. Figure 6.14 shows eyeOS, "Open Source Cloud Computing's Web Desktop." Another popular Web OS is icloud, which calls itself your online computer. A Web OS doesn't handle the hardware functions of a true operating system, but it's a platform that provides access to applications, file sharing, collaboration, and security without the need to install any software on your computer.

Find Out MORE

Is a Web OS for you? Use the Internet to find out about three different Web OS platforms. Compare prices and features, and read about any case studies or examples on each website. Pick one, and sign up for a free trial. Spend some time looking around. Do you think you'll continue to use this service? What are the advantages to using a Web OS? Can you think of any disadvantages? Which Web operating systems did you use?

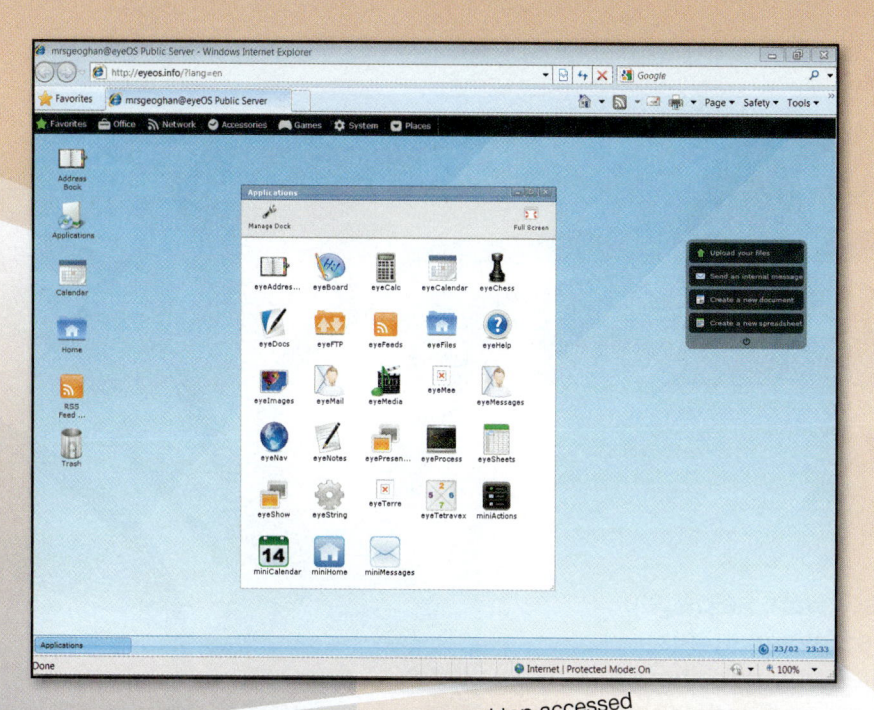

FIGURE 6.14 The eyeOS Web desktop accessed via your browser has a familiar interface design.

As technology becomes more mobile, smaller, faster, and less tethered to the desk, alternative operating systems become an important way for us to interface with our files and applications. Developers know this and strive to create the best interfaces—ones we can learn to use easily and come to depend upon quickly.

Key Terms

embedded operating system

Web OS

Running Project

What's the embedded OS on your favorite handheld device? What are some of the features that you like about it? Are there any features that are missing? What features do you (or would you) use the most often?

Two Things You Need to Know

- Embedded OSs are small and specialized for devices such as GPS, ATMs, and cell phones.
- A Web OS is a virtual desktop that provides access to your applications and documents through a Web browser.

Utilities YOU SHOULD USE

5 OBJECTIVE
List and explain important disk utility software.

System software isn't just the operating system. Utility software helps you maintain your computer and is also considered system software. In this article, we look at some of the most important disk utilities that you should use. Security software such as antivirus software, firewalls, and antimalware software are also considered utility software and are discussed in the chapter on security and privacy.

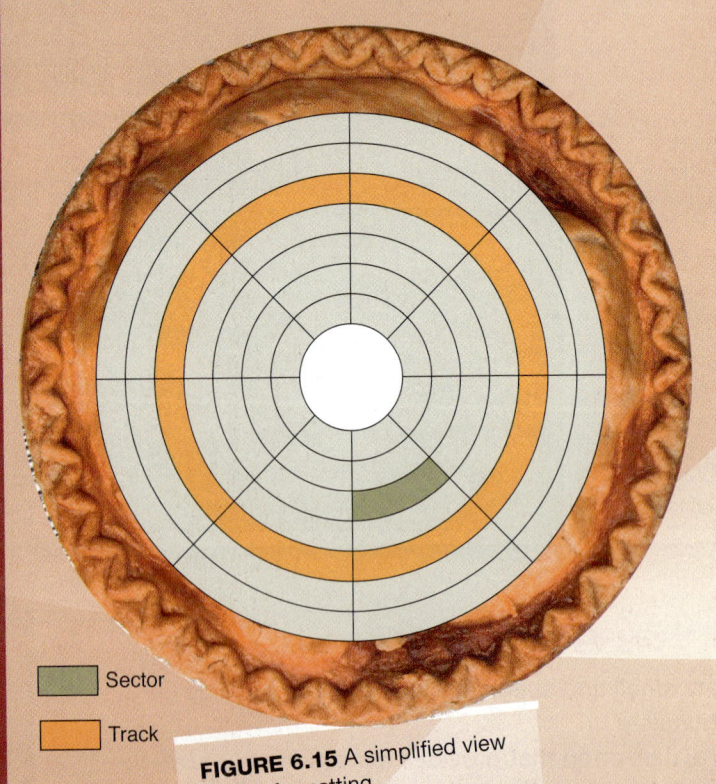

■ Sector
■ Track

FIGURE 6.15 A simplified view of disk formatting

WHY USE UTILITIES?

Hard disks today are very large and can hold a lot of information. It's important to keep your disks healthy to keep your system running efficiently and to protect the files stored on them. When a disk is first **formatted** to hold files, a set of concentric circles called tracks are created. The disk is then divided up like a pie into sectors (see Figure 6.15). The files are stored in blocks of sectors, called "clusters." This physical, low-level formatting occurs when the disk in manufactured. Think of this like a library full of empty bookshelves. The second part of formatting a disk is called high-level formatting. High-level formatting sets up the **file system** of the disk. You can think of it like a library catalog. When you save files to your disk, the file system keeps track of what you saved and where you saved it. The file system used on hard disks in Windows 7 is the NTFS file system. External disks or those from older versions of Windows may be formatted with the FAT file system instead.

UTILITIES FOR DISK HEALTH

Windows includes several disk utilities to help you maintain your disks: Check Disk, Disk Defragmenter, Disk Cleanup, and Backup. The Backup utility is discussed in the chapter on file management. To open these tools, first open the Computer window from the Start menu and then right-click on the disk you want to work with. From the context menu, choose *Properties* to open the Properties dialog box for the disk.

CHECK DISK Disk-checking utilities monitor the health of the file system on a disk. To check a disk for errors in Windows, in the disk's Properties dialog box, click the Tools tab and then click *Check now*. The Check Disk utility (see Figure 6.16) has two options: *Automatically fix file system errors* (which is checked by default) and *Scan for and attempt recovery of bad sectors* (which is not checked by default). When you click Start, you get a message that states that Windows can't check the disk while it's in use and an option to schedule a disk check. You should schedule the disk check to run the next time Windows starts. Because the process can take a while on a large disk, I usually run this overnight.

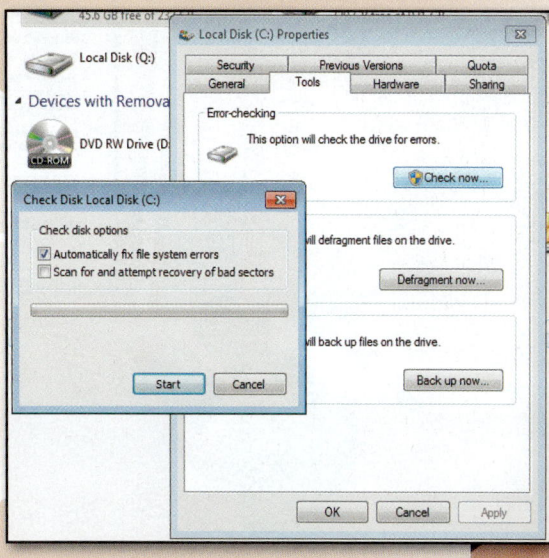

FIGURE 6.16 The Windows Check Disk utility can check both the file system and the physical health of the disk.

Click Analyze disk to determine the percentage of disk fragmentation.

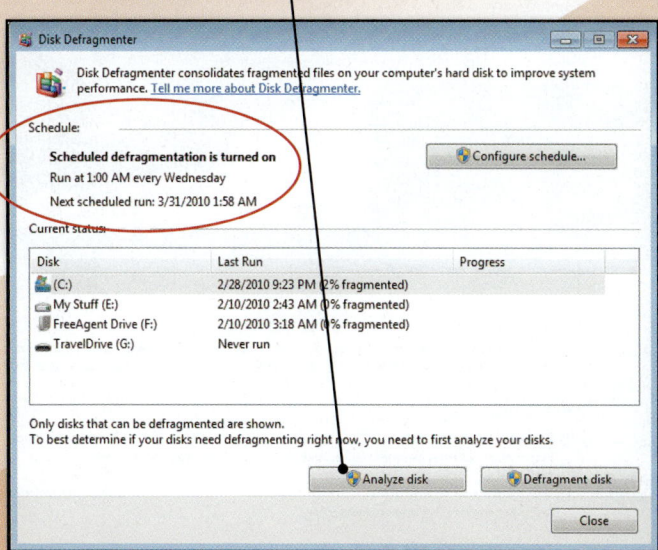

FIGURE 6.17 The Windows Disk Defragmenter is scheduled to run automatically.

DISK DEFRAGMENTER

Over time, the disk can become messy as files are created, edited, saved, and deleted. Staying with the library analogy, as books are checked out, lost, purchased, misplaced, and returned, the shelves can become disorganized and require someone to periodically go through and clean them up. In addition to being unorganized, files that are fragmented are broken into small pieces that are stored in nonadjacent or noncontiguous clusters on the disk. This is referred to as **file fragmentation**. A disk **defragmenter** is a utility that rearranges the fragmented files on your disk to improve efficiency.

Windows 7 comes with a built-in Disk Defragmenter utility that, by default, runs automatically on a weekly basis. You can also run it manually if you need to. Microsoft recommends that you defragment a drive that's more than 10% fragmented. Figure 6.17 shows the Disk Defragmenter utility. Like the Disk Check utility, the Disk Defragmenter can be accessed from the Tools tab of the disk's Properties dialog box.

Chapter 6 | 241

DISK CLEANUP

Back to the library. Over time, books become damaged, old, outdated, duplicated, and obsolete. A librarian will go through the stacks of books and remove those books. A disk cleanup utility looks for files that can be safely deleted to free up disk space so you have more space to store your files and to help keep your system running efficiently. The Windows Disk Cleanup utility is on the General tab of the disk's Properties dialog box. Click the Disk Cleanup button to begin. Figure 6.18 shows the result of running the Disk Cleanup utility. During the first part of the process, the disk is analyzed and the results can be reviewed by the user. When you click on each file type listed, a description of these files displays. You should read each description carefully to help you decide which files you can delete safely. In this example, the first two types of files are checked by default and the total amount of disk space I would gain is a meager 51.7 MB. If I choose to delete the Office Setup Files, I can free up another 250 MB of space, but the description recommends that I do not remove them unless I always have access to the original installation media. To proceed with the cleanup, click OK.

FIGURE 6.18 The Windows Disk Cleanup utility identifies files that you might choose to delete to free up disk space.

The first two items are checked by default.

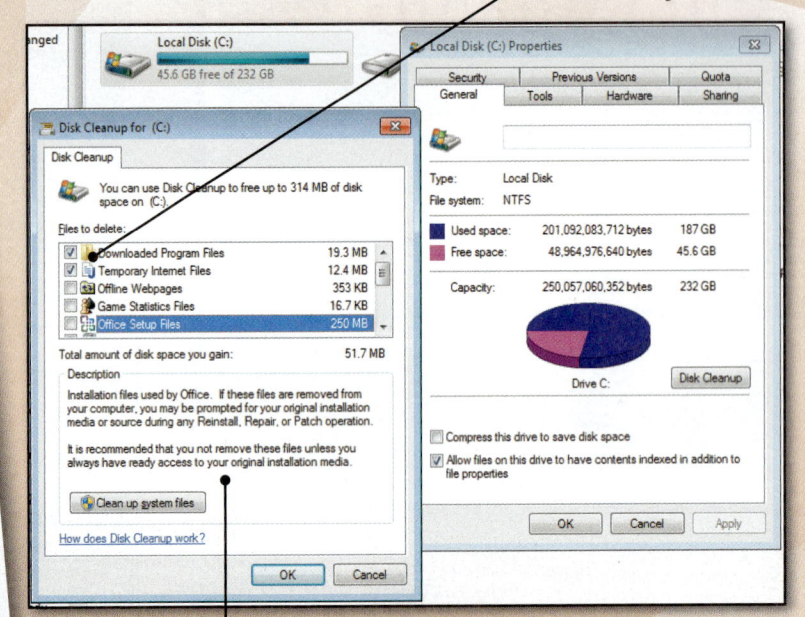

The description for Office Setup Files recommends against deleting them.

GREEN COMPUTING

POWER MANAGEMENT

Did you know that you could cut the energy used by your computer in half, saving between $25–75 a year in energy costs, by using its power management features? That would save more than lowering your home thermostat by 2 degrees or replacing 6 regular light bulbs with compact fluorescents (CFLs). Putting your computer into a low power mode can save on home cooling costs and even prolong the life of your notebook battery.

Energy Star power management features are standard in both Windows and Mac operating systems. Activating these settings is easy and saves both money and resources. The EPA recommends setting computers to sleep or hibernate after 30 to 60 minutes of inactivity. To save even more, set monitors to sleep after 5 to 20 minutes of inactivity. And don't use screensavers—they actually increase energy use!

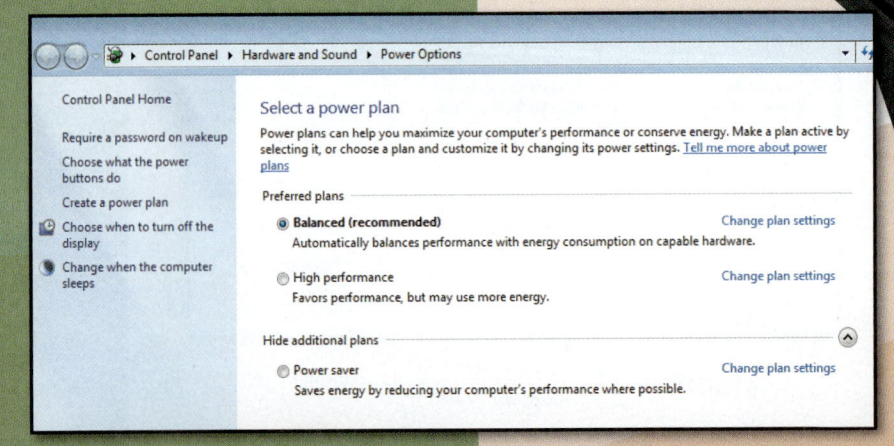

Find Out MORE

Is defragmenting a disk really necessary? Some people say no. Use the Internet to research the controversy. Do you agree with the contention? Why or why not? What Web pages did you find supporting this argument? What credentials does the author have that makes you trust the information you found? Make sure you're using recent information.

The utilities discussed here are included with Windows; however, there are also third-party versions available. The important thing is to remember to use them. Like changing the oil in your car and checking the tire pressure, regular maintenance of your computer will keep it running more efficiently and last longer.

Key Terms

defragmenter

file fragmentation

file system

format

Running Project

Open the disk properties for your primary hard drive (C). What's the disk file system? What is its capacity, and how much disk space is used? Run a Disk Defragmenter analysis. When was the disk last defragmented? What percentage of the disk is currently fragmented?

Four Things You Need to Know

- Utility software helps you to maintain your computer.
- You format a disk to prepare it to hold data.
- Files that are broken up and stored in noncontiguous clusters are considered to be fragmented.
- NTFS is the file system used on Windows-formatted hard drives.

What Can I Do With KNOWLEDGE ABOUT SYSTEM SOFTWARE?

OBJECTIVE 6
Identify the certifications and careers related to system software.

Every personal computer has an operating system, so there will always be work for folks who can install and troubleshoot OS problems. Certifications related to network operating systems are discussed in the networking chapter.

MICROSOFT CERTIFIED TECHNOLOGY SPECIALIST CERTIFICATION

The Microsoft Certified Technology Specialist (MCTS) certification is one way to show your expertise in Windows operating systems. There are currently 16 different MCTS certifications (see Figure 6.19) that you can earn. You must pass one exam for each certification. You can learn more about each certification from the Microsoft website (**microsoft.com/learning/en/us/certification/mcts.aspx**).

- Business Desktop Deployment
- Connected Home Integrator
- Windows Embedded CE 6.0: Application Development
- Microsoft Windows Embedded Standard 2009, Development
- Windows Essential Business Server 2008, Configuration
- Windows Mobile 5.0, Applications
- Windows Mobile 5.0, Implementing and Managing
- Windows Server 2003 Hosted Environments, Configuration and Management
- Windows Server 2008 Active Directory Configuration
- Windows Server 2008 Network Infrastructure Configuration
- Windows Server 2008 Applications Infrastructure Configuration
- Windows Server Virtualization, Configuration
- Windows Small Business Server 2008, Configuration
- Windows Vista – Configuration
- Windows 7 – Configuration
- Windows Internals

FIGURE 6.19 MCTS certifications

MICROSOFT CERTIFIED IT PROFESSIONAL

After you earn an MCTS certification, Microsoft offers another certification called Microsoft Certified IT Professional (MCITP). Each of these certifications (see Figure 6.20) requires you to pass a second exam and is geared toward support technicians with 2 years of experience in the field.

FIGURE 6.20 MCITP certifications

Enterprise Desktop Support Technician 7
Enterprise Desktop Administrator 7
Consumer Support Technician
Enterprise Support Technician

LINUX AND MAC CERTIFICATIONS

Linux certifications are offered by several different organizations, including:

- CompTIA (Linux +)
- Novell (Certified Linux Administrator (CLA) and Certified Linux Desktop Administrator (CLDA)
- Red Hat (Red Hat Certified Technician (RHCT)
- Linux Professional Institute (Linux Professional Institute Certified [LPIC] Level 1–3).

Several Mac OS X certifications are offered through Apple. The first-level certification is Apple Certified Support Professional (ACSP), which requires you to pass one exam. This exam is also required in order to earn higher-level Apple certifications.

JOB OPPORTUNITIES

An entry-level IT job that requires good OS skills is a computer support specialist working at a help desk (see Figure 6.21). Help desk specialists are the folks you speak with when you call or e-mail for tech support. Computer support specialists assist people with computer problems—both hardware and software related. As you can imagine, a good foundation in operating systems is a must. According to the U.S. Bureau of Labor Statistics, by 2016, the demand for help desk jobs will increase by 18 percent.

Certifications and careers that involve computer operating systems abound, and as computers and handheld devices become essential business tools, the demand for support specialists will continue to grow.

FIGURE 6.21 A computer support specialist working at a help desk needs a good foundation in operating systems.

SYSTEM SOFTWARE

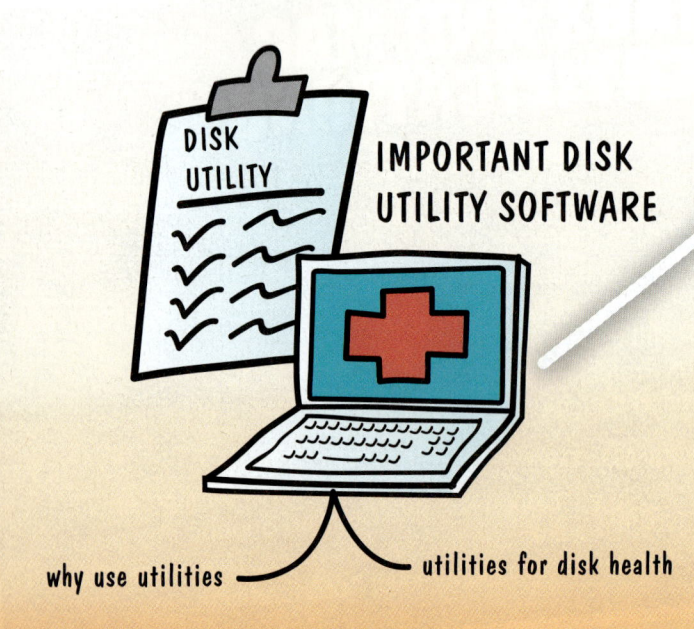

6. CAREERS AND CERTIFICATION
- microsoft certified technology specialist
- microsoft certified IT professional
- linux certification
- job opportunities

5. IMPORTANT DISK UTILITY SOFTWARE
- why use utilities
- utilities for disk health

4. SPECIALIZED OPERATING SYSTEMS
- embedded operating systems
- web operating systems

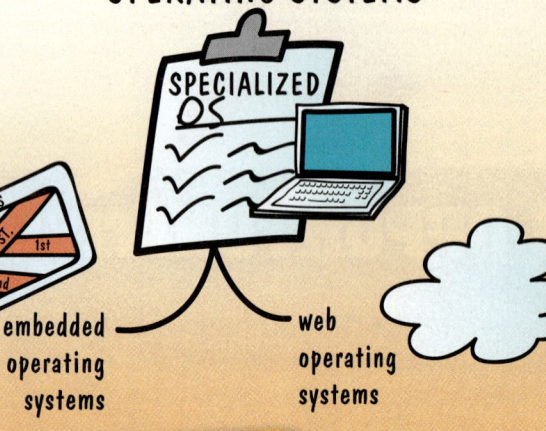

Objectives Recap

1. Explain what an operating system does. (p. 224)
2. Compare the most common stand-alone operating systems. (p. 228)
3. Compare the most common network operating systems. (p. 234)
4. Compare specialized operating systems. (p. 236)
5. List and explain important disk utility software. (p. 240)
6. Identify the certifications and careers related to system software. (p. 244)

Key Terms

application programming interface (API) **227**
beta version **231**
defragmenter **241**
device driver **226**
embedded operating system **236**
file fragmentation **241**
file system **240**
format **240**
graphical user interface (GUI) **224**
Linux **230**
Mac OS X **230**
Microsoft Windows **228**
multitasking **225**
network operating system (NOS) **234**
open source **230**
operating system (OS) **224**
Plug and Play (PnP) **226**
system software **224**
Web OS **238**

WHAT AN OPERATING SYSTEM DOES

1

- manages resources
- manages and controls hardware
- interacts with software
- provides user interface

NETWORK OPERATING SYSTEMS

2

windows server, apache, UNIX, linux

STANDALONE OPERATING SYSTEMS

3

mac, linux, windows

Summary

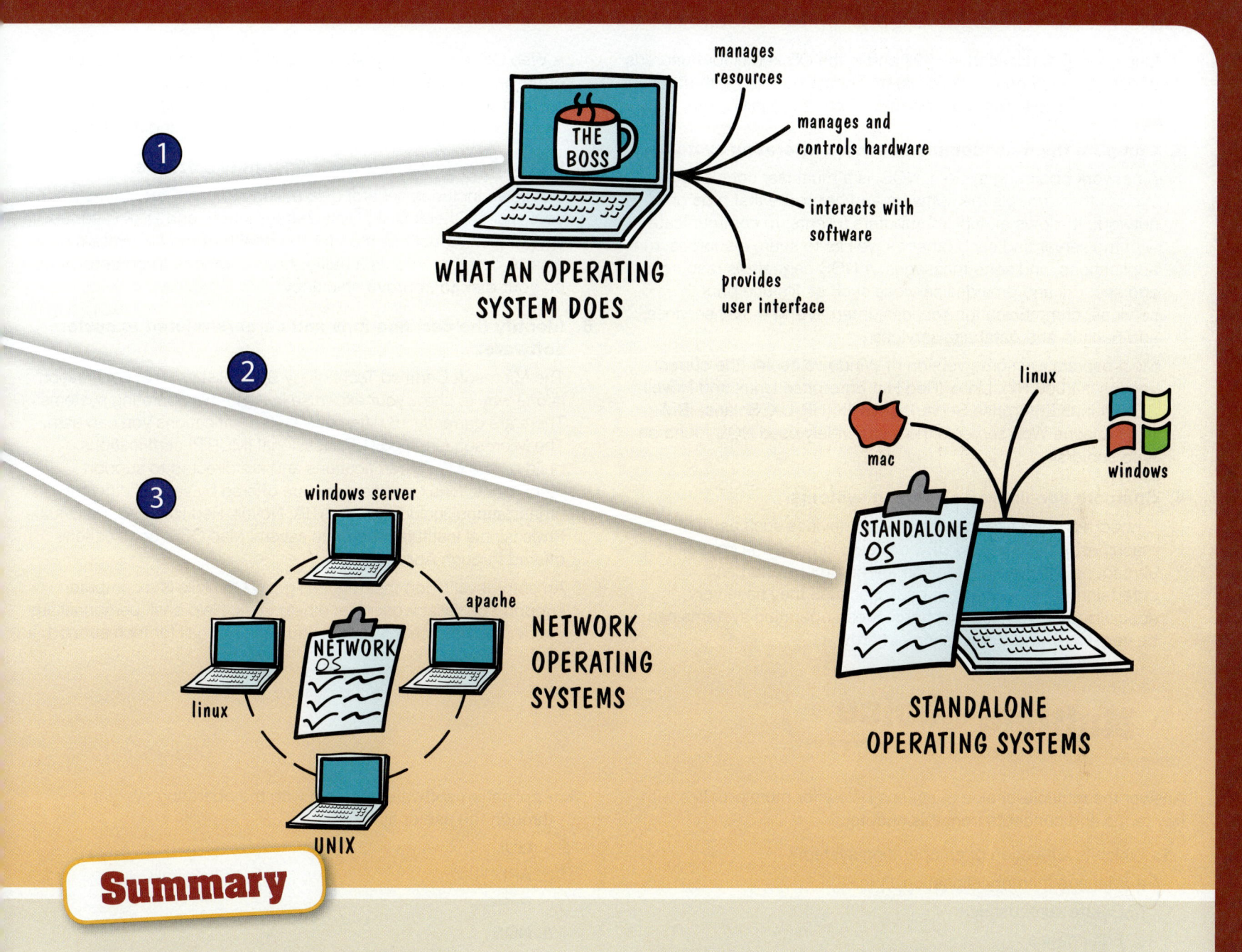

1. **Explain what an operating system does.**

    The operating system (OS) is the most important type of system software because it provides the user with the interface to communicate with the hardware and other software on the computer. The operating system also manages the allocation of memory and processing resources to both hardware and software, manages and controls hardware using Plug and Play and device drivers, and provides services to applications through the use of an application programming interface (API).

2. **Compare the most common stand-alone operating systems.**

    The three most common stand-alone operating systems are Microsoft Windows, Mac OS X, and Linux.

    Windows has been around since 1985, and the current version is Windows 7. Windows is installed on over 90 percent of personal computers.

    The Mac OS has been around since the first Mac computer was released in 1984. The Mac OS only runs on Mac computers, which currently make up about 5 percent of the total personal computer market. The current version is Mac OS X 10.6 Snow Leopard.

Linux was first released in 1991 and is the OS kernel for hundreds of different distributions (distros) that come bundled with utilities and applications. The most popular Linux distro is Ubuntu.

3. **Compare the most common network operating systems.**

   A network operating system (NOS) is a multiuser operating system that controls the software and hardware that runs on a network. It allows multiple computers (clients) to communicate with the server and each other as well as to share resources, run applications, and send messages. A NOS centralizes resources and security and provides services such as file and print services, communication services, Internet and e-mail services, and backup and database services.

   Most servers run some version of Windows server (the current version is 2008 R2), Linux (Red Hat Enterprise Linux and Novell SUSE Linux Enterprise Server), or UNIX (HP-UX, Solaris, IBM AIX). Apache Web server is the most widely used NOS found on Web servers.

4. **Compare specialized operating systems.**

   Embedded operating systems run on devices such as ATM machines, smartphones, GPS devices, video game consoles, ultrasound machines, and even the communication and entertainment system in your car. Because they have very specialized and limited functions, these operating systems can be very small and run on simpler hardware.

A Web OS is a virtual desktop you interact with through your browser. It doesn't matter what desktop operating system you're running. As long as you have a Web browser, you can even use an old, obsolete computer to access your files and applications.

5. **List and explain important disk utility software.**

   Windows includes several disk utilities to help you maintain your disks: Check Disk, Disk Defragmenter, and Disk Cleanup. Disk-checking utilities monitor the health of the file system on a disk. A defragmenter is a utility that rearranges fragmented files on your disk to improve efficiency.

6. **Identify the certifications and careers related to system software.**

   The Microsoft Certified Technology Specialist (MCTS) certification is one way to show your expertise in Windows operating systems. There are currently 16 different MCTS certifications you can earn. The Microsoft Certified IT Professional (MCITP) certifications build on the MCTS certifications and are directed to support technicians. Linux certifications are offered by several different organizations, including CompTIA, Novell, Red Hat, and the Linux Professional Institute. There are several Mac OS X certifications offered through Apple.

   An entry-level IT job that requires good OS skills is a computer support specialist working at a help desk. Help desk personnel are the people you speak to when you call or e-mail for tech support.

Multiple Choice

Answer the multiple-choice questions below for more practice with key terms and concepts from this chapter.

1. Which is a function of an operating system?
   - a. Manage memory allocation
   - b. Create spreadsheets
   - c. Edit images
   - d. Browse the Internet

2. What OS feature makes installing new hardware easy?
   - a. GUI
   - b. API
   - c. Plug and Play
   - d. Multi-touch

3. Application software interacts with the operating system through the use of a(n) _____.
   - a. GUI
   - b. API
   - c. PnP
   - d. NOS

4. Which operating system is found on most personal computers?
   - a. Microsoft Windows
   - b. Mac OS X
   - c. Linux
   - d. UNIX

5. A disadvantage of Mac OS X is that _____.
   - a. it does not have a GUI
   - b. it only runs on Mac computers
   - c. it can't be updated over the Internet
   - d. it can't be used in a home network

6. Which is the most popular NOS found on Web servers?
   a. Windows NT
   b. SUSE Enterprise
   c. Red Hat Enterprise
   d. Apache ✓
7. On what type of device might you find an embedded OS?
   a. Desktop computer
   b. Smartphone ✓
   c. Notebook computer
   d. Server
8. Which is *not* a feature of a Web OS?
   a. Access to applications
   b. Hardware management ✓
   c. File sharing
   d. Security

9. What is the process of preparing a disk for storing files called?
   a. File system sectoring
   b. Defragmenting
   c. Disk cleanup
   d. Formatting ✓
10. What utility should you use to reorganize the files on your disk to improve efficiency?
    a. Disk Defragmenter ✓
    b. Disk Checker
    c. Disk Cleanup
    d. Disk Properties

True or False

Answer the following questions with T for true or F for false for more practice with key terms and concepts from this chapter.

F 1. You can use a computer without an operating system installed.
T 2. Multitasking is the ability to do more than one task at a time.
T 3. Each running application is assigned its own area of memory by the OS.
F 4. Many people don't use Linux because it requires high-end hardware to run.
F 5. A network operating system is necessary to set up a peer-to-peer network.

F 6. A Web OS requires you to install special software on your computer.
T 7. Formatting a disk divides the disk into tracks and sectors to store data in.
T 8. The Disk Cleanup utility identifies files that you might choose to delete to free up disk space.
F 9. Using a screensaver reduces energy consumption on your computer.
T 10. Because it's open source, there are no Linux certifications.

Fill in the Blank

Fill in the blanks with key terms and concepts from this chapter.

1. A(n) **GUI** allows a user to point and click on objects to initiate commands.
2. An OS communicates with hardware by means of a(n) **device driver**.
3. The most common desktop operating system is **Windows**.
4. Snow Leopard is the current version of **Mac OS X 10.6**.
5. Ubuntu is the most popular desktop version of **Linux**.

6. Manufacturers sometimes release a pre-release or **beta version** of software before the final version is released.
7. A(n) **NOS** runs on servers in a client-server network.
8. The OS on a cell phone is referred to as a(n) **embedded OS**.
9. A(n) **Web OS** is a virtual desktop that runs in a browser.
10. The **file system** of a disk keeps track of what files are saved and where they're stored on the disk.

Running Project

. . . The Finish Line

Use your answers to the previous sections of the running project. Assume that you just got a new computer with no software on it. What operating system and version would you install? Select one utility that you consider indispensable to have. Which program did you pick and why?

Write a report describing your selections and responding to the questions raised. Save your file as **Lastname_Firstname_ch06_Project**, and submit it to your instructor as directed.

File Management

Utility software such as disk defragmenters and cleanup utilities help you keep your computer running efficiently. In this activity, you'll use the Disk Cleanup utility to examine some of the files on your computer.

1. Open the Computer window from the Start menu or desktop. What items are listed under *Hard Disk Drives*? Right-click on the C: drive, and choose *Properties* from the context menu. What is the capacity of the disk? How much free space is currently available?

2. Click the Disk Cleanup button. Allow the Disk Cleanup utility to analyze your system. When it's finished, take a screen shot of this dialog box, and paste it into a document.

3. Click on each of the categories of files listed, and read the descriptions in the bottom of the dialog box. What types of files are included in Downloaded Program Files and Temporary Internet Files? What are Temporary Files, and is it safe to delete them? What other categories of files are listed? Which ones have check marks next to them?

4. How much space could you free up if you cleaned up all the files found? Save your file as **Lastname_Firstname_ch06_Cleanup**, and submit it as directed by your instructor.

Critical Thinking 1

Windows Home Server is a network operating system geared toward home users that have more than one computer. Use the Internet to find out about the costs and features of Windows Home Server.

1. Would you buy it? Does it offer a true NOS or is it something else? What is the advantage of using Windows Home Server instead of a simple peer-to-peer network in your home?

2. Write up a two- to three-paragraph summary that includes the answers to the questions above. Save the file as **Lastname_Firstname_ch06_Home_Server**, and submit it as directed by your instructor.

Critical Thinking 2

Your school is still running Windows Vista in the computer lab. It's considering upgrading to Windows 7. As a user of the computer lab, you've been asked to give some input into the decision process.

1. Use the Internet to research the improvements in Windows 7 over Windows Vista. What are the improvements you feel are the most important? Do they require any special hardware or software to be installed?

2. Do you recommend the school upgrade the computer lab? Give two reasons supporting your recommendation.

3. Write up a one-page summary that includes the answers to the questions above. Save the file as **Lastname_Firstname_ch06_Windows_Upgrade**, and submit your assignment as directed by your instructor.

Do It Yourself 1

Utility software is important to protect and maintain your computer. In this activity, you'll examine your computer to determine what type of utility software is installed on it and if it's properly protected.

1. Open the Action Center by clicking on the white flag in the notification area of the Windows taskbar.
2. If necessary, click the arrow next to Security to open that section. What is your status for each category? Are there any important notices? What software is reported for virus protection and spyware?
3. If necessary, click the arrow next to Maintenance to open that section. What is your status for each category? Are there any important notices?
4. Write up your answers to the questions above. Include a screen shot of the Action Center. Save your file as **Lastname_Firstname_ch06_ActionCenter**, and submit your work as directed by your instructor.

Do It Yourself 2

In this exercise, you'll perform a disk check on your flash drive.

1. Insert your flash drive into the computer. If necessary, wait until Windows finishes installing drivers. Close any windows that open automatically.
2. From the Start menu, open the Computer window. Right-click on your flash drive, and choose *Properties*. Open your word processor, and type your answers to the following questions: What file system is on the disk? What's the capacity, and how much free space is on the disk? Take a screen shot of the Properties dialog box, and paste it into your document.
3. Click the Tools tab and click *Check now*. Make sure that only the first box is checked, and click Start. When the scan is finished, click on *See Details*, and take a screen shot of the results. Paste it into your document.
4. Write up your answers to the questions. Save the file as **Lastname_Firstname_ch06_Disk_Check**, and submit your work as directed by your instructor.

Ethical Dilemma

Miriam works at a small company and was just passed over for a promotion, which was given to a new employee Bill because he has a certification. Bill lets it slip that he easily passed the test because he paid $50 for a study guide that had all the test answers in it.

1. Miriam is confused. She has the experience in the company, but Bill got the job because he has the certification. What should she do? Should she report Bill to her employer? To the certification testing center? Borrow the questions and take the exam herself? What would you do?
2. Because this has been a common issue in the past, the certification tests have become stricter and more difficult to cheat on, but it still happens. Use the Internet to find out the penalty for cheating on one of the industry exams mentioned in the chapter.
3. Write up a one-page summary that includes the answers to the questions above. Save the file as **Lastname_Firstname_ch06_Certification**, and submit it as directed by your instructor.

On the Web 1

In this activity, you'll compare the hardware requirements for different versions of Windows.

1. Use the Internet to research the hardware requirements for each of the following versions of Windows: Windows 3.1, Windows 95, Windows 98, Windows XP, Windows Vista, and Windows 7. When there are multiple versions of the OS, choose the original release and the Home (or Home Premium) version.

2. Create a table like the one below.

Windows Version	Year Released	Minimum Processor	Minimum Memory	Minimum Free Disk Space	Optical Disc Type	Other Requirements
Windows 3.1						
Windows 95						
Windows 98						
Windows XP						
Windows Vista						
Windows 7						

3. What websites did you use to locate this information? Save the file as **Lastname_Firstname_ch06_Versions**, and submit your work as directed by your instructor.

On the Web 2

There are literally hundreds of Linux distros available.

1. Search the Web for a list of the 10 most popular Linux distros. List the top 5 distros and their most important features in a table or list.

2. Where did you find your information? Why did you choose this website for your information? What makes you believe it to be reliable?

3. Write up your answers. Save the file as **Lastname_Firstname_ch06_Distros**, and submit your file as directed by your instructor.

Collaboration 1

Instructors: Divide the class into groups of three to five members, and assign each group one topic for this project. The topics include: Windows 7, Mac OS X Snow Leopard, and Ubuntu Linux. For larger classes, assign multiple groups the same operating system.

The Project: Each team is to prepare a commercial that includes an explanation of its operating system and special features that aren't included in this book. Teams must use at least three references, only one of which may be this textbook. Use Google Docs to prepare the outline and script of your commercial, and provide documentation that all team members have contributed to the project. For more on using Google Docs, see Appendix C.

Students: Before beginning this project, discuss the roles each group member will play. Choose a team name, which you'll use in submitting your commercial. Be sure to divide the work among your members, and pick someone to present your project. You may find it helpful to elect a team leader who can direct your activities and ensure that all team contributions are collated through Google Docs.

Outcome: You're to prepare a commercial on your assigned topic. The presentation may be no longer than 2 minutes. You may videotape it or perform it live for your class. On the first page of your written outline, be sure to include the name of your commercial and a list of all team members. Turn in a final version of your outline and script named as **Teamname_ch06_OS_Script**. Submit your project to your instructor as directed.

Collaboration 2

Instructors: Divide the class into six groups, and assign each group one type of embedded OS for this project. The topics include: iPhone OS, Windows Mobile 7, Palm webOS, Symbian, BlackBerry, and Android.

The Project: Each team is to prepare a multimedia presentation or poster for its OS. The presentation should be designed to educate consumers about the OS features. Teams must use at least three references, only one of which may be this textbook. Use Google Docs to plan the presentation, and provide documentation that all team members have contributed to the project. For more on using Google Docs, see Appendix C.

Students: Before beginning this project, discuss the roles each group member will play. Choose a team name, which you'll use in submitting your presentation. Be sure to divide the work among your members, and pick someone to present your project. You may find it helpful to elect a team leader who can direct your activities and ensure that all team contributions are collated through Google Docs.

Outcome: You're to prepare a multimedia presentation or poster on your assigned topic in PowerPoint (or another tool if approved by your instructor) and present it to your class. The presentation may be no longer than 3 minutes and should contain 5 to 7 slides. On the first slide or the back of the poster, be sure to include the name of your presentation and a list of all team members. Turn in a final version of your presentation named as **Teamname_ch06_Embedded** and your Google Docs file showing your collaboration named as **Teamname_ch06_Embedded_Collaboration**. Submit your project to your instructor as directed.

Blogging

Blog about your favorite computer utility or the one that you consider the most important. In your write-up, provide the type of computer you have and the operating system you're using. Outline the things your program does well and things it could do better.

Visit at least two of your classmates' blogs on this topic. On the blogs you visit, provide three to five sentences to convince your classmate to try your program.

Create a document that includes your blog URL and the URLs of the two blogs you commented on. Save the file as **Lastname_Firstname_ch06_Utility_Blog**, and submit the document to your instructor as directed.

CHAPTER 7
The Internet

Running Project

In this chapter, you'll learn about the Internet. Look for project instructions as you complete each article. For most, there's a series of questions for you to research. At the conclusion of the chapter, you're asked to submit your responses to the questions raised.

f Become our friend on Facebook

OBJECTIVES

1. Recognize the importance of the Internet. (p. 256)
2. Compare types of Internet connections. (p. 260)
3. Compare popular Web browsers. (p. 266)
4. Demonstrate how to navigate the Web. (p. 276)
5. Discuss how to evaluate the credibility of information found on the Web. (p. 280)
6. Identify the certifications and careers related to the Internet. (p. 282)

IN THIS CHAPTER

If you're a typical college-aged student, then the Internet has always been around. It has become such a part of our everyday lives that you may already know a lot about it. But there's so much to know that most folks only scratch the surface. The goal of this chapter is to introduce you to the wide variety of tools and information that's literally at your fingertips. When you've finished this chapter, you'll have a broad understanding of the Internet as a whole as well as a good idea of the parts of the Internet that you find particularly useful. You'll have researched, evaluated, and discovered why the Web is so important in today's society and why you need to be fluent in the tools and language of the Internet to be an educated consumer, a better student, and a valuable employee.

Did Al Gore INVENT THE INTERNET?

OBJECTIVE 1
Recognize the importance of the Internet.

Al Gore invented the Internet? Well, no, not really. Al Gore didn't *invent* the Internet, but early on, he recognized its potential and, as a congressman and vice president, promoted its development through legislation. In 2005, he received a Webby Lifetime Achievement Award for his contributions (**Webbyawards.com**). He was one of the first politicians to see the potential of the Internet.

HOW IT ALL GOT STARTED

In 1957, the Soviet Union launched the first space satellite: Sputnik. The United States and the Soviet Union were engaged in a political conflict—called the Cold War—at the time, and this launch led to fears that the United States was falling behind in the technology race. In 1958, President Eisenhower created the Advanced Research Projects Agency (ARPA) to jump-start U.S. technology for the military. One of ARPA's early projects was to create a Galactic Network that would connect smaller networks around the world.

The Internet started as a U.S. Department of Defense ARPA project in the 1960s to design a communications system that had multiple pathways through which information could travel so that losing one part of the system (for example, in a nuclear strike) wouldn't cripple the whole thing. It took about 10 years to develop the technology. The original system was called **ARPANET** and only had four nodes on it (see Figure 7.1). The four nodes were at UCLA, the Stanford Research Institute (SRI), the University of Utah in Salt Lake City, and UCSB (UC Santa Barbara).

FIGURE 7.1 This original drawing of ARPANET shows the first four nodes at UCLA, UCSB, SRI, and the University of Utah. Today's Internet has many millions of nodes, as illustrated on the Internet map (right) captured on January 16, 2010.

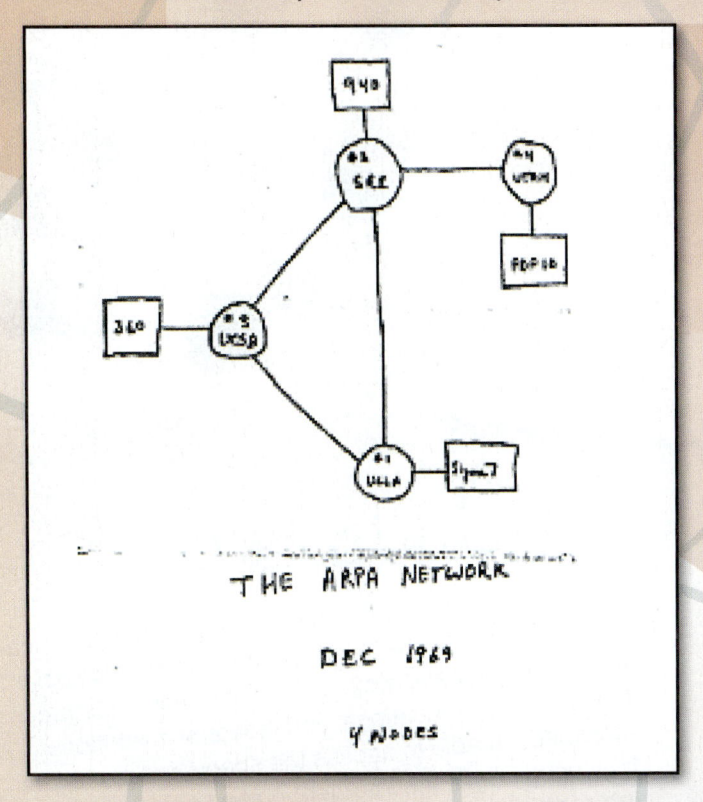

In 1979, the National Science Foundation (NSF) created CSNET to connect the computer science departments at universities using the ARPANET technology. In the mid-1980s, the NSF created NSFNET, giving other academic disciplines access to supercomputing centers and connecting smaller networks together. By the late 1980s, NSFNET was the primary **Internet backbone**—the high-speed connection points between networks. In 1995, NSF decommissioned the NSF backbone, the Internet backbone was privatized, and the first five large Network Access Points (NAPs) that made up the new backbone were established in Chicago, New Jersey, San Francisco, San Jose, and Washington, D.C. Today, the backbone of the Internet is composed of **Internet Exchange Points** around the world.

WORLD WIDE WEB

Most people use the terms "Internet" and "World Wide Web" interchangeably, but they are, in fact, two different things. The **Internet** is the physical entity—a network of computer networks. The World Wide Web, or just Web, is just one way that information moves on the Internet—such as e-mail or file transfer, both of which were around long before the Web was. Instant messaging, P2P (peer-2-peer) file sharing, and VoIP (voice over IP) are other ways that you might use the Internet.

257

In 1991, Tim Berners-Lee and CERN released the hypertext system we know as the **World Wide Web**. **Hypertext** is text that contains links to other text and allows you to navigate through pieces of information by using the links, known as **hyperlinks**, that connect them. The milestone of having a million Internet nodes (networks or ISPs) was reached in 1992, and commercial sites, such as Pizza Hut, began to appear. The first White House website was launched in 1994. In 1993, a group of graduate students led by Marc Andreeson released the Mosaic point-and-click graphical browser for the Web, which later became Netscape. These events led to a user-friendly Internet. A couple years later, Windows 95 was released, and AOL and CompuServe began offering Internet access. As personal computers dropped in price and became more powerful, the Internet grew at an incredible rate, with an estimated 1.6 billion (1650 million) users at the beginning of 2010 (see Figure 7.2). Indeed, it's growing even as you read this article.

FIGURE 7.2 The growth of the Internet: internetworldstats.com/emarketing.htm

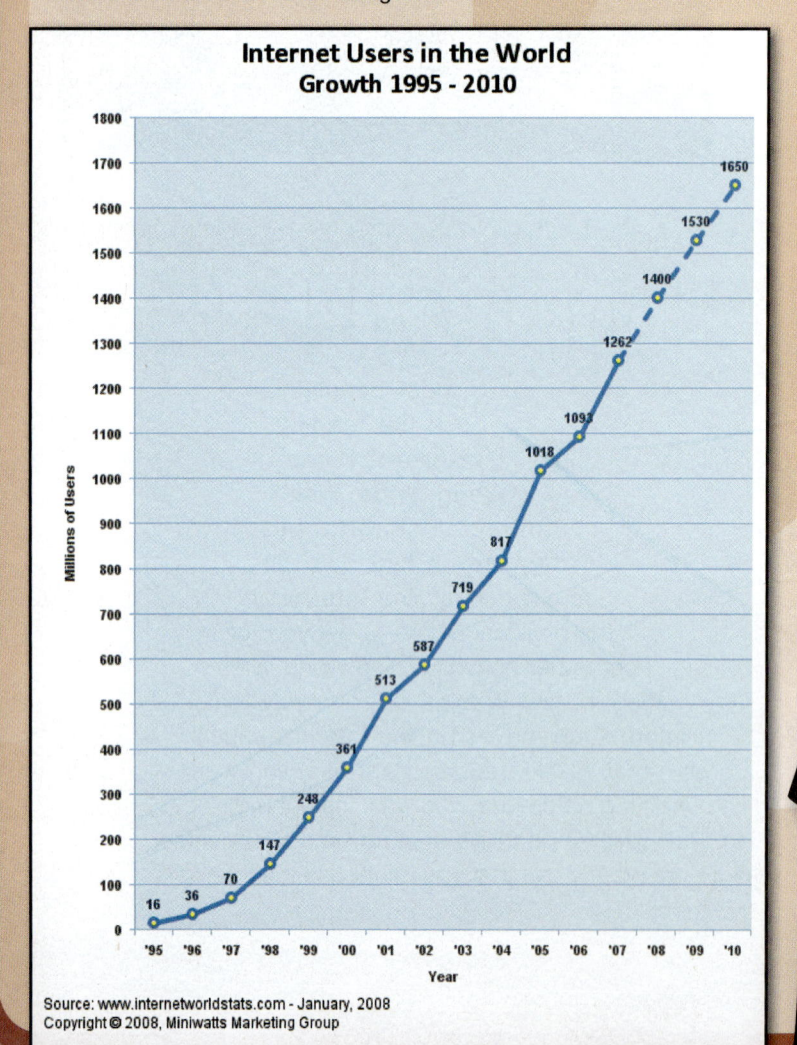

INTERNET2 (I2)

The original uses of the Internet—research and education—have been overtaken by commercial and social uses. Even as bandwidth and the Internet infrastructure increase, educational and research institutions have been unable to access the speed and resources they need. Thus, the Internet2 project was born. **Internet2 (I2)** is a second Internet designed for education, research, and collaboration, very much like how it all began—only faster. In 1995, when NSFNET was decommissioned, there was a small remnant retained just for research called the Very High Speed Backbone Network Service (vBNS), which later evolved into the Internet2 project. While the Internet is composed of a mix of older telephone cables and newer fiber-optics, the I2 backbone is all fiber. The data travels much faster and is less prone to corruption.

Find Out MORE

Wondering what your favorite website used to look like? The Internet Archive Wayback Machine can show you. Go to **archive.org**, and enter the address of the website you want to see. The archives only go back to 1996—so you can't see the original Pizza Hut or White House site, but you can see the 1996 versions. Type in the address of your school's website, and click Take Me Back. Click on several available dates to see how it has changed over time. Try a few other sites that you visit regularly.

Membership in I2 is limited to colleges, universities, other educational institutions, museums and art galleries, libraries, hospitals, and other organizations that work with them. It's a pretty small group, and that's one of the reasons it's so fast. Collaboration, streaming video, and Web conferencing are just some of the applications that benefit from the faster speed. Figure 7.3 shows the muse K20 connectivity survey map.

FIGURE 7.3 Schools around the country are connected to I2.

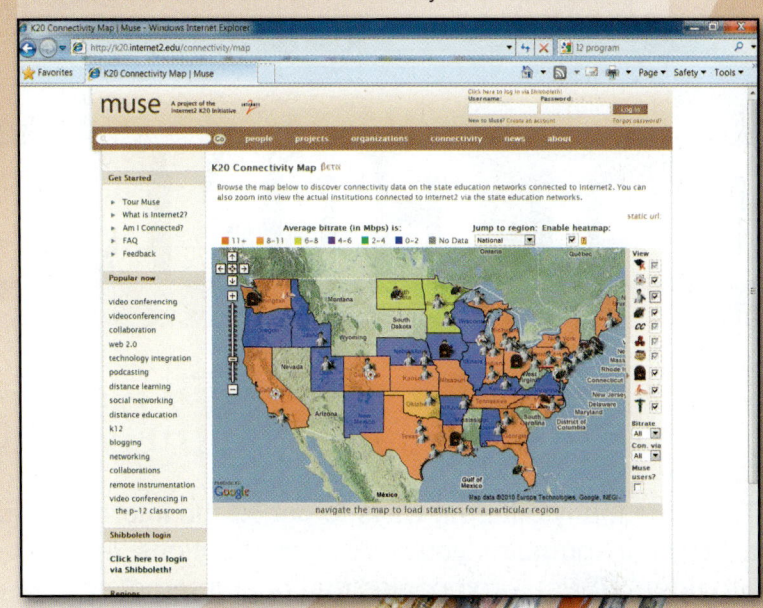

Key Terms

ARPANET

hyperlink

hypertext

Internet

Internet2 (I2)

Internet backbone

Internet Exchange Points

World Wide Web

Running Project

Does your school participate in the I2 project? Ask your librarian or instructor. If yes—what features does your school use? If not—why not?

From its earliest inception, the Internet was designed to be a place for collaboration and information sharing. Today, it's an integral part of education, business, and communication. Even if you don't spend a lot of time surfing the Web, it's hard to deny the impact it has on your life.

3 Things You Need to Know

- ARPANET was the original Internet.
- Hypertext is used to navigate the World Wide Web by using hyperlinks.
- Internet2 is a second Internet designed for education, research, and collaboration.

Get CONNECTED

OBJECTIVE 2
Compare types of Internet connections.

There are many different ways to get on the Internet. If you have a personal computer, you have several options. **Internet service providers (ISPs)**—companies that offer Internet access—offer many different plans from which to choose. The options available to you depend on where you live and how much you have to spend.

SO, HOW DO YOU GET CONNECTED?

A good place to find local ISPs is by searching the Web. If you don't have access at home, most schools and libraries offer free access (see Figure 7.4). Search for a list of ISPs that offer service in your area; there are many websites that compare services and prices for you. Before you begin your search, read the rest of this article to learn about the questions you should ask when comparing packages.

Ask yourself what you need based on how you use the Internet. Do you just check e-mail and look up recipes? If so, a slower connection might work for you. But if you play games, share photos, or watch videos, then you'll need a faster connection. So, what are your options? Speed is essentially the data transfer rate and is measured in kilobits or megabits per second (Kbps or Mbps). For this measurement, the higher the number, the better.

FIGURE 7.4 Most schools and libraries provide free Internet access.

DIAL-UP The least expensive type of connection is usually **dial-up**. With a dial-up connection, you use your regular phone lines to connect to the network. Plans range from about $10 to $30 per month. There are even some companies that will give you free access for up to 10 hours a month. This might be a good backup plan to have in case your normal connection should become unavailable. I have this set up on my notebook for when I travel in case there's no another access where I am. For some people, a dial-up connection may be the only option available. Dial-up can be very slow, maxing out at 56 Kbps (kilobits per second), especially if you're trying to download a file or watch a video. Another drawback is that the connection ties up your phone line while you're online.

BROADBAND If you're looking for more speed, then you have several options: cable, DSL, FiOS, and wireless technologies. The FCC defines **broadband** as anything over 200 Kbps, which is at least four times faster than dial-up and often significantly more than that. Availability, speed, and costs vary depending on where you live. You'll have to do some research to get the best price and service.

Cable Internet access is generally offered by your cable TV provider and uses the same wires to carry both signals. Some cable companies also offer digital phone service. This requires older cable systems to be upgraded, so it's not universally available. Cable speeds range from 1 Mbps (megabit per second) to 50 Mbps but are typically 8 to 20 Mbps. One drawback to using cable Internet access is that you share the cable with your neighbors. This could potentially negatively impact your Internet speed if many neighbors are online at the same time.

DSL (digital subscriber line) uses telephone lines to carry digital signals. Unlike your normal phone line that's designed to carry analog signals (sound), DSL lines are designed to carry digital signals and thus are much faster than ordinary telephone lines. DSL averages speeds of 384 Kbps to 7 Mbps, which is slower than cable; however, it's generally less expensive. One of the biggest problems with DSL is its distance limitations. You must be within 3 miles of the DSL service provider's facilities. The further away you are, the slower your connection will be.

FiOS (Fiber Optic Service) is the fastest of the three broadband alternatives, with top speeds of 50Mbps—but at a premium. FiOS can cost two to three times as much as DSL or cable for the highest speeds. FiOS can carry Internet, TV, and phone calls to your home over fiber-optic cable and is available in limited areas—those where the fiber-optic cable has been installed. Unlike cable and DSL lines, which many people already have, FiOS requires a contractor to lay a fiber-optic conduit directly to the home, which can be costly and involve digging up your lawn.

WIRELESS What if you live in a rural or remote area without cable, DSL, or FiOS access? Are you stuck with dial-up? What about if you're on the road? There are several wireless alternatives available too.

WiMAX Mobile Internet includes 3G and 4G service that allow you to connect to the Internet using cellular networks. The signals are transmitted by a series of towers; thus, coverage isn't universal. 3G, or third-generation, access was launched in 2001 and was the first wireless technology that offered reasonably fast data transfer speeds. The first 4G networks began appearing in 2009 and offer even faster data rates. One advantage of using WiMAX is the fact that you can take it with you—almost anywhere. Coverage maps are available on the providers' websites, allowing you to verify coverage exists where you need it before making the commitment. Although we tend to think about 3G/4G in terms of smartphones, they can be used on personal computers with a special adapter. In some cases, the smartphone can serve as a wireless access point to share the connection with other devices. Special modems make 4G available at home too. Top speeds are considered broadband and can potentially equal those associated with wired broadband service.

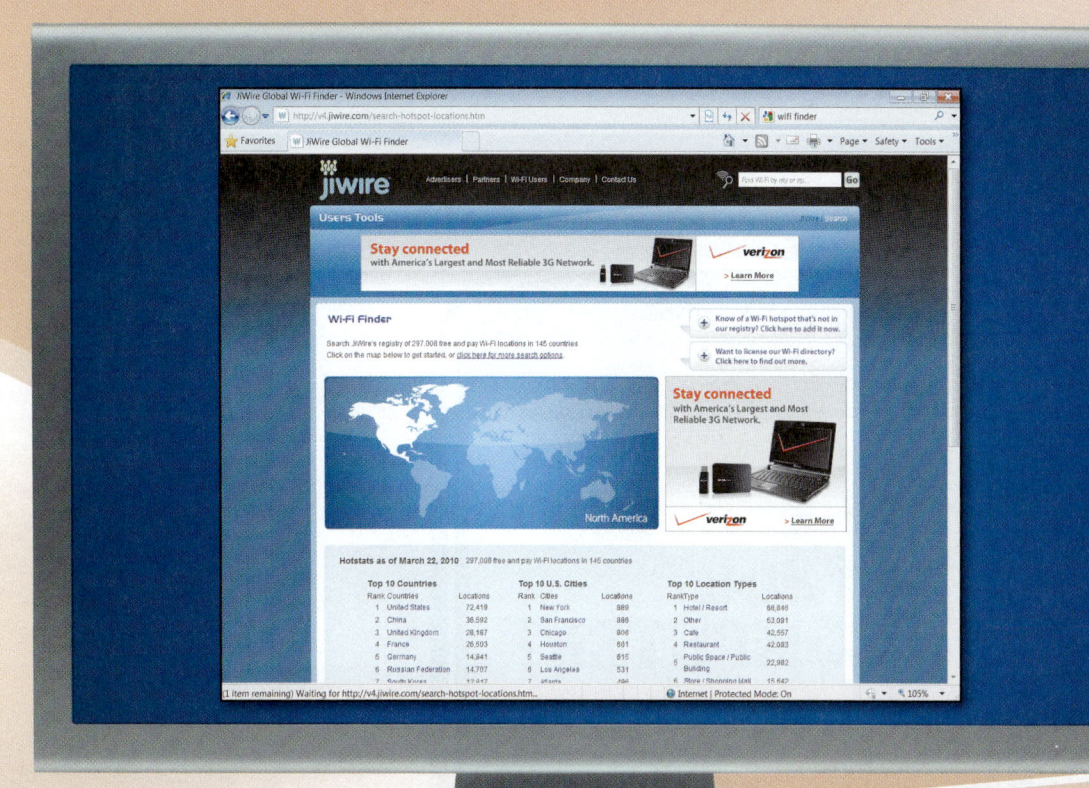

FIGURE 7.5 Jiwire's WiFi Finder can help you locate public hotspots.

Satellite Internet access is a more global and more expensive option. Satellite service speeds are comparable to DSL. You need a clear view of the southern sky, where the communications satellites are positioned, and weather conditions can affect your service. You would probably only consider satellite if there were no other option available where you live.

Municipal WiFi is offered in some cities and towns. CBS Mobile Zone is available in central Manhattan. Wireless Philadelphia currently covers most of the city for free. WiFi **hotspots**, both free and fee-based, are available in many public locations, such as airports, schools, hotels, and restaurants. You can find hotspots by using a website such as jiwire.com (see Figure 7.5). **WiFi** is the same type of wireless networking you may have set up in your home.

Find Out MORE

The National Broadband Plan—Connecting America—is an ambitious plan to assure that all Americans have fast, affordable Internet access. Go to **www.broadband.gov** to find out why the U.S. government considers this so important. What is the status of this project? On the home page, run the Consumer Broadband Test to test your speed. Are your results what you would expect based on the type of Internet connection you have? If not, why do you think there's such a discrepancy?

CONNECTING WITHOUT A COMPUTER?

Today, most cell phones offer at least a limited ability to connect to the Internet. Smartphones, PDAs, video game consoles, and even your media player may be able to connect via cellular or WiFi too. The Amazon Kindle includes free 3G Internet access to shop for and download books and to access Wikipedia. These devices generally have small screens and limited keyboards, which can make using them more difficult. However, they're becoming more powerful and easier to use. Many people rely on such devices as their primary Internet access device. While only about 25 percent of the world's population has personal computers, over 60 percent have cell phones.

Satellite phones connect to satellites instead of cellular towers, making them useful in places where cell service is lacking, such as remote locations. They need a clear view of the sky and don't work well indoors. Satellite phones and satellite phone services are very expensive.

78%

Key Terms

broadband

cable Internet access

dial-up

DSL (digital subscriber line)

FiOS (Fiber Optic Service)

hotspot

municipal WiFi

satellite Internet access

WiFi

WiMAX Mobile Internet

According to the FCC, in 2010, 78 percent of adults in the United States are Internet users, and 65 percent of adults have home broadband access. For those who don't have broadband at home, cost and inaccessibility are often cited as the reasons. Of course, there are always some people that just aren't interested—they don't find any reason to have Internet access at home. But for the rest of us, not having a good Internet connection just isn't an option.

Running Project

Research two types of Internet access that are available where you live. Create a table like the one below to compare the features of each.

PROVIDER	SERVICE TYPE	SPEED UPSTREAM/ DOWNSTREAM	COST	EXTRAS	OTHER

3 Things You Need to Know

- Dial-up is the slowest type of Internet access.
- Broadband Internet access includes cable, DSL, FiOS, and WiMAX.
- The type of Internet access you choose largely depends on where you live.

Surf's UP

3 OBJECTIVE
Compare popular Web browsers.

Some people use the Internet strictly for e-mail, others for day-trading, and others for work. Some folks have specific websites that they visit regularly, while others like to surf and explore. However you use the Web, you need the right tools to access it and enjoy the content. In this article, we discuss the software you need.

BROWSERS

Most information on the Web is in the form of basic **Web pages**, which are written in **HTML (hypertext markup language)**. HTML is the authoring language that defines the structure of a Web page. **Web browsers**, such as Microsoft Internet Explorer and Mozilla Firefox, are programs that interpret the HTML to display Web pages as you browse the Internet. Although these are the most widely used browsers for personal computers, there are actually many alternatives, including Chrome, Opera, and Safari. The first Web browser, Mosaic, was released in 1993. Mosaic eventually became Netscape Navigator, which dominated the market until Microsoft got in the game.

INTERNET EXPLORER First released in 1995, Internet Explorer (IE) has become the leading Web browser. IE is included with Windows, so there's no special download needed. As of this writing, IE8 is the current version, and IE9 is being developed. Figure 7.6 shows a Smithsonian Institute Web page displayed in IE8.

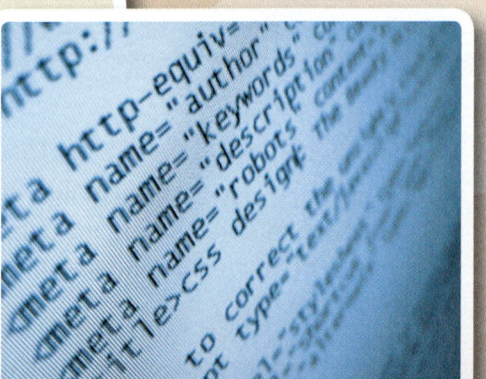

Some important features of Internet Explorer are:

- **Navigation buttons:** Provide a means to navigate back and forward through browsed Web pages
- **Address bar:** Contains the Web address of the current Web page
- **Search box:** Allows you to search the Web from your current Web page without having to go to a search provider's website first
- **Favorites bar:** Allows you to save Web addresses, giving you easy access to your favorite websites. Favorites are sometimes called bookmarks.
- **Tabbed browsing:** Allows you to have multiple Web pages open in tabs
- **Command bar:** Contains easy access to most settings and features of IE

These features are fairly common across most browsers.

FIGURE 7.6 Internet Explorer 8

(Labels: Navigation buttons, Favorites bar, Address bar, Search box, Command bar, Tabbed browsing)

FIREFOX The first version of Mozilla Firefox was released in 2004. At the time, Internet Explorer had become the dominant Web browser and Netscape was at the end of its life. By 2007, Firefox had approximately 16 percent of the market share. By the beginning of 2010, Firefox has increased its market share to about 24 percent. Figure 7.7 shows weather.com in Firefox.

If you compare the Firefox image with the IE image, you'll see that they're very similar. Many people use IE simply because it comes with Windows. Firefox is free and easy to install; however, it requires you to go out and download it.

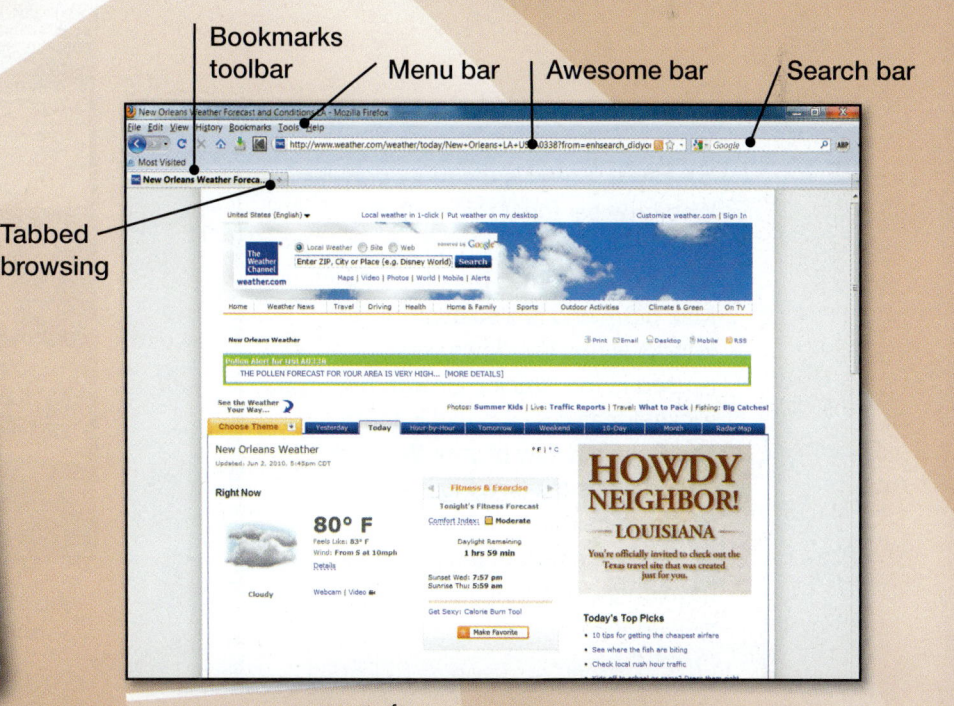

FIGURE 7.7 Mozilla Firefox

(Labels: Bookmarks toolbar, Menu bar, Awesome bar, Search bar, Tabbed browsing)

Chapter 7 | 267

CHROME The newest browser is Google Chrome (see Figure 7.8). Released in 2008, Google Chrome has about a 6 percent market share as of this writing. Comparing it to the previous images, you'll see that it has a streamlined interface but is still very similar to both IE and Firefox. Chrome's main focus is on speed, and it does load Web pages faster than other browsers; but it's still not as full-featured as Firefox and IE.

FIGURE 7.8 Google Chrome

SAFARI Safari is the most popular Web browser for Macs but has an overall market share of about 5 percent. It comes bundled with Mac OS X and is also available for Windows (the Windows version is used in this article). One of the slickest features of Safari is the Top Sites preview of your 24 most visited websites (see Figure 7.9). Safari places stars in the corners of the thumbnails of the sites that have changed since the last time you viewed them.

FIGURE 7.9 The Windows version of Safari

MOBILE BROWSERS Small screen devices, such as PDAs and cell phones, use **mobile browsers**, which are sometimes called **microbrowsers** (see Figure 7.10). IE, Firefox, Safari, and Opera all come in mobile versions. Other microbrowsers are proprietary—such as the Kindle, Android, and Blackberry browsers.

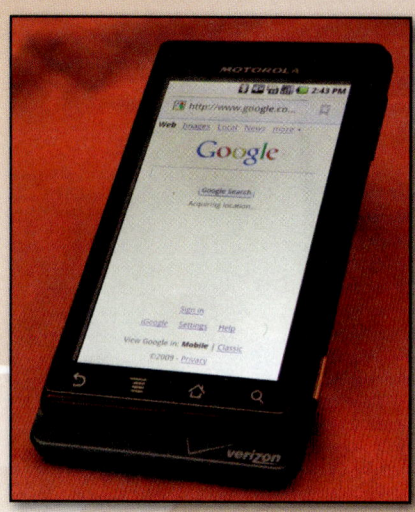

FIGURE 7.10 Microbrowsers are optimized for small screens.

CONFIGURING YOUR WEB BROWSER

The first time you open any browser, it will have default settings, such as the home page and search provider, but you can (and should) customize it for your own use. In this example, we'll look at IE8, but the same basic concepts apply to most browsers.

SETTING THE HOME PAGE The term **home page** has several meanings. It can mean the first page of a website, but in this case, it means the Web page that appears when you first open your browser. The default home page for IE is msn.com unless your computer manufacturer or ISP has altered it, in which case it is probably the company home page. You can set any page you want as your home page. In fact, because most browsers support tabbed browsing, you can actually set multiple home pages. Think about the things that you do as soon as you open your browser. Do you check Facebook? Web mail? Weather? Stock prices? Traffic? These are the things that will help you choose your home page(s). I have three home pages: one for my iGoogle page, one for Facebook, and one for my work e-mail (see Figure 7.11).

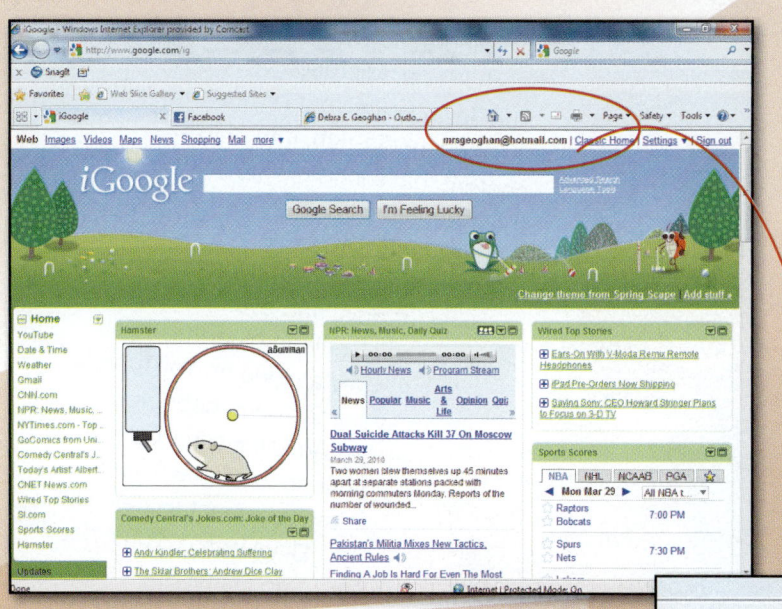

Click the house icon to go to your home page. Click the arrow next to it to add or change your home page(s).

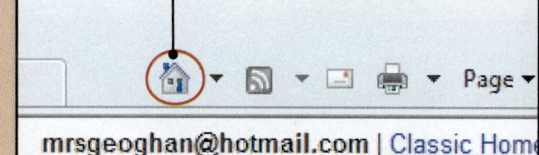

FIGURE 7.11 My home pages in IE8

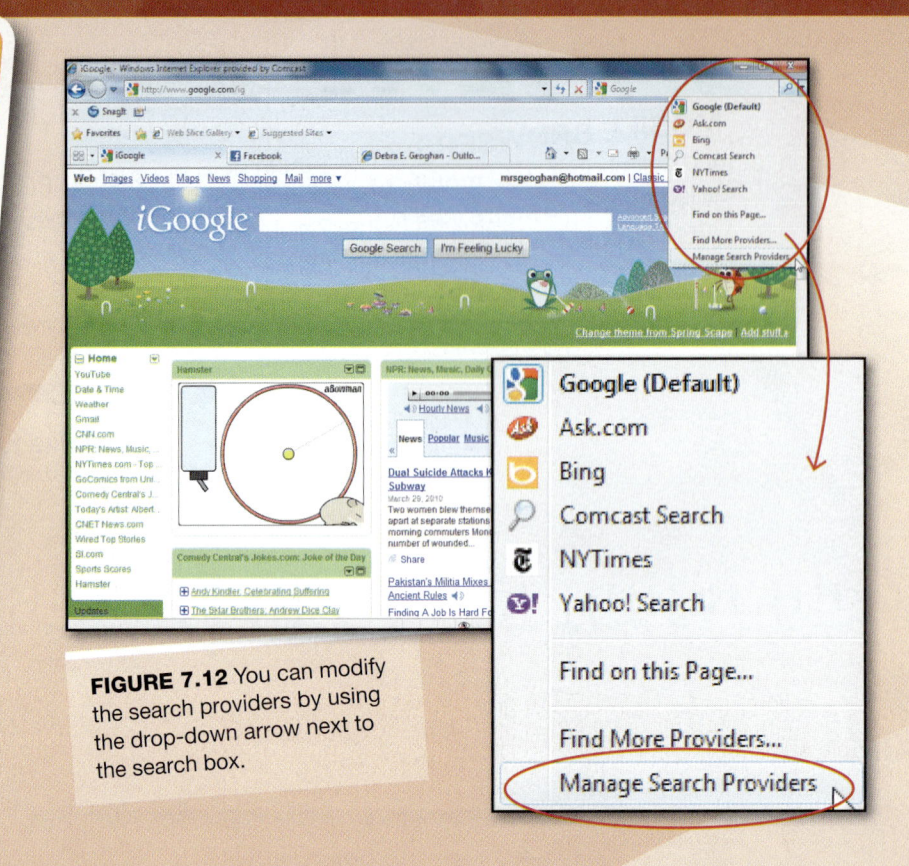

SETTING THE SEARCH PROVIDERS When you type a search term in the search box in IE, what search provider is used? By default, the search provider will either be Microsoft Bing or the provider your computer manufacturer or ISP chose. But as with your home page(s), you can modify this to your own favorites. Click the arrow next to the search box, and you'll see what search providers are already set up. You can choose any one of them during a search by clicking the name from the list, but if you want to change which is the default, choose *Manage Search Providers* from the menu. If your favorite isn't in the list, choose *Find More Providers* instead (see Figure 7.12).

FIGURE 7.12 You can modify the search providers by using the drop-down arrow next to the search box.

ADD-ONS, PLUG-INS, AND TOOLBARS

You can extend the functionality of your Web browser by installing add-ons, plug-ins, extensions, and toolbars. The term "extension" tends to be used to refer to all of them. The distinction between the terms "add-on" and "plug-in" varies by browser. A **plug-in** is a third-party program, such as Adobe Reader. An **add-on** is created for a specific browser to add features to it. Firefox is the king of add-ons—there are hundreds of them available. My favorites allow me to capture video from the Web and block ads. IE has a smaller number of add-ons, but some of my favorites give me quick access to maps and shopping. Adding a toolbar to your browser gives you quick access to the features of the application that installed it.

Plug-in software, such as Adobe Flash Player, Microsoft Silverlight, and Sun Java, helps your browser to display the multimedia-rich, interactive, dynamic content that's increasingly common on the Internet. You don't need a plug-in to view a static Web page of text, such as a Wikipedia page; but dynamic content, videos, games, and even the flashy ads you see all rely on plug-ins. If you try to view a video on YouTube or play games on Facebook, you need Adobe Flash Player. If your school uses a learning management system like Blackboard, you'll need to install Sun Java on your computer. Installing plug-ins is quick and free.

Internet Explorer

Mozilla Firefox

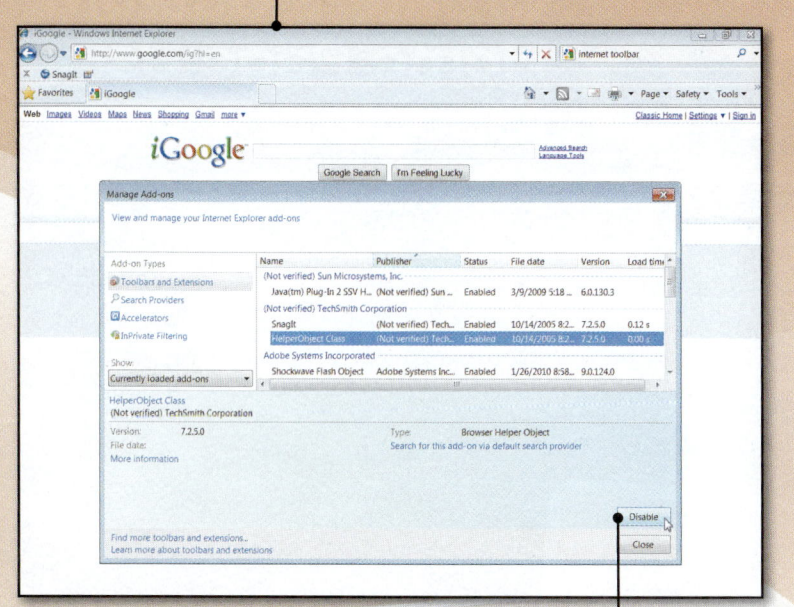

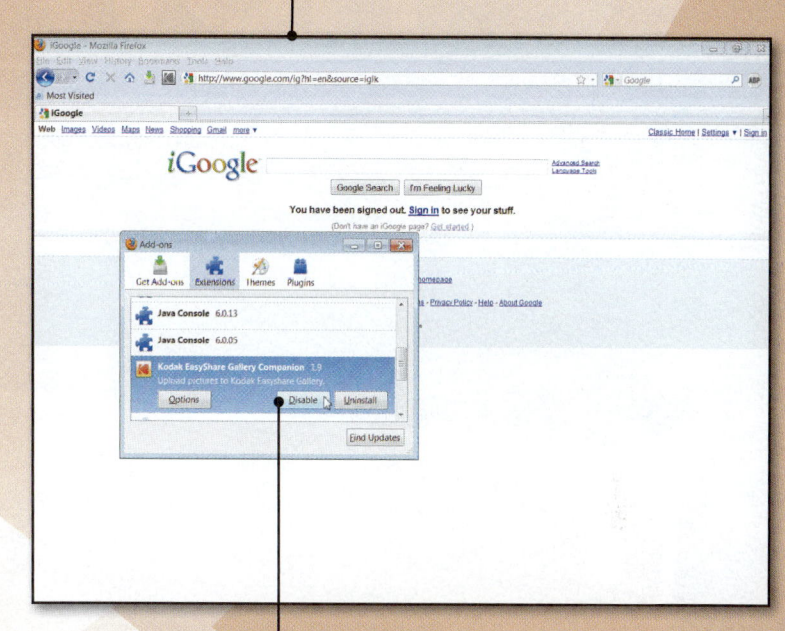

FIGURE 7.13 Managing IE and Firefox add-ons

Select an add-on, and click Disable to stop it from running.

Select an add-on, and click Disable to stop it from running.

To see which add-ons and plug-ins are installed on your computer in IE, open the Tools menu, and click *Manage Add-ons*. In Firefox, choose *Add-ons* from the Tools menu. Figure 7.13 shows some of the add-ons installed on my IE and Firefox browsers. From this window, you can disable add-ons that you don't want.

For many people, choosing a browser is largely a matter of using whatever is available or preinstalled on their device. You do, however, have options if you're not happy with that choice. Also, remember that you can and should customize your browser to fit your needs. Make it work for you, and you'll enjoy the experience even more.

Key Terms

add-on

home page

HTML (hypertext markup language)

mobile browser (microbrowser)

plug-in

Web browser

Web page

Running Project

Research the version and market shares of the top five Web browsers. How has this changed since this article was written? Are there any in the current list of five that were not mentioned in this book?

3 Things You Need to Know

- The most popular Web browsers are: Internet Explorer, Firefox, Chrome, and Safari.
- You can customize the home page and other settings in most browsers.
- Add-ons and plug-ins extend the functionality of Web browsers.

HOW TO Create a Custom Home Page Using iGoogle

When you open your Internet browser, your home page displays. This home page can be any Web page you want. In fact, with browsers that support tabs, you can have multiple home pages. The default home page for your browser is set by the browser publisher, the computer manufacturer, or your ISP, but you're not locked in to the choices they made for you. In this activity, you learn how to create a personalized home page using iGoogle.

1 If necessary, first create a Google account. You'll need one if you want to keep the customizations we're going to do in this exercise. Creating a Google account is easy. Just go to **Google.com**, click *Sign in*, and click *Create an account now*. Answer a few questions, and you're all set. Now that you have a Google account, you can create an iGoogle page that aggregates many of your favorite Web features on your home page. Here's a picture of mine: But of course, this is customized for me—not you. Follow the steps below to create your own iGoogle page.

2 Go to **igoogle.com**. The first time that you log in to iGoogle, the *Create your own homepage in under 30 seconds* screen is displayed. Click the check boxes for the content that interests you (don't worry—you can change these later), select a theme (you can also change this later), enter your country and zip code, and click *See your page*. If you already have an iGoogle page, skip to step 3.

Voilà! You have an iGoogle page! You can leave it just as it is or you can customize it further by modifying the gadgets on the page.

CLICK CHECK BOXES FOR YOUR INTERESTS.

SELECT A THEME.

ENTER LOCATION INFORMATION.

SEE YOUR PAGE.

Chapter 7 | 273

CUSTOMIZE OR CLOSE A GADGET USING THE ICONS ON THE TOP BAR.

YOU CAN DRAG A GADGET TO A NEW LOCATION.

3 You can rearrange the elements simply by dragging and dropping them. Spend a few minutes looking at the items that Google selected for you. Are they what you would have picked? Move them around, and close the gadgets that you don't want.

CHANGE THEME | ADD STUFF

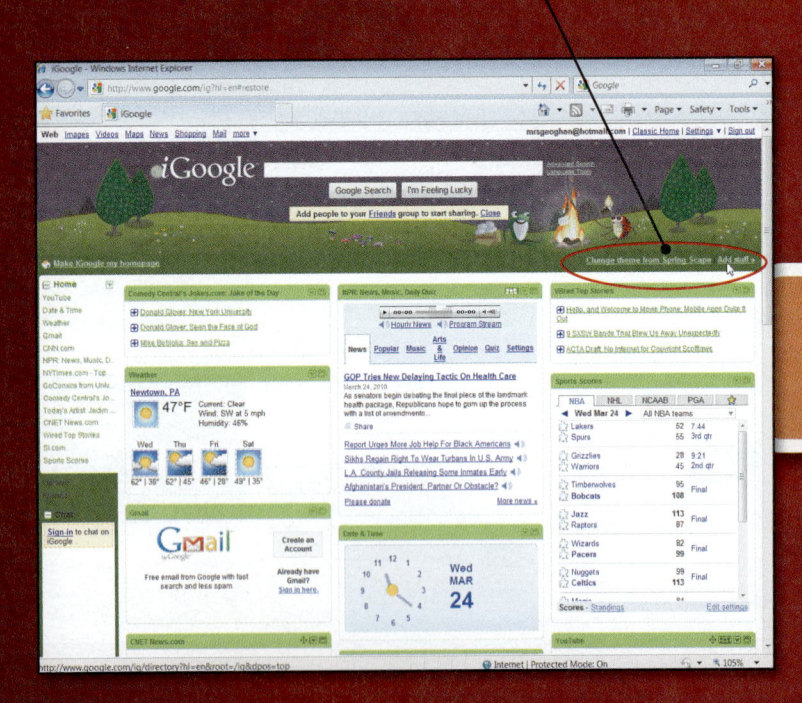

4 Let's add some new content. In the upper-right corner, click *Add stuff* (notice this is where you can also select a new theme).

HOW TO

274

5 The Gadget Gallery lists many different gadgets you can add to your page. Browse around or use the search feature to find a few that you like, and add them to your page. I added the hamster—totally useless but amusing.

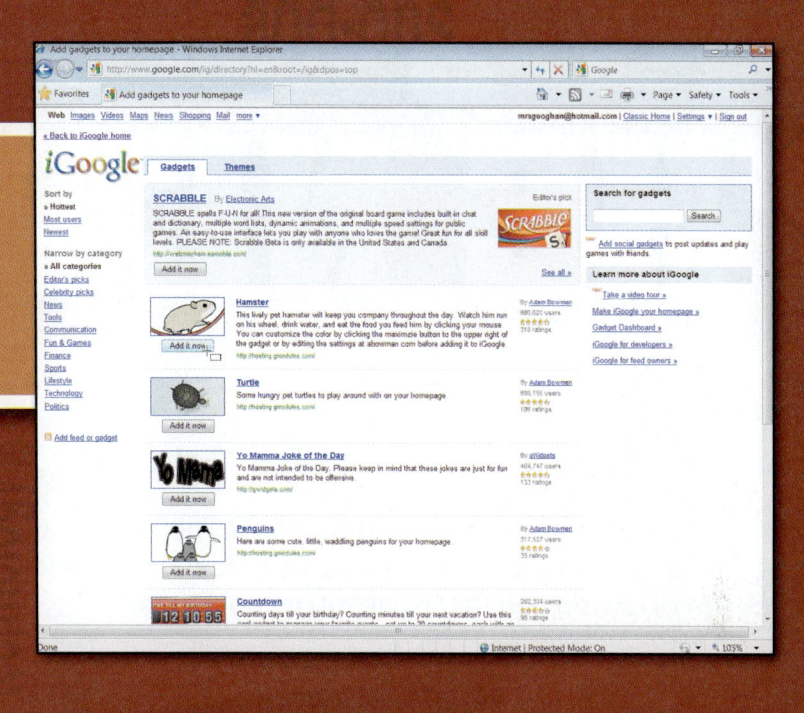

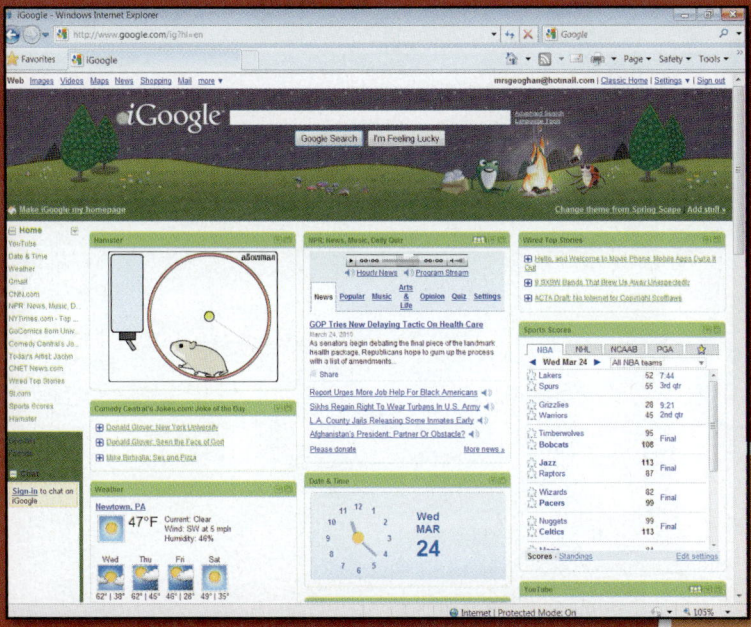

6 Once you've finished customizing your iGoogle page, open a new document, and explain the steps you took to create your page. Which gadgets did you add/delete and why? Take a screen shot of your page, and paste it into the document. Save the file as **Lastname_Firstname_ch07_HowTo**, and submit it as directed by your instructor.

Navigating THE NET

4 OBJECTIVE
Demonstrate how to navigate the Web.

Congratulations—you're connected. Now what? There's so much information out there, it can be overwhelming. How do you know where to start? How do you find what you're looking for?

WEB ADDRESSES

Let's start with the basics of how navigation works. There are two ways to move around the Web. First, you can type in the **URL (uniform resource locator)** or address of the website you want to visit (such as **http://www.google.com**) or you can follow links embedded in Web pages (remember Tim Berners-Lee) from one place to the next. Most people do both. A **website** consists of one or more Web pages that all are located in the same place. The home page of a website is the main or starting page. It's the page you see when you type in the Web address for a site.

Let's look at the parts of a URL.

http://www.google.com

http is the protocol that tells your computer what type of page you're looking at. This is almost always http (a Web page) but can be https (a secure Web page), ftp (file transfer protocol), or others. It is so likely to be http that you can actually leave this part of the address out when you type it.

http://www.google.**com**

.com is known as the **top-level domain (TLD)** and represents the type of website you're visiting. Common TLDs are .com (commercial), .edu (educational), and .gov (government). Today, there are so many websites that more TLDs are needed. Websites outside the United States often have a country code TLD, such as .ca (Canada) or .af (Afghanistan).

http://www.**google**.com

The **domain name** precedes the TLD and is sometimes called the second-level domain. In our example, google is the domain name. The domain name represents a company or product name and makes it easy for us to remember the address.

http://**www**.google.com

The *www* represents the computer on the google domain and is called the third-level domain. It is common to name the computer www, so this part of the URL is also often omitted.

276 | OBJECTIVE 4

So, typing http://www.google.com or merely google.com will result in the same thing. And from there, the fun begins. In this book, the http://www part of a URL is generally omitted.

When you visit other pages on a website, the URL will have an additional part after the TLD. For example, to view the page about the band Tom Petty and the Heartbreakers on Facebook, you can type **facebook.com/TomPetty**.

ICANN (Internet Corporation for Assigned Names and Numbers) coordinates the Internet naming system. Computers speak in numbers, so computers on the Internet are assigned **IP (Internet protocol) addresses**. Like phone numbers, these IP addresses must be unique.

FIGURE 7.14 The Domain Name System is a directory system for the Internet.

IP addresses are composed of numbers, which can be hard for a person to remember, so the DNS system was developed. **DNS (Domain Name System)** allows us to use a friendly name like flickr.com instead of an IP address like 165.193.123.253 to contact a website. DNS works like a telephone directory. When you enter a URL in your browser, your computer requests the IP address of the computer. Your DNS server, which is probably provided by your ISP, locates the IP address information and sends it back to your computer, which then uses it to address your request (see Figure 7.14).

Find Out MORE

Check out the current list of TLDs at the iana.org website. What are some of the gTLDs in the list that are less common? What is the difference between a ccTLD and a gTLD?

SMART SEARCHING

When did Google become a verb? The verb google—to use the Google search engine to obtain information about (as a person) on the World Wide Web—was added to the Merriam-Webster Dictionary in 2001. With billions of Web pages on the Internet, how do you begin to find what you're looking for, and when you do find it, how can you trust it? Searching for information on the Internet is a crucial skill in today's world. While it may seem that everything you want to know is on Google, the fact is that Google only covers part of the Internet. Also, when you type in a search like the words dog care in a search page such as Google, you'll likely get *millions* of results or hits. So, the first part of the puzzle is knowing how to ask the right question.

Let's use Google in our example. Typing in the word eagles on the Google website today got me 37 million hits (see Figure 7.15). Because the Web is constantly changing, if you perform the same search today, your numbers will probably be different. So, where do I start? A good approach is to look at the first few hits and see if what you want is there. If not, it's time to think about a better way to ask the question. To narrow down the results, I can add some more keywords to the search. The first few hits using the word eagles got me the football team and the rock band. I need to be more specific in my query if I'm really interested in the kind of eagles that fly! I can do this by adding more terms to my search, such as birds, raptors, or bald. To get narrower search results, I can use the advanced search tool to filter the results. I can add or exclude terms as well as specify a language and date, among other things. The advanced search options are fairly common for different search sites too.

You can also use Boolean operators to refine your search. Figure 7.16 shows the eagles search using various Boolean operators.

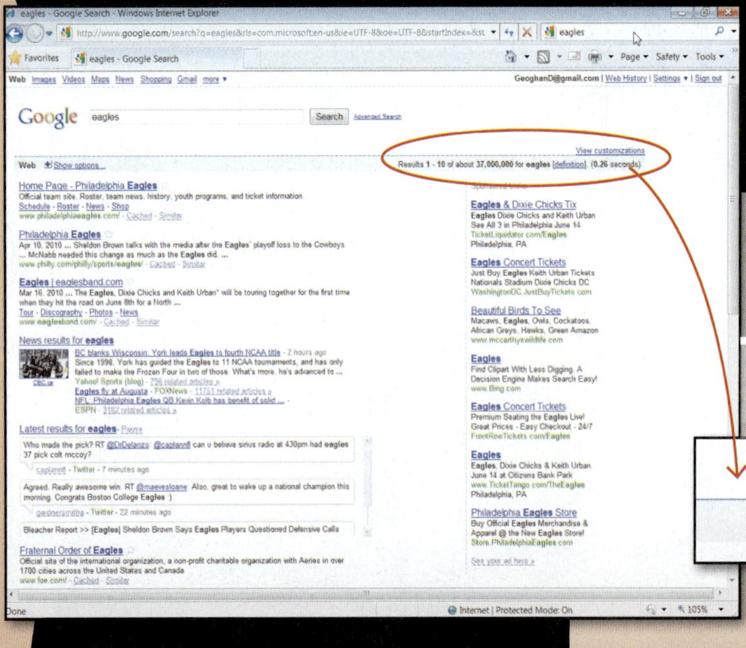

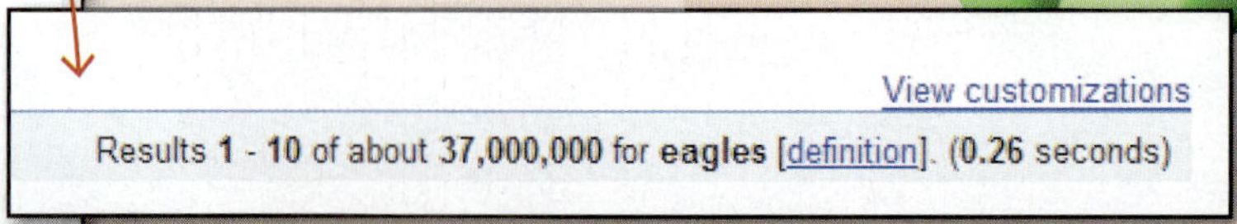

FIGURE 7.15 My Google results for the search term eagles

FIGURE 7.16 Using search filters in Google

TERMS	SEARCH FILTER/ BOOLEAN OPERATOR	RESULTS
eagles	None	37,000,000
eagles AND birds	AND	5,720,000
eagles OR birds	OR	142,000,000

What's the difference between search tools? **Search engines** are huge databases. They send out software (called spiders or bots) to crawl the Web and gather information, which is then indexed. Because the Web is dynamic and constantly changing, this method helps the search engine stay up-to-date. Some search engines also accept submissions, and others use both methods to gather information. There are even metasearch engines that search other search engines. There may also be differences in the way the information is classified and categorized.

There are so many places to search for information that it can be hard to figure out where to start. Contrary to popular belief, Google doesn't index the entire Web, so it's wise to become familiar with at least a couple of other search tools you can use.

Key Terms

domain name

DNS (Domain Name System)

IP (Internet protocol) address

search engine

top-level domain (TLD)

URL (uniform resource locator)

website

Running Project

Think Google and Yahoo! are the only search engines around? Try googling to see how many you get. How many of them have you used in the past? Select two that look interesting, and search for the name of your favorite sports team on each. Did you get the same results? How were they different? Read the About section of the search tool to determine how content is added. You can usually find this link at the bottom of a Web page. What are some of the unique features of each?

5 Things You Need to Know

- A Web address is also known as a URL.
- TLDs are .com, .edu, .gov, and so on.
- DNS allows us to use URLs instead of IP addresses to access websites.
- Every node on the Internet has a unique IP address.
- Search engines are databases that index the Web.

Would I LIE TO YOU?

5 OBJECTIVE
Discuss how to evaluate the credibility of information found on the Web.

So, now that you have your three million hits, how do you know what to believe? The Internet is full of **user-generated content**—content that has been written by everyday users. While there's a lot of wonderful content out there, the truth is anyone can say anything. You need to be able to evaluate the information you find. There are many clues to look for when deciding whether a website is one that you can trust. Here are just a few.

WHO WROTE IT?

Do you believe everything you hear? Or everything you read? Do you evaluate the credentials of the people that you take advice from? How did Bernie Madoff scam so many people? He was convincing. He was believable, and nobody questioned his results until it was too late—even though what he promised was too good to be true. Be a skeptic when evaluating information you find on the Internet.

Look at the URL. Ask yourself: Is it a restricted TLD like .edu or .gov or a general one like .com? Take a look at **www.nasa.gov** and **nasa.com**, and compare them (see Figure 7.17). The .com version isn't the true NASA website. Because we're in the habit of typing .com not .gov, many times we end up at a site we didn't intend to. Some organizations go so far as to own both domains so you can't make that mistake—for example, you can reach the U.S. Post Office website by typing usps.com or usps.gov. A restricted TLD such as .edu or .gov gives some authority to a site, but even that's not a guarantee that the author is credible.

For more information, read the home page and About Us page, and look for the credentials of the author or organization. Ask yourself if there are any conflicts of interest or obvious biases. Is there contact information? How up-to-date is the website? You can usually find this information at the bottom of the home page. If you can't find any of this information, it should raise a red flag.

Stick to well-known sources for important information. If you're looking up health advice, WebMD and the American Cancer Society websites are trustworthy authorities. On the other hand, **skipyourselfhealthy.info** may not be. Then again—it might, but you'll need to do a bit of research before you can be sure.

FIGURE 7.17 The NASA website, which is part of the restricted TLD .gov, is quite different from the nasa.com website.

I typed nasa.com, but ended up here instead.

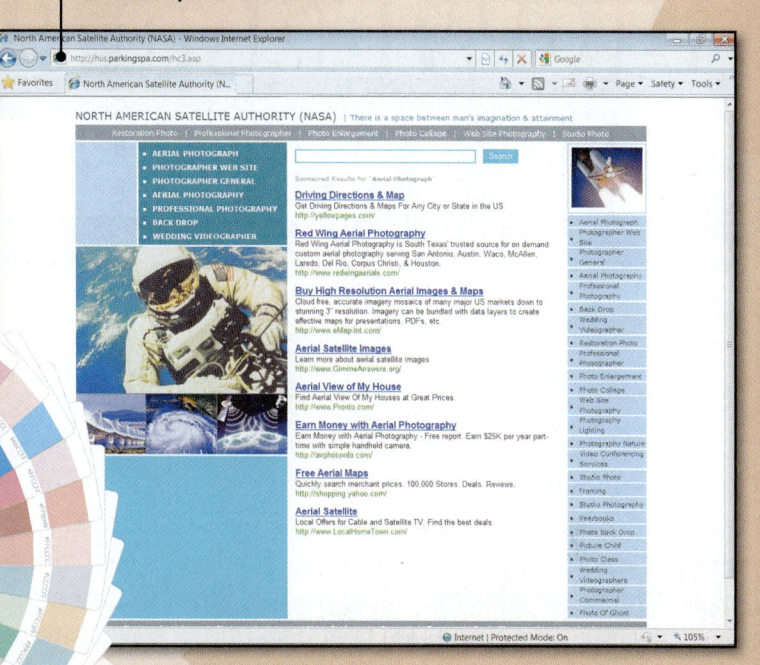

WHAT ABOUT THE DESIGN?

Look at the design of the site, including its sophistication, grammar, and spelling. What impression do you get from the site? But don't be fooled—a well-designed and executed site can still have bad information, and a poorly designed site might have really good information.

Finally, take a look at other sites. Does this information match what you can find on other sites that cover the same topics? Does it make sense? This is really key. If it's too good to be true, it probably is.

Critically evaluating the information you find on a website is a skill that takes time to master. It may not be a big deal if you believe a website that says you should eat tofu to make your hair grow (although it probably won't work), but if you follow advice to invest all your money and it turns out to be a scam, then it will be a huge deal.

Key Term

user-generated content

Running Project

Compare these two websites: **www.mypyramid.gov** and **www.foodpyramid.com**. Use the guidelines discussed in this article to evaluate and compare the two.

4 Things You Need to Know

- User-generated content means anybody can create content on the Web.
- Use the home page, contact information, and About pages of a website to look for credentials of the author or organization.
- Restricted TLDs include .gov and .edu., and they add some credibility to the content.
- Good website design doesn't guarantee credible website content.

Chapter 7 | 281

What Can I Do With Knowledge About THE INTERNET?

6 OBJECTIVE
Identify the certifications and careers related to the Internet.

Just about any career that requires research relies on the Internet is some ways, and most businesses have a Web presence. Creating a website and effectively using the underlying technologies requires employees with lots of technical skills. When most people want to find a business, they start on the Web, so companies that don't have a website or have a poorly designed website are at a disadvantage.

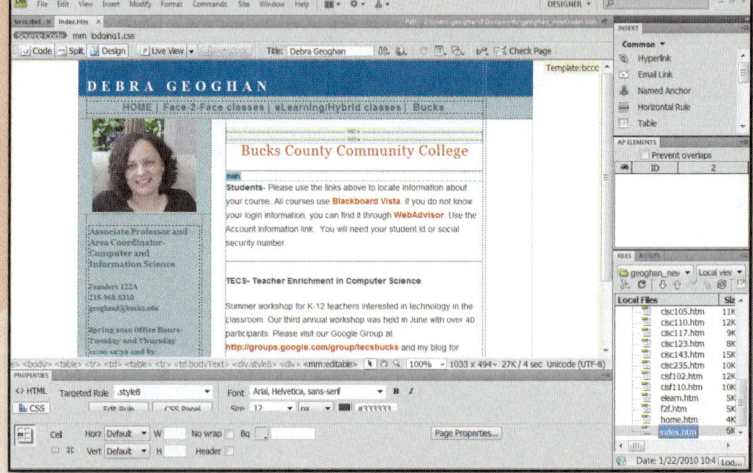

WEB DESIGNER

The person that decides how a website will look is called the Web designer. If the website is simple, the Web designer may also be the person that creates the website. If you have ever created your own Web page, then you were the designer.

Today, it's pretty easy to create a basic website. There are software programs, templates, and websites that can help you make something quickly and easily. Figure 7.18 shows my school Web page being edited using Adobe Dreamweaver. The design was created from a template included with the software. A professional Web designer, however, goes beyond the basics and creates designs from scratch that are customized and branded for a business.

FIGURE 7.18 A simple, template-based Web page created using Adobe Dreamweaver

A Web designer needs to have a good understanding of the capabilities of the Web to design an interesting, dynamic, and professional site. Some Web designers are self-taught; others have degrees in graphic arts, computer science, e-business, or marketing.

WEB DEVELOPER

A Web developer is a computer programmer or software engineer that specializes in creating Web applications using technologies like JavaScript, PHP, and Ajax to create dynamic and interactive websites (see Figure 7.19). This career generally requires at least a four-year degree. The career outlook for this field is very good because businesses are increasingly moving toward using Internet applications. According to the *Occupational Outlook Handbook* website, computer software engineering job prospects are projected to rapidly grow over the 2008–2018 decade.

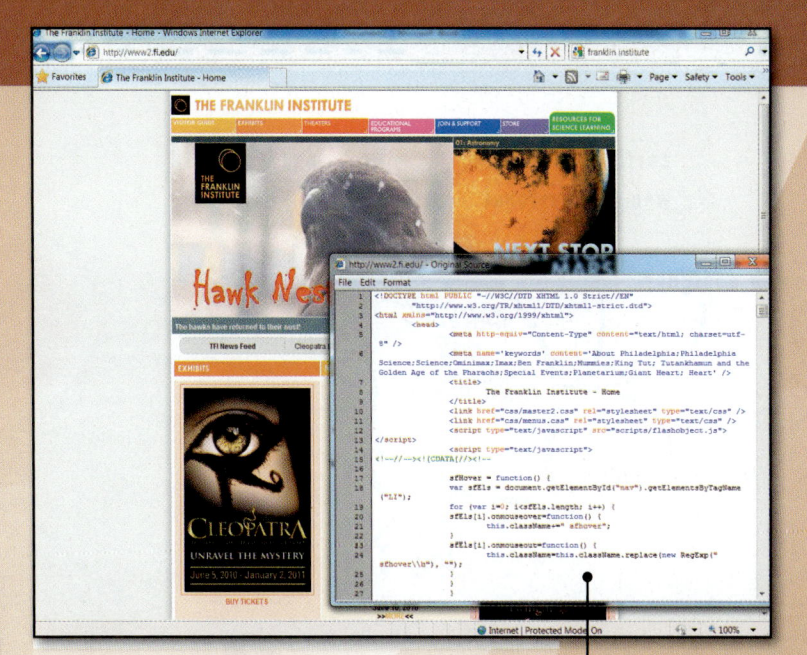

FIGURE 7.19 This dynamic Web page was developed using technologies such as JavaScript. The source code for this Web page shows the use of scripting.

GREEN COMPUTING

TELECOMMUTING TO SAVE

As I write this, I'm sitting in my family room in my pajamas. I'm one of the millions of Americans that telecommute at least part-time. I do go in to school a few days a week to teach classes, but I also teach many online classes, especially in the summer, which allows me to work from home. It saves me a few days' worth of gas, which really adds up. So, it's better for the environment to keep my car off the road, and it's better for my wallet too.

Not every job lends itself to telecommuting, but according to one site created to provide resources to telecommuters, businesses, and individuals, if just 50 percent of the people that could work from home did so just half of the time, in the United States, we would:

- Save over $650 billion a year
- Reduce greenhouse gases by the equivalent of taking 9 million cars off the road
- Reduce oil imports by 37%

Businesses that encourage telecommuting can also save on real estate expenses. Fewer employees onsite means smaller office space requirements and lower utility bills. Sun Microsystems has a large telecommuting program that saves over 5,000-kilowatt hours per year for each person who works from home just two days a week.

CIW (CERTIFIED INTERNET WEB PROFESSIONAL)

The CIW (Certified Internet Web Professional) certification program is a vendor-neutral program of certifications that can help you show a prospective employer the skills that you have. Figure 7.20 shows the CIW certification program, beginning with the CIW Associate certification, which covers basic knowledge of Internet technologies, Web authoring with XHTML, project management, and network infrastructure and troubleshooting.

FIGURE 7.20 The Certified Internet Web Professional certification track

THE INTERNET

CAREERS AND CERTIFICATION ⑥
- certified internet web professional
- web designer
- web developer

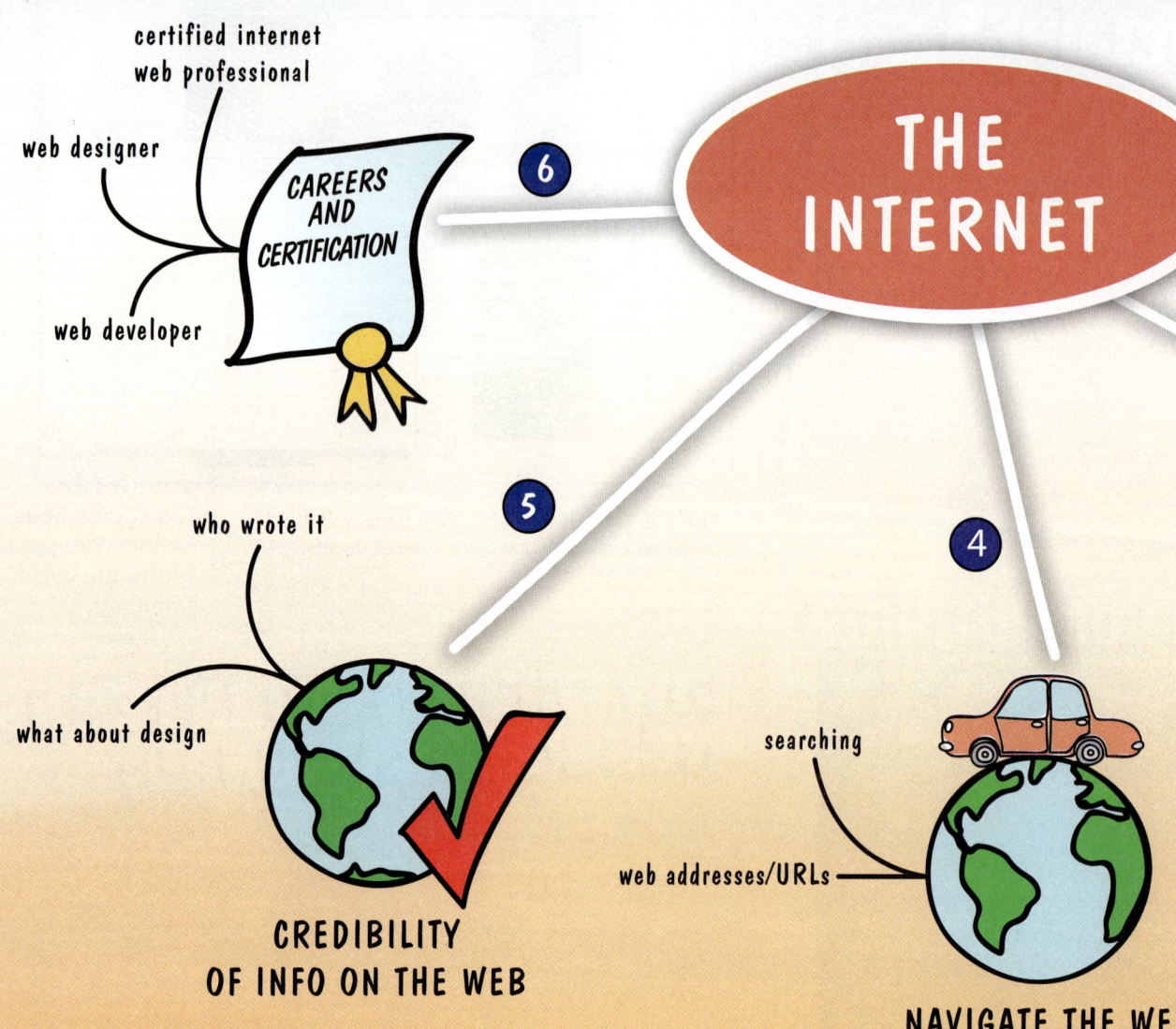

CREDIBILITY OF INFO ON THE WEB ⑤
- who wrote it
- what about design

NAVIGATE THE WEB ④
- searching
- web addresses/URLs

Objectives Recap

1. Recognize the importance of the Internet. (p. 256)
2. Compare types of Internet connections. (p. 260)
3. Compare popular Web browsers. (p. 266)
4. Demonstrate how to navigate the Web. (p. 276)
5. Discuss how to evaluate the credibility of information found on the Web. (p. 280)
6. Identify the certifications and careers related to the Internet. (p. 282)

Key Terms

- add-on 270
- ARPANET 256
- broadband 261
- cable Internet access 261
- dial-up 261
- domain name 276
- DNS (Domain Name System) 277
- DSL (digital subscriber line) 262
- FiOS (Fiber Optic Service) 262
- home page 269
- hotspot 263
- HTML (hypertext markup language) 266
- hyperlink 258
- hypertext 258
- Internet 257
- Internet2 (I2) 258
- Internet backbone 257

1. IMPORTANCE OF THE INTERNET
- ARAPNET
- how it all got started
- world wide web
- internet 2

2. INTERNET CONNECTIONS
- dial up
- broadband
- wireless

3. WEB BROWSERS
- configuration
- add-ons
- plug-ins
- browsers
- mobile browsers

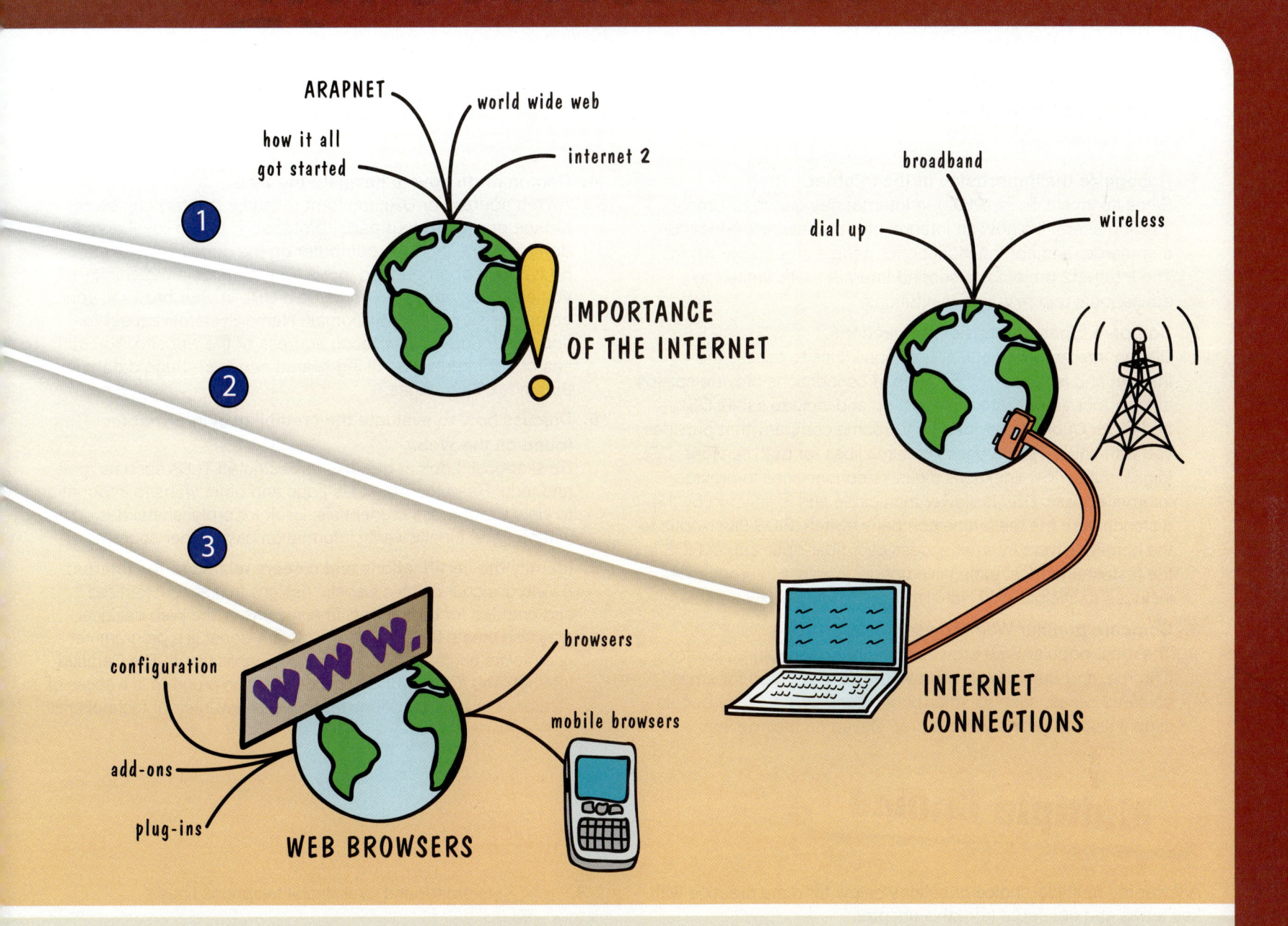

Internet Exchange Points **257**
Internet service provider (ISP) **260**
IP (Internet protocol) address **277**
mobile browser (microbrowser) **269**
municipal WiFi **263**
plug-in **270**
satellite Internet access **263**
search engine **279**
top-level domain (TLD) **276**

URL (uniform resource locator) **276**
user-generated content **280**
Web browser **266**
Web page **266**
website **276**
WiFi **263**
WiMAX Mobile Internet **262**
World Wide Web **258**

Summary

1. **Recognize the importance of the Internet.**
   Since its invention in 1969, the Internet has grown to almost 2 billion users. It's now an integral part of research, education, commerce, and communication for people around the world. The Internet2 project is a second Internet that's limited to educational and research institutions.

2. **Compare types of Internet connections.**
   Dial-up Internet uses regular telephone lines to access the Internet and is very slow. Broadband connections provide speeds at least four times faster than dial-up and include cable, DSL, and FiOS. Cable is provided by the same company that provides you with cable TV and uses the same lines for both services. DSL (digital subscriber line) uses digital telephone lines to provide Internet access. DSL is slower than cable and is affected by the distance from the telephone company switch. FiOS (fiber-optic to the home) delivers Internet access over fiber-optic cable. FiOS is the fastest and most expensive option. Wireless Internet access includes municipal WiFi, satellite, and 3G/4G cellular service.

3. **Compare popular Web browsers.**
   The most popular Web browsers are Internet Explorer, Firefox, Chrome, and Safari. Mobile browsers are optimized for small screen devices, such as smartphones and PDAs. Many people simply use the browser that's preinstalled on their device.

4. **Demonstrate how to navigate the Web.**
   A Web address or URL (uniform resource locator) can be broken down into four parts: protocol, TLD (top-level domain), domain name, and the computer on the domain. URLs can be typed in or embedded into a Web page as a hyperlink that you can click on. When you type a URL in your browser, your computer sends a DNS (Domain Name System) request to find the IP (Internet protocol) address of the website. You can search for information using search engines—huge databases that index Web pages.

5. **Discuss how to evaluate the credibility of information found on the Web.**
   Be skeptical. Look at the URL for restricted TLDs such as .gov and .edu. Read the About Us page and other website information to view the author's credentials. Look for professional design and writing style. Finally, verify information using other sources.

6. **Identify the certifications and careers related to the Internet.**
   A Web designer creates website designs that are customized and branded for businesses. In some cases, the Web designer may also create the website. A Web developer is a programmer or software engineer that creates Web applications. The Certified Internet Web (CIW) Professional certification program is a series of vendor-neutral certifications that cover many Internet technologies.

Multiple Choice

Answer the multiple-choice questions below for more practice with key terms and concepts from this chapter.

1. The original Internet was called
   a. ARPANET.
   b. CSNET.
   c. NSFNET.
   d. Internet2.

2. The fastest broadband Internet service is
   a. cable.
   b. DSL.
   c. WiMAX.
   d. FiOS.

3. _____ is broadband over digital telephone lines.
   a. Cable
   b. DSL
   c. WiMAX
   d. FiOS

4. The most popular Web browser today is
   a. Internet Explorer.
   b. Firefox.
   c. Chrome.
   d. Safari.

5. You can view multiple Web pages in most browsers using
   a. add-ons.
   b. plug-ins.
   c. extensions.
   d. tabs. ✓

6. A(n) _____ is a third-party program that extends the functionality of a Web browser.
   a. add-on ✓
   b. plug-in ✓
   c. extension
   d. microbrowser

7. The extensions .com, .gov, and .edu are examples of
   a. websites.
   b. domains.
   c. TLDs (top-level domains). ✓
   d. protocols.

8. The _____ allows you to type a URL in your browser instead of an IP address.
   a. DNS (Domain Name System) ✓
   b. TLD (top-level domain)
   c. Hypertext
   d. ICANN

9. One way to evaluate a website's credibility is to look for a _____ TLD.
   a. .com
   b. restricted ✓
   c. cc
   d. .net

10. Check the _____ page on a website for the credentials of the author or organization.
    a. home
    b. contact
    c. About Us
    d. All the above ✓

True or False

Answer the following questions with T for true or F for false for more practice with key terms and concepts from this chapter.

F 1. Al Gore invented the Internet.
T 2. There are five Internet Exchange Points around the world.
F/T 3. The Internet2 project evolved from the original NSFNET.
T 4. Outside of your home, you share your cable with your neighbors.
F 5. Because it uses satellites, WiMAX is available in remote locations.
T 6. You can easily change your browser's home page.
T 7. Adobe Flash Player in needed to watch videos on YouTube.
T 8. It's generally not necessary to type http:// when entering a URL in your browser.
T 9. Every node on the Internet must have a unique IP address.
F 10. Google is an index of the entire Web.

Fill in the Blank

Fill in the blanks with key terms and concepts from this chapter.

1. The ____*Internet backbone*____ is the high-speed connection point between networks.
2. ____*Hypertext*____ allows you to navigate through information by using the ____*hyperlink*____ that connect them.
3. ____*ISPs*____ are companies that offer Internet access.
4. Internet access that exceeds 200 Kbps is considered ____*broadband*____
5. The Internet access method that allows 3G and 4G access is called _____. *WiMAX   Mobile Internet*
6. Basic Web pages are written in ____*HTML*____.
7. ____*Microbrowsers*____ are optimized for small screen devices.
8. The ____*home page*____ is the Web page that appears when you open your browser.
9. The ____*TLD*____ .com is assigned to commercial websites.
10. You need to critically evaluate ____*user-generated content*____ because anyone can say anything.

Running Project

...The Finish Line

Use your answers to the previous sections of the project. Why is the Internet important to you, and why is it important to be knowledgeable about it? Write a report describing how you use the Internet in your daily life and respond to the questions raised. Save your file as **Lastname_Firstname_ch07_Project**, and submit it to your instructor as directed.

Critical Thinking 1

Anthony is a technician at a local community college. He's setting up new computers for a computer lab on campus. He's trying to decide which browsers and add-ons are needed on these computers.

1. Think about the courses that you have taken or are currently taking. Do they require you to use the Internet? If so, for what purposes? Are there technical requirements for specific browsers?
2. Based on this information, write up your recommendation for Anthony in a two- to three-paragraph essay. Which browsers should he install and why? What add-ons or plug-ins will he need to install?
3. Save your file as **Lastname_Firstname_ch07_Lab**, and submit it as directed by your instructor.

Critical Thinking 2

A new neighbor just moved in and needs to get Internet access. She asks you for advice.

1. What type of service do you have? Use the Internet to determine which broadband services are available where you live.
2. What questions should you ask your neighbor to help her make a choice?
3. Write up a summary of the services available and the questions you would ask your neighbor. Save the file as **Lastname_Firstname_ch07_Internet_Access**, and submit it as directed by your instructor.

Do It Yourself 1

The actual Internet access speed that you get is rarely as high as your ISP advertises. In this activity, you'll use an online speed test to measure your speed.

1. Open your favorite browser. For this activity, close anything else that uses Internet access, such as your e-mail or instant messaging programs. Close all but a single tab in your browser.

2. Navigate to one of the following websites: **speakeasy.net/ speedtest**, **dslreports.com/stest**, or **speedtest.net**, and run a speed test on your connection. Because results can fluctuate, run your test at least two or three times. Try to use different servers if you're given the option. Take a screen shot of the results screen for each of your tests.

3. Write up a summary of your results. How do the results compare to your expected speeds? Paste your screen shots into a word processing document. Save the file as **Lastname_ Firstname_ch07_Speed_Test**, and submit it as directed by your instructor.

Ethical Dilemma

In the early days of the Web, it was common practice to buy up domain names to resell them. Speculators would buy domain names that they anticipated would be worth a lot of money to them. This practice is known as cybersquatting.

1. Intentionally buying a domain name that's the same as a trademark another company owns (for example, Avon or Hertz, which were both victims) for the purpose of selling it to the trademark owner at profit is a trademark infringement, but what about something that's not trademarked but still recognizable— like a catchphrase or a person's name? Is it legal to grab up these domain? Is it ethical? What about changing the TLD (nasa.com for example)?

2. Suppose you purchase a domain name for your own use, and it turns out that a company wants to buy it from you? Is it legal to sell it to them? At a profit?

3. Type up your answers, save the file as **Lastname_Firstname_ ch07_Ethics,** and submit it as directed by your instructor.

Do It Yourself 2

There are many different search engines you can use to find information on the Web. In this activity, you'll perform a search using Bing and refine your search using advanced options.

1. Open your browser, and go to **bing.com**. In the search box, type **Bengal tigers**, and press Enter.

2. Open a new document, take a screen shot of this page, and paste it into the document. How many results did you get? Is this a practical number of results?

3. Click *Advanced* next to the results. Add the word *zoo* to the search. How does this affect the results? Type *white* and select *None of these terms* to exclude it from the search. How are the results affected? Take a screen shot of the results, and paste it into the document.

4. Type up your answers, save the file as **Lastname_Firstname_ ch07_Bing**, and submit it as directed by your instructor.

On the Web 1

Many websites will allow you to personalize the content that you see. Choose one of the following websites: espn.com, yahoo.com, msn.com, or use your ISP's home page. Join and customize the site.

1. If necessary, create an account on your chosen website and log in. What personalization and customizations are available to you?

2. Create your personal page on the site. What items did you choose to modify, add, or delete?

3. Type up your answers, take a screen shot of your customized page, and paste it in your document. Save the file as **Lastname_Firstname_ch07_My_Page**, and submit it as directed by your instructor.

On the Web 2

Your brother just got a cool new smartphone and wants to add a second mobile browser to it. Go to **download.com**.

1. In the Search box, type **browser**, choose *Mobile* from the drop-down list, and press Enter. How many options are there? What are the two highest rated? How much do they cost?
2. What options do you recommend? Type up your answers, save the file as **Lastname_Firstname_ch07_Mobile**, and submit it as directed by your instructor.

Collaboration 1

Instructors: Divide the class into four groups, and assign each group one topic for this project. The topics include cable, DSL, FiOS, and WiMAX 4G.

The Project: Each team is to prepare a poster for its method of accessing the Internet. Teams must use at least three references, only one of which may be this textbook. Use Google Docs to prepare the final version of your presentation and provide documentation that all team members have contributed to the project. For more on using Google Docs, see Appendix C.

Students: Before beginning this project, discuss the roles each group member will play. Choose a team name, which you'll use in submitting your presentation. Be sure to divide the work among your members, and pick someone to present your project. You may find it helpful to elect a team leader who can direct your activities and ensure that all team contributions are collated through Google Docs.

Outcome: You're to prepare your poster using any tool that your instructor approves. In addition, turn in a final version of your Google doc showing your collaboration named **Teamname_ch07_Internet_Access**. Submit your presentation to your instructor as directed.

Collaboration 2

Instructors: Divide the class into four groups, and assign each group one browser for this project. The topics include Internet Explorer, Firefox, Chrome, and Safari.

The Project: Each team is to prepare a multimedia commercial for its browser. The presentation should be designed to convince a consumer to use the browser. Teams must use at least three references, only one of which may be this textbook. Use Google Docs to plan the presentation and provide documentation that all team members have contributed to the project. For more on using Google Docs, see Appendix C.

Students: Before beginning this project, discuss the roles each group member will play. Choose a team name, which you'll use in submitting your presentation. Be sure to divide the work among your members, and pick someone to present your project. You may find it helpful to elect a team leader who can direct your activities and ensure that all team contributions are collated through Google Docs.

Outcome: You're to prepare a multimedia presentation on your assigned topic in PowerPoint (or another tool if approved by your instructor) and present it to your class. The presentation may be no longer than 3 minutes and should contain 5 to 7 slides. On the first slide, be sure to include the name of your presentation and a list of all team members. Turn in a final version of your presentation named as **Teamname_ch07_Browser_Wars** and your Google Docs file showing your collaboration named as **Teamname_ ch07_Browser_ Wars_Collaboration**. Submit your presentation to your instructor as directed.

Blogging

1. Blog about your Web browser choices. What browser(s) do you normally use at home? School? Work? On what devices? Why do you use those browser(s)?

2. Visit at least two of your classmates' blogs on this topic. On the blogs you visit, provide three to five sentences with suggestions of why they might consider switching to a different browser.

3. Create a document that includes your blog URL and the URLs of the two blogs you commented on. Save the file as **Lastname_Firstname_ch07_Browser_Blog**. Submit the file to your instructor as directed.

CHAPTER 8

Communicating
Sharing: The S

Running Project

In this project, you explore online communication. Look for instructions as you complete each article. For most, there's a series of questions for you to research. At the conclusion of the chapter, you're asked to submit your responses to the questions raised.

and Social Web

Become our friend on Facebook

OBJECTIVES

1. Compare different forms of synchronous online communication. (p. 294)
2. Demonstrate how to use e-mail effectively. (p. 298)
3. Discuss the roles of social media in today's society. (p. 304)
4. Locate user-generated content in the form of a blog or podcast. (p. 314)
5. Discuss how wikis and other social media sites rely on the wisdom of the crowd. (p. 318)
6. Explain the influence of social media on e-commerce. (p. 322)
7. Identify the careers related to online communication. (p. 324)

IN THIS CHAPTER

The first thing I do every morning when I come downstairs is open my browser. I have two home page tabs. The first is my iGoogle page, which includes my e-mail, groups, and the RSS feeds from my favorite blogs, news, and sports websites. The second tab is Facebook. I can find out everything I need to start my day in just a few minutes. Online communication has become an integral part of my life—and probably yours too. In this chapter, we look at the world of online communication and the impact it has on society.

Talk TO ME

OBJECTIVE 1
Compare different forms of synchronous online communication.

Want to talk to someone right now? That's what chat and instant messaging allow you to do. The term **synchronous online communication** means communication that happens in real-time, with two (or more) people online at the same time. Face-to-face conversations or telephone calls are examples of synchronous communication. Online synchronous communication tools let us communicate in real-time on the Web.

CHAT AND IM

Online **chat** allows you to talk to multiple people at the same time in a chat room. **Instant messaging (IM)** allows you to talk to one person at a time, although most IM software will also support group chats. The line between chat and IM has blurred over the years. For example, Facebook chat is really a form of IM by the definition used here.

CHAT You can find chat rooms that are geared toward common interests, such as travel or cooking, or more general chats for people that just want to talk. There are chats that are moderated, where a moderator screens all content, or unmoderated, where anything goes. There are many chat rooms that are adult in nature, and unfortunately, sexual predators often find their victims in such chat rooms. That said, it's important to put safety first when using chat rooms (or any form of online communication for that matter).

Traditional chat rooms are text-based, persistent, and users come and go, often not knowing each other. You can find Web-based chat rooms using sites such as Chat Avenue or Talk City. Client-based chats require you to install client software in order to access them. Some instant messaging programs, such as Yahoo! Messenger, allow you to join and create chat rooms. In Figure 8.1, I'm in the process of joining a Yahoo! chat room. You can see the list of categories of rooms that are available. You can also create your own chat room from here, which can be public or private (limited to users that you invite).

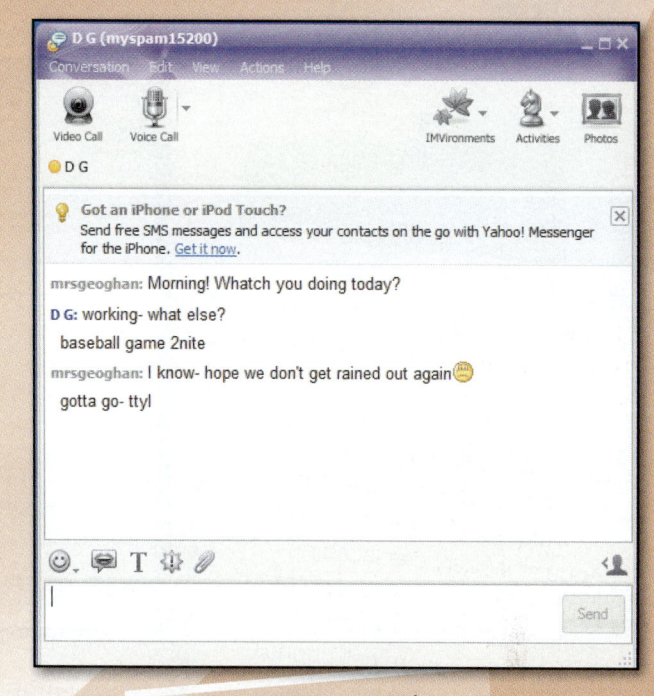

FIGURE 8.1 Joining a chat room using Yahoo! Messenger

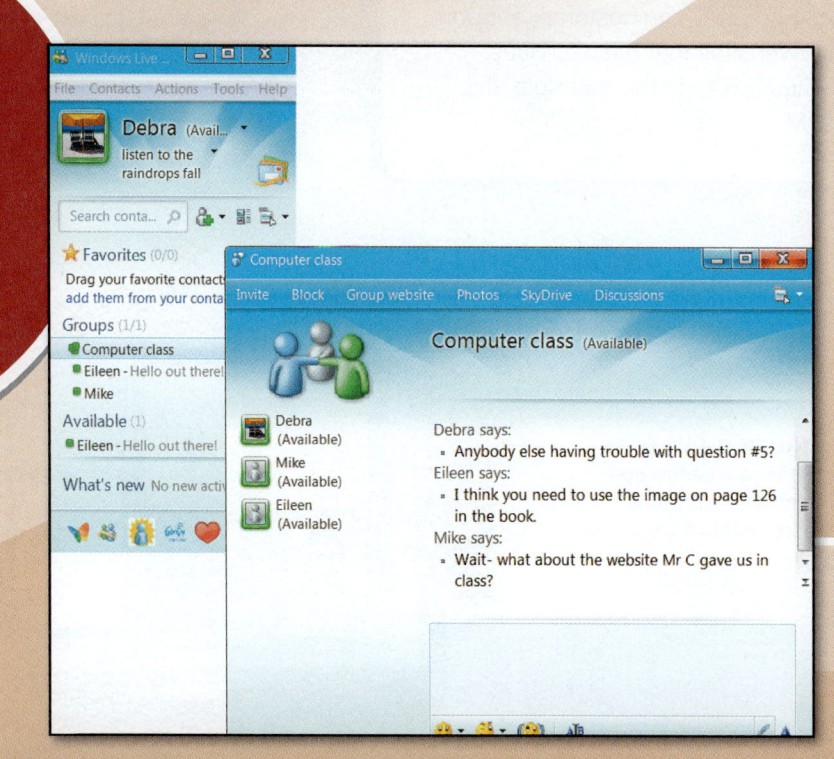

Chat is a great way to talk with people in real time. It is perfect for a class discussion or getting a group of family members together to plan a reunion. Figure 8.2 shows students in a computer class studying together using the Group feature of Windows Messenger to hold a chat.

FIGURE 8.2 Windows Messenger allows you to chat with multiple users by creating a group.

INSTANT MESSAGING

Instant-messaging (IM) sessions happen between buddies and disappear when they end, although some IM software will allow you to save the text of your conversation. There are Web-based IM tools, but many popular IM services, such as AIM or Google Talk, use client software that the user must install first. Modern cell phones also often have IM capabilities. Figure 8.3 shows several different IM clients and the Trillian client. Trillian—and other programs like it—allow you to access all your separate accounts in one place.

Windows Live Messenger | **Google Talk** | **Yahoo! Messenger** | **AIM**

FIGURE 8.3 The Trillian client replaces the need for all the separate clients behind it (Windows Live Messenger, Google Talk, Yahoo! Messenger, and AIM) as well as Facebook and Twitter.

Today, businesses are finding IM and chat to be useful tools for holding meetings and providing customer support. This is often the case with websites that offer services, such as Internet access (Figure 8.4). In this example, the term "chat" really means IM.

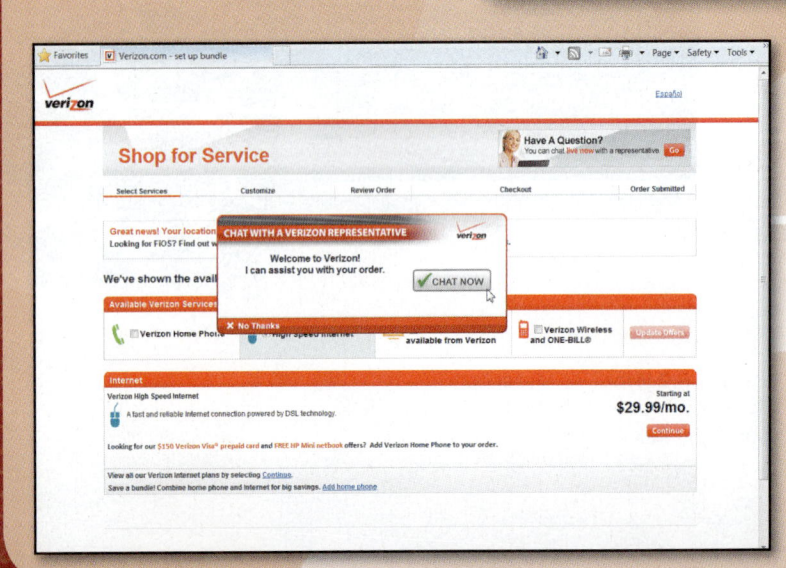

FIGURE 8.4 Websites, like Verizon, allow you to chat via IM with a representative.

VoIP

You can even make phone calls over the Internet. **VoIP (voice over IP)** allows phone calls to be transmitted over the Internet instead of via traditional phone lines. If you have broadband Internet access, your Internet Service Provider (ISP) may also offer VoIP phone service.

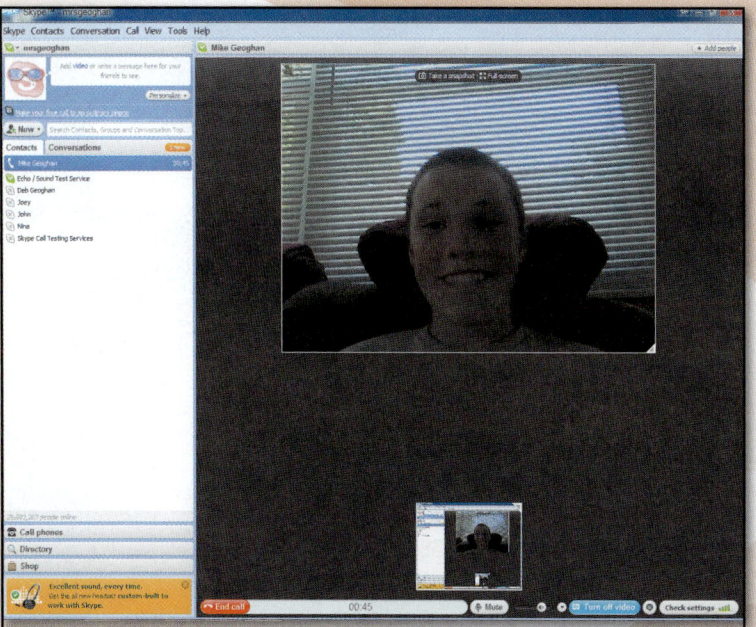

A service like Skype (see Figure 8.5) allows you to place calls to other Skype users for free or to regular phones for a small fee. Using a service like Skype allows you to make calls anywhere you have Internet access, even if you don't have phone service. You can even video chat if you have a webcam on your computer. Using Skype to talk to friends and family that are in other countries can save a lot of money over traditional telephone calls. My cousin, who lives in Australia, talks regularly with his sisters here in the United States, and his children are able to keep in touch with their faraway grandparents.

FIGURE 8.5 Using Skype to talk to my son

Using the tools discussed in this article, you can communicate with people online in real time. These tools have made it easier (and cheaper) than ever to get instant help or advice and keep in touch with friends and family both near and far.

Key Terms

chat

instant messaging

synchronous online communication

VoIP (voice over IP)

Running Project

Use the Internet to research chat/IM safety rules for kids. Create a list of five rules you consider the most important when it comes to keeping kids safe.

3 Things You Need to Know
- Chat rooms can have many people in them at one time.
- IM occurs between two people at a time.
- VoIP uses the Internet to make phone calls.

Leave a MESSAGE

2 OBJECTIVE
Demonstrate how to use e-mail effectively.

Asynchronous forms of communication don't require the participants to be online at the same time. Like leaving a voicemail or sending a letter, **asynchronous online communication** technology lets you send a message that the receiver can access later.

HOW DO YOU READ AND SEND E-MAIL?

At its roots, the Internet was designed for communicating and sharing. One of the first applications of it was e-mail, which quickly became the most widely used Internet application. Using e-mail to communicate has become an essential business skill.

E-mail is a system of sending electronic messages using store-and-forward technology. That means an e-mail server holds your messages until you request them. Thus, someone can send you an e-mail message even if you're not online at the time. There are two ways to access e-mail: using an e-mail client on your computer (or PDA, cell phone, or some other device) or reading it online through a webmail interface. When you use an e-mail client, such as Outlook, Windows Live Mail, or Thunderbird, the e-mail server sends a copy of the message to you. This makes it available to read even after you disconnect from the Internet. The advantage to using a webmail interface is that your e-mail is available to you from anywhere whenever you're online: home, school, vacation, or work.

298 | OBJECTIVE 2

Today, it makes sense to have multiple e-mail accounts. This allows you to keep your private, work, school, etc., accounts separate. Think about the impression you'd make if you sent a job inquiry from cutiepie_cupcake@hotmail.com. I have one account just for shopping websites, another for friends and family, and yet another at work. One very important thing to remember about e-mail is that it's not secure. As it travels from your computer over the Internet, it can be read by hackers along the way. Copies of the message exist on servers and routers it crosses on its journey, and those copies can be retrieved long after you've deleted the message from your Inbox. Your e-mail provider might scan your messages to deliver you targeted advertising, and your employer or school network administrator might also read your e-mail. A good analogy is to think of e-mail as a postcard, not a letter in a sealed envelope.

Your ISP can provide you with at least one (and maybe up to 10) e-mail accounts. Your employer or school may provide you with another. There are also many places where you can sign up for a free e-mail account, such as Yahoo!, Google, and Windows Live. Figure 8.6 shows how easy it is to create a free Hotmail account on Windows Live. The hardest part of the process is getting the letters of the captcha right. A **captcha** (Completely Automated Public Turing Test to Tell Computers and Humans Apart) is a series of letters and numbers that are distorted in some way. This makes them difficult for automated software to read but relatively easy for humans to read.

FIGURE 8.6 Creating a free Hotmail e-mail account

1. On the live.com home page, click Sign up.

2. Type your desired username, and click Check availability.

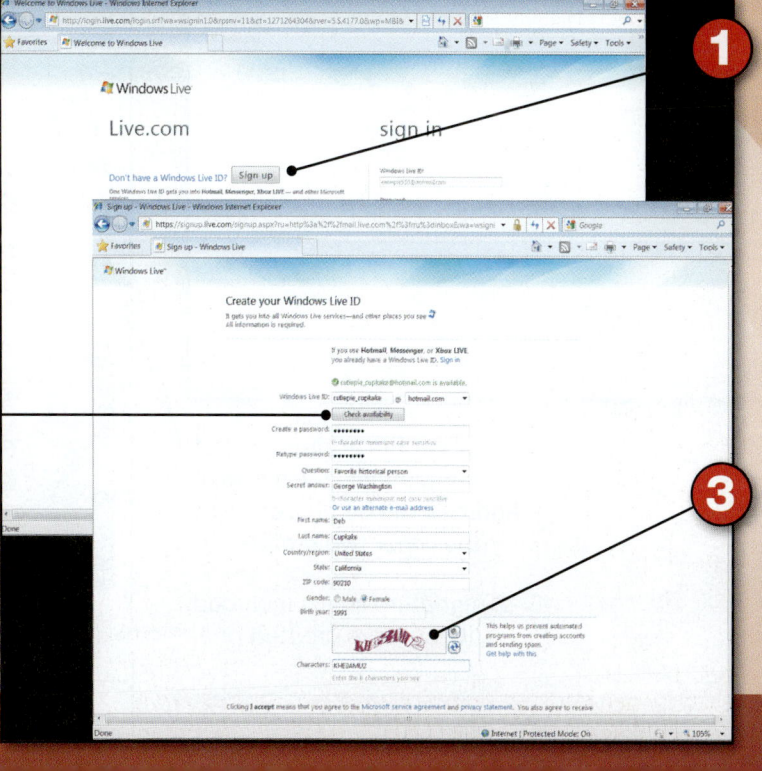

3. A captcha prevents automated systems from creating accounts.

Accessing your new Hotmail account is easy. Just log in to the live.com website and click on the Mail link (see Figure 8.7). New e-mail messages are in your Inbox. You can read a message by double-clicking on it.

You can also use an e-mail program such as Windows Live Mail, Mozilla Thunderbird, or Microsoft Outlook to read your e-mail on your computer. In a business environment, a program like Outlook is a critical tool, but many home users don't feel the need for a local e-mail program. Figure 8.8 shows Thunderbird configured for the same Hotmail account.

FIGURE 8.7 Accessing a webmail account

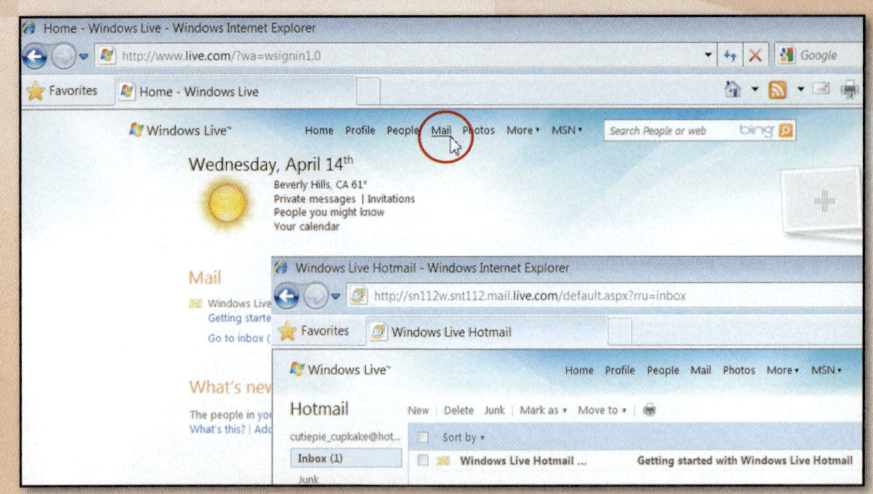

FIGURE 8.8 The Mozilla Thunderbird e-mail client

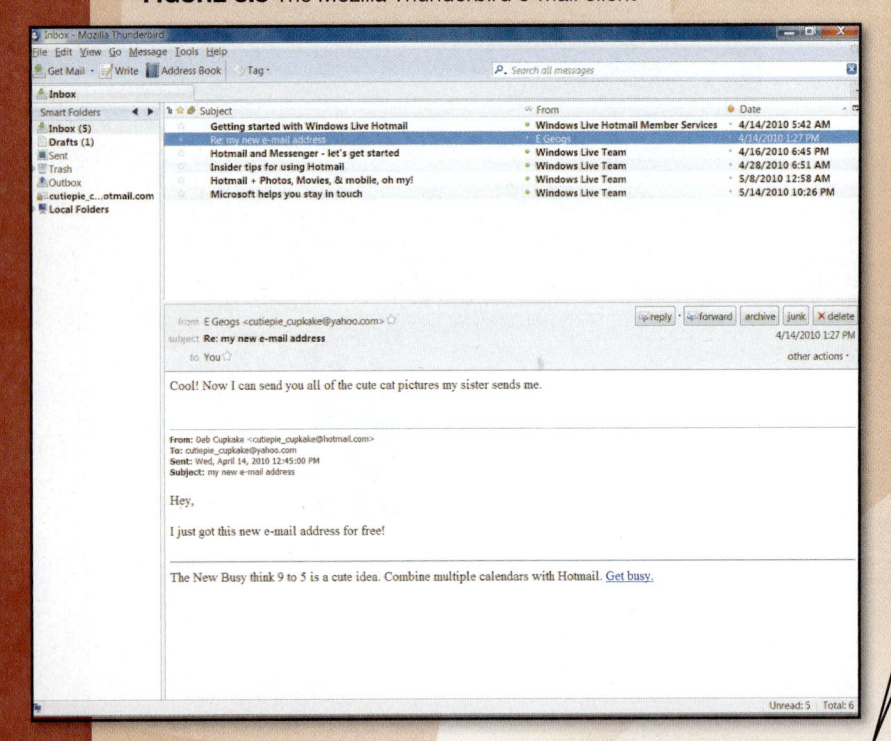

An e-mail message has some distinct parts that you should be familiar with. Figure 8.9 has some of the important parts of a new e-mail message labeled. This message has not yet been sent.

FIGURE 8.9 Composing an e-mail message

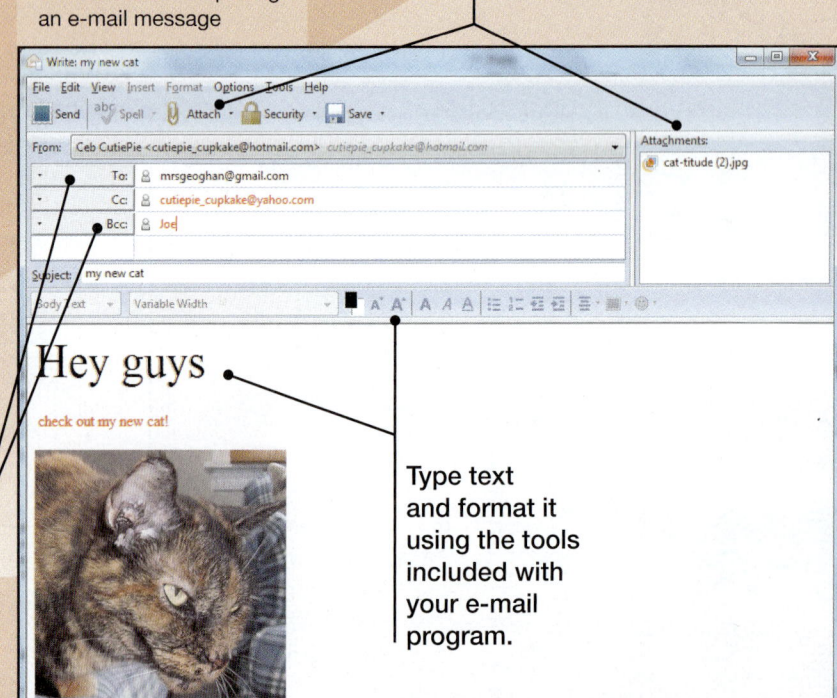

Add attachments only if necessary.

Type text and format it using the tools included with your e-mail program.

Enter the address(es) of recipient(s). Joe's e-mail address will be hidden from the other two recipients.

A signature line is included if you have created one.

The most important part of the message is the address. If you don't address it correctly, the message will not reach its recipient. There are three address fields that you can use: To, Cc, and Bcc. To: is the field you normally use when sending an e-mail to someone. Cc:, which stands for carbon copy, is the field you use to send to someone who's not the main addressee a copy—so he or she know about a conversation, for example. It's like an FYI and generally means that a reply isn't expected. Functionally, there's no real difference in the way the message is sent or received. Bcc:, however, has an important difference. Did you ever have an e-mail message forwarded to you that includes the addresses of dozens of other people? The sender should have used the Bcc field, not the To: or Cc: fields, to send that message. The B stands for blind. When you send an e-mail out to several people, using the Bcc field keeps the addresses private.

Use the Subject line of an e-mail message to give the recipient some idea of the content of the e-mail. The body of the message should contain the rest of the information. This message includes some formatted text and an image. Not all e-mail programs will let you format text or include images, and not everybody will be able to view those elements. You need to use an e-mail program that's configured to read HTML e-mail messages in order for those elements to be visible. An e-mail program that's configured to view only text e-mail messages will only see the text in this message.

A signature line is a block of text that's automatically put at the end of the messages that you compose. It can be a very simple message that just includes your name, but in business, it will usually contain more contact information and perhaps a privacy statement of some type. You need to create the signature and activate it in order for it to appear on your e-mail messages.

Find Out MORE

Is using Bcc: really protecting anyone? Use the Internet to find out if there are ways to decode the Bcc to see the e-mail addresses it hides.

When you receive an e-mail message, you have the ability to reply to the message or forward it (see Figure 8.10). When you choose Reply, your response is sent back to the original sender. If you choose Reply all (or Reply to All, depending on the e-mail program), then the response is sent to all the addressees of the original message and the original sender. The subject line for a Reply will include Re: before the original subject. If you want to send the message to someone else, then you would use the Forward option, which allows you to select new addresses and put Fw: before the subject.

FIGURE 8.10 Replying to an e-mail

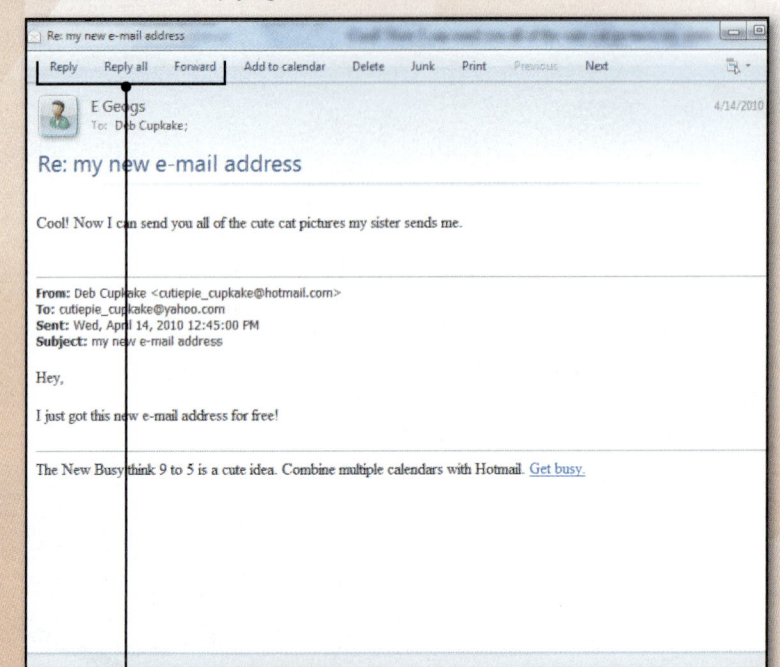

Choose Reply, Reply all, or Forward to respond to an e-mail message.

FORUMS AND DISCUSSION BOARDS

Forums, also known as discussion boards or message boards, were one of the first forms of social media. They're conversations much like chat but are not in real time. There are forums for people with common interests, such as sports, pets, travel, or video games. Many technology and product websites include forums, which may be used as a support system. Some websites refer to a forum as a community.

Participants post comments and questions, usually about a particular topic or problem, and other participants respond. Each conversation is called a thread, and the responses are posts. Forums are a great place to get help with problems, ask for advice, or just communicate with folks with similar interests. Threads can be searched and read long after the initial conversation has ended. Most forums are moderated and require you to create an account before you're allowed to post. Figure 8.11 shows the home page of the Ubuntu forums.

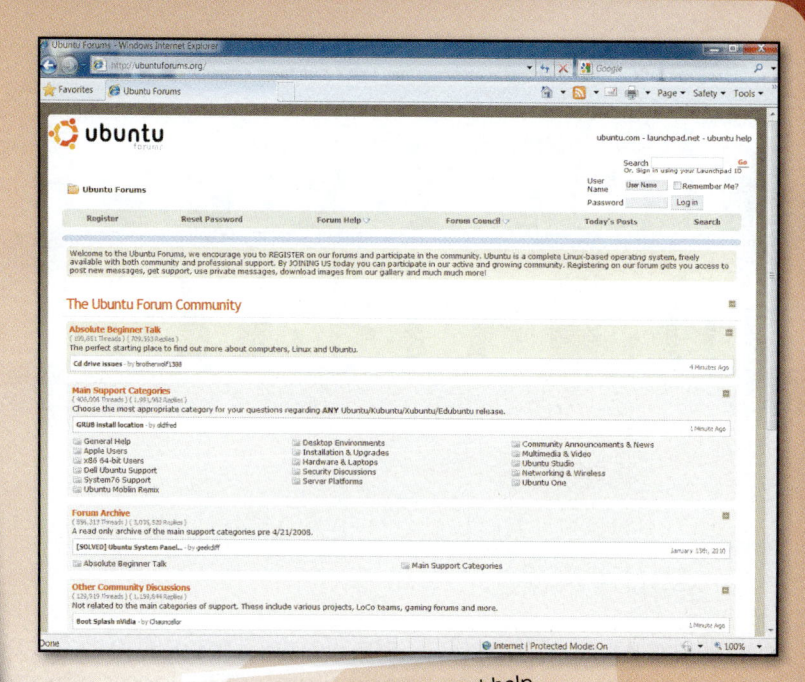

FIGURE 8.11 Users can get help and information about Ubuntu through The Ubuntu Forum Community.

The advantage to using e-mail or a forum over chat or IM is that the conversations have a longer life span. You can save e-mails indefinitely as long as you have the storage space, and forums can persist for years after a thread is started. These tools have become critical ways to communicate in all types of businesses.

Key Terms

asynchronous online communication

captcha

e-mail

forum

Running Project

Visit **tripadvisor.com** and click on Forums. Select a destination that you have visited in the past. Read some of the threads. Select a thread that you would like to reply to. Do you agree with the replies posted? Would you find them helpful if you were deciding whether to visit this location?

5 Things You Need to Know

- E-mail is a store-and-forward technology that doesn't require you to be online when someone sends it to you.
- Webmail allows you to access your e-mail from anywhere.
- You shouldn't expect that your e-mail is private.
- A captcha assures that a person and not a machine is creating an account.
- Forums are online discussion boards.

There's a Place FOR EVERYONE...

3 OBJECTIVE
Discuss the roles of social media in today's society.

So many ways to connect with people! Forums and e-mail are old technologies, having been around almost as long as the Internet itself, but recently, newer technologies have emerged. These new tools are sometimes called **Web 2.0** and are changing the way we communicate and collaborate on the Web. These new tools rely on the wisdom of the crowd. What's important, interesting, or relevant is no longer decided by a few people sitting around a table but by the crowd of participants. Collectively, these tools—which enable users to create user-generated content, connect, network, and share—are called **social media**.

SOCIAL NETWORK SITES

Social networks, such as Facebook, MySpace, and LinkedIn, are online communities that combine many of the features of the other online tools we have discussed. Social networks allow you to chat in real time and to post messages for all to see or to send a personal message similar to an e-mail. There are hundreds of social networking sites. Some focus on business, others are language- or location-specific, and still others are available where anything goes. Social networking allows you to keep in touch with old friends and make new ones.

FACEBOOK AND MYSPACE The first social network sites began in the late 1990s, and today, there are literally hundreds of them. Facebook and MySpace are two of the most popular. MySpace was launched in 2003, and Facebook was launched in 2004 for Harvard students and in 2006 for the rest of us. Today, these two sites have hundreds of millions of users worldwide. Users create a profile that includes some personal information, pictures, and interests and then they connect with other users or friends. You can also join groups within the network that interest you. For some people, using a social network is all about the number of "Friends" that they have, but for others, it is a way to stay in touch with people.

I have accounts on many different social websites and use different accounts for my personal and professional communication. I have different friends on each and post different information on each. For example, on my professional profile, I might post a link to an interesting tech article (see Figure 8.12) and join a group related to technology or education. Because my personal profile is private, only my friends can see what I post there. I play games, post pictures, and chat with friends on my private profile. I belong to several groups that match my interests, such as the neighborhood I grew up in and martial arts.

FIGURE 8.12 My professional profile only has posts and information that I want to be public.

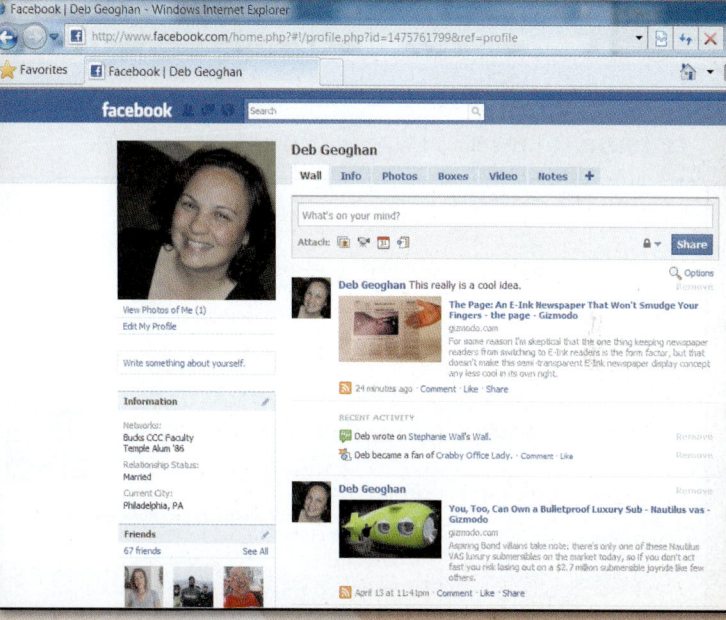

If you have friends that tag you in their photos, even if your profile is private, you may be sharing more than you meant to. Be sure to use the security and privacy settings to keep your private life private, and consider creating a second public profile. Many employers will expect you to be technically literate and use social networking tools, so not having one could be a negative. I have had people tell me that they received friend requests from people that interviewed them for jobs and internships and from bosses at work. These are the people that should be in your public social network.

Chapter 8 | 305

BUSINESS SOCIAL NETWORKS Facebook and MySpace are great for making connections with friends and family, but for a more business-centered social network, consider a site such as LinkedIn. LinkedIn is designed for business connections. Figure 8.13 shows my LinkedIn profile. There are no games or silly applications, no place to post photos (except a profile image), and no chat. You have connections instead of friends. LinkedIn—or other business social networks that relate to your field of interest—should be part of your personal brand.

FIGURE 8.13 LinkedIn is a business-oriented social network.

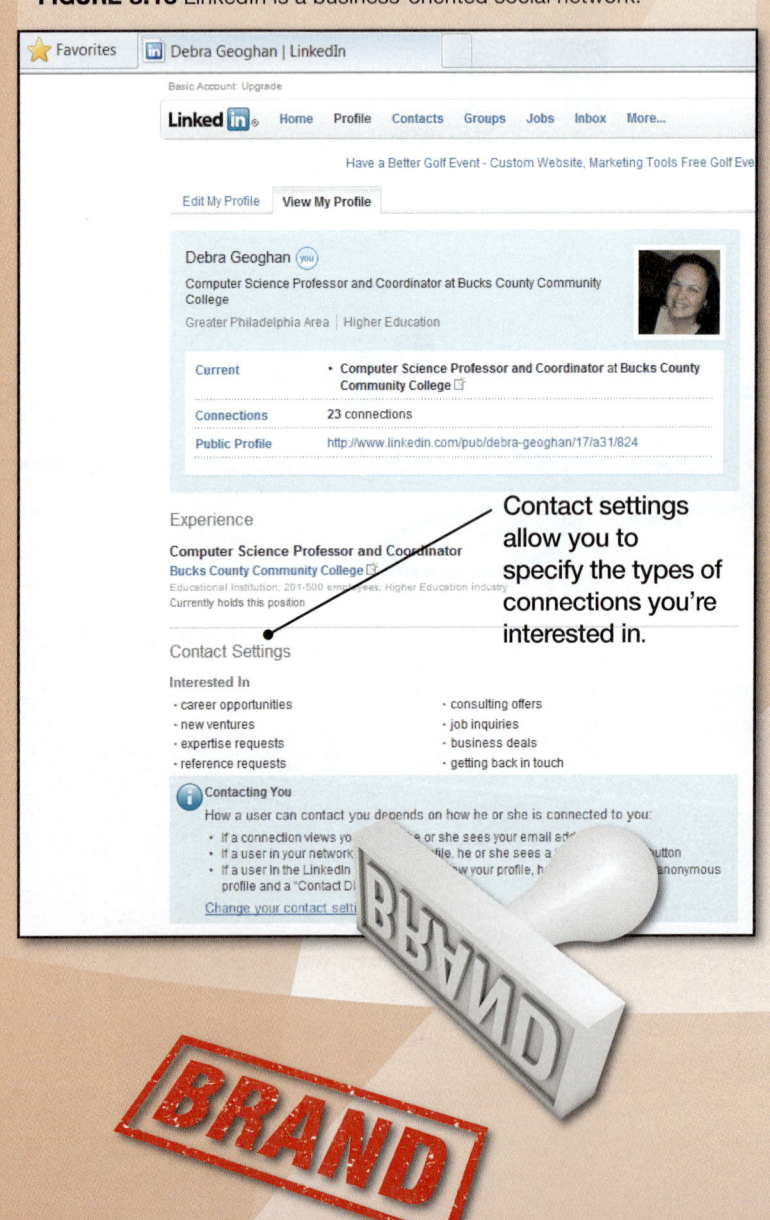

Contact settings allow you to specify the types of connections you're interested in.

VIRTUAL WORLDS Virtual communities, such as Second Life and Webkinz, and multiplayer games allow you to interact with people in real time using an **avatar**, or virtual body. Some schools even offer virtual classes in Second Life. Figure 8.14 shows my avatar entering the Penn State virtual campus.

FIGURE 8.14 Second Life allows you to enter a virtual world using an avatar.

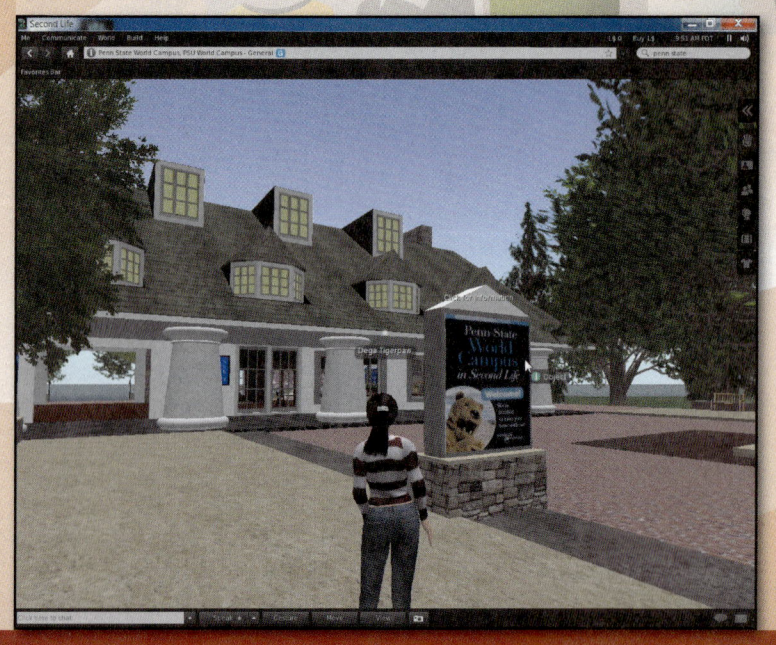

SOCIAL VIDEO, IMAGE, AND MUSIC SITES

Social sharing sites, such as YouTube, Flickr, and Last.fm, allow anyone to create and share media. These sites are outside of social networks like Facebook, although you can also share their content within them. One of the key features of these sites is the ability to tag items. This tagging, or **folksonomy**, makes the sharing even more social, as users begin to tag not just their own creations but also those of others.

VIDEO Let's face it: Everyone knows about YouTube. It's the largest online video hosting site in the world. It's also social in the sense that you can subscribe to other user's channels, send messages, and recommend videos. A **viral video** is one that becomes extremely popular because of recommendations and social sharing. Figure 8.15 shows a viral video from YouTube. There are other video sharing sites, including CollegeHumor, Vimeo, TeacherTube, and even Facebook and Flickr. Sites like Hulu don't host user-created content but are still social in that they keep track of the popularity of videos and have users review and discuss the videos.

FIGURE 8.15 YouTube is the largest video sharing network in the world.

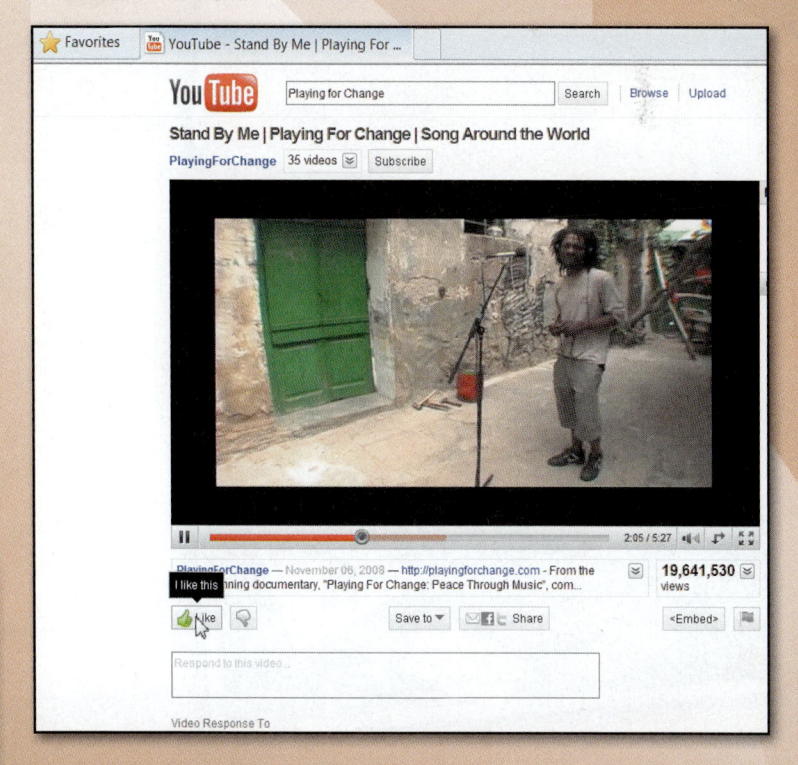

Find Out MORE

Some companies have virtual tours on Second Life. Use the Internet to find out which companies are using it and why.

FIGURE 8.16 A Flickr image showing its tags and comment field

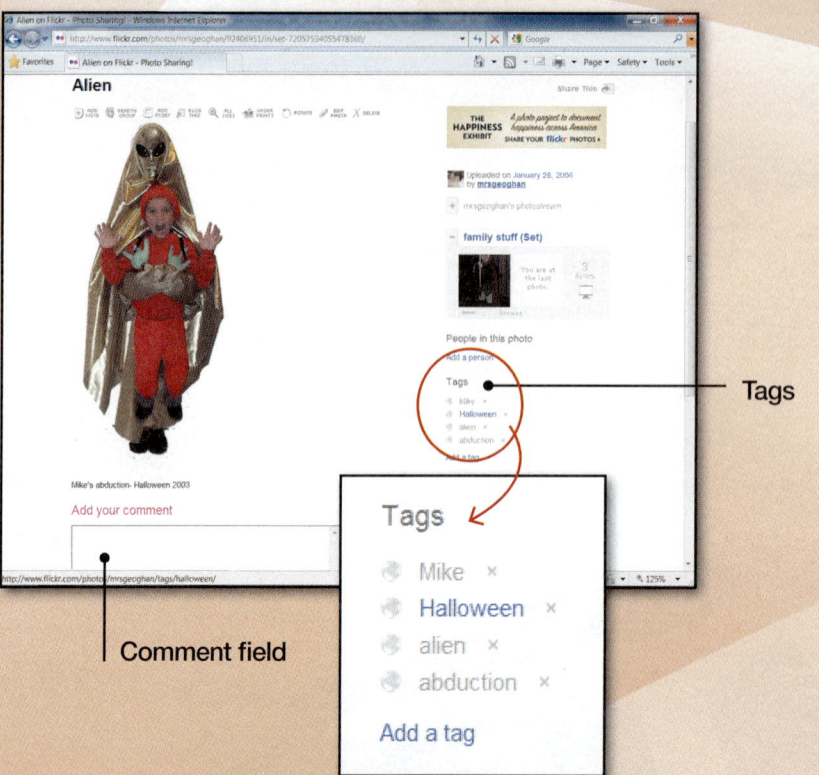

IMAGES Flickr is the largest image sharing site. With a free account, you can post up to 200 images. You can mark your pictures as private or make them public. You can adjust the copyright to allow others to use your images legally. Images can be tagged, allowing you to search for something that interests you. Other popular photo sharing sites include Picasa and Photobucket. To share your photos, create an account (Flickr will let you use your Yahoo account, and Picasa uses your Google account), log in, and begin uploading your images. You can tag them with appropriate categories to make them easier to find using a search. In Figure 8.16, the image is tagged with Mike, Halloween, alien, and abduction. You can also comment on and share images that you like.

MUSIC What is more social than music? There are lots of places on the Web to find music, but if you want a social experience, create an account on a site such as Last.fm or Pandora. These sites recommend music to you based on what you listen to. With Last.fm, you can browse users with similar music tastes and discover what they're listening to. You can mark tracks as "loved," which will help you get recommendations. The more you listen to and love tracks, the more recommendations you will get. You can add tag and shouts (comments) to music you like. Figure 8.17 shows the artist page for Andrea Bocelli, with links to concerts, albums, videos, and similar artists. I can tag and share this page easily using the tag and share buttons. This page was recommended to me because I have Andrea Bocelli music in my personal collection.

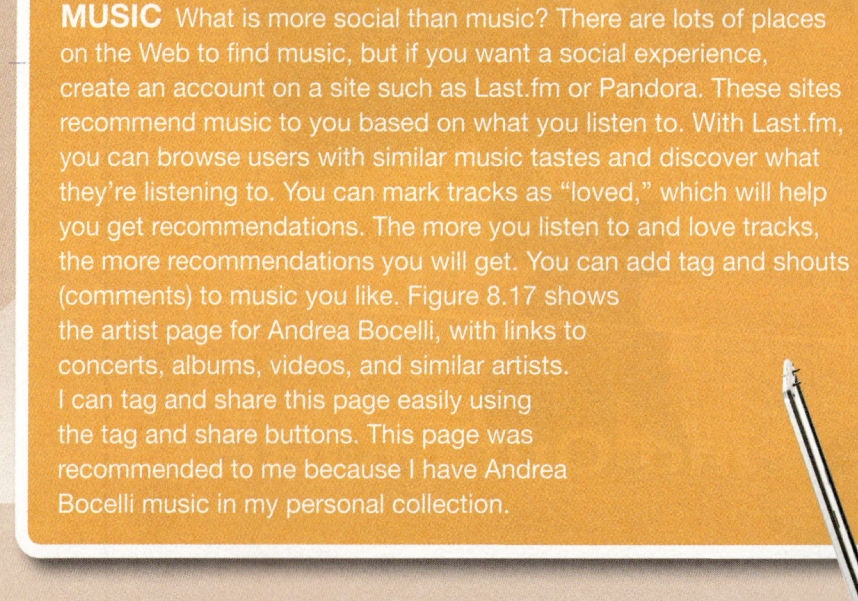

FIGURE 8.17 Last.fm is a social music site.

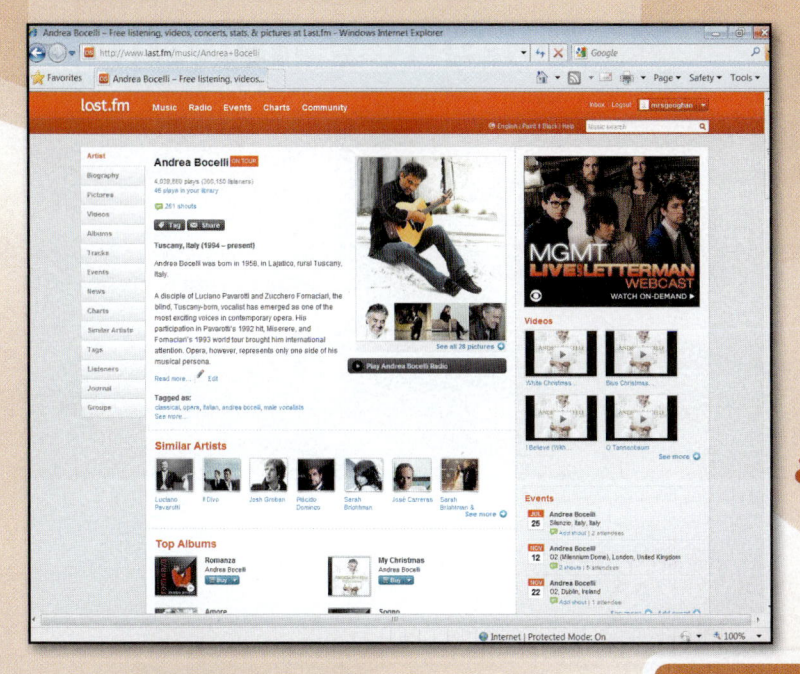

It's really important to think about your digital footprint. Your **digital footprint** is all the information that someone could find out about you by searching the Web, including social network sites. Remember that once something has been posted on the Web, it's almost impossible to completely get rid of it. Suppose you were a prospective employer. Would you hire someone that has compromising pictures on Facebook? You need to develop your own brand and make sure that anything that's publically viewable fits into that brand.

Key Terms

avatar

digital footprint

folksonomy

social media

social network

Web 2.0

viral video

Running Project

Imagine that you're a prospective employer. Search the Web and major social networks to see what they would find. Log out of your social networking sites to see how an outsider would view you. How is your brand? Would you hire yourself? Was it easy to find things that you would rather keep private?

4 Things You Need to Know

- Social networks are online communities where people connect with each other.
- Video, image, and music sharing sites allow users to post their creations on the Web for others to see and use.
- Tagging, or folksonomy, creates a way to search for content on social websites.
- You should be very careful about your digital footprint.

HOW TO Create an Avatar

Most social websites allow you to upload a picture for your profile, but what if you don't want to use an actual image of yourself? You can use a website like WeeWorld to create an avatar that you can use instead.

1 Go to **weeworld.com** and click *Create your WeeMee.*

2 Select your body features and click *Get dressed now.*

310 | HOW TO

3 Dress your avatar using the menu on the left and choosing items from the middle of the screen.

4 Click on More stuff and add accessories and change your environment. Click *Save me now!*

5 Register your WeeMee.

FILL OUT THE REGISTRATION FORM.

Chapter 8 | 311

6 Click *Export*.

7 Click *Facebook, Twitter, MySpace, blogs*.

8 Choose *Facebook* from the drop-down list and click *Next*.

9 Select *Small (96 x 96px)* and click *Next*.

10 Save the file to your computer and click *Finish*.

You can now use this image for your profile picture on Facebook and many other websites by uploading it to your profile.

Chapter 8

313

Get Your WORD OUT

4 OBJECTIVE
Locate user-generated content in the form of a blog or podcast.

User-generated content is the content created not by professional writers and photographers but by the rest of us. It includes the videos and photos we take and post online, but it also includes what we write and say.

BLOGS

A **blog** (weblog) is like an online journal. It's a Web page that's created with simple blog tools that anyone can set up and pretty much talk about whatever they like. Vlogs, or video blogs, are just that—video journals instead of text. The idea is the same either way. The difference between just creating a Web page and writing a blog is that blogs can be interactive. Your readers can post comments about your blog posts.

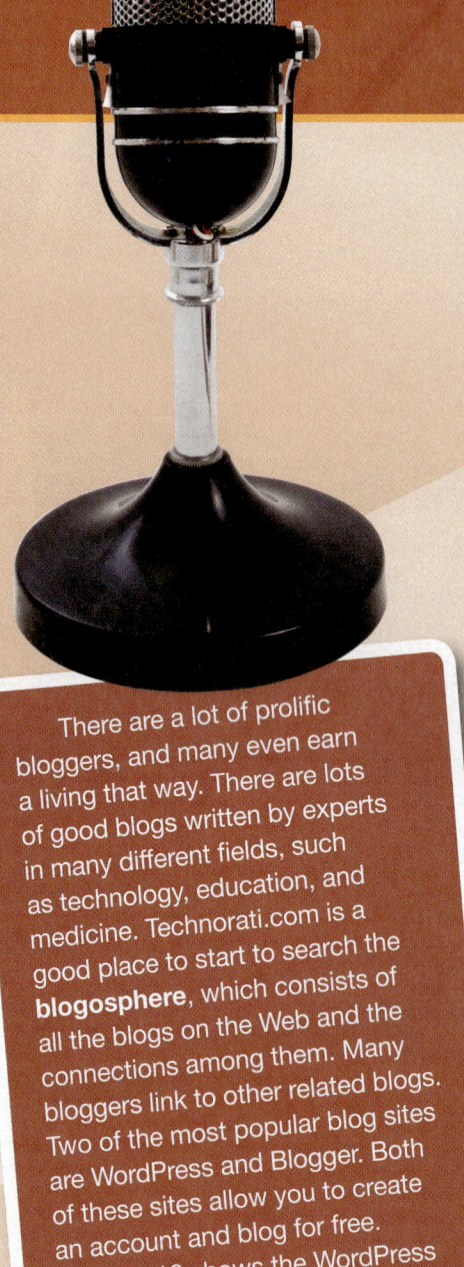

There are a lot of prolific bloggers, and many even earn a living that way. There are lots of good blogs written by experts in many different fields, such as technology, education, and medicine. Technorati.com is a good place to start to search the **blogosphere**, which consists of all the blogs on the Web and the connections among them. Many bloggers link to other related blogs. Two of the most popular blog sites are WordPress and Blogger. Both of these sites allow you to create an account and blog for free. Figure 8.18 shows the WordPress blog Technology 4 Teachers.

FIGURE 8.18 A blog for teachers created with WordPress

Microblogging sites like Twitter are a more social form of blogging where posts are typically limited to 140 characters and users post updates frequently. Posts can be public or restricted to a group of users; sent from computers, cell phones, and text messages; and they can be received the same ways. Twitter posts are called tweets and answer the question: What are you doing? Instead of friends, Twitter users have followers. Unlike most social networks, you don't have to ask for permission to follow someone (although they can block you). In Figure 8.19, you can see my Twitter page, with recent tweets from some of the folks I follow.

FIGURE 8.19 Twitter tweets are limited to 140 characters each.

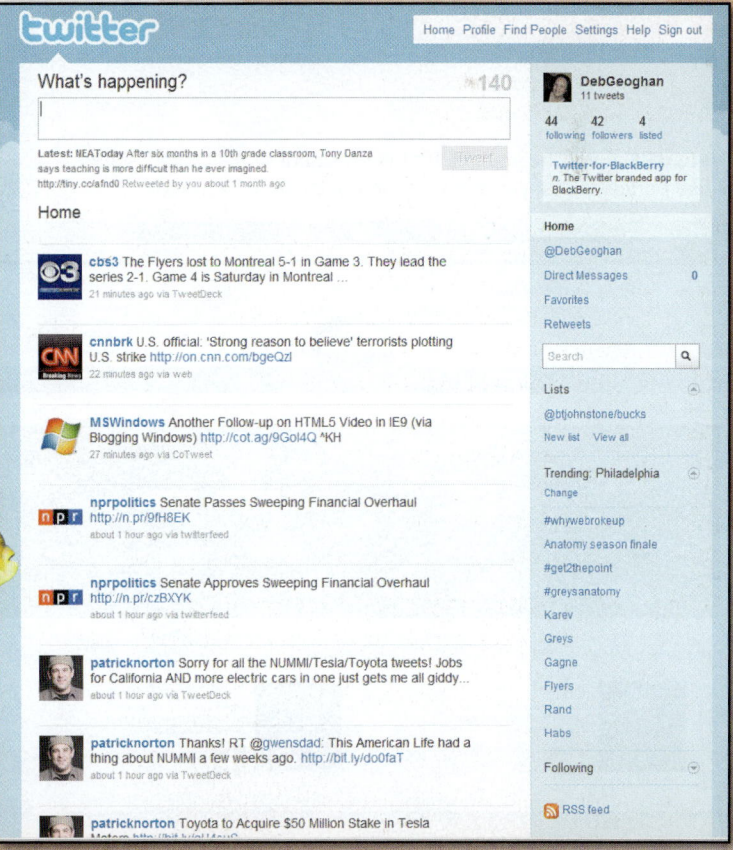

PODCASTS

A **podcast** is a digital media file of a prerecorded radio- and TV-like show that's distributed over the Web to be downloaded and listened to (or watched) on a computer or portable media player. Podcasts allow both time shifting (listening on your own schedule) and location shifting (taking it with you).

You can find podcasts using a **podcast client** or media player program, such as iTunes or Winamp, and download single episodes or subscribe to a podcast that's part of a series. There are hundreds of thousands of podcasts available. Two good sites to find podcasts are podcast.com and podcastalley.com. The White House (Figure 8.20) and the *New York Times* both produce regular podcasts that you can listen to using a podcast client or directly from their websites.

FIGURE 8.20 The website for the President of the United States has podcasts that you can listen to right in your browser.

RSS

So, how do you keep up with all your favorite websites? **RSS (Really Simple Syndication)** is a format used for distributing Web feeds that change frequently—for example, blogs, podcasts, and news. RSS saves you time by sending you the updates on the sites you subscribe to. Subscribing to the RSS feeds of your favorite blogs, podcasts, and other websites will bring the information right to you. You need a feed reader, such as Internet Explorer or Google Reader. To add a subscription, you usually just click the RSS icon at the top of the page.

Key Terms

- blog
- blogosphere
- microblogging
- podcast
- podcast client
- RSS (Really Simple Syndication)
- user-generated content

Running Project

Search for a podcast about a topic that interests you. Find out as much as you can about the podcast and its creators. Listen to an episode and write up a short summary of the contents. Did you enjoy it? Would you subscribe to it? Recommend it to a friend? Do you feel this is a good way to get this information? Explain your answers.

4 Things You Need to Know

- Anybody can create a blog to talk about almost anything.
- A microblog site restricts the length of posts.
- Podcasts are radio- and TV-like shows that you can download and listen to or watch anytime.
- You can subscribe to the RSS feed of blogs, podcasts, and other sites to be notified of new content.

The Wisdom OF THE CROWD

5 OBJECTIVE
Discuss how wikis and other social media sites rely on the wisdom of the crowd.

One of the most interesting aspects of the social uses of the Web is the idea of the wisdom of the crowd—the idea of trusting the collective opinion of a crowd of people rather than that of an expert. Sites such as Digg, reddit, and Slashdot allow users to share content and Web pages they find interesting. **Wikis** are websites that allow users to edit content, even if it was written by someone else. Review sites such as Yelp give us a voice and a place to get advice and recommendations from other folks that are just like us.

WIKIS

Wikis differ from blogs and podcasts in that they're designed for collaboration. Not just posting responses to another post but actually editing the content. The most well-known wiki is Wikipedia (see Figure 8.21), which is a massive free encyclopedia that is written by . . . anyone. What? How can you trust something that anyone can edit? Well, that's part of the design. The thought is that if many people are involved in a wiki, then the person that knows the right information will (eventually) be the one to write or edit it. In less than 10 years, Wikipedia grew to over 3 million articles in English alone. Wikipedia is a great place to start but is generally frowned upon for use as a source in academic research.

FIGURE 8.21 The Wikipedia main page

Wikipedia is the most well-known wiki, but it's not the only one. Wikis abound and are often used as a way for a community to develop instructions. For example, wikiHow (see Figure 8.22) is a website that contains how-to wikis on thousands of topics. You can read, write, or edit an existing wikiHow article or request that someone else write one if you can't find what you're looking for.

FIGURE 8.22 wikiHow has thousands of articles.

SOCIAL REVIEW SITES

Social review sites such as TripAdvisor, epinions, and Yelp let users review hotels, movies, games, books, and other products and services. I don't go anywhere without checking out some reviews first. I prefer reviews from regular people, not just expert food critics. Figure 8.23 shows the Yelp page for a restaurant that I enjoyed just the other day. The reviews here helped me choose this spot, and the food was great. There were other places in the area that I could have tried, but the reviews for this place helped me decide. I used the Yelp application on my smartphone, so I was able to get the information when I was right in the area.

FIGURE 8.23 The Yelp page for a local restaurant

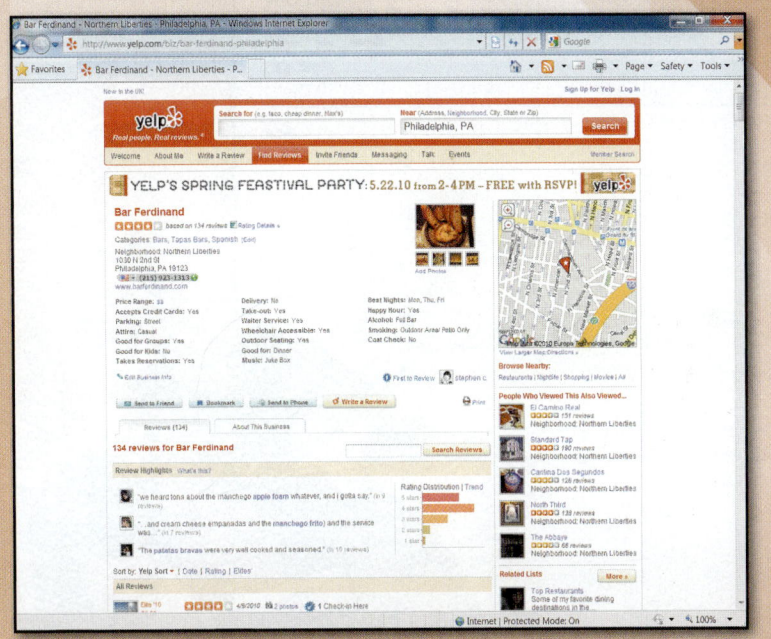

Chapter 8 | 319

SOCIAL BOOKMARKING AND NEWS SITES

Social bookmarking sites allow you to save and share your bookmarks or favorites online. Delicious allows you to not only save and share your bookmarks online but to also search the bookmarks of others. It's a great way to quickly find out what other people find interesting and important right now. Figure 8.24 shows the Delicious Web page with the current list of most recently bookmarked sites. StumbleUpon discovers websites based on your interests. When you sign up, you indicate topics that interest you. Then, as you visit websites, you can click the StumbleUpon button to be taken to a similar site. You can click I like this to improve the pages you stumble onto.

Social news sites are different than traditional media news sites in that at least some of the content is submitted by users. It's interactive in a way that traditional media isn't. It's like having millions of friends sharing their finds with you. Content that's submitted more frequently or gets the most votes is promoted to the front page.

FIGURE 8.24 The Delicious Fresh Bookmarks tab shows the most recent items that users have bookmarked.

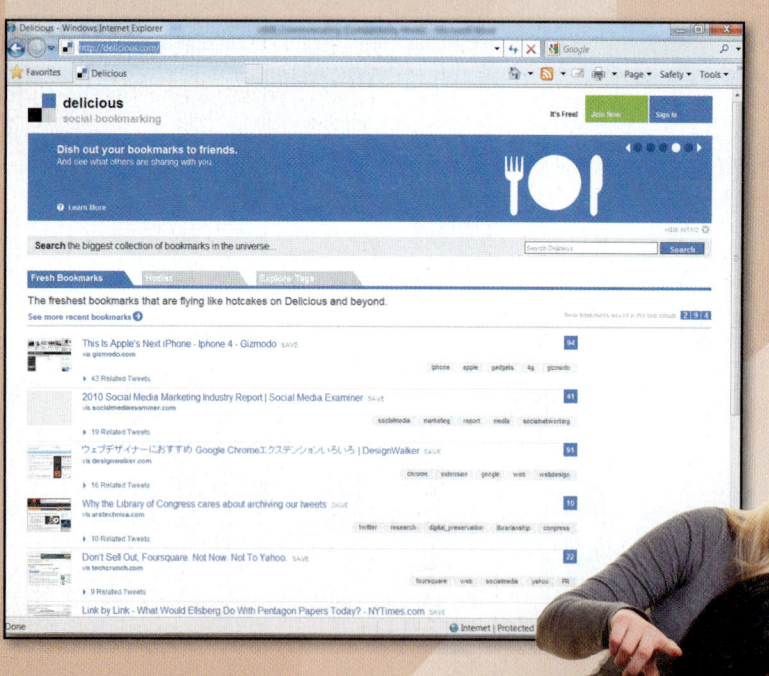

Two of the most popular social news sites are reddit and Digg. Digg doesn't publish *any* content but allows the community to submit content they discover on the Web and puts it in one place for everyone to see and to discuss. Slashdot, which focuses primarily on technology topics, does produce its content but also accepts submissions from its readers. Boudica is a social news site for women that works very much like Digg. Whatever your interests, there's probably a social news site for you.

Relying on the wisdom of the crowd is much like asking your friends, family, and co-workers for advice. Did you enjoy the movie? Where should I go for the best ice cream? How do you change the oil in your car? Everybody's an expert in something. The Web just makes it easier for us to find and share that expertise with each other. But just a word of caution: Like anything else you read on the Web, be critical in your evaluation of the credibility and reliability of its author.

ETHICS

Some people create multiple accounts on social bookmarking and news sites so they can promote their own content. For example, a blogger might create several accounts on Digg and use each one to Digg a blog post, thereby artificially raising its popularity on Digg and driving more traffic to it. This violates the Digg terms of use. But what if the blogger had all his friends and family members create accounts and Digg his post? Is it ethical? Does it violate the terms of use? Is it fair to other bloggers?

Key Terms

social bookmarking site

social news site

social review site

wiki

Running Project

Go to the Wikipedia home page. Locate the page Editorial administration, oversight, and management. How does Wikipedia assure that the content is correct? What procedures are in place to remove or correct mistakes?

3 Things You Need to Know

- Social media relies on the wisdom of the crowd rather than that of an expert.
- A wiki can be edited by anybody.
- Social bookmarking and news helps users find content that others recommend.

E-Commerce

OBJECTIVE 6
Explain the influence of social media on e-commerce.

As we've seen, social media sites are used by businesses to provide support and interaction to customers. **Social media marketing (SMM)** is the practice of using social media sites to sell products and services.

TYPES OF E-COMMERCE

E-commerce is business on the Web and is often broken into three categories: B2B, B2C, and C2C, where B stands for business and C stands for consumer. B2B, or business to business, services are ones that a business provides for another; for example, Google Checkout service or website design B2B services on the Web allow smaller companies to have a Web presence or store without needing to have the in-house expertise or expense. The small startup company Urge Essentials (see Figure 8.25) is able to have a professional-looking website and sophisticated shopping cart system because of B2B services it purchases from other companies.

FIGURE 8.25 The website design and shopping cart are B2B services used by this small company.

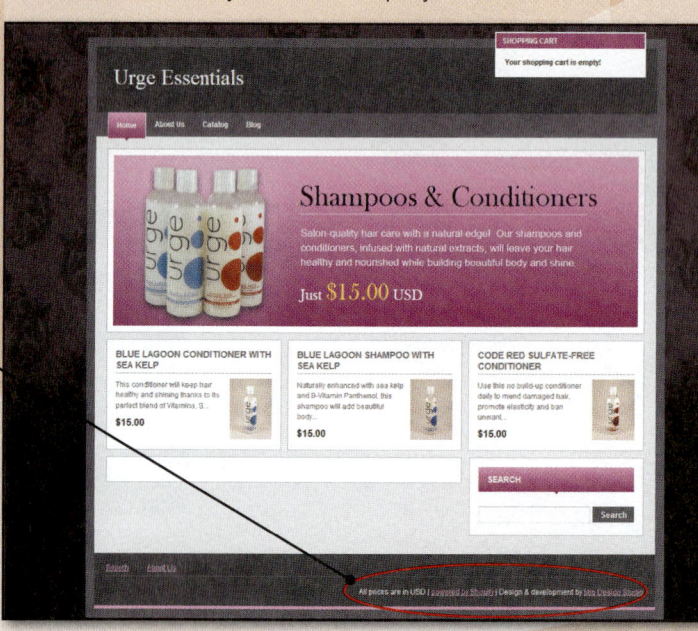

B2B services include a shopping cart and website design.

B2C, or business to consumer, is the most familiar form of e-commerce. Amazon.com, Overstock.com, and most brick-and-mortar retailers sell their goods and services online to you and me (see Figure 8.26). This form of e-commerce has grown exponentially since Pizza Hut offered pizza ordering on its website in 1994. B2C companies leverage social media to help customers find out about their products.

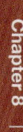

FIGURE 8.26 Amazon.com is the largest B2C website in the world.

FIGURE 8.27 The eBay community adds social media to the world's largest C2C site.

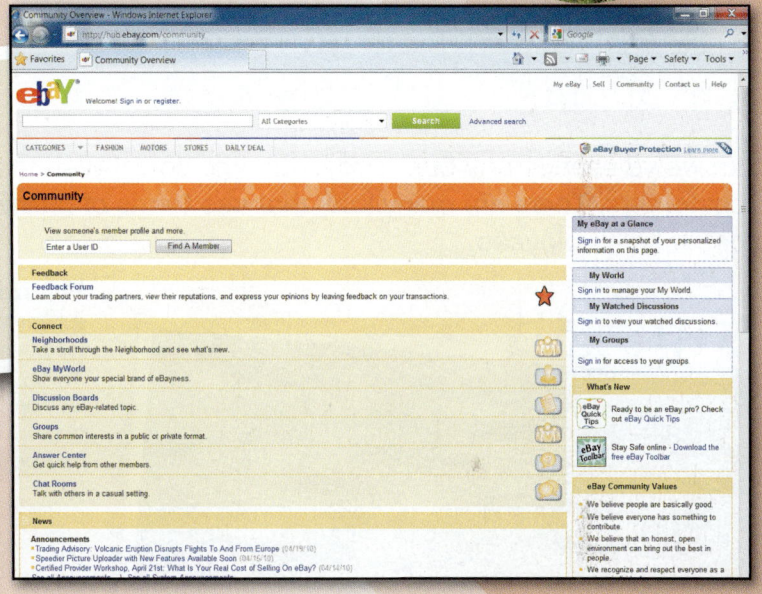

The third form of e-commerce is C2C, or consumer to consumer, electronic commerce. Websites such as eBay and Craig's List have created a global yard sale, where you can find, sell, or trade virtually anything. eBay has a seller rating system that helps ensure honest transactions and a community (see Figure 8.27) that includes discussion boards, groups, and chats. An unscrupulous seller will quickly get a bad reputation, and a top-rated seller will see more sales as a result.

HOW SAFE IS MY CREDIT CARD?

E-commerce on the Web requires you to hand over some sensitive information. So, is it okay to shop online? Yes, but just as you wouldn't leave your doors unlocked, you need to be sure that you're shopping wisely. Shop at well-known sites or use third-party payment sites such as Google Checkout and PayPal to protect credit card information. Make sure you're on a secure website when completing transactions. Look at your browser's address bar. If the URL begins with https, then the site is using SSL security. You'll also notice a padlock that indicates a secure site. Clicking on the padlock will open a security report about the website.

Key Terms

e-commerce

social media marketing

Running Project

Visit Amazon.com. What are two ways that Amazon uses social media marketing? Can you find any other ways? How is this experience different from shopping in a store?

2 Things You Need to Know

- E-commerce is business on the Web.
- Social media marketing (SMM) uses social media sites to sell products and services.

What Can I Do WITH KNOWLEDGE ABOUT ONLINE COMMUNICATION?

7 OBJECTIVE
Identify the careers related to online communication.

As we've seen, many businesses use the social Web to reach and support customers. There are many jobs that use forms of online communication between employees.

BLOGGER

Although most blogs are personal in nature and earn the writer no compensation, some lucky folks are professional bloggers. These bloggers may be paid by a company to blog about a product or provide news or reviews, and their blogs are usually part of a bigger website. Some professional bloggers use their blogs to drive customers to their other products. Successful bloggers monetize the content on their sites in several ways, including placing ads and links to other sites. It takes a lot of time and work to write a good blog and even more to make money while doing it. Figure 8.28 shows a blog that I read every day.

FIGURE 8.28
A professional blog may earn money by using Google AdSense to place ads and links on it.

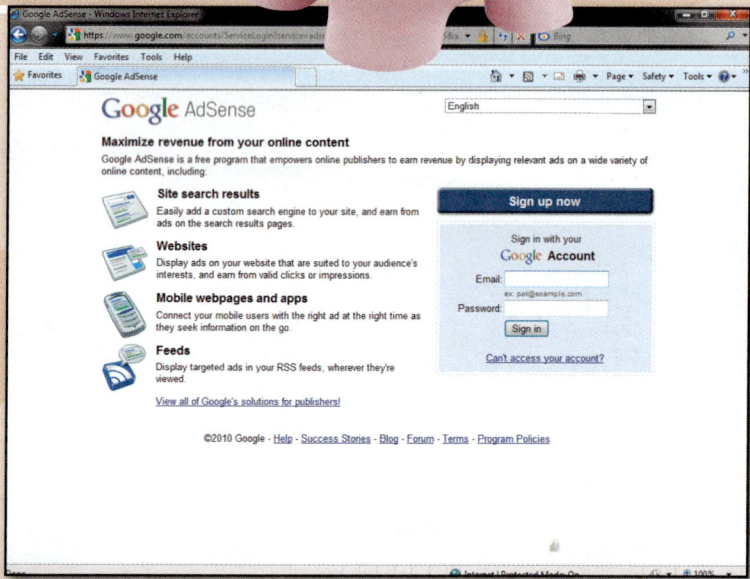

SOCIAL MEDIA MARKETER

Creating a good social media marketing (SMM) campaign requires someone with both marketing skills and technical skills. Simply sending mass e-mail messages results in a very low response rate, but a good SMM campaign can reach more people and result in a much higher response rate. An SMM campaign might include creating fan pages and ads on social network sites, contests on Twitter, or a video that's so funny that it goes viral. This is a relatively new field, and there's lots of room for creative people with new ideas.

Figure 8.29 shows the Twitter page for WholeRecipes. This is a brilliant SMM that doesn't specifically suggest consumers go shopping at Whole Foods market but simply provides interesting recipes every day. Of course, the hope is that you'll go buy the ingredients at your local Whole Foods market, and some people do.

No matter what field you go into, knowing how to use online communication tools is a useful skill to have.

FIGURE 8.29 A social media marketer develops marketing campaigns that use social media sites such as Twitter to reach customers.

GREEN COMPUTING

RAISING SOCIAL AWARENESS

How much paper mail do you receive every week? And how much of it do you actually read? The cost of a direct-mail campaign is huge, and many people simply toss what they see as junk mail in the trash anyway, so the costs are also large in terms of the environment. SMM isn't just for businesses but can also be used to raise awareness of important issues.

Not long ago, women all over Facebook posted one word status updates. White, red, gray, black. What was going on? Women were sharing a message with each other that said: "Some fun is going on. . . . Just write the color of your bra in your status. Just the color; nothing else. It will be neat to see if this will spread the wings of breast cancer awareness. It will be fun to see how long it takes before people wonder why all the girls have a color in their status. . . . Haha."

The message quickly spread, and thousands of women (and even some men) responded. The idea was to raise social awareness about breast cancer. Did it work? Well, it certainly didn't do any harm, and the story was also picked up by the news media. So, a simple act of social networking resulted in raising social awareness. The beauty of the idea was that it got women thinking about something we usually prefer not to at no cost to the environment. Facebook has an application called Causes that can be used to raise both awareness and funds for social causes without printing a single piece of paper.

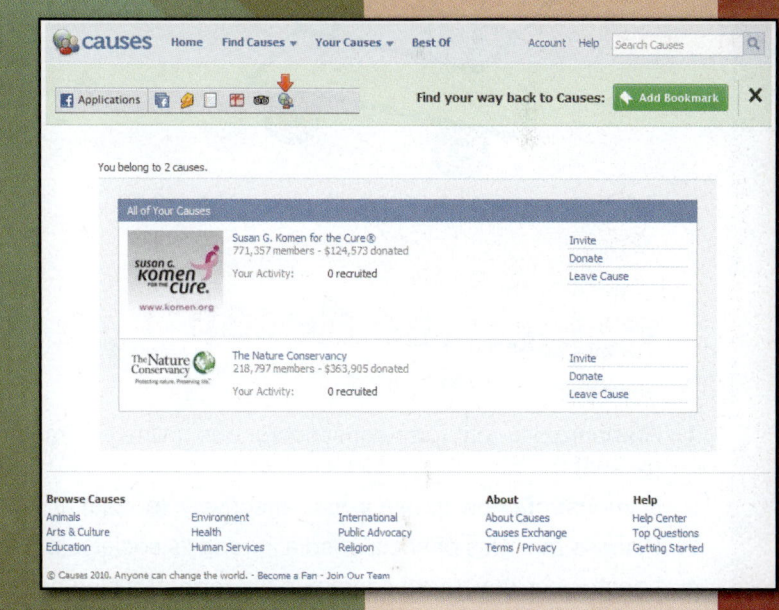

Chapter 8

325

COMMUNICATING & SHARING: THE SOCIAL WEB

CAREERS AND CERTIFICATION — blogger, social media marketer

SOCIAL MEDIA AND E-COMMERCE — types of e-commerce, credit card safety

WIKIS AND OTHER SOCIAL MEDIA — wikis, social review sites, social bookmarking sites

Objectives Recap

1. Compare different forms of synchronous online communication. (p. 294)
2. Demonstrate how to use e-mail effectively. (p. 298)
3. Discuss the roles of social media in today's society. (p. 304)
4. Locate user-generated content in the form of a blog or podcast. (p. 314)
5. Discuss how wikis and other social media sites rely on the wisdom of the crowd. (p. 318)
6. Explain the influence of social media on e-commerce. (p. 322)
7. Identify the careers related to online communication. (p. 324)

Key Terms

asynchronous online communication 298
avatar 306
blog 314
blogosphere 314
captcha 299
chat 294
digital footprint 309
e-commerce 322
e-mail 298
folksonomy 307
forum 302
instant messaging (IM) 294
microblogging 315
podcast 316
podcast client 316
RSS (Really Simple Syndication) 317
social bookmarking site 320
social media 304

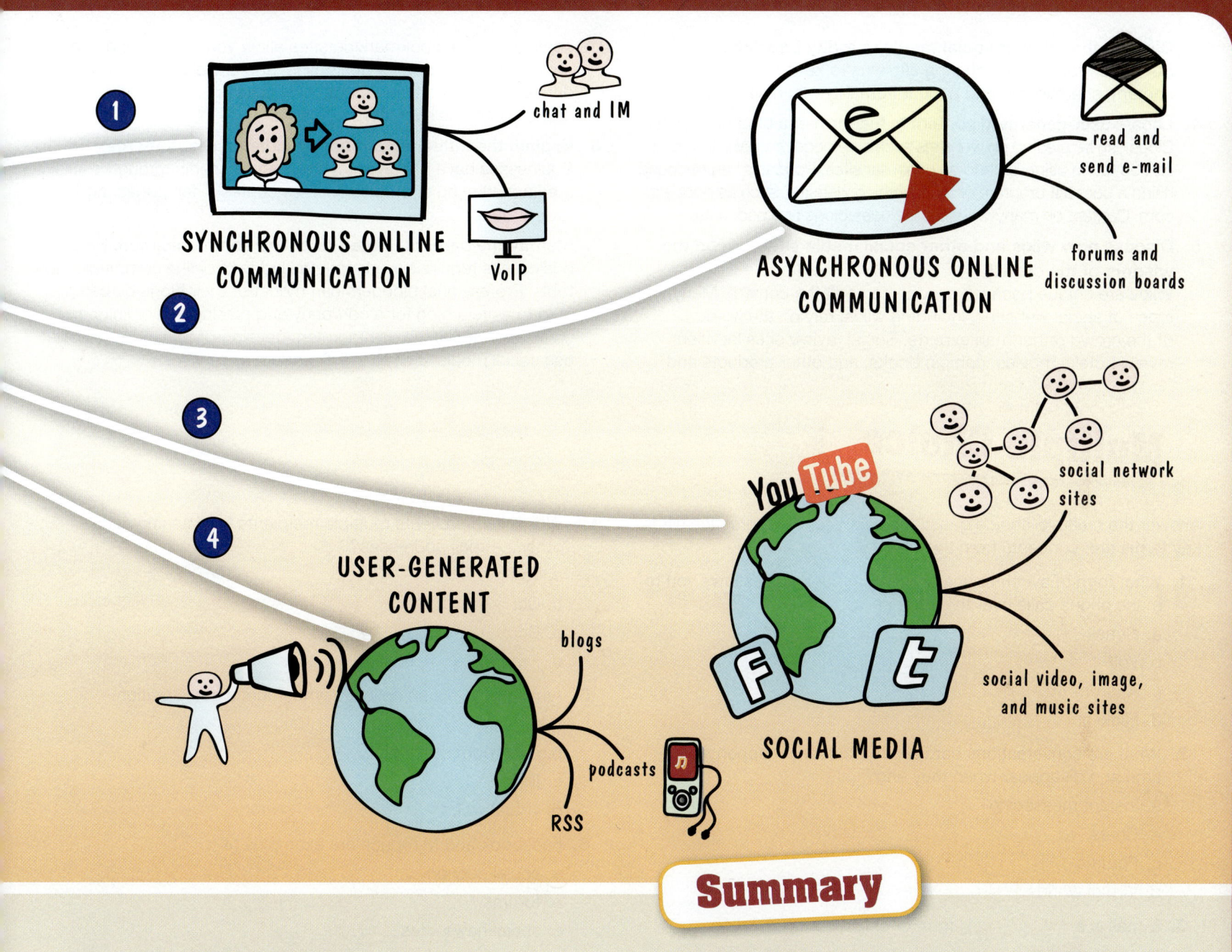

① **SYNCHRONOUS ONLINE COMMUNICATION**
- chat and IM
- VoIP

ASYNCHRONOUS ONLINE COMMUNICATION
- read and send e-mail
- forums and discussion boards

②

③ **USER-GENERATED CONTENT**
- blogs
- podcasts
- RSS

④ **SOCIAL MEDIA**
- social network sites
- social video, image, and music sites

Summary

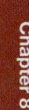

social media marketing (SMM) **322**
social network **304**
social news site **320**
social review site **319**
synchronous online communication **294**
user-generated content **314**
viral video **307**
VoIP (voice over IP) **297**
Web 2.0 **304**
wiki **318**

1. **Compare different forms of synchronous online communication.**
   Synchronous communication happens in real time. Chat usually involves more than two people having a conversation in a chat room and is usually text-based. Instant messaging is similar to chat, but the conversation is between only two people. The terms IM and chat are often used interchangeably. VoIP service uses the Internet to place phone calls.

2. **Demonstrate how to use e-mail effectively.**
   E-mail is an asynchronous, store-and-forward technology. You can access e-mail using webmail or a desktop e-mail program. You shouldn't expect that your e-mail is private.

3. **Discuss the roles of social media in today's society.**
   Social networking and sharing allow us to keep in touch, create content, share ideas, and benefit from the expertise of others.

4. **Locate user-generated content in the form of a blog or podcast.**
   Blogs can be created on websites such as Blogger and WordPress and can be found using Technorati or similar sites. Podcasts can be found using a podcast program or by searching websites such as podcast.com. Content on many websites includes blogs and podcasts.

5. **Discuss how wikis and other social media sites rely on the wisdom of the crowd.**
   Wikis are unique because anyone can edit the content. Many types of social websites, including wikis, rely on the wisdom of the crowd rather than experts. Social review sites let users review hotels, movies, games, books, and other products and services; social bookmarking sites allow you to save and share your bookmarks or favorites online; and social news sites are different from traditional media news sites in that at least some of the content is submitted by users.

6. **Explain the influence of social media on e-commerce.**
   Businesses have begun to leverage social media through social media marketing strategies such as contests, fan pages, and review sites.

7. **Identify the careers related to online communication.** Most businesses require a working knowledge of online communication tools. Professional bloggers can monetize their blogs by being paid to write a blog for a company and placing ads or links on their sites. Social media marketers develop SMM campaigns that use social media sites to sell a product or service.

Multiple Choice

Answer the multiple-choice questions below for more practice with key terms and concepts from this chapter.

1. What form of synchronous online communication allows you to make phone calls over the Internet?
   a. E-mail
   b. VoIP
   c. A forum
   d. Flickr

2. What are conversations between buddies that happen in real time and disappear when they end?
   a. Instant messaging
   b. Chats
   c. Forums
   d. Virtual worlds

3. E-mail is a _____ form of online communication.
   a. synchronous
   b. real-time
   c. private
   d. store-and-forward

4. Which field prevents multiple recipients from seeing each other's e-mail addresses?
   a. To:
   b. Cc:
   c. Bcc:
   d. Fw:

5. A(n) _____ is an online, asynchronous conversation.
   a. forum
   b. chat room
   c. IM
   d. virtual world

6. Facebook and MySpace are examples of
   a. social networks.
   b. forums.
   c. social news sites.
   d. social media marketing.

7. You can use a virtual body or _____ to interact with others online.
   a. screen name
   b. profile
   c. client
   d. avatar

8. Your _____ is all the information that someone could find out about you by searching the Web, including social network sites.
   a. profile
   b. digital footprint ← *(circled)*
   c. avatar
   d. captcha

9. What service is used to distribute Web feeds to subscribers?
   a. RSS ← *(circled)*
   b. E-mail
   c. Podcasts
   d. Folksonomy

10. Which type of social media allows users to edit content, even if it was written by someone else?
    a. Blog
    b. Forum
    c. Podcast
    d. Wiki ← *(circled)*

True or False

Answer the following questions with T for true or F for false for more practice with key terms and concepts from this chapter.

- **T** 1. Synchronous online communication happens in real time.
- **F** 2. E-mail is private and can't be read by others.
- **F** 3. You can have only one profile on a social network.
- **F** 4. A viral video spreads computer viruses.
- **T** 5. Microblog posts are typically limited to 140 characters.
- **F** 6. You must use special software to read blogs.
- **T** 7. You can listen to some podcasts directly from their websites without a podcast client.
- **F** 8. Like a blog, a wiki usually has only one author.
- **T** 9. Social news sites include content that's submitted by users.
- **F** 10. Social media marketing is designed to get more subscribers on social networks.

Fill in the Blank

Fill in the blanks with key terms and concepts from this chapter.

1. Online __chat__ allows you to talk to multiple people at the same time in real time.
2. __asynchronous online communication__ technology lets you send a message that the receiver can access later.
3. A(n) __captcha__ is a series of letters and numbers that are distorted in some way.
4. Collectively, the tools that enable users to create user-generated content, connect, network, and share are called __social media__.
5. __folksonomy__ is the social tagging of Web media.
6. The __blogosphere__ consists of all the blogs on the Web and the connections between them.
7. A __viral__ video becomes extremely popular because of recommendations and social sharing.
8. A(n) __podcast__ is a digital media file of a prerecorded radio- or TV-like show that is distributed over the Web.
9. __Social bookmarking sites__ sites allow you to save and share your favorites online.
10. __E-commerce__ is doing business on the Web.

Running Project

... The Finish Line
Use your answers from the previous sections of the chapter project to discuss the impact of social network on society. How has it changed the way we keep in touch with others? Do business? How has it personally changed the way you connect with others?

Write a report responding to the questions raised. Save your file as **Lastname_Firstname_ch08_Project**, and submit it to your instructor as directed.

File Management

Social sharing sites allow you to put your videos and images online. To help organize this content, the sites use social tagging. For this activity, you'll create tags for a group of images provided with this book.

1. Navigate to the folder where you're keeping your student files for this chapter. Look at the 21 images in the folder. Create a table like the one below. For each image, list at least two tags that you would use to tag the file. Try to use the same tags for multiple files.

Image	Tag1	Tag2

2. Go to the Flickr website, and search for the three tags that you used the most often in your table. Do you find images that are similar to the ones you tagged? Do you think you did a good job of tagging them?
3. Save your file as **Lastname_Firstname_ch08_Tags**, and submit it as directed by your instructor.

Critical Thinking 1

Visit a social network site mentioned in this book that you don't normally use. Read the information about membership and the privacy policy.

1. What are the basic rules or terms for membership? What type of behavior is unacceptable? Do you feel your information is adequately protected under the privacy policy?
2. Will the network allow you to view profiles without becoming a member? If yes, look around to see what profiles you can view. Did you see exactly what you were expecting? Did anything disappoint you?
3. Type up your answers, save the file as **Lastname_Firstname_ch08_Social_Behavior**, and submit it as directed by your instructor.

Critical Thinking 2

Think about the way you use social networks and why you use them.

1. What social networks do you belong to? Do you use them all regularly? Are there some that you never use? Why do you belong to these networks?
2. Think about the network that you use the most. What are the five features you use most frequently? Why? What are the five you use the least? Why?
3. Have you set your privacy settings to keep your personal information protected? When was the last time you checked and updated them? Have the terms of service changed since you first joined this network?
4. Type up your answers, save the file as **Lastname_Firstname_ch08_My_Networks**, and submit it as directed by your instructor.

Do It Yourself 1

Instant messaging and chatting have become popular tools for businesses to provide services to customers. Some libraries also offer virtual librarians that you can chat with live online.

1. If your school or local library provides this service, use it to ask them about the success of this service. Take a screen shot of your conversation. If you don't have a local library that uses chat/IM, then use the Internet to find another library that does.
2. Type up your answers, and save the file as **Lastname_Firstname_ch08_Library**. Submit your work as directed by your instructor.

Do It Yourself 2

Some websites require you to provide an e-mail address to register. While it's okay to use your normal e-mail on sites that you trust and want communication from, it's a good idea to have a separate e-mail address just to use for those sites that you don't want to hear from again.

1. Go to **yahoo.com**, and click *New here?* Sign Up. (If you're already logged in to Yahoo!, sign out first).
2. Fill in the form. Click *Create My Account*.
3. Take a screen shot of the Congratulations page. Save the image as **Lastname_Firstname_ch08_Email**, and submit it as directed by your instructor.

Ethical Dilemma

Your digital footprint says a lot about you, but not everything is true or accurate. When you're a college (or high school) student, it's hard to think about the impact your digital life will have on future employment. Some potential employers will search the Web looking for information on job applicants.

1. Is it ethical for a potential employer to use the Internet this way? Is it legal? What if an angry ex-boyfriend or ex-girlfriend posted some things pretending to be you? How might this affect your chances for employment? Do you think it's okay to post things that make you look good, even if they're not true?
2. Type up your answers, save the file as **Lastname_Firstname_ch08_Digital_Footprint**, and submit your work as directed by your instructor.

On the Web 1

There are literally hundreds of social networks on the Web today. Use the Internet to find a list of social networks.

1. How many did you find? Select one that you do not use that sounds interesting. Research more about it. When was it founded? Where is it located? How many members does it have? Does it cater to special interests? What features make it unique?
2. Type up your answers, save the file as **Lastname_Firstname_ch08_Social_Network**, and submit your work as directed by your instructor.

On the Web 2

Social news sites are a great way to find out what other people think is important. Visit **Slashdot.com**, and look on the Recent page.

1. What are some of the recent stories? Select two that you think are interesting or important, and write a short summary of each. Why did you select these stories?
2. Type up your answers, save the file as **Lastname_Firstname_ch08_Slashdot**, and submit your work as directed by your instructor.

Collaboration 1

With a group of three to five students, create a podcast on a current technology topic of mutual interest to the group. You must receive approval for your topic from your instructor. Use a social news site to locate possible topics.

Instructors: Divide the class into groups of three to four students, and approve the topics they propose.

The Project: Each team is to prepare a script for the podcast. Teams must use at least three references, only one of which may be this textbook. Use Google Docs to prepare the final version of your script, and provide documentation that all team members have contributed to the project. For more on using Google Docs, see Appendix C. Record the podcast using an audio tool such as Audacity or Windows Sound Recorder.

Students: Before beginning this project, discuss the roles each group member will play. Choose a team name, which you'll use in submitting your materials. Be sure to divide the work among your members. You may find it helpful to elect a team leader who can direct your activities and ensure that all team contributions are collated through Google Docs.

Outcome: Record the podcast using the script you've written. The podcast should be 3 to 5 minutes long. Save this podcast as **Teamname_ch08_Podcast**.

Turn in a final text version of your script named as **Teamname_ch08_Podcast_Script** and your Google Docs file showing your collaboration named as **Teamname_ch08_Podcast_Collaboration**. Be sure to include the name of your podcast and a listing of all team members. Submit your presentation to your instructor as directed.

Collaboration 2

With a group of three to five students, research the history of social networks. Create a timeline showing five to seven important milestones of this development. Use a free online timeline generator, a drawing program, a word processor, or a presentation tool to create your timeline. Present your findings to the class.

Instructors: Divide the class into groups of three to five students.

The Project: Each team is to research the history of social networks. Create a timeline showing five to seven important milestones of this development. Teams must use at least three references, only one of which may be this textbook. Use Google Docs to plan the presentation, and provide documentation that all team members have contributed to the project. For more on using Google Docs, see Appendix C.

Students: Before beginning this project, discuss the roles each group member will play. Choose a team name, which you'll use in submitting your presentation. Be sure to divide the work among your members, and pick someone to present your project. You may find it helpful to elect a team leader who can direct your activities and ensure that all team contributions are collated through Google Docs.

Outcome: Use a free online timeline generator, a drawing program, a word processor, or a presentation tool to create your timeline, and present it to your class. The presentation may be no longer than 3 minutes and should contain 5 to 7 milestones. Turn in a final version of your presentation named as **Teamname_ch08_Timeline** and your Google Docs file showing your collaboration named as **Teamname_ch08_Timeline_Collaboration**. Be sure to include the name of your presentation and a listing of all team members. Submit your presentation to your instructor as directed.

Blogging

1. Blog about the impact of online communication in your lifetime. In your write-up, talk about the technology that has been developed since you were born. What do you expect to change in the next 10 years? The next 20 years?

2. Visit at least two of your classmates' blogs on this topic. On the blogs you visit, comment on their ideas, and compare them to what you have written.

3. Create a document that includes your blog URL and the URLs of the two blogs you commented on. Save the file as **Lastname_Firstname_ch08_Pace_Blog**. Submit the document to your instructor as directed.

CHAPTER 9
Networks and Communi...

Running Project

In this chapter, you'll learn about computer networks and communication. Look for instructions as you complete each article. For most, there is a series of questions for you to research. At the conclusion of this chapter you're asked to submit your responses to the questions raised.

Become our friend on Facebook

...cation

OBJECTIVES

1. Discuss the importance of computer networks. (p. 336)
2. Compare different types of LANs and WANs. (p. 348)
3. List and describe the hardware used in both wired and wireless networks. (p. 352)
4. List and describe the software and protocols used in both wired and wireless networks. (p. 358)
5. Explain how to protect a network. (p. 364)
6. Identify the certifications and careers related to computer networks. (p. 366)

IN THIS CHAPTER

The Internet is the largest computer network in the world, but it is actually a network of networks. On a much smaller scale, most of the computers that you use at school and in the workplace are part of a network, and it is very likely that you also have a network at home. But only a few years ago, that was not the case. In this chapter, you'll learn about different kinds of computer networks.

From Sneakernet TO HOTSPOTS

OBJECTIVE 1
Discuss the importance of computer networks.

A **computer network** is two or more computers that share resources. **Network resources** can be software, hardware, or files. Computer networks save us both time and money and make it easier for us to work, increasing productivity. Before computers were connected in networks, moving files between them involved physically putting them on a disk and carrying the disk to the new machine. This is wistfully referred to as "sneakernet."

PEER-TO-PEER NETWORKS

Figure 9.1 shows a small peer-to-peer network that you might have set up at home. A **peer-to-peer network (P2P)** is one in which each computer is considered equal. Each device can share its resources with every other device, and there's no centralized authority. In this example, the computers might share music (files) and a printer (hardware). They don't necessarily have to connect to the Internet at all. This is the simplest type of network you can set up. Computers in a P2P network belong to a **workgroup**.

FIGURE 9.1 A simple peer-to-peer network between two computers

Most P2P networks are found in homes or small businesses. They are easy to set up and configure and offer basic file and print sharing. A peer-to-peer network doesn't require a NOS (network operating system). While your personal operating system has networking features, the files and services that are shared between your home computers aren't centralized. Windows 7 has the Network and Sharing Center to help you configure your sharing options (see Figure 9.2). For example, if you have a printer in your house that's connected to your desktop computer, that printer can easily be shared with your notebook computer through your home network. The biggest problem with this type of network is that the computer that's sharing a resource must be turned on and accessible by the other computers in the network. If your desktop computer is turned off or in sleep mode, then the notebook will be unable to print.

FIGURE 9.2 The Windows 7 Network and Sharing Center window allows you to view and configure your network.

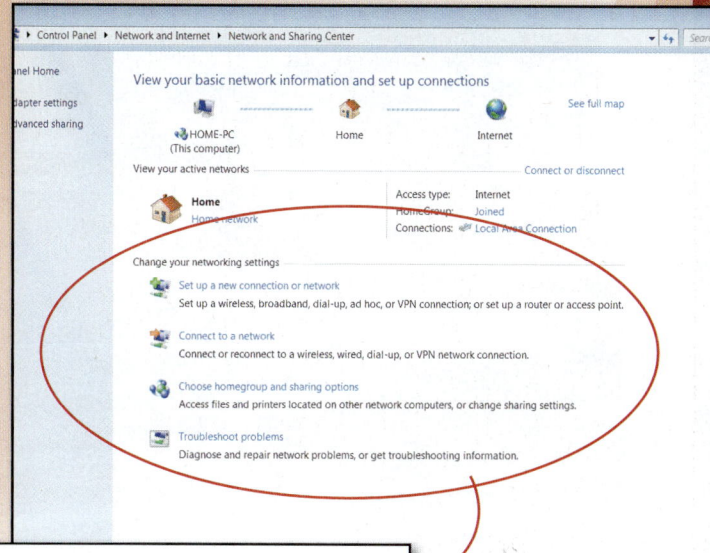

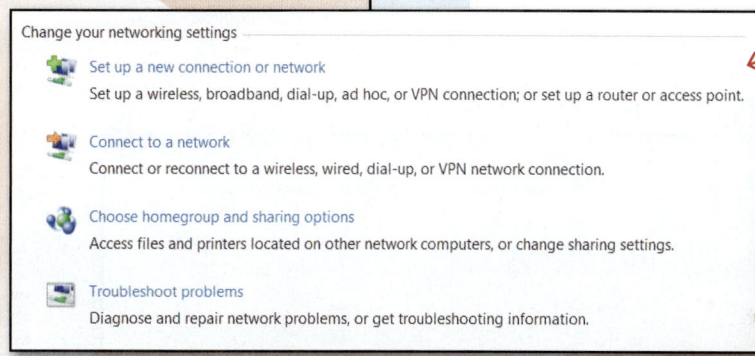

FIGURE 9.3 This network map from a Windows 7 computer shows the computers and other devices detected on this network.

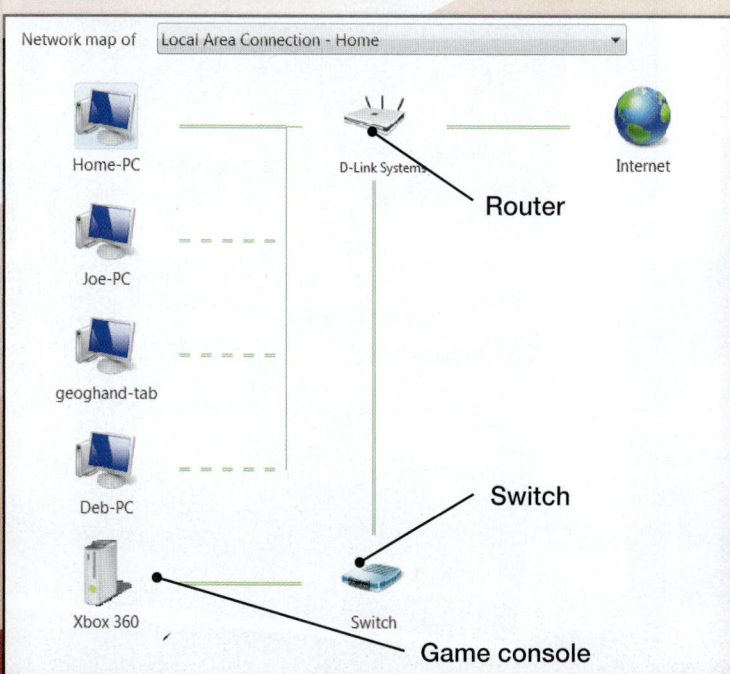

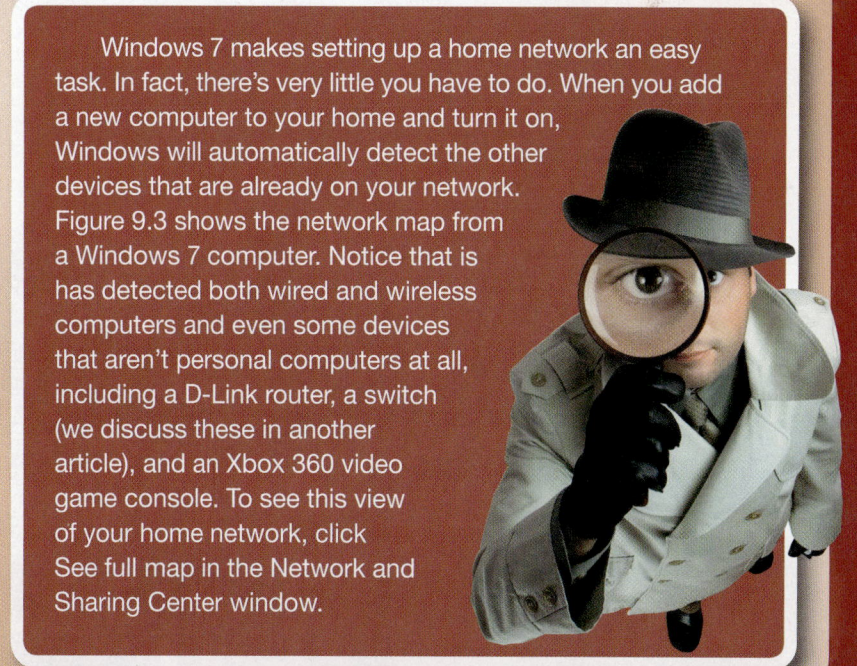

Windows 7 makes setting up a home network an easy task. In fact, there's very little you have to do. When you add a new computer to your home and turn it on, Windows will automatically detect the other devices that are already on your network. Figure 9.3 shows the network map from a Windows 7 computer. Notice that is has detected both wired and wireless computers and even some devices that aren't personal computers at all, including a D-Link router, a switch (we discuss these in another article), and an Xbox 360 video game console. To see this view of your home network, click See full map in the Network and Sharing Center window.

Windows 7 comes with a new networking feature called homegroup. A **homegroup** is a simple way to network a group of Windows 7 computers that are all on the same home network. Members of a homegroup automatically share their picture, music, and video libraries and printers with each other without any additional configuration on your part. You can create a homegroup if your computer is running Windows 7 Home Premium, Professional, Ultimate, or Enterprise. Once you create a homegroup, Windows will create a password that you can then use to join all your other Windows 7 computers to the homegroup. In Figure 9.4, you can see my homegroup setup in the Windows Explorer window. In the navigation pane, GEOGHAND-TAB is visible under Network but does not appear under Homegroup. This is because GEOGHAND-TAB is running Windows Vista and cannot join a homegroup. In order to share resources with this computer, I must use a workgroup, which requires more configuration.

HOME SWEET HOME

FIGURE 9.4 My homegroup and network computers

Members of the homegroup

Computers on the network

Setting up shared resources using a homegroup is easier than using a regular workgroup. You can choose to share Pictures, Music, Videos, Documents, and Printers. By default, Documents are not shared, but you can easily change this setting. The How To exercise in this chapter demonstrates how to do this. If you have computers running other versions of Windows or Linux or Mac computers, then you will need to use a workgroup to share resources between them. Setting up the shares in a workgroup is not difficult but takes a bit more work than setting up a homegroup. Computers in a workgroup need to have the same workgroup and account information configured. By default, Windows computers belong to the workgroup called "workgroup." Mac and Linux computers will need to be configured with the same workgroup name to be able to access the resources (see Figure 9.5).

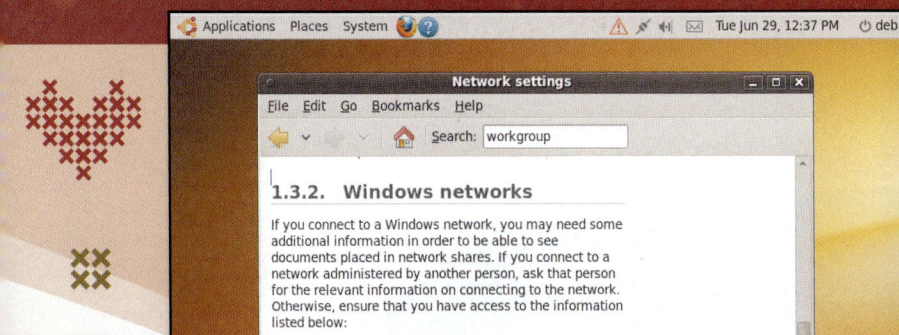

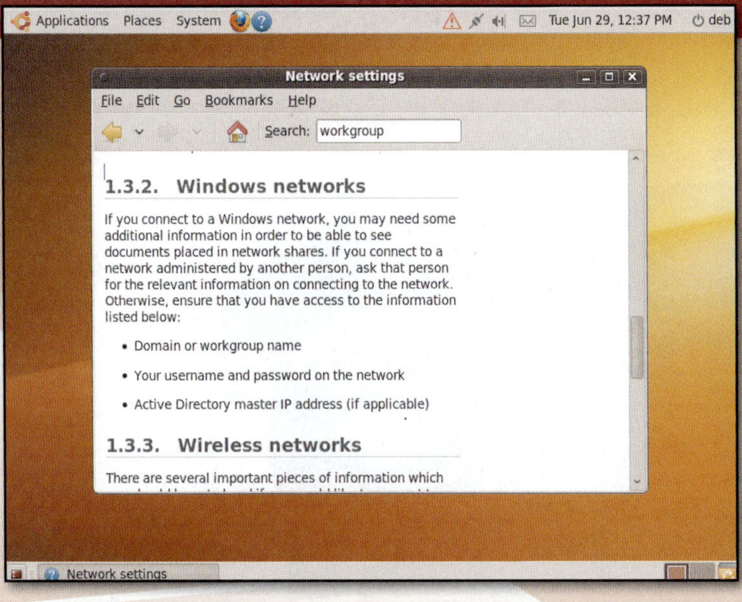

FIGURE 9.5 An Ubuntu Linux computer will need to have account and workgroup information configured to join a Windows workgroup.

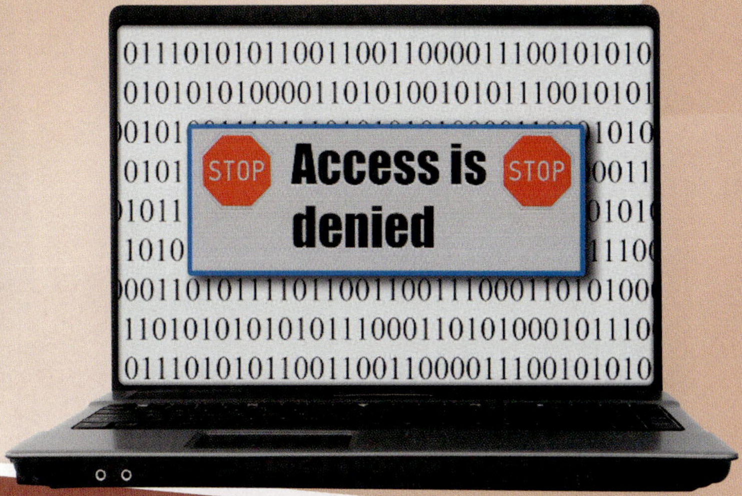

To share a resource with computers in your workgroup, right-click the item to be shared and choose Share with (see Figure 9.6). Click *Specific people* to open the File Sharing dialog box. In the File Sharing dialog box, choose the users you want to give access to from the drop-down list box and click *Add*. You can grant read or read/write access to this folder. You can also remove users from this list.

FIGURE 9.6 Use the File Sharing dialog box to grant access to your files.

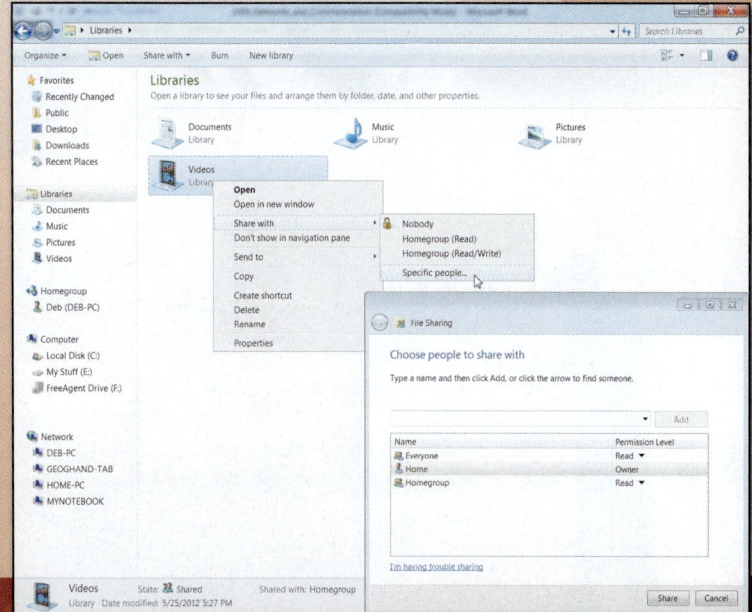

CLIENT-SERVER NETWORKS

P2P networks are fine for homes and very small businesses, but they have two major drawbacks. First, they're limited to a small number of devices, and second, they provide no centralization of resources and security. In most business settings, a client-server network is a better choice.

A **client-server network** is one that has at least one server at its center (see Figure 9.7). The server provides a way to centralize the network management, resources, and security. In a client-server network, users log in to the network instead of their local computers and are granted access to resources based on that login.

FIGURE 9.7
A client-server network with centralized servers

Find Out MORE

Windows Home Server is a network operating system specifically designed to be used on a home network. Use the Internet to find out more about it. What features does it include? What are the hardware requirements? How much does it cost? Is it worth it?

A **server** is a multiuser computer system that runs a network operating system (NOS) and provides services—such as Internet access, e-mail, or file and print services—to client systems. The personal computers and other devices that connect to the server are called **clients**. Servers range from very small to massive enterprise level systems that serve hundreds of thousands of clients.

Key Terms

client

client-server network

computer network

homegroup

network resource

peer-to-peer network (P2P)

server

workgroup

Running Project

Examine the network settings on your computer as described in this article. Does it belong to a workgroup? A homegroup? A client-server network? What resources does it share? Include a screen shot of the Network and Sharing Center and any other screen that you used to find this information.

3 Things You Need to Know

- A computer network is two or more computers that share resources, such as software, hardware, or files.
- A peer-to-peer network (P2P) is one in which each computer belongs to the same workgroup and is considered an equal.
- A client-server network is one that has at least one server at its center that provides centralized management, resources, and security.

HOW TO Share Files and Printers using a Windows Homegroup

The Windows 7 homegroup is an easy way to share files and printers on your home network. In this How To, you'll examine your current homegroup settings and share resources on your network. (Note that in a school network, security settings may prevent you from being able to perform this exercise). Before you begin, create a blank document to record your answers.

PART A—CREATE A HOMEGROUP

First, check to see if your computer belongs to a homegroup. Open Windows Explorer from the taskbar or Start menu, and click *Homegroup* in the navigation pane. If there is no existing homegroup, Windows will give you the opportunity to create one. (Computers running Windows 7 Home Basic edition can join but can't create a homegroup). If you see this message, click *Create a homegroup*. Take a screen shot of this window, and paste it into your document. If you do not see the option to *Create a homegroup*, skip to Part B.

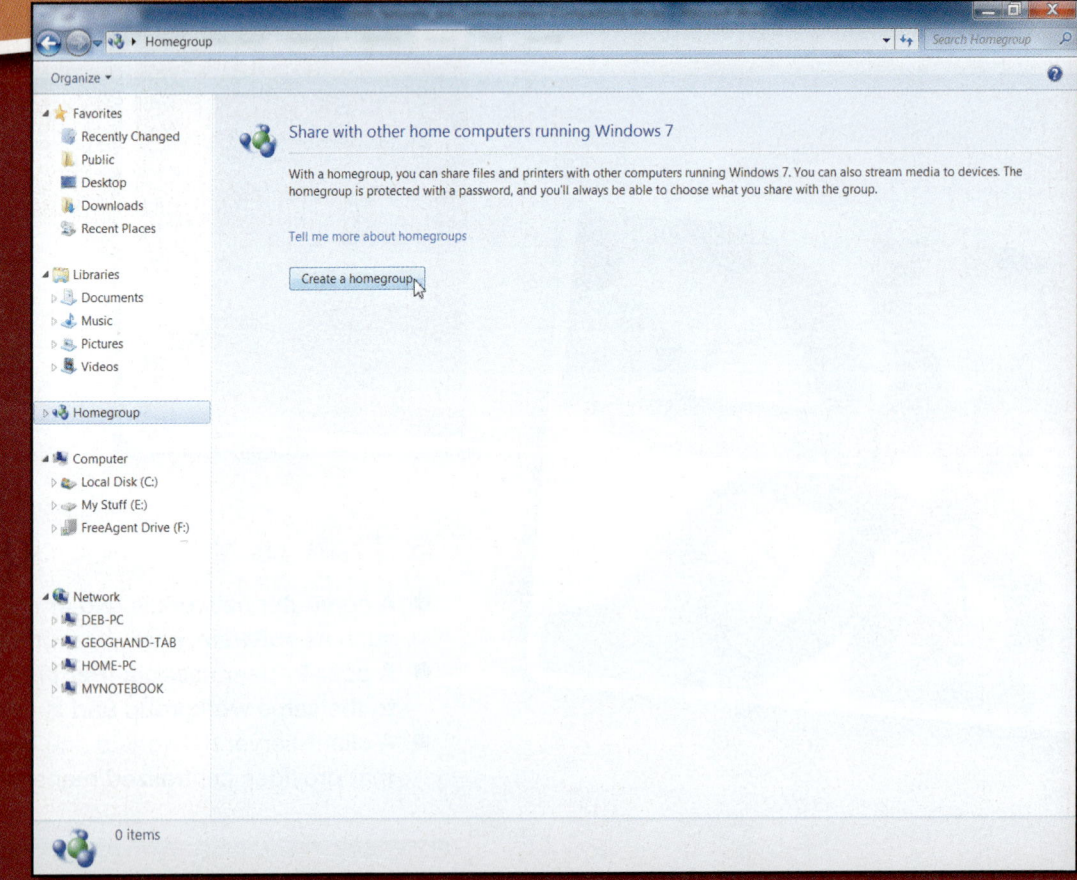

2 Choose what you want to share and then click *Next*. Which resources were shared by default? Which resources did you choose to share?

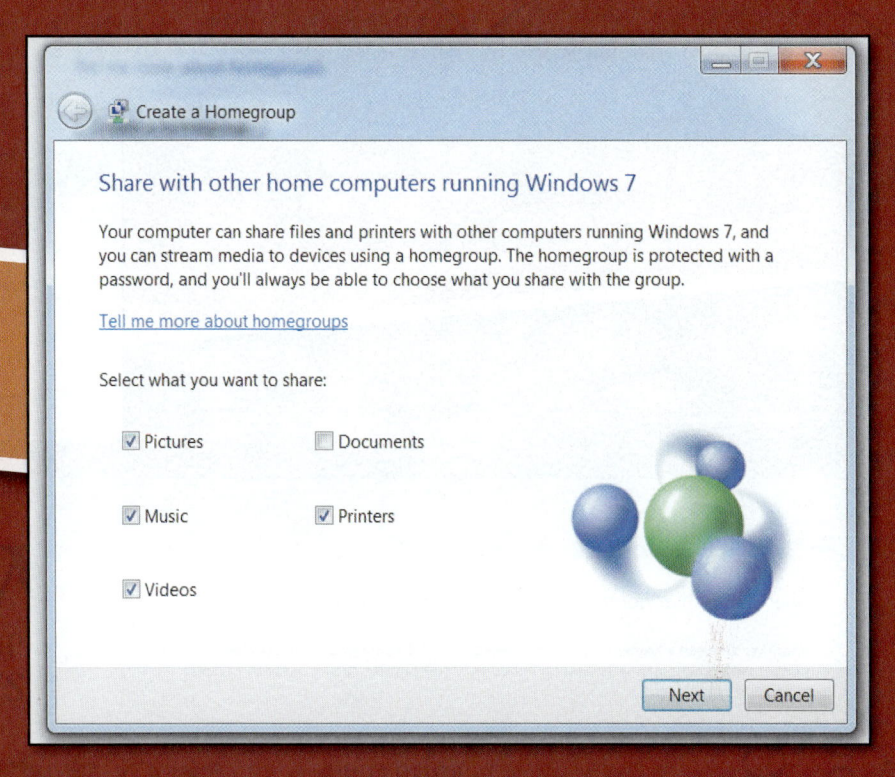

Create a Homegroup

Share with other home computers running Windows 7

Your computer can share files and printers with other computers running Windows 7, and you can stream media to devices using a homegroup. The homegroup is protected with a password, and you'll always be able to choose what you share with the group.

Tell me more about homegroups

Select what you want to share:

- ☑ Pictures
- ☐ Documents
- ☑ Music
- ☑ Printers
- ☑ Videos

[Next] [Cancel]

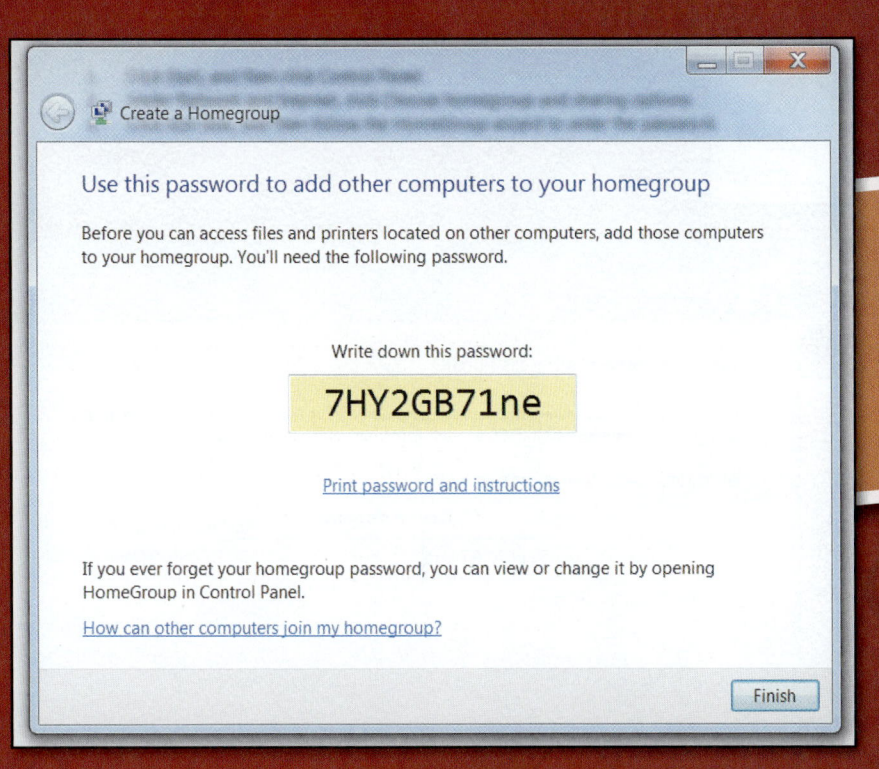

Create a Homegroup

Use this password to add other computers to your homegroup

Before you can access files and printers located on other computers, add those computers to your homegroup. You'll need the following password.

Write down this password:

7HY2GB71ne

Print password and instructions

If you ever forget your homegroup password, you can view or change it by opening HomeGroup in Control Panel.

How can other computers join my homegroup?

[Finish]

3 A homegroup password is automatically generated. Use this password on your other Windows 7 computers to join the homegroup.

Chapter 9 | 343

PART B—JOIN A HOMEGROUP

1 Open Windows Explorer from the taskbar or Start menu, and click *Homegroup* in the navigation pane. If you don't belong to a homegroup but Windows detects one, you'll see the message *Share with other home computers running Windows 7*. Click *Join now*. (If you already belong to a homegroup, skip to Part C).

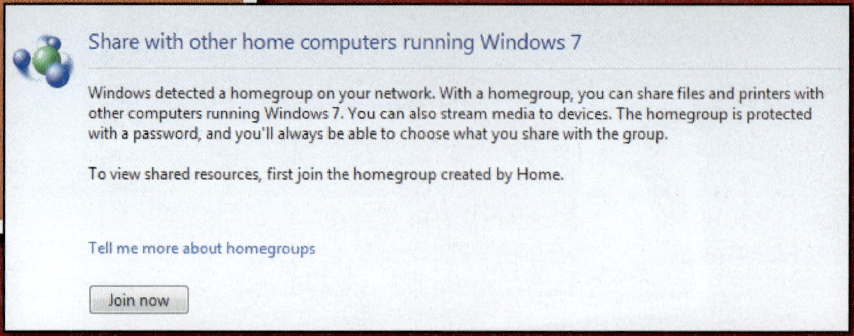

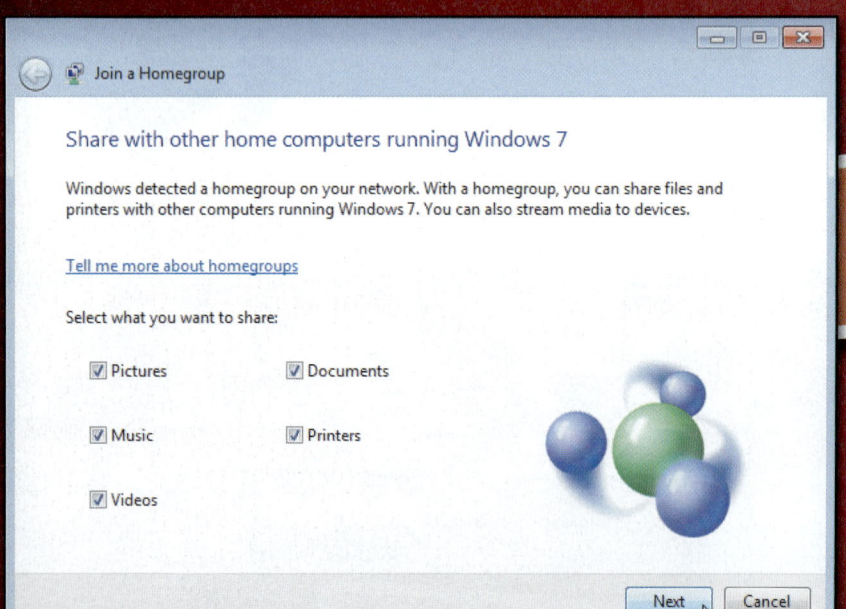

2 Choose what you want to share, and click *Next*.

3 You'll need the homegroup password to continue. Enter the homegroup password, and click *Next*. (If you don't have the homegroup password, you can find it on any computer that belongs to the homegroup by opening the Network and Sharing Center and clicking *Choose homegroup and sharing options* and then clicking *View or print the homegroup password*.)

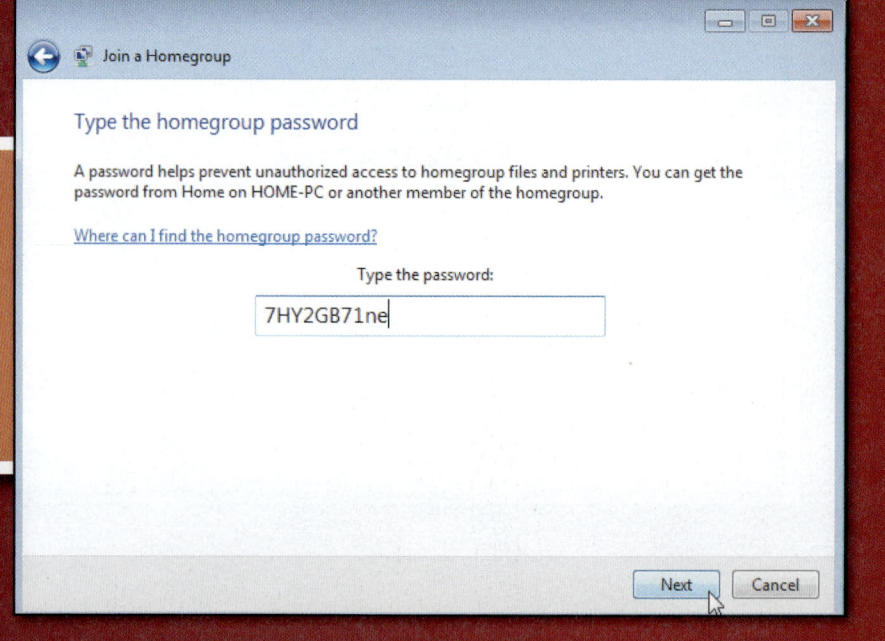

4 Click *Finish*.

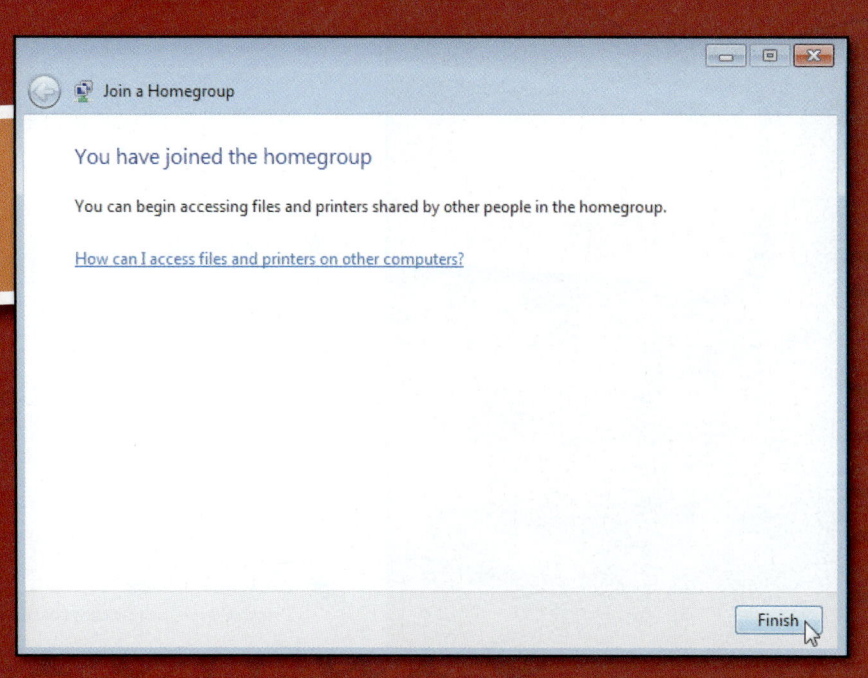

PART C—EXAMINE HOMEGROUP SETTINGS

1 On a computer that belongs to a homegroup, open the Network and Sharing Center by clicking the network icon on the taskbar.

2 Click *Choose homegroup and sharing options*.

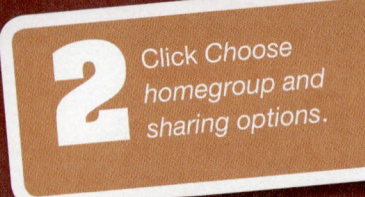

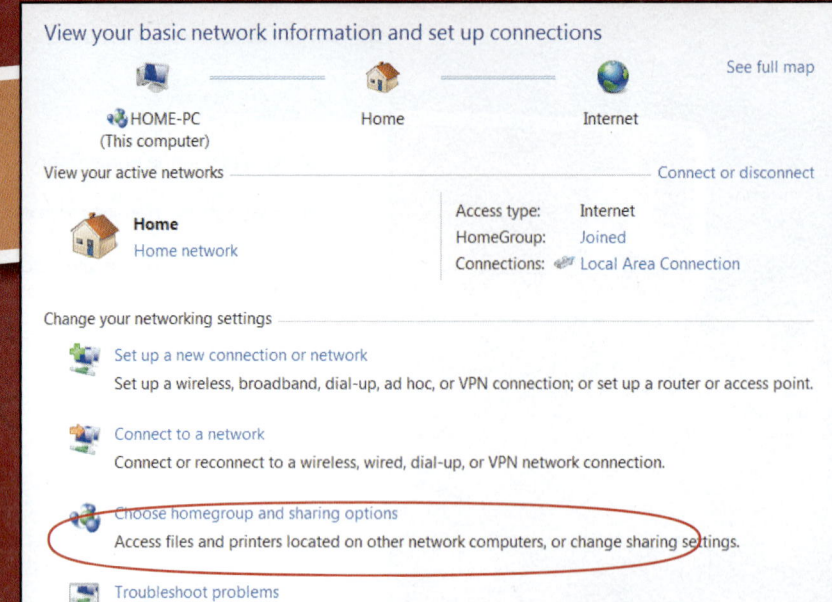

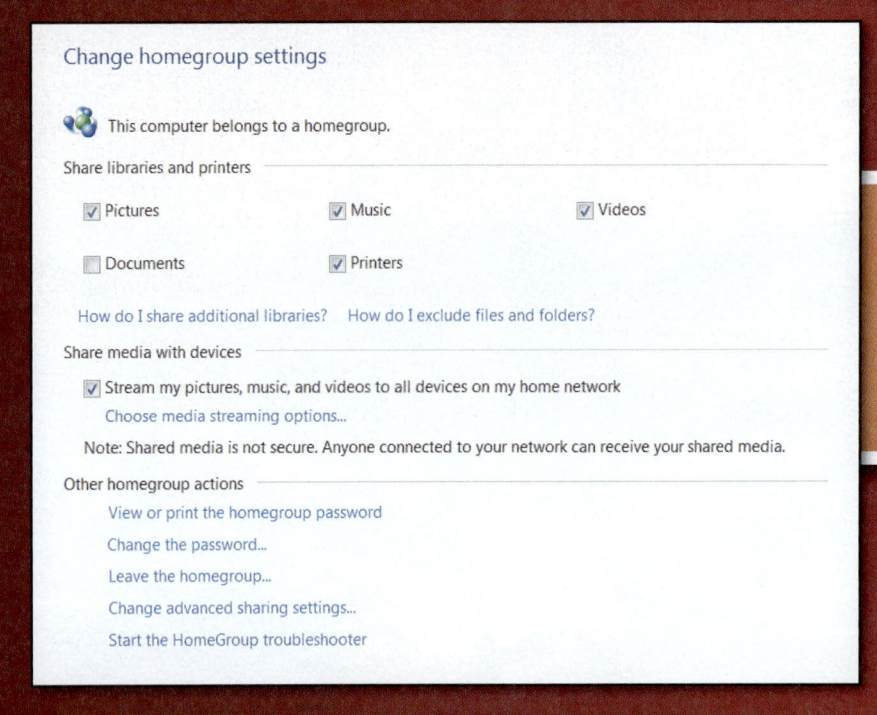

3 Under *Share libraries and printers*, check the resources that you want to share. Take a screen shot of this window, paste it into your document, and then click *Save changes* at the bottom of the page.

4 Click *Choose media streaming options*. If necessary, click *Turn on media streaming* in the next window.

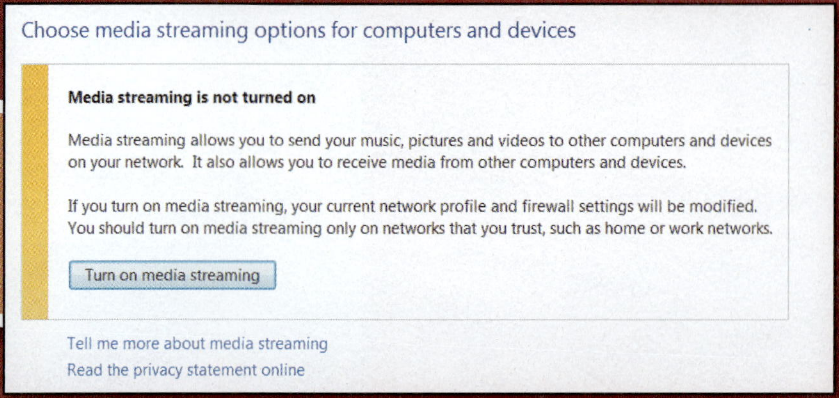

HOW TO

346

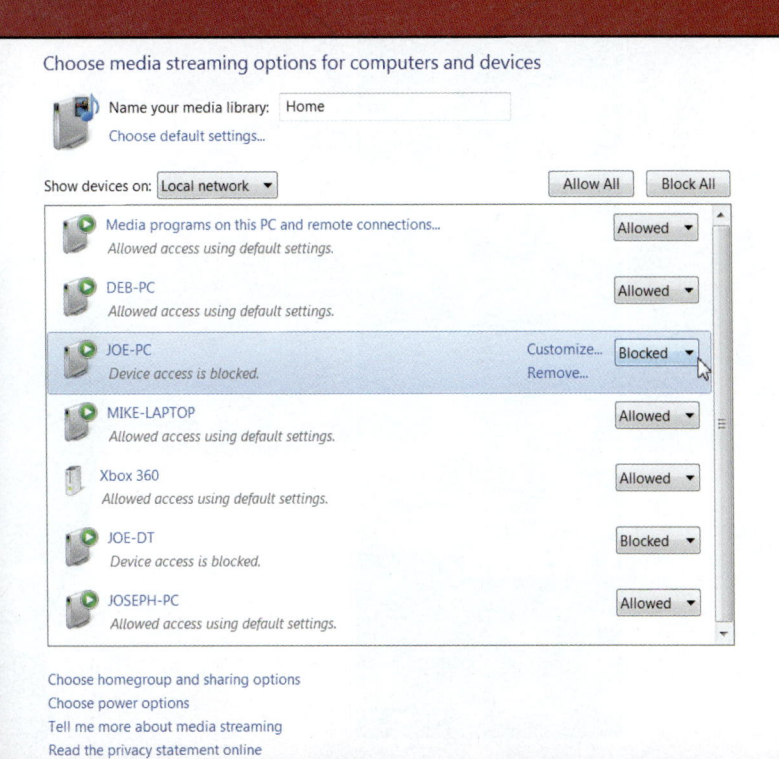

5 Take a screen shot of the *Media streaming options* window. Are there any devices that are blocked?

6 Click *OK* to return to the Change homegroup settings window. Click *Change advanced sharing settings*. Examine the settings for the Home or Work profile and the Public network profile (you'll need to scroll down to see this). How are they different? How are they the same?

7 Answer the questions posed, save this file as **Lastname_Firstname_Ch09_HowTo**, and submit it to your instructor as directed.

LANS and WANS

2 OBJECTIVE
Compare different types of LANs and WANs.

Networks come in many different shapes and sizes. In this article, we discuss some of the most common types of networks you'll find in both homes and businesses.

SMALL NETWORKS

A **local area network (LAN)** is a network that has all connected devices or nodes located in the same physical location. On a small scale, a home network is a LAN. In a business, a LAN might consist of a single room, a floor, a building, or an entire campus. A home LAN is likely to be a peer-to-peer network, whereas a business LAN is more likely to be a client-server network and consist of computers, printers, and servers as well as the network hardware that connects them (see Figure 9.8). Devices on a LAN are connected using switches.

FIGURE 9.8
A client-server LAN configuration

A LAN that consists of devices connected by Bluetooth, such as a PDA and a computer, is referred to as a **personal area network (PAN)** or **piconet**. Bluetooth has a very limited range of only about 10 to 100 meters (30 to 300 feet). The most common Bluetooth radio used for personal electronics is a low-power Class 2 radio, with a range of 30 feet and a data transfer rate of up to 3 Mbps. Bluetooth is designed to be easy to use, allowing devices to talk to each other securely over short distances. Each device in a piconet can connect to up to seven other devices at a time. Some common devices that might use Bluetooth include mice, keyboards, interactive white boards, headsets, cell phones, PDAs, cameras, media players, video game consoles, and printers. A **wireless LAN (WLAN)** is one that uses WiFi to transmit data. WiFi has a much larger range, higher speeds, better security, and supports more devices than Bluetooth, but it is also more expensive and complicated to set up.

A home LAN uses the same Ethernet standards and equipment used in larger business networks. **Ethernet** defines the way data is transmitted over a local area network. Although there are other network standards, Ethernet is by far the most widely implemented. Standards are important because they assure that equipment that is made by different companies will be able to work together. Ethernet networks transmit signals over twisted-pair cable, fiber-optic cable, and WiFi at data transmissions speeds of 10 Mbps to as much as 10 Gbps. The maximum speed depends on the type of media and capability of the network hardware on the LAN. Most home networks use 100 Mbps Ethernet.

LARGE NETWORKS

A **wide area network (WAN)** is a network that spans multiple locations and connects multiple LANs over dedicated lines using routers. A college that has multiple campuses would need to use WAN connections between them (see Figure 9.9). WAN technologies are slower and more expensive than LAN technologies. At home, the WAN you connect to is the Internet, and the port on your router that connects to the modem is labeled WAN port, distinguishing it from the LAN ports your other devices connect to.

FIGURE 9.9 A WAN connects LANs located at different locations.

What if you need to connect to your work network from home or while on the road? Because you're located in a different location, you must use a WAN connection to access your work network, but it wouldn't be practical for a business to provide its employees dedicated WAN lines from every offsite location. Instead, companies use a special type of connection called a **virtual private network (VPN)** (see Figure 9.10). A VPN creates a private network through the public network (Internet), allowing remote users to access a LAN securely without needing dedicated lines. This is much less expensive and more practical for businesses, and in some cases, a VPN even replaces the need for dedicated lines completely. VPNs use encryption to ensure the data is secure as it travels through the public network.

FIGURE 9.10 A VPN creates a virtual private network through the public Internet.

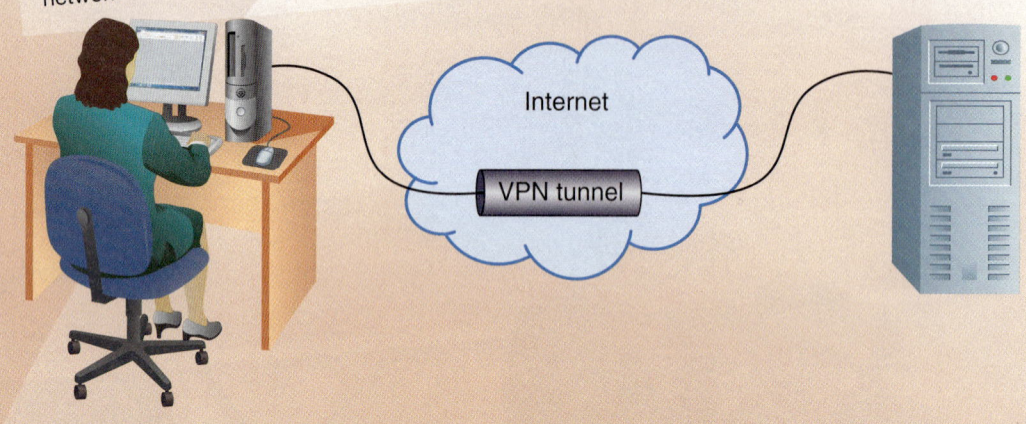

Somewhere in between a LAN and a WAN is an enterprise network. In a business that is too large and has too many computers to manage a single LAN practically, there may be multiple LANs located in the same location. These LANs are connected to each other using routers—technically making them WANs. This hybrid is sometimes called a **campus area network (CAN)**. A network that covers a single geographic area—such as Wireless Philadelphia, which provides WiFi access over much of the city—is called a **metropolitan area network (MAN)**.

Companies that have massive amounts of information to move and store may have a **storage area network (SAN)** between the data storage devices and the servers on a network, making the data accessible to all servers in the SAN. Normal users are not part of the SAN but are able to access the information through the LAN servers.

Cellular networks use cell towers to transmit voice and data over large distances. The newest 3G and 4G networks have speeds that have made these networks a practical way for people on the move to connect to network resources, including the Internet and corporate VPNs from almost anywhere in the world.

Computer networks range from two personal computers sharing a printer to large enterprise networks to the Internet. The larger and more complex networks require more hardware, configuration, and expertise to manage, but they all have the same basic purpose: to share resources.

Key Terms

campus area network (CAN)

cellular network

Ethernet

local area network (LAN)

metropolitan area network (MAN)

personal area network (PAN)

piconet

storage area network (SAN)

virtual private network (VPN)

wide area network (WAN)

wireless LAN (WLAN)

Running Project

Make a list of networks that you use. Include home, cellular, work, and school networks. Label each as a LAN, WAN, or one of the other network types described in this article. List the devices you use to connect to each. What resources do you access?

5 Things You Need to Know

- A local area network (LAN) is a network that has all its nodes located in the same physical location.
- Wireless network types include Bluetooth personal area networks (PAN), WiFi wireless LANs (WLAN), and cellular networks.
- Ethernet is the standard that defines the way data is transmitted over a LAN.
- A wide area network (WAN) is a network that spans multiple locations and connects multiple LANs.
- A VPN creates a private network through the public network (Internet).

The Networking HARDWARE STORE

OBJECTIVE 3
List and describe the hardware used in both wired and wireless networks.

Every network has two major components: hardware to create the physical connections between devices and software to configure the resources and security. In this article, we look at the hardware needed to create different types of networks.

NETWORK ADAPTERS

The hardware needed to set up a peer-to-peer network is much less complicated than what is needed in a client-server network. The simplest P2P network can consist of two devices sharing files using a wireless connection. For example, you can beam data from a smartphone or PDA directly to your computer or go head-to-head against a buddy by connecting your Nintendo DS games. Larger networks with many types of devices require extra hardware to connect them.

Each device that connects to a network must have some type of network adapter (see Figure 9.11). A **network adapter** is a communication device used to establish a connection with a network. Most personal computers today come with a built-in Ethernet adapter. This type of connection, called an RJ-45, looks like a slightly larger phone jack. The cable used for this type of connection is called twisted-pair, Ethernet cable, or sometimes Cat-5 (or Cat-6). Depending on the size of the network you're connecting to, the other end of the cable might plug into a wall jack, a switch, a router, or a modem.

FIGURE 9.11 A built-in Ethernet adapter connected to an Ethernet cable (left) and a USB wireless adapter (right)

There are several advantages to using a wired network connection, including speed, location, and security. Network speed is measured in bits per second. Wired Ethernet connections can reach speeds of 1,000 megabits per second (also known as Gigabit Ethernet). Most home Ethernet connections use FastEthernet connections, which equal 100 Mbps. No wireless technology can currently reach the 1 Gbps speed, but some can equal or exceed the 100 Mbps speed. Another advantage is that a wired connection is less subject to interference and can travel long distances without slowing. A wireless connection that is 150 Mbps at close range might drop to less than half that speed at a distance of 300 feet. Buildings and other structures can slow or even prevent a wireless connection from working. Finally, a wired connection is more secure than a wireless connection, especially if the wireless connection is not configured with strong security settings.

There are several types of wireless network adapters. The WiFi networks found in homes and public hotspots use the IEEE 802.11 standards. The 802.11 standards ensure that devices developed by different vendors will work with each other. Most notebook computers today come with a built-in wireless adapter. A USB wireless adapter can easily be connected to a desktop or notebook computer that does not have one built in. Wireless printers can be connected to a network directly, eliminating the need to be shared from an individual computer. Figure 9.12 compares the speeds of the most common types of WiFi connections. The Wi-Fi Alliance certifies wireless devices to ensure interoperability. A WiFi network is also called a WLAN or Wireless Local Area Network. When two wireless devices connect to each other directly, they create an **ad hoc network**. In an **infrastructure wireless network**, devices connect through a wireless access point. A 3G or 4G adapter can be built into a smartphone or notebook computer and can be connected by USB to any computer, allowing you to use the cellular network for network access.

FIGURE 9.12 A comparison of WiFi standards

802.11 STANDARD	MAXIMUM SPEED	DATE INTRODUCED
802.11b	11 Mbps	1999
802.11g	54 Mbps	2003
802.11n	300 Mbps	2009

To view the network adapters that are installed on your computer, click the network icon on the taskbar, and click *Open Network and Sharing Center*. In the left pane, click *Change adapter settings*. This opens the Network Connections window, which lists all the network adapters on the machine and the status of each (see Figure 9.13). From here, you can manage your connections. This figure displays a 3G adapter, a Bluetooth adapter, a modem, a wired Ethernet adapter (Local Area Connection), and a wireless adapter. Most computers don't have all these.

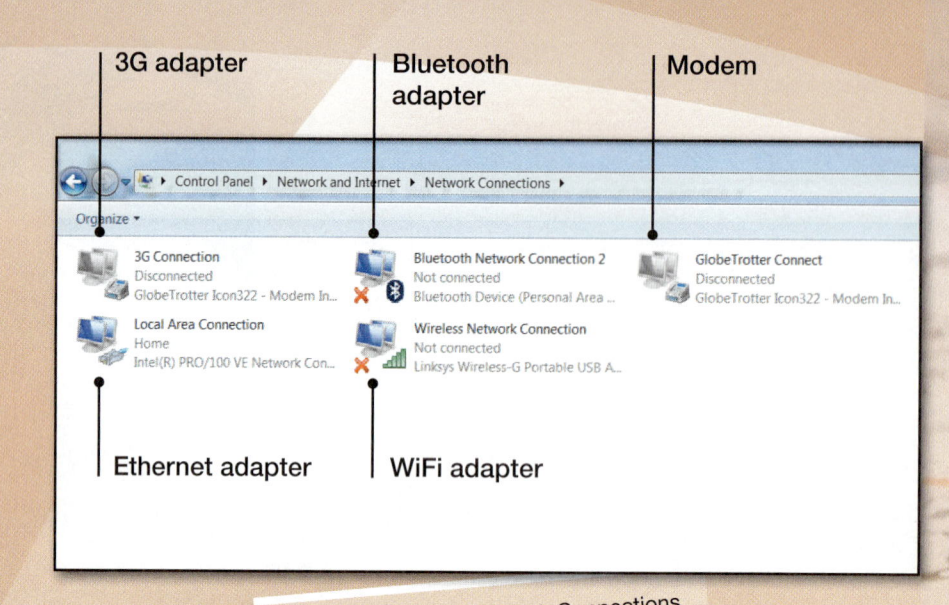

FIGURE 9.13 The Network Connections window shows several types of network adapters installed on this computer.

NETWORK HARDWARE

To create networks with more resources and devices, you'll need some additional hardware. The first device on a network is usually the device that connects to the Internet. If you use a dial-up connection, this is a traditional **modem**. Cable and DSL have special digital modems, and FiOS has an **optical network terminal (ONT)**. You can connect your computer directly to a modem or ONT, but you can share the connection with other devices more easily if you use a router instead.

A business network consists of routers, switches, wireless access points, and firewalls. Your home router serves all these functions. A **router** is a device that connects two or more networks together—for example, your home network and the Internet. A router uses address information to correctly route the data packets it receives. In a home network, the router is a convergence device that serves several functions: It shares the Internet connection, provides IP addresses to the other devices on the network, and, if configured correctly, provides security for your network.

OBJECTIVE 3

354

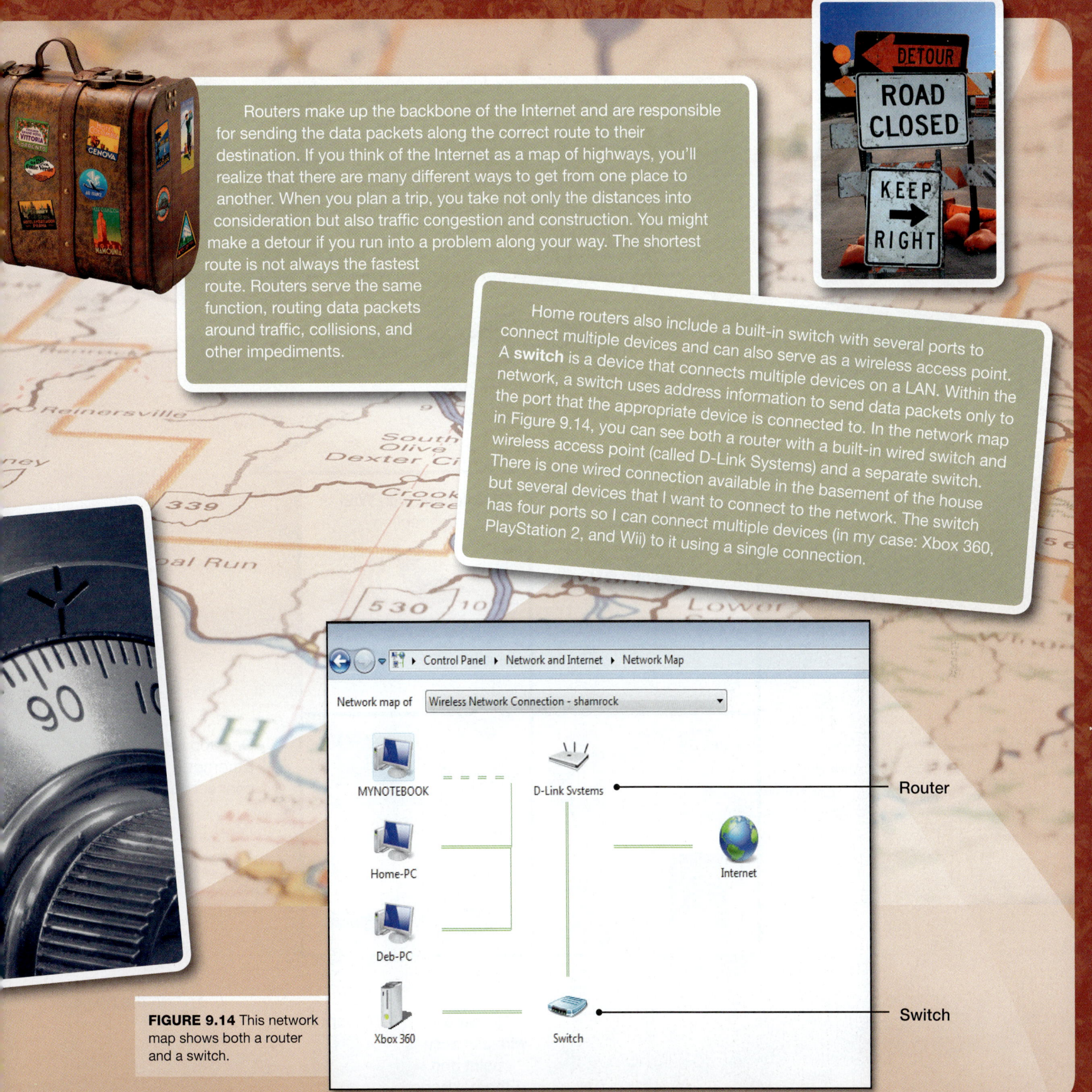

Routers make up the backbone of the Internet and are responsible for sending the data packets along the correct route to their destination. If you think of the Internet as a map of highways, you'll realize that there are many different ways to get from one place to another. When you plan a trip, you take not only the distances into consideration but also traffic congestion and construction. You might make a detour if you run into a problem along your way. The shortest route is not always the fastest route. Routers serve the same function, routing data packets around traffic, collisions, and other impediments.

Home routers also include a built-in switch with several ports to connect multiple devices and can also serve as a wireless access point. A **switch** is a device that connects multiple devices on a LAN. Within the network, a switch uses address information to send data packets only to the port that the appropriate device is connected to. In the network map in Figure 9.14, you can see both a router with a built-in wired switch and wireless access point (called D-Link Systems) and a separate switch. There is one wired connection available in the basement of the house but several devices that I want to connect to the network. The switch has four ports so I can connect multiple devices (in my case: Xbox 360, PlayStation 2, and Wii) to it using a single connection.

FIGURE 9.14 This network map shows both a router and a switch.

To set up a WiFi network, you'll need a wireless access point. A **wireless access point (WAP)** is a device that allows wireless devices to join a network much like a switch. It can be built into a router or it can be a separate device. In a large wireless network, there may be many WAPs installed. In a home, one or two is usually enough to provide coverage, but in a larger building, many WAPs may be needed. Figure 9.15 shows a home network that includes both wired and wireless devices.

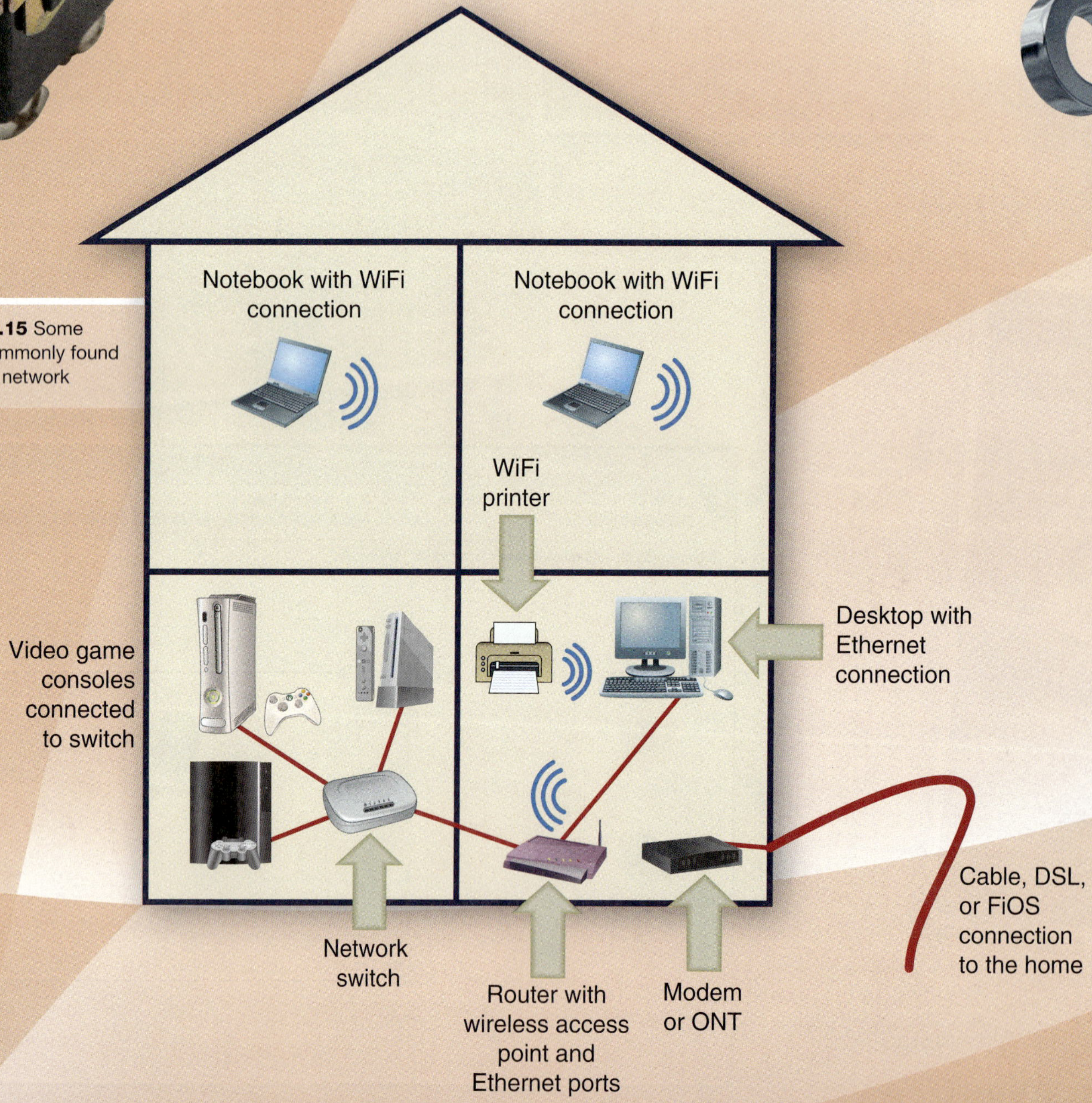

FIGURE 9.15 Some devices commonly found on a home network

- Notebook with WiFi connection
- Notebook with WiFi connection
- WiFi printer
- Desktop with Ethernet connection
- Video game consoles connected to switch
- Network switch
- Router with wireless access point and Ethernet ports
- Modem or ONT
- Cable, DSL, or FiOS connection to the home

A **firewall** is a device that blocks unauthorized access to a network. There are both software firewalls, such as the one included with Windows 7, and hardware firewalls. A hardware firewall may be part of a router or a stand-alone device. Firewalls can check both outgoing and incoming data packets. A firewall can be configured with filters to allow/deny various kinds of traffic. Firewall filters can be based on IP address, protocol type, domain names, and other criteria. For example, a firewall might block access to certain websites or deny Internet access to certain computers during certain hours. Incoming packets that try to access restricted data will be denied access to the network.

The larger and more complex a network, the more hardware is necessary to assure the flow of data. These devices work together to transmit and filter data packets around the network and eventually to their destination. Without the network hardware, computers could not connect to each other.

Key Terms

ad hoc network

firewall

infrastructure wireless network

modem

network adapter

optical network terminal (ONT)

router

switch

wireless access point (WAP)

Running Project

Open the Network Connections window as described in this article. What adapters are installed on your computer? What type of networks do they connect to? Which of them are connected now? Include a screen shot of the window.

4 Things You Need to Know

- Each device that connects to a network must have a network adapter.
- The first device on a network connects to the Internet, typically a modem or optical network terminal (ONT).
- A router connects two or more networks together; a switch connects multiple devices on a network.
- A firewall blocks unauthorized access to a network.

The Softer SIDE

OBJECTIVE 4
List and describe the software and protocols used in both wired and wireless networks.

Network hardware allows devices to physically connect to each other, but it's the software and protocols that allow them to communicate with and understand each other. In this article, we look at network operating systems, communication software, and protocols that make a network work.

PEER-TO-PEER NETWORK SOFTWARE

No special software is required to create a simple peer-to-peer network. Modern desktop operating systems have networking capabilities built into them. When Windows 7 is installed on a computer, it includes a feature called Client for Microsoft Networks, which allows it to remotely access files and printers on a Microsoft network. To verify that the Client for Microsoft Networks is installed on your computer, you can view the network adapters that are installed on a Windows 7 computer. Open the Network and Sharing Center from the taskbar, click *Change adapter settings* in the left pane, right-click the active adapter, and choose *Properties* to open the properties dialog box for the connection (see Figure 9.16).

FIGURE 9.16 The properties for the Local Area Connection shows the Client is installed.

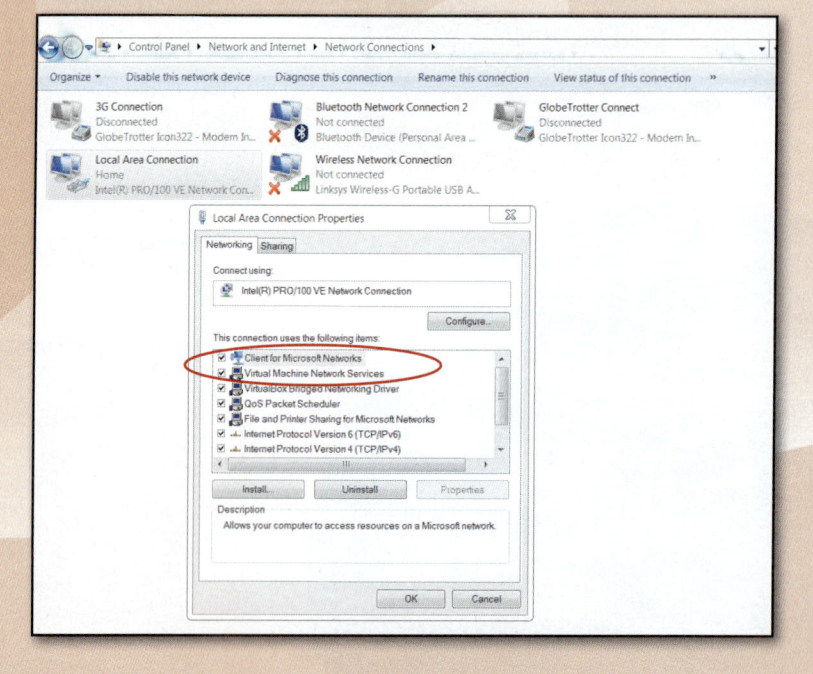

Using the workgroup feature of Windows 7 allows you to share and remotely access files on a Windows network. To connect computers running Mac OS X to a Windows network, you may need to change some configuration settings on the Mac. In particular, you'll need to be sure the Mac belongs to the same workgroup as the Windows computers and has account information configured. The Mac OS includes Windows File Sharing, and its network discovery tool should locate your Windows computers automatically. It's also possible to include a Linux computer on a Windows network, but each version has a somewhat different method to do so. Figure 9.17 shows an Ubuntu Linux computer connecting to a Windows network as part of the workgroup. If your network consists of computers running the same OS, then network configuration should be easy. These computers are able to detect and share resources with each other with little or no configuration on your part.

FIGURE 9.17 An Ubuntu Linux computer can detect a Windows workgroup.

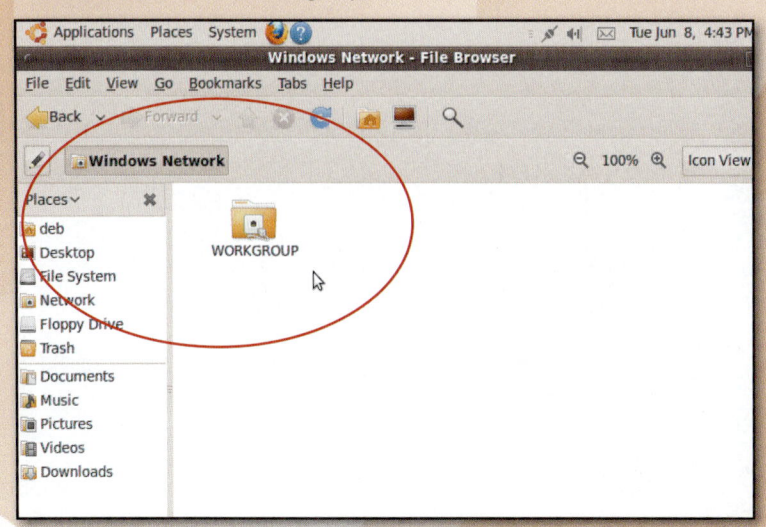

CLIENT-SERVER NETWORK SOFTWARE

As the name implies, both client software and server software are needed on a client-server network. The client software makes requests, and the server software fulfills them.

In a network where the servers run the Microsoft Server OS, Windows clients don't need any special client software for basic file and print services. Instead, they use the same Client for Microsoft Networks used in peer-to-peer networks to connect to the servers. A **domain** is a network composed of a group of clients and servers under the control of one central security database on a special server called the domain controller. You only need to log in to the domain once to have access to all the servers in the domain. So, in a network with multiple servers, you don't need to log in to each one individually. The security database includes your user information—who you are, what your password is, and what your access and restrictions are.

Clients log in to a server and request access to resources. For many types of servers, a special client is needed. When you use your Web browser to access your e-mail, it serves as an e-mail client. The browser can also act as an FTP client (when you download a file), a database client (when you access your bank transactions), and, of course, an HTTP client when you access a Web page. Other client software you may use includes VPN software, desktop e-mail programs, instant messaging/chat programs, and even video and photo software that include an upload feature.

Server software is also known as a network operating system. A **network operating system (NOS)** is a multiuser operating system that controls the software and hardware that runs on a network. It allows multiple computers (clients) to communicate with the server and each other, to share resources, run applications, and send messages. A NOS centralizes resources and security and provides services such as file and print services, communication services, Internet and e-mail services, and backup and database services to the client computers.

FIGURE 9.18 Using a Web browser as an e-mail client

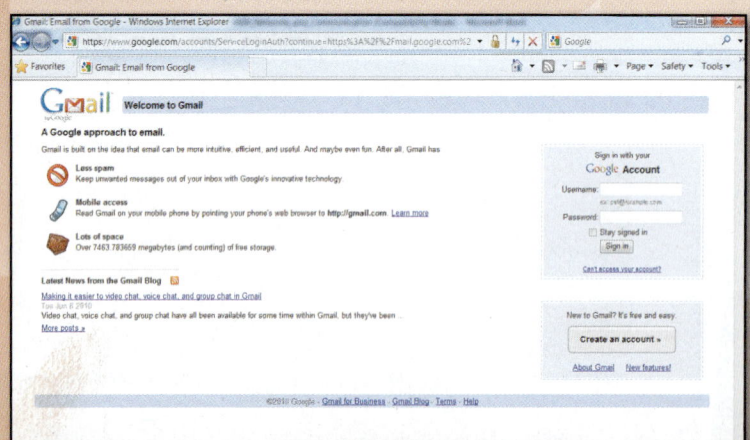

Servers are classified by the type of services they provide. Some common services are file and print services, e-mail, database, Web, chat, audio/video, and applications. Whenever you log in to a website such as Facebook or Gmail (see Figure 9.18), you're connecting to a server.

The most common network operating systems are Microsoft Windows Server (2003, 2008), Linux servers (Red Hat, SUSE), UNIX servers (HP-UX, IBM AIX, Sun Solaris), and Novell servers (Netware, SUSE).

NETWORK PROTOCOLS

Network hardware is what allows devices to connect to each other, but network protocols allow them to communicate. **Protocols** define the rules for communication between devices. These rules determine how data is formatted, transmitted, received, and acknowledged. Without protocols, devices could be physically connected and still unable to communicate.

Think about a meeting between two people. When you walk into the meeting, you greet the other person, perhaps shake hands, and exchange names. There are mutually agreed-upon protocols as to how you begin a "conversation" between devices begins. This ensures that both are ready to communicate and agree on how to proceed. During the meeting, you also follow rules: what to say, how to say it, what language to speak, what's appropriate, and what's not. Protocols also define how devices converse in much the same way. Finally, at the end of your meeting, you likely stand up, shake hands, say goodbye, and depart. Protocols also define the method to end an electronic conversation.

FIGURE 9.19 Protocols define how two devices (or people) communicate.

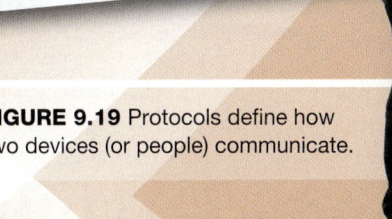

Although there are hundreds of different protocols, the most important ones belong to the **TCP/IP protocol stack**. This is a suite of protocols that define everything from how to transfer files (FTP) and Web pages (HTTP) to sending (SMTP) and receiving (POP) e-mail. **TCP** stands for transmission control protocol, and it's responsible for assuring that data packets are transmitted reliably. **IP** stands for Internet protocol, and it's responsible for addressing and routing packets to their destination. Both pieces are needed for data to move between devices. Figure 9.20 lists some of the important protocols in the TCP/IP stack and their functions.

FIGURE 9.20 Some important network protocols in the TCP/IP stack

PROTOCOL	FUNCTION
TCP (transmission control protocol)	Assuring that data packets are transmitted reliably
IP (Internet protocol)	Addressing and routing packets to their destination
HTTP (hypertext transfer protocol)	Requesting/delivering Web pages
FTP (file transfer protocol)	Transferring files between computers
POP (post office protocol)	Receiving e-mail
SMTP (simple mail transfer protocol)	Sending e-mail
DHCP (dynamic host configuration protocol)	Requesting/receiving an IP address from a DHCP server
DNS (domain name system)	Resolving domain names to IP addresses

TCP/IP is the protocol stack that runs on the Internet, and because of this, it's also the protocol stack that runs on most LANs. TCP/IP is the default protocol stack installed on Windows, Mac, and Linux computers, and it's what allows them to communicate with each other easily. Figure 9.21 shows the adapter properties for the Local Area Connection. You can see that both TCP/IPv6 and TCP/IPv4 are installed. Currently, TCP/IP version 4 is used on the Internet and most LANs. Although many devices don't currently support TCP/IP version 6, it is slowly being implemented and will eventually replace version 4 altogether. By default, Windows computers are set to Obtain an IP address automatically using the DHCP protocol (see Figure 9.21). The computer sends out a DHCP request that's answered by a DHCP server (likely a router at home). Every computer on the network must have a unique IP address. This automatic configuration makes it easy to create a home network.

FIGURE 9.21 Windows computers are set to use DHCP to obtain an IP address.

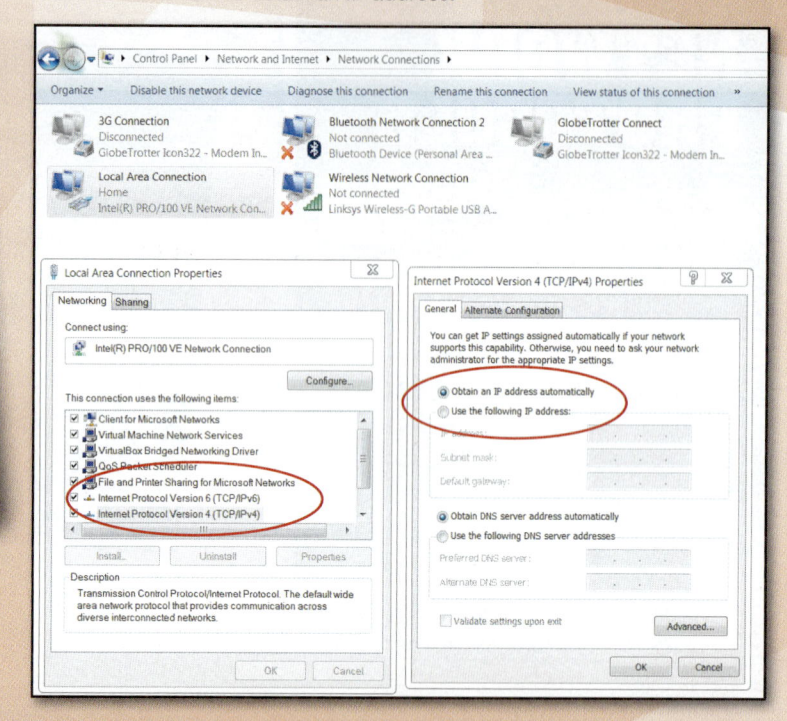

GREEN COMPUTING

SERVER VIRTUALIZATION

Technically, the term *server* refers to the server software on a computer, not to the hardware it runs on. So, a network server computer might actually run mail server, Web server, and file and print server software. The advantage to this is that a single physical computer can be several different servers at once. Server computers are high-end, with fast processors and lots of storage. Sometimes, the computer's capabilities aren't fully utilized, and its processors are idle much of the time. Virtualization takes advantage of this unused resource. A good example might be running both a Microsoft Exchange e-mail server and an Apache Web server on the same computer. Each virtual server runs in its own space, sharing the hardware but not necessarily interacting with each other in any way. To the client, they appear to be separate servers.

Server virtualization is a big component of cloud computing. A company that offers IaaS (Infrastructure as a Service) can set up virtual servers for many small companies on a large enterprise server. This saves money and reduces the amount of hardware (and thus e-waste) needed for each business. Keeping servers in one location can also save in cooling and electric costs. IaaS is not just good for small companies. Joyent, one of the largest IaaS providers, hosts the social network LinkedIn and the online retailer Gilt Groupe.

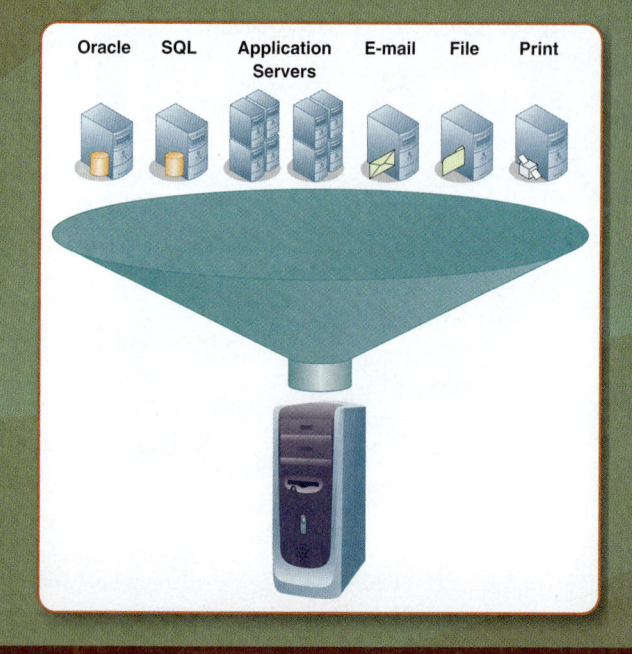

Find Out MORE

Before the need for Internet access necessitated the use of TCP/IP, Mac computers used different protocols to talk to each other. Use the Internet to find out how they did this.

As with any computer system, the hardware of a network is useless without the software to make it work. In a network, that software also includes protocols to define the rules of communication. Together, the hardware, software, and protocols allow devices to share resources securely, efficiently, and (hopefully) easily.

Key Terms

domain

IP (Internet protocol)

network operating system (NOS)

protocol

TCP (transmission control protocol)

TCP/IP protocol stack

Running Project

Make a list of the networks you use. Include home, cellular, work, and school networks. List the software clients that you use to connect to each. What resources do you access? Do you use different clients to access different resources?

5 Things You Need to Know

- Peer-to-peer computers are able to detect and share resources with each other with little or no configuration.
- A domain is a network composed of a group of clients and servers under the control of the domain controller.
- Clients log in to a server and request access to resources.
- Server software allows clients to communicate with the server to share resources, run applications, and send messages.
- Protocols define the rules for communication between devices. TCP/IP is the protocol stack that runs on the Internet and on most LANs.

Protecting YOUR NETWORK

5 OBJECTIVE
Explain how to protect a network.

A few years ago, network security was only a concern to network administrators in large businesses; but today, with networks everywhere, it has become a larger problem. Just as you use layers of security at home—fences, door locks, alarm systems, and even guard dogs—the same approach should be used with network security.

LAYER 1— THE FENCE

In a network, the fence is the hardware at the access point to your network (see Figure 9.22). In a home network, the firewall is probably part of your router. In a business, the firewall is a stand-alone device. The firewall examines the data packets as they enter or leave your network and will deny access to traffic based on rules the network administrator defines. It also shields your computers from direct access to the Internet, hiding them from hackers looking for an easy target.

LAYER 2—DOOR LOCKS

In a network, door locks are represented by the network configuration determining what's shared and who's granted access to it. Your usernames should have strong passwords that are hard to crack, and each user should be granted access only to what they need (see Figure 9.23).

FIGURE 9.22 A firewall protects the network.

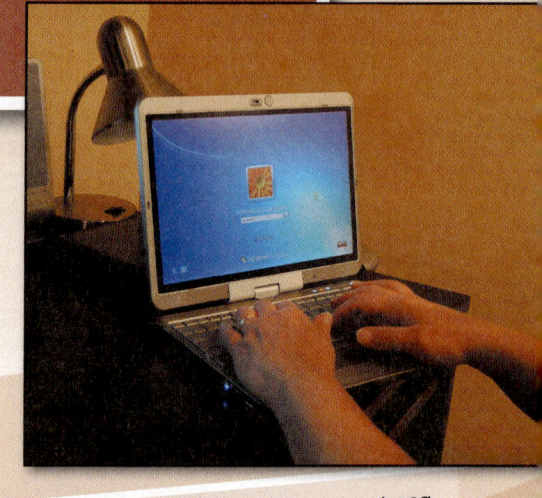

FIGURE 9.23 Users should use strong passwords to access a network.

LAYER 3—ALARM SYSTEMS

The alarm system on a computer network includes software-based firewalls and antivirus and antimalware software on the individual computers on the network (see Figure 9.24). If an intruder somehow breaches your network, software will detect unauthorized actions and prevent them.

LAYER 4—GUARD DOGS

The network administrator (on a home network, that's you) needs to be diligent in keeping the systems on the network up to date and secure. It's critical that the software on personal computers is kept up to date. Unpatched systems are easy targets for hackers and can allow them access into your network. Although you can never be completely secure, it *is* possible to make your home so difficult to break into to that the thief moves on to an easier target. That's also the goal with network security.

Security

Network firewall	On
Windows Firewall is actively protecting your computer.	
Windows Update	On
Windows will automatically install updates as they become available.	
Virus protection	On
AVG Anti-Virus Free reports that it is up to date and virus scanning is on.	
Spyware and unwanted software protection	On
AVG Anti-Virus Free reports that it is turned on.	
View installed antispyware programs	
Internet security settings	OK
All Internet security settings are set to their recommended levels.	

FIGURE 9.24 Each computer on the network should have its own up-to-date security software installed.

ETHICS

The term **piggybacking** means using an open wireless network to access the Internet without permission. If an access point is left unsecured, "Why not?"

In some places, it's illegal to use a network without authorization, but many statutes—if they exist at all—are vague. It's virtually impossible to detect someone that's piggybacking. Still, it's unethical to use someone's connection without his or her knowledge.

The practice of **wardriving** is related and means driving around and locating open wireless access points. There are communities on the Internet where wardrivers post maps of the open networks they find, along with free software that makes it easy to locate wireless networks. Wardrivers don't actually access the wireless networks, so the practice isn't illegal—but is it ethical? You decide.

Key Terms

piggybacking

wardriving

4 Things You Need to Know

- A firewall examines the data packets as they enter or leave your network.
- Network users should have strong passwords that are hard to crack and be granted access only to what they need.
- Individual computers on the network must be protected with firewalls and antivirus and antimalware software.
- Systems on the network must be kept up to date and secure.

What Can I Do WITH KNOWLEDGE ABOUT COMPUTER NETWORKS?

OBJECTIVE 6 Identify the certifications and careers related to computer networks.

You'll find computer networks in every type of business, and knowing how to access network resources is a critical skill for most employees. However, there are some technical certifications and careers that require more extensive knowledge and skills.

COMPTIA CERTIFICATIONS

An entry-level certification in network technologies is the CompTIA Network+ certification. This is a vendor-neutral certification that's widely accepted in the industry. The certification demonstrates skills in "managing, maintaining, troubleshooting, installing and configuring basic network infrastructure." This certification is also accepted as part of the certification programs from other companies, such as Microsoft and Cisco. There's no formal education requirement, although there are recommended courses offered through many sources, including colleges, technical schools, and online.

CompTIA also offers other network-related certifications, including Security+, Server+, and Linux+.

MICROSOFT CERTIFICATIONS

Microsoft offers a variety of different certification paths. Microsoft Certified Technology Specialist (MCTS) is awarded for each exam a candidate passes. There are six network-related MCTS exams that can be later applied to a higher-level certification. Microsoft recommends that candidates have at least one year of experience before taking the exams.

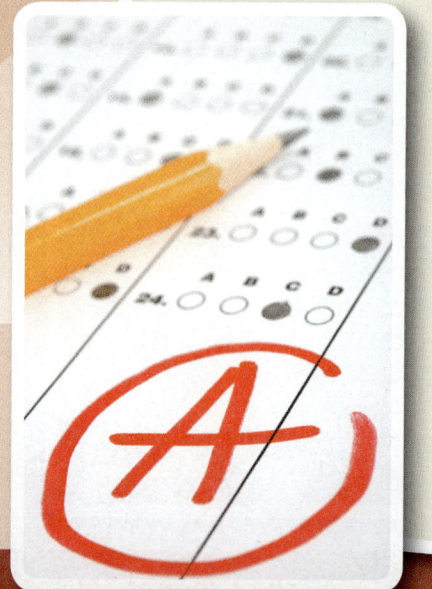

The MCITP (Microsoft Certified IT Professional) program includes two different network-related programs: MCITP: Server Administrator (which requires passing three exams) and MCITP: Enterprise Administrator (which require passing four exams). These programs are designed for a person with several years of experience. A person pursuing a career in networking could begin with the first two exams, which are common to both certifications.

CISCO CERTIFICATIONS

Cisco is a company that builds network hardware, such as routers, switches, and firewalls. Managing and configuring these systems requires a high level of skill. Cisco certifications are well-respected in the industry.

There are five levels (Entry, Associate, Professional, Expert, and Architect) and eight tracks of certification in the Cisco system. Each level builds on the previous certification, so you can start out as a Cisco Certified Entry Networking Technician (CCENT) by passing a single exam.

NETWORK ADMINISTRATOR

A network administrator is the person responsible for managing the hardware and software on a network (see Figure 9.25). The job may also include troubleshooting and security. Although not required, a two- or four-year college degree is helpful in this field, as are certifications. According to **Salary.com**, the average salary for an experienced person in this field is about $62,000. As with any technical field, you should expect to continue your training to keep up with the changes in technology. An entry-level person may be called a network technician rather than an administrator.

FIGURE 9.25 A network administrator managing a server

The importance of networks and connectivity for most businesses requires employees that are experts at making networks secure and reliable. The *Occupational Outlook Handbook* predicts that network-related jobs will grow faster than the average for all occupations over the next decade, so considering a career in this field might be a good choice for you.

NETWORKS AND COMMUNICATION

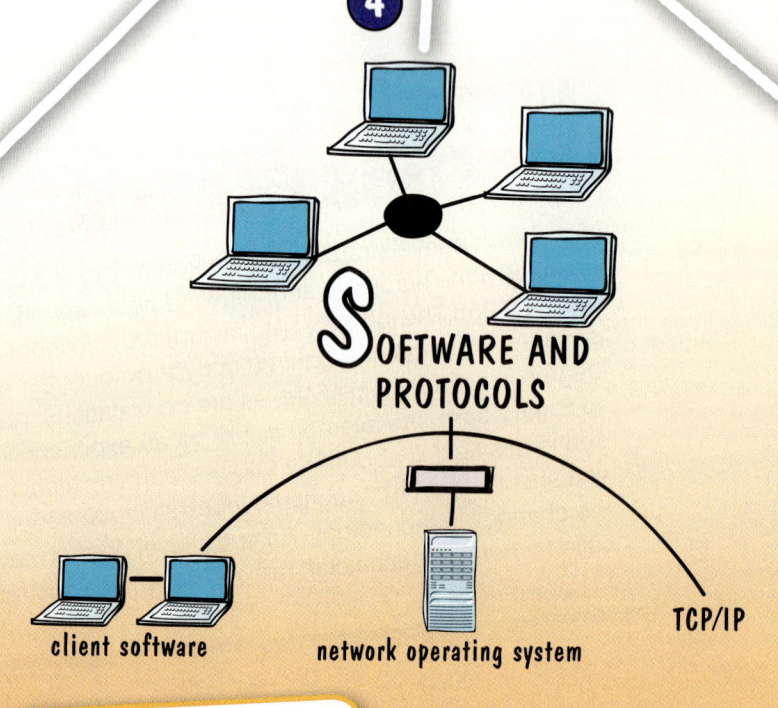

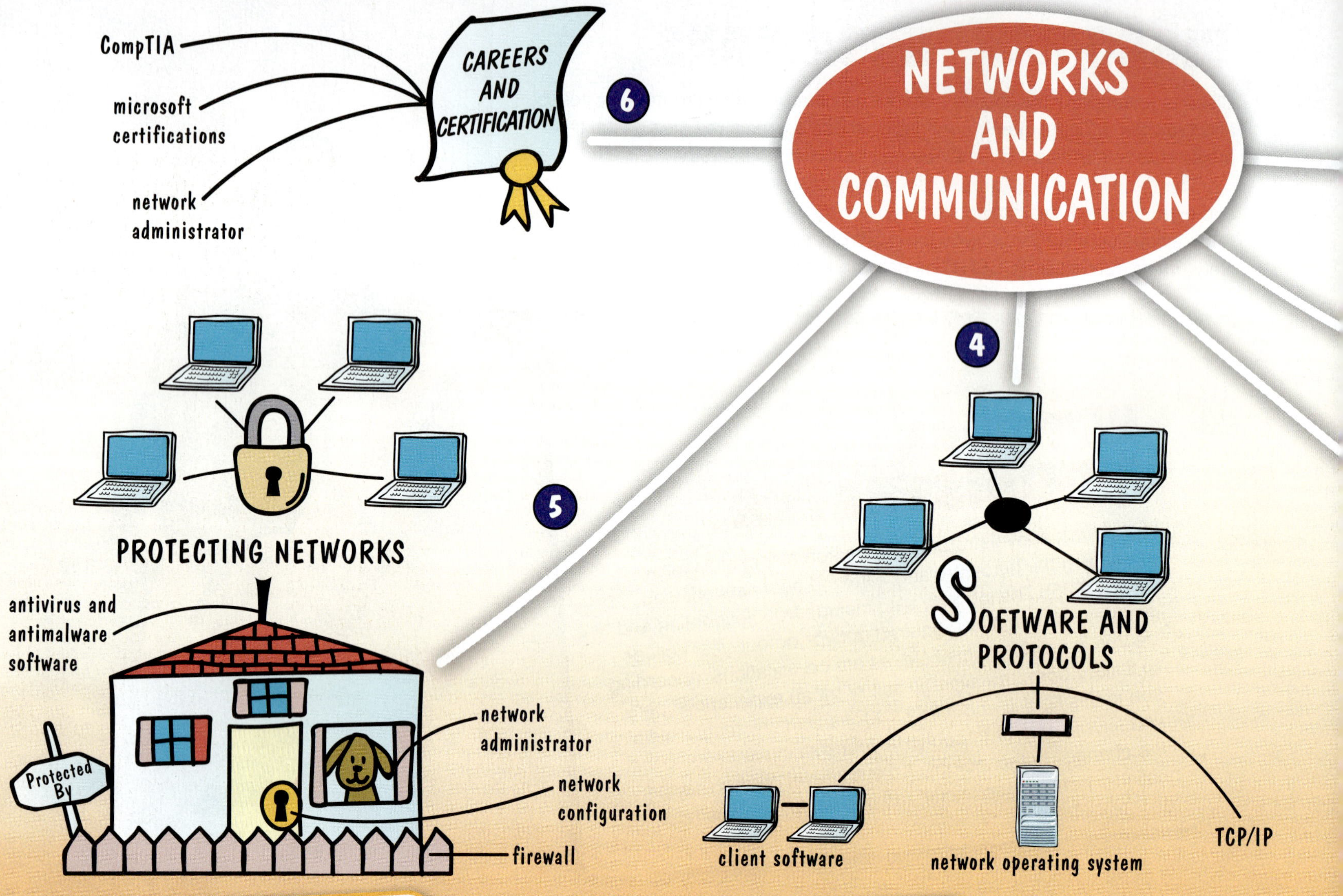

6 CAREERS AND CERTIFICATION
- CompTIA
- microsoft certifications
- network administrator

5 PROTECTING NETWORKS
- antivirus and antimalware software
- network administrator
- network configuration
- firewall

4 SOFTWARE AND PROTOCOLS
- client software
- network operating system
- TCP/IP

Objectives Recap

1. Discuss the importance of computer networks. (p. 336)
2. Compare different types of LANs and WANs. (p. 348)
3. List and describe the hardware used in both wired and wireless networks. (p. 352)
4. List and describe the software and protocols used in both wired and wireless networks. (p. 358)
5. Explain how to protect a network. (p. 364)
6. Identify the certifications and careers related to computer networks. (p. 366)

Key Terms

ad hoc network **353**
campus area network (CAN) **350**
cellular network **351**
client **341**
client-server network **340**
computer network **336**
domain **359**
Ethernet **349**
firewall **357**
homegroup **338**
infrastructure wireless network **353**
IP (Internet protocol) **361**
local area network (LAN) **348**
metropolitan area network (MAN) **350**
modem **354**

1. COMPUTER NETWORKS

- peer-to-peer
- client-server

2. Types of LANS and WANS

- LAN
- WAN

3. Hardware

- switch
- wireless access point
- firewall
- router
- modem

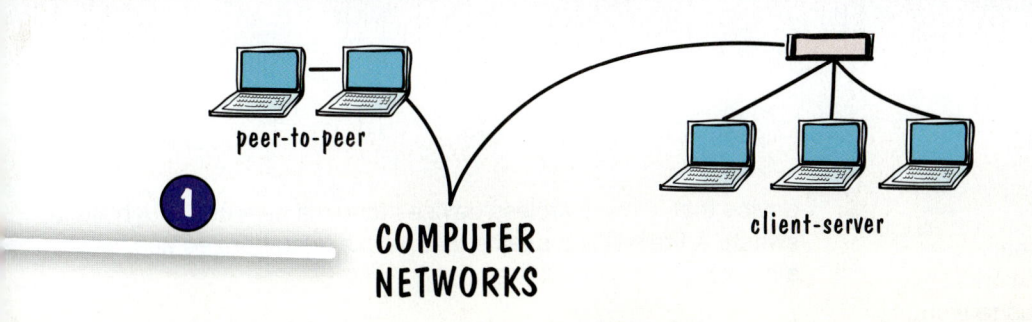

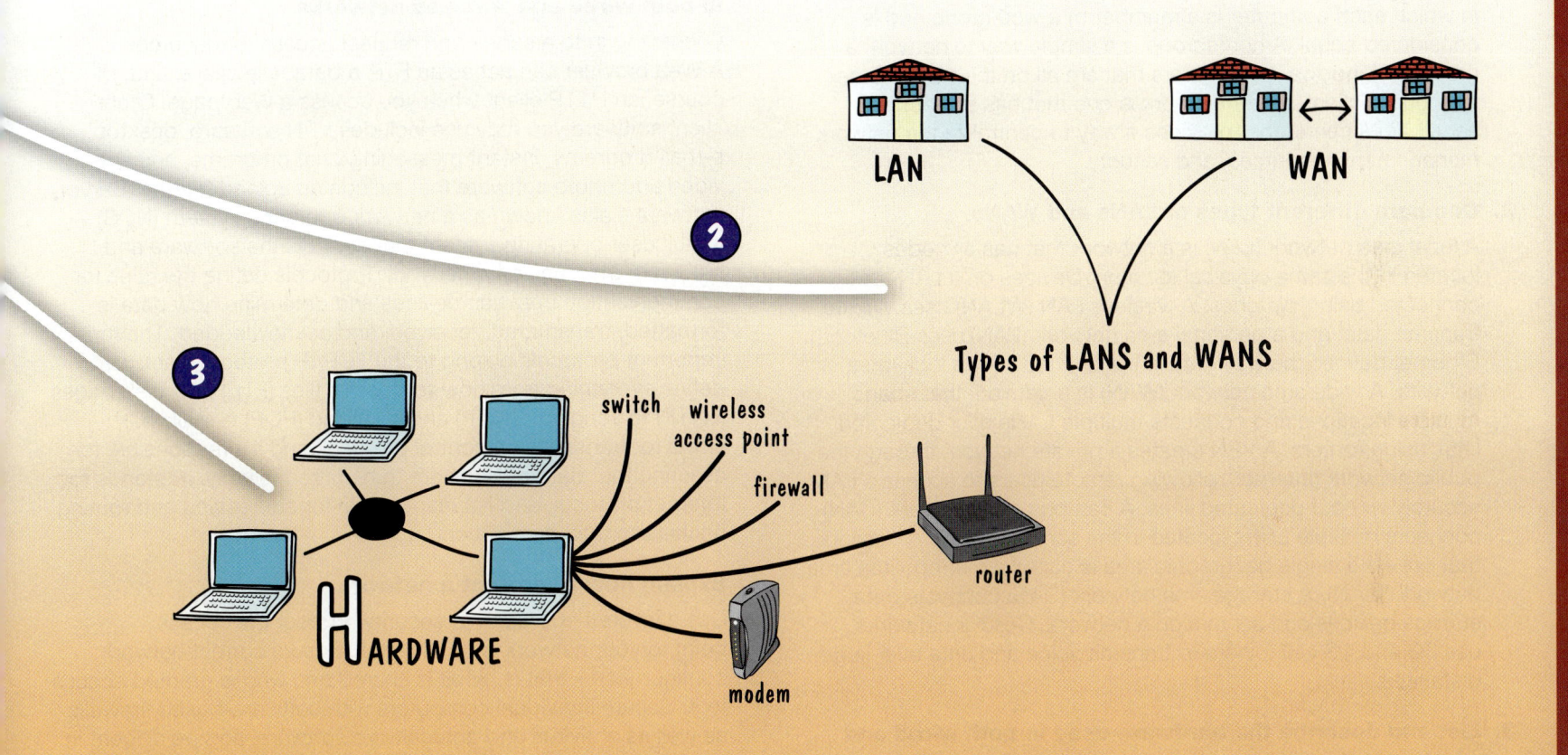

network adapter **352**
network operating system (NOS) **360**
network resource **336**
optical network terminal (ONT) **354**
peer-to-peer network (P2P) **336**
personal area network (PAN) **349**
piconet **349**

piggybacking **365**
protocol **361**
router **354**
server **341**
storage area network (SAN) **350**
switch **355**
TCP (transmission control protocol) **361**

TCP/IP protocol stack **361**
virtual private network (VPN) **350**
wardriving **365**
wide area network (WAN) **349**
wireless access point (WAP) **356**
wireless LAN (WLAN) **349**
workgroup **336**

Summary

1. **Discuss the importance of computer networks.**

   A computer network is two or more computers that share resources: software, hardware, or files. Computer networks save us both time and money and make it easier for us to work, increasing productivity. A peer-to-peer network (P2P) is one in which each computer is a member of a workgroup and is considered equal. A homegroup is a simple way to network a group of Windows 7 computers that are all on the same home network. A client-server network is one that has at least one server at its center that provides a way to centralize the network management, resources, and security.

2. **Compare different types of LANs and WANs.**

   A local area network (LAN) is a network that has all nodes located in the same physical location. Devices on a LAN are connected using switches. A wireless LAN (WLAN) uses WiFi to transmit data, and a personal area network (PAN) uses Bluetooth. Ethernet defines the way data is transmitted over a local area network. A wide area network (WAN) is a network that spans multiple locations and connects multiple LANs over dedicated lines using routers. A VPN creates a private network through the public network (Internet), allowing remote users to access a LAN securely without dedicated lines. A campus area network (CAN) connects multiple LANs located in the same location. A network that covers a single geographic area is called a metropolitan area network (MAN). A storage area network (SAN) connects data storage devices and servers on a network. Cellular networks use 3G and 4G cell towers to transmit voice and data over large distances.

3. **List and describe the hardware used in both wired and wireless networks.**

   Each device that connects to a network must have a network adapter. The first device on a network is usually the device that connects to the Internet: a modem or optical network terminal (ONT). A business network consists of routers, switches, wireless access points, and firewalls. Your home router serves all these functions. A router is a device that connects two or more networks together. It uses address information to correctly route the data packets it receives. A switch is a device that connects multiple devices on a LAN. A wireless access point (WAP) is a device that allows wireless devices to join a network, much like a switch. A firewall is a device that blocks unauthorized access to a network.

4. **List and describe the software and protocols used in both wired and wireless networks.**

   Clients log in to a server and request access to resources. A Web browser can act as an FTP, a database client, and, of course, an HTTP client when you access a Web page. Other client software you may use includes VPN software, desktop e-mail programs, instant messaging/chat programs, and even video and photo software that include an upload feature. Server software—also known as a network operating system (NOS)—is a multiuser operating system that controls the software and hardware that runs on a network. Protocols define the rules for communication between devices and determine how data is formatted, transmitted, received, and acknowledged. The most important protocols belong to the TCP/IP protocol stack and define everything from how to transfer files (FTP) and Web pages (HTTP) to sending (SMTP) and receiving (POP) e-mail. TCP stand for transmission control protocol, and it's responsible for assuring that data packets are transmitted reliably. IP stands for Internet protocol, and it's responsible for addressing and routing packets to their destination.

5. **Explain how to protect a network.**

   Use a layered approach to security. Protect the access point to your network with a firewall. Ensure correct network configuration—that is, what is shared and who is granted access to it. Secure individual computers with software-based firewalls as well as antivirus and antimalware software, and be diligent in keeping the systems on the network up to date and secure.

6. **Identify the certifications and careers related to computer networks.**

   There are dozens of network certifications from CompTIA, Microsoft, and Cisco to name a few. Network administrators are well-paid technicians that manage the hardware and software on a network. The role may also include troubleshooting and security. Jobs in this field are predicted to grow at a rapid pace over the next decade.

Multiple Choice

Answer the multiple-choice questions below for more practice with key terms and concepts from this chapter.

1. Computers in a peer-to-peer network belong to a _____.
   a. workgroup ✓
   b. domain
   c. personal area network
   d. piconet

2. Which resources are not shared by default in a homegroup?
   a. Pictures and videos
   b. Music
   c. Documents ✓
   d. Printers

3. Which type of wireless LAN uses WiFi to transmit data?
   a. PAN
   b. MAN
   c. VPN
   d. WLAN ✓

4. Which type of network spans multiple locations and connects multiple networks?
   a. MAN
   b. WAN ✓
   c. LAN
   d. VPN

5. Which type of network creates a private network through a public network?
   a. PAN
   b. CAN
   c. VPN ✓
   d. Piconet

6. When two wireless devices connect to each other directly, they form a(n) _____.
   a. ad hoc network ✓
   b. infrastructure wireless network
   c. WAN
   d. virtual private network

7. The device needed to connect to a FiOS network is called a(n) _____.
   a. modem
   b. router
   c. optical network terminal ✓
   d. access point

8. A(n) _____ connects multiple devices on a LAN.
   a. modem
   b. switch ✓
   c. firewall
   d. ONT

9. Which protocol is responsible for addressing and routing packets to their destination?
   a. TCP
   b. IP ✓
   c. POP
   d. SMTP

10. Which device examines data packets as they enter and leave a network and denies unauthorized packets access?
    a. Modem
    b. Switch
    c. Router
    d. Firewall ✓

True or False

Answer the following questions with T for true or F for false for more practice with key terms and concepts from this chapter.

_T_ 1. In a peer-to-peer network, each computer is considered equal.
_T_ 2. Once you create a homegroup, computers running any version of Windows can join it.
_T_ 3. It's possible to share files between computers running Windows, Mac OS X, and Linux.
___ 4. Normal users aren't part of a storage area network (SAN).
_F_ 5. A wireless connection is more secure than a wired connection.
_T_ 6. Computers can have multiple network adapters installed at one time.
_T_ 7. A router is a device that connects two or more networks together.
_F_ 8. You must install special software to create a peer-to-peer network.
_T_ 9. TCP/IP is the default protocol installed on Linux computers.
_F_ 10. Computers behind a firewall on a network don't need to have any additional security software installed.

Fill in the Blank

Fill in the blanks with key terms and concepts from this chapter.

1. _Network resources_ include software, hardware, and files.
2. A(n) _homegroup_ is a simple way to network a group of Windows 7 computers.
3. A(n) _client-server network_ has at least one server at its center.
4. The computers and other devices that connect to a server area are called _clients_.
5. A(n) _LAN_ is a network that has all devices located in the same physical location.
6. _Ethernet_ defines the way data is transmitted over a local area network.
7. Every device on a network must have a(n) _network adapter_ to establish a connection with a network.
8. A(n) _firewall_ is a device that blocks unauthorized access to a network.
9. A group of clients and servers under the control of one central security database is called a(n) _domain_.
10. _Protocol_ define the rules for communication between devices.

Running Project

... The Finish Line

Assume that you just moved into a new house with several roommates. Use your answers to the previous sections of the project to help you decide the best type of network setup to use so you can all share an Internet connection and printer as well as stream media files. Describe the hardware and software requirements for your setup. What other devices might you also connect to the network?

Write a report describing your selections and responding to the questions raised. Save your file as **Lastname_Firstname_ch09_Project**, and submit it to your instructor as directed.

File Management

1. Open the Computer window from the Windows Start menu. Are there any items listed under the Network location? If so, what are they?
2. Search Help and Support for **Map network drive**. Click on *Create a shortcut to (map) a network drive*. What's the purpose of mapping a drive? Read through the article (but don't perform the steps described). To what other places can you create shortcuts?
3. Type up your answers, save the file as **Lastname_Firstname_ch09_Map**, and submit the assignment as directed by your instructor.

Critical Thinking 1

You're starting a home retail business. You'll have three employees that will need to share files (including company records, customer information, inventory, and financial information), Internet access, and a printer.

1. Use a word processor to create a table like the one below, comparing the three types of network setups for your business. (Note: WordPad doesn't include the ability to create tables.)
2. In the same document, write your conclusion in a two- to three-paragraph essay. Which setup should you use and why? What hardware and software will you need to purchase to use the setup?
3. Save your file as **Lastname_Firstname_ch09_Smallbiz_Network**, and submit both your table and essay as directed by your instructor.

	Homegroup	Workgroup	Client-Server
Hardware required			
Software required			
Ease of setup			
Important features			
Security			
Support			

Critical Thinking 2

You work for a school that teaches computer networking. Your boss wants to find an effective way to virtualize different servers so students can learn to work with each of them.

1. Use the Internet to research three different virtualization platforms. Compare costs, licensing, hardware, and software requirements for each. Which do you recommend to your boss and why?
2. Read the EULA (end-user license agreement) for each. Are there different restrictions for personal users vs. educational and business users? What are they?
3. Write up your answers, save the file as **Lastname_Firstname_ch09_Virtualization**, and submit your work as directed by your instructor.

Do It Yourself 1

Windows 7 provides many details about your computer through a variety of built-in utilities. For this exercise, you'll use the network properties to examine your IP address.

1. Open the Network and Sharing Center from the taskbar or Control Panel window. On the right side, click on a connection. Click *Details* in the Status dialog box.
2. What's your IP address? Take a screen shot of this dialog box. What other information is available here? Click *Close* to return to the Status dialog box.
3. Click *Properties*, and examine the items that are installed for this adapter (don't change anything). Take a screen shot of this properties dialog box. Click each item in the list, and read the description in the box. What is the purpose of each?
4. Type up your answers, include the screen shots requested, save the file as **Lastname_Firstname_ch09_Adapter**, and submit the assignment as directed by your instructor.

Do It Yourself 2

Most of us use multiple networks at home, work, and school. In this exercise, you'll examine a network you use and the devices that are part of it.

1. Make a diagram of a network you use. If you don't have a home network, you may draw a friend's network or one you work on at school or work instead. You can use a program such as MS Paint, Google SketchUp, or even PowerPoint to create the diagram. Be sure to label the devices (including printers, cell phones, game consoles, and so on).
2. If your network connects to the Internet, label the LAN and WAN parts.
3. Save the file as **Lastname_Firstname_ch09_My_Network**, and submit it as directed by your instructor.

Ethical Dilemma

A popular technology reporter received a call from an upset listener, Tina. Tina had been accessing the Internet with her notebook for months but was suddenly unable to connect. The reporter asked her some questions to help her troubleshoot the problem. Did she try turning off her router and turning it back on? No—she didn't have a router. What about a wireless access point? Nope—she didn't have one of those either. Did she call her ISP for help? You guessed it—she didn't have one of those either! After some more questions, the reporter finally realized that Tina had been piggybacking off her neighbor's wireless network.

1. Tina was very upset to have lost her Internet connection, and a few days later, it was restored. There's no way for her neighbor to know that Tina is using the connection. Is it acceptable for Tina to continue to use her neighbor's network now that she's aware of what she's doing?
2. Look up the laws where you live. Is it legal? Is it ethical? Would you do it?
3. Type up your answers, save the file as **Lastname_Firstname_ch09_Piggyback**, and submit it as directed by your instructor.

On the Web 1

E-mail is one system that most of us use that relies on servers. To access your e-mail using a desktop e-mail client or smartphone, you may need to configure the settings for the incoming and outgoing e-mail servers.

1. What is your e-mail provider? Go to the home page of your e-mail provider, and locate the help feature (for Gmail, Yahoo! Mail, and Hotmail, this is in the upper-right corner of the window). Search the help to find out if it is possible to use a desktop e-mail client (such as Outlook, Windows Live Mail, or Thunderbird) to access your e-mail. Is there a cost for this service?
2. What are the settings for the incoming mail server and outgoing mail server? Are they the same? Are there any other settings that you must change? Is there a different method for accessing it using a mobile device?
3. Type up your answers, save the file as **Lastname_Firstname_ch09_Mail_Servers**, and submit it as directed by your instructor.

On the Web 2

Joyent is one of the largest IaaS providers on the Internet.

1. Go to the Joyent website (**joyent.com**). What are some of the companies that use Joyent? Research the pricing plans.
2. Research the cost and features for Amazon EC2 (**aws.amazon.com/ec2**). How does it compare to Joyent? Which would you recommend for a small business and why?
3. Compare the total cost for these services. Are they worth the cost? Type up your answers, save the file as **Lastname_Firstname_ch09_IaaS**, and submit it as directed by your instructor.

Collaboration 1

Instructors: Divide the class into small groups, and provide each group with a large piece of paper or poster board or access to computers.

The Project: Each team is to prepare a Venn diagram that compares the features of peer-to-peer and client-server networks. Teams must use at least three references, only one of which may be this textbook.

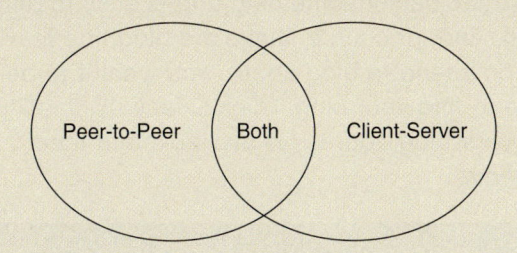

Students: Before beginning this project, discuss the roles each group member will play. Choose a team name, which you'll use in submitting your presentation. Be sure to divide the work among your members, and pick someone to present your project. You may find it helpful to elect a team leader who can direct your activities and ensure that all team members contribute to the project.

Outcome: You're to prepare a Venn diagram using a large piece of paper or a computer drawing program. The diagram must have at least four items in each of the three areas of the diagram. Present your findings to the class. Be sure to include a listing of all team members. Turn in your diagram named as **Teamname_ch09_Venn_Diagram**. Submit your presentation to your instructor as directed.

Collaboration 2

Instructors: Divide the class into five groups, and assign each group one type of network for this project: PAN, CAN, MAN, WLAN, and VPN.

The Project: Each team is to prepare a multimedia presentation for its network type. The presentation should be designed to educate consumers about the network type. Teams must use at least three references, only one of which may be this textbook. Use Google Docs to plan the presentation and provide documentation that all team members have contributed to the project. For more on using Google Docs, see Appendix C.

Students: Before beginning this project, discuss the roles each group member will play. Choose a team name, which you'll use in submitting your presentation. Be sure to divide the work among your members, and pick someone to present your project. You may find it helpful to elect a team leader who can direct your activities and ensure that all team contributions are collated through Google Docs.

Outcome: You're to prepare a multimedia presentation on your assigned topic in PowerPoint (or another tool if approved by your instructor) and present it to your class. The presentation may be no longer than 3 minutes and should contain 5 to 7 slides. On the first slide, be sure to include the name of your presentation and a listing of all team members. Turn in a final version of your presentation named as **Teamname_ch09_Networks** and your Google Docs file showing your collaboration named as **Teamname_ch09_Network_Collaboration**. Submit your presentation to your instructor as directed.

Blogging

1. Blog about the network that you connect to the most often. In your write-up, provide the type of devices you use to connect to it. Outline the things that you use the network for the most. What other resources would you like to be able to access through it?
2. Visit at least two of your classmates' blogs on this topic. On the blogs you visit, comment on the differences and similarities of your posts.
3. Create a document that includes your blog URL and the URLs of the two blogs you commented on. Save the file as **Lastname_Firstname_ch09_Network_Blog**. Submit the document to your instructor as directed.

Appendix

Appendix A

Blogger

A blog (short for Web log) is like an online journal. It's a Web page that's created with simple blog tools that anyone can set up, and bloggers can talk about whatever they like. The difference between just creating a Web page and writing a blog is that blogs can be interactive. Your readers can post comments about your blog posts.

Setting up a blog is pretty easy. You don't need to know how to create a Web page. The blogging tools do all the work for you. One website for creating free blogs is Blogger.com. To use Blogger, you need to have a Google account.

1. Open your browser, and go to **Blogger.com**. Use your Google account to log in to Blogger. (If you don't have a Google account, you can create one as part of the Blogger signup.) Sign in and then click *Create a Blog*.

2. On the *Sign up for Blogger* screen, type a display name (this is how your posts will be signed, so think about what you want to display—your real name or a pen name perhaps), select a notification preference, read and accept the Terms of Service, and then click *Continue*.

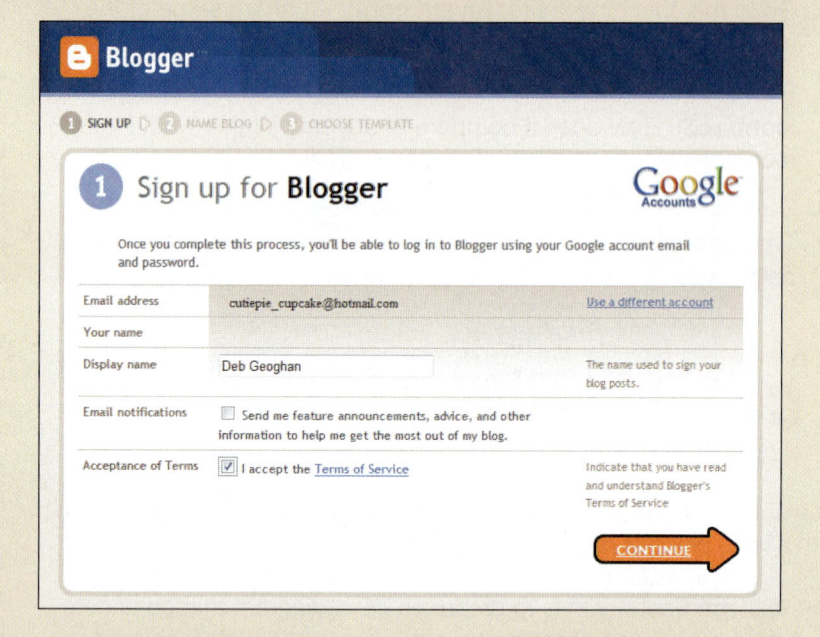

3. On the *Name your blog* screen, create a blog title and address. Try to select something that is easy to remember (and spell). And, of course, make the blog title fit with the content you intend to blog about. You want it to be easy for people to find your blog. Click *Check Availability* to be sure that your blog address is available and then click *Continue*.

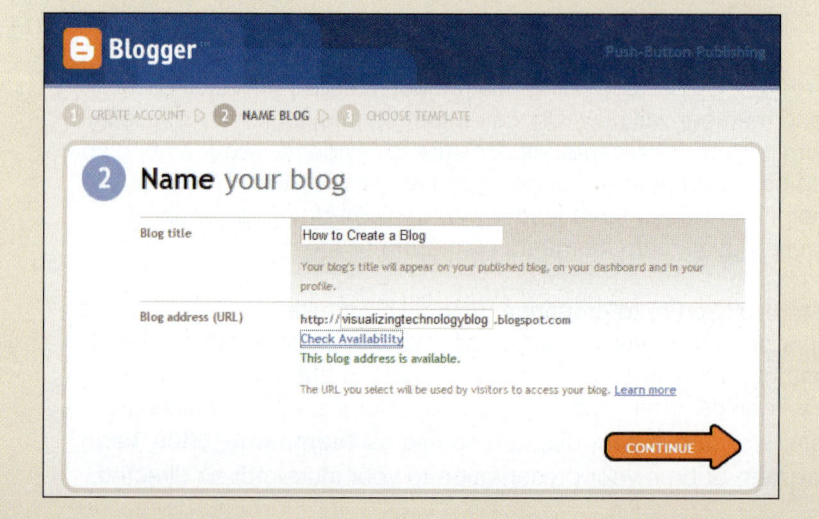

4. Choose a starter template that visually complements the style and content of your blog. Don't worry—you can change or customize it later. Click *Continue*.

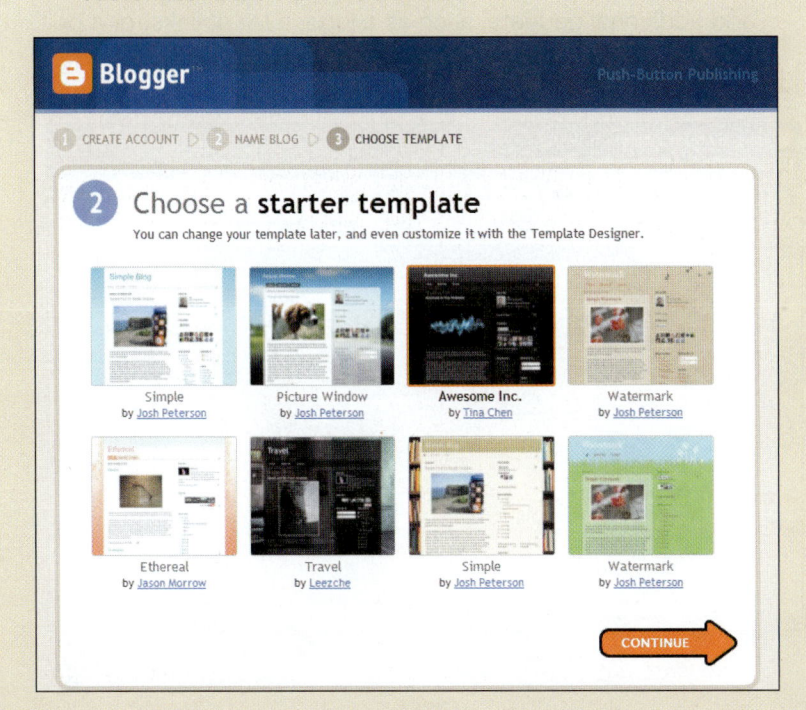

5. You now have a blog. Click *Start Blogging*.

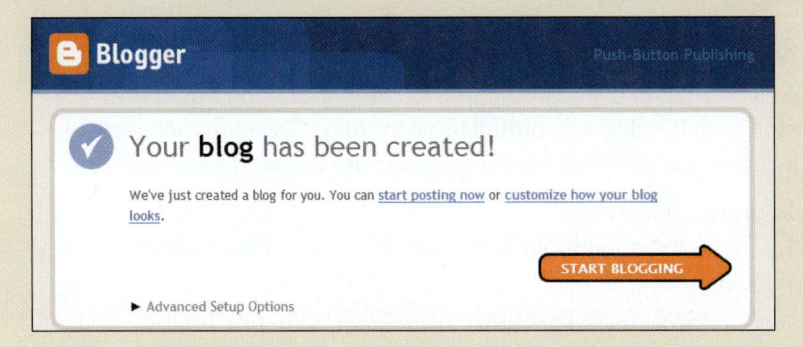

6. Your blog dashboard is where you manage your blog. The first tab—Posting—is where you compose and format your blog postings. You can use the formatting toolbar to add styles, links, images, and videos to your post. Under *Post Options*, you can allow comments (the default) and even schedule a post for a future date and time. Labels (also called "tags") help your readers find posts that are related. When you're satisfied with your post, click *Publish Post*. Congratulations—you're a blogger!

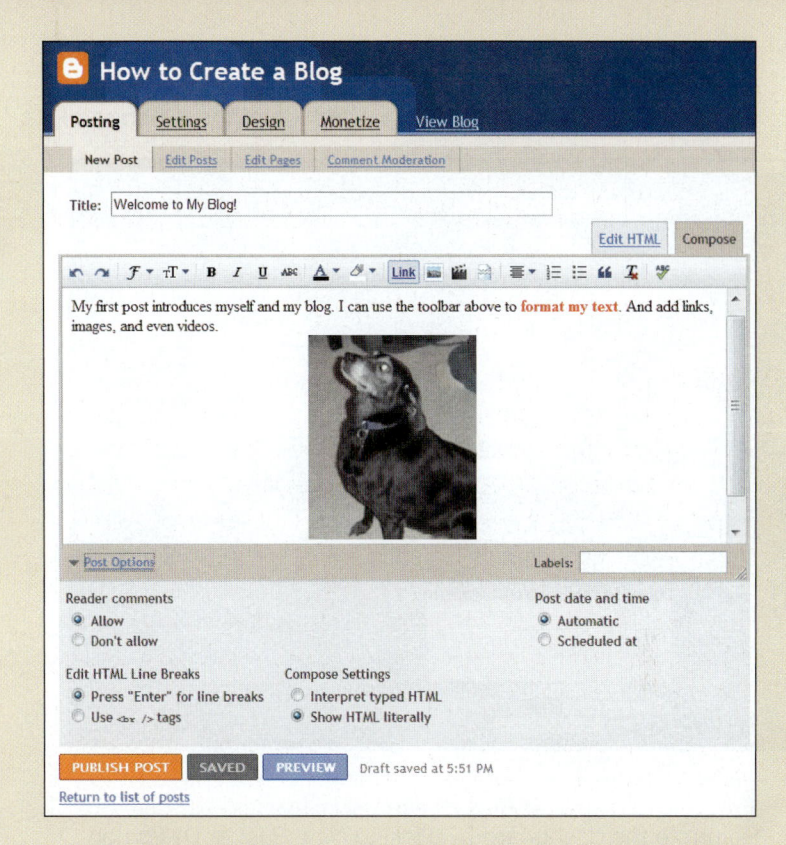

7. Click *View Post* to display your blog in the template you selected. If you allowed comments (the default), a *Post a Comment* box will be displayed for each post. This allows your readers to interact with you. The layout will vary depending on the template you chose, but most will include a list of followers and a blog archive. Type your comment in the white box and then click *Post Comment* to post a comment to the blog.

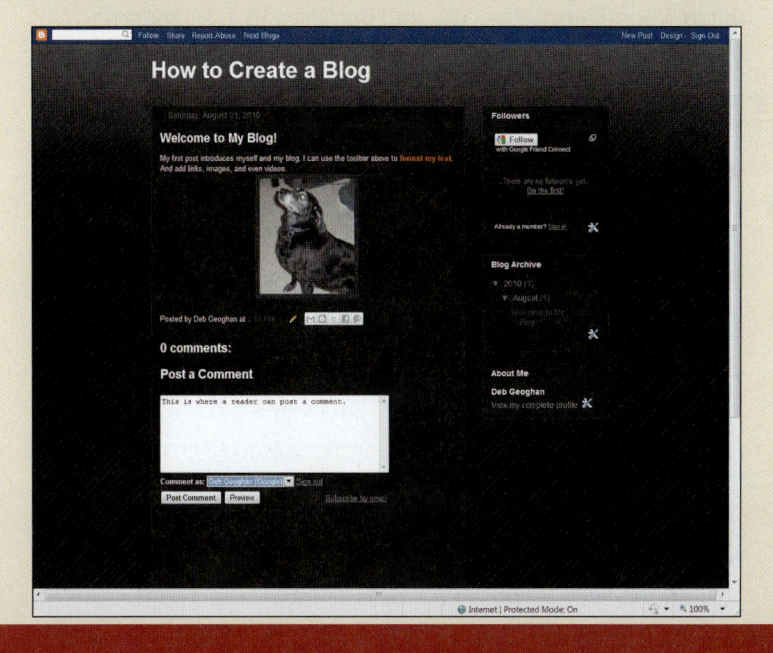

8. Posted comments are listed below the blog post (unless you change it in the *Comment Settings* section of the dashboard).

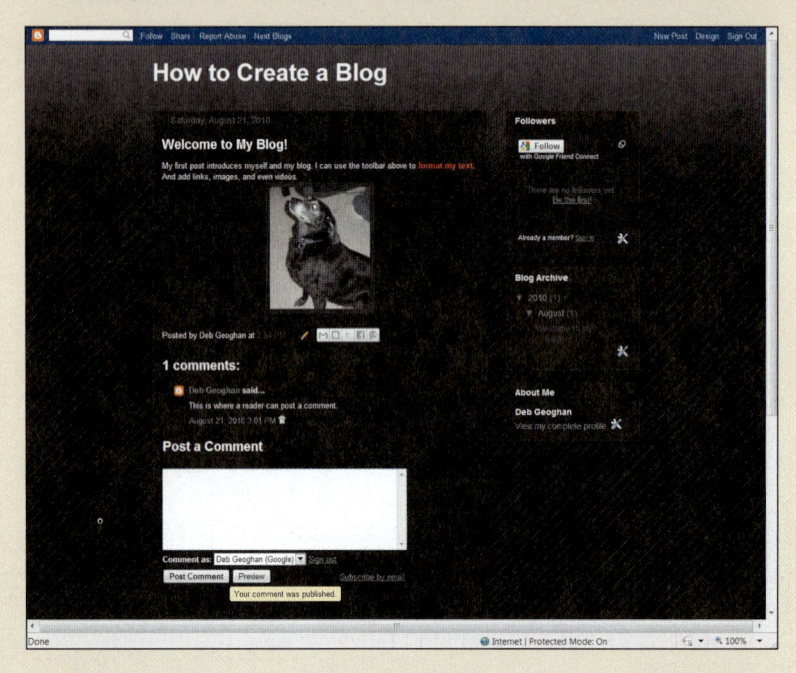

9. Return to the dashboard by clicking *New Post* or *Design* on the top right of your blog. The Settings tab of the dashboard has nine different options. You can explore those as you need them. The last section—Permissions—is what allows you to set up multiple authors. This is a great way for a group of people to create a collaborative blog. You can also make your blog private by specifying just who can (and can't) access it. So, for example, if your blog is a class project, you can limit readers to just your classmates. You can name up to 100 readers. By default, your blog is public and can be read by anyone.

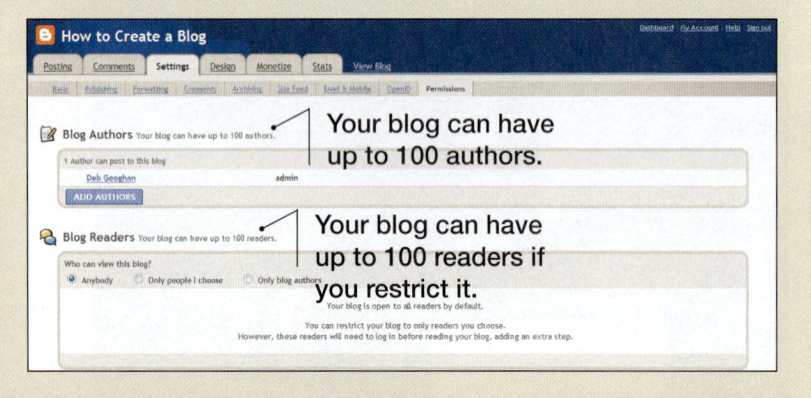

10. Click the Design tab to customize the way your blog looks. You can choose a new template, move elements around, and add additional gadgets, such as a logo, a list of links, or a poll. When you're finished making design changes, click *Save*—and you're all set.

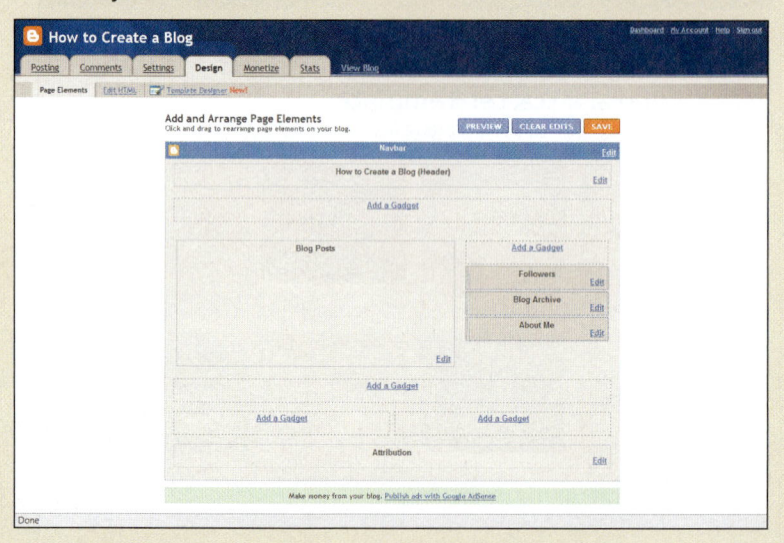

Appendix B

Mind Maps

A mind map is a visual tool that's useful for taking notes and studying. It helps you organize information using images and keywords and to see how the pieces are related to each other.

To draw a mind map:
1. Write the main topic in the center of the page and then put a circle around it.
2. For each major subtopic, draw a line radiating out from the center.
3. Draw branches off the subtopics as you dig deeper into the material.
4. Draw dotted connecting lines between branches that are related.

Use single words and simple phrases, color, and images to help clarify the material.

Mind maps are used throughout this book to outline the basic structure of each chapter, but you can build on those beginning maps to delve deeper into the material. The figure at the top of the next page shows the mind map for Chapter 2. We can build on it by adding more detail to the branches.

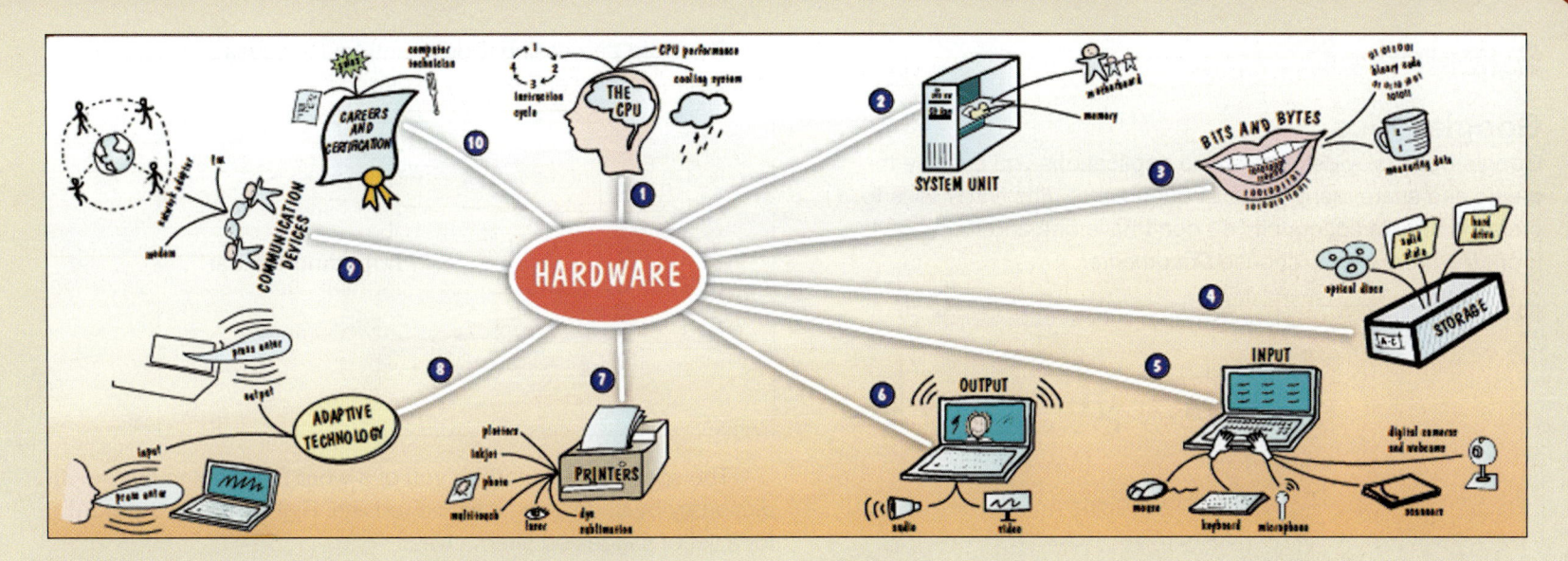

The printer branch is a good place to expand. What topics and concepts would you list on the printer branch? Look at the chapter, and you'll see many choices that you might put here. The next figure shows some ideas you might include on your map of this branch. We could draw a connection between PictBridge on the printer branch and the digital camera on the input branch as well as the solid-state storage (memory card) on the storage branch.

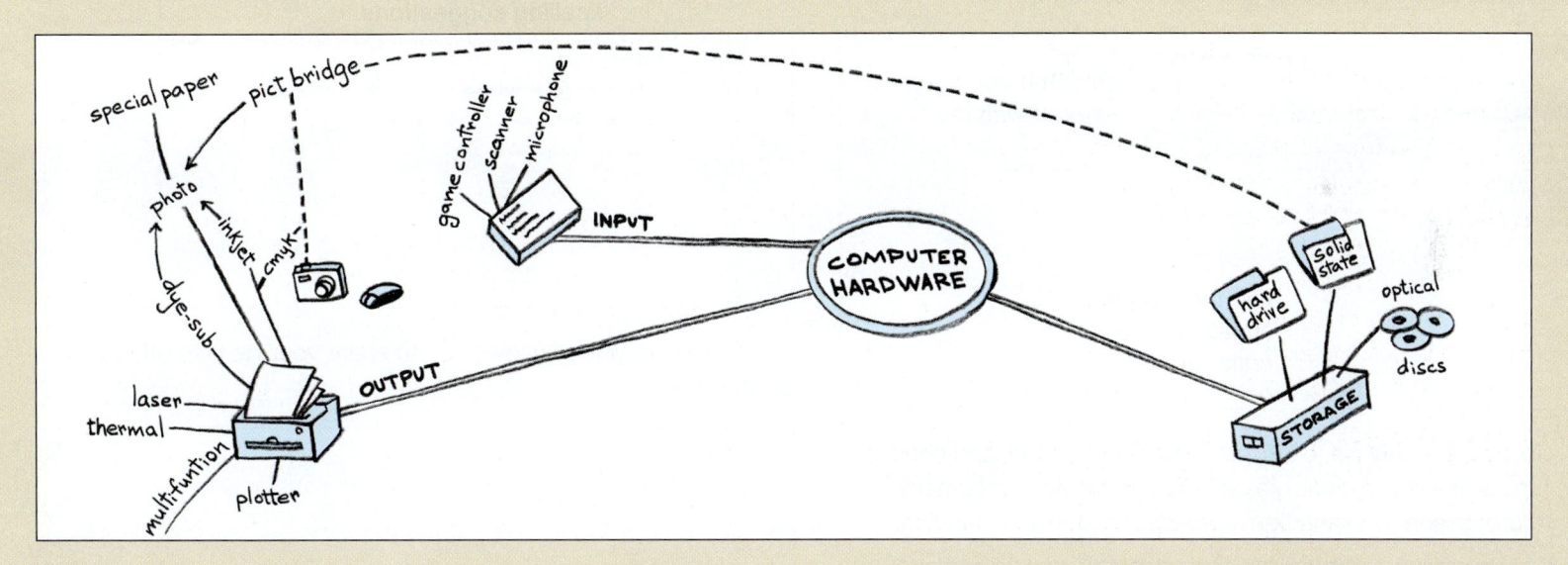

Because mind maps are used to help you remember and connect information, there's no right or wrong answer. Some people like to hand-draw mind maps; others use software to make maps cleaner. Mind maps help you review material and see connections between the topics. They're one tool you could use to take notes and study.

Appendix C

Google Docs

Google Docs provides free online applications you can use to create and share many types of documents. The first step is to create a Google account if you don't have one and then sign in. From the more menu, choose *Documents*.

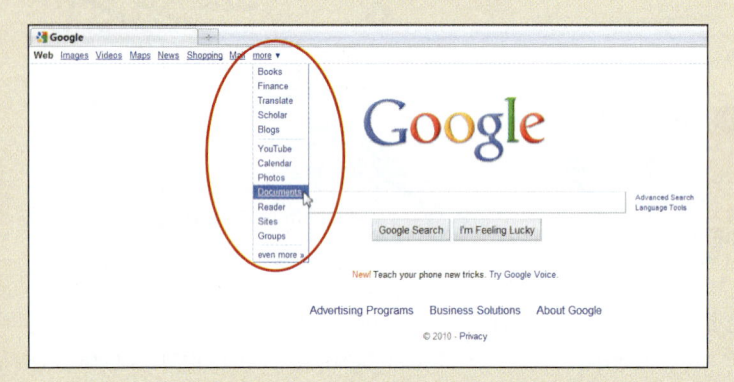

On the Google Docs page, you can see the files you've created and shared as well as files others have shared with you.

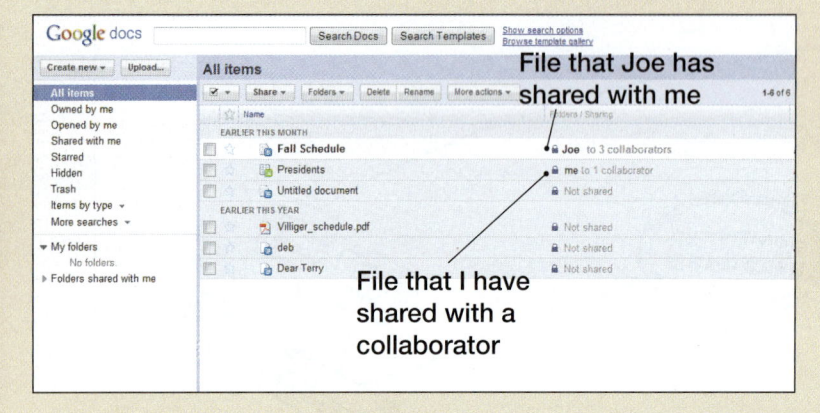

To create a new file, click the *Create new* button, and choose the type of file you wish to create. You can create a document (word processor), presentation, spreadsheet, form, or drawing.

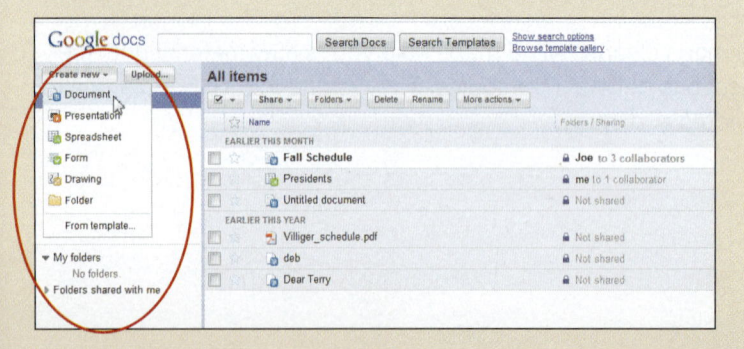

The word processing (Document) tool includes standard formatting options and is easy to use.

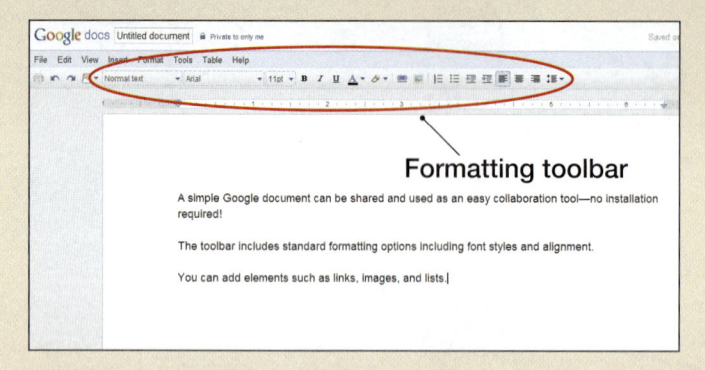

The spell-checker notifies you of a word that's not in the dictionary by underlining it with a red line. Right-click on the word for a list of suggested alternatives.

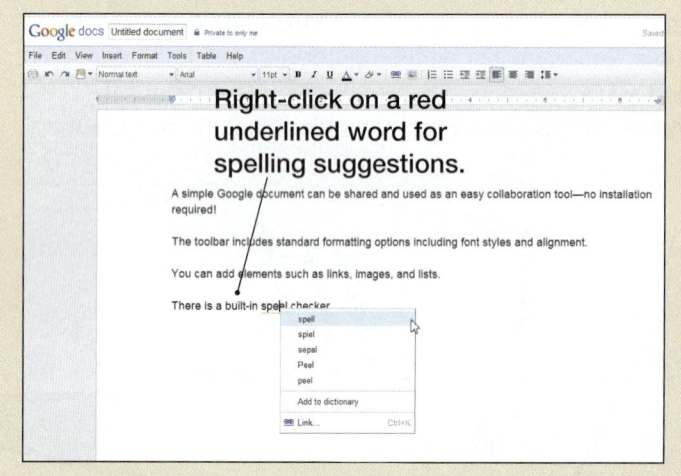

The *Share* button allows you to share your file with others for collaboration.

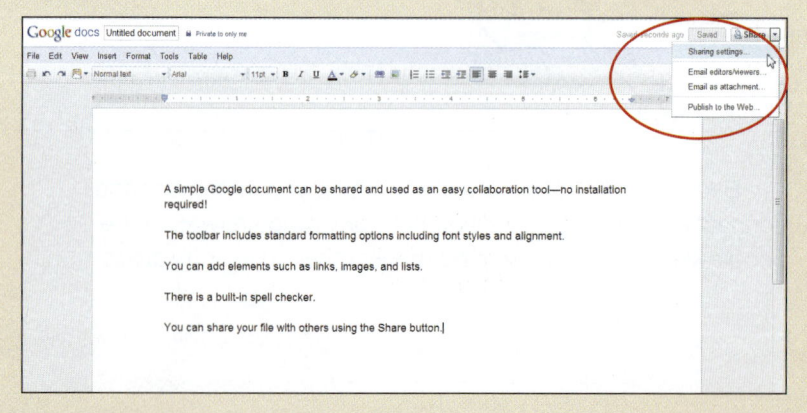

To work on a shared file, simply open it from the Google Docs file list. From the File menu, choose *See revision history* to see each revision of the document.

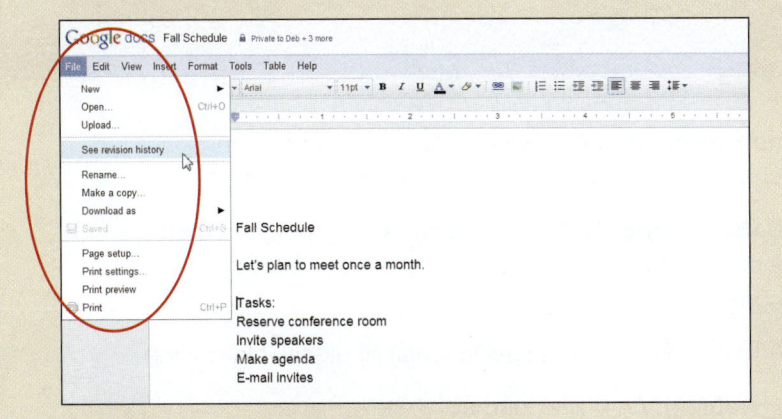

You can add a comment by selecting a word or phrase and then choosing *Comment* from the Insert menu.

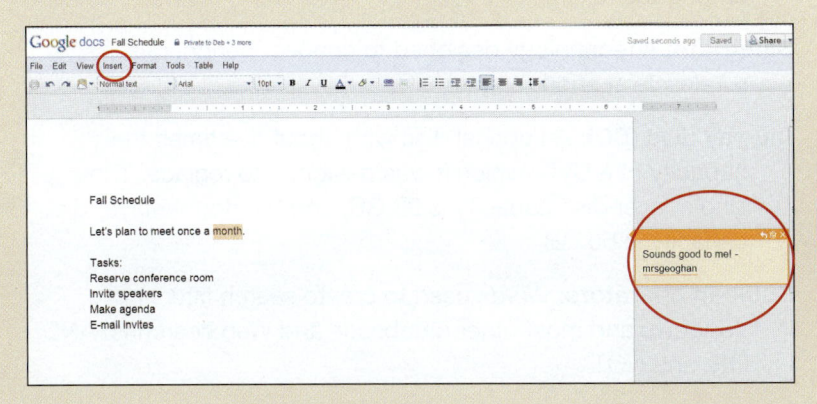

You can collaborate in real time. A list of people working on the document displays in the upper-right corner, and you'll see their edits in real time.

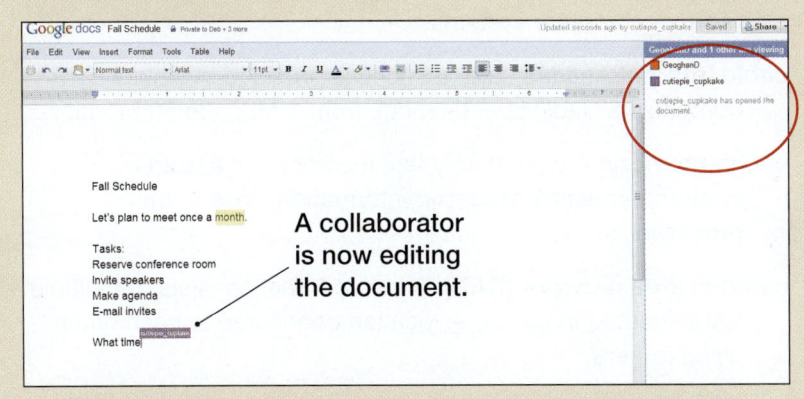

Open the list to view and chat with collaborators in the current session.

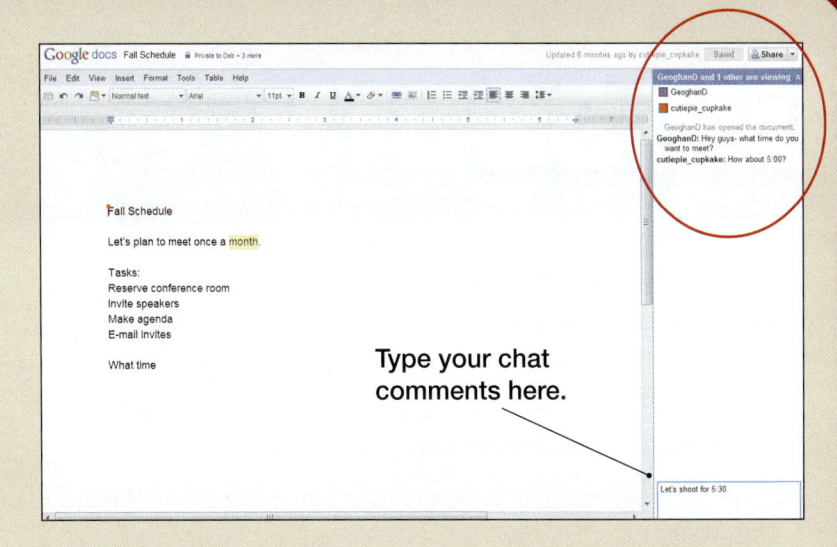

You can download the file into many popular formats, including Microsoft Office formats, by choosing *Download* as from the File menu.

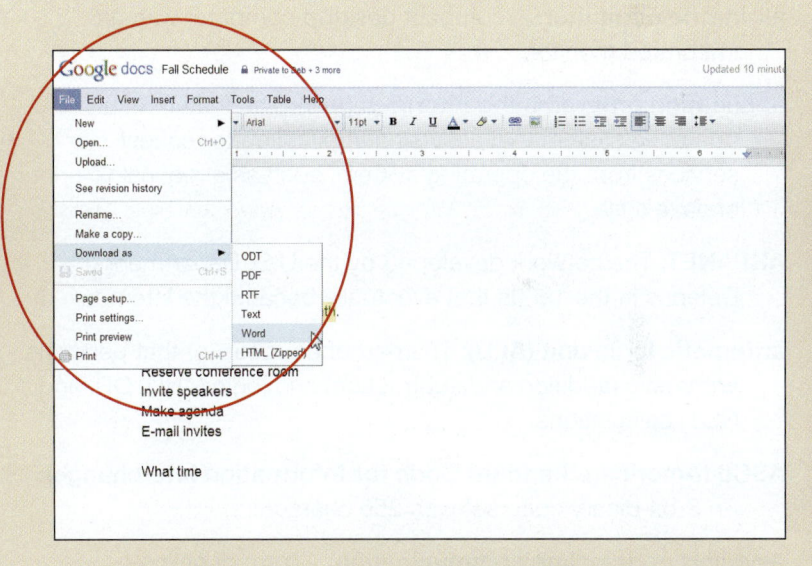

Using Google Docs is an easy way to quickly create and share documents with others. There's no software to purchase or install; it all runs right from your browser. Google Docs is an example of a SaaS (Software-as-a-Service) application. It doesn't matter if you have a PC and your friend has a Mac. Because collaboration is so easy, you can work on the file together even if you're not in the same location.

Glossary

adaptive technology: Software and hardware used by individuals with disabilities to interact with technology. Also called assistive technology.

ad hoc network: A network created when two wireless devices connect to each other directly.

add-on: An application that extends the functionality of a Web browser.

AGP (accelerated graphics port): The standard analog video port on computers manufactured before 2009.

all-in-one computer: A compact desktop computer with an integrated monitor.

application programming interface (API): The feature of an operating system that allows an application to request services from the operating system, such as a request to print or save a file.

ARPANET: The network developed by the U.S. Department of Defense in the 1960s that eventually became the Internet.

arithmetic logic unit (ALU): The part of a processor that performs arithmetic (addition and subtraction) and logic (AND, OR, and NOT) calculations.

ASCII (American Standard Code for Information Interchange): An 8-bit binary code set with 256 characters.

asynchronous online communication: A form of online communication that does not require the participants to be online at the same time—for example, e-mail.

avatar: A virtual body used online.

back up: The process of copying files to another location for protection.

beta version: A pre-release version of software.

binary code: A code that represents digital data as a series of 0s and 1s that can be understood by a computer.

binary number system (base 2): The base 2 number system that only has the digits 0 and 1.

biometric scanner: A scanner that measures human characteristics such as fingerprints and eye retinas.

BIOS (Basic Input Output System): A program stored on a chip on the motherboard that's used to start up the computer.

bit: A binary digit. It's the smallest unit of digital information.

blog (weblog): An online journal.

blogosphere: All the blogs on the Web and the connections among them.

Bluetooth: A technology designed to connect peripherals wirelessly at short ranges.

Blu-ray disc (BD): An optical disc with about five times the capacity of a DVD, which it was designed to replace. The single-layer disc capacity is 25 GB, and the double-layer disc capacity is 50 GB.

Boolean operators: Words used to create search filters in Windows and most other databases and Web searches: AND, OR, and NOT.

broadband: Internet access that exceeds 200 Kbps. Examples include cable, DSL, FiOS, and WiMAX.

byte: Equal to 8 bits and used to represent a single character in modern computer systems.

cable Internet access: Internet access provided by cable companies. Cable speeds range from 1 Mbps to 50 Mbps.

cache memory: A type of very fast memory that's used to store frequently accessed information close to the processor.

campus area network (CAN): A network that consists of multiple LANs located in the same location connected to each other using routers.

cell: The intersection of a row and a column in a spreadsheet.

cellular network: A network that uses cell towers to transmit voice and data over large distances.

CPU (central processing unit): The brain of a computer; housed inside the system unit on the motherboard. It consists of two parts: the arithmetic logic unit and the control unit.

chat: A real-time online conversation between multiple people at the same time in a chat room.

client: A personal computer or other device that connects to a server.

client-server network: A network that has at least one server at its center. Users log in to the network instead of their local computers and are granted access to resources based on that login.

clock speed: The speed at which the processer executes the instruction cycle.

cloud computing: Moves the processing and storage off your desktop and business hardware and puts it in the cloud—on the Internet. Cloud computing consists of three parts: Infrastructure-as-a-Service (IaaS), Platform-as-a-Service (PaaS), and Software-as-a-Service (SaaS).

CMYK: The standard ink colors used by printers: cyan, magenta, yellow, and key (black).

communication device: A device that serves as both an input and output device and allows you to connect to other devices on a network or to the Internet. These include network adapters, modems, and fax devices.

CD (compact disc): The oldest type of optical disc in use today, with a storage capacity of about 700 MB.

CMOS (complementary metal oxide semiconductor): A volatile form of memory that uses a small battery to provide it with power to keep the data in memory even when the computer is turned off. It stores settings that are used by the BIOS.

captcha (Completely Automated Public Turing Test to Tell Computers and Humans Apart): A series of letters and numbers that are distorted in some way. This makes them difficult for automated software to read but relatively easy for humans to read.

compression: The process of making files smaller to conserve disk space and make them easier to transfer.

computer: A programmable machine that converts raw data into useful information.

computer network: Two or more computers that share resources including software, hardware, or files.

control unit: The part of the processor that manages the movement of data through the CPU.

convergence: The integration of technology on multifunction devices, such as smartphones, that has accustomed us to carrying technology with us.

CRT monitor: A legacy technology that uses a cathode ray tube to excite phosphor particles coating a glass screen to light up the pixels.

data: The unprocessed, or raw form, of information.

data bus: The wires on the motherboard over which information flows between the components of the computer.

default program: The program that's associated with a particular file type that automatically opens when a file of that type is double-clicked.

defragmenter: A disk utility that reorganizes fragmented files on a disk.

desktop computer: A personal computer that's designed to sit on a user's desk.

device driver: A piece of software that enhances the capabilities of the operating system, enabling it to communicate with hardware.

dial-up: Internet access over ordinary telephone lines. The maximum speed of dial-up is 56 Kbps.

digital footprint: All the information that someone could find out about you by searching the Web, including social network sites.

DLP (digital light-processing) projector: A projector that uses hundreds of thousands of tiny swiveling mirrors to create an image. They produce high-contrast images with deep blacks but are limited by having weaker reds and yellows.

domain: A network composed of a group of clients and servers under the control of one central security database on a special server called the domain controller.

DRM (digital rights management): A technology that is applied to digital media files, such as music, eBooks, and videos, to impose restrictions on the use of these files.

D-SLR (digital single lens reflex camera): A digital camera that uses interchangeable lenses, can be manually focused, and can cost thousands of dollars. D-SLR cameras give the user more control than point-and-shoot cameras.

DSL (digital subscriber line): Internet access over telephone lines designed to carry digital signals. DSL speeds range from 384 Kbps to 7 Mbps.

DVD (digital video disc/digital versatile disc): An optical disc that can hold about 4.7 GB of information (single-layer [SL]). Double-layer (DL) DVDs have a second layer to store data and can hold about 8.5 GB.

distributed computing: The distribution of the processing of a task across a group of computers.

document management system: The ability to save, share, search, and audit electronic documents throughout their life cycle.

domain name: The part of a URL that precedes the TLD and is sometimes called the second-level domain. The domain name represents a company or product name and makes it easy to remember the address.

DNS (Domain Name System): The service that allows you to use a friendly name, such as flickr.com, instead of an IP address, such as 165.193.123.253, to contact a website.

donationware: A form of freeware where the developers accept donations, either for themselves or for a nonprofit organization.

drive controller: Located on the motherboard, it provides a drive interface, which connects disk drives to the processor.

dye-sublimation printer: A printer that uses heat to turn solid dye into a gas that is then transferred to special paper.

e-commerce: Business on the Web; often broken into three categories: B2B, B2C, and C2C, where B stands for business and C stands for consumer.

ENIAC (Electronic Numerical Integrator and Computer): The first working, digital, general-purpose computer.

e-mail: A system of sending electronic messages using store-and-forward technology.

embedded computer: A specialized computer found in ordinary devices, such as gasoline pumps, supermarket checkouts, traffic lights, and home appliances.

embedded operating system: A specialized operating system that runs on GPS devices, ATMs, smartphones, and other devices.

EULA (end-user license agreement): License agreement between the software user and the software publisher.

EIDE (enhanced integrated drive electronics): A legacy drive interface found on the motherboard of older personal computers.

ergonomics: The study of the relationship between workers and their workspaces.

Ethernet: The most commonly used standard that defines the way data is transmitted over a local area network.

expansion card: A card that plugs directly into an expansion slot on a motherboard and allows you to connect additional peripheral devices to a computer. Video cards, sound cards, network cards, TV tuners, and modems are common expansion cards. Also called adapter cards.

e-waste: Old computers, cell phones, TVs, VCRs, and other electronic devices, some of which are considered hazardous.

FiOS (Fiber Optic Service): Internet access over fiber optic cables. FiOS speed ranges up to 50 Mbps.

file extension: The second part of the file name. The extension is assigned by the program that is used to create the file and is used by the operating system to determine the type of file.

file fragmentation: Unorganized files that are broken into small pieces that are stored in nonadjacent or noncontiguous clusters on the disk.

file management: The processes of opening, closing, saving, naming, deleting, and organizing digital files.

file name: The property of a file that's used to identify it using a name and file extension.

file property: Information about a file, such as authors, size, type, and date, which can be used to organize, sort, and find files more easily.

file system: Keeps track of what files are saved and where they're stored on the disk.

FireWire: A hot-swappable port that can connect up to 63 devices per port. It also allows for peer-to-peer communication between devices, such as two video cameras, without the use of a computer. Also known as IEEE 1394.

flash drive: A small, portable, solid-state drive that can hold up to 128 GB of information. They have become the standard for transporting data. Also called key drives, thumb drives, pen drives, or jump drives.

flash memory: The technology used by solid-state storage devices, such as flash drives and memory cards, to store data. The data is stored on a chip.

flowchart: A graphic view of an algorithm.

folder: A container used to store and organize files on a computer.

folksonomy: The social tagging of Web media.

format: The process of preparing a disk to store files by dividing it into tracks and sectors and setting up the file system.

forum: An online, asynchronous conversation, also known as a discussion board.

freeware: Software that can be used at no cost for an unlimited period of time.

game controller: A type of input device that's used to interact with video games.

Gantt chart: A chart used in project management to show a project schedule.

gigahertz (GHz): Used to measure the speed at which a processer executes the information cycle. A GHz is equal to one billion cycles per second.

GPS (global positioning system): A system of 24 satellites that transmit signals that can be picked up by a receiver on the ground and used to determine the receiver's current location, time, and velocity through triangulation of the signals.

graphical user interface (GUI): The interface between a user and the computer. A GUI allows a user to point to and click on objects, such as icons and buttons, to initiate commands.

green computing: The efficient and eco-friendly use of computers and other electronics.

grid computing: Distributed computing using a few computers in one location.

handheld: See mobile device.

hard drive: The main mass-storage device in a computer. A form of nonvolatile storage; when the computer is powered off, the data isn't lost. The primary hard drive holds the operating system, programs, and data files. Also called hard disks or hard disk drives.

hardware: The physical components of a computer.

headphones: An output device that converts digital signals into sound. They come in several different sizes and styles, ranging from tiny earbuds that fit inside your ear to full-size headphones that completely cover your outer ear. Headphones that also include a microphone are called headsets.

hierarchy: The folder structure created by Windows is a hierarchy. There are folders within folders, known as subfolders or children.

homegroup: A simple way to network a group of Windows 7 computers that are all on the same home network.

home page: 1. The Web page that appears when you first open your browser. 2. The home page of a website is the main or starting page.

hotspot: A public wireless access point often available in public locations, such as airports, schools, hotels, and restaurants.

hot-swappable: A device that can be plugged and unplugged without turning off the computer.

IEEE 1394: See FireWire.

hyperlink: A connection between pieces of information in documents written using hypertext.

hypertext: Text that contains links to other text and allows you to navigate through pieces of information by using the links that connect them.

HTML (hypertext markup language): The authoring language that defines the structure of a Web page.

information: The processed, useful form of data.

information processing cycle (IPC): The process a computer uses to convert data into information. The four steps of the IPC are input, processing, storage, and output.

Infrastructure-as-a-Service (IaaS): Part of cloud computing. IaaS is the use of Internet-based servers.

infrastructure wireless network: A wireless network in which devices connect through a wireless access point.

inkjet printer: The most common personal printer, the inkjet works by spraying droplets of ink onto paper.

input device: A device that's used to get data into the computer system so it can be processed.

instant messaging (IM): A real-time online conversation between two people.

instruction cycle: The steps a CPU uses to process data: fetch, decode, execute, also store. Also known as the fetch-and-execute cycle or the machine cycle.

integrated circuit: A silicon chip that contains a large number of tiny transistors.

Internet: The global network of computer networks.

Internet backbone: The high-speed connection point between networks that make up the Internet.

Internet Exchange Points: The backbone of the modern Internet.

Internet2 (I2): A second Internet designed for education, research, and collaboration.

IP (Internet protocol): The protocol responsible for addressing and routing packets to their destination.

IP (Internet protocol) address: A unique numeric address assigned to each node on a network.

Internet service provider (ISP): A company that offers Internet access.

joystick: An input device mounted on a base that consists of a stick, buttons, and sometimes a trigger. Typically used as a game controller, especially in flight-simulator games, a joystick may also be used for such tasks as controlling robotic machinery in a factory.

keyboard: An input device that consists of alphabet keys, numeric keys, and other specialized keys.

keypad: A small keyboard that doesn't contain all the alphabet keys.

laser printer: The most common type of printer found in schools and businesses. They use a laser beam to draw an image on a drum. The image is electrostatically charged and attracts a dry ink called toner. The drum is then rolled over paper, and the toner is deposited on the paper. Finally, the paper is heated, bonding the ink to it.

legacy technology: Old technology that's still used alongside its more modern replacement, typically because it still works and is cost-effective.

LCD (liquid crystal display): The most common type of display found on desktop and notebook computers. They consist of two layers of glass that are glued together with a layer of liquid crystals between them. When electricity is passed through the individual crystals, it causes them to pass or block light to create an image.

LCD projector: A projector that passes light through a prism, which divides the light into three beams—red, green, and blue—which are then passed through an LCD screen.

library: Designed to help you organize your files. There are four libraries: Documents, Music, Pictures, and Videos. You can use these folders to gather files that are located in different locations.

Linux: An open source operating system distribution that contains the Linux kernel and bundled utilities and applications.

local area network (LAN): A network that has all connected devices or nodes located in the same physical location.

lossless compression: Uses a compression algorithm that looks for the redundancy in a file and creates an encoded file by removing the redundant information. When the file is decompressed, all the information from the original file is restored.

lossy compression: Uses a compression algorithm on files that contain more information than humans can typically discern (typically images, audio, and video files). That extra information is removed from the file. It's not possible to decompress this file, as the information has been removed from the file.

Mac: A personal computer manufactured by Apple. Also referred to as a Macintosh.

Mac OS X: The operating system installed on Macintosh computers.

mainframe: A large multiuser computer that can perform millions of transactions in a day.

memory: Temporary storage that's used by a computer to hold instructions and data.

memory card: A form of solid-state storage used to expand the storage of digital cameras, video games, and other devices.

metropolitan area network (MAN): A network that covers a single geographic area.

microblogging: A form of blogging where posts are limited to 140 characters and users post updates frequently. Twitter is a microblog site.

microphone: An input device that converts sound into digital signals and is used to chat in real time or as part of voice-recognition applications used in video games and for dictating text.

microprocessor: The chip that contains the central processing unit (CPU) of a computer.

Microsoft Windows: The operating system found on most personal computers.

minicomputer: The smallest multiuser computer. Users connect to a minicomputer via dumb terminals, which have no processing capabilities of their own.

mobile browser (microbrowser): A microbrowser optimized for small screen devices, such as smartphones and PDAs.

mobile device: A device such as a PDA (personal digital assistant), Pocket PC, or smartphone. A pocket-sized computer we carry with us wherever we go.

modem: A communication device used to connect a computer to a telephone line, modems are most often used for dial-up Internet access. Modem is short for modulator-demodulator. A modem modulates digital data into an analog signal that can be transmitted over a phone line and, on the receiving end, demodulates the analog signal back into a digital data.

monitor: A video output device that works by lighting up pixels on a screen. Each pixel contains three colors: red, green, and blue (RGB). From that base, all colors can be created by varying the intensities of the three colors.

Moore's Law: An observation made by Gordon Moore in 1965 that the number of transistors that can be placed on an integrated circuit had doubled roughly every 2 years. The current trend is closer to doubling every 18 months and is expected to continue for another 10 to 20 years.

motherboard: The main circuit board of a computer. It houses the CPU, drive controllers and interfaces, expansion slots, data buses, ports and connectors, BIOS, and memory and may also include integrated peripherals, such as video, sound, and network cards. It provides the way for devices to attach to your computer.

mouse: An input device that allows a user to interact with objects by moving a pointer, also called a cursor, on the computer screen. It may include one or more buttons and a scroll wheel and works by moving across a smooth surface to signal movement of the pointer.

MP3: MPEG-1 Audio Layer 3. A common audio file type used for music files. MP3 is a lossy form of compression that works by removing some of the detail. There is a trade-off between file size and quality.

MP3 player: A handheld device that allows you to carry with you thousands of songs and podcasts, so you can listen to them wherever you are. Also called portable media player if it supports photos and videos.

multi-core processor: A processor that consists of two or more processors integrated on a single chip. Multi-core processing increases the processing speed over single-core processors and reduces energy consumption over multiple separate processors.

multifunction device: A printer device with a built-in scanner and sometimes fax capabilities. Also known as an all-in-one printer.

multimedia: The integration of text, graphics, video, animation, and sound content.

multitasking: The ability to do more than one task at a time.

multiuser computer: A system that allows multiple, simultaneous users to connect to it, allowing for centralized resources and security. Multiuser computers are also more powerful than personal computers.

municipal WiFi: Wireless Internet access available in some cities and towns.

netbook: A lightweight, inexpensive notebook computer designed primarily for Internet access. Netbooks have built-in wireless capabilities but have small screens and offer limited computing power and storage.

network adapter: A communication device used to establish a connection with a network. The adapter may be onboard, an expansion card, or a USB device and may be wired or wireless.

network operating system (NOS): A specialized operating system found on servers in a client-server network that provides services requested by the client computers, such as file services, printing services, centralized security, and communication services.

notebook: A portable personal computer. Also referred to as a laptop.

office application suite: A suite of productivity applications—such as a word processor, spreadsheet, presentation program, database, and personal information manager—integrated into a single package.

open source: Software that has its source code published and made available to the public, enabling anyone to copy, modify and redistribute it without paying fees.

operating system (OS): The system software that provides the user with the interface to communicate with the hardware and software on a computer. A computer can't run without an operating system installed.

optical disc: A form of removable storage. Data is stored on these discs using a laser to either melt the disc material or change the color of embedded dye. A laser can read the variations as binary data.

optical network terminal (ONT): The device that connects a LAN to a FiOS network.

OLED (organic light-emitting diode): A new technology used in monitors that are composed of extremely thin panels of organic molecules sandwiched between two electrodes.

output device: A device that returns information to the user.

parallel processing: The use of multiple processors or multi-core processors to divide up the work.

path: The sequence of folders to a file or folder.

PC: A small microprocessor-based computer designed to be used by one person at a time.

PCI (peripheral component interconnect): The most common type of expansion slot on a motherboard that an expansion card plugs into.

PCI express (PCIe): A faster version of PCI that's typically used to connect a video card.

peer-to-peer network (P2P): A network in which each computer is considered equal. Each device can share its resources with every other device, and there's no centralized authority.

peripheral device: The components that serve the input, output, and storage functions of a computer system.

personal area network (PAN): A LAN that consists of devices connected by Bluetooth. Also called a piconet.

personal computer: See PC.

PDA (personal digital assistant): A small, handheld computer that is designed for business instead of entertainment and will typically have a calendar, contacts organizer, calculator, and other business applications.

PIM (personal information manager): A program used to manage e-mail, calendar, and tasks and is often part of an office suite.

photo printer: A printer designed to print high-quality photos on special photo paper. Photo printers can be inkjet printers that use special ink cartridges or dye-sublimation printers, which produce lab-quality prints.

piconet: See personal area network (PAN).

PictBridge: An industry standard that allows a camera to connect directly to a printer, usually by a USB connection or special dock.

piggybacking: Using an open wireless network to access the Internet without permission.

pipelining: A method used by a single processor to improve performance. As soon as the first instruction has moved from the fetch to the decode stage, the processor fetches the next instruction.

pixel: A single point on a display screen. Short for picture elements. Each pixel contains three colors: red, green, and blue (RGB). From that base, all colors can be created by varying the intensities of the three colors.

plasma monitor: A large display type that works by passing an electric current through gas sealed in thousands of cells inside the screen. The current excites the gas, which in turn excites the phosphors that coat the screen to pass light through an image.

plotter: A printer that uses one or more pens to draw an image on a roll of paper.

Plug and Play (PnP): An operating system feature that allows you to easily add new hardware to a computer system. When you plug in a new piece of hardware, the OS detects it and helps you set it up.

plug-in: A third-party program that extends the functionality of a browser.

podcast: A prerecorded radio- and TV-like show that you can download and listen to or watch any time.

podcast client: A program used to locate, subscribe to, and play podcasts.

point-and-shoot camera: The simplest, least expensive digital camera type and has the fewest features.

port: A way to connect a peripheral device to a motherboard.

portable apps: Application software that can be run from a flash drive.

portable media player: A handheld device that allows you to carry with you thousands of songs and podcasts (and perhaps photos, videos, and games), so you can listen to them wherever you are. Also called MP3 player.

processor: See CPU.

project management software: An application designed to help you to complete projects, keep within your budget, stay on schedule, and collaborate with others.

projector: A video output device typically used when making a presentation or sharing media with a group in such places as classrooms, businesses, and home theaters because they can produce larger output than a monitor.

prosumer: A contraction of "professional" and "consumer;" refers to someone that is not a professional photographer, but has enough interest or expertise to require a camera with some professional features.

protocol: The rules for communication between devices, which determine how data is formatted, transmitted, received, and acknowledged.

PS/2 port: A legacy port used to connect a keyboard and mouse.

Public folder: In Windows, the folder that is common to all users and provides an easy way to share files between them.

RAM (random access memory): A form of volatile memory that holds the operating systems, programs, and data the computer is currently using. Any information left in memory is lost when the power is turned off.

ROM (read-only memory): A nonvolatile form of memory that doesn't need power to keep its data.

RSS (Really Simple Syndication): A format used for distributing Web feeds that change frequently—for example, blogs, podcasts, and news—to subscribers.

resolution: 1. The number of horizontal pixels by vertical pixels, for example 1280 × 1024 or 1024 × 768, on a display screen. The higher the resolution, the sharper the image. 2. The measure of the number of pixels in an image, expressed in megapixels.

retail software: The user pays a fee to use the software for an unlimited period of time.

RFID tag: A tag that can be read by an RFID (radio frequency identification) scanner. It contains a tiny antenna for receiving and sending a radio frequency signal.

satellite Internet access: A means of connecting to the Internet using communication satellites.

scanner: An input device that can increase the speed and accuracy of data entry and convert information into a digital format that can be saved, copied, and manipulated.

screen capture: A software tool that allows you to create a video of what happens on your computer screen.

search engine: A database that indexes the Web.

serial and parallel ports: Legacy ports used to connect peripheral devices to a computer.

SATA (serial ATA): The standard internal drive interface.

server: A multiuser computer system that runs a network operating system (NOS) and provides services—such as Internet access, e-mail, or file and print services—to client systems.

shareware: Software offered in trial form or for a limited period that allows the user to try it out before purchasing a license.

shutter lag: The time between pressing the shutter button and the camera snapping the picture.

smartphone: A multifunction device that blends phone, PDA, and portable media player features. Popular in both the business and personal markets.

social bookmarking site: A site that allows you to save and share your bookmarks or favorites online.

social media: A collection of tools that enable users to create user-generated content, connect, network, and share.

social media marketing (SMM): The practice of using social media sites to sell products and services.

social network: An online community that combines many of the features of the other online tools.

social news site: An online news site that allows the community to submit content they discover on the Web and puts it in one place for everyone to see and to discuss.

social review site: A website where users review hotels, movies, games, books, and other products and services.

Software-as-a-Service (SaaS): Part of cloud computing. SaaS is the delivery of applications—or Web apps—over the Internet.

solid-state storage: A nonmechanical form of storage that uses flash memory to store data on a chip.

sound card: An expansion card that provides audio connections for both input devices (microphones and synthesizers) and output devices (speakers and headphones).

speakers: An output device that converts digital signals from a computer or media player into sound.

speech recognition: A feature that allows users to use a computer without a keyboard by speaking commands. It can be used for such tasks as automatically providing customer service through a call center, dialing a cell phone, or even dictating a term paper.

spreadsheet: An application that creates electronic worksheets composed of rows and columns. Spreadsheets are used for mathematical applications, such as budgeting, grade books, and inventory. Spreadsheets are also very good at organizing data so it can be sorted, filtered, and rearranged, making them useful for things that don't involve calculations, such as address lists and schedules.

storage area network (SAN): A network between the data storage devices and the servers on a network that makes the data accessible to all servers in the SAN. Normal users are not part of the SAN but are able to access the information through the LAN servers.

streaming: Media, such as video or audio, begins to play immediately as it is being received and does not require the whole file to be downloaded to your computer first.

stylus: A special pen-like input tool used by tablet computers, graphic design tablets, PDAs, and other handheld devices.

supercomputer: A very expensive computer system that's used to perform complex mathematical calculations, such as those used in weather forecasting and medical research.

switch: A device that connects multiple devices on a LAN and uses address information to send data packets only to the port that the appropriate device is connected to.

synchronous online communication: A form of online communication that requires the participants to be online at the same time—for example, chat and instant messaging.

system requirements: The minimum hardware and software specifications required to run a software application.

system unit: The case that encloses and protects the power supply, motherboard, CPU, and memory of a computer. It also has drive bays to hold the storage devices and openings for peripheral devices to connect to expansion cards on the motherboard.

tablet PC: A type of notebook computer that has a screen that can swivel to fold into what resembles a notepad or tablet. They include a special digital pen or stylus that allows the user to write directly on the screen.

tagging: Labeling images or files with keywords to make it easier to organize and search for them.

thermal printer: A printer that creates an image by heating specially coated heat-sensitive paper, which changes color where the heat is applied.

top-level domain (TLD): The suffix, such as .com or .edu, that follows the domain name in a URL.

touchpad: An input device typically found on a notebook computer instead of a mouse. Motion is detected by moving your finger across the touch-sensitive surface.

touchscreen: An input device that can accept input from a finger or stylus.

transistor: A tiny electric switch used in second-generation computers.

TCP (transmission control protocol): The protocol responsible for assuring that data packets are transmitted reliably on a network.

TCP/IP protocol stack: A suite of protocols that defines everything from how to transfer files (FTP) and Web pages (HTTP) to sending (SMTP) and receiving (POP) e-mail. TCP/IP is the protocol stack that runs on the Internet, and because of this, it's also the protocol stack that runs on most LANs.

ubiquitous computing (ubicomp): Technology recedes into the background and becomes part of our environment.

Unicode: An extended ASCII set that has become the standard on the Internet and includes codes for most of the world's written languages, mathematical systems, and special characters. It has codes for over 100,000 characters.

URL (uniform resource locator): An address, such as http://google.com, that consists of three main parts: protocol (http), domain name (google), and top-level domain (.com).

USB (universal serial bus): A standard port type that's used to connect many kinds of devices, including printers, mice, keyboards, digital cameras, cell phones, and external drives. Up to 127 devices can share a single USB port.

USB hub: A device used to connect multiple USB devices to a single USB port.

user-generated content: Web content created by ordinary users.

vacuum tube: A tube that resembles an incandescent light bulb and was used in first-generation computers.

video card: An expansion card that provides the data signal and connection for a monitor or projector. It may also include input ports to connect a TV tuner or another video device to the system.

video game system: A computer that's designed primarily to play games.

viral video: A video that becomes extremely popular because of recommendations and social sharing.

virtual private network (VPN): A private network through the public network (Internet) that allows remote users to access a LAN securely. Such networks use encryption to ensure data security.

VoIP (voice over IP): A service that allows phone calls to be transmitted over the Internet instead of traditional phone lines.

volunteer computing: A form of distributed computing that relies on the processing power of hundreds or thousands of volunteers' personal computers.

wardriving: The practice of driving around and locating open wireless access points.

wearable: A computer designed to be worn on the body.

Web 2.0: New technologies used to communicate and collaborate on the Web. Web 2.0 tools rely of the wisdom of the crowd and enable users to create user-generated content, connect, and network. They are also called social media.

webcam: A specialized video camera that provides visual input for online communication, such as Web conferencing or chatting.

Web browser: A program that interprets HTML to display Web pages as you browse the Internet.

Web page: Information on the Internet, written in HTML, that can be viewed with a Web browser.

webcasting: Broadcasting on the Web.

Web OS: A virtual desktop that can be accessed using a Web browser.

website: One or more related Web pages that are all located in the same place.

wide area network (WAN): A network that spans multiple locations and connects multiple LANs over dedicated lines using routers.

WiFi (wireless fidelity): The type of wireless network found in homes and public hotspots.

wiki: A website that allows users to edit content, even if it was written by someone else.

WiMAX Mobile Internet: A means of connecting to the Internet using cellular networks that provides 3G and 4G service.

Windows Experience Index: A rating system that assesses the operating system version, processor type and speed, and amount of memory installed as well as your video card performance to determine the types of software that your computer can run.

Windows Explorer: The window you use to look at a library or folder on a Windows computer.

wireless access point (WAP): A device that allows wireless devices to join a network much like a switch.

wireless LAN (WLAN): A network that uses WiFi to transmit data.

word processor: An application that is used to create, edit, and format text documents. The documents can also contain images.

workgroup: The devices in a peer-to-peer network.

workstation: A high-end desktop computer or one that's attached to a network in a business setting.

World Wide Web: The hypertext system of information on the Internet that allows you to navigate through pieces of information by using hyperlinks that connect them.

WYSIWYG (what you see is what you get): The layout on the computer screen shows the document layout as it would appear when printed.

Zoom: Making objects appear closer (telephoto) or farther (wide-angle) away.

Index

A

AAC files, 152
accelerated graphics port (AGP), 47
accounting software, 186, 186 fig. 5.7
A+ certification (CompTIA), 84, 85
ADA (Americans with Disabilities Act), 78, 81
Ada computer language, 5
adaptive technology, 78–81, 78 fig. 2.48, 91, 93
add-ons, 270–71, 271 fig. 7.13
address bar in Windows Explorer, 102 fig. 3.3–3.4
ad hoc networks, 353
Adobe software. *See* specific product names
Advanced Research Projects Agency (ARPA), 256
advanced search options, 278
AGP (accelerated graphics port), 47
AIM, 296 fig. 8.3
Ajax, 283
algorithms, 116–17
all-in-one computers, 10, 10 fig. 1.9, 13
all-in-one printers, 77
ALU (arithmetic logic unit), 42, 42 fig. 2.2
Amazon.com, 322, 323 fig. 8.26
Amazon Kindle, 264, 269
American Standard Code for Information Interchange (ASCII), 54, 54 fig. 2.17, 55
Americans with Disabilities Act (ADA), 78, 81
analog signals, 82, 83, 83 fig. 2.52
Analytical Engine, 4–5
Andreeson, Marc, 258
Android (Google), 237, 237 fig. 6.14, 269
AOL, 258
API (application programming interface), 227, 227 fig. 6.4
Apollo Guidance Computer, 8
Apple, 12, 18, 49, 153–54, 164–65, 165 fig. 4.13, 224, 229
Apple Certified Support Professional (ACSP), 245
application programming interface (API), 227, 227 fig. 6.4
application software. *See* business productivity software; personal software; software
arithmetic logic unit (ALU), 42, 42 fig. 2.2, 45
ARPA (Advanced Research Projects Agency), 256
ARPANET, 256–57, 257 fig. 7.1, 259
ASCII (American Standard Code for Information Interchange), 54, 54 fig. 2.17, 55
assistive technology, 78–81, 78 fig. 2.48, 93
asynchronous online communication, 298–303
ATMs, 236, 239
audio files, 152–55, 171
audio output devices, 72–73, 91
audio ports, 48 fig. 2.11, 49, 72
auto mechanics, 29, 29 fig. 1.24
avatars, 306, 306 fig. 8.14, 310–13

B

B2B (business to business) e-commerce, 322, 322 fig. 8.25
B2C (business to consumer) e-commerce, 322, 323 fig.8.26
Babbage, Charles, 4, 5
backing up files, 112–15, 131
bar code readers, 64, 64 fig. 2.34
Basecamp, 187, 220
basic input output system (BIOS), 49, 51
Bcc field in e-mail, 301
Berners-Lee, Tim, 258
beta versions, 231, 231 fig. 6.10
binary codes, 52–53, 53 fig. 2.16, 82, 90
binary number system (base 2), 52, 55
binary storage capacity prefixes, 54, 55 fig. 2.18
Bing (Microsoft), 270, 289
bioinformatics, 28, 28 fig. 1.23
biometric scanners, 65, 65 fig. 2.36
BIOS (basic input output system), 49, 51
bits (b), 53, 54, 55
Blackberry, 166, 237 fig. 6.14, 269
Blackboard Learning System, 295, 295 fig. 8.2
Blogger, 341
bloggers, professional, 324, 324 fig. 8.28
blogosphere, 314
blogs, 314–15, 317, 324, 324 fig. 8.28, 328

Bluetooth, 48, 49, 72, 349, 351
Blu-ray discs, 56, 57, 57 fig. 2.21
Boole, George, 125
Boolean operators, 125, 125 fig. 3.26, 278, 279 fig. 7.16
Boot Camp, 12
Boudica, 320
Braille-writing devices, 79, 80
broadband Internet access, 261, 265
browsers, 258, 266–75, 286
burning CDs, 154
business productivity software, 180–87
  office application suites, 180–85
  other business software, 186–87
business to business (B2B) e-commerce, 322, 322 fig. 8.25
business to consumer (B2C) e-commerce, 322, 323 fig. 8.26
bytes (B), 53, 54, 55

C

C2C (consumer to consumer) e-commerce, 322, 323, 323 fig. 8.27
cable Internet access, 261
cable modems, 83
cache memory, 51
campus area networks (CAN), 350
captcha, 299, 299 fig. 8.6, 303
careers, 28–29, 84–85, 128–29, 168–69, 212–13, 244–45, 282–83, 324–25, 366–67
cathode ray tube (CRT) monitors, 69, 69 fig. 2.38, 71, 166
CCFL (cold cathode fluorescent lamps), 69
CD (compact discs), 56, 57, 57 fig. 2.21, 152, 153, 154
cell phones, 19, 25, 57, 58, 60, 152, 157, 166, 264, 296. *See also* smartphones
cells in spreadsheets, 182
cellular networks, 262, 264, 351, 353
central processing unit (CPU), 8, 42–45, 42 fig. 2.1, 46, 46 fig. 2.8, 51, 90

CERN, 16 fig. 1.14, 258
certifications, 29, 84, 128–29, 212–13, 244–45, 283, 366–67
Certified Internet Web Professional (CIW), 283, 283 fig. 7.20
chat and chat rooms, 294–95, 295 fig. 8.1–8.2, 296, 296 fig. 8.4, 297
Chrome OS (Google), 231, 231 fig. 6.10
Chrome Web browser (Google), 266, 268, 268 fig. 7.8
Cisco certifications, 367
CIW (Certified Internet Web Professional), 283, 283 fig. 7.20
ClearType Text Tuner, 94
Client for Microsoft Networks, 358, 358 fig. 9.16, 359
clients and client software, 15, 341, 359–60, 363
client-server networks, 234–35, 235 fig. 6.12, 340–41, 340 fig. 9.7, 348, 348 fig. 9.8, 359–60, 363
clock speed, 43
cloud computing, 210–11, 216, 362
CMOS (complementary metal oxide semiconductor) chips, 49
CMYK, 74, fig. 2.43
CNET website, 209, 209 fig. 5.27, 220
cold cathode fluorescent lamps (CCFL), 69
collage creation, 193 fig. 5.17
colorjive, 196, 196 fig. 5.21
command-line user interface, 224–25, 225 fig. 6.1
communication devices, 82–83, 91
complementary metal oxide semiconductor (CMOS) chips, 49
compression of files, 116–21, 131, 152, 155
CompTIA certifications, 84, 85, 245, 366
CompuServe, 258
computer hardware. *See* hardware
computer networks, 336–67. *See also* wireless networks
  careers, 366–67
  client-server, 234–35, 340–41, 348, 360–61, 363
  hardware, 352–57
  LANs and WANs, 348–51
  peer-to-peer, 336–39, 342–47, 358–59, 363
  protection of, 364–65
  software, 358–63
computers, introduction to, 4–31
  careers, 28–29
  creating screenshots, 30–31
  defined, 4, 5
  ergonomics, 22–23, 37
  history of, 6–9
  multiuser, 14–17
  other devices, 18–21
  personal, 10–13
  ubiquitous computing, 24–27
computer sales careers, 85
computer support specialists, 245, 245 fig. 6.22
computer technician careers, 85, 85 fig. 2.53
Connecting America (National Broadband Plan), 263
Consumer Broadband Test, 263
consumer to consumer (C2C) e-commerce, 322, 323, 323 fig. 8.27
control unit, 42, 45
convergence, 25, 25 fig. 1.22, 27, 34
cooling systems and fans, 45, 45 fig. 2.6–2.7, 46, 46 fig. 2.8
copy machines, 77
copyright, 150, 153
cost of software, 207, 209
CPU (central processing unit), 8, 42–45, 42 fig. 2.1, 46, 46 fig. 2.8, 51, 90, 225
Craig's List, 323
Creative Commons (CC), 150
CRT (cathode ray tube) monitors, 69, 69 fig. 2.38, 71, 166
CSNET, 257
cybersquatting, 289

D

data, 5
database software, 184, 184 fig. 5.5
data buses, 47, 51
DCMA (Digital Millennium Copyright Act), 153
DDR2 and DDR3, 50
DDR (double data rate) SDRAM, 50
decimal number system, 52
decimal storage capacity prefixes, 54, 55 fig. 2.18
decompression of files, 116, 118, 119
default programs, 126–27, 131
defragmenters, 241, 241 fig. 6.18
Delicious, 320, 320 fig. 8.24
Dell computers, 95
desktop computers, 10, 10 fig.1.9, 13, 69
Details pane of Windows Explorer, 103, 103 fig. 3.6, 107 fig. 2.12, 110 , 110 fig. 3.15
device drivers, 226, 226 fig. 6.3
DHCP (dynamic host configuration protocol), 361 fig. 9.20, 362, 362 fig. 9.21
dial-up Internet access, 82, 83, 261, 265
Digg, 320, 321
digital cameras, 64, 67, 74, 75 fig. 2.44, 77, 140–47, 149, 171
digital devices, 140–69
  careers, 168–69
  digital cameras, 64, 67, 74, 75 fig. 2.44, 77, 140–47, 149, 171
  iPods and MP3 players, 153–54, 164–65
  PDAs and smartphones, 166–67
  video cameras, 157
  webcams, 11, 64 fig. 2.33, 67, 156–57, 159
digital divide, 37
digital footprints, 309
digital light-processing (DLP) projectors, 70, 71 fig. 2.40, 73
Digital Millennium Copyright Act (DCMA), 153
digital rights management (DRM), 153, 155
digital signals, 82, 83, 83 fig. 2.52
digital single-lens reflex cameras (DSLR), 141, 143, 143 fig. 4.4
digital subscriber line (DSL), 262
digital visual interface (DVI) ports, 71, 71 fig. 2.41
digital zoom, 141, 143, 143 fig. 4.3
DIMM (dual in-line memory module), 50, 50 fig. 2.15
disabilities, aid for individuals with, 79–81, 93, 155
discussion boards, 302–3, 303 fig. 8.11
disk-checking, 241, 241 fig. 6.17
disk cleanup, 242
disk defragmentation, 241, 241 fig. 6.18
disk formatting, 240, 240 fig. 6.16
disk utilities, 240–43, 248
disposable cameras, 142
distributed computing, 16, 17
DLP (digital light-processing) projectors, 70, 71 fig. 2.40, 73
DMCP (Document Management Certified Professional), 128
DMS (document management systems), 186, 187
DNS (Domain Name System), 277, 277 fig. 7.14, 279, 361 fig. 9.20

Index | 393

document creation, 198–201
Document Management Certified Professional (DMCP), 128
document management systems (DMS), 186, 187
domain names, 276
Domain Name System (DNS), 277, 277 fig. 7.14, 279, 361 fig. 9.20
domains, 359, 363
donationware, 207
double data rate (DDR) SDRAM, 50
downloading software, 208–9
Dragon NaturallySpeaking, 79
Dreamweaver (Adobe), 282, 282 fig. 7.18
drive bays, 46, 46 fig. 2.8
drive controllers and interfaces, 47
DRM (digital rights management), 153, 155
DS and DSi (Nintendo), 21
DSL (digital subscriber line), 262
DSL modems, 83
DSLR (digital single-lens reflex cameras), 141, 143, 143 fig. 4.4
DTV (digital TV), 83
dual in-line memory module (DIMM), 50, 50 fig. 2.15
DVD (digital versatile/video discs), 56, 57, 57 fig. 2.21, 157
DVD authoring, 158, 168
DVI (digital visual interface) ports, 71, 71 fig. 2.41
Dvorak keyboard layout, 61, 61 fig. 2.28
dye-sublimation printers, 74, 75, 77
dynamic host configuration protocol (DHCP), 361 fig. 9.20, 362, 362 fig. 9.21
dynamic Web pages, 283, 283 fig. 7.19

E

eBay, 323, 323 fig. 8.27
eBooks and eBook readers, 153, 167
e-commerce, 322–23, 328
eCycling, 166
Edison, Thomas, 159
educational and reference software, 195–96, 197
EIDE (enhanced integrated drive electronics) controllers, 47, 47 fig. 2.9–2.10
Electronic Numerical Integrator and Computer (ENIAC), 7, 7 fig. 1.4
Electronic Product Environmental Assessment Tool (EPEAT), 76, 95
e-mail, 298–302, 303, 327

e-mail clients, 298, 360, 360 fig. 9.18
e-mail messages, 300–302, 300 fig. 8.9, 302 fig. 8.10
embedded computers, 24, 24 fig. 1.21, 27
embedded operating systems, 236–37, 248
end-user licensing agreements (EULAs), 206, 209, 231
energy consumption, 94
Energy Star-rated devices, 76
engineering careers, 169, 169 fig. 4.17
enhanced integrated drive electronics (EIDE) controllers, 47, 47 fig. 2.9–2.10
ENIAC (Electronic Numerical Integrator and Computer), 7, 7 fig. 1.4
enterprise networks, 350, 351
enterprise servers, 15, 15 fig. 1.13, 17
entertainment software, 191–94, 197
Environmental Protection Agency (EPA), 124, 166
EPEAT (Electronic Product Environmental Assessment Tool), 76, 95
ergonomic keyboards, 62, 62 fig. 2.29
ergonomics, 22–23, 23 fig. 1.20, 34, 37, 62
Ethernet, 349, 351
Ethernet connections, 82, 82 fig. 2.51, 352, 352 fig. 9.11, 356 fig. 9.15
Ethernet ports, 48 fig. 2.11, 49, 356 fig. 9.15
ethics, 81, 153, 231, 321, 365
EULAs (end-user licensing agreements), 206, 209, 231
e-waste, 166
Excel (Microsoft), 182, 182 fig. 5.3
expansion cards, 46, 46 fig. 2.8, 47, 47 fig. 2.10, 72, 82
Explorer (Windows), 102–3, 102 fig. 3.3–3.4, 103 fig. 3.5–3.7, 106, 106 fig. 3.10, 110, 110 fig. 3.15, 118 fig. 3.21, 123 fig. 3.23
extensions, Web browser, 270–71
external hard drives, 58, 113 fig. 3.18, 114
Eye-Fi, 145
eyeOS, 238, 239 fig. 6.15

F

Facebook, 294, 304, 305 fig. 8.12, 307, 313, 325
facial recognition, 192, 192 fig. 5.15
Family Tree Maker, 195, 195 fig. 5.20
fax devices, 77, 83
Federal Records Management, 129
fetch-and-execute cycle, 42, 42 fig. 2.2

Fiber Optic Service (FiOS), 262
fields, database, 184
file compression, 116–21, 117 fig. 3.20, 131, 152, 155
file extensions, 108–11, 109 fig. 3.14, 126–27
file fragmentation, 241
file list area of Windows Explorer, 102, 102 fig. 3.3
file management, 100–129. *See also* Explorer
backup files, 112–15
careers, 128–29, 129 fig. 3.31
changing default programs, 126–27
copying and moving files, 106, 106 fig. 3.10
defined, 100
file compression, 116–21, 152, 155
file extensions, 108–11, 126–27
file names, 108–9, 111
file properties, 109, 110 fig. 3.15, 111
folders and libraries, 100–101, 104–6, 107
file names, 108–9, 108 fig. 3.13, 111
file properties, 109, 110 fig. 3.15, 111
file sharing, peer to peer, 257, 336–37, 339, 339 fig. 9.6, 342–47
file systems, 240
financial software, 186, 186 fig. 5.7, 190
fingerprint scanners, 65, 65 fig. 2.36
FiOS (Fiber Optic Service), 262
Firefox (Mozilla), 267, 267 fig. 7.7, 269, 270, 271, 271 fig. 7.13
firewalls, 357, 364–65, 364 fig. 9.22
FireWire (IEEE 1394) connections, 49, 56, 58, 64, 73
FireWire connectors, 49, 49 fig. 2.14, 145, 147, 149
FireWire ports, 48 fig. 2.11
first-generation computers, 6, 7 fig. 1.3
flash drives, 58, 58 fig. 2.22, 64, 104, 104 fig. 3.8, 113 fig. 3.18, 197
flash media players, 165, 165 fig. 4.13, 167
flash memory, 57, 141, 157, 165
Flash Player (Adobe), 270
flatbed scanners, 64
flat-panel monitors, 69–70, 69 fig. 2.38, 70 fig. 2.39
Flickr, 149, 150, 150 fig. 4.8, 307, 308, 308 fig. 8.16
folders, 100–101, 104–6, 107, 131
folksonomy, 307, 309
formatting disks, 240, 240 fig. 6.16

forums, 302–3, 303 fig. 8.11
4G networks, 262, 351
fourth-generation computers, 8
freeware, 207
FTP, 276, 361 fig. 9.20

G

gadgets, 274–75
gaming. *See* video gaming
Gantt chart, 187, 187 fig. 5.8
genealogy software, 195, 195 fig. 5.20
geocaching, 19
geotagging images, 150, 150 fig. 4.8, 193, 193 fig. 5.17
GHz (gigahertz), 43
global positioning system (GPS), 18, 19, 19 fig. 1.16, 21, 236, 237, 239
Google, 231, 278–79, 278 fig. 7.15, 279 fig. 7.16
Google accounts, 272
Google Checkout service, 322, 323
Google Docs, 189, 189 fig. 5.10
Google Talk, 296 fig. 8.3
Gore, Al, 256
GPS (global positioning system), 18, 19, 19 fig. 1.16, 21, 236, 237, 239
GPU (graphics processing unit), 72
graphical user interface (GUI), 224–25, 225 fig. 6.1, 227, 229, 230
graphic designers, 168, 169 fig. 4.16
graphic design tablets, 63, 63 fig. 2.32
graphics processing units (GPU), 72
green computing, 26, 76, 94, 124, 166, 211, 242, 283, 325, 362
grid computing, 16
GUI (graphical user interface), 224–25, 225 fig. 6.1, 227, 229, 230

H

Hackintosh, 231
handhelds, 18–19, 21, 21 fig. 1.19, 164–67
handheld scanners, 64, 64 fig. 2.34
hard drive media players, 165 fig. 4.13, 167
hard drives, 58–59, 59 fig. 2.25, 157
hardware, 42–87
  adaptive technology, 78–81
  assessing, 86–87
  binary coding, 52–55
  careers, 84–85
  communication devices, 82–83
  CPU, 42–45
  defined, 41
  input devices, 60–67
  management and control of, 226
  in networks, 352–57, 370
  output devices, 68–77
  storage devices, 56–59
  system unit and motherboard, 46–51
Hawking, Stephen, 78 fig. 2.48
headphones, 72, 73
health care careers, 168, 168 fig. 4.15
heart-rate monitors, 18
heat sinks, 45, 45 fig. 2.6
hierarchy for folder structure, 101, 102, 107
high-definition video and data, 57
home and landscape design software, 196, 196 fig. 5.21
homegroups, 338, 338 fig. 9.4, 342–47
home networks, 348, 349, 356 fig. 9.15, 364
home page (Web browser), 269, 269 fig. 7.11, 272–75
home page (website), 276
Hotmail accounts, 299–300, 299 fig. 8.6, 300 fig. 8.7
hot-swappable devices, 48, 49
HTML (hypertext markup language), 266
HTTP, 276, 361 fig. 9.20
HTTPS, 276
Hulu, 307
hyperlinks, 258, 276
hypertext, 258, 259
hypertext markup language (HTML), 266

I

I2 (Internet2), 258–59, 259 fig. 7.3
IaaS (Infrastructure-as-a-Service), 210, 362
ICANN (Internet Corporation for Assigned Names and Numbers), 277
icloud, 238
IE. *See* Internet Explorer
IEEE 802.11, 353, 353 fig. 9.12
IEEE 1394. *See* FireWire
iGoogle, 272–75
IM (instant messaging), 156, 257, 294, 296, 296 fig. 8.3–8.4, 297
image sharing, 308, 308 fig. 8.16
image stabilization, 142, 143 fig. 4.3
iMovie (Apple), 158, 194
index of files, 122, 125
Industrial Revolution, 4, 5, 6
information, 5
Information Age, 6
information evaluation, 280–81, 286
information processing cycle (IPC), 5, 5 fig. 1.2
Infrastructure-as-a-Service (IaaS), 210, 362
infrastructure wireless networks, 353
inkjet printers, 74, 77
input, 5, 5 fig. 1.2
input devices, 60–67, 79, 79 fig. 2.49, 82–83, 90–91
instant messaging (IM), 156, 257, 294, 296, 296 fig. 8.3–8.4, 297
instruction cycle, 42, 42 fig. 2.2, 45
intangible outputs, 73
integrated circuits, 8, 8 fig. 1.6, 9
integrated monitors, 10 fig. 1.9
Intel, 9 fig. 1.8, 44
internal hard drives, 58, 113 fig. 3.18
International Supercomputing Conference, 38
Internet, 256–83
  careers, 282–83
  and cellular networks, 351
  connection types, 260–65
  evaluating information, 280–81
  growth of, 258 fig. 7.2
  importance of, 256–59
  navigation, 276–79
  and routers, 355
  and virtual private networks, 350
  Web browser types, 266–75
Internet2 (I2), 258–59, 259 fig. 7.3
Internet access, 82–83, 165, 167, 260–65, 261 fig. 7.4, 286
Internet Archive Wayback Machine, 258
Internet backbone, 257
Internet Corporation for Assigned Names and Numbers (ICANN), 277
Internet Exchange Points, 257
Internet Explorer (IE), 229, 266–67, 267 fig. 7.6, 269–70, 269 fig. 7.11, 270 fig. 7.12, 271, 271 fig. 7.13

Index | 395

Internet Protocol (IP) addresses, 277, 279, 362 fig. 9.21
Internet service providers (ISPs), 260, 297, 299
IP (Internet protocol), 361, 361 fig. 9.20
IP addresses, 277, 279, 362 fig. 9.21
IPC (information processing cycle), 5, 5 fig. 1.2
iPhone (Apple), 166, 166 fig. 4.14, 237, 237 fig. 6.14
iPods (Apple), 153–54, 164–65, 165 fig. 4.13
ISPs (Internet service providers), 260, 297, 299
iTunes (Apple), 152, 153–54, 154 fig. 4.9, 207, 316

J

Jacquard, Joseph Marie, and Jacquard loom, 4, 5
Java (Sun), 270
Javascript, 283, 283 fig. 7.19
jiwire.com, 263 fig. 7.5
Joyent, 362, 375
joysticks, 67, 79

K

keyboards, 60–62, 61 fig. 2.27, 67, 79
keypads, 62, 62 fig. 2.30
keys, special, 60, 61, 61 fig. 2.27
keystroke shortcuts, 61
Kindle (Amazon), 264, 269
King, Augusta Ada (Countess of Lovelace), 5, 5 fig. 1.1
Kodak Gallery, 149, 149 fig. 4.7, 150

L

LANs (local area networks), 348–49, 348 fig. 9.8, 349 fig. 9.9, 350, 351, 370
laptop computers. See notebook computers
Large Icons view in Windows Explorer, 103, 103 fig. 3.7
laser printers, 76, 76 fig. 2.46, 77
lasers, 56, 56 fig. 2.19, 59
Last.fm, 308, 309 fig. 8.17

layers of network security, 364–65
LCD (liquid crystal display) monitors, 69, 69 fig. 2.38, 70, 70 fig. 2.39, 73
LCD projectors, 71, 71 fig. 2.40, 73
LED (light-emitting diodes), 63, 69
legacy technology, 69, 71
lenses, digital camera, 141, 143
libraries, 101, 101 fig. 3.2, 107
licensing, software, 206–7, 209
life sciences professionals, 128
light-emitting diodes (LED), 63, 69
LinkedIn, 306, 306 fig. 8.13, 362
links. See hyperlinks
Linux certifications, 245
Linux operating system distros, 10, 13, 44, 230–31, 234 fig. 6.11, 235, 237. See also Ubuntu Linux computers
Linux servers, 231, 234 fig. 6.11, 360
liquid cooling systems, 45, 45 fig. 2.7
liquid crystal display (LCD) monitors, 69, 69 fig. 2.38, 70, 70 fig. 2.39, 73
local area networks (LANs), 348–49, 348 fig. 9.8, 349 fig. 9.9, 350, 351, 370
lossless compression, 116, 119
lossy compression, 116, 119, 152
Lovelace, Ada, 5

M

machine cycle, 42, 42 fig. 2.2
Macintosh computers, 10, 12, 12 fig. 1.11, 13, 229, 338, 359
Macintosh operating system, 10, 11, 12, 13, 44, 229–30, 229 fig. 6.7. See also specific versions
Mac OS 8, 229, 229 fig. 6.7
Mac OS 9 (Mac Classic), 229, 229 fig. 6.7
Mac OS X, 230, 231, 237. See also Mac OS X 10.6 Snow Leopard
Mac OS X 10. 6 Snow Leopard, 12, 230, 230 fig. 6.8
Mac OS X certifications, 245
MacSpeech Dictate, 79
Mac System 7, 229, 229 fig. 6.7
magnetic strip readers, 65, 65 fig. 2.35
Magnifier, 80 fig. 2.50
mainframes, 15, 17
MakeUseOf.com, 196
MAN (metropolitan area networks), 350

MCAS (Microsoft Certified Application Specialist), 212, 212 fig. 5.29
MCDST certification, 29
MCITP certifications, 245, 245 fig. 6.21, 336
MCTS certifications, 244, 244 fig. 6.20, 366
media management software, 153–54, 155, 191, 191 fig. 5.14
media players, portable, 153–54, 164–65, 165 fig. 4.13, 166, 167, 172, 264
megabytes (MB), 54, 55
memory, 49, 50–51, 72, 225
memory boards, 50
memory cards, 58, 58 fig. 2.23, 59 fig. 2.24, 141, 144, 144 fig. 4.5, 147, 149, 157
memory slots, 47 fig. 2.10
metasearch engines, 279
metropolitan area networks (MAN), 350
mice, 63, 63 fig. 2.31, 67, 79
microblogging, 315, 315 fig. 8.19, 317
microbrowsers, 269, 269 fig. 7.10
microphones, 66, 67
microprocessors, 8, 9
Microsoft Certified Application Specialist (MCAS), 212, 212 fig. 5.29
Microsoft Certified Desktop Support Technician (MCDST) certification, 29
Microsoft Certified IT Professional (MCITP), 245, 245 fig. 6.21, 366
Microsoft Certified Technology Specialist Certifications (MCTS), 244, 244 fig. 6.20, 366
Microsoft Office, 180, 188, 189
Microsoft operating system user interfaces, 225 fig. 6.1
Microsoft Windows. See Windows
midrange servers, 15, 17
minicomputers, 15, 17
mini-DVDs, 157
Mint.com, 190, 190 fig. 5.12
MMS (Multimedia Messaging Service), 167
mobile browsers, 269, 269 fig. 7.10
mobile devices, 18–19, 21, 21 fig. 1.19, 164–67
modems, 82–83, 354, 356 fig. 9.15, 357
Moneydance (The Infinite Kind), 190
monitors, 10 fig. 1.9, 68–70, 73, 80
Moore, Gordon, 8
Moore's Law, 6, 8–9, 9 fig. 1.7–1.8, 34
Mosaic, 258, 266
motherboards, 42, 42 fig. 2.1, 46, 46 fig. 2.8, 47, 47 fig. 2.10, 48, 48 fig. 2.11, 49, 51, 73, 90

motion-sensing controllers, 20
mouse. *See* mice
Mouse Keys, 79
MP3 files, 152, 155
MP3 players, 153–54, 164–65, 165 fig. 4.13
multi-core processors, 44, 45
multifunction devices, 77, 83, 166–67
multimedia, 140–69
  defined, 139
  audio files, 152–55
  careers, 168–69
  and digital mobile devices, 164–67
  photos, creating and transferring, 140–47
  photos, editing and sharing, 148–51
  videos, 156–63
Multimedia Messaging Service (MMS), 167
multiple processors, 44, 44 fig. 2.5
multitasking, 225
multiuser computers, 14–17, 34. *See also* network operating systems; servers
municipal WiFi, 263
muse K20 connectivity survey map, 259 fig. 7.3
music sharing, 308, 308 fig. 8.17
MySpace, 304

N

NAP (Network Access Points), 257
National Broadband Plan (Connecting America), 263
navigation, Web, 276–79, 286
Navigation pane of Windows Explorer, 103, 103 fig. 3.5
netbooks, 11, 11 fig. 1.10, 13, 230
Netcraft, 235
Netscape, 258, 266, 267
Network Access Points (NAP), 257
network adapters, 82, 82 fig. 2.51, 83, 352–54, 352 fig. 9.11, 357
network administrators, 367, 367 fig. 9.25
network backup storage, 113 fig. 3.18
network hardware, 354–57, 370
network maps, 337, 337 fig. 9.3, 355, 355 fig. 9.14
network operating systems (NOS), 234–35, 234 fig. 6.11, 248, 340, 341, 360
network protection/security, 364–65, 370

network protocols, 361–63, 361 fig. 9.19–9.20, 363, 370
network resources, 336
networks. *See* computer networks; social networks; wireless networks
network software, 358–60
Nobel Prize in physics (2000), 8
nonvolatile memory or storage, 49, 58
NOS (network operating systems), 234–35, 234 fig. 6.11, 248, 340, 341, 360
notebook (laptop) computers, 11, 11 fig. 1.10, 13, 69, 73
Novell certifications, 245
Novell servers, 234 fig. 6.11, 360
NPR, 316, 316 fig. 8.20
NSFNET, 257, 258
NTFS file system, 240, 243

O

OBD (onboard diagnostics port), 29, 29 fig. 1.24
Odyssey game console, 20
Office (Microsoft), 180, 188, 189
office application suites, 180–85, 187, 188–89
OLED (organic light-emitting diode) monitors, 70
onboard diagnostics port (OBD), 29, 29 fig. 1.24
online alternative office suites, 189
online backup services, 115
online communication, 294–303. *See also* social media
  asynchronous online communication, 298–303
  synchronous online communication, 294–97, 327
online photo editing, 149, 149 fig. 4.7
online printing and sharing, 150, 151
ONT (optical network terminal), 354, 356 fig. 9.15, 357
OpenOffice.org, 180, 188 fig. 5.9, 207
Open Source Initiative (OSI), 207
open source software, 188, 207, 209, 230, 231
Opera, 266, 269
operating systems (OS). *See also* specific operating systems
  embedded, 236–37
  functions of, 224–27
  network (NOS), 234–35, 340, 341, 360
  parallel processing, 44, 45
  stand-alone, 228–31
  Web OS, 237, 238–39

optical discs, 56, 113 fig. 3.18, fig. 56 fig. 2.19–2.20
optical network terminal (ONT), 354, 356 fig. 9.15, 357
optical scanners, 64, 64 fig. 2.34, 77, 83
optical zoom, 141, 142, 143, 143 fig. 4.3
organic light-emitting diode (OLED) monitors, 70
OS. *See* operating systems
OSI (Open Source Initiative), 207
ouput devices
  adaptive, 80, 80 fig. 2.50, 91
  audio and video, 68–73, 91
  communication devices, 82–83, 91
  printers, 74–77, 91
Outlook (Microsoft), 185, 185 fig. 5.6, 207
output, 5, 5 fig. 1.2
overclocking processors, 43

P

P2P (peer-to-peer) file sharing, 257, 336–37, 339, 339 fig. 9.6
P2P (peer-to-peer) networks, 235, 336–39, 336 fig. 9.1, 341, 348, 358–59, 363
PaaS (Platform-as-a-Service), 210
Paget, Chris, 95
paint color online apps, 196, 196 fig. 5.21
Palm webOS, 237, 237 fig. 6.14
PAN (personal area networks), 349, 351
paperless offices, 124
parallel ports, 48, 48 fig. 2.11
parallel processing, 44, 44 fig. 2.4, 45
Passages from the Life of a Philosopher (Babbage), 4
passwords, 364, 364 fig. 9.23, 365
path (to a file or folder), 101
PayPal, 323
PCI and PCI express slots, 47, 47 fig. 2.10
PCs, 10, 11, 12, 12 fig. 1.11, 13, 224, 231
PDA (personal digital assistants), 18, 21, 166, 167, 168, 168 fig. 4.15, 172, 264
peer-2-peer (P2P) file sharing, 257, 336–37, 339, 339 fig. 9.6
peer-to-peer networks (P2P), 235, 336–39, 336 fig. 9.1, 341, 348, 358–59, 363

Index | 397

peripheral component interconnect (PCI and PCI express) slots, 47, 47 fig. 2.10
peripheral devices, 41, 62, 62 fig. 2.30
personal area networks (PAN), 349, 351
personal computers
　as clients, 15
　monitors, 69, 73
　operating systems, 228–31
　types and characteristics, 10–13, 34
　and volunteer computing, 16–17
personal digital assistants (PDA), 18, 21, 166, 167, 168, 168 fig. 4.15, 172, 264
personal information managers (PIM), 185, 185 fig. 5.6, 187
personal software, 188–97
　educational and reference, 195–96
　entertainment and multimedia, 191–94
　finance and tax preparation, 190–91
　office application suites, 188–89
　portable apps, 197
photo editing software, 148, 151, 192–93
photojournalism, 169, 169 fig. 4.18
photo kiosks, 149, 151
photo printers, 59 fig. 2.24, 74, 75 fig. 2.44, 149
photos
　editing and printing, 148–51, 172, 192–93, 192 fig. 5.16
　sharing, 308, 308 fig. 8.16
　transferring, 144–47, 171
Photoshop (Adobe), 148, 207, 213
Picasa (Google), 148, 192–94, 192 fig. 5.15–5.16, 193 fig. 5.17, 308
piconets, 349
PictBridge-enabled cameras, 74, 75 fig. 2.44, 77, 149
piggybacking, 365
PIM (personal information managers), 185, 185 fig. 5.6, 187
pipelining, 43, 43 fig. 2.3, 44, 45
pixels, 68, 73
plasma monitors, 69, 70, 70 fig. 2.39
Platform-as-a-Service (PaaS), 210
Playstation 3 (Sony), 20, 152
Playstation Portable (PSP), 21
plotters, 77, 77 fig. 2.47
Plug and Play (PnP), 226, 227, 228
plug-ins, 270–71
PnP (Plug and Play), 226, 227, 228

podcast clients, 316
podcasts, 154, 154 fig. 4.9, 176, 316, 316 fig. 8.20, 317, 328
point-and-shoot cameras, 142, 143, 143 fig. 4.3
pointing devices, 63, 79
Point-of-Sale terminals, 62, 62 fig. 2.30
PONG video game, 20, 20 fig. 1.18
POP (post office protocol), 361 fig. 9.20
portable apps, 197, 197 fig. 5.22
portable media players, 153–54, 164–65, 165 fig. 4.13, 166, 167, 172, 264
ports, 48, 48 fig 2.11
post office protocol (POP), 361 fig. 9.20
power management, 242
Powerpoint (Microsoft), 183, 183 fig. 5.4, 189, 189 fig. 5.11
Power Settings, 94
power supply, 46, 46 fig. 2.8
Premiere Elements (Adobe), 194, 194 fig. 5.18
presentation software, 183, 183 fig. 5.4, 188, 189
printers, 59 fig. 2.24, 74–77, 91
printer sharing, 336, 337, 338, 342–47
processing, 5, 5 fig. 1.2
processing speed and power, 8, 9, 11, 43, 44
processors (CPU), 8, 42–45, 42 fig. 2.1, 46, 46 fig. 2.8, 51, 90, 225
professional profiles, 305–6, 305 fig. 8.12, 306 fig. 8.13
Project (Microsoft), 187, 187 fig. 5.8
project management software, 187, 187 fig. 5.8
projectors, 70–71, 71 fig. 2.40, 73
Properties dialog box in Windows Explorer, 110, 111 fig. 3.16
proprietary software licenses, 207
prosumer digital cameras, 142, 143 fig. 4.3
protocols, 361–63, 361 fig. 9.19–9.20, 363, 370
PS/2 ports, 48, 48 fig. 2.11
PSP (Playstation Portable), 21
public folders, 100

Q

Quickbooks (Intuit), 186, 186 fig. 5.7
Quicken (Intuit), 190
QWERTY keyboard layout, 60, 60 fig. 2.26, 61 fig. 2.28

R

RAM (random access memory), 50, 51
read-only memory (ROM), 49, 56
read/write head, 59, 59 fig. 2.25
Really Simple Syndication (RSS), 317
recordable (+R/-R) optical discs, 56
records, database, 184
Red Hat Certified Technician (RHCT), 245
Red Hat Enterprise Linux servers, 231, 234 fig. 6.11
Remote Media Streaming, 229
resolution, display, 68, 73
resolution, image, 140, 141 fig. 4.1, 143, 143 fig. 4.3
resource management, 225, 225 fig. 6.2
restricted TLDs, 280–81, 281 fig. 7.17
retail software, 207
rewritable (+RW/-RW) optical discs, 56
RFID passport program, 65, 65 fig. 2.35, 95
RFID scanners and tags, 65, 65 fig. 2.35
RHCT (Red Hat Certified Technician), 245
ripping CDs, 152, 153
RJ-45 connections, 352
Roddenberry, Gene, 27
ROM (read-only memory), 49, 56
routers, 354–57, 355 fig. 9.14, 356 fig. 9.15
RSS (Really Simple Syndication), 317

S

SaaS (Software-as-a-Service), 210, 211, 211 fig. 5.28
Safari, 266, 268, 268 fig. 7.9, 269
SAN (storage area networks), 350
SATA (Serial ATA) controllers, 47, 47 fig. 2.9–2.10
satellite Internet access, 263
satellite phones, 264
Save As dialog box, 105, 105 fig. 3.9
scanners, 64–65, 67, 77, 83
science careers, 28, 28 fig. 1.23, 128, 169, 169 fig. 4.17
screen capture, 156, 159
screen magnification, 80, 80 fig. 2.50
scripting, 283 fig. 7.19
SDRAM (synchronous dynamic random access memory), 50

search boxes, 102, 102 fig. 3.3, 122, 123 fig. 3.23, 125
search engines, 278–79, 289
search filters, 278, 279 fig. 7.16
searching for files, 122–25, 123 fig. 3.23–3.24, 124 fig. 3.25, 131
search providers, setting, 270, 270 fig. 7.12
Search Results window, 123 fig. 3.23–3.24
second-generation computers, 8
second-level domain, 276
Second Life, 306, 306 fig. 8.14
security, 240, 364–65, 365 fig. 9.24, 370
Semiconductor Industry Association, 8
Serial ATA (SATA) controllers, 47, 47 fig. 2.9–2.10
serial ports, 48
servers and server software, 14, 14 fig. 1.12, 15, 17, 44, 231, 234 fig. 6.11, 340–41, 359–60, 363
server virtualization, 362
Set Default Programs window, 126–27, 126 fig. 3.28
SETI@home, 17, 17 fig. 1.15
7-Zip, 118, 207
shareware, 207
Sholes, Christopher, 60
Short Message Service (SMS), 167
shutter lag, 142, 143, 143 fig. 4.3
signature lines, 301
Silverlight (Microsoft), 270
simple mail transfer protocol (SMTP), 361 fig. 9.20
Skype, 297, 297 fig. 8.5
Slashdot, 320
small outline dual in-line memory module (SODIMM), 50, 50 fig. 2.15
smart appliances, 26
smart homes, 26
smartphone operating systems, 237 fig. 6.14
smartphones, 18, 21, 166, 166 fig. 4.14, 167, 172, 262, 264
Smithsonian Institution, 150
SMM (social media marketing), 322, 323, 324–25, 325 fig. 8.29
SMS (Short Message Service), 167
SMTP (simple mail transfer protocol), 361 fig. 9.20
sneakernet, 336
Snipping Tool, 30–31
social bookmarking sites, 320, 320 fig. 8.24, 321
social media, 304–25. *See also* online communication

blogs, 314–15, 317, 324
careers, 324–25
and e-commerce, 322–23
podcasts, 154, 176, 316, 317
and social causes, 325
social image sites, 308, 308 fig. 8.16
social music sites, 308, 309 fig. 8.17
social network sites, 304–6
social news, review, and bookmarking sites, 319–21
social video sites, 307, 307 fig. 8.15
virtual worlds and avatars, 306, 306 fig. 8.14, 310–13
wikis, 318–19
social media marketers, 324–25, 325 fig. 8.29
social media marketing (SMM), 322, 323, 324–25, 325 fig. 8.29
social networks, 304–6, 309
social news sites, 320, 321
social review sites, 319, 319 fig. 8.23
social Web. *See* online communication; social media
SODIMM (small outline dual in-line memory module), 50, 50 fig. 2.15
software. *See also* business productivity software; personal software; system software
assessing compatibility, 202–5
assistive technology, 78–81
careers, 212–13
cloud computing, 210–11
media, 153–54
in networks, 358–63, 370
obtaining, 206–9
photo editing, 148, 151, 192–93
screen capture, 156, 159
security, 240, 365
updating, 232–33
video editing, 158, 194
Software-as-a-Service (SaaS), 210, 211, 211 fig. 5.28
software certifications, 212–13
software download websites, 209, 209 fig. 5.27
software engineering, 283
software trainers, 213, 213 fig. 5.30
solid-stage storage, 57, 59
Sony Vegas Movie Studio, 158, 194
sound cards, 72, 73, 73 fig. 2.42

source codes, 283 fig. 7.19
space availability, 202, 202 fig. 5.23
speakers, 72, 73
specialized operating systems, 236–39, 248
speech recognition, 66, 79, 80, 155
spreadsheet software, 182, 188, 189
stand-alone operating systems, 228–31, 247–48
Start menu, searching from, 122, 124, 124 fig. 3.25
Sticky Keys, 79
storage, 5, 5 fig. 1.2
storage area networks (SAN), 350
storage capacity, 8, 11, 57, 57 fig. 2.21, 59
storage devices, 56–59, 90
storage of digital images, 141
streaming, 157
StumbleUpon, 320
styluses, 63, 63 fig. 2.32
supercomputers, 16, 16 fig. 1.14, 17, 38, 44
SUSE Linux Enterprise Server, 234 fig. 6.11
S-Video (super video) ports, 71, 71 fig. 2.41
Swiss Flash USB knife, 58, 58 fig. 2.22
switches, 355, 355 fig. 9.14, 356 fig. 9.15, 357
Symbian, 237 fig. 6.14
synchronous dynamic random access memory (SDRAM), 50
synchronous online communication, 294–97, 327
System Control Panel (Windows), 86–87, 203, 203 fig. 5.24–5.35
system requirements, 204–5, 204 fig. 5.26
system software, 224–45
careers, 244–45
network operating systems (NOS), 234–35, 340, 341, 360
operating system functions, 224–27
specialized operating systems, 236–39
stand-alone operating systems, 228–31
updating, 232–33, 365
utilities, 240–43
system specifications, 202–3, 205
system unit, 46, 46 fig. 2.8, 51, 90

T

tablets, 11, 13, 167, 168
tagging, 145, 150, 307, 308, 308 fig. 8.16, 309
tangible output, 77
tax preparation software, 190

Index | 399

TCP (transmission control protocol), 361, 361 fig. 9.20
TCP/IP protocol stack, 361–62, 361 fig. 9.20, 363
Technorati.com, 314
telecommuting, 283
telephone lines, 82, 83
thermal printers, 75, 75 fig. 2.45, 77
third-generation computers, 8
third-level domain, 276
3G networks, 262, 264, 351
Thunderbird (Mozilla), 300, 300 fig. 8.8
TLDs (top-level domains), 276, 279, 280
T-Mobile G1 (HTC), 166, 166 fig. 4.14
toner, 76
toolbars, 102, 270
top-level domains (TLDs), 276, 279, 280
Top Sites preview (Safari), 268, 268 fig. 7.9
Torvald, Linus, 230
touch input, 63
touchpads, 63, 63 fig. 2.31
touch screens, 63, 79, 79 fig. 2.49
transistors, 8, 8 fig. 1.5, 9, 9 fig. 1.8
transmission control protocol (TCP), 361, 361 fig. 9.20
Trillian client, 296, 296 fig. 8.3
trip planning software, 195
TurboTax (Intuit), 190, 191 fig. 5.13, 207
Twitter, 315, 315 fig. 8.19, 325, 325 fig. 8.29

U

ubiquitous computing (ubicomp), 24–27, 34
Ubuntu Forum Community, 303 fig. 8.11
Ubuntu Linux computers, 230, 230 fig. 6.9, 338, 339 fig. 9.5, 359, 359 fig. 9.17
Unicode, 54, 54 fig. 2.17, 55
uniform resource locators (URL), 276–77, 279
UNIX, 229, 234 fig. 6.11, 235
UNIX servers, 234 fig. 6.11, 360
URL (uniform resource locators), 276–77, 279
USB card readers, 58, 59 fig. 2.24
USB (Universal Serial Bus) connections, 48, 56, 58, 62, 64, 73, 82
USB connectors, 48, 48 fig. 2.13, 145, 147, 149
USB hubs, 48, 48 fig. 2.12
USB ports, 48, 48 fig. 2.11, 72
USB wireless adapters, 352 fig. 9.11, 353

user folders, 100, 100 fig. 3.1, 107
user-generated content, 280, 281, 314–17, 328
user interfaces, 224–25, 225 fig. 6.1
utility software, 240–43, 248

V

vacuum tubes, 6, 7, 8 fig. 1.5, 9
vBNS (Very High Speed Backbone Network Service), 258
Verizon, 296, 296 fig. 8.4
Very High Speed Backbone Network Service (vBNS), 258
VGA (video graphics array) ports, 71, 71 fig. 2.41
video cameras, 157
video cards, 71, 71 fig. 2.41, 73
video chat, 297
video conferencing, 156, 159
video creation and sharing, 156–63, 172, 194, 307, 307 fig. 8.15
video editing software, 158, 194, 194 fig. 5.18
video game consoles, 20, 21, 49, 236, 264
video game controllers, 20, 66 fig. 2.37, 67
video gaming, 20–21, 20 fig. 1.18, 21 fig. 1.19, 194, 194 fig. 5.19, 204 fig. 5.26
video graphics array (VGA) ports, 71, 71 fig. 2.41
video ouput devices, 68–71, 91
video ports, 48 fig. 2.11, 49, 71, 71 fig. 2.41
video projectors, 70–71, 71 fig. 2.40, 73
video RAM (VRAM), 72
Views button and menu in Windows Explorer, 103, 103 fig. 3.7, 107 fig. 3.11, 110 fig. 3.15
viral video, 307, 307 fig. 8.15
virtual librarians, 331
virtual private networks (VPNs), 350, 350 fig. 9.10, 351
virtual worlds, 306, 306 fig. 8.14
vlogs, 314
voice over IP (VoIP), 257, 297, 297 fig. 8.5
voice-recognition. *See* speech recognition
VoIP (voice over IP), 257, 297, 297 fig. 8.5
volatile memory, 49, 50, 51
volunteer computing, 16–17, 38
volunteering, 29
voting machines, 79 fig. 2.49
VPNs (virtual private networks), 350, 350 fig. 9.10, 351
VRAM (video RAM), 72

W

WAN (wide area networks), 349–50, 349 fig. 9.9, 351, 370
WAP (wireless access points), 355 fig. 9.14, 356, 356 fig. 9.15
wardriving, 365
wearables, 19, 19 fig. 1.17, 21
weather forecasting, 16
Web 2.0, 304
Web addresses, 276–77, 279
Web applications, 211, 211 fig. 5.28, 283
Web Apps (Microsoft Office), 189, 189 fig. 511
Web browsers, 258, 266–75, 286
Webby Lifetime Achievement Award, 256
webcams, 11, 64 fig. 2.33, 67, 156–57, 159, 297
webcasting, 157, 157 fig. 4.11, 159
Web crawling, 279
Web designers, 282
Web developers, 283
webmail, 298, 300, 300 fig. 8.7, 303
Web navigation, 276–79, 286
Web OS (operating systems), 237, 238–39, 248
Web pages, 266, 276, 283, 283 fig. 7.19
Web searching, 278–79
website design, 281, 282
websites, 276, 280–81, 282–83
WeeWorld, 310–13
Whiteboard feature, 295, 295 fig. 8.2
whiteboards, interactive, 63
wide area networks (WAN), 349–50, 349 fig. 9.9, 351, 370
widescreen displays, 11
WiFi hotspots, 263, 263 fig. 7.5
WiFi networks, 82, 82 fig. 2.51, 145, 147, 263, 349, 350, 351, 353, 356, 356 fig. 9.15
WiFi standards, 353, 353 fig. 9.12
Wii (Nintendo), 20, 152
wikiHow, 319, 319 fig. 8.22
Wikipedia, 318, 318 fig. 8.21
wikis, 318–19, 318 fig. 8.21, 319 fig. 8.22, 321
WiMAX Mobile Internet, 262
Winamp Media Player, 153–54, 316
Winamp Remote, 154, 155 fig. 4.10
Windows 7
   Action Center, 112, 112 fig. 3.17
   Backup utility, 112–14, 113 fig. 3.18, 114 fig. 3.19, 241
   Check Disk utility, 241, 241 fig. 6.17

ClearType Text Tuner, 94
Client for Microsoft Networks, 358, 358 fig. 9.16, 359
Default Programs control panel, 126–27, 126 fig. 3.27–3.28, 127 fig. 3.29–3.30
desktop, 229 fig. 6.6
and DHCP protocol, 362, 362 fig. 9.21
Disk Cleanup utility, 242, 242 fig. 6.19
Disk Defragmenter, 241, 241 fig. 6.18
Experience Index, 203, 203 fig. 5.25, 205
Explorer, 102–3, 102 fig. 3.3–3.4, 103 fig. 3.5–3.7, 106, 106 fig. 3.10, 110, 110 fig. 3.15, 118 fig. 3.21, 123 fig. 3.23
File Sharing, 339, 339 fig. 9.6, 359
homegroups, 338, 338 fig. 9.4, 342–47
Home Server, 250, 340
Live Messenger, 296 fig. 8.3
Live Movie Maker, 160–63, 194
Live Photo Gallery, 126 fig. 3.28, 127, 127 fig. 3.29–3.30, 148
Magnifier, 80, 80 fig. 2.50
Media Center, 191, 191 fig. 5.14
Media Player, 153–54
network access, 235, 235 fig. 6.12–6.13
Network and Sharing Center, 337, 337 fig. 9.2–9.3, 344–47, 358
Network Connections window, 354, 354 fig. 9.13
networking features, 337–39, 358–59
new hardware installation, 226 fig. 6.3
NTFS file system, 240, 243
parallel processing, 44
photo transfer, 144–46, 146 fig. 4.6
Search feature, 122–24
Snipping Tool, 30–31

speech recognition, 79
System Control Panel, 86–87, 203, 203 fig. 5.24–5.35
Touch, 11, 229
Update, 232–33
ZIP format and archives, 117–19, 117 fig. 3.20, 118 fig. 3.21–3.22
Windows 95, 226, 228 fig. 6.5, 229, 258
Windows 98, 228 fig. 6.5, 229
Windows Embedded CE, 237, 237 fig. 6.14
Windows Media Audio files (WMA), 153
Windows Mobile, 237, 237 fig. 6.14
Windows operating system, 10, 12, 13, 228, 228 fig. 6.5, 231, 237. *See also* specific versions
Windows Server, 234 fig. 6.11, 235, 360
Windows Vista, 228, 228 fig. 6.5
Windows XP, 228, 228 fig. 6.5
wired cards, 82, 82 fig. 2.51
wired network adapters, 352–53, 354
wireless access points (WAP), 355 fig. 9.14, 356, 356 fig. 9.15
wireless cards, 82, 82 fig. 2.51
wireless Internet connections, 262–64
wireless LANs (WLAN). *See* WiFi networks
wireless networks
 adapters, 352, 353–54, 354 fig. 9.13
 cellular networks, 262, 264, 351
 personal area networks (PAN), 349, 351
 piggybacking and wardriving, 365
 WiFi networks, 82, 145, 147, 263, 349, 350, 351, 353, 356
wireless transfer of photos, 145, 147
WLAN (wireless LANs). *See* WiFi networks
Word (Microsoft), 180–81, 181 fig. 5.1–5.2

WordPad (Microsoft), 198–201
WordPress, 314, 315 fig. 8.18
word processing, 180–81, 181 fig. 5.1–5.2, 188, 189, 198–201
workgroups, 336, 338–39, 339 fig. 9.5–9.6, 359
workstations, 10
World Community Grid, 38
World of Warcraft, 44, 194, 204, 204 fig. 5.26
World Wide Web, 257–58
WYSIWYG, 181

X

Xbox 360 (Microsoft), 20

Y

Yahoo! accounts, 331
Yahoo! Messenger, 295, 295 fig. 8.1, 296 fig. 8.3
Yelp, 319, 319 fig. 8.23
YouTube, 158, 158 fig. 4.12, 159, 307, 307 fig. 8.15

Z

ZIP format and archives, 117–19, 117 fig. 3.20, 118 fig. 3.21–3.22
Zip Zip's Memory Bricks, 58, 58 fig. 2.22
Zoho Docs, 189, 189 fig. 5.10
zoom, 141, 141 fig. 4.2, 142, 143, 143 fig. 4.3
Zune (Microsoft), 165, 165 fig. 4.13

Photo Credits

01-01UN: ©LJSphotography/Alamy
01-02UN: COMPUTER SCREEN CONCEPTS/MARK SYKES/ALAMY
01-03UN: igorkosh\Shutterstock
01-04UN: ©Csaba Zsarnowszky/Alamy
01-04: CORBIS- NY
01-05UN: Goncharuk\Shutterstock
01-06UN: Dariush M.\Shutterstock
01-06: lek2481\Shutterstock
01-07UN: Nitr\Shutterstock
01-08UN: ©Blend Images/SuperStock
01-09UN: ©Forrest Smyth/Alamy
01-09: ShaUN: Lowe\iStockphoto.com
01-010UN: ©LouisBerk.com/Alamy
01-011UN: ©LAMB/Alamy
01-012UN: androfroll\Shutterstock
01-12: Alex Slobodkin\iStockphoto.com
01-013UN: ©Alyson Aliano/SuperStock
01-13: David H. Lewis\iStockphoto.com
01-014UN: ©Clearviewstock/Alamy
01-015UN: ©Heymo Vehse/Alamy
01-016UN: yuyangc\Shutterstock
01-16: edobric\Shutterstock
01-017UN: Edcel Mayo\Shutterstock
01-018UN: ©Finnbarr Webster/Alamy

01-019UN: ©Kuman Sriskandan/Alamy
01-19A: ©Myrleen Pearson/Alamy
01-19a: AzureLaRoux\iStockphoto.com
01-19b: Andy Dean\Shutterstock
01-020UN: jUN: jie\Shutterstock
01-021UN: ©Design Pics/SuperStock
01-21a: mbbirdy\iStockphoto.com
01-21b: iStockphoto.com
01-21c: Amanda Rohde\iStockphoto.com
01-022UN: ©Tetra Images/SuperStock
01-22a: adventtr\iStockphoto.com
01-22b: Flemming Hansen\iStockphoto.com
01-22c: bluestocking\iStockphoto.com
01-22d: iStockphoto.com
01-22e: bpablo\iStockphoto.com
01-023UN: ©age fotostock/SuperStock
01-024UN: ©D Hurst/Alamy
01-24e: arattansi\iStockphoto.com
01-027UN: ©Jeff Greenbeerg/Alamy
01-028UN: ©UN: ited Archives GmbH/Alamy/KPA Honorar & Belege
01-029UN: Julien Tromeur\Shutterstock
01-030UN: ©Exactostock/SuperStock
01-031UN: ©Sebastian Kaulitzki/Alamy

01-032UN: ©i love images/health and wellbeing/Alamy
01-033UN: Alex Segre\Alamy Images
01-034UN: ©John Tomaselli/Alamy
01-035UN: ©Paul Rapson
01-037UN: LesPalenik\Shutterstock
01-038UN: ©ONOKY-Photononstop/Alamy/Fabrice Lerouge
01-039UN: ©ArcadeImages/Alamy
01-040UN: ©Chris Willson/Alamy
01-043UN: kontur-vid\Shutterstock
01-044UN: © axel leschinski/Alamy
01-045UN: ©Jon Helgason
01-047UN: ©David Burton/Alamay
01-048UN: ©Stuwdamdorp/Alamy
01-049UN: ©Ian Dagnall/Alamy
01-050UN: ©Juice Images/Alamy
01-051UN: ©Adrian Sherratt/Alamy
01-052UN: ©Adrian Sherratt/Alamy
01-054UN: ©moodboard/SuperStock
01-055UN: ©Exactostock/SuperStock
01-056UN: ©Simone Brandt/Alamy
01-057UN: ©Sean Gladwell/Alamy
01-058UN: ©Nikreates/Alamy
01-059UN: Michael Shake\Shutterstock

01-060UN: ©Jim West/Alamy
01-061UN: ©Jon Helgason/Alamy
01-062UN: taelove7\Shutterstock
01-63UN: The Art Gallery Collection\Alamy Images
01-064UN: ©JFTL IMAGES/Alamy
01-065UN: ©Fancy/Alamy/FancyVeerSet8
01-HT01: geopaul\iStockphoto.com

02-01UN: hely\Shutterstock
02-02UN: ©picturesbyrob/Alamy/fc1
02-04UN: © jon challicom/alamy
02-04: Dmitriy Shironosov\Shutterstock
02-05UN: © D Hurst/Alamy
02-05: demarcomedia\Shutterstock
02-06: thumb\Shutterstock
02-07UN: Wth\Shutterstock
02-07: dubbs\iStockphoto.com
02-08: Tihis\Shutterstock
02-09UN: © Mark Sykes/Alamy
02-09: Alberto Perez Velga\Shutterstock
02-010UN: © Charles Mistral/Alamy
02-10a: Norman: Chan\Shutterstock
02-10b: Sergei Devyatkin\Shutterstock
02-011UN: © UpperCut Images/Alamy
02-11: Valentin Mosichev\Shutterstock

02-012UN: OneSmallSquare\Shutterstock
02-12: Norman Chan\Shutterstock
02-013UN: grzym\Shutterstock
02-13: Samantha Craddock\iStockphoto.com
02-014UN: © Best View Stock/Alamy
02-14: Tonis Pan\Shutterstock
02-015UN: Tatiana Popova\Shutterstock
02-016UN: Thomas Moens\Shutterstock
02-16: winterling\iStockphoto.com
02-017UN: Thomas Moens\Shutterstock
02-018UN: © D Hurst/Alamy
02-019UN: LiudmllaKorsakova\Shutterstock
02-19: Dino Ablakovich\iStockphoto.com
02-020UN: imagewell\Shutterstock
02-20: janprchal\Shutterstock
02-021UN: © philipus/Alamy
02-022UN: © Atlaspix/Alamy
02-023UN: © Enigma/Alamy
02-024UN: © PaulPaladin/Alamy
02-24a: Josch\Shutterstock
02-24b: Serg64\Shutterstock
02-025UN: © Clearviewstock/Alamy
02-25: KLH49\iStockphoto.com
02-027UN: ©oliver leedham/Alamy
02-028UN: ©Hugh Threlfall/Alamy
02-029UN: ©BlueMoon Stock/Maciej Frolow/Alamy
02-29: Ximagination\Shutterstock
02-030UN: ©Andrew Paterson/Alamy
02-30a: IDAL\Shutterstock
02-30b: Courtney Keating\Shutterstock

02-031UN: ©CreativeAct-Toys/Games series/Alamy
02-31a: Yellowj\Shutterstock
02-31b: Vasily Pindyurin\iStockphoto.com
02-032UN: ©Peter Dazeley/Alamy
02-32A: Slaven \Shutterstock
02-033UN: ©Eyebyte/Alamy
02-33: mammamaart\iStockphoto.com
02-034UN: ©Frederic SUN: e/Alamy
02-34: Anatoly Vartanov\iStockphoto.com
02-035UN: ©Westend61 GmbH/Alamy/Julian Rupp
02-35a: Timothy W. Stone\Shutterstock
02-35b: Nazdravie\iStockphoto.com
02-036UN: ©Dave Cameron/Alamy
02-36: Dino Ablakovic\iStockphoto.com
02-037UN: Marco Rullkoetter\Shutterstock
02-37a: iStockphoto.com
02-37b: NWphotoguy\iStockphoto.com
02-37c: Marcelo Pinheiro\iStockphoto.com
02-038UN: ©Alex Segre/Alamy
02-039UN: ©David Kilpatrick/Alamy
02-040UN: pics721\Shutterstock
02-041UN: ©Losevsky Pavel/Alamy
02-042UN: ©Sebastian Kaulitzki/Alamy
02-42: lexiks\Shutterstock
02-043UN: ©Blend Images/Colin Anderson/Alamy
02-43: Guanta\Shutterstock

02-044UN: ©Stocksearch/Alamy
02-045UN: vaizan\Shutterstock
02-45: jabejon\iStockphoto.com
02-046UN: ©RTimages/Alamy
02-46: Shutterstock
02-047UN: ©Leonid Nyshko/Alamy
02-47: Getty Images, Inc.
02-048UN: ©John Woodworth/Alamy
02-049UN: ©catnap/Alamy
02-49: lisafx\iStockphoto.com
02-050UN: ©Tom McNemar/Alamy
02-051UN: © D Hurst/Alamy
02-51a: VisualField\iStockphoto.com
02-52b: EdBockStock\Shutterstock
02-052UN: ©RubberBall/Alamy/Mike Kemp
02-053UN: ©Picture Contact/Alamy/Maarten Udema
02-054UN: ©D Hurst/Alamy
02-055UN: ©Stuart Walker/Alamy
02-057UN: ©Ton Koene/Picture Contact/Alamy
02-058UN: ©Monalyn Gracia/Fancy/Alamy
02-061UN: ©David Cantrille/Alamy
02-062UN: ©Yuri Arcurs/INSADCO Photography/Alamy
02-063UN: ©Ron Chapple Stock/Alamy
02-064UN: ©david pearson/Alamy
02-066UN: ©Mike Kemp/RubberBall/Alamy
02-067UN: ©Judith Collins/Alamy
02-069UN: D. Hurst\Alamy Images Royalty Free
02-070UN: RTimages\Alamy Images Royalty Free
02-072UN: © Cusp/SuperStock

02-073UN: © Exactostock/SuperStock
02-074UN: iStockphoto.com
02-075UN: © fStop/SuperStock
02-076UN: © Andres Rodriguez/MediaMagnet/SuperStock
02-077UN: © Glasshouse Images/SupterStock
02-079UN: © Blend Images/SuperStock
02-07IUN: Ingo Schulz/Imagebroker/Alamy
02-081UN: © Terry Harris PCL/SuperStock
02-083UN: J. R. Ripper\Alamy Images
02-084UN: smartstock\iStockphoto.com
02-085UN: Nlp\Shutterstock
02-086UN: Exactostock\Superstock Royalty Free
02-087UN: Larry Lilac\Alamy Images Royalty Free
02-087UNa: Helene Rogers\Alamy Images
02-087UNb: Exactostock\Superstock Royalty Free
02-087UNc: Darryl Jacobson\SuperStock, Inc.
02-087UNd: K-PHOTOS\Alamy Images
02-087UNe: Petr Student\Shutterstock
02-087UNf: Exactostock\Superstock Royalty Free
02-087UNg: Christophe Testi\Shutterstock
03-01UN: Tomasz Piotrowski\Alamy Images
03-02UN: Indigo Photo Agency\Alamy Images
03-03UN: Bryan Mullennix\Alamy Images

Photo Credits | 403

03-04UN: Larry Lilac\Alamy Images Royalty Free
03-06UN: Sean Gladwell 39\Alamy Images Royalty Free
03-07UN: Fancy\Alamy Images Royalty Free
03-08: Kacso Sandor\Shutterstock
03-09UN: Barry Mason\Alamy Images
03-011UN: Andres Rodriguez\Alamy Images Royalty Free
03-012UN: Image Source\Alamy Images Royalty Free
03-014UN: Vince Clements\Alamy Images Royalty Free
03-015UN: MBI\Alamy Images Royalty Free
03-016UN: Kheng Ho Toh\Alamy Images Royalty Free
03-017UN: F1online digitale Bildagentur GmbH\Alamy Images
03-018UN: D.Hurst\Alamy Images Royalty Free
03-019UN: Jon Helgason\Alamy Images Royalty Free
03-020UN: David Robertson\Alamy Images
03-021UN: Darryl Brooks\Alamy Images Royalty Free
03-023UN: Editorial Image, LLC\Alamy Images
03-024UN: Catalin Petolea\Alamy Images Royalty Free
03-025UN: RubberBall\Alamy Images Royalty Free
03-026UN: ImageState\Alamy Images Royalty Free
03-027UN: imagebroker\Alamy Images Royalty Free
03-028UN: K-PHOTOS\Alamy Images
03-029UN: NiMo85\Alamy Images

03-030UN: Andrzej Tokarski\Alamy Images Royalty Free
03-031UN: Metta foto\Alamy Images Royalty Free
03-032UN: Vince Clements\Alamy Images Royalty Free
03-033UN: Gary Lucken\Alamy Images
03-034UN: Images-USA\Alamy Images Royalty Free
03-037UN: NG YEW KEONG\Alamy Images Royalty Free
03-038UN: SUN: NYphotography.com\Alamy Images
03-039UN: Jon Helgason\Alamy Images Royalty Free
03-040UN: Maurice Savage\Alamy Images
03-041UN: Alamy Images Royalty Free
03-042UN: Tracy Martinez\Alamy Images Royalty Free
03-043UN: Blend Images\Alamy Images Royalty Free
03-044UN: Edd Westmacott\Alamy Images
03-045UN: Kirsty Pargeter\Alamy Images Royalty Free
03-046UN: RubberBall\Superstock Royalty Free
03-047UN: Neal & Molly Jansen\SuperStock, Inc.
03-048UN: Exactostock\Superstock Royalty Free
03-049UN: Pixtal\Superstock Royalty Free
03-050UN: Lucidio Studio, Inc.\Superstock Royalty Free
03-051UN: image100\Superstock Royalty Free
03-052UN: moodboard\Superstock Royalty Free
03-53UN: D. Hurst\Alamy Images Royalty Free

03-54UN: Corbis RF\Alamy Images Royalty Free
03-55UN: Tom Gril\Alamy\Corbis Super RF
03-56UN: Lawrenc Manning\Corbis Premium RF\Alamy
03-57UN: D. Hurst\Alamy Images
GC-03: Sharon Day\Shutterstock

04-01UN: Abstract backgroUN:ds\Alamy Images Royalty Free
04-02UN: RTimages/Alamy
04-03UN: Maksymenko 1/Alamy
04-04UN: Christoph Weihs/Alamy
04-04a: Murat Baysan\Shutterstock
04-04b: Roman Sigaev\Shutterstock
04-05UN: Christopher King/Alamy
04-06UN: mangostock\Shutterstock
04-07UN: DigitalDarrell/Alamy
04-08UN: Marvin woodyatt/Alamy
04-09UN: Alex Genovese\Alamy Images Royalty Free
04-09UN: Joshua Kristal\Alamy Images
04-10UN: Jonathan Brown\Alamy Images Royalty Free
04-11UN: Ingram Publishing\Superstock Royalty Free
04-12UN: SuperStock RF\Superstock Royalty Free
04-13UN: Ron Chapple Photography Inc./MediaMagnet/SuperStock
04-14UN: ST-images\Alamy Images
04-14B: Stefan Glebowski\Shutterstock
04-14C: Hugh Threlfall\Alamy Images

04-15UN: Ron Hayes\Alamy Images Royalty Free
04-15: iStockphoto.com
04-16UN: Image Source/Alamy
04-16: Wojtek Kryczka\iStockphoto.com
04-17UN: oliver leedham/Alamy
04-17: e_rasmus\iStockphoto.com
04-18UN: David J Green - technology/Almay
04-19UN: BrUN: o Sinnah/Alamy
04-20UN: BrUN: o Sinnah/Alamy
04-21UN: graficart.net/Alamy
04-22UN: Corbis/SuperStock
04-23UN: bikerriderlondon\Shutterstock
04-24UN: Photosani\Shutterstock
04-25UN: Maridav\Shutterstock
04-26UN: Frances M Roberts/Alamy
04-27UN: Frances M Roberts/Alamy
04-28UN: Wendy White/Alamy
04-29UN: Ariel Skelley/Blend Images/Alamy
04-30UN: sciencephotos/Alamy
04-31UN: David Buffington/Blend Images/Alamy
04-32UN: IndigoMoods/Alamy
04-33UN: Clover/amana images inc/Alamy
04-34UN: Michael Weber/imagebroker/Alamy
04-35UN: Jacqui Dracup/Alamy
04-36UN: Redfx/Alamy
04-37UN: Realimage/Alamy
04-38UN: Malcolm Fairman/Alamy
04-39UN: world map/Alamy
04-40UN: Isolated objects/Alamy
04-41UN: Streetfly Stock/Alamy
04-42UN: iStockphoto.com

04-43UN: PSL Images/Alamy
04-44UN: Image Source/Alamy
04-45UN: Greg Vivash/Alamy
04-46UN: Dennis Hallinan/Alamy
04-47UN: CreativeAct - Technology series/Alamy
04-48UN: Nadja Antonova\Shutterstock
04-49UN: Andrew Paterson\Alamy Images
04-50UN: Peter Alvey\Alamy Images
04-51UN: Plush Studios/TNC/Blend Images/Alamy
04-52UN: Indigo\Alamy Images
04-52aUN: Blend Images\Alamy Images Royalty Free
04-53UN: haveseen\Shutterstock
04-54UN: Hatonthestove\Alamy Images
04-55UN: David Hancock\Alamy Images
04-56UN: David YoUN: g-Wolff\Alamy Images
04-57UN: Sean Gladwell\Alamy Images Royalty Free
04-58UN: Brian Elliott\Alamy Images
04-59UN: Greg Balfour Evans\Alamy Images
04-60UN: sciencephotos\Alamy Images
04-61UN: Steve Cukrov\Shutterstock
04-62UN: Shay Velich/PhotoStock-Israel/Alamy
04-63UN: Image Source\Superstock Royalty Free
04-64UN: SuperStock RF\Superstock Royalty Free
04-65UN: SuperStock RF\Superstock Royalty Free
04-66UN: Paul B. Moore\Shutterstock

04-67UN: keith van-Loen\Alamy Images
04-68UN: Lourens Smak\Alamy Images
04-70UN: Aiste Miseviciute\Alamy Images Royalty Free
04-71UN: Bill Bachmann\Alamy Images
04-72UN: D. Hurst\Alamy Images Royalty Free
04-73UN: GraficallyMinded\Alamy Images Royalty Free
04-74UN: D. Hurst\Alamy Images
04-75UN: D. Hurst\Alamy Images
04-76UN: Vince Clements\Alamy Images Royalty Free
04-77UN: D. Hurst\Alamy Images Royalty Free
04-78UN: Lifestyle pictures\Alamy Images
04-79UN: Juice Images\Alamy Images Royalty Free
04-80UN: Corbis Premium RF/Alamy
04-81UN: Sharon Day\Shutterstock
04-82UN: Morgan Lane Photography \Shutterstock
04-83UN: D. Hurst\Alamy Images Royalty Free
04-85UN: Blue Moon Sock\Superstock Royalty Free
04-86UN: iStockphoto.com
04-87UN: iStockphoto.com
04-88UN: Eric Carr\Alamy Images
04-89UN: Exactostock\Superstock Royalty Free
GC-04:Shutterstock

05-001UN: Donald Sawvel\Shutterstock
05-002UN: Ellen Isaacs /Alamy

05-005UN: Wendy White/Alamy
05-006UN: SkillUp\Shutterstock
05-007UN: Darryl Jacobson\Superstock Royalty Free
05-008UN: Elena Kharichkina\Shutterstock
05-009UN: Dennis Hallinan\Alamy Images
05-010UN: Moculskly Stanislav\Shutterstock
05-011UN: D.Hurst/Alamy
05-012UN: Chad McDermott
05-013UN: Aleksey Oleynikov
05-014UN: Djordje Radivojevic
05-015UN: Image Source/Alamy
05-016UN: Francesco Ridolfi\Shutterstock
05-017UN: mikeledray\Shutterstock
05-018UN: D.Hurst/Alamy
05-019UN: Natalia Siverina\Shutterstock
05-020UN: Beaux Arts\Alamy Images
05-021UN: vnlit\Shutterstock
05-022UN: David McGlynn/Alamy
05-023UN: Lordprice Collection/Alamy
05-024UN: Clynt Garnham Technology/Alamy
05-025UN: ollirg\Shutterstock
05-026UN: ajt\Shutterstock
05-027UN: LAMB/Alamy
05-029UN: wideweb\Shutterstock
05-030UN: Digifoto Blue/Alamy
05-031UN: Studiomode/Alamy
05-032UN: Index Stock\SuperStock, Inc.
05-033UN: Lesley Sandles\Alamy Images
05-034UN: Imagewell\Shutterstock

05-035UN: Westermann\Alamy Images
05-036UN: Peter Titmuss\Alamy Images
05-037UN: AST Fotoworks\Alamy Images
05-038UN: Randy Duchaine\Alamy Images Royalty Free
05-040UN: Geoff du Feu\Alamy Images Royalty Free
05-041UN: 2020WEB\Alamy Images
05-042UN: Tom Payne\Alamy Images
05-043UN: Andrew Paterson\Alamy Images
05-044UN: John A. Anderson\Shutterstock
05-045UN: Panom\Shutterstock
05-046UN: David Tan\Shutterstock
05-048UN: Anton Prado\Alamy Images Royalty Free
05-049UN: Kurhan\Shutterstock
05-050UN: Studio51\Alamy Images
05-30: Monkey Business Images\Shutterstock
05-51UN: ZTS\Shutterstock

06-001UN: Lisa F. YoUN: g\Shutterstock
06-02: SVLumagraphica\Shutterstock
06-003UN: idesign\Shutterstock
06-004UN: Mongolka\Shutterstock
06-005UN: Kavione\Shutterstock
06-006UN: vieloryb\Shutterstock
06-007UN: spectral design\Shutterstock
06-008UN: Serggod\Shutterstock

Photo Credits | 405

06-009UN: Michael D. Brown\Shutterstock
06-010UN: wrangler\Shutterstock
06-011UN: PixAchi\Shutterstock
06-013UN: Gelpi\Shutterstock
06-014UN: HomeStudio\Shutterstock
06-016UN: ED-HAR\Shutterstock
06-017UN: leonardo255\Shutterstock
06-018UN: fotofermer\Shutterstock
06-019UN: Paul Paladain\Shutterstock
06-020UN: Feng yu\Shutterstock
06-022UN: Robert Milek\Shutterstock
06-023UN: Dominator\Shutterstock
06-23: Chris Curtis\Shutterstock
06-02UN: Michele Perbellini\Shutterstock
06-025UN: Kokhanchikov\Shutterstock
06-027UN: Viktor Gmyria\Shutterstock
06-028UN: Barone Firenze\Shutterstock
06-030UN: crisimatei\iStockphoto.com
06-031UN: Nisangha\iStockphoto.com
06-032UN: Zaptik\Shutterstock
06-033UN: italianestro\Shutterstock
06-034UN: Brian A. Jackson\Shutterstock
06-036UN: Nicholas Piccillo\Shutterstock
06-037UN: Kirbvzz\iStockphoto.com
06-038UN: lfong\Shutterstock
06-039UN: Kirsty Pargeter\Shutterstock

06-040UN: gualtiero boffi\Shutterstock
06-041UN: bmaki\Shutterstock
06-042UN: iStockphoto.com
06-044UN: Dietmar Hopfl\Shutterstock
06-045UN: Nayashkova Olga\Shutterstock
06-046UN: B. Melo\Shutterstock
06-46UN: Christopher Elwell\Shutterstock
06-47UN: Photazz\iStockphoto.com
06-49UN: Kacso Sandor\Shutterstock

07-001UN: stocklight\Shutterstock
07-002UN: Ford Prefect\Shutterstock
07-003UN: Ford Prefect\Shutterstock
07-004UN: Eugene Buchko\Shutterstock
07-04: Martin Heitner\SuperStock, Inc.
07-005UN: slart\Shutterstock
07-006UN: arkasha1905\Shutterstock
07-007: Harris Shiffman\Shutterstock
07-008UN: val lawless\Shutterstock
07-009UN: Slavoljub Pantelic\Shutterstock
07-011UN: tr3gin\Shutterstock
07-012UN: Lawrence Roberg\Shutterstock
07-013UN: Kim Seidi\Shutterstock
07-014UN: Tatiana Popova\Shutterstock
07-015UN: beto Gomez\Shutterstock
07-016UN: diebarbieri\Shutterstock

07-017UN: RTimages\Alamy Images
07-018UN: Oleg Nekhaev\Shutterstock
07-019UN: Nowik\Shutterstock
07-020UN: Gerry Boughan\Shutterstock
07-022UN: imagefactory\Shutterstock
07-023UN: tatniz\Shutterstock
07-027UN: Michal Mrozek\Shutterstock
07-028UN: glo\Shutterstock
07-029UN: rtguest\Shutterstock
07-030:Jaimie Duplass\Shutterstock
07-031UN: Marc Van Vuren\Shutterstock
07-032UN: karen roach\Shutterstock
07-033UN: Maridav\Shutterstock
07-034UN: HomeStudio\Shutterstock
07-035UN: Zlatko Guzmic\Shutterstock
07-036UN: mostafa fawzy\Shutterstock
07-038UN: RTimages\Shutterstock
07-039UN: Stephen Coburn\Shutterstock
07-040UN: sircommy\Shutterstock
07-041UN: stephen rudolph\Shutterstock
07-31UN: iStockphoto.com
07-37UN: 3911854\Shutterstock
GC-07: Robin Wong\Alamy Images

08-01UN: Blaj Gabriel\Shutterstock
08-002UN: Mandy Godbehear\Shutterstock

08-003UN: Adrian Niederhauser\Shutterstock
08-005UN: Germany Feng\Shutterstock
08-006UN: Pokomeda\Shutterstock
08-007UN: Andresr\Shutterstock
08-008UN: IKO\Shutterstock
08-009UN: Slavoljub Pantelic\Shutterstock
08-010UN: Ximagination\Shutterstock
08-011UN: Travel Bug\Shutterstock
08-012UN: Sharon Day\Shutterstock
08-013UN: RosyBlack\Shutterstock
08-014UN: R.Gino Santa Maria\Shutterstock
08-015UN: juliengrondin\Shutterstock
08-016UN: mostafa fawzy\Shutterstock
08-017UN: Galushko Sergey\Shutterstock
08-018UN: bhathaway\Shutterstock
08-019UN: Viorl Sima\Shutterstock
08-021UN: Amid\Shutterstock
08-022UN: IQoncept\Shutterstock
08-023UN: HomeStudio\Shutterstock
08-024UN: Lasse Kristensen\Shutterstock
08-025UN: tommistock\Shutterstock
08-026UN: Victor Correla\Shutterstock
08-027UN: TokyoLights\Shutterstock
08-028UN: Kokhanchikov\Shutterstock

08-029UN: C.\Shutterstock
08-031UN: ARENA Creative\Shutterstock
08-032UN: Edyta Pawlowska\Shutterstock
08-034UN: Moneca\Shutterstock
08-035UN: Ralf Juergen Kraft\Shutterstock
08-036UN: Janet Faye Hastings\Shutterstock
08-037UN: Shutterstock
08-038UN: Dmitry Rukhlenko\Shutterstock
08-039UN: Yuri Arcurs\Shutterstock
08-040UN: sextoacto\Shutterstock
08-042UN: Svemir\Shutterstock
08-043UN: photogl\Shutterstock
08-044UN: swinner\Shutterstock
08-045UN: SeDmi\Shutterstock
08-046UN: Robert Kneschke\Shutterstock
08-047UN: M. UN: al Ozmen\Shutterstock
08-048UN: Pefkos\Shutterstock
08-049UN: Mark Poprocki\Shutterstock
08-050UN: Diamond_images\Shutterstock
08-051UN: jokerpro\Shutterstock
08-052UN: Robyn Mackenzie\Shutterstock

08-053UN: Richard Peterson\Shutterstock
08-54UN: italianestro\Shutterstock
08-55UN: CROX\Shutterstock
08-56UN: M.Dykstra\Shutterstock
08-57UN: DSGpro\iStockphoto.com

09-01UN: Steven Newton\Shutterstock
09-01a: ArtmannWitte\Shutterstock
09-02UN: Susan Chiang\Shutterstock
09-03UN: Tomasz Trojanowski\Shutterstock
09-04UN: Morgan Lane Photography\Shutterstock
09-05UN: Susan Montgomery\Shutterstock
09-06UN: Vanessa Nel\Shutterstock
09-07: Vladru\Shutterstock
09-07a: Lev Olkha\Shutterstock
09-08: jaddingt\Shutterstock
09-08a: thumb\Shutterstock
09-09UN: alphaspirit\Shutterstock
09-10UN: StockLite\Shutterstock
09-11A: Mike Flippo\Shutterstock
09-11B: kzww\Shutterstock
09-11UN: Dmitry Nikolaev\Shutterstock

09-12UN: juliengrondin\Shutterstock
09-13UN: Andresr\Shutterstock
09-14UN: Marsel82\Shutterstock
09-15UN: Aleksandar Mijatovic\Shutterstock
09-16UN: JinYoUN: g Lee\Shutterstock
09-17UN: JinYoUN: g Lee\Shutterstock
09-18UN: Pontus Edenberg\Shutterstock
09-19UN: Petoo\Shutterstock
09-20UN: Shutterstock
09-21UN: Tish1\Shutterstock
09-22: Palto\Shutterstock
09-22a: Tatiana Popova\Shutterstock
09-23UN: ARENA Creative\Shutterstock
09-24UN: Norman Chan\Shutterstock
09-25UN: Robyn Mackenzie\Shutterstock
09-25a: Yurchyks\Shutterstock
09-26UN: Danny Smythe\Shutterstock
09-27UN: Stephen VanHorn\Shutterstock
09-28UN: David E Waid\Shutterstock
09-29UN: Nata-Lia\Shutterstock

09-30UN: Sashkin\Shutterstock
09-31UN: CarUN: tu\Shutterstock
09-32UN: Chris Hellyar\Shutterstock
09-33UN: Palto\Shutterstock
09-34UN: Goodluz\Shutterstock
09-35UN: Yegor Korzh\Shutterstock
09-36UN: Kinetic Imagery\Shutterstock
09-37UN: Péter Gudella\Shutterstock
09-38UN: Sebastian Tomus\Shutterstock
09-39UN: Jaimie Duplass\Shutterstock
09-40UN: photomak\Shutterstock
09-41UN: mmaxer\Shutterstock
09-42UN: Ljupco Smokovski\Shutterstock
09-43UN: thumb\Shutterstock
09-44UN: Vixit\Shutterstock
09-45UN: iofoto\Shutterstock

8.19, 8.29: © Twitter. Used by Permission
8.25: © Urge Essentials, www.urgeessentials.com
9.2–9.6, How to 9.1–9.13, 9.21, 9.24: Used with permission from Microsoft.
9.18: Used with permission from Google, Inc.